APPLIED MATH FOR DERIVATIVES

A Non-Quant Guide to the Valuation and Modeling of Financial Derivatives

APPLIED MATH FOR DERIVATIVES

A Non-Quant Guide to the Valuation and Modeling of Financial Derivatives

John Martin

John Wiley & Sons (Asia) Pte Ltd

Singapore • New York • Chichester • Brisbane • Toronto • Weinheim

Originally published by IFR Publishing under the title, *Derivatives Maths: A User's Guide to the Valuation of Financial Derivative Instruments*

This revised and updated edition published in 2001 by
John Wiley & Sons (Asia) Pte Ltd
2 Clementi Loop, #02-01, Singapore 129809

Published by arrangement with John S. Martin

Other Wiley Editorial Offices
John Wiley & Sons, Inc., 605 Third Avenue, New York, NY 10158-0012, USA
John Wiley & Sons Ltd, Baffins Lane, Chichester, West Sussex PO19 1UD, England
John Wiley & Sons (Canada) Ltd, 22 Worcester Road, Rexdale, Ontario M9W 1L1, Canada
John Wiley & Sons Australia Ltd, 33 Park Road (PO Box 1226), Milton, Queensland 4064, Australia
Wiley-VCH, Pappelallee 3, 69469 Weinheim, Germany

Library of Congress Cataloging in Publication Data
Martin, John, 1964-
Applied math for derivatives: a non-quant guide to the valuation and modeling of financial derivatives/John Martin.
p.cm. – (Wiley finance series)
Includes index.
ISBN 0-471-47902-0 (cloth: alk. paper)
1. Derivative securities – Valuation. I. Title. II. Series.
HG 6024.M374 2001
332.63'228—dc21

2001026004

Typeset in 11 points Times by Cepha Imaging Pvt Ltd, India
Printed in Singapore by Saik Wah Press Pte Ltd
10 9 8 7 6 5 4 3 2 1

TABLE OF CONTENTS

Acknowledgments

When I started working as a consultant in risk management in 1994 it was often difficult to explain to my friends and colleagues what I did and, more importantly, why clients should employ me. In a remarkably short timeframe, risk management has developed into a "kosher" career path and a whole industry and body of literature has developed in the last half decade. For me, while the issues and solutions are more complex, the building blocks of what we do as risk managers is based around derivative pricing and financial engineering concepts—and I still find I go back to the basic principals set out in this book on an almost daily basis.

I would like to thank everyone who helped me along my rather chequered path including my parents (the Edna and Ian referred to in the book), Warren Hogan, my professor at Sydney University, and my various bosses over the years including Stephen Grenville, David Mortimer, Les Hosking, Ric Spooner, John Meacock, Rob Ward and Conor O'Dowd. I particularly want to thank Satyajit Das who acted as a mentor and guide since our crazy days together at TNT Global Treasury in the late 1980s and early 1990s. Rather surprisingly, Adrian Blundell-Wignall deserves a mention as he unintentionally convinced me that life as a research economist was a dead end.

John Wiley & Sons have been particularly patient with the completion of this book. Thanks also to my current employer, PricewaterhouseCoopers, and all of my colleagues within the financial risk management practice.

Jenny Wilbow from MultiText Solutions did a wonderful job of technical editing and transforming the material into a workbook.

My most important acknowledgment is to my wife, Jen, who has always proved a source of wisdom and sound advice. Despite my persistent over commitment, work-a-holism and downright peculiar behaviour, she still cares for me—for that I am truly thankful.

PREFACE

This book provides an integrated approach to the valuation of financial derivative instruments over a wide range of asset classes. It is aimed at market practitioners, market observers and students who have a general understanding of derivative instruments and who wish to obtain a more thorough understanding of the valuation characteristics of derivatives.

This book is designed in a "workbook" format so it may be used as both a training and reference tool. The material is arranged so that it can be read from cover to cover by those wishing to learn the intricacies of derivative pricing and valuation, and it can also be easily accessed by experienced market practitioners who need a refresher on the mechanics of a particular derivative instrument. For every instrument covered, there is a discussion regarding its valuation characteristics, real life applications and at least one worked example or case study.

The emphasis of this book is to demystify derivative instruments and to explain valuation principles as simply as possible. This book is not aimed at "quants;" it is for the use of the general financial community. To assist in this process, the "building block" valuation approach is used; that is, instruments are broken down into their simpler pricing concepts, which are more familiar to readers, such as bond pricing, internal rate of return and net present values. The fundamental premise of the book is that in order to value instruments correctly we must first understood their economics (i.e., potential live cash flows) and then do the mathematics.

The book is divided into four parts:

Part 1: Getting Started. The aim of part one is to provide an overview of derivatives and derivative valuation concepts. Chapter 1 provides an introduction to derivatives and derivatives markets. Chapter 2 lays the foundations for derivative valuation and discusses the relationship between physical assets and their derivatives, in order to highlight the key variables in pricing and valuing derivatives.

Part 2: Forwards and Futures. Forwards and futures are the most important category of derivative, representing the largest portion of outstanding derivative volume. Forward pricing and valuation also represent a key element in the pricing and valuation of the more complex derivative types: swaps and options. Part 2 investigates the pricing and valuation characteristics of interest rate, foreign exchange and equity forwards.

Part 3: Swaps. Part 3 follows on from the valuation concepts developed for forward instruments. The key characteristics of swap transactions are examined and then applied to interest rate, currency and equity swaps.

Part 4: Options. In order to accurately price options, we need to understand the mathematical tools that are available to enable us to develop robust pricing and valuation models. The focus of this part is unashamedly pragmatic: we develop straightforward pricing and valuation techniques. A range of models are developed, primarily in a Black-Scholes environment, that can be applied to equity, foreign exchange and interest rate options.

By the end of this book, the reader will have the tools to:

- describe the various types and functions of derivatives and derivative markets;
- apply mathematical calculations and market conventions to accurately price and value forwards, swaps and options;
- develop effective pricing and valuation models for forwards, swaps and options;
- critically analyze the appropriateness and effectiveness of various derivative pricing and valuation models.

This book also comes with a disk containing some of the more complex pricing and valuation spreadsheets. Those chapters where the figures are included in the disk are indicated with a 🖫. As an added service to readers from time to time amended or updated spreadsheets will be made available on the PricewaterhouseCoopers Global Risk Management Solutions website www.pwcglobal.com/risk and so to the Financial Risks Management section.

Each chapter also contains a self-test set of questions, answers to these questions can be found on the enclosed disk.

Part 1

Getting Started

CHAPTER 1

INTRODUCTION

OVERVIEW

This introductory chapter is designed to create a context and lay the foundations for the rest of the book.

By the end of this chapter we will have:

- an understanding of the forces driving the evolution of derivatives;
- an appreciation of the size and scope of derivative instruments and markets;
- identified the various types and functions of derivatives.

1.1 THE DERIVATIVES MARKET

The spectacular growth in derivatives in the last couple of decades is an extension of the rapid and continuing structural changes that have been occurring in global financial markets since the 1970s. These changes include:

- the global deregulation of financial institutions and markets;
- the development of highly integrated global financial securities and currency markets;
- the trend away from traditional intermediated financial transactions toward the securitization of credit;
- the emergence of pooled fund managers aiming to maximize short-term returns;
- the impact of rapid technological development on data processing and modeling complexity.

The effect of these changes is that financial assets can be bought and sold at very short notice and financial prices are subject to substantial volatility as international market players respond to the release of relevant information. As *Figure 1.1* shows, the strong growth in the use of derivatives has been a consistent trend since the early 1980s and far from being isolated transactions,

Figure 1.1
Estimated Global Derivative Outstandings

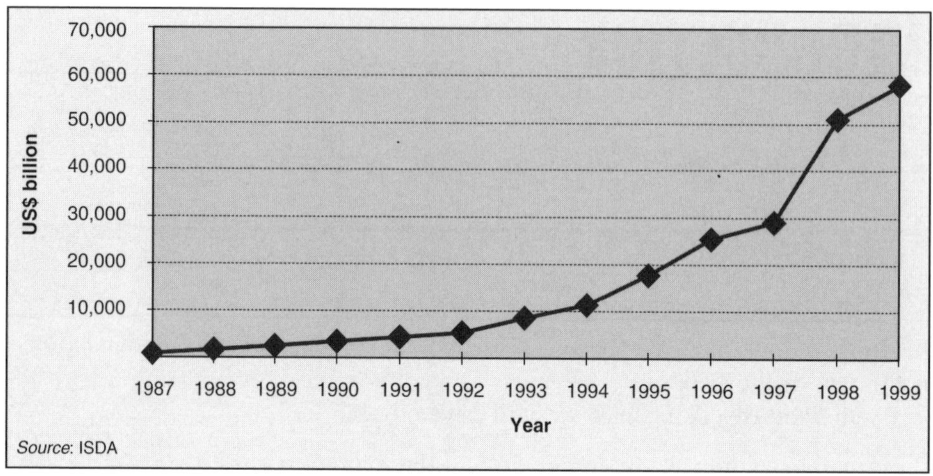

derivatives now form an integral part of financial operations for most corporations and financial institutions.

Derivatives are employed primarily to reduce, rather than increase, an organization's exposure to risk. Essentially, derivatives have developed as a means of making decisions in the face of uncertainty. Volatile financial market prices in the 1970s meant that managing exposures and devising methods to reduce exposures to financial prices became a primary concern for many organizations. This process is described as *market risk management.* Derivatives provide a low-cost and off-balance sheet method of isolating exposure to financial prices and taking an offsetting position to hedge that exposure.

This book divides derivatives into three major groups:

- **Forwards** An agreement to buy or sell an underlying financial instrument at some time in the future. Futures contracts are a standardized subset of forward contracts. We discuss forwards in Part 2 of this book.

- **Swaps** An agreement whereby two parties agree to exchange a future series of cash flows either in the same or different currencies. We discuss swaps in Part 3 of this book.

- **Options** An agreement that gives the purchaser of the option the right, but not the obligation, to buy (a call option) or sell (a put option) an underlying financial instrument at some time in the future. We discuss options in Part 4 of this book.

Within these groups, derivative instruments are divided further into three market, or asset, types:

- interest rate
- foreign exchange
- equity

collectively defined as *financial derivatives*. Many of the concepts covered in this book can be applied to other market types, such as commodities, credit and property; however, these are beyond the scope of material covered in this book.

In the following chapters, we will analyze the pricing and valuation aspects of various derivative instruments within the categories defined above.

1.1.1 Forwards

Forwards and futures represent the largest derivative type by global outstanding face value and volume.

Foreign exchange and interest rate products dominate forward transactions, with most of this volume comprising over-the-counter (OTC) foreign exchange forwards and exchange-traded (ET) interest rate futures. The volume of ET interest rate futures is considerably higher than OTC interest rate forwards. This reflects the fact that short-term and long-term interest rate futures are the primary forward interest rate instrument in most currencies, whereas OTC forwards tend to be for more specialized use. The volume of equity forwards is relatively low and consists mainly of stock index futures.

Many FX forward transactions are actually not outright forwards at all, but constitute part of an FX swap transaction. The global swap market is expanding and the largest FX market, London, continues to grow at a rapid rate compared to its nearest rivals, the US and Japan. This reflects London's historical position as a global financial centre and its location between European and North American time zones. In terms of geographical regions, the importance of Europe continues to grow and it now represents more than half the total global volume.

1.1.2 Swaps

Interest rate swaps are a fundamental aspect of most corporations' asset and liability interest rate risk management. Swap transactions tend to be used by end users of medium- to long-term exposures. The futures market volume tends to be driven by financial intermediaries and fund managers.

While the original swap transactions in the 1970s were currency swaps, the importance of currency swaps relative to interest rate swaps has declined steadily since the mid-1980s--by the late 1990s, interest rate swap outstandings are nearly 15 times that of currency swap. Another development since the mid-1980s has been the decline in the *relative* importance of the US dollar swap market. This was primarily the result of the development and strong growth of interest rate swap markets in European and Asian markets.

1.1.3 Options

The level of turnover in options generally remains lower than that of forwards, futures and swaps. This is because financial institutions traditionally use interest rate products to manage risk.

A feature of global option volume is that while the *value* of OTC options outstanding is significantly higher than ET options, ET option transactions are a significantly larger proportion of total *volume*—this is due to the fact that, as mentioned previously, OTC option transactions tend to be more specialized and are usually tailor-made to high net-worth individuals and organizations and ET options are the standardized, more accessible contracts.

The bulk of equity options trading is based on the US exchanges, where there are more than 1,000 contracts. The US markets represent 74% of volume by contract.

In line with derivatives generally, the bulk of options traded globally are mainly on interest rate products. Unlike equity and interest rate options, the bulk of currency option volume is OTC. This corresponds to the fact that business in the underlying spot and forward FX contracts is primarily OTC.

The Bank for International Settlements (BIS) conducts a triennial survey (the last one was conducted in 1998, the next one will be in 2001) on OTC global derivatives and foreign exchange. The preliminary findings from this survey are reproduced in the appendix for this chapter.

The graphs in *Figure 1.2* summarize some of the results from the latest survey, illustrating the relative sizes of the OTC derivative markets by instrument and asset type.

While these figures do not capture exchange-traded derivatives, they do reflect the general profile total of derivatives outstanding. Some of the interesting features include:

- the enormous growth in the value of derivatives outstanding (78% over the 3-year period);
- a continuation of the general increase in importance of more sophisticated derivatives (swaps and options) over forwards—in 1998 forwards represented less than half of outstandings;
- options have shown the strongest growth—up 128% over the three years;
- while the original driver of derivative activity in the 1980s and early 1990s, the relative share of FX derivatives is declining. In 1998, more than two-thirds of outstandings were in interest rate derivatives;

Figure 1.2
OTC Derivatives Outstanding
Foreign Exchange, Interest Rate and Equity Derivatives[1]

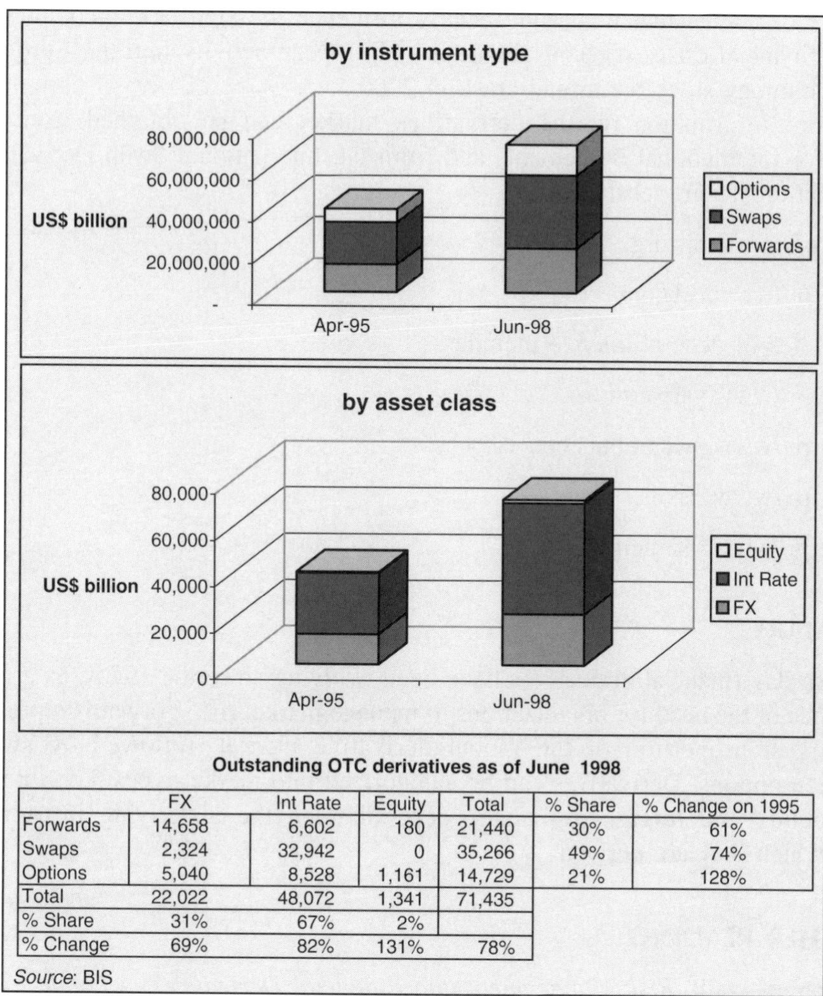

Outstanding OTC derivatives as of June 1998

	FX	Int Rate	Equity	Total	% Share	% Change on 1995
Forwards	14,658	6,602	180	21,440	30%	61%
Swaps	2,324	32,942	0	35,266	49%	74%
Options	5,040	8,528	1,161	14,729	21%	128%
Total	22,022	48,072	1,341	71,435		
% Share	31%	67%	2%			
% Change	69%	82%	131%	78%		

Source: BIS

- while coming from a fairly low base, the strongest growth by asset class has been in equities. While the data is not shown in this table, a similar growth story is occurring in OTC commodity derivatives.

The broad conclusion from this analysis is that derivatives markets are maturing. Increasingly, the derivatives transactions that are being executed

[1] ISDA and BIS statistical data are from different sources and therefore they cannot be easily reconciled; however, both serve as an indication for the relative sizes of both OTC and exchange-traded derivatives.

are more sophisticated and in some of the less "plain vanilla" asset classes (e.g., equities and commodities).

It should be noted that since the publication of the survey there have been a number of events that may significantly influence the statistics, including the Asian financial crisis, the consolidation of European activity into the Euro and the technology stock boom and crash in 2000.

More information on the derivatives market can be obtained from the Bank for International Settlements and from the International Swap Derivatives Association. Their websites are:

- http://www.bis.org
- http://www.isda.org

Other sites of general interest include:

- http://www.garp.com
- http://www.pwcglobal.com/risk
- http://www.risk.net
- http://www.riskmetrics.com

SUMMARY

Modern-day financial derivatives have been evolving since the 1970s, as a consequence of the need for organizations to manage market risk. Forwards represent the largest proportion of the global derivative market, followed by swaps and then options. Derivatives can be categorized into market types, i.e., interest rate, equity and foreign exchange—depending on the underlying instrument from which they are derived.

FURTHER READING

- Das, Satyajit. *Risk Management and Financial Derivatives: A Guide to the Mathematics*, McGraw Hill, March 1998.
- Das, Satyajit. *Swaps and Financial Derivatives*, 2nd edition, LBC, 1994.
- Hull, John C. *Options, Futures and Other Derivatives with Disk*, 4th edition, Prentice-Hall Incorporated, July 1999.
- Hull, John C. and Alan White. *Hull-White on Derivatives*, Risk Books, June 1996.
- Natenberg, Sheldon. *Option Volatility and Pricing: Advanced Trading Strategies and Techniques*, Probus Publishing Co., August 1994.

- *From Black-Scholes to Black Holes: New frontiers in options*, Risk Books, published in association with FINEX, September 1992.

SELF-TEST QUESTIONS

1. How do you explain the popularity of forwards compared to swaps and options, as a risk management tool in the modern organization?
2. Explain why the *value* of OTC options outstanding is much higher than ET options, whereas ET options comprise a much greater proportion of total option *volume.*
3. What is the driving force behind the growth of the global swaps market?
4. There were two significant economic events that occurred *after* the printing of the Bank for International Settlements 1998 central survey on foreign exchange and derivatives market activity. What were they and how might they have affected the shape and direction of global derivatives?

APPENDIX

BANK FOR INTERNATIONAL SETTLEMENTS

P.O. BOX, 4002 BASEL, SWITZERLAND

PRESS RELEASE

CENTRAL BANK SURVEY OF FOREIGN EXCHANGE AND DERIVATIVES MARKET ACTIVITY IN APRIL 1998: PRELIMINARY GLOBAL DATA

The BIS is releasing today preliminary global turnover data from the latest Triennial Central Bank Survey of Foreign Exchange and Derivatives Market Activity in April 1998. It follows the publication of national data by participating central banks and monetary authorities on September 29, 1998. The geographical coverage of the new survey was significantly expanded (from 26 countries in 1995 to 43 countries), but, in order to reduce the reporting burden, the coverage of derivatives was limited to over-the-counter (OTC) currency and interest rate instruments. Therefore, it excludes exchange-traded business, information on which is regularly collected by the BIS from the exchanges themselves, as well as smaller OTC market segments such as equity, commodity and credit-related products. In addition, although the reporting of OTC *turnover data* for April 1998 is consistent with earlier surveys, information pertaining to *amounts outstanding* applied to end-June, rather than end-March as hitherto, and is not yet available. This change in reporting date was made to ensure consistency with the new regular reporting of consolidated derivatives market statistics in the G-10 countries which was also introduced at end-June 1998 and preliminary data for which will be released later this year. The BIS will publish the final global results on both foreign exchange and derivatives turnover and amounts outstanding in the spring of 1999.

After allowing for the double-counting resulting from local and cross-border inter-dealer transactions and for estimated gaps in reporting, the average daily turnover in "traditional" global foreign exchange instruments (spot transactions, outright forwards and foreign exchange swaps) can be estimated at US$1,490 billion in April 1998, compared with US$1,190 billion in April 1995.[1] Although the rate of growth in other OTC foreign exchange derivative instruments (currency swaps and options) was considerably higher than in traditional ones, they remained, at US$97 billion, a small fraction of overall trading. Meanwhile,

[1] Data adjusted for local double-counting are referred to as "net-gross," while those adjusted for both local and cross-border double-counting are referred to as "net-net."

Summary of Global Activity in Foreign Exchange Markets*
(average daily turnover in billions of US dollars)

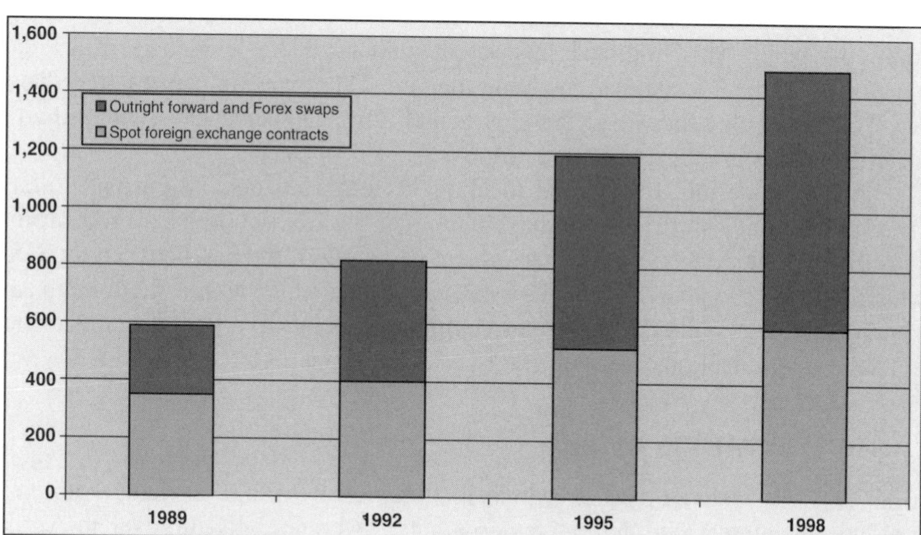

* Adjusted for local and cross-border double-counting (net-net). Includes estimates for gaps in reporting.

the notional value of transactions in interest rate derivatives, i.e., forward rate agreements (FRAs), swaps and options, amounted to US$265 billion, compared with US$151 billion in 1995.

1 TRADITIONAL FOREIGN EXCHANGE MARKET

In the traditional segment of the foreign exchange market, percentage changes in turnover in the two latest 3-year periods (1992–95 and 1995–98) show a considerable deceleration in the rate of expansion in current dollar terms (from 45% to 260%). Between April 1995 and April 1998, however, the dollar rebounded strongly (in particular, it appreciated by more than 50% vis-à-vis the yen, which correspondingly reduced the dollar value of yen transactions). Adjusted for differences in the dollar value of nondollar transactions, growth accelerated from 29% to 46%. Forward instruments consolidated their leading position, pushing the share of spot turnover down further (to 40%, from 44% in 1995). Within the former group, foreign exchange swaps continued to overshadow outright forwards by a large margin. At the same time, the market continued to show a predominance of inter-dealer business (63%) and cross-border transactions (54%).

In current dollar terms, the breakdown by currency reveals another increase in the role of the dollar on one side of transactions (from 83% in April 1995 to 87%).[2] However, at constant exchange rates, the share of the dollar actually declined (to 76%). There was, in particular, a strong pick-up in yen business (from 24% to an exchange-rate-adjusted share of 29%) and in a large number of small currencies. This finding is consistent with anecdotal evidence of a wide range of investment strategies involving the yen. There was, in contrast, a reduction in currency plays between core continental European currencies (with a sharp fall in Deutsche mark/French franc turnover).

When considering, finally, the location of forex business in current dollar terms, the currency shifts seem to have benefited the UK (whose share rose from 30% to 32%). At the same time, there was a widening of the gap between the US (which ranked second at 18% of the total) and Japan (third with a share reduced from 10% to 8%), although such relative movements partly reflect differences in exchange rate valuations between the two reporting periods.

2 OTC DERIVATIVES MARKET

In the OTC derivatives market (which includes other foreign exchange derivatives and all interest rate derivatives contracts), average daily turnover in April 1998 was, at US$ 362 billion, 85% higher than in April 1995, the first period for which such data were reported. Interest rate products continued to outweigh forex instruments (accounting for 73% of total turnover), attracting a growing proportion of end-users. For its part, OTC forex business was boosted by option transactions. The currency breakdown indicates that contracts between the dollar and the yen, as well as those involving the Deutsche mark against a wide range of currencies, were the most actively traded.

Expansion in the interest rate segment of the market was driven by the growing popularity of single-currency swaps. Of note was the almost seven-fold increase in DM-denominated swaps, which often acted as counterparts to cash and derivatives transactions involving other EU currencies, as well as a proxy for the euro. The fact that the survey was conducted just before the announcement concerning the initial participation in European monetary union, which was followed by a flattening of the main European swap curves and a moderation of arbitrage transactions, may have also played a role. As a result, the German currency overtook the dollar as the most important currency of denomination in swaps (with shares of 30% and 23% respectively). Meanwhile, strategies based on yen interest rates slackened, in a context of historically low levels of interest rates and reduced market volatility.

Finally, the breakdown by reporting centre shows that the share of OTC derivatives business conducted in the UK rose from 27% in 1995 to 36%, with the

[2] Counting both currency sides of every foreign exchange transaction means that the currency breakdown sums to 200% of the aggregate.

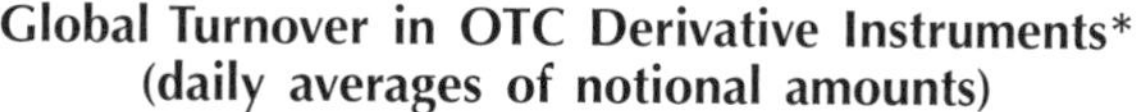

Global Turnover in OTC Derivative Instruments*
(daily averages of notional amounts)

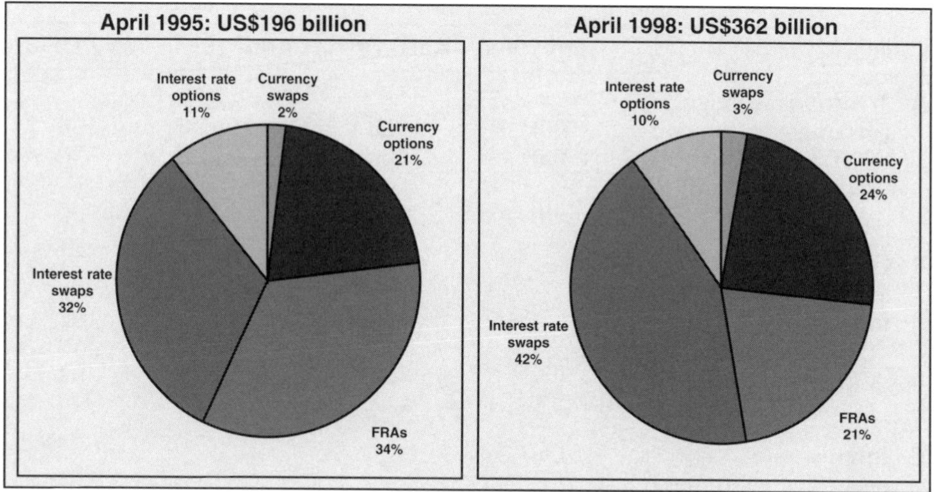

* Excluding traditional foreign exchange instruments (outright forwards and foreign exchange swaps) and adjusted for local and cross-border double-counting (net-net).

growing buoyancy of European currency transactions more than compensating for the more subdued pace of activity in the yen. While the US maintains its rank as the next most important location (at 19%), France overtook Japan as number three, with Germany replacing Singapore in fifth position. The fall in the market share of Singapore (from 7% to 2%) should probably be seen in relation to the drying-up of liquidity in instruments based on the yen and a number of other Asian currencies.

Table 1
The Global Foreign Exchange and Over-The-Counter Derivatives Markets[1]
(average daily turnover in billions of US dollars; notional amounts for derivatives)

Category	April 1989	April 1992	April 1995	April 1998
A. Traditional foreign exchange instruments	**590**	**820**	**1,190**	**1,490**
Spot transactions[2]	350	400	520	590
Outright forwards and forex swaps[2]	240	420	670	900
B. Other foreign exchange derivative instruments	**–**	**–**	**45**	**97**
Currency swaps	–	–	4	10
Options	–	–	41	87
Other	–	–	1	0
C. Interest rate derivative instruments	**–**	**–**	**151**	**265**
FRAs	–	–	66	74
Swaps	–	–	63	155
Options	–	–	21	36
Other	–	–	2	0
D. Total B+C	**–**	**–**	**196**	**362**
Memorandum items: exchange-traded derivatives[3]				
Currency instruments	***13***	***14***	***17***	***12***
Interest rate instruments	***374***	***640***	***1,205***	***1,360***

[1] Adjusted for local and cross-border double-counting.
[2] Includes estimates for gaps in reporting.
[3] *Sources*: Futures Industry Association and various futures and options exchanges.

Table 2
Measures of Global Traditional Foreign Exchange Market Activity[1]
(average daily turnover in billions of US dollars)

Category	April 1989	April 1992	April 1995	April 1998
Total reported gross turnover	**907**	**1,293**	**1,864**	**2,337**
Adjustment for local double-counting[2]	−189	−217	−293	−366
Total reported turnover net of local double-counting (net-gross)	**718**	**1,076**	**1,572**	**1,971**
Adjustment for cross-border double-counting[2]	−184	−291	−435	−537
Total reported "net-net" turnover	**534**	**785**	**1,137**	**1,434**
of which: cross-border transactions	–	392	611	768
Estimated gaps in reporting[3]	56	35	53	56
Estimated global turnover	**590**	**820**	**1,190**	**1,490**

[1] Data include spot transactions, outright forwards and foreign exchange swaps. Number of reporting countries in 1989: 21; in both 1992 and 1995: 26; and in 1998: 43.
[2] The adjustments have in principle been made by halving positions vis-à-vis other local reporting dealers and other reporting dealers abroad respectively.
[3] Includes estimates for less than full coverage within individual reporting countries and for underreporting of activity involving nonreporting countries.

Table 3
Currency Distribution of Global Traditional Foreign Exchange Market Activity[1]
(percentage shares of average daily turnover)

Currency	April 1989	April 1992	April 1995	April 1998
US dollar	90	82	83	87
Deutsche mark[2]	27	40	37	30
Japanese yen	27	23	24	21
Pound sterling	15	14	10	11
French franc	2	4	8	5
Swiss franc	10	9	7	7
Canadian dollar	1	3	3	4
Australian dollar	2	2	3	3
ECU and other EMS currencies	4	12	15	17
Other currencies	22	11	10	15
All currencies	**200**	**200**	**200**	**200**

[1] Whenever reported on one side of transactions. The figures relate to reported "net-net" turnover, i.e., they are adjusted for both local and cross-border double-counting, except for 1989 data, which are available only on a "gross-gross" basis.
[2] Data for April 1989 exclude domestic trading involving the Deutsche mark in Germany.

Table 4
Geographical Distribution of Global Traditional Foreign Exchange Market Activity[1] (average daily turnover in billions of US dollars)

Country	April 1989		April 1992		April 1995		April 1998	
	Amount	Percentage share	Amount	Percentage share	Amount	Percentage share	Amount	Percentage share
Argentina	–	–	–	–	–	–	2.2	0
Australia	28.9	4	29.0	3	39.5	3	46.6	2
Austria	–	–	4.4	0	13.3	1	10.5	1
Bahrain	3.0	0	3.5	0	3.1	0	2.4	0
Belgium	10.4	1	15.7	1	28.1	2	26.5	1
Brazil[2]	–	–	–	–	–	–	0.4	0
Canada	15.0	2	21.9	2	29.8	2	36.8	2
Chile	–	–	–	–	–	–	1.3	0
China[2]	–	–	–	–	–	–	0.2	0
Czech Republic	–	–	–	–	–	–	0.5	0
Denmark	12.8	2	26.6	2	30.5	2	27.3	1
Finland[3]	3.4	0	6.8	1	5.3	0	4.2	0
France	23.2	3	33.3	3	58.0	4	71.9	4
Germany	–	–	55.0	5	76.2	5	94.3	5
Greece	0.4	0	1.1	0	3.3	0	7.2	0
Hong Kong	48.8	7	60.3	6	90.2	6	78.6	4
Hungary	–	–	–	–	–	–	1.4	0
India	–	–	–	–	–	–	2.4	0
Indonesia	–	–	–	–	–	–	1.5	0
Ireland	5.2	1	5.9	1	4.9	0	10.1	1
Italy	10.3	1	15.5	1	23.2	1	28.2	1
Japan	110.8	15	120.2	11	161.3	10	148.6	8
Luxembourg	–	–	13.2	1	19.1	1	22.2	1
Malaysia	–	–	–	–	–	–	1.1	0
Mexico	–	–	–	–	–	–	8.6	0
Netherlands	12.9	2	19.6	2	25.5	2	41.0	2
New Zealand	–	–	4.2	0	7.1	0	6.9	0
Norway	4.3	1	5.2	0	7.6	0	8.8	0
Philippines	–	–	–	–	–	–	0.8	0
Poland	–	–	–	–	–	–	1.3	0
Portugal	0.9	0	1.3	0	2.4	0	4.4	0
Russia	–	–	–	–	–	–	6.8	0
Saudi Arabia	–	–	–	–	–	–	2.3	0
Singapore	55.0	8	73.6	7	105.4	7	139.0	7
South Africa	–	–	3.4	0	5.0	0	8.8	0
South Korea	–	–	–	–	–	–	3.5	0
Spain	4.4	1	12.3	1	18.3	1	19.3	1
Sweden	13.0	2	21.3	2	19.9	1	15.4	1
Switzerland	56.0	8	65.5	6	86.5	6	81.7	4
Taiwan	–	–	–	–	–	–	4.8	0
Thailand	–	–	–	–	–	–	3.0	0
United Kingdom	184.0	26	290.5	27	463.8	30	637.3	32
United States	115.2	16	166.9	16	244.4	16	350.9	18
Total "net-gross" turnover	**717.9**	**100**	**1,076.2**	**100**	**1,571.8**	**100**	**1,971.0**	**100**

[1] Data are adjusted for local double-counting (net-gross). Estimated coverage of the foreign exchange market ranged between 90% and 100% in most countries, and between 66% and 80% in a few countries.

[2] Data only cover spot transactions.

[3] Data for 1992 not adjusted for local double-counting.

Table 5
Global Reported Turnover in Over-The-Counter Derivatives by Currency and Type of Instrument (daily averages of notional amounts in billions of US dollars)

A. Foreign exchange contracts

Category	Currency swaps and options		Memorandum items: Outright forwards and forex swaps	
	April 1989	April 1992	April 1995	April 1998
Total reported gross turnover	**67**	**150**	**1,047**	**1,421**
Adjustment for local double-counting	–7	–20	–155	–215
Total reported "net-gross" turnover	**60**	**130**	**892**	**1,207**
Adjustment for cross-border double-counting	–16	–34	–249	–344
Total reported "net-net" turnover	**44**	**97**	**643**	**862**
of which: cross-border	27	56	348	479
US dollar vs other currencies	34	77	595	803
Deutsche mark	11	18	111	146
Japanese yen	14	36	154	146
Pound sterling	1	4	52	79
Other EMS currencies	4	8	143	217
Other	4	10	135	215
Deutsche mark vs other currencies[1]	8	17	31	36
Japanese yen	2	5	5	6
Pound sterling	1	5	3	6
Other EMS currencies	4	2	16	12
Other	1	4	7	12
Japanese yen vs other currencies[2]	0	1	6	5
Other currency pairs	2	2	11	17

[1] Excluding the US dollar.
[2] Excluding the US dollar and the Deutsche mark.

(Table continued)

B. Interest rate contracts

Category	All instruments		of which FRAs		of which Swaps	
	April 1995	April 1998	April 1995	April 1998	April 1995	April 1998
Total reported gross turnover	**254**	**415**	**114**	**120**	**104**	**242**
Adjustment for local double-counting	−45	−71	−21	−24	−20	−40
Total reported "net-gross" turnover	**209**	**344**	**93**	**97**	**84**	**201**
Adjustment for cross-border double-counting	−57	−78	−28	−22	−22	−47
Total reported "net-net" turnover	**151**	**265**	**66**	**74**	**63**	**155**
of which: cross-border	78	132	38	35	30	79
US dollar	41	71	18	23	17	36
Deutsche mark	18	63	9	9	7	47
Japanese yen	35	27	9	3	17	14
Other	58	104	30	39	22	58

Table 6
Geographical Distribution of Global Over-The-Counter Derivatives Market Activity*
(average daily turnover of notional amounts in billions of US dollars)

Country	April 1995		April 1998	
	Notional amounts	Percentage share	National amounts	Percentage share
Australia	3.8	1	4.6	1
Austria	2.3	1	4.6	1
Bahrain	4.1	2	0.4	0
Belgium	6.2	2	5.7	1
Canada	5.3	2	7.5	2
Denmark	3.9	1	4.9	1
Finland	1.8	1	2.4	0
France	22.3	8	45.8	10
Germany	13.8	5	34.4	7
Greece	0.1	0	0.0	0
Hong Kong	4.3	2	3.8	1
Indonesia	–	–	0.2	0
Ireland	1.5	1	2.4	1
Italy	2.4	1	4.4	1
Japan	32.8	12	42.1	9
Luxembourg	2.2	1	2.6	1
Mexico	–	–	0.2	0
Netherlands	5.2	2	5.3	1
New Zealand	0.2	0	0.5	0
Norway	1.5	1	2.9	1
Portugal	0.1	0	1.0	0
Russia	–	–	0.1	0
Saudi Arabia	–	–	0.3	0
Singapore	18.1	7	11.3	2
South Africa	0.4	0	0.8	0
South Korea	–	–	0.1	0
Spain	3.6	1	3.5	1
Sweden	2.3	1	4.3	1
Switzerland	4.4	2	15.8	3
Taiwan	–	–	0.3	0
Thailand	–	–	0.1	0
United Kingdom	73.8	27	170.8	36
United States	53.2	20	90.9	19
Total "net-gross" turnover	**269.5**	**100**	**474.0**	**100**

* Adjusted for local double-counting (net-gross). Estimated coverage of the derivatives market in individual countries ranged between 75% and 100%. Excluding outright forwards and foreign exchange swaps.

Source: Bank for International Settlements, April 1998. Reproduced with permission.

CHAPTER 2

FUNDAMENTALS OF DERIVATIVE VALUATION

OVERVIEW

In this chapter, we discuss the concept of derivative valuation and outline the steps necessary to construct appropriate valuation models.

By the end of this chapter we will have:

- identified the relationship between the underlying physical security and its derivative in order to accurately price the derivative;
- distinguished between the *value* and the *price* of a derivative;
- identified the fundamental elements involved in valuing derivatives and creating derivative valuation models.

2.1 THE IMPORTANCE OF VALUATION

Derivative valuation is, at the most fundamental level, the mathematical exercise of determining the cash flows and obligations generated by a derivative contract. More importantly, however, valuation is concerned with determining the relative cost or benefit of using a derivative instrument, both at the time the instrument is executed and during its life. For the purpose of this book, the simple definition of the *value* of a derivative is:

> *The value of a derivative is the amount of cash that has to be paid or received today in exchange for that instrument.*

As we mentioned in Chapter 1, derivatives are a fundamental aspect of the operation of the modern business. Derivatives are used to *add value* to an organization. Derivative valuation is, therefore, the process of *quantifying* the extent to which derivative transactions add or reduce the value of an organization. Without adequate valuation methods, we cannot assess whether a derivative adds to or reduces the value of an organization. Therefore, valuation of derivatives is a fundamental aspect of derivative usage.

The key risk in modern financial markets is uncertainty, and decision-making involves an assessment of the relative return versus the risk of making that return. A decision on a particular project or strategy will be dependent on an entity's perceived attitude to risk versus return. So, if the risk represented by an exposure is too great, derivatives can add value by reducing risk even though there might be a cost in doing so.

The ways in which derivatives can add value are varied and depend on the preferences and risk profile of the individual organization. Some of these areas may include:

Arbitrage Activities:

- lowering the cost of borrowing
- increasing the return on assets
- exploiting mispricing between markets
- taking advantage of differences in regulatory treatment of on- and off-balance sheet instruments that have the same economic characteristics

Risk Management:

- reducing asset and liability mismatch
- reducing future cash flow uncertainty
- creating strategic exposures to markets

Income Generation:

- proprietary trading
- market-making
- providing a client service

Risk Management

Traditionally, financial texts have focused on arbitrage activities as the main function of derivative instruments, such as swaps and futures. While prevalent in the early 1980s, these arbitrage opportunities are now limited.

The major driving force behind current derivative usage is in the area of risk management. The focus in most corporations is risk reduction, which suggests that if a firm uses derivatives to reduce the future variability of its profits, then investors are willing to pay more for that firm today (i.e., a higher share price). Common examples of risk-reducing activities include "fixing" interest costs using interest rate swaps or hedging foreign currency exposures using foreign exchange forward transactions.

Risk management, however, is not just about reducing risk. It also involves *managing* the risk profile of an organization to meet its strategic objectives. For organizations such as fund managers, derivatives can represent a low-cost method of assuming desired exposures to particular assets. An example of this is purchasing stock index futures to obtain an exposure to equity markets. The added value of using stock futures relative to buying a physical stock portfolio is the speed of execution, liquidity and the substantially lower transaction costs.

While derivatives represent a highly competitive market place, some players generate significant incomes from derivatives market making and proprietary trading. However, given the competitive nature of the marketplace, there is significant pressure on market makers to develop more sophisticated products in the hope that trading margins will be improved.

2.2 DERIVATIVES AND CASH MARKETS

A key component in calculating the value of a derivative is the underlying cash or physical financial instrument to which the performance of the derivative is linked. The usual starting point in any valuation is determining the current market price of the underlying cash instrument and, in some instances, the likely distribution of the underlying price in the future.

Cash market instruments are usually distinguished from derivatives in that they are instruments that can be exchanged directly into cash and typically accrue income. Cash instruments can be divided into four general asset classes:[1]

- interest rate
- foreign exchange
- equity
- commodity

We shall focus on the derivative instruments for the first three financial asset classes. Many of the models, particularly the equity pricing models, can however, be applied to commodity markets.

In order for a derivative market to exist, a cash market must also exist. In fact, a derivative market offers an alternative method of trading the cash market, usually in the future and without requiring legal ownership of the underlying cash asset. In most markets, with the exception of equity markets, the first derivatives to develop were forward contracts, as market participants developed a means of offsetting the risk associated with buying or selling the underlying cash instrument at some time in the future. Swaps can be viewed as a consecutive

[1] This is a definition of present value, thus the value of a derivative is its present value.

series of forward contracts which develop in conjunction with forward markets. Options-based forward contracts typically develop later than forward and swaps markets and the volume of these instruments is substantially lower than forward-based derivatives. This evolution from cash to derivative instruments is represented diagrammatically in *Figure 2.1*.

While *Figure 2.1* is valid for the interest rate and foreign exchange markets in most countries, some equity markets have omitted the forward instrument stage. In particular, where derivatives on individual shares consist primarily of options, there is very little trading in forward instruments in individual shares and all forward trading is forwards on broad-based indices.[2] Also, while *Figure 2.1* suggests that the cash market volume is greater than derivative market turnover in many markets, turnover in forwards and futures is actually considerably higher than the underlying cash market. This is reflected in the Australian dollar financial markets in *Figure 2.2*, which shows that in all markets, except equities, more than half the market turnover is in forwards and swaps.

The global volume of derivatives in each asset class tends to reflect the underlying cash market liquidity. As we mentioned in Chapter 1, while there has been substantial growth in the volume of derivatives across all asset classes, interest rate derivatives dominate global volume.

Figure 2.1
Cash and Derivative Market Inter-Relationships

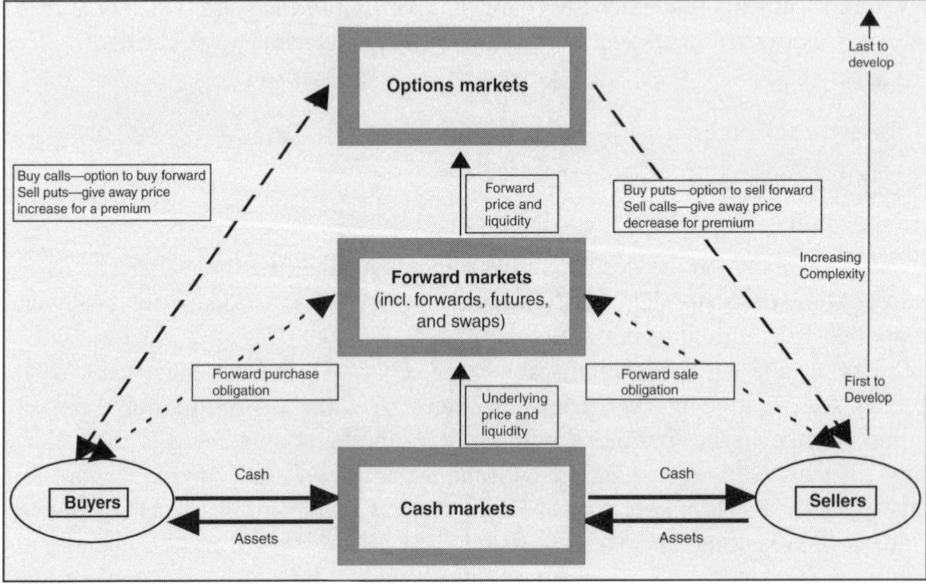

[2] Some explanations for this phenomenon are discussed in Chapter 13 on equity options.

Figure 2.2
Australian Financial Markets — Summary of Total Market Turnover 1998/99

A$ Trillion					
	Interest Rate	FX	Equities	Total	% Total
Cash	3.56	8.31	0.28	12.15	32%
Forwards[2]	3.64	10.85	–	14.49	38%
Futures	9.17	–	0.27	9.43	25%
Swaps	0.46	0.12	–	0.58	2%
ET Options	0.68	–	0.10	0.78	2%
OTC Options	0.05	0.65	0.01	0.72	2%
Total	17.56	19.93	0.65	38.14	100%
Cash	3.56	8.31	0.28	12.15	32%
Forwards/Swaps	13.27	10.96	0.27	24.50	64%
Options	0.73	0.65	0.11	1.50	4%
Forwards/Swaps % Share	76%	55%	41%	64%	
Option % Share	4%	3%	17%	4%	

Source: Australian Financial Markets Association (with adjustments by the author).

Notes:

(1) The exchange-traded equity option volume figures have been adjusted from the data in the original AFMA report that reported just the premium value of equity option value. In order to constrast this with other instruments, an implied face value has been calculated.

(2) Includes repos and FX swaps.

As we examine the valuation requirements for different derivative types, we shall also examine the inter-relationships between cash and derivative markets.

2.3 DISTINGUISHING BETWEEN VALUE AND PRICE

The aim of derivative valuation is to determine the cash value, or replacement cost, of a derivative from given market prices such as bond prices, security yields and foreign exchange rates. In general terms, this involves taking financial market prices as a given and then applying them to an appropriate mathematical formula to produce the valuation.

In this book we distinguish between the *price* and *value* of a derivative. We have already defined the *value* of a derivative as the amount of cash that would be paid or received today in exchange for that instrument.

For the purpose of this book, the *price* of a derivative is represented by:

The price of a derivative is represented by the current market quotation or rate of exchange for a derivative.

For example, in the case of an interest rate swap, the current price is expressed as a fixed swap interest rate, whereas the value of an existing swap is defined by the present value of the difference between the future cash flows created by the original traded fixed swap rate and the current swap rate. In the case of an option, the current value of an open contract is defined by the cash value of the difference between the original traded premium and the current market premium.

Note

Price and value are interlinked concepts where *price* is the method of market quotation for the derivative and the *value* of an open contract is a function of the derivative's original traded price and the current market price.

The relationship between price and value can be expressed mathematically:

$$\text{Value} = \Omega\,(P_T, P_C)$$

Where:

Ω is some form of mathematical process such as a present value or option pricing calculation

P_T is the original traded price of the derivative

P_C is the current market price of the derivative.

To illustrate this idea with an example, we can extend the price and valuation relationship to physical financial assets such as bonds. Suppose we purchase a 10-year bond with a yield to maturity of 7% pa, this yield to maturity is a market price and does not actually tell us how much cash we will require to settle the bond purchase. To determine the cash value of the instrument we need to apply a mathematical process, in this case the bond formula, which converts the future cash flows of a bond into a present value amount.[3]

[3] For more on the bond formula, see Chapter 3, Section 3.4.1.

Value = Bond price (7% pa)

The reason for distinguishing between the concepts of price and value is to emphasize that there are always two steps in determining the value of a derivative. The first step is to determine the current market price of a derivative and the second step is to convert this price into a value. Typically, the pricing calculation involves determining the likely future movements in the price of the physical instrument underlying the derivative. This calculation is considerably more complex for an option than for a forward or a swap. Usually, the valuation step involves a present value or time value of money calculation, and this is often considerably more complex for a swap than for a forward or an option.

In the following chapters, we will distinguish between the pricing and valuation steps for each derivative and we will break down the complex components into simple calculations.

While valuation is conceptually straightforward, in practice it can be a difficult and complex process. This complexity may stem from:

- the number of cash flows generated by a derivative;
- the fact that these cash flows may be contingent on specific events taking place;
- the ability to derive the current market price of an instrument.

2.4 WHAT ARE THE ELEMENTS OF DERIVATIVE VALUATION?

The fundamental element of derivative valuation is the price of the physical or cash financial instrument that underlies the derivative instrument. However, if we view the question more generally and ask what are all of the elements that need to be incorporated into a derivative pricing and valuation model, we come up with the following four "cornerstones" of accurate valuation that form the foundations for the models constructed in this book.

- **Financial market prices** A derivative instrument is often a complex construction of underlying physical instruments. When valuing a derivative we need access to all of the interest rates, exchange rates and prices comprising the derivative.
- **The time value of money** All derivatives have the potential of creating obligations, such as cash flows, in the future. A key aspect of all financial transactions is that cash flows occurring at different times have different values. When valuing derivatives, we need to ensure that we have taken into account the time value of money.

- **The law of equivalent value** All derivatives can be broken down into combinations of physical instruments and/or other derivatives. The concept behind equivalent value is that the value of a derivative should always equal the sum of the value of its components. It is called a law because it should always hold true, if it does not hold true then risk-free arbitrage profits can be made by breaking derivatives into components. Most financial engineering and arbitrage strategies revolve around equivalent value and we will use this concept extensively when deriving pricing and valuation models.
- **Uncertainty** The future cannot be predicted with certainty. Derivatives create obligations in this uncertain future and consequently derivative pric-ing and valuation models must incorporate uncertainty when required. This is a feature of option pricing models; however, it also plays a part in the pricing of other derivative instruments.

Whenever we construct a model, we must ensure that all four of the above elements have been incorporated. If they have not, then we cannot be sure of the accuracy of the model. Ensuring all of the elements are covered does not guarantee a perfect valuation model, but it does ensure that the model is reasonably accurate and robust.

> ***Note***
> A common source of error in derivative valuation models is the failure to give due consideration to the time value of money. Therefore, if a forward contract generates a profit or loss one year into the future, the value of that contract is not just the profit or loss, it is the *present value* of that profit or loss.

2.5 DEVELOPING PRICING AND VALUATION MODELS

When developing pricing and valuation models, we need to ensure that the four cornerstones outlined in Section 2.3 are incorporated. The first part of this process is to ensure that we understand the basic valuation drivers of a specific derivative instrument. In particular, we need to know what type of obligation has been created; that is, whether the derivative instrument is a forward, swap, option or combination of all three.

To assist in this process, this book divides the derivative valuation component into three parts: forwards, swaps and options. This allows us to develop generalized tools that can be fine-tuned for the specific terms of a contract or the nature of the underlying instrument. We divide each type of instrument into the asset class of the specific underlying instrument. Using this distinction, each part of the book is divided into four chapters: the first is a general description of the instrument type, while the following three deal specifically with the requirements for pricing and valuing derivatives on interest rate, currency and equity instruments.

The approach we take when developing a pricing and valuation model for each derivative instrument is to follow these steps:

- **Establish the contract terms** How does the contract work? What is the underlying instrument and what are the future rights and obligations it creates? This first step sets out the scope of the contract and the underlying financial market prices that will determine the price and value of a derivative. It also indicates the role uncertainty plays in the pricing of a derivative—if any of the contract rights or obligations are contingent (as with an option) then we know we must incorporate a way of modeling uncertainty.
- **Create synthetic replication** How can the instrument be synthetically replicated using physical financial instruments and/or using other types of derivatives? This step is a direct application of equivalent value: we explicitly look for the components, or building blocks, of a derivative instrument. As the name implies, synthetic replication is simply a term for combining cash and derivative financial instruments to create another financial instrument. In terms of valuation, it is ensuring that, we abide by equivalent value and it also identifies all of the financial market prices that combine to determine a derivative's price or value.
- **Calculate the derivative price** Using synthetic replication, we determine the current market price of a derivative using the concept of equivalent value—the value of a derivative should be equivalent to its component parts.
- **Calculate the derivative value** Once a current market price is determined, we compare the cash flows created by existing contracts to the cash flows created at the current market price. The present value of these differences is the value of the derivative. This usually involves actually calculating the cash values of the rights and obligations set out in step one and applying time value of money calculations.

Note

In general, the models created in steps three and four of this process are spreadsheet models. A full description of all of the formulae used is provided with each model. While these models will apply to most spreadsheet packages, the models are specifically created for Microsoft Excel version 5.04.[4] A disk containing selected samples of the models developed in this book is enclosed in the back cover.

[4] In most cases, the models are backwardly compatible with Excel Version 4.0 and can certainly be used with higher versions of Excel such as V7.0.

SUMMARY

This chapter identified the relationship between a derivative's price and its value. The price refers to the derivative's market quotation or rate of exchange and the value is the amount of money that must be paid or received *today* for the derivative, i.e., the derivative's present value. We outlined the four "cornerstones," or elements, that must be incorporated into any robust derivative valuation model:

- financial prices;
- time value of money;
- law of equivalent value;
- uncertainty.

We also identified the four "steps" necessary in performing a derivative valuation:

- establishing the contract terms;
- creating a synthetic replication;
- calculating the derivative's price;
- calculating the derivative's value.

SELF-TEST QUESTIONS

1. How do you express mathematically, the relationship between the *price* and the *value* of a derivative? Explain this relationship.
2. Explain the meaning of "time value of money."
3. "Derivatives are a risk management tool in the modern corporation, as opposed to purely a means of exploiting arbitrage opportunities." Discuss this statement.
4. Explain what is meant by *synthetic replication.*
5. Identify the four "steps" involved in developing derivative pricing and valuation models.

CHAPTER 3

A REVIEW OF FINANCIAL MATH

OVERVIEW

In this chapter, we review the fundamental financial mathematics concepts necessary to value derivatives. By the end of this chapter we will have:

- distinguished between present value and future value;
- applied the concept of time value of money and nominal versus effective interest rates;
- applied appropriate formulae to calculate the prices of short-term money market and long-term capital market securities;
- identified the risk management concepts of duration, convexity and point value of a basis point (PVBP).

3.1 DEVELOPING VALUATION TOOLS

Before we can value financial derivatives we need to understand the valuation formulae for the underlying physical financial instruments. In this chapter, we will review the mathematics required to value a wide range of money and capital market instruments, which will be applied in later chapters of this book. Derivative valuation requires adjustments to be made for the passing of time and for the interpolation of actual financial prices. These adjustments will be dealt with in the discussion on the time value of money and the yield curve in this chapter. We will also be developing the basic mathematical terminology we will use throughout the book.

3.2 TIME VALUE OF MONEY AND PRESENT VALUE FORMULAE

The time value of money (TVM) refers to the difference in the value of cash today and in the future. This concept allows us to quantify the relative values of cash flows occurring at different times. It is an essential component in the calculation of the value of financial instruments. It is also an important consideration in derivative valuation where multiple cash flows occur at different times and need to be converted to an equivalent amount at one point in time.

Present and future values are key elements in derivative valuation and form the basis of the TVM concept. A fundamental aspect of all financial transactions is that receiving cash today is more valuable then receiving it in the future. If a lender provides funds to a borrower, it requires the payment of interest as well as the repayment of the principal amount. The primary reasons motivating the payment of interest include the fact that the lender forgoes all other uses of the cash, the eroding effect of inflation on purchasing power and the risk that the principal will not be repaid.[1]

The level of interest rates is the index that we use for determining prevailing TVM. These interest rates are determined by the relative supply of funds for financing and the demand for those funds. Though there is no generic interest rate, for every type of financing transaction, there is potentially a different rate of interest. In any financially deregulated economy, this results in the very large range of interest rates, each with its own supply and demand dynamics. Interest rates are distinguished by the nature of the underlying transaction and focus on three characteristics:

- type of instrument
- creditworthiness of the borrower
- term to expiry and/or interest reset.

> ***Note***
> An important aspect of valuation is applying the *appropriate* interest rate. For example, valuing a fixed-rate loan to a highly speculative company using a government bond rate is inappropriate; an adjustment must be made reflecting the relative creditworthiness of the borrower.

It is worth noting that while all individuals and organizations are likely to have different TVMs, it is the rate at which we can currently lend and borrow the underlying financial transaction that is important for valuation purposes.[2] This becomes particularly important when we start to consider the interest rates used when valuing capital market instruments and derivatives. Using the wrong interest rate will lead to a wrong valuation. Most financial math formulae are a form of present value calculation; that is, these formulae identify the future cash

[1] For more on the determinants of interest rates, see Van Horne, James C. *Financial Markets: Rates and Flows*, Prientice Hall, July 2000.

[2] The focus of valuation is to determine current market values. If an individual's TVM is different to the current market interest rate, it will give rise to an opportunity gain or loss; however, this takes us away from our focus of valuation to financial theory.

flows of a financial instrument and then calculate the value at which these instruments could be exchanged for cash today.

3.2.1 Simple Interest

Simple interest is the difference between the value of cash today and cash at some date in the future. It is expressed as a "flat" amount as opposed to the "annualized" amount and compounding is ignored. For example, if we invest US$100 today and we receive US$111 in seven months' time, the simple interest rate is 11%.

Formula: Simple Interest

$$FV = PV \times (1 + r)$$

If we rearrange terms, we can solve for the other variables

$$PV = FV/(1 + r)$$
$$r = FV/PV - 1$$

Where:

FV = future value
PV = principal (present value)
r = interest rate per annum as a percentage.

Simple interest is useful for comparison of different investments over the same period because it avoids any compounding differences. The return on the investment is calculated by comparing cash flows at the beginning and at the end of the investment period. The investment return is the simple interest received over the period.

3.2.2 Compound Interest

It is very unusual to find a financial asset providing interest in a simple interest form. In most cases, interest is expressed in an annualized form and it is assumed that interest is paid periodically. In order to determine the value of this type of instrument, the annualized interest rate needs to be adjusted for the frequency with which interest is paid. This will take account the fact that interest is earned on interest prior to the expiry of the financial instrument (that is, compounding of interest). The compounding process is explained by calculating the future value amount in the example in *Figure 3.1*.

Figure 3.1 expressed mathematically is shown in the compound interest formula on the following page. Note that this model assumes that interest

Figure 3.1
Compounding Example

$100 is invested in a financial instrument which expires in 1 year and pays 10% pa semi-annually. What is the future value of this investment?

A semi-annual payment pays interest every half-year. In this example, the cash flows will be the initial investment of $100, a $5 payment at the end of 6 months and 1 year, and the principal repayment at the end of the year.

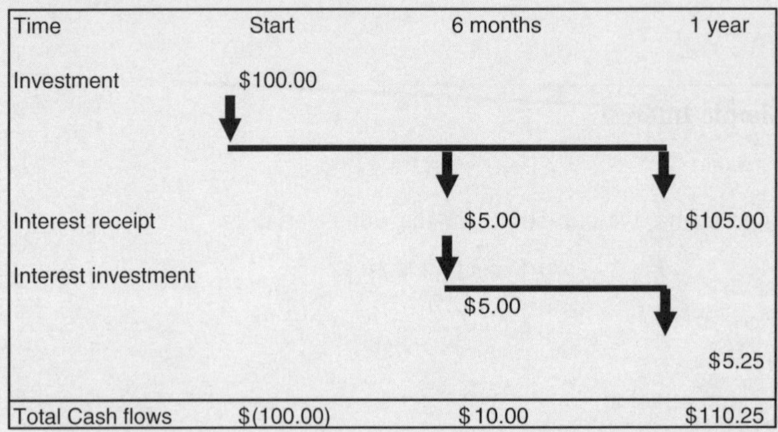

The total value (or the future value) at the end of the year is $110.25—assuming that we can reainvest the $5 received at the end of 6 months at 10% pa.

Formula: Compound Interest

$$FV = PV \times (1 + r/m)^n$$

If we rearrange terms, we can solve for the other variables

$$PV = FV/(1 + r/m)^n$$

$$r = ((FV/PV)^{1/n} - 1) \times m$$

Where:

FV = future value
PV = principal (present value)
r = interest rate per annum as a percentage
n = number of periods over which investment held
m = number of interest payments per annum.

Related Microsoft Excel functions:

FV: *FV*(rate, nper, pmt, pv, type)
PV: *PV*(rate, nper, pmt, fv, type)

payments can be re-invested at the same interest rate that is earned on the underlying instrument. This assumption can lead to valuation problems that will be highlighted in the section on zero-coupon interest rates.

Compounding is a key concept and will be used regularly in our valuation models. It allows us to determine the *present value of a single cash flow* at some date in the future, providing we know the appropriate interest rate that should be applied to this cash flow. The compound interest formula forms the basis for most short-term money market and bond formulae.

3.2.3 Effective, Nominal and Continuous Interest Rates

The compound interest formula highlights the fact that the payment frequency underlying an interest rate influences present and future valuation calculations; that is, for a given interest rate, the more interest payments per annum, the greater the compounding effect and the higher the future value or lower the present value. A common error in any valuation is the application of an interest rate with the wrong payment frequency when calculating a present value. When using an interest rate, we need to know the underlying payment frequency assumption. If the interest frequency is not appropriate for our calculation, we must *adjust* the interest rate. The need for this adjustment has led to the distinction between *nominal* and *effective* interest rates. An effective interest rate for a defined interest payment frequency is the simple interest for that payment frequency. For example, an investment paying interest quarterly at a nominal rate of 12% pa has an effective quarterly interest rate of 3%. An effective interest rate for a given period explains the difference between the present and future value of an investment held for that period. If we invest US$100 at an effective rate of 12%, then we know at the end of the year the future value will be US$112.

With a nominal interest rate, the period and interest frequency are different. Generally, this involves quoting an interest rate as an annualized rate when the interest frequency is less than a year. The net effect is that the interest rate needs to be adjusted in order to determine the difference between a present and future value amount.

In practice, interest rates are expressed as an annualized number. This means that an interest rate with an annual interest payment frequency is the effective rate and all other interest payment frequencies are nominal rates. For the purposes of valuation, we need to be able to convert nominal to effective rates or interest rates from one nominal basis to another nominal basis (for example, converting from quarterly to semi-annual). The formulae necessary for these conversions appears on page 36.

The simplest method of converting an interest rate from one payment frequency to another is to convert to an effective annual rate and then to convert to the desired nominal rate. *Figure 3.2* provides an example of this process.

Figure 3.2
Adjusting Nominal Interest Rates

Suppose an investment earns a nominal quarterly interest rate of 8% pa. Calculate this interest rate as a nominal semi-annual rate.

The quickest method of performing this calculation is to break it into two steps: first convert to an effective rate and then convert to a semi-annual nominal rate.

Step 1: Convert from a nominal quarterly to an effective annual interest rate

r_m = 8.0000%
m = 4

r_1 = (1 + 0.08/4) ^ 4 −1
= 8.2432%

Step 2: Convert from an effective annual to a nominal semi-annual interest rate

r_1 = 8.2432%
m = 2

r_m = ((0.082432 + 1) ^ (1/2) −1) × F21
= 8.080%

One method of avoiding these compounding complexities is to use continuously compounding interest rates. A continuously compounding interest rate assumes that interest is paid continuously rather than at discrete monthly or quarterly intervals.[3] A continuously compounding rate is equivalent to a daily

Formula: Nominal and Effective Interest Rates

$$r_1 = (1 + r_m/m)^m - 1$$

If we rearrange terms, we can solve for the other variables

$$r_m = ((r_1 + 1)^{1/m} - 1) \times m$$

Where:

r_1 = effective annual interest rate per annum
r_m = nominal interest (with m frequency) per annum
m = number of interest payments per annum.

Related Microsoft Excel functions:

r_1: EFFECT(nominal_rate, npery)
r_m: NOMINAL(effect_rate, npery)

[3] Put another way, the interest frequency (m) is infinite.

interest rate, because the benefits from compounding by second, minute and hour are very small for most levels of interest rates.

The advantage of continuously compounding interest rates is that all the effective and nominal conversions can be ignored and also present values can be more simply calculated using the exponential function. In a number of pricing models, all interest rates are converted to continuous rates before being used and all calculations use continuous rates. The formula for converting compounding rates to continuous rates is provided below.

Formula: Continuous Compounding

$$r = \ln(1 + r_m/m) \times m$$

If we rearrange terms, we can solve for the other variables

$$r_m = (\exp(r/m) - 1) \times m$$

Where:

r = interest rate with continuous compounding per annum
r_m = nominal interest (with m frequency) per annum
m = number of interest payments per annum
ln = natural logarithm function
exp = exponential function (the inverse of a natural logarithm).

Related MS Excel Functions

ln: LN(number)
exp: EXP(number)

To see an example of a spreadsheet that converts to continuous compounding refer to *Figure 5.5* in Section 5.2.3.

Figure 3.3 compares continuously compounded, nominal and effective rates for three different interest rate scenarios.

Note
A continuous rate is always lower than nominal and effective interest rates. The difference is more noticeable in higher interest rates.

To calculate a future value using a continuous rate, we multiply the present value by the exponent of the number of years multiplied by the continuous interest rate:

$$FV = PV \times \exp(r \times n)$$

Figure 3.3
Nominal, Effective and Continuous Interest Rates

The same interest rate under five different compounding assumptions.

	1	2	3
Continuously compounded	5.0000%	10.0000%	15.0000%
Nominal monthly	5.0104%	10.0418%	15.0941%
Nominal quarterly	5.0314%	10.1260%	15.2848%
Nominal semi-annual	5.0630%	10.2542%	15.5768%
Effective annual	5.1271%	10.5171%	16.1834%

This can be rearranged to solve for a present value of a future cash flow as follows:

$$PV = FV \times \exp(-r \times n)$$

This particular present-value formula appears regularly in option pricing models such as the Black-Scholes model, which is examined in Part 4 of this book.

3.3 VALUING SHORT-TERM MONEY MARKET INSTRUMENTS

In most currencies, the short-term money market refers to the market for debt instruments with a maturity of six months or less. Each currency, however, has its own money market conventions and securities.

Short-term money market instruments are less complex to value than long-term, or capital market instruments, mainly due to the smaller number of cash flows involved.

Most money market instruments pay all interest at maturity—there is no intermediate interest payment or coupon. Most of the valuation differences arise

Figure 3.4
Money Market Instrument Cash flows

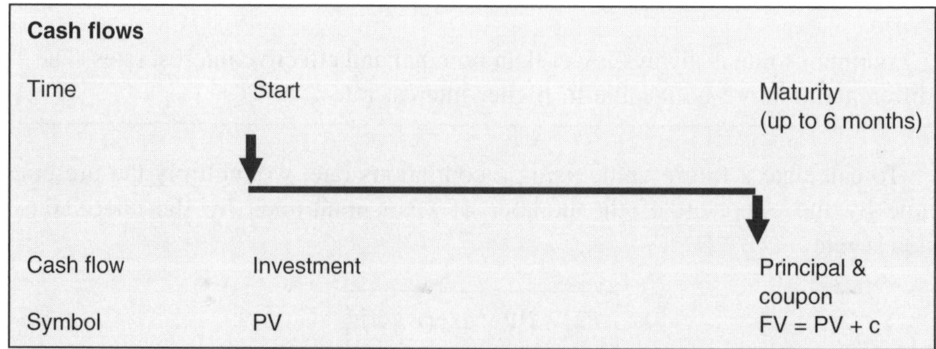

from the method in which interest is calculated and whether or not the instrument is traded at a discount to face value.

The major characteristics of money market instruments are summarized in *Figure 3.4.*

While the cash flow profile of a money market instrument is straightforward, differing conventions around the world complicate the valuation process. Some examples of these conventions are set out in the following table:

Some Important Money Market Valuation Conventions

Area	Characteristic	Comment
Cash flow	Discount security	A security trades at a discount, if the face value only is repaid at maturity. Investors earn interest by investing (PV) an amount less than the face value (FV) of the instrument. This is a common feature of instruments traded in secondary markets such as commercial paper or bank bills.
	Coupon	Some money market instruments pay a coupon prior to maturity. In this case, a bond pricing formula can be used. This is occasionally a feature of money market instruments issued by governments.
Interest	Day count	Day count refers to the number of days assumed to occur in a year. In money market instruments there are generally two options: an assumed 360 or 365 days a year. Interest is calculated by dividing the actual number of days elapsed by the assumed number of days a year (often the two methods are summarized as "A/360" or "A/365" respectively). A/360 is commonly used in the US and Europe, while A/365 is widely used in Japan, UK, Canada, Australia and New Zealand.
	Yield or discount method	In a discount security, the present value can be calculated using either the "yield" or "discount" method. Under the yield method, the interest accrued is based on the present value of the instrument, while under the discount method, it is based on the face value. Both formulae are provided below. The discount method is widely used in US dollar markets, while the yield method is often used in European currencies as well as Australia and New Zealand.

In the following sections, we examine three different kinds of formulae for short-term money market instruments:

- term deposits
- discount securities — yield method
- discount securities — discount method.

As well as examining the mathematics used to value short-term money market instruments, we will discuss the impact of valuation conventions highlighted in the table on page 39.

3.3.1 Valuing Term Deposits

In the case of a deposit, the principal amount invested and repaid is the same. All interest is accrued based on the face value of the deposit. In the case of a term deposit, interest is paid at the end of the deposit. In some currencies, for example Australian and New Zealand dollars, deposits made overnight or for one week, or less than a week receive interest at the end of the calendar-month in which the deposit was made.

Calculating the future value of a term deposit is a form of simple interest as is shown by the formula below:

Financial Math: Term Deposit

$$FV = A \times (1 + c \times d/D)$$

If we rearrange terms we can solve for the other variables

$$PV = FV/(1 + r \times f/D)$$

$$r = (FV/PV - 1) \times D/f$$

Where:

A = principal or face value of the instrument
FV = future value
PV = present value
c = coupon rate as a percent pa
r = current interest rate or yield as a percent pa
d = number of days of original deposit
D = day count basis (360 or 365)
f = number of days to maturity of the deposit.

Primary and Secondary Value

The important feature of this model is that we have two interest rates.

The first, referred to as the coupon rate, is the rate at which interest accrues on the instrument. In the case of the term deposit, the coupon is the interest rate at which the deposit was originally made.

The second rate is referred to as the current interest rate or yield. This is the market interest rate for the remaining term to expiry of the deposit. This yield represents the rate that we used to determine the present value of the deposit. This distinction is similar to the concept of primary and secondary value that we discussed in Chapter 2; the coupon determines the primary value of the deposit and the yield determines the secondary value. In accounting terms, we

Figure 3.5
The Present Value of a Term Deposit

Suppose $1 m is invested in a term deposit for 180 days at a rate of 7% pa. Calculate the future value of the deposit.

$$\begin{aligned} FV &= PV \times (1 + c \times d/D) \\ &= 1{,}000{,}000 \times (1 + 0.07 \times 180/365) \\ &= 1{,}034{,}521 \end{aligned}$$

On the day that the deposit is made interest rates rise by 1% pa. What is the value of the term deposit?

$$\begin{aligned} PV &= FV/(1 + r \times f/D) \\ &= 1{,}034{,}521/(1 + 0.08 \times 180/365) \\ &= 995{,}256 \\ &\quad (4{,}744) \end{aligned}$$

This present value calculation reveals that, due to the rise in interest rates, this deposit has realised a capital loss today of $4,744.

On any day over the life of the term deposit, the value of the deposit is likely to differ from the the original value of the instrument, due to changes in interest rates.

The following graph displays the value of the deposit over it's term to maturity. The present value changes are due to movements in yield and the passing of time. The value at the coupon rate changes due to the passing of time. The difference between these two amounts represents the current gain or loss on the deposit.

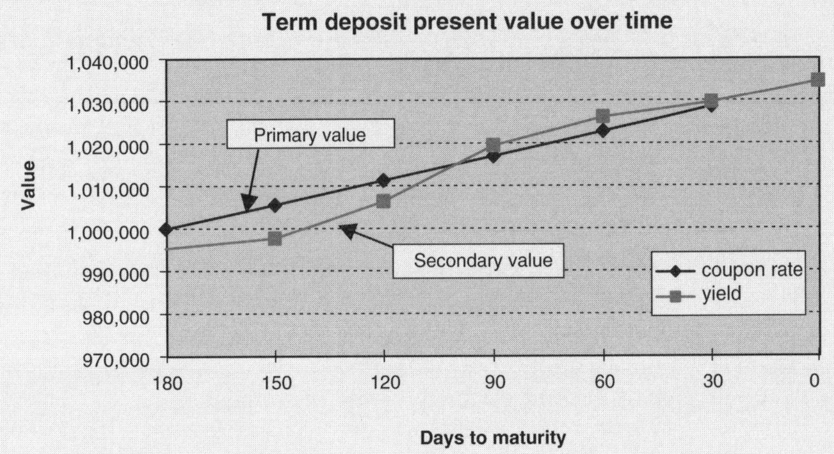

could say the coupon determines the "book" value of an instrument, while the yield determines the market value of an instrument—and the difference between the two amounts represents the current gain and loss on a financial instrument.

From a valuation perspective, the coupon rate is a fixed cash flow that is part of the term deposit, whereas the yield is a market-determined price that determines the present value of the deposit. At the time the deposit is made, the coupon rate and current interest rate is the same. As time passes, the coupon remains fixed and the current interest rate varies depending on prevailing market conditions. This is illustrated in *Figure 3.5*, where the present value of a term deposit is calculated over the life of a term deposit using both the coupon rate and prevailing market yield.

This distinction between primary and secondary values is the same for all financial instruments, including derivatives. It is a fundamental aspect of mark-to-market calculations and is a starting point for quantifying the risk of a financial instrument. We will come across this concept regularly during the remaining chapters of the book.

3.3.2 The Yield Method

Discount securities are a widely used form of short-term money market instruments, since they can be easily traded in a secondary market. Except for the interest rate, the other two variables required in the valuation of discount securities—face value and days to maturity—are given. Therefore, market participants only need to agree on the interest rate for the present value of the security to be determined.

Using the yield method, interest is accrued on the amount originally invested in the security. The yield formula for discount securities is as follows:

Financial Math: Discount Security — Yield Method

$$PV = A/(1 + r \times f/D)$$

If we rearrange terms, we can solve for the other variables

$$FV = A$$

$$r = (FV/PV - 1) \times D/f)$$

Where:

A = principal or face value of the instrument
FV = future value
PV = present value
r = current interest rate or yield as a percent pa
D = day count basis (360 or 365)
f = number of days to maturity of the instrument.

Examples of instruments using this formula are A$ and NZ$ bank-accepted bills and certificates of deposit.

For example, suppose that we wish to purchase a discount security with a face value of $10 million, 96 days to maturity on an A/360-day basis and using the yield method. If we agree to a yield of 5.65% pa then the calculation is as follows:

$$
\begin{aligned}
PV &= A/(1 + r \times d/D) \\
&= 10{,}000{,}000/(1 + 0.0565 \times 96/360) \\
&= 9{,}851{,}570
\end{aligned}
$$

If held to maturity, the interest earned on the security US$148,430. As expected, it gives a return, or yield, to maturity of:

$$
\begin{aligned}
r &= 148{,}430/9{,}851{,}570 \times 360/96 \\
&= 5.65\%\ \text{pa}
\end{aligned}
$$

This shows that the yield and interest rate on this type of instrument are the same.

> ***Note***
> The yield method is essentially the bond formula (see Section 3.4) when only one coupon remains to be paid. This is useful when choosing between investing in a short-term money market instrument or a bond close to maturity, as the yields can be directly compared.

3.3.3 The Discount Method

The discount method is another widely used form of short-term security valuation. However, unlike the yield method, the interest rate and the yield on the security are *not* the same. This is because the interest amount is calculated based on the face value of the security, rather than the original amount invested. As a result, the interest rate is always *less* than the yield. This can be seen from the formula and example on page 44.

Discount Security — Discount Method

$$PV = A \times (1 - r \times f/D)$$

If we rearrange terms, we can solve for the other variables

$$FV = A$$

$$r = ((FV/PV - 1) \times D/f)$$

Where:

A = principal or face value of the instrument
FV = future value
PV = present value
r = current interest rate or yield as a percent pa
D = day count basis (360 or 365)
f = number of days to maturity of the deposit.

Examples of instruments using this formula: domestic US dollar commercial paper market, common in the Euro-commercial paper market across all currencies.

As a comparison, let us use the previous example, but this time apply the discount method using a yield of 5.65% pa. The calculation is as follows:

$$\begin{aligned} PV &= A \times (1 - r \times d/D) \\ &= 10{,}000{,}000 \times (1 - 0.0565 \times 96/360) \\ &= 9{,}849{,}333 \end{aligned}$$

If held to maturity, the interest earned on the security US$150,667. The interest amount is higher, because it is based on the face value rather than the original investment amount, which gives a return, or yield to maturity of:

$$\begin{aligned} r &= 150{,}667/9{,}849{,}333 \times 360/96 \\ &= 5.74\% \text{ pa} \end{aligned}$$

or effectively 0.09% pa more than the interest rate.

3.3.4 Converting the Discount Method to the Yield Method

A common problem faced by money market participants is comparing the relative returns offered by securities using discount and yield method interest rates. As we saw in Section 3.3.3, the interest rates on these two types of instruments are not comparable. The formula below provides a simple means of converting these two methods to allow an accurate comparison:

Financial Math: Conversion from Discount to Yield Method

$$r = (D \times i)/(D - i \times f)$$

Where:

r = yield as a percent pa
i = discount interest rate as a percent pa
D = day count basis (360 or 365)
f = number of days to maturity of the instrument.

Some examples of discount to yield conversions are provided in *Figure 3.6*.

Figure 3.6
Discount to Yield Method Conversion

Calculate the yield to maturity on a discount security with a current discount method interest rate of 6.5% pa and 150 days to maturity (A/360-day basis).

$r = (D \times i)/(D - i \times f)$
$= (360 \times 0.065)/(360 - 0.065 \times 150)$
$= 6.6809\%$

The table below calculates the yield to maturity of this security based on a range of discount method interest rates.

Discount method interest rate	Yield to maturity
5.00%	5.1064%
6.00%	6.1538%
7.00%	7.2103%
8.00%	8.2759%
9.00%	9.3506%
10.00%	10.4348%
11.00%	11.5284%
12.00%	12.6316%

3.4 VALUING LONG-TERM CAPITAL MARKET INSTRUMENTS

Generally, capital market instruments refer to securities with a term to maturity of greater than six months. Apart from the difference in time, the distinction between "money" and "capital" markets is largely arbitrary and is historically based. In most countries, prior to financial deregulation, the majority of investments were held to maturity and there was a distinction between short-term instruments as either a place to put short-term excess cash or fund working capital requirements, and long-term securities as a way of financing capital expenditures. As a result of the development of secondary markets, both money and capital markets are liquid and both markets are used for raising capital. However, the distinction is still useful for valuation purposes as it allows us to recognize the difference in relative complexity of the instruments traded in the two markets.

The most common form of capital market security is the bond, typically a security with a term to maturity of several years when issued, which pays a regular fixed interest coupon. These securities also include floating-rate securities such as the floating rate note (FRN).

In this section, we shall focus on the valuation of bonds and FRNs. These models will provide tools for pricing fixed-rate and floating-rate financial instruments. In modern capital markets, there is considerable variety in the characteristics of instruments issued. These differences, however, can usually be valued as an extension of these general models.

3.4.1 Bond Valuation

In its basic form, a bond provides its owner with the right to receive a stream of coupons during the life of the bond with the repayment of principal at expiry. These cash flows are fixed over the life of the bond. *Figure 3.7* displays the cash flow profile of a bond.

Figure 3.7
Bond Cash flows

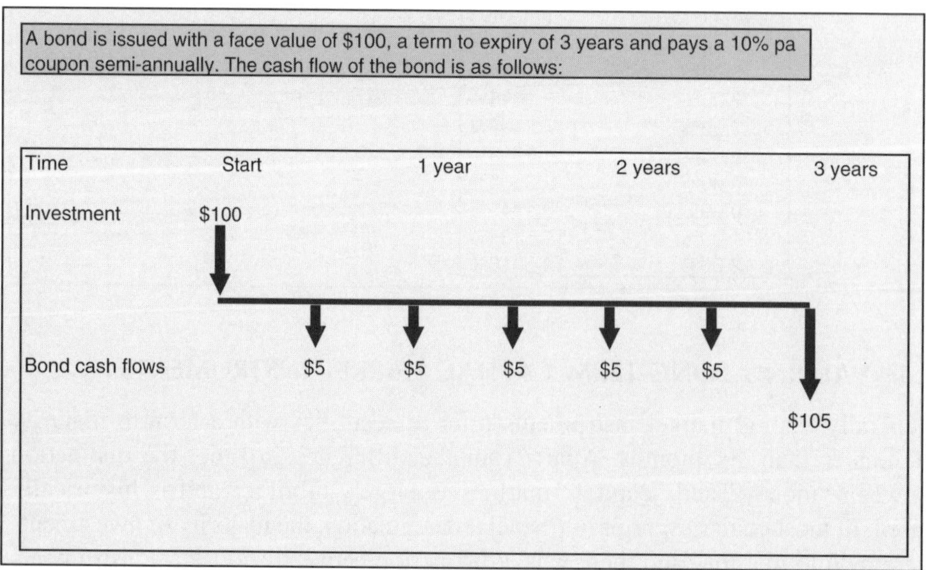

Understanding the valuation of bonds is essential to understanding the valuation of derivative instruments. This is particularly the case with swaps, where bond mathematics is often used and we are often required to alter the bond formula. In the following section, we will work through the derivation of the bond formula.

Given each of the cash flows generated by a bond is a fixed amount at a known time in the future, and providing we can determine an appropriate interest rate, a bond value can be determined by applying the present-value of a single amount. While this is true, if we hold a 30-year US Treasury bond with semi-annual coupons, we would need to perform 60 present-value calculations. Instead, the bond formula makes use of another financial math concept, the *present value of an annuity* to considerably simplify the calculation.

An annuity is a stream of known future cash flows—like the coupon stream of a bond. We know the present value of a coupon stream for n period is given by the following formula:

$$PV = c/(1 + r/m) + c/(1 + r/m)^2 + \cdots + c/(1 + r/m)^n$$

This can be algebraically rearranged to derive the following formula:[4]

$$PV = c \times (1 - 1/(1 + r/m)^n)/(r/m)$$

which can be simplified to:

$$PV = c \times (1 - v^n)/(r/m)$$
$$\text{where} \quad v^n = 1/(1 + r/m)^n$$

If we apply this annuity formula to the coupon and also the present value of the principal amount at maturity, we are able to value a bond. The only additional step is adjusting for accrued interest conventions as demonstrated in the following formula on page 48.

Some example calculations using the bond formula are provided in *Figure 3.8* on page 49.

It is worth noting that in most bond markets, the bond is traded in terms of its current "clean" (also referred to as "capital") price. In Australia, New Zealand and Sweden, bonds are traded according to their yield to maturity. In either case,

[4] If you are interested in the derivation of this formula, see Marshall (1989) p. 78.

Financial Math: Valuing a Bond

Calculating the value per US$100 of face value:

$$PV = v^{f/d} \times (c \times (1 + a_n) + 100 \times v^n)$$

Other calculations:

Accrued interest $= (d - f)/d \times c$

"Dirty" price $= PV$

"Clean" price $= PV -$ accrued interest

Where:

r = yield to maturity as a percent pa

c = coupon paid per period per US$100 face value

n = the number of periods to maturity excluding the next n payment date

m = the number of coupon payments pa

d = number of days from the last coupon payment date to the next coupon payment date

f = number of days from the valuation date to the next coupon payment date

v = $1/(1 + r/m)$

a_n = $(1 - v^n)/(r/m)$.

Related Microsoft Excel functions:

PV: PRICE (settlement, maturity, rate, yld, redemption, frequency, basis)

r: YIELD (settlement, maturity, rate, pr, redemption, frequency, basis)

Interest:ACCRINT (issue, first_interest, settlement, rate, par, frequency, basis)

the same formula is used except that where bonds are traded using price, the formula is solved for yield.

While the bond formula can be used to value a large proportion of "straight" bond issues, there are a number of considerations that need to be made when valuing any bond, including the day count basis and odd coupons.

Day Count Basis

As stated above, day count basis refers to the assumed number of days in a year. In the money market calculations, these can be either 360 or 365. In bond markets there are four main day count alternatives. The table on page 50 summarizes the main conventions while the example in *Figure 3.8* calculates the day count and accrued interest on a bond using each basis.

Figure 3.8
Using the Bond Formula

Suppose you have invested in the following bond:

Bond details	
Settlement date	23-Mar-01
Maturity date	15-Aug-03
Coupon	10.00%
Payment frequency	2

Calculate the value of the bond and the accrued interest assuming a yield to maturity of 8% pa. (Note: assume actual/actual basis.)

r = 0.08
v = 0.96153846
c = 5
n = 4
f = 145
d = 181

LCD = 15-Feb-01
NCD = 15-Aug-01

PV = 105.2698

Accrued interest = 0.9945

Clean price = 104.2753

Price at different yields

Yield to maturity	Clean price
6%	108.8086
8%	104.2753
10%	99.9807
12%	95.9097

Different Day Count Conventions

Day count basis	Description
30/360	This calculation assumes a year has 360 days comprised of 12 months with 30 days each. In the bond calculation, d is given by the number of months between payment dates multiplied by 30 days. The coupon paid is always the annual coupon rate divided by the payment frequency. Determining $(d-f)$ is more complex as each part month needs to be treated, as if there are 30 days. This type of interest convention is common in Europe and is often referred to as the annual coupon basis.
Actual/Actual	The interest accrual is based on the actual number of days elapsed since the last interest payment date $(d-f)$ in an interest period divided by the actual number of days between the last and next interest payment dates (d). The coupon paid is always the annual coupon rate divided by the payment frequency. This method is commonly used in English-speaking countries and includes instruments such as US Treasury Bonds, A$ and NZ$ government issues and UK Gilts.
Actual/360	This method is also referred to as the US Money Market basis because interest is calculated in the same way as for US dollar money market instruments. The interest accrual is based on the actual number of days elapsed since the last interest payment date $(d-f)$ in an interest period divided by an assumed 360 days a year (d). In this method, the coupon payment is not always an even amount.
Actual/365	As for Actual/360 except d is 365 days per annum.

Different Day Count Conventions

Understanding the differences between these methods and knowing how to generate the cash flows created by each alternative is essential for valuing swaps. While Actual/360 and Actual/365 bonds are less common than the other two methods in the bond market, they are, in fact, very commonplace in interest rate swap transactions. *Figure 3.9* shows the differences in accrued interest on bonds with the various day count conventions.

Figure 3.9
Different Day Count Basis

Using the bond shown below, calculate the accrued interest on the settlement date using the four different day count methods.

Bond details

Settlement date	18-May-00
Maturity date	11-Feb-04
Coupon	10.00%
Payment frequency	2

Intermediate calculations

Last coupon date	11-Feb-00	
Next coupon date	11-Aug-00	
Actual days in coupon period	182	
Actual days elapsed	97	
30/360 days in coupon period	6 × 30 =	180
30/360 days elapsed	19 + 30 + 30 + 18 =	97

Accrued Interest calculation

Accrued interest = $(d - f)/d \times c$

Calculation method	Coupon c	Days accrued $(d - f)$	Days in period d	Accrued interest
30/360	5	97	180	2.6944
Actual/Actual	5	96	181	2.6519
A/360	10	96	360	2.6667
A/365	10	96	365	2.6301

Odd Coupons

Another common complicating factor in bond valuation is that the actual first coupon period may be longer or shorter than the payment frequency of the bond would suggest. This arises because bond issues are often made on noncoupon dates. If the issue is made close to what would normally be a coupon date, the issuer may elect to skip this coupon date and any interest accrued from the following interest payment, to reduce administration. This is a *long* coupon date.

On the other hand, the issuer may elect to pay the coupon on the shorter coupon, but it will only pay the accrued interest amount, not the full coupon—a *short* coupon period. In either a long or short coupon period, the underlying mechanics of the bond are the same except that the initial coupon payment will be larger or smaller than the coupon for the remainder of the issue. Further, the time till the next interest payment date (f) and the interest period (d) will be longer or shorter than the day count basis would suggest. If we adjust the formula accordingly we have:

$$v_1^{f/d} \times (c_1 + c \times a_n + 100 \times v^n)$$

Where c_1 is the first odd coupon amount per US\$100 per period, v_1 uses the yield adjusted for the number of days in the odd interest period.

The values of f and d have the same meaning; however, they will relate to the first odd coupon period. An example of this adjustment is shown in *Figure 3.10.*

3.4.2 Floating Rate Note (FRN) Valuation

An FRN is a debt instrument that pays a regular interest amount until its maturity. Unlike a bond, however, the interest payment varies over the life of the instrument as it is reset against a short-term interest rate benchmark at each interest payment date. An FRN is a combination of a money market instrument and a bond: while it pays a coupon based on money market interest rates, like a bond, it repays the principal at maturity and it also pays a fixed interest rate margin until maturity.

In the case of a bond, valuation consists of present valuing a series of known cash flows. With an FRN, the only cash flows we know are the coupon interest payment at the end of the current interest payment period and the repayment of principal at maturity—all of the intermediate coupon payments are unknown. This is shown in *Figure 3.11*, which represents the cash flows of an FRN.

Initially, it appears as though we would need to estimate each of the future floating interest rates to determine the FRN coupon. We can avoid this complexity by breaking the valuation down into three components:

- current interest
- annuity stream
- par bond.

Figure 3.12 divides the FRN into these three components.

Figure 3.10
Odd Coupon Periods

The following bond has a long first coupon period, the coupon due on 15-Feb-00 will be combined with the August coupon.

Bond details	
Issue date	15-Jan-00
Settlement date	23-Mar-00
Maturity date	15-Aug-08
Coupon	8.00%
Payment frequency	2

Calculate the value of the bond and the accrued interest assuming a yield to maturity of 8% pa.

r	=	0.08
r/m	=	0.04
$r \times d/365$		0.046684932
v	=	0.961538462
v_1	=	0.955397341
c_1	=	4.668493151
c	=	4
n	=	16
f	=	145
d	=	213
LCD	=	15-Jan-00
NCD	=	15-Aug-00
PV	=	101.4673
Accrued interest	=	1.4904
Clean price	=	99.9769

Current Interest

This component is the known interest amount which will be paid at the end of the current interest period once the interest rate has been set. If the valuation date is an interest payment date and the new interest rate has not been set, or if this interest period is "ex-interest," (i.e., interest will not be paid for the current coupon period) then this interest amount is zero.

Figure 3.11
FRN Cash flows

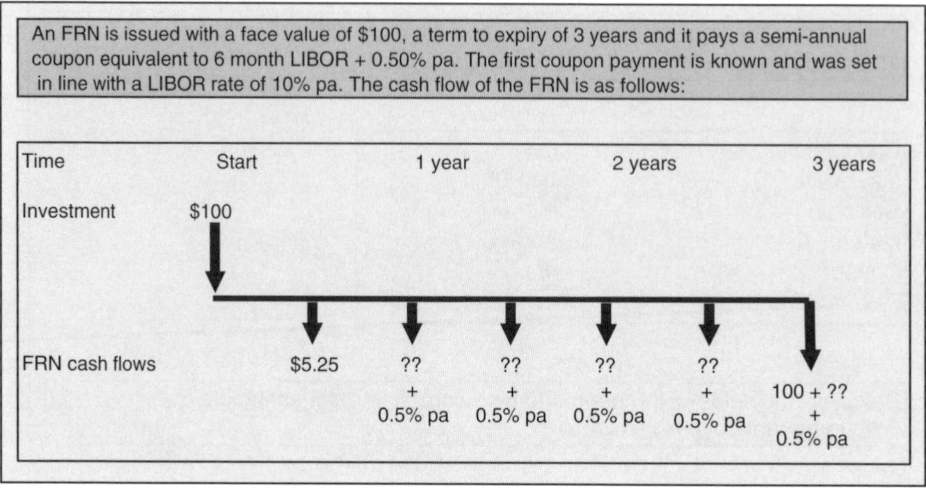

Figure 3.12
FRN Components

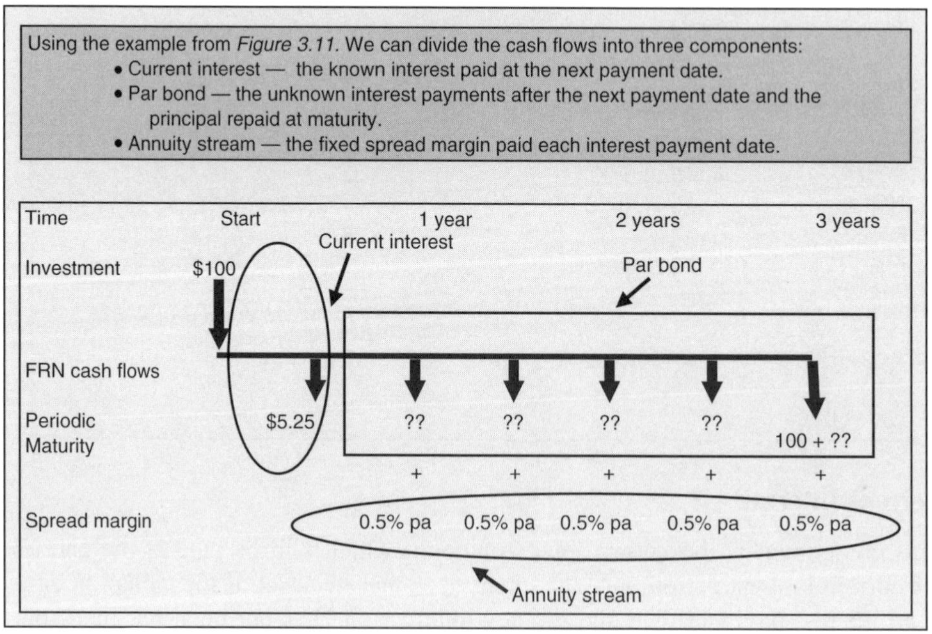

If the interest period is "cum" interest (interest will be paid for the current coupon period) and the interest rate has been set, the interest rate can be calculated. At the beginning of each interest period, the base interest rate (b) will be determined according to a floating rate index such as LIBOR. The interest margin (IM) will then be added (in some cases deducted) from this base rate to determine the coupon interest rate. The coupon payment is then calculated per US\$100 of face value by multiplying this coupon rate by the number of days in the interest period (d) divided by the day count basis (D) of 360 or 365. We can express this as follows:

$$\text{Interest} = (b + \text{IM}) \times d/D \times 100$$

This is equivalent to the interest received on a term deposit and can be valued using the compound interest present value formula.

Annuity Stream

The annuity stream refers to the IM stream over the life of the FRN. While the base interest is unknown, the IM is fixed over the life of the FRN and can be likened to a very low coupon stream on a bond.

The magnitude of the IM reflects the relative creditworthiness of the borrower and also the term of the FRN. Just like interest rates, IMs change over time and when determining the present value of an FRN, we need to incorporate changes in the IM. When valuing an FRN, the IM is compared to the prevailing margin at which the market is trading—this is referred to as the trading margin or TM. If the TM is lower than the IM, there will be a positive cash flow over the remaining life of the FRN equivalent to this difference. If the TM is higher than the IM, then it creates a negative cash flow equivalent to this difference.

Using a bond analogy, we can use the present value of an annuity formula to value the net coupon created by the IM and TM. The IM for the current interest period has already been included in the current interest calculation, hence, it can be ignored in this annuity calculation. As a result, for our purposes we wish to determine the value of all IMs after the next coupon date. We can express this as follows:

$$\text{Annuity stream} = (\text{IM} - \text{TM})/m \times a_n$$

Par Bond

If we remove the current interest and IM annuity stream, we are left with the unknown coupon payments after the current interest period and the principal repayment at maturity. Which we can express as follows:

$$c/(1+r/m)+c/(1+r/m)^2+\cdots+(c+100)/(1+r)^n$$

Where:

c represents the unknown future coupons

r represents the rate at which the coupons are present valued.

This seemingly complex FRN cash flow has a simple outcome. If we look at the formula above, both the values for c and r are estimates of the floating interest rate applying between the next interest period at maturity—that means that while they are unknown, the two interest rates (c and r) are the same. Therefore, all of the cash flows after the current interest period can be likened to a par security—a security where the annualized coupon and yield to maturity are the same.

A feature of par securities is that the present value is the same as the future or principal amount. We can express this as follows:

$$100=c/(1+r)+c/(1+r)^2+\cdots+(c+100)/(1+r)^n$$

provided that, $c=r$

The net result of this reasoning is that we can treat all of these remaining cash flows as a par security as at the next interest payment date. So, for an FRN with a face value of US$100, the value of these cash flows will be US$100 on the next coupon date.

Combining these three elements provides an FRN value as at the next interest payment date. To provide the present value, all three elements need to be added together and then present valued. The interest rate used for the present value should also include the TM. The complete formula is provided on page 57.

A bond has just one yield to maturity, an FRN effectively has *three* types of yield to maturity to incorporate:

- r_b
- r_s and
- TM.

It is important to use the correct yield. The value of r_b is the current rate for the interest index used to determine b from the valuation date to the next interest payment date. If an FRN is based on six-month LIBOR and we are valuing this

Financial Math: Valuing an FRN

Calculating the value per US$100 of face value:

$$PV = \frac{100 \times ((b + \mathrm{IM}) \times d/D + (\mathrm{IM} - \mathrm{TM}) / m \times a_n + 1)}{1 + (r_b + \mathrm{TM}) \times f/D}$$

Other calculations

Accrued interest $= (b + \mathrm{IM}) \times (d - f)/D$

Where:

- r_b = current yield to next interest payment date % pa (e.g., LIBOR)
- r_s = current yield to maturity of the FRN on a security that is equivalent to the security underlying the interest rate (e.g., swap rate)
- b = interest rate set at last interest payment date or issue date % pa
- IM = IM paid relative to b fixed in FRN % pa
- TM = current interest margin paid relative to b % pa
- m = interest payment frequency pa
- n = the number of periods to maturity excluding the next payment date
- d = number of days from the last coupon payment date to the next coupon payment date
- D = days pa (360 or 365)
- f = number of days from the valuation date to the next coupon payment date
- v = $1/(1 + r_s/m)$
- a_n = $(1 - v^n)/(r_s/m)$.

FRN with three months to the next payment date, r_b will be the 3-month LIBOR rate.

Selecting r_s can be a little more difficult. In valuing an FRN, we are determining its replacement cost; r_s is the base rate used to present value the fixed IM cash flows and it needs to reflect our estimate of the floating interest rate over the remaining life of the FRN. If the floating interest rate is based on a common index such as LIBOR, then the swap interest rate prevailing to the maturity of the FRN is appropriate. Obtaining this estimate for less common floating indices, i.e., indices that are not used by the swap market, is difficult.

Figure 3.13 calculates the present value of a FRN.

Figure 3.13
Using the FRN Formula

Suppose you have invested in the following FRN:	
Maturity date	15-Aug-00
Interest margin (IM) % pa	0.5000
Last interest index reset (b) % pa	8.0000
Interest frequency	2
Day count	365

Value the FRN on 15-Jun-2000 given the following inputs:	
Settlement date	15-Jun-00
Current traded margin (TM)	0.2500
Current floating rate (rb)	6.5000
Current swap rate (rs)	7.6000
Current FRN market price per $100 face value	**103.8873**

3.5 INTEREST RATE RISK CALCULATIONS

Valuation of financial assets is the first step in the risk management process. Once the current value of an asset is known, we can examine how this value will change in response to changes in market conditions.

Three important, and commonly used, risk management concepts are:

- duration
- convexity
- point value of a basis point (PVBP).

In this section, we will look at each of these three concepts and examine the mathematics involved.

3.5.1 Duration

Duration is a concept commonly used to describe the effective life of bonds. It is a method of assessing the risk profile of different bonds regardless of differences in term to expiry, coupon rates and yields to maturity.[5]

[5] For more detail on duration, Hull (1991) pp. 124–134.

The duration of an interest-bearing security can be defined as the:

> *The duration of an interest-bearing weighted average time to the receipt of the cash flows—both principal and interest—generated by that security.*

It is expressed mathematically as follows:

Financial Math: Duration

The duration for each US$100 of face value on a coupon date is given by:

$$\text{Duration} = \frac{(c/(1+r/m) + c \times 2/(1+r/m)^2 + \cdots + (c+100) \times n/(1+r/m)^n)}{PV \times m}$$

Modified duration is calculated as follows:

$$\text{Duration}_{\text{MOD}} = \frac{\text{Duration}}{(1+r/m)}$$

Where:

r = yield to maturity as a percent pa
c = coupon paid per period per US$100 face value
n = the number of periods to maturity excluding the next n
m = the number of coupon payments pa
PV = the current PV per US$100.

Related Microsoft Excel functions:

Duration: DURATION (settlement, maturity, rate, yld, redemption, frequency, basis)

We take the bond pricing formula and weight each cash flow by the time factor for each cash flow. The net effect of the calculation is to generate a weighted average time to maturity of the bond. It is worth noting that a zero-coupon security, such as a money market instrument, will have an equivalent term to maturity and duration. *Figure 3.14* provides a duration calculation example.

From a risk management perspective, duration is useful because it provides an estimate of the percentage change in the present value of a security arising from a change in yield to maturity. To perform these estimates, we make use of modified duration as follows:

$$\text{Price \% change} = -\text{Duration}_{\text{MOD}} \times \text{yield change}$$

Figure 3.14
Duration and Convexity

Calculate the price, duration and convexity of the following bond:

Settlement date	15-Nov-00
Maturity date	15-Aug-06
Coupon rate %	8.0000
Number of periods/year—(1, 2 or 4)	2
Yield %	7.0000
Day count basis	Act/Act

Price ex interest	104.6504
Accrued interest	2.0000
Price cum interest	106.6504
Duration	4.6607
Modified duration	4.5031
Convexity (for each 0.01 % change in yield)	3.0155
PVBP per $100 face value	0.0480

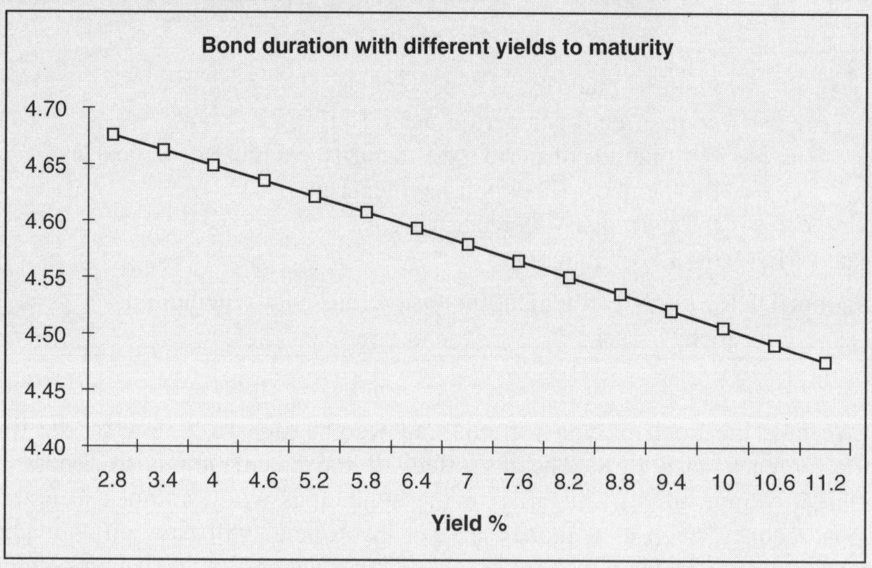

Example

Suppose a bond has a duration of 8.5 years, pays interest annually and has a current yield to maturity of 10% pa. What is the likely percentage change in price from a 1% rise in yield?

$$\text{Price \% change} = -8.5/(1+0.10) \times 0.01$$
$$= -0.0772$$

The price will therefore, fall by 7.72%. These estimates need to be treated with caution, as the duration of a bond is not constant (as is shown by the duration graph in *Figure 3.14*). The estimate is accurate for small changes in yield, such as ±0.01% pa; however, the larger the change, the less accurate the measurement.

The duration concept is an essential part of financial risk management. It is a similar concept to the delta of an option, and it serves a similar purpose as the delta in determining the hedge requirements for bond portfolios. Most interest-bearing securities either have constant duration (zero-coupon securities) or a duration that increases with a fall in interest rates (i.e., most coupon-paying securities). These properties are referred to as nonconvex and positive convexity respectively.

3.5.2 Convexity

As we noted in the previous section, duration is not constant. For a coupon-paying bond, the duration increases as yields fall and decreases as yields rise. This relationship is described as convexity and can be seen in *Figure 3.14.* In this graph, at any given point, convexity is the slope of the duration curve. At a yield of 7% pa, convexity is 3.0155, which means that a 0.01% pa change in yield will alter duration by around 0.0003 years. Convexity can be viewed as the change in duration caused by a change in yield or, said mathematically, as the second derivative of the change in bond price arising from a change in yield.

A security displays convexity when it has more than one cash flow over time. As can be seen from the duration calculation in Section 3.5.1, as interest rates rise, the present value of cash flows with longer to maturity are reduced more than the cash flows closer to maturity. This means that the relative time weighting of later cash flows in the duration calculation falls at a greater rate than nearer cash flows. This is explained in the following example.

Example

Assume that an annual bond pays a coupon of 10% pa and has two years to expiry. Calculate the duration at 10% pa:

$$\begin{aligned}\text{Duration}_{10\%} &= (10/(1+0.10) + (110 \times 2)/(1+0.10)^2)/(100 \times 1)\\ &= (10/1.1 + 110 \times 2/1.21)/(100 \times 1)\\ &= (9.0909 + 181.8181)/(100 \times 1)\\ &= 1.9091 \text{ years}\end{aligned}$$

Recalculate the duration at 20% pa:

$$\begin{aligned}\text{Duration}_{20\%} &= (10/(1+0.20)+(110\times 2)/(1+0.20)^2)/(84.7222\times 1)\\ &= (10/1.20+110\times 2/1.44)/(84.7222\times 1)\\ &= (8.3333+152.7778)/(84.7222\times 1)\\ &= 1.9016 \text{ years}\end{aligned}$$

This example reveals that duration has declined by 0.0075 years. Although this is a small amount, it highlights the cause of convexity. When the yield increased to 20%, the present value of the cash flow decreased by an equal amount in both the bond price (the denominator of the calculation) and the duration (the numerator). The duration weighting of time is, however, also reduced in the second cash flow in the duration calculation; that is, the weighting of 2 was present valued using a factor of 1.21 at 10% pa and 1.44 at 20% pa. This means that as interest rates *increase* the importance of later cash flows decreases at a greater rate than near term cash flows.

> ***Note***
> Most coupon-bearing securities have positive convexity, while zero-coupon securities have zero convexity because their duration is constant, regardless of yield to maturity.

We will come across the notion of convexity often in the following chapters. It can be viewed as a similar concept to the gamma of an option, which will be discussed in Chaper 12.

3.5.3 Point Value of a Basis Point (PVBP)

The concept of point value of a basis point (PVBP) is closely related to the concept of duration, in that it is the dollar value change in the price of an interest-bearing security, arising from a one basis point (0.01% pa) change in yield. Other names for this concept include: dollar value of 1 basis point (DVO1), tick value, bond volatility from a 1 basis point yield change and the hedge ratio. The latter two names can easily be confused with other important concepts and will not be used in this book.

Whereas duration is a measure of percentage price sensitivity for a very small change in yield, PVBP is a dollar value for a discrete change. The procedure for calculating a PVBP for almost all financial assets and financial derivatives is to calculate the present value of the instrument at current market prices and then to recalculate the present value after increasing yields by 1 basis point; that is:

$$\text{PVBP} = \text{present value at } r - \text{present value at } (r + 0.01\% \text{ pa})$$

In the bond example in *Figure 3.14*, the PVBP per US$100 is 0.048. This means that a 1 basis point increase in yield results in a decrease in price of 4.8 cents. To compare the PVBP to the duration, we need to convert it to a percentage by dividing by the current present value and dividing by 1 basis point:

$$\begin{aligned}\text{PVBP as a percentage} &= 0.048/(104.6504)/0.0001 \\ &= 4.5878\end{aligned}$$

As we can see, this is close to the duration calculation.

While PVBP as a concept is straightforward for cash instruments, it is considerably more complex for derivative instruments where the present value is dependant on more than one yield.

The PVBP is widely used as a hedging tool by market participants, because it provides a simple means of comparing the valuation sensitivities of different instruments. For example, if a bank buys a bond with a PVBP of US$2,000 and it wishes to hedge this by selling futures contracts with a PVBP of US$100, then the appropriate number of futures contracts to sell is 20 (i.e., US$2,000/US$100). This method of calculating the hedge requirement is referred to as the "hedge ratio":

$$\text{Hedge ratio} = \frac{\text{PVBP}_A}{\text{PVBP}_H}$$

Where:

PVBP_A is the sensitivity of the asset to be hedged.
PVBP_H is the sensitivity of the instrument used as the hedge.
This calculation is also sometimes called a "volatility match."

Although this type of hedging approach does have a number of limitations, if the two instruments are not perfectly correlated, it represents a robust first step in hedging an exposure. We will investigate some of these limitations in later chapters.

Most interest-bearing financial assets have a "positive" PVBP; that is, a PVBP that rises with a fall in yield. As we saw with duration, most interest-bearing securities have zero or positive convexity. Duration is a percentage value, so even for an instrument with constant duration, the dollar value of that duration (i.e., the PVBP) must *increase* as the present value of that security increases with a fall in interest rates. There are a number of commonly used short-term futures contracts (e.g., Eurodollars) that have a *constant* PVBP and the impact of this is discussed in Chapter 5.

3.6 APPLYING FINANCIAL MATH

Financial math refers to formulae used to value financial assets such as debt securities. Formulae have been developed in order to calculate the current cash value of these financial assets using present-value models. It is important to bear in mind that formulae have been designed for specific securities. When using these formulae, it is possible that the security being valued has different characteristics to the "standard" formula for that type of security.

To assist in identifying the differences between a standard formula and a specific security to be valued, it is useful to break the calculation into four steps:

1. cash flows
2. interest rate
3. present value calculation
4. adjustments.

These steps occur in all of the financial math formulae outlined so far in this book. All securities have cash flows and have an interest rate that represents the rate at which we can buy or sell the security. Depending on the nature of the cash flows of the security, we will apply an appropriate present value calculation and then make any adjustments necessary for conventions, such as interest accrual.

A detailed description of each of these four steps is provided below:

Step 1

Identify cash flows: All financial instruments create future cash flows; these will be the subject of valuation where they can be predicted in advance (e.g., bond coupons and principal flows).

Step 2

Identify the interest rate: If cash flows are to be present valued then an investor must be indifferent to receiving the calculated amount of cash today or in the future. This means that the interest rate used to perform the present value must represent the market interest rate required for the types of cash flows identified in *Step 1*. For example, if we are valuing a 3-year government security paying a fixed annual coupon, then we must present value the cash flows from this security using a 3-year government yield to maturity.

Step 3

Present value the cash flows using the interest rate: Using the appropriate mathematical formula, calculate the present value of the future cash flows.

Step 4

Adjust for interest accrual: Depending on the interest payment convention of the security, adjust the present value calculated in *Step 3* for interest accruals.

When valuing a nonstandard security, it is a useful exercise to review each of these steps in the calculation and look for exceptions to the standard formula. If any differences are identified, we need to alter the formula accordingly. While the possible adjustments can be wide-ranging, it is usually possible to use the general structure of the standard formula and insert an appropriate adjustment. An example of an adjustment to the standard bond formula is provided in *Figure 3.15*.

Figure 3.15
Example Adjustment to the Bond Formula

Difference	Calculation Step	Adjustment
Coupon based on actual days elapsed in a year rather than dividing the annual coupon by the number of periods per annum.	1. Cash flows	Calculate each coupon based on the number of days that have elapsed and present value each coupon.
	2. Interest rate	The interest rate should be for the actual number of days elapsed in a year, not an assumed 360 or 365.
	3. Present value calculation	Each coupon should be present valued individually rather than using the annuity formula.
	4. Accrual adjustment	The interest accrual must be calculated as the coupon rate as a percentage by the actual number of days in the coupon period divided by the actual number of days in the year.

Understanding this valuation process can be useful for physical securities and it becomes an essential part of derivative valuation where there is a very wide variety of pricing conventions. The aim of an adjustment is to avoid too much additional complexity and calculation time. This involves making a minimum number of changes to the standard formulae, and if possible, making the adjustment using other standard calculations. For example, in the present value calculation step in *Figure 3.15*, each of the present values would be calculated using the compound interest formula from Section 3.2.2.

SUMMARY

This chapter explained some basic financial mathematical concepts, which are fundamental for the accurate pricing and valuing of any financial security. The time value of money refers to the fact that money paid or received *now* has a higher value than money to be paid or received in the *future*. This forms the basis of present and future value calculations. Nominal, effective and continuously compounding interest rates are also important concepts and accurate comparison depends upon using the same basis for calculations. We also discussed the derivation of short-term money market and long-term capital market security pricing calculations and we introduced the concepts of duration, convexity and PVBP, as important interest rate risk measurement techniques.

FURTHER READING

Marshall, John. *Money Equals Maths*, Allen & Unwin Australia Pty Ltd 1989.

Das, Satyajit. *Risk Management and Financial Derivatives: A Guide to the Mathematics*, McGraw Hill March 1998.

SELF-TEST QUESTIONS

1. Calculate the future value of $100,000 invested at 6.00% compounded quarterly.

2. Assume an investment earns a nominal semi-annual interest rate of 7.50% pa. What would be the nominal quarterly interest rate?

3. Calculate the future value of $500,000 invested at 5.75% using continuous compounding.

4. A US dollar commercial paper security has a face value of US$1,000,000, a yield of 6.25% and 180 days until maturity. Calculate the present value of this security.

5. Calculate the clean price of the following bond:

Issuer	US Government
Face value	$5,000,000
Coupon	8.00%
Yield	8.50%
Settlement date	Jan 9, 2001
Maturity date	Apr 15, 2010

6. What would be the clean price of the bond above, if its yield is 9.00%?

7. Calculate the price of the following FRN quoted as per $100 face value:

Maturity date	December 15, 2005
Interest margin (IM)	0.6000%
Last interest rate index reset (% pa)	7.75%
Interest frequency	2
Day count	365
Settlement date	Oct 15, 2000
Current traded margin (TM)	0.3000%
Current floating rate	5.5000%
Current swap rate	6.1500%

8. Samantha is a fixed-interest trader and she buys a bond with a PVBP of US$1,800. Bond futures currently have a PVBP of US$200. How many futures contracts does Samantha need to sell in order to affect the hedge?

9. Explain the difference between the *yield* and the *discount* methods of pricing short-term money market securities.

Part 2

Forwards and Futures

CHAPTER 4

The Role of Forward Markets

OVERVIEW

In this chapter, we will discuss forward pricing and valuation issues. By the end of this chapter we will have:

- described the key elements of forward pricing;
- understood the concepts of cash flow timing and the cost of carry;
- applied forward pricing calculations to derive forward prices;
- reviewed the key valuation differences between forwards and futures.

4.1 INTRODUCTION

A forward is an obligation to buy or sell a financial instrument or physical commodity at some date in the future at an agreed price. For our purposes, forwards include over-the-counter (OTC) forward contracts and exchange-traded (ET) futures contracts. The following instruments are included in these two groups that make up forwards:

- foreign exchange forward contracts
- forward rate agreements
- forward bonds
- short-term interest rate futures
- bond futures
- stock index futures
- commodity futures contracts.

Forward contracts represent a starting point for all derivative valuation. As we will see in Parts 3 and 4 of this book, swaps and options can be grouped into portfolios of forward contracts. As a consequence, the valuation of these more complex instruments will be based partly on the forward valuation techniques developed in the following three chapters.

4.2 FORWARD VERSUS CASH TRANSACTIONS

Distinguishing between when a transaction is a cash transaction and when it is a forward transaction is important. We might expect any transaction that settles today to be a cash transaction and anything settling from tomorrow onward to be a forward. Unfortunately, this is not always the case and depending on the underlying financial asset, a cash transaction can range from today for a money market transaction to several weeks, or longer in some securities markets. Some examples of cash instrument settlement days are listed below.

Cash market	Settlement date
Money market transactions	Today
Euromarkets	Today + 2 business days
Foreign exchange	Today + 2 business days
Stock exchanges	Today + 3 business days
Crude oil	Today + 1 month
Some property markets	Today + 6 weeks

All of these represent cash transactions. The market conventions applying to the settlement of these transactions differ, however, according to the individual country. The market convention usually reflects the ease with which settlement can be arranged and/or the relative complexity of changing ownership of a financial asset. For example, money market instruments in most currencies are lodged on electronic networks where both payment and transfer of ownership can occur in a matter of minutes—i.e., same day settlement. However, where change of ownership involves different time zones and bank accounts, such as foreign exchange, or the shipment of commodities in the oil market, or the completion of legal documentation as in property, the time to settlement is necessarily longer.

When considering a forward, the market convention for the time to settlement underlying a cash or spot price has to be known. A forward transaction does not commence until the settlement day passes the cash settlement date. So, in the foreign exchange market, a forward is a transaction that settles after two business days.

4.3 FORWARD PRICE AND VALUATION

A forward contract gives us the right to buy or sell an underlying financial asset at some date after the cash settlement date at an agreed price. The advantage of forward contracts is that they provide a means of fixing the price of an asset, regardless of movements in the cash price between the trade date and the settlement date. Forwards are therefore a means of hedging against adverse market movements.

As in the cash market, a forward price is agreed between the buyer and seller to reflect the relative cost or benefit to both parties of delaying settlement of that transaction. Once this price is agreed, the market replacement cost, or the value of reversing that transaction, will also change as market conditions change. This is an important feature of forwards and derivative valuation in general. There are always two questions to be answered with regards to valuation:

- What is the forward price?
- What is the value of an open transaction based on this price?

The forward price and cash price are usually different. When valuing a forward transaction, we first need to determine the prevailing market price of a forward, and then determine the present value based on that forward price. This is simplified in futures markets, as a transparent forward price is the subject of trading and, in liquid markets, is a fair reflection of the price at which open contracts can be reversed.

Determining the forward price is not only a requirement of valuation, it is also an essential tool in comparing different forward instruments, such as forwards and futures, from the perspective of a market-maker, arbitrager or hedger. For example, suppose we know that the true "fair" forward price of a security is US$100 and the futures market is trading at US$99. This suggests that an arbitrage opportunity of US$1 exists if we buy the futures contract and enter into another contract to sell it forward. Likewise, if we are a market-maker in forward instruments, we need to be able to calculate a constantly updated forward price to quote to our clients. Forward pricing, forward instrument valuation and a comparison between futures and forwards are discussed later in this chapter.

Terminology

Term	Description
Valuation date	The date on which a valuation is being performed (usually today).
Forward expiry date	The date on which the forward contract expires and the obligation to buy or sell forward falls due.
Forward settlement date	The date on which the forward obligations arising from the forward contract must be settled in cash (usually the forward expiry date or soon after).
Forward period	The number of days between the valuation date and the forward expiry date.
Cash or spot price	The price paid on the valuation date for a cash purchase of the underlying asset.
Forward price	The price agreed to be paid for the underlying asset on the forward expiry date.
Asset income	The income paid to the owner of a financial asset, usually during the forward period. Examples of asset income include coupons and dividends.

4.4 DERIVING THE FORWARD PRICE

The easiest way to understand forward pricing is to break it down into its underlying components. Like most derivatives, forward transactions can be reproduced by a series of physical positions.

Calculating the forward price is the same as asking the question—how much should I pay to buy something in the future? To remove the complications sometimes presented by financial instruments, it often easier to understand derivative pricing using a tangible good such as a piece of artwork. In both of the following examples we ignore any compounding effects and we assume that there are no other benefits from the asset apart from those described.

Example 1

Suppose an art dealer offers to sell you a painting today for US$1 million or US$1.2 million in one year's time. Would you buy it today or in one year? Assume the current 1-year interest rate is 10% pa.

In *Figure 4.1* the problem is represented diagrammatically. The art dealer is offering to buy the painting at a cash price of US$1 million or a forward price of US$1.2 million. We wish to take the deal that is most financially beneficial to us.

A useful way of looking at the transaction is in terms of the cash and asset balances. If we buy the painting today, we give up US$1 million. This is financed either by borrowing the funds or reducing the existing cash balance, which at the end of the year incurs an interest cost or reduces interest income by US$0.1 million. While the forward purchase avoids spending cash today, it requires paying US$1.2 million in one year. At the end of one year, both deals give us the same asset, however the cash cost of the forward purchase is US$0.1 million higher than the spot purchase—therefore we would prefer to buy the painting today.

This example illustrates an important concept:

> *A forward transaction can be replicated by purchasing the asset today and borrowing the money to finance it.*

The "fair" forward price is therefore the cash price plus the interest cost over the life of the forward transaction. In this example, the fair 1-year forward price is US$1.1 million.

This example shows the forward price of an asset that provides no cash return in the form of coupons or dividends. Most financial assets provide an income, so we need to incorporate that into our pricing framework. In the following example, we use another tangible asset.

Figure 4.1
Buying a Painting Forward

Your relative position can be summarized by looking at your asset and cash balances:

Spot purchase	**Balance**	**Cash flows**	**Balance**
Assets	Painting		Painting
Cash	–$1 m	–$0.1 m	–$1.1 m
Forward purchase — 1 Year			
Assets	0		Painting
Cash	0		–$1.2 m
Net cash difference of today versus forward			+$0.1 m

Example 2

You are given the opportunity to buy a warehouse as an investment for US$1 million today or US$1.1 million in one year's time. Would you buy it today or in one year? Assume the warehouse is currently earning rental income of 2% pa and you can borrow US dollar for one year at 14% pa.

This time we need to take account of the cash income. In this case, if we buy the property today, we receive US$0.02 million in income, which we do not receive if we purchase the warehouse forward. The rent has the effect of reducing the net cost of "carrying" that property.

Using the same cash balance approach as in the above example, we can see from *Figure 4.2* that while the rental income reduces the net cost of buying the

Figure 4.2
Buying a Warehouse Forward

Spot purchase	**Balance**	**Net Cash flows**	**Balance**
Assets	Warehouse		Warehouse
Cash	–$1 m	–$0.12 m	–$1.1 m
Forward purchase — 1 Year			
Assets	0		Warehouse
Cash	0		–$1.1 m
Net cash difference of today versus forward			–$0.02 m

property, the net cash cost, and the "fair" forward price, at the end of the year, is US$1.12 million. So, in this example we would buy the property forward.

4.5 SOME CONCLUSIONS ABOUT FORWARD PRICING

The two examples in Section 4.4 illustrate the fundamentals of forward pricing. The "fair value" forward price indicates the price at which buyers and sellers are indifferent to buying and selling the underlying asset today or in the future, based on the current market cash price, cost of financing the asset and the expected return on the asset. In other words, the forward price is essentially a summary of the net financial obligations of owning an asset.

The examples also highlight four of the key features of forward prices:

- **Replication** A forward purchase of an asset can be replicated by buying the asset in the cash market, financing the purchase by borrowing the cash required and then receiving any asset income.
- **Fair price** The "fair" forward price is given by the cash price plus the net cost of financing the asset over the term of the forward contract.
- **Interest effect** The interest cost tends to *increase* the forward price versus the cash price.
- **Dividend or coupon effect** Any cash return on the asset over the term of the forward contract tends to *decrease* the forward price versus the cash price.

These four general rules should apply to all forward prices on financial assets, regardless of whether it is an interest rate, foreign exchange or equity product, provided they operate in freely operating markets. It is worth noting that these relationships start to break down when we move away from financial assets, particularly to consumable commodities such as agricultural and energy products. This is because the decision to have the physical commodity today or in the future is not just a financial or investment decision; the decision to buy a commodity today or in the future also has to take into consideration *when* the commodity is required for consumption.

The examples in Section 4.4 were from the point of view of a forward purchase; however, the same logic applies to a forward sale except it works in reverse. In Example 1, if we agree to sell the painting forward, we forego receiving the cash today and any interest earned over the year. Correspondingly, if we sell the painting forward, we want to ensure that we will receive a cash amount that is, at least, equivalent to the cash price plus interest—giving us the same price as suggested by the "buy" example.

The forward price can be "synthetically replicated" using physical transactions. This would be achieved by buying today and borrowing funds in order to finance the purchase over the forward term. There are two main limitations of this method compared to using derivatives. First, the transaction costs of the physical replication are often greater due to the number of extra "legs" and also physical transactions often have higher execution costs than derivatives. Second, forward transactions are a future commitment and are off-balance sheet. The transactions in the physical replication are included in the balance sheet, which has the effect of increasing assets and liabilities and possibly increasing capital costs.

4.6 CASH FLOW TIMING AND THE COST OF CARRY

A cash and forward purchase provides *ownership* of the asset at different times. Providing the only benefit offered by these assets is their income stream and the repayment of principal in debt instruments, this benefit of ownership, now or in the future, is only notional.[1] The forward price incorporates both the net interest cost of holding the asset as well as the asset return. As a result, the difference between cash and forward transactions is only a difference of cash flow profiles:

- **Cash purchase cash flow profile** requires cash today, but it will provide income between today and the forward date.
- **Cash sale cash flow profile** receives cash today but will miss out on any income between today and the forward date.
- **Forward purchase cash flow profile** does not require cash till the forward settlement date and as such misses out on any asset income.
- **Forward sale cash flow profile** forgoes receiving cash till the forward settlement date; however, it will provide income between today and the forward date.

These cash flow profiles illustrate an important part of the use of forward transactions. Any of the four cash flow profiles represent the exchange of cash and an asset. However, if opposite spot and forward transactions are combined (e.g., a spot sale and a forward purchase) then two offsetting cash flows at different points in time are created. In effect, we are creating transactions using an underlying financial asset, which have the cash flow profile of a borrowing or lending. This is a fundamental driving force in forward markets globally and is a key function of transactions such as repos (see Chapter 5) and foreign exchange swaps (see Chapter 6).

[1] This is an important condition of forward pricing. If there are other tangible or intangible benefits of owning an asset, such as the appreciation of artwork, or the ability to use it for consumption, then, unless these factors can be quantified, the forward price is unknown.

Example

Suppose you are the chief financial officer of a small merchant bank that owns US$100 million of liquid government securities. Your organization requires US$100 million in short-term funds over the next three months. The traditional way to finance this would be to borrow in the short-term money market. However, the problem with borrowing funds is that it is influenced by credit status, which in turn affects the actual *cost* of the borrowing. As a small bank, your board of directors does not think this is a viable solution and, in addition, it does not wish to increase the leaverage, or gearing, levels of the bank.

If, however, you entered into an agreement to sell the securities today and then buy them back in three months, you have created the underlying borrowing required. Further, the ability to raise the funds, and the cost of those funds, is primarily determined by the government securities, as opposed to your own credit rating. This type of transaction is often described as "security lending," "sell and buy," "repurchase or reciprocal purchase agreement (repo)," or as a "liquidity swap"—we will refer to it a "repurchase agreement." Both the money market and "sell and buy" transactions are summarized in *Figure 4.3.* The cash flows are identical, although the balance sheet and gearing consequences are very different—with the money market doubling total assets and liabilities while the other security transaction only affects the composition, not the total assets and liabilities.

Whereas the cost of borrowing in the money market is determined by its interest rate, in the security transaction, it will be determined by the difference between the spot and forward price. As we discussed earlier, the forward price of securities is determined by the current cash price plus the net cost of financing those positions. Government securities can be used as collateral in the forward purchase, so the implied interest cost will be lower than the cost of direct money market borrowing.

Repurchase agreements are a balance sheet-efficient and potentially low-cost form of financing for large holders of financial assets. For example, an investment bank that is a market-maker in securities and that holds large bond portfolios will use repurchase agreements to finance its bond holdings in a similar way to the example in *Figure 4.3.* We will discuss the intricacies of repurchase agreements in Chapters 5 and 6.

Cost of Carry

The key pricing concept in forward transactions is the net financing cost of creating a synthetic replica using cash instruments. The usual terminology for this net financing cost is the "cost of carry."

$$\text{Forward price} = \text{Cash price} + \text{Cost of carry}$$
$$\text{Cost of carry} = \text{Interest cost} - \text{Asset income}$$

Figure 4.3
Using Forwards to Raise Finance

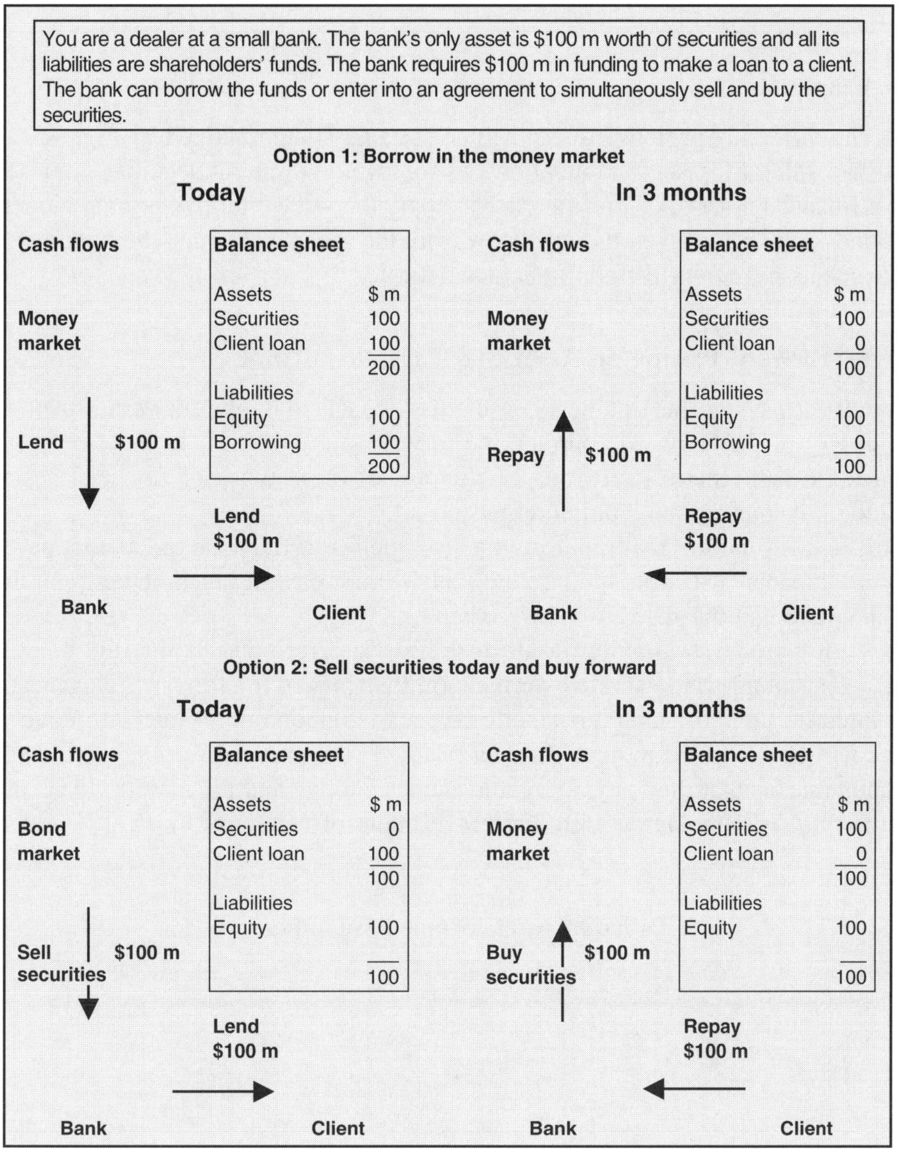

4.7 FORWARD PRICING FORMULAE

In this section we will develop three formulae for pricing forward transactions. These formulae vary depending on the nature of the income steam generated by the underlying financial asset during the period of time to the forward expiry date.

The three forms considered are assets that pay:

- no income
- constant income
- lumpy income.

The difference in these three income streams is summarized in *Figure 4.4*. Distinguishing by asset income allows us to develop three models that can price most financial assets. As a result, we can apply the same "lumpy" pricing models to bonds and shares, even though, apart from the income streams, the underlying instruments have very different characteristics.

4.7.1 Forward Pricing an Asset that Pays No Income

If the asset pays *no* income between the day we calculate the forward price and the expiry of that forward contract, the forward price is equal to the cash price adjusted for the interest cost only. Examples of these types of financial assets include precious metals, commodities and art.

It is worth noting that this formula also applies to financial assets that pay a "lumpy income" (Section 4.7.3 below) but will not pay any income between the pricing date and the forward expiry date.

An important assumption in all of the forward formulae is that the interest rate, r, is a simple interest rate over the term to expiry of the forward. This means the interest rate in the model is an effective zero-coupon rate. While zero-coupon rates will be discussed in detail in later chapters, the important point about zero-coupon rates is that they pay *no* interest between today and the maturity date and there is *no* risk associated with the reinvestment of coupons.

Figure 4.4
Different Asset Income Assumptions

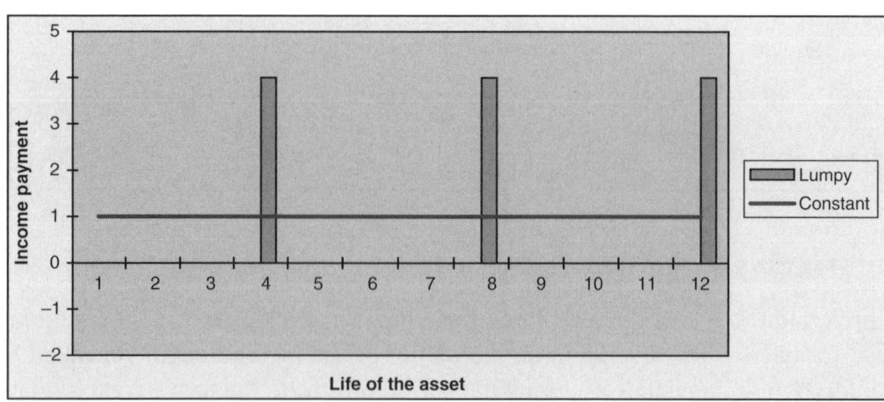

Forward Price: Asset Pays No Income

Using simple interest, the calculation is as follows:

$$F = S \times (1 + r \times f/D)$$

Where:

F = forward price
S = cash or spot price of the underlying instrument
r = interest rate to forward date (preferably zero-coupon rate)
D = day count basis (365 or 360)
f = number of days to the forward expiry date.

In practice, most money market instruments are zero-coupon. So pricing forward transactions with up to six months to expiry is accurate. For longer terms, pricing using a coupon paying interest rate should be viewed as an estimate—accurate pricing requires zero-coupon yields.

4.7.2 Forward Pricing an Asset that Pays Constant Income

The assumption in this formula is that the underlying financial asset pays income at a *constant* rate over the life of the forward contract. In practice this means the asset will pay income for every day that it is held. Examples of this type of instrument include discount money market instruments, foreign exchange and broad-based equity indices.

Forward Price: Asset Pays Constant Income

Using simple interest, the calculation is as follows:

$$F = S \times (1 + (r - q) \times f/D)$$

Where:

F = forward price
S = cash or spot price of the underlying instrument
r = interest rate to the forward expiry date
D = day count basis (365 or 360)
f = number of days to the forward expiry date
q = asset income expressed as a % pa.

4.7.3 Forward Pricing an Asset that Pays "Lumpy" Income

The assumption in this formula is that the underlying financial asset pays income only at *certain points* over its life. Typically, the asset income is accrued over a period and then paid at the end of the period—this gives a "lumpy" appearance to the income cash flows. The important consideration in forward pricing is the number of income payments that will occur during the life of the forward contract.

Examples of this type of instrument include bonds and shares.

Forward Price: Asset Pays "Lumpy" Income

Using simple interest and one income payment, the calculation is as follows:

$$F = S \times (1 + r_1 \times f_1/D) - c \times (1 + r_2 \times f_2/D)$$

Where:

F = forward price
S = cash or spot price of the underlying instrument
r_1 = interest rate to the forward expiry date
r_2 = interest rate between the income payment and forward expiry dates
D = day count basis (365 or 360)
f_1 = number of days to the forward expiry date
f_2 = number of days between the income payment and forward expiry dates
c = asset income expressed in the same units as the cash price.

Figure 4.5 illustrates the forward price calculated for securities with each of the three asset income assumptions.

As the results demonstrate, the nature of the income payment has a considerable impact on the forward price. The "rule of thumb" of the cost of carry concept reveals that where the asset income exceeds the cost of financing the security, the forward price is *lower* than the cash price.

4.8 VALUATION OF FORWARD CONTRACTS

Now that we are able to generate a forward price, we can determine the *present value* of open forward contracts. We divide this calculation into two steps:

- determining the value on the forward expiry date;
- determining the present value.

Figure 4.5
Forward Price Example

You intend to buy a security 180 days forward. The current spot price is $90 and the 6 month interest rate is 6.7% pa (A/360). Calculate the forward price under the following three asset income scenarios:

- no income
- income paid at rate of 8% pa on a constant basis
- a lump sum of $4.50 will be paid in 91 days — assume the 3 month interest rate in three months is also 6.7% pa

(i) No income

$S = \$90 \quad r = 0.067 \quad f = 180 \quad D = 360$

$$F = S \times (1 + r \times f/D)$$
$$= 90 \times (1 + 0.067 \times 180/360)$$
$$= 93.015$$

(ii) Income = 8% pa constant

$S = \$90 \quad r = 0.067 \quad f = 180 \quad D = 360 \quad q = 0.08$

$$F = S \times (1 + (r-q) \times f/D)$$
$$= 90 \times (1 + (0.067-0.08) \times 180/360)$$
$$= 89.415$$

(iii) Income = Lump sum payment of $4.50

$S = \$90 \quad r_1 = 0.067 \quad r_2 = 0.067 \quad f_1 = 180 \quad f_2 = 89 \quad D = 360 \quad c = 4.50$

$$F = S \times (1 + r_1 \times f_1/D) - c \times (1 + r_2 \times f_2/D)$$
$$= 90 \times (1 + 0.067 \times 180/360) - 4.5 \times (1 + 0.067 \times 89/360)$$
$$= 88.44046$$

4.8.1 Valuation on the Forward Expiry Date — The Forward Value

In Chapter 3 we examined the financial mathematics of financial assets. We saw that value is determined by the present value of all future coupon and principal cash flows. As a result, the present value generally represented a premium or discount to the face value of the asset. This is not the case, however, with forward contracts. When a forward contract is initially executed, its value is zero, and the forward price can change to be positive or negative.

A forward contract represents a *commitment* to purchase or sell a financial asset; it is not a financial asset in its own right. Unlike a financial asset, which has value arising from future cash flows, the value of a forward contract only arises from the obligation to buy or sell the underlying asset.

When a bond is purchased forward, the cash flows consist of a cash payment on the forward settlement date and also cash receipts in the form of coupons and principal repayments over the remaining life of the bond.

At the time a forward contract is executed, the forward price and the value of all of the future cash flows created by the bond after the forward expiry date are equal. However, as interest rates change, the relative values of the forward price and all of the future cash flows are different. This relationship for a forward purchase of a bond contract can be summarized as follows:

> Forward value = Forward bond value – Forward contract price
>
> Where:
>
> Forward bond value is the value of all of the cash flows created by the bond after the forward expiry date.
>
> Forward contract price is the price agreed under the forward contract.

As the forward price is fixed, the contract value will change as the forward bond value changes. If the yield to maturity on the bond falls (increasing the forward bond value) then the forward contract value will rise above zero, and if bond yields rise, the forward contract value will fall below zero.

Over the life of the contract, the forward contract price is fixed. The forward bond value is calculated by determining the current forward price using the appropriate formula outlined in Section 4.7. For example, if the forward contract price was US$110 and the current forward price is US$120, the value of a forward purchase on the forward expiry date would be positive US$10.

The value at the forward expiry date is the *difference between the forward contract price and the current forward price*. This relationship is valid for all forward contracts and it also explains the risk profile, or potential for profit or loss, of a forward contract. It is described as the "pay-off" of the forward contract and the graphical representation as a "pay-off diagram." We will utilize this concept regularly in our investigation of derivative value.

Figure 4.6 provides an example of a full forward pricing and valuation exercise. It also illustrates the sensitivity of the contract value to changes in the current forward price using a pay-off graph.

4.8.2 Valuation Today — The Present Value

When dealing with forward contracts, we must make clear whether we are calculating forward or present values. This is an important consideration when comparing futures and forwards and is discussed in Section 4.9 below. A common mistake in using forward contracts is to forget that the forward valuation occurs on the forward expiry date. As we know from the TVM, cash today is worth more than cash in the future. The implication is that, depending on the time period involved, the forward valuation overstates the true present value.

Calculating the present value of a forward contract is performed using one of the present value formulae illustrated from Chapter 3. If we can apply a simple interest rate, then the present value of the forward contract value is:

$$\text{Present value} = \text{Forward value}/(1 + r \times f/D)$$

Where:

r is a simple interest zero-coupon rate between today and the forward expiry date.

As already noted, if the interest rate that is being used is a money market interest rate, it is already a zero-coupon interest rate and can be entered directly into this calculation.

The distinction between forward and present values is demonstrated in *Figure 4.6*.

4.9 VALUATION DIFFERENCES BETWEEN FORWARDS AND FUTURES

Futures contracts are a standardized form of forward contract and can be defined as:

> *A futures contract is a commitment to buy or sell a fixed amount of an underlying financial asset, at a single date in the future.*

> **Note**
> An OTC and a futures contract with the same forward expiry date should have the same forward price.

While the pricing and valuation methodologies for the forwards and futures are similar, there are some key differences that need to be considered. In the following two chapters, we will deal with specific differences between comparable OTC and ET futures contracts.

The differences between OTC and ET futures contracts arise from the fact that futures contracts are subject to daily mark-to-markets (i.e., the price is calculated based on the daily market price) and upfront initial margins. These

Figure 4.6
Forward Price and Valuation

You have entered into the forward contract discussed in *Figure 4.5*, where the asset pays no income at a price of $93.015. You decide to calculate the value of this contract after 30 days have passed. In that time, interest rates have risen to 8% pa and the cash price of the security has declined to $84.2. Calculate the current forward price, the forward valuation and then the present value of this contract.

Current forward price:

$S = \$84.2 \quad r = 0.08 \quad f = 150 \quad D = 360$

$$
\begin{aligned}
F &= S \times (1 + r \times f/D) \\
&= 84.2 \times (1 + 0.08 \times 150/360) \\
&= \underline{87.0067} \\
&\quad \underline{87.0119} \qquad 0.0052
\end{aligned}
$$

Value at forward expiry date:

$$
\begin{aligned}
\text{Forward value} &= \text{Current forward price} - \text{Forward contract price} \\
&= 87.8333 - 93.0150 \\
&= -6.0083
\end{aligned}
$$

Present value of forward contract:

$$
\begin{aligned}
\text{Present value} &= \text{Forward value}/(1 + r \times f/D) \\
&= -6.0083/(1 + 0.08 \times 150/360) \\
&= -5.814484
\end{aligned}
$$

Profit and loss risk profile of the forward contract — the pay-off diagram:

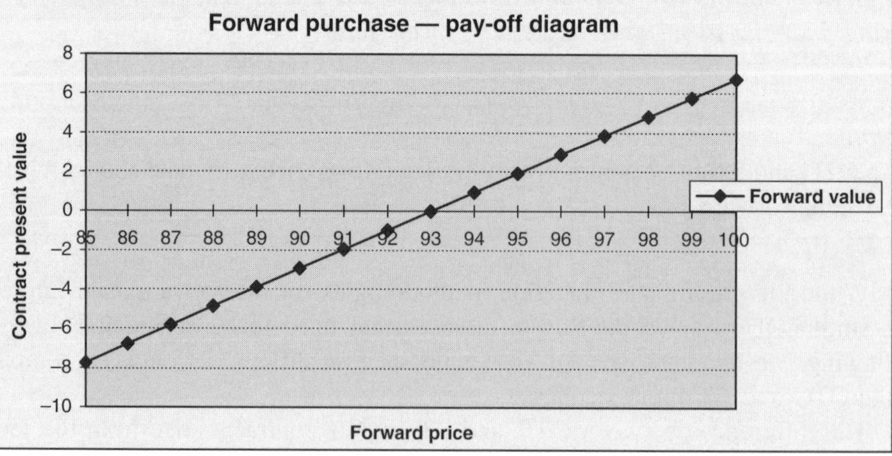

margining requirements exist to minimize the risk for position-takers. The effect of these margins is to alter the valuation of futures versus forwards because they create cash flows prior to the forward expiry date.

> ***Note***
> In terms of the forward valuation/present valuation distinction in Section 4.8, a futures contract generates *present values* rather than *forward values*.

4.9.1 The Impact of Daily Mark-to-Markets on Valuation

While equivalent forward and futures contracts have the same value at the forward expiry date, it is often not realized that prior to the expiry date they have different present values. It is still common practice in many organizations to directly compare the valuations of forward and futures contracts without recognizing this fundamental difference.

The valuation effect of daily mark-to-markets is to create a cash flow timing difference. In essence, the forward values are being paid early. On any given day, the present value of a futures contract (represented by the mark-to-market gain or loss) is the same as the forward value on an equivalent forward contract.

Example

Suppose we buy identical futures and forward contracts for expiry in one year. The difference between the current forward price and the purchase price of the contracts equals a value equivalent to US\$100 profit. The present value of these two instruments will reflect the relative timing of the values. If the 1-year rate is 10% then the present values are:

$$\begin{aligned}\text{Futures profit} &= \text{US\$100}\\ \text{Forward profit} &= \text{US\$100}/(1+10\%)\\ &= \text{US\$90.91}\end{aligned}$$

The difference in these values is important, as the futures contract demonstrates greater sensitivity to movements in the forward price. In this example, for every US\$1 movement in the forward value, the futures contract will generate a present value change of US\$1 while the present value of the forward contract will only change by US\$0.9091.[2]

[2] This will be discussed further in Chapter 5—in particular see Section 5.3.3.

4.9.2 The Impact of Initial Margins on Valuation

Initial margins are a security deposit that must be paid by both buyers and sellers of futures contract to the clearinghouse of a futures exchange. These initial margins are held to cover any losses incurred by a defaulting position holder. The initial margins are set to cover the losses generated by a very large movement in the futures price over a 24-hour period. As a result the more volatile the futures price, the higher the level of initial margins.[3]

The impact of initial margins on valuation depends on the level of initial margins and the rules of the relevant futures exchange clearinghouse with respect to the types of collateral allowed (e.g., cash, government securities, precious metals and shares) and it also depends on the interest payment policy. The cost effective of initial margins can be divided into two categories:

- interest cost
- capital cost.

Interest Cost

Assume the clearinghouse only accepts cash as the initial margin. The cost of the initial margin is equivalent to the interest differential between the cost of funding the initial margin deposit and the interest paid on that deposit by the clearinghouse:

Interest cost = Initial margin × (Funding cost − Clearinghouse rate)

Example

Suppose you enter a futures contract with a face value of US$100 million and an initial margin requirement of US$3 million. Your company borrows at the overnight money market rate while the clearinghouse pays the overnight rate minus 0.50% pa on your initial margin deposit. The additional funding cost of this initial margin is equivalent to 0.75% pa or US$15,000 annually. In terms of the total contract value, this has increased the cost of funding the position by 0.015% pa, or 1.5 basis points.

To incorporate the interest cost into the forward pricing formula we need to *increase the cost of carry* to reflect the additional funding cost of the initial margin. In this example we would therefore add 1.5 basis points to the interest rate, which will have very little effect on the forward price, as is shown in the calculation below, where the forward price from *Figure 4.8* is recalculated using an interest rate of 8.015% pa:

[3] For more detail on how initial margins are derived, see the appendix to Chapter 13.

$$
\begin{aligned}
F &= S \times (1 + r \times f/D) \\
&= 84.2 \times (1 + 0.08015 \times 150/360) \\
&= 87.0119
\end{aligned}
$$

This represents a change in the forward price of 0.0052—a minimal impact on the price. Often the interest cost is ignored by market participants because it is viewed as relatively unimportant.

If the clearinghouse accepts the lodgement of other forms of collateral such as bonds shares, and money market instruments, without imposing any charges—a common practice in most large exchanges—then the interest cost will be the difference between the return on the asset and the organization's cost of funds.

It is quite common for financial institutions to consider that providing securities as initial margin collateral incurs no cost. This is because they already hold the assets used for collateral for regulatory or investment reasons—they are simply re-using existing assets.

Capital Cost

Whether initial margin collateral is in the form of cash or some form of security, there is a capital cost. By providing this collateral to the clearinghouse, the position-taker is potentially transferring ownership of the assets and there is the possibility that those assets will not be repaid—initial margins represent a credit risk to the clearinghouse and some capital has to be set aside for that possibility.

The capital cost will depend on the capital allocation policies of the organization involved. However, for a bank, the Bank for International Settlements' (BIS) capital adequacy standards view the initial margins deposited with the clearinghouse as a deposit with a corporation—requiring an allocation of capital equivalent to 8% of the deposit. Given the assumed cost of capital of an organization, we can calculate the capital cost as follows:

$$
\text{Capital cost} = \text{Initial margin} \times 8\% \times \text{Cost of capital}
$$

So, in the example above, if the cost of capital is assumed to be 20% pa, the annual capital cost is as follows:

$$
\begin{aligned}
\text{Capital cost} &= \$3{,}000{,}000 \times 8\% \times 20\% \\
&= \$48{,}000 \text{ pa}
\end{aligned}
$$

In the same manner as the interest cost, the capital cost is considered an additional cost in financing the futures position and increases the cost of carry. As with the interest cost, the capital cost is often viewed as too small to worry about and is ignored by some market participants.

SUMMARY

Forward pricing and valuation is fundamental to all derivative pricing and valuation, because all derivative instruments can be broken down conceptually into various kinds of forward transactions. Consequently, the concepts outlined in this chapter form the basis for valuation techniques covered throughout this book. Forward pricing occurs *after* the cash settlement date has taken place and this varies according to the types of securities and differing market conventions. This chapter discussed the four main features of forward pricing:

- replication
- fair price
- interest effect
- coupon or yield effect.

We saw how forwards can be synthetically replicated in the physical market and the benefits of the derivative transactions compared to the physical transactions. We also examined how forward pricing and valuation takes into account various cash flow profiles.

SELF-TEST QUESTIONS

1. Lotza Money Inc. will need to purchase a security in 80 days. It expects security prices to rise within that time frame, so it decides to hedge this risk by buying forward. The current spot security price is US$75 and the semi-annual interest rate is 7.55% pa (A/360). Calculate the price of the 180-day forward for the security.
2. What would be the forward price if the synthetic replication was on an asset that paid continuous income at the rate of 6.00% pa?
3. Explain the *key* difference, in terms of pricing, between forwards and futures.
4. Assume you are considering either purchasing an apartment in the city for US$1,200,000 today, or you can purchase it for US$1,300,000 in one year's time. Assume the apartment currently earns rental income of 4% pa and you are able to borrow funds at 12% pa. Would you choose to purchase now or in one year's time? Show all workings.

5. What is the cost of carry of the transaction in Question 4 above?
6. Assume a forward contract price is US$200 and the current forward price is US$220. What would be the value of a forward purchase on the forward expiry date?
7. Explain the relationship between forwards and futures contracts.
8. How does daily mark-to-marketing effect the valuation of futures contracts?

CHAPTER 5

INTEREST RATE FORWARDS

The models developed in this chapter are saved as Microsoft Excel™ files in the enclosed disk.

OVERVIEW

This chapter develops pricing and valuation models for the four major forms of interest rate forwards:

- forward rate agreements (FRAs)
- short-term interest rate futures
- bond forwards
- bond futures.

5.1 INTRODUCTION

As we saw in Chapter 1, interest rate forwards and futures represent the largest single category of volume in financial derivatives. This reflects the importance of these instruments as a day-to-day hedging and trading tool for financial markets participants.

In this chapter, we will develop pricing and valuation models for forward and futures contracts on interest-bearing financial assets.[1] These models will be divided into categories reflecting the different characteristics of forwards on short-term and long-term debt securities.

Our starting point is the generalized models developed in Chapter 4 that shall be adapted to the specific cash flow and convention characteristics of each instrument.

[1] Another description of the underlying assets is "debt securities."

5.2 FORWARD RATE AGREEMENTS (FRAS)

5.2.1 General Description

Forward rate agreements (FRAs) are the predominant form of OTC forward on short-term interest rate securities. They represent an agreement between two parties to "fix" the interest rate on an underlying short-term security at a future date. FRAs do not have physical delivery; instead, any profits and losses are realized by way of a cash settlement at the end of the forward period. While the underlying instrument in an FRA is usually a short-term instrument with a term of three or six months the forward period can range from one month to several years. An FRA is agreed in terms of a forward interest rate as opposed to a forward price and the pricing formula must be adjusted to reflect this.

In most countries, the liquidity of FRAs is very high with most financial institutions providing market-making services. Standard documentation and dealing terms and conditions have been developed in most countries, reflecting the level of activity.[2] A summary of the general terms and conditions is provided in *Figure 5.1*.

Figure 5.1
General FRA Terms and Conditions

Item	Description
Broken period	A settlement period which differs in length from that used in fixing the interest settlement rate.
Buyer/borrower	The party wishing to protect against a rise in interest rates.
Cash settlement	There is no delivery under an FRA, instead any profits or losses are realized as a cash settlement on the settlement date.
Contract amount	The notional sum on which the FRA is based (i.e., the principal).
Contract/trade date	The date, the FRA is entered into.
Contract rate	The rate of interest agreed between the parties on the contract date (i.e., the Forward rate).
Maturity date	The date that the settlement period ends (i.e., the maturity date of the security which notionally underlies the FRA).
Run	The period or term of the notional underlying security, usually three or six months.
Seller/lender	The party wishing to protect against a fall in interest rates.
Settlement date	The expiry of the forward period, the start of the notional underlying security and the day the settlement sum is paid.
Settlement period	The term of the notional underlying security represented by the number of days between the settlement date and the maturity date.
Settlement rate	The mean rate quoted by the specified reference banks for the settlement period of the notional underlying security. In US$-based FRAs this is commonly given by the Reuters page "LIBO."
Settlement sum	The amount representing the difference between interest calculated at the contract rate and the settlement rate.
Source: British Bankers Association and Australian Financial Markets Association AFMA	

[2] Examples of this documentation and terms and conditions can be obtained from most bankers' associations or the local branch of ISDA in the relevant country or the ISDA web site. Otherwise see Das (1994) pp. 89–96.

In an FRA, the two parties agree to the interest rate (the forward rate) applying to a notional principal amount of an underlying money market security at a forward settlement date. Depending on how the relevant interest rate moves between the trade date and the forward settlement date, one of the parties will owe the other party a net settlement amount equivalent to the difference between the forward rate and the actual rate for the forward settlement date. The party that benefits from a *fall* in interest rates is defined as the lender or seller of the FRA. The other party, which benefits from a *rise* in interest rates, is the borrower or buyer of the FRA.

FRAs are normally quoted in terms of monthly combinations of the time to the forward settlement date and the time to maturity of the notional underlying security. For example, an FRA with one month to forward settlement on a 3-month security is referred to as a "1 × 4." On quote vendor services such as Reuters and Bloomberg, FRA dealers generally provide indications of FRA rates in terms of the standard combinations as follows:

Tenor	**Rate**	**Description of Forward**
1 × 4	7.35	A 3-month security starting in one month
3 × 6	7.25	A 3-month security starting in three months
6 × 9	7.23	A 3-month security starting in six months
3 × 9	7.24	A 6-month security starting in three months
6 × 12	7.20	A 6-month security starting in six months

An example of an FRA transaction starting in three months on a 3-month security is summarized in *Figure 5.2.*

Figure 5.2
A 3 × 6 Forward Rate Agreement

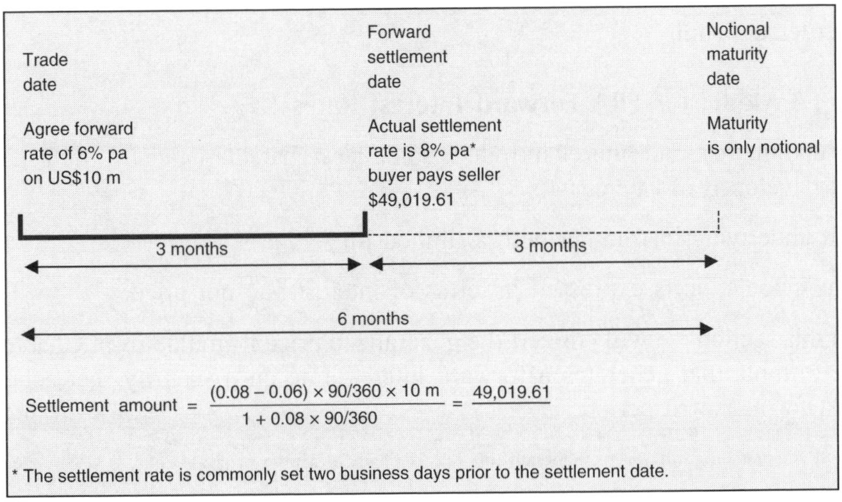

Trade date

Agree forward rate of 6% pa on US$10 m

Forward settlement date

Actual settlement rate is 8% pa* buyer pays seller $49,019.61

Notional maturity date

Maturity is only notional

3 months

3 months

6 months

$$\text{Settlement amount} = \frac{(0.08 - 0.06) \times 90/360 \times 10\text{ m}}{1 + 0.08 \times 90/360} = \underline{49{,}019.61}$$

* The settlement rate is commonly set two business days prior to the settlement date.

5.2.2 Synthetic Replication of an FRA

To understand the pricing of FRAs, we will look at how an FRA can be synthetically replicated using cash instruments. In the example in *Figure 5.3*, the buyer/borrower is agreeing to the interest rate of a 3-month borrowing commencing in three months' time. This can be replicated by borrowing on the trade date for six months and investing the funds raised for three months, until the forward settlement date, as is shown in *Figure 5.3*.

As with any forward transaction, a cost of carry will be created depending on the difference between the 3- and 6-month interest rates. The forward interest rate will be given by the 6-month interest rate adjusted for the cost of carry. For example, if the 6-month interest rate is 5.75% pa and the three month rate is 5.5% pa, the cost of carry is 0.25% pa.[3] The forward interest rate is consequently 6.00% pa. At the end of three months there has been a net interest cost of US$6,250, which effectively means the principal amount of the original borrowing remaining is US$9,993,750.

To replicate the cash settlement of the FRA on the forward settlement date, the borrowing is repaid three months early using the principal amount available at three months. The cost of repaying this borrowing is the present value of the principal or interest accrued at the end of the borrowing. The net cash flow arising from repaying the borrowing is US$48,897.06, or approximately the same as the same strategy using an FRA in *Figure 5.3*.

Using the terminology developed in Chapter 4:

- the forward rate in this example is the forward price and is derived using the cost of carry concept;
- the settlement sum or amount is the same as the forward value;
- the present value of an FRA is given by taking the present value of the settlement sum.

5.2.3 A Model for FRA Forward Interest Rates

FRAs and interest rate futures introduce some new characteristics for the general model developed in Chapter 4:

- an underlying instrument with a limited life;
- the calculation is expressed in terms of interest rate not price.

In this section we will convert the generalized price formulae from Chapter 4 into a formula that generates a forward interest rate on a security that accrues interest for a limited period.

[3] To avoid compounding differences, although this rate is fixed for a term of six months, it is compounded quarterly.

Figure 5.3
Synthetic Replication of an FRA Buyer/Borrower Position

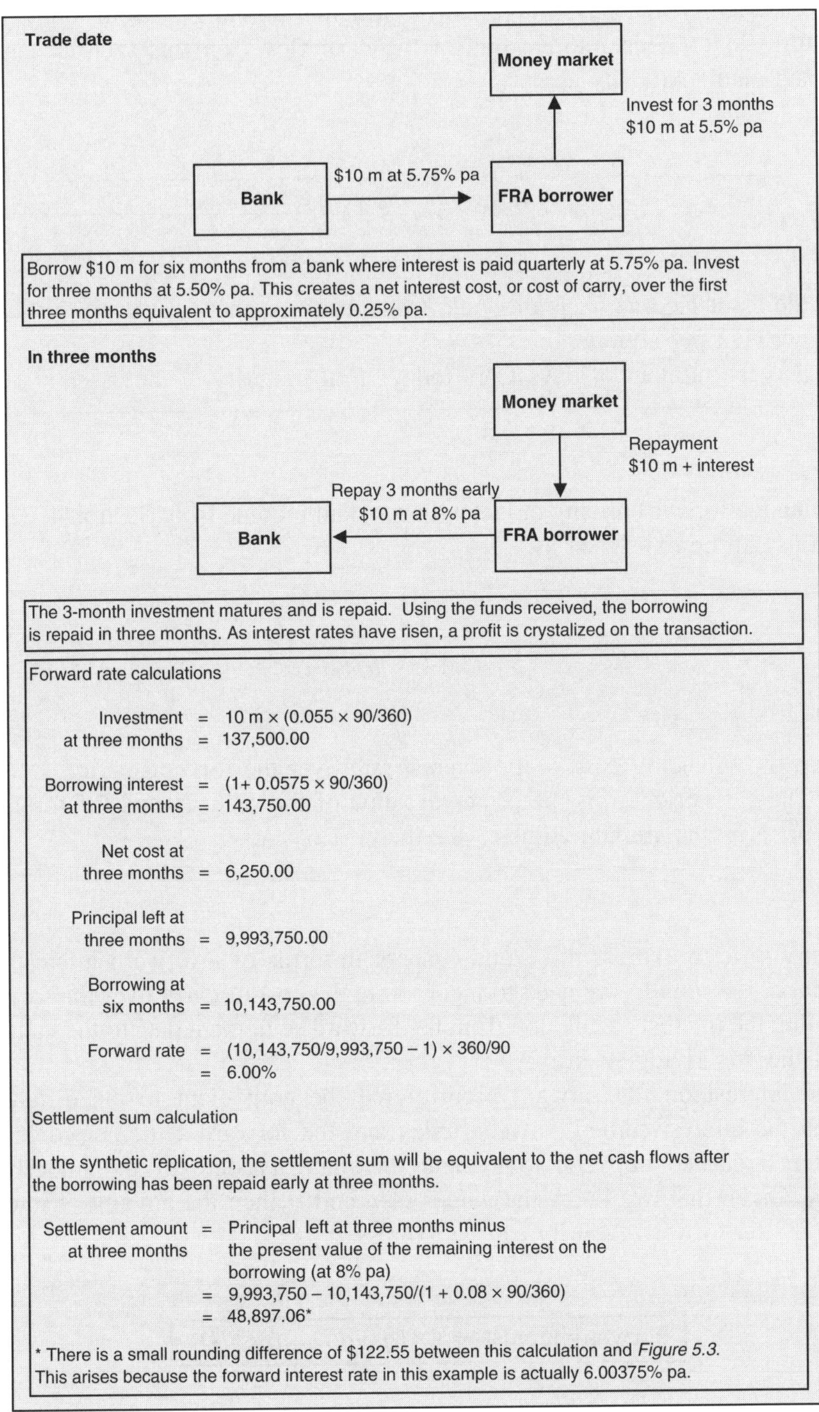

FRAs are instruments in which the underlying asset is cash providing a constant income in the form of interest payments. We know that the underlying asset is a security that pays interest on a principal amount, S, from today, until its maturity date. This future value of the cash flows on this security can be expressed mathematically as:

$$FV = S \times (1 + q \times d/D)$$

Where:

the asset income, q, is the yield to maturity on the asset expressed as a per cent per annum.
d is the number of days from today, until maturity of the asset.

Using the forward pricing model with constant income from Section 4.7.2, we know this can be expressed as:

$$F = S \times (1 + (r - q) \times f/D)$$

Where:

r, the financing cost, is the interest rate over the forward period.
The cash price, S, is the principal value of the security and the forward price is this amount adjusted for the cost of carry.

Our aim is to express this same concept in terms of a forward interest rate calculation. Essentially, we need to incorporate the cost of carry over the forward period into the interest calculation from the forward settlement date to the maturity date of the underlying security.

The interest on the forward security will be equivalent to the difference between the interest earned between today and the forward settlement date and the interest earned between today and the maturity date of the underlying security. Given that, we know the values of q and r, then the amount of interest earned by the forward security can be expressed as:

$$\text{Forward interest} = S \times (q \times d/D - r \times f/D)$$

The forward interest rate can then be expressed as:

$$\text{Forward rate} = \frac{\text{Forward interest}}{\text{Forward price}} \times \frac{D}{(d-f)}$$

If we insert the formulae above, then we have:

$$\text{Forward rate} = \frac{S \times (q \times d/D - r \times f/D)}{S \times (1 + (r-q) \times f/D)} \times \frac{D}{(d-f)}$$

which simplifies to:

$$\text{Forward rate } (r_f) = \frac{(q \times d/D - r \times f/D)}{(1 + (r-q) \times f/D)} \times \frac{D}{(d-f)}$$

This formula approximates the calculation performed in *Figure 5.4*. However, it ignores the timing of cash flows and the compounding of interest. In most forward interest rate calculations, interest rates r and q have different compounding frequencies, which means they cannot be directly compared.

A common method of avoiding the compounding problem is to convert the interest rates into continuously compounding interest rates (see Section 3.2.3). This avoids any compounding differences and simplifies the forward rate calculation.

Figure 5.4
Forward Rate Agreement Calculator

Spreadsheet example

Field	Cell	Cell : Formula
Inputs		
Trade date	01-Nov-00	$E$8 :
Forward settlement date	30-Jan-01	$E$9 :
Underlying maturity date	30-Apr-01	$E$10 :
Spot rate to forward settlement date %	5.5000	$E$11 :
Frequency (1, 2 or 4)	4	$E$12 :
Interest rate for maturity %	5.8050	$E$13 :
Frequency (1, 2 or 4)	2	$E$14 :
Outputs		
Term to forward settlement in days (f)	90	$E$16 : =+E9–E8
Term to maturity in days(d)	90	$E$17 : =+E10–E9
Continuous rate to settlement date % (r)	5.4625	$E$18 : =LN(E11/(E12*100)+1)*E12*100
Continuous rate to maturity % (q)	5.7224	$E$19 : =LN(E13/(E14*100)+1)*E14*100
Forward rate % —continuous compounding	**5.9822**	**$E$20 : =(+E19*(E10–E8)–E18*(E9–E8))/(E10–E9)**
—quarterly compounding	6.0271	$E$21 : =4*(EXP($E$20/(4*100))–1)*100
—s.annual compounding	6.0725	$E$22 : =2*(EXP($E$20/(2*100))–1)*100
—annual compounding	6.1647	$E$23 : =(EXP($E$20/100)–1)*100

We know that the future value of using a continuous rate is as follows:

$$FV = S \times \exp(q \times d/D)$$

Further, we know that the future value of an amount invested for the full term, d, and an amount invested for the combined term of f and $(d-f)$ must be the same. Using the future value formula, we can express this as follows:

$$S \times \exp(q \times d/D) = S \times \exp(r \times f/D + r_f \times (d-f)/D)$$

If we cancel S and take the natural logarithm of both sides of this equation, this simplifies to:

Forward Interest Rate: Continuous Compounding

$$r_f = \frac{q \times d/D - r \times f/D}{d/D - f/D}$$

Where:

r_f = forward interest rate % pa
r = interest rate to the forward settlement date % pa
q = interest rate to the maturity date % pa
D = day count basis (360 or 365)
f = number of days to the forward expiry date
d = number of days to the maturity date of the underlying security.

Examples of underlying assets: FRAs and short-term interest rate futures.

Market interest rates are rarely quoted in continuously compounded form; to use this model, we need to convert to and from continuously compounded rates. Refer to Section 3.3.3 for the conversion calculations. *Figure 5.5* provides an example of a spreadsheet that calculates forward interest rates using the continuous compounding method.

The approach in this model is to take the interest rates based on market rates, and adjust them to continuous rates to calculate the forward rate. Once the continuously compounded rate has been calculated, this can be re-converted to any compounding basis required.

5.2.4 A Model for FRA Valuation

The value of an FRA on the forward settlement date is the difference between the agreed contract rate in the FRA and the prevailing reference interest rate for the remaining term to maturity of the underlying security (the settlement rate).

Figure 5.5
Forward and Present Value of an FRA

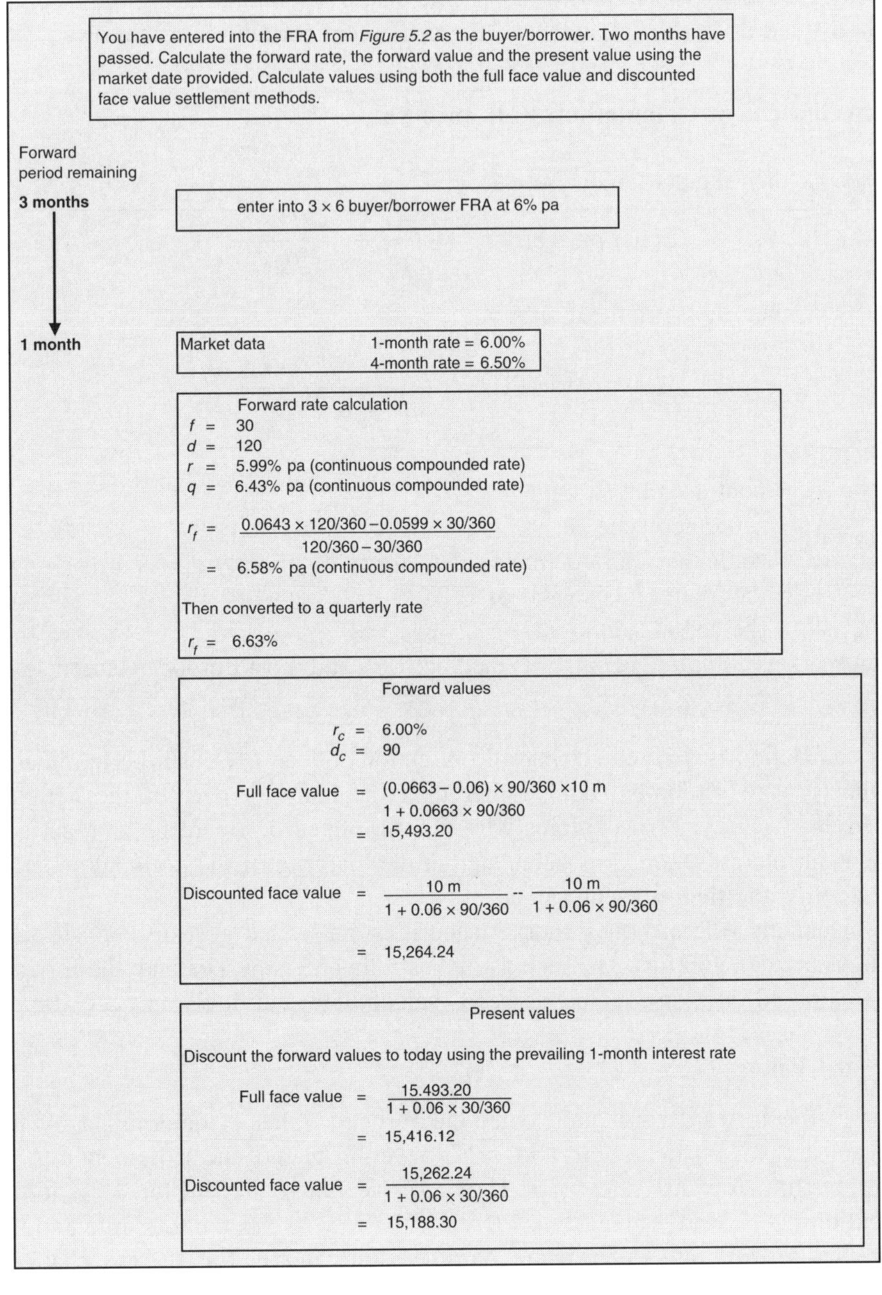

There are two general methods of calculating the forward amount, depending on the conventions in the money market.[4] In most markets, where money market securities are traded in terms of face value or are discounted using the discount method, such as in the US and UK, the settlement formula is as follows:

FRA Settlement Calculation: Full Face Value

If $r_s > r_c$, then the settlement sum is:

$$\text{Seller pays buyer} = \frac{(r_s - r_c) \times d_c / D \times S}{1 + r_c \times d_c / D}$$

If $r_s < r_c$, then the settlement sum is:

$$\text{Buyer pays seller} = \frac{(r_c - r_s) \times d_c / D \times S}{1 + r_c \times d_c / D}$$

Where:

r_c = contract rate % pa
r_s = settlement rate % pa
d_c = settlement period (days till maturity of underlying security)
D = day count basis (360 or 365)
S = the contract amount.

FRA markets commonly using this method: US$ and most European currencies.

This calculation is derived so that all obligations of the FRA can be terminated on the forward settlement date, rather than the maturity date of the notional underlying security. That explains why the difference between the contract and settlement interest amounts is calculated at the maturity of the notional underlying security and then present valued.

In markets where money market securities are traded at a discount to face value using the yield method, such as in Australia and New Zealand, the forward value is based on a discounted proceeds calculation as follows on page 103.

Forward Value

Prior to the forward settlement date, the forward value is determined by the relevant settlement calculations above. However, instead of the settlement rate, r_s, the prevailing forward rate, r_f, is used. As we noted in Chapter 4, at initial execution the forward value of an FRA will be zero as the contract rate and the prevailing forward rate are the same. As time passes and the forward rate changes,

[4] For a review of the different money market conventions, see Chapter 3 Section 3.3.

FRA Settlement Calculation: Discounted Face Value

If $r_s > r_c$, then the settlement sum is:

$$\text{Seller pays buyer} = \frac{S}{1 + r_c \times d_c/D} - \frac{S}{1 + r_s \times d_c/D}$$

If $r_s < r_c$, then the settlement sum is:

$$\text{Buyer pay seller} = \frac{S}{1 + r_c \times d_c/D} - \frac{S}{1 + r_s \times d_c/D}$$

Where:

r_c = contract rate % pa
r_s = settlement rate % pa
d_c = settlement period (days till maturity of underlying security)
D = day count basis (360 or 365)
S = the contract amount.

FRA markets commonly using this method: A$ and NZ$

so will the forward value of the FRA. To illustrate this point, *Figure 5.5* extends the previous example and examines the change in the value of the FRA contract over the forward period using both settlement calculations.

Present Value

The present value of an FRA is easily calculated, once the forward value has been generated using the standard present value formulae. An example of this calculation is provided in *Figure 5.6.*

As already noted, the present value should be calculated using a zero-coupon interest rate.

5.2.5 FRA Risk Characteristics[5]

An FRA is the right to purchase or sell a short-term money market instrument at some date in the future. Correspondingly, the sensitivity to movements in interest rates of an FRA is very similar to the underlying money market instruments.

In the case of an FRA, the duration and convexity is equivalent to the underlying instrument. The PVBP, however, is less than that of the underlying instrument. An FRA generates gains and losses on the forward settlement date equivalent to the underlying security. However, these amounts are present valued in the PVBP and so are consequently smaller.

[5] To review the concepts in this section, go to Chapter 3, Section 3.5.

Figure 5.6
Synthetic Replication of a Sold Eurodollar Futures Position

In the following example, the forward interest rate provided by a sold Eurodollar position is compared to the forward interest rate provided by a Forward Rate Agreement. The Eurodollar contract has a term of 90 days and it expires in one year. It is sold today at a price of 92.74. Over the year, interest rates fall and the futures price converges to a 3-month rate of 5% pa. The table summarizes the resulting cash flows by quarter.

To simplify the analysis, all interest rates are continuously compounded and converted to a 365-day basis. Also the futures price is assumed to remain steady until the end of the quarter at which time it falls to the price shown in the table.

Dates	
Trade date	Oct-24-01
Forward settle	Oct-24-02
Maturity date	Jan-22-03

Market rates	
Overnight/3-month/1-year =	6.00%
1.25 year rate =	6.25%

Implied FRA rate calculations		
f	365	
d	455	Forward rate = 7.2639%
r	6.00%	
q	6.25%	

		Interest rates			Synthetic replication		Futures replication				
	Qtr	Overnight rate and 3 mth rate	Futures price	Current fwd rate	Borrow for 1.25 years @ 6.25%	Invest for 1 year	Mark-to-market	Funding requirement	interest on initial margins (o/n—1% pa)	Quarterly interest	Total interest
Today	0	6.00%	92.74	7.26%	1,000,000.00	(1,000,000.00)		(500.00)			
	1	6.75%	92.30	7.70%			1,100.00	600.00	8.51	18.72001	
	2	7.50%	91.86	8.14%			1,100.00	1,718.72	9.46	41.99346	
	3	8.25%	91.42	8.58%			1,100.00	2,860.71	10.42	70.03446	
Forward	4	9.00%	91.00	9.00%		1,061,836.55	1,050.00	3,980.75	11.38	101.9596	
maturity	5	9.00%			(1,081,026.40)			4,082.71	11.38	104.2797	336.9872

Effective forward rate from futures contract		
Investment return after 1 year	=	1,061,836.55
Initial borrowings after 1.25 years	=	1,081,026.40
Extra funding cost of futures	=	(336.99)
Total borrowings after 1.25 years	=	1,080,689.41
Effective interest cost	=	7.1374%
Difference between FRA and futures	=	−0.1264%

An example of the PVBP is provided later in the chapter in *Figure 5.10* where an FRA PVBP is calculated and compared to short-term interest rate futures contracts.

5.3 SHORT-TERM INTEREST RATE FUTURES

5.3.1 General Description

Short-term interest rate futures represent standardized, exchange-traded forward contracts on money market instruments. In general, most major currencies have one futures contract on a tradeable short-term money market instrument such as a bank deposit or bank bill. The pricing and valuation of these instruments is very similar to FRAs and the two markets can often be viewed as direct substitutes. The global volume in these instruments is enormous, representing the largest single category of futures contract.

The benchmark contract for short-term interest rate futures is the Eurodollar contract traded on the Chicago Mercantile Exchange (CME). The Eurodollar contract is the most heavily traded, reflecting its status as the primary hedging vehicle for short- to medium-term exposures. It is also traded on the London International Financial Futures and Options Exchange (LIFFE) and the Singapore Exchange. The Singapore Exchange contract is fungible with the CME contract, which means contracts traded on the two exchanges can be offset against each other.

The Eurodollar contract was the first global short-term futures contract listed in 1981. Most other short-term interest rate futures contracts have been a copy of the Eurodollar contract with only different currency, settlement interest rate and face value. The Australian and New Zealand dollar bank bill contracts traded on the Sydney Futures Exchange (SFE) are the only contracts that have different valuation formulae.

In order to familiarize ourselves with short-term interest rate contracts, we will firstly review the features of the Eurodollar contract and then examine the differences with other contracts.

Eurodollars

The Eurodollar is a cash-settled contract on a 3-month Eurodollar time deposit. The name "Eurodollar" derives from the fact that it is a forward contract on a US dollar money market instrument traded in Europe (or London to be more specific). The importance of the contract reflects the importance of the US dollar in global financing and the willingness of US-based market participants to use futures.

The CME lists contracts to expire in quarterly resets in March, June, September and December. Currently, there are 40 consecutive quarters listed; that is, expiries out to ten years. The Eurodollar is mainly traded by corporations, banks and fund managers with short-term interest rate exposures. However, a substantial driving force behind Eurodollar volumes is from organizations with medium-term exposures such as interest rate swap market-makers.

The Eurodollar contract expires on the third Monday of the delivery month and is cash-settled against 3-month LIBOR rates in a similar way to a US dollar FRA. If the current month is not a quarterly delivery month, then a single spot contract is also listed to ensure traders have a very short-term instrument. For example, after the March contract expires an April contract is listed. This spot contract concept is currently only offered on the Eurodollar.

The price of a contract is expressed as:

$$\text{Futures price} = 100 - \text{Interest rate} \times 100$$

So, if the current interest rate for a Eurodollar deposit starting on the futures expiry date is 5.00% pa, then the futures price is 95.00. The aim of quoting in terms of price rather than yield is primarily to keep interest rate contracts in line with other price-based contracts on bonds, shares and commodities.

A buyer of a Eurodollar contract gains, if the futures price rises (interest rate falls) above the price at which they purchase it and the seller gains if the price falls (interest rate rises).

> ***Note***
> Be careful, when comparing futures to FRAs as the terminology is opposite—a Eurodollar futures *buyer* is equivalent to an FRA *seller/lender* because they both benefit from a *fall* in interest rates.

The major features of the Eurodollar contract are summarized below:

Summary of Eurodollar Futures Specifications

Feature	Description
Underlying	90-day Eurodollar time deposit
Face value	US$1,000,000
Delivery months	March, June, September, December and spot month
Delivery method	Cash settled
Settlement rate	LIBOR rate for 3-month Eurodollar deposits on the last trading day
Last trading day	Third Wednesday of the delivery month
Quotation method	100 minus the rate of interest
Valuation formula	Term deposit
Tick size	The value of each price point is US$25
Margining	Initial margin (currently US$500/contract) and daily mark-to-market

The details of most of the other short-term interest rate contracts are similar except for differing face values as is summarized below:

Contract	Exchange	Face Value
90-day T-Bills	CME	1,000,000
Bank accepted bills	SFE	1,000,000
3-month Euro-Swiss franc	LIFFE	1,000,000
1 and 3-month Euribor futures	EUREX	1,000,000
3-month Euro	LIFFE	1,000,000
3-month sterling interest rate	LIFFE	500,000
3-month Euro-yen	TIFFE	100,000,000

For most contracts, the underlying instrument is the same as the Eurodollar; that is, a 3-month deposit on a discount security where interest is calculated using the discount method (see Section 3.3.2).[6] However, in the case of the SFE contract, the underlying instrument is a bank bill, which is a discount security, and is valued using the yield formula (see Section 3.3.2). This has an impact on valuation and will be discussed in Section 5.3.3.

5.3.2 A Model for Futures Prices

The price of a futures contract is equal to 100 minus the forward interest rate. So, the futures pricing model is based on the forward pricing models from Chapter 4 and the FRA model from Section 5.2.3.

The method of synthetically replicating a futures contract is exactly the same as an FRA (see Section 5.2.2). However, as we have already noted, futures contracts have a different cash flow profile to similar forward contracts, because of initial margins and the daily mark-to-market of gains and losses.[7] Futures may need to incorporate a small funding cost to take into account the initial margin, however, the impact of the mark-to-market is unknown, as it will depend on the level of interest rates over the life of the futures contract.

In summary, the short-term futures contract price is primarily determined by the prevailing forward rate using the formula in Section 5.2.3. There is, however, an element of the interest rate that will not be known, until expiry of the contracts, due to the unknown funding requirements during the life of the contract. This can be summarized as follows:

[6] It may not be obvious that the Eurodollar futures contract assumes an underlying discount security. However, the fact that interest amounts on the Eurodollar are effectively paid on the start date of the underlying security, without any discounting of interest (as with the FRA formula), means that the Eurodollar must be viewed as a discount security using the discount interest calculation method.

[7] See Chapter 4, Section 4.9 for a more detailed discussion on this point.

Futures price = 100 – (Forward Rate + Funding adjustment)

For contracts with a forward period of up to six months, the differences between short-term interest rate futures and FRAs are very small, as well as unknown, and can often be ignored.[8] However, for longer term futures, consideration should be given to incorporating the possible funding consequences of a futures contract; however, this is purely an estimate. It is common for market users to estimate the worst-case funding cost requirement and to incorporate that into their estimate of the effective forward rate given by short-term interest rates.

Figure 5.6 gives an example of the impact that the funding requirements of a futures contract can have on the effective forward rate. In this case, we examine the synthetic replication of a single sold Eurodollar contract. As with the FRA synthetic replication, we borrow until the maturity date of the underlying asset (1.25 years) and invest for the forward period (year). The additional complication of the futures contract is the upfront initial margin of US$500 and the mark-to-markets based on the prevailing forward price. In this example, the Eurodollar future is sold at a price of 92.74 with one year until expiry. It is assumed that the forward price increases over the life of the futures contract to settle at 95.00 (a 3-month interest rate of 5.00% pa). As well as the initial margin, this generates substantial funding requirements for a sold position. The interest cost of funding these cash flows is incorporated into the effective futures forward rate calculation. Here, the effective interest rate on the Eurodollar futures contract exceeds the equivalent FRA forward rate by nearly 10 basis points.

The difference between the FRA and the effective forward rate in the futures contract is dependant on the movement of interest rates over the forward period. The effective forward rate in *Figure 5.6* is calculated for a range of outcomes in *Figure 5.7*.

It is important to realize that these funding problems affect both buyers and sellers of futures contracts. The effective forward rates achieved are the same, but they have a different outcome. For a seller, if interest rates fall, the higher effective forward rate increases its cost of borrowing. However, for a buyer, if interest rates fall, the higher effective forward rate represents an improvement in their investment yield.

This difference in cash flows also gives rise to "convexity adjustments" when hedging OTC products such as FRAs and swaps. This issue will be discussed in the following section on valuation.

[8] In this case, the spreadsheet model provided in *Figure 5.4* is appropriate.

Figure 5.7
Effective Futures Rate Over a Range of Outcomes

Using the example from *Figure 5.6*. The effective forward rate given by the futures contract is calculated for a range of final 3 month interest rates.

3-month rate after 1 year	Effective futures rate	FRA/futures difference
5%	7.3620%	0.0981%
6%	7.3273%	0.0634%
7%	7.2784%	0.0146%
8%	7.2152%	−0.0487%
9%	7.1374%	−0.1264%

It is important to note that these funding issues also face the buyer of a futures contract. However, in the case of the buyer, a fall in rates generates positive cash flows and improves the effective forward interest rate.

5.3.3 Valuation of Short-Term Interest Rate Futures Contracts

As we saw in Chapter 4, the valuation of futures contracts can be a source of considerable confusion. It is important to remember that futures contracts have a constant PVBP—there is no distinction between present and future values. However, with cash financial assets and OTC derivatives there is a difference between the present and future values, equivalent to the TVM.

In this section, we will consider the formula for determining the value of a futures contract and then we will examine the impact of constant PVBP when used for the valuation of FRAs.

Contract Values

All open futures contracts are subject to at least a daily mark-to-market, sometimes more.[9] Whenever a mark-to-market is made, the valuation method is unchanged and is based on the same formula used to determine the final settlement value of the futures contract. In the case of the Eurodollars contract, the underlying security is the interest on a 90-day deposit—each point change in the futures price is equivalent to a 0.01% change in the interest rate in the underlying security. We can then express the value of this type of contract mathematically as:

[9] Some exchanges such as the CME and CBOT mark-to-market twice a day, once at the close of business and once at the end of morning trading. Most exchange clearinghouses require "intra-day" margins when market conditions are volatile—effectively marking-to-market during the day.

$$\text{Contract value}_{ED} = \text{Face value} \times (100 - \text{Price}) \times d/D/100$$

where "price" refers to the prevailing futures price.

So if the futures price is 96.24, then the contract value of a Eurodollar contract is:

$$= 1{,}000{,}000 \times (100 - 96.24) \times 90/360/100$$
$$= 9{,}400.$$

On any given day, the mark-to-market gain or loss will be equivalent to the difference in the contract value at the previous mark-to-market price and today's market price.

Most market participants recognize that the contract value formula always implies a constant PVBP, commonly known as the "tick value" in futures markets, equivalent to US$25—regardless of the time to expiry of the futures contract. As we saw in Section 3.5.3, this is quite an unusual feature, and is commonly referred to as "nonconvexity." In fact it represents a form of slightly negative convexity, as convexity relates to the percentage change in price and in these contracts the PVBP is declining as a percentage of the present value as interest rates fall. It is more appropriate to describe this property as "nondollar convexity."

This formula can be applied to all short-term interest rate contracts except the SFE bank bill contract. Here the contract value is given by a discount security formula using the yield method:

$$\text{Contract value}_{BB} = FV/(1 + (100 - \text{Price}) \times d/D/100)$$

In the case of the SFE contract, a price of 96.24 is:

$$= 1{,}000{,}000/(1 + (100 - 96.24) \times 90/365/100)$$
$$= 990{,}813.93.$$

In these instruments the PVBP is not constant, it changes slightly according to the level of interest rates. In the previous example the tick value is US$24.21; however, at a price of 86.24, the tick value is US$23.06. In practice, most market participants assume the tick value is approximately US$24. Because of the underlying yield discount method, bank bill futures contracts display a "positive" PVBP relationship, because PVBP rises with a fall in yields. It is important to realize that this convexity results from the valuation of the underlying 3-month bank bill contract. It is not related to the term to forward expiry at all and it is a reflection of the bank bill's convexity on the futures expiry date. As such, it shares the same property as the Eurodollar contract: at a given yield the PVBP of the futures contract will be the same regardless of the number of days to the futures expiry date. In the following section, we will refer to this property as "constant PVBP."

TVM Hedge Ratios and Convexity Adjustments

It appears that futures contracts do not comply with TVM rules. At a given yield the value of a contract is the same today as in the future—there seems to be no compensation for the passing of time. Of course, this is not the case. We need to remember that futures contracts represent a highly structured form of financial derivative. The constant PVBP is a result of the risk management practices of exchange clearinghouses; it has not been specifically designed to work this way.

> ***Note***
> One of the fundamental elements of valuation is that all derivatives must comply with the TVM characteristics for which they are being used. Therefore, when using futures contracts to hedge an instrument such as OTC derivatives, the number of futures contracts needs to be adjusted in accordance with the TVM characteristics of the instrument being hedged. This is an extremely important rule and if it is not followed, it will lead to over- or under-hedging.

In this section we will consider using short-term interest rate futures to hedge FRAs. For a futures contract and an FRA with the same forward settlement date and notional maturity date, the forward interest rate represented is very similar—with differences only arising due to the funding consequences of the futures contract. As market interest rates change, the current forward interest rate used to determine the FRA rates and futures prices can be viewed as identical. Any differences in the two contracts will result from the different treatment of present values.

This is highlighted in *Figure 5.8*, where the PVBP of an A$ FRA and equivalent bank bill futures contract is compared. While the future value is the same, the FRA PVBP is lower, reflecting the TVM. If we wish to hedge the FRA with futures contracts the aim is to ensure that any profits and losses today on the FRA are offset by the futures contracts. To determine the appropriate number of futures contracts to hedge the FRA should equal the PVBPs of the two instruments; in this case, 91 contracts. This equating of PVBPs is the same concept as the hedge ratio introduced in Chapter 3. Note that as time passes, the PVBP of

Figure 5.8
Futures and FRAs: Dealing with Different PVBPs

It is the 13th of June 2002. Calculate today's PVBP on a bank accepted bill futures (BAB) contract and FRA listed below for face values of A$1 m. Using this information, if you had bought $100 m face value of FRAs, how many futures contracts would you sell to hedge the price risk?

Current market data

Instrument	Tenor	Underlying days	Expiry date	Current yield	PVBP yield
1. FRA	15/18	90	13-Sep-02	7.58%	7.59%
2. BAB	Sep-02	90	13-Sep-02	7.58%	7.59%

Note: Zero-coupon rate to Sep13 2002 = 7.90%

Calculations

Instrument	Current value	PVBP value	Future value	Present value	PVBP
1. FRA	981,652.51	981,628.75	(23.76)	(21.60)	21.60
2. BAB	981,652.51	981,628.75	(23.76)	(23.76)	23.76
		Difference		(2.16)	

Number of futures contracts to hedge $100 m FRAs.

We assume that the futures price and FRA are very closely correlated, and then apply the hedge ratio formula developed in Section 3.5.3.

Hedge ratio = PVBP(FRA) / PVBP
= 21.60/23.76
= 0.9092

So for every $1 face value of FRA, we would sell 0.9099 BAB contracts.

Number of contracts = FRA face value × hedge ratio/BAB face value
= $100,000,000 × 0.9093/$1,000,000
= 90.92
= 91 contracts (rounded to nearest whole contract)

the FRA will increase toward the futures PVBP and the number of futures contracts will need to increase correspondingly.

This analysis suggests that FRAs and futures can be equated by adjusting for the differences in PVBP. However, there is also the "convexity adjustment," which takes into account the differences in the convexity characteristics of futures contracts and other closely related OTC derivatives. It recognizes that interest earned on futures mark-to-markets is negatively correlated with the futures price; that is, as interest rates fall, futures prices rise. From the point of view of a short-seller of futures contracts this means, if interest rates fall, then they will pay mark-to-market losses. However, the interest rate to fund these losses will be *lower* than the rate prevailing when the transaction was executed. On the other hand, if interest rates rise, the seller receives mark-to-market profits and earns a *higher* rate of investment interest. This creates a natural bias in futures contracts that favors short-sellers whether interest rates rise or fall. This bias works against a buyer of short-term futures contracts.

As with the funding adjustment the consequences of this convexity effect are not known until the expiry of the futures contracts. Estimating the convexity adjustment depends on determining an expected path for interest rates over the life of the futures contract—not a straightforward task. As with the funding adjustment it is advisable to estimate the net convexity approach and convert it into a forward interest rate equivalent. The implied futures yield should then be equivalent to the FRA rate plus the convexity adjustment.

Figure 5.9 shows how the convexity adjustment can be calculated. It illustrates the outcome of the previous hedging example, assuming interest rates either increase or decrease by 1% pa. This example assumes that the zero-coupon and forward rates rise or fall by 1% pa on the first day and this rate does not change, an unrealistic assumption in the real world. Estimating the effect of convexity is quite complex for a small increase in accuracy and as such it is generally only of concern to FRA and swap market-makers.

> ***Note***
> In practice, the convexity adjustment amount is ignored for forward periods of up to one year. For longer forward terms the adjustment is in the order of one or two basis points, gradually rising as the forward period increases.

A Complete Futures Pricing Model

If we incorporate all the special features of a futures contract relative to a forward contract, we can summarize the "complete" short-term interest rate futures pricing model as follows:

$$\text{Futures price} = 100 - (\text{Forward rate} + \text{Funding adjustment} + \text{Convexity adjustment})$$

5.4 FORWARD BONDS

5.4.1 General Description

Forward bonds are an OTC forward contract on fixed-interest bonds and are similar to an FRA on a long-term interest rate security. In a forward bond agreement, two parties agree to deliver a specified bond series at a future date. While

Figure 5.9
Futures and FRAs: Estimating Convexity Adjustments

To see the effect of the convexity adjustment, let us look at the cash flows generated by the transactions in *Figure 5.8.* We will examine the cashflows' impact, if interest rates rose by 1% pa or fell by 1% pa on the trade date and then stayed there till the forward expiry and we will examine the relative costs of futures and FRAs.

Original transactions — June 13, 2002

Instrument	Amount		Forward settlement	Maturity date	Traded rate/ price
1. FRA	100,000,000	Seller/investor	13-Sep-02	12-Dec-02	7.58%
2. BAB	91 contracts	Seller	13-Sep-02	12-Dec-02	92.42

Interest rates

	Original	After 1% rise	After 1% fall
FRA	7.58%	8.58%	6.58%
BAB	7.58%	8.58%	6.58%
1 1/4 year rate	7.90%	8.90%	6.90%

Calculations for 1% rise in rates

Instrument	Traded value value (1)	Settlement value	Settlement amount	Present value (2)
1. FRA	98,165,251.11	98,162,875.07	(2,376.05)	(2,160.62)
2. BAB	(89,330,378.51)	(89,328,216.31)	2,162.20	2,162.20
		Difference		1.58

Calculations for 1% fall in rates

Instrument	Traded value value (1)	Settlement value	Settlement amount	Present value (2)
1. FRA	98,165,251.11	98,403,437.92	238,186.80	216,591.24
2. BAB	(89,330,378.51)	(89,547,128.51)	(216,749.99)	(216,749.99)
		Difference		(158.75)

Notes: (1) A long position is shown as a positive, a short position as negative.
(2) The futures present value is the mark-to-market, where a gain is positive and a loss is negative.

Transaction cash flows and net benefit of futures

Date/cash flows		Interest rates up 1% pa		Interest rates down 1% pa	
		Futures	FRA	Futures	FRA
Trade date	13-Jun-02				
Traded contract value		(89,330,379)		(89,330,379)	
Value after rate change		(89,328,216)		(89,547,129)	
Mark-to-market		2,163		(216,750)	
Expiry date	13-Sep-02				
Settlement		0	(2,376.05)	0	238,186.80
Interest on mark-to-market		243.25		(18,853.23)	
Total future value		2,406.25	(2,376.05)	(235,603.22)	238,186.80
Futures benefit — $		30.21		2,583.58	
Futures benefit — % pa		0.0001%		0.0105%	
Futures benefit — bp		0.01		1.05	

This example displays the futures/FRA convexity effect. Given the simple scenario used, the convexity adjustment suggests that the futures yield should be a little more than 1 bp greater than the FRA rate.

FRAs relate to a generic money market interest rate, such as LIBOR, forward bond agreements relate to a specific bond issue. Every forward bond agreement must reflect the characteristics (such as issuer, maturity date, coupon and yield) of the underlying bond. This variety of issues, combined with the more complex valuation formula, tend to make forward bonds more complex and specialized transaction than FRAs.

Typically, the forward bond market revolves around government and other high-quality bond issues, as there is already considerable activity in the underlying securities. As we will see, cash, forward and futures transactions in the bond market are closely related.

5.4.2 Synthetic Replication of Forward Bonds

A forward bond purchase can be synthetically replicated in the same way as an FRA by purchasing the security today and financing the bond for the forward period. This is illustrated in *Figure 5.10*.

As with all forward transactions, the forward price represents the current cash price adjusted for the cost of carry. In this case the cost of carry is the difference between the coupons received on the bond and the cost of financing the bond:

Cost of carry = Financing cost – Bond coupons

A common mistake in forward bond calculations is to use the yield to maturity as the asset return instead of the bond coupon. A forward calculation is concerned with actual cash flows that take place during the forward term—the yield to maturity reflects the asset return over the whole life of the underlying security.

The example in *Figure 5.10* uses a money market interest rate to determine the financing cost and this provides an estimate only. The credit quality of a government bond, for example, is higher than for most money market instruments. In a synthetic forward purchase the buyer could offer the bond as security and borrow at an interest rate appropriate to the *credit quality* of the bond. This will be discussed more in Section 5.4.5 on repurchase agreements.

5.4.3 A Model for Forward Bond Prices

The synthetic replication indicates that the forward bond price complies with the "lumpy" income model developed in Section 4.7.3, where the lumpy income is the coupon payment on the bond. If the bond does not pay any coupon during the forward period, we use the "no income" model from Section 4.7.1.

Figure 5.10
Synthetic Replication of a Forward Bond Purchase

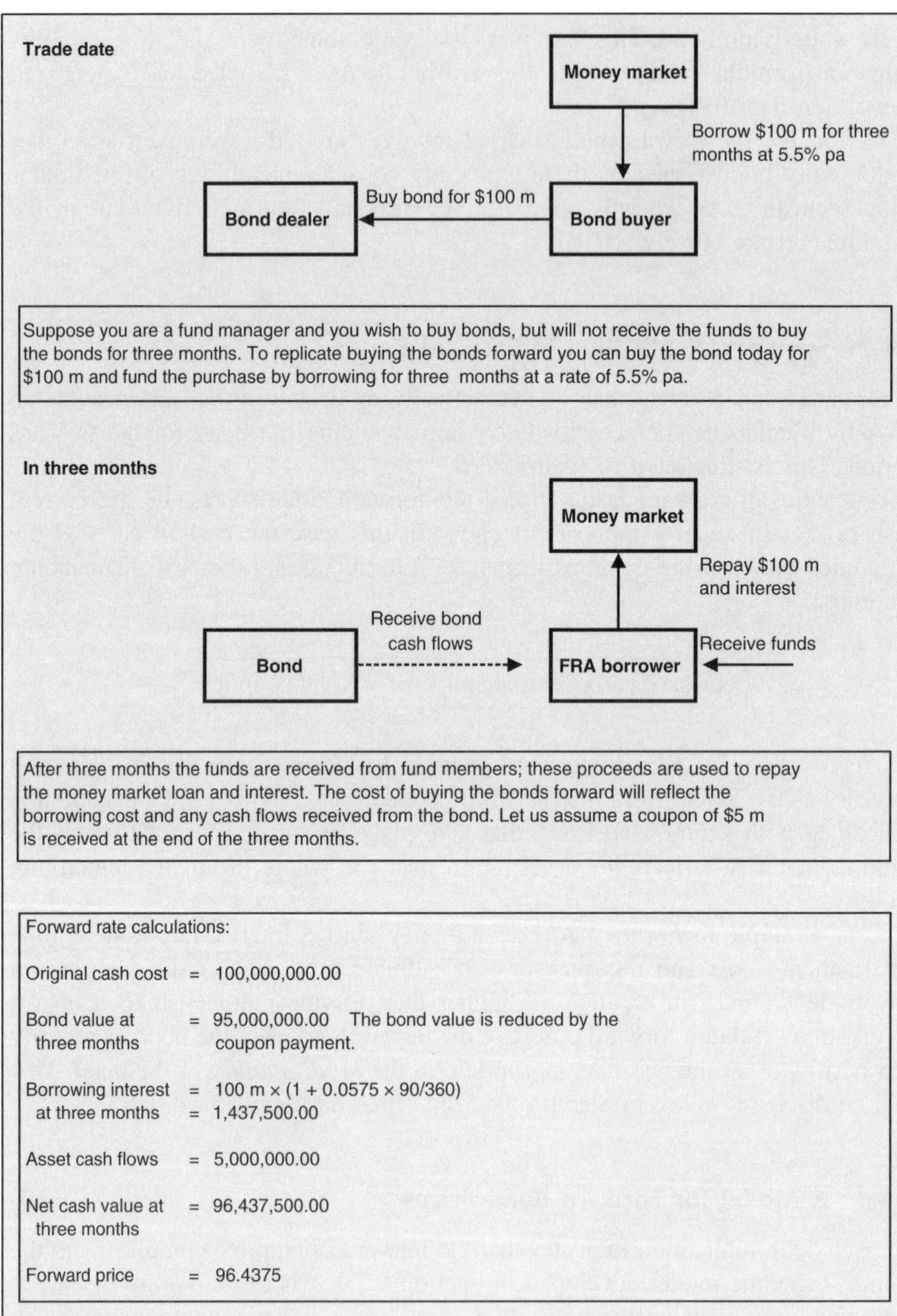

Forward Bond Price Model — One Coupon Payment

The forward price per US$100 can be expressed as:

$$F = S \times (1 + r_1 \times f_1/D) - c \times (1 + r_2 \times f_2/D)$$

Where:

- F = forward price per US$100 face value including accrued interest (dirty price)
- S = cash bond price including accrued interest
- r_1 = interest rate to the forward expiry date
- r_2 = interest rate between the coupon payment and forward expiry dates
- D = day count basis (360 or 365)
- f_1 = number of days to the forward expiry date
- f_2 = number of days between the coupon payment and forward expiry dates
- c = periodic coupon payment per US$100 of face value.

It is interesting to note that the forward calculation is based purely on cash flows between today and the forward settlement date. Apart from calculating the initial cash price, S, there is no reference to the bond pricing formula. As with all forward calculations, the aim of the model is to reflect the cash flow consequence of entering into a forward transaction.

This formula calculates the forward price. To determine the forward yield, we must enter the forward price into the bond price calculator and solve for the yield on the forward settlement date. This yield will reflect the cost of carry; however, it is not just a function of the difference between the financing cost and coupon rate—it also reflects the timing and payment of coupons.

This model only allows the incorporation of one coupon payment. Including other coupon payments is simply a matter of calculating the future value of each extra coupon using the same methodology as the first coupon. In practice, the bulk of forward bond transactions have a forward term of three months or less, so encountering more than one coupon is uncommon.

The best way of building forward bond pricing models is to combine them with a cash bond price calculator. This allows the current cash price to be automatically generated, as well as the next coupon dates and coupon amounts. An example of a forward bond pricing spreadsheet is provided in *Figure 5.11*. It assumes that the two short-term interest rates, r_1 and r_2, are the same.

To appreciate the impact of the coupon, *Figure 5.12* takes the bond in *Figure 5.11*, but with different coupons. While the yield to maturity and financing rate on each bond is the same, the forward yield at each coupon level is different.

> ***Note***
> In general, as the coupon rate increases the absolute level of the cost of carry also increases.

5.4.4 A Model for Forward Bond Valuation

The forward value of a forward bond is the difference between the contract price in the forward bond agreement and the prevailing forward bond price:

$$\text{Forward value} = \text{Forward bond price} - \text{Contract price}$$

Figure 5.11
Forward Bond Price and Yield Calculator

Spreadsheet example

Field	Cell	Cell Address: Formula (blank for input cells)
Inputs		
Trade date	20-Dec-98	$F$11 :
Forward settlement date	15-Jun-99	$F$12 :
Maturity date	15-Jul-02	$F$13 :
Coupon rate %	8.0000	$F$14 :
Number of periods/year (1, 2 or 4)	2	$F$15 :
Current yield to maturity	6.0000	$F$16 :
Repo rate till fwd settlement	4.8500	$F$17 :
Repo rate day count basis (360 or 365)	365	$F$18 :
30/360 days count (y or n)	y	$F$19 :
Underlying bond details		
Settlement date	20-Dec-98	$F$22 : =F11
Fwd date	15-Jun-99	$F$23 : =F12
Maturity date	15-Jul-02	$F$24 : =F13
Last coupon date	15-Jul-98	$F$25 : =COUPPCD(F22,F24,F28,F30)
Next coupon date 1	15-Jan-99	$F$26 : =COUPNCD(F22,F24,F28,F30)
Coupon rate %	8.0000	$F$27 : =F14
Number of periods/year (1,2 or 4)	2.0000	$F$28 : =F15
Current yield to maturity % pa	6.0000	$F$29 : =F16
MS excel day count method	0	$F$30 : =IF(F19="n",1,0)
Clean price	106.3342	$F$31 : =PRICE(F22,F24,F27/100,F29/100,100,F28,F30)
Accrued Interest at trade date	3.4444	$F$32 : =IF(F22=F25,0,ACCRINT(F25,F26,F22,F27,1,F28,F30))
Financing (or repo) details		
Current financing rate	4.85	$F$35 : =F17
Repo rate day count	365	$F$36 : =F18
Dirty bond price on trade date	109.7787	$F$37 : =F32+F31
Number of coupons during repo	1	$F$38 : =IF(F23>F26,1,0)
Number of repo days in forward period	177	$F$39 : =F23−F22
Number of days from coupon date to fwd date	151	$F$40 : =IF(F38=1,F23−F26,0)
Repo finance cost of bond	112.3606	$F$41 : =F37*(1+F35/(F36*100)*F39)
Forward price calculation		
Cumulative coupon 1 value at forward date	4.0803	$F$44 : =F27/F28*(1+F35/(100*F36)*F40)*F38
Dirty forward price	108.2803	$F$45 : =F41−F44
Last coupon at forward date	15-Jan-99	$F$46 : =COUPPCD(F23,F24,F28,F30)
Next coupon date at forward date	15-Jul-99	$F$47 : =COUPNCD(F23,F24,F28,F30)
Accrued interest at forward date	3.3333	$F$48 : =ACCRINT(F46,F47,F23,F27,1,F28,F30)
Clean forward price	104.9470	$F$49 : =F45−F48
Forward yield % pa	6.2093	$F$50 : =YIELD(F12,F13,F14/100,F49,100,F15,F30)*100

Note: Model requires MS Excel "Analysis Toolpak" add-in.

Figure 5.12
The Impact of Coupons on Forward Bond Yields

Using the example in *Figure 5.11*, determine the impact on the forward yield of different coupon levels leaving all other inputs unchanged.

Original bond

Trade date	20-Dec-98
Forward settlement date	15-Jun-99
Maturity date	15-Jul-02
Coupon rate %	8
Number of periods/year (1,2 or 4)	2
Cash yield to maturity % pa	6
Financing/repo rate % pa	4.85
Forward price	104.947
Forward yield % pa	6.209304
Yield cost of carry	–0.209304

Impact of coupons

Coupon % pa	Forward yield % pa	Cost of carry % pa
4	6.1973	(0.1973)
8	6.2093	(0.2093)
12	6.2199	(0.2199)
16	6.2292	(0.2292)

When determining the present value of the forward bond, we need to be wary of the discounting interest rate used. While it is common practice to use the prevailing short-term money market rate to the forward term to determine the present value, it is not strictly correct. Determining the present value involves converting a known future cash flow with specific characteristics into a known amount today. The forward bond forward value is characterized by the difference between the current forward price and the contract price. However, these cash flows are also dependant on the characteristics of the underlying bond, most notably the credit quality of the bond. Consequently, the interest rate used to present value these cash flows should be a short-term interest rate on the bond. For example, the interest rate used for government bonds should be equivalent to a Treasury bill rate, while the interest rate for bank bonds should be the same as bank-related money market instruments.

In summary, the present value interest rate should be the same as the financing interest rate, r_1, used in the forward bond price formula. On a simple interest basis the formula is as follows:

$$\text{Present value} = \text{Forward value}/(1 + r_1 \times f/D)$$

In *Figure 5.13*, an existing forward bond position is marked-to-market by calculating the current forward price and then determining the forward and present value of the forward bond. The forward value can be determined with reference to the dirty or clean price of the bond. Either method is acceptable as the difference in the two is accrued interest. In this example, we use the clean price, which gives the capital gain or loss on the position.

5.4.5 Repurchase Agreements

In any forward bond market, a large proportion of forward transactions are linked to repurchase (repo) and reverse repurchase (reverse repo) agreements. In some markets, it is estimated that the majority of bond dealers' transactions are some form of repo or reverse repo. The bulk of bond repos are very short-term, in the order of one day to one week. Even in very liquid markets, such as the US Treasury bond market, repos for longer than six months are relatively rare.

A repo involves one counterparty and is the simultaneous execution of the sale of a cash bond and the purchase of a forward bond; that is, it is an agreement to sell a bond today and repurchase it at a date in the future at a fixed price.[10] A reverse repo is the simultaneous purchase of a cash bond and the sale of a forward bond. A repo is arranged so that the sale of the bond today is at the prevailing cash price for the bond and the future repurchase of the bond is based on the forward bond price. Given that, we know the cash price of the bond, the forward period and the coupon on the bond, the only unknown variable in a repo is the financing interest rate. This makes the financing interest rate the key variable in any repurchase agreement and explains why this financing interest rate in the forward pricing formula is referred to as the repo rate.[11]

Figure 5.14 diagrammatically illustrates the mechanics of a repo.

As discussed in Chapter 4, the effect of a repo is to shift cash flows from one point in time to another; it does not actually change the participant's exposure to

[10] Other names for repo transactions include buy-backs, reciprocal purchase agreements and bond-lending. All have similar economic results, although the mechanics can be different. For more detail see Shanahan, T., "The Repo Market," *Journal of International Securities Markets*, Summer 1991.

[11] In some markets, this is referred to as the cash or term rate. Both of these terms can be confused with other interest rates, so they will be avoided in the remainder of this book.

Figure 5.13
Forward Bond Valuation

Suppose you have purchased forward $100 m face value of bonds on the following basis:

Original forward purchase

Trade date	17-Jun-99
Forward settlement date	02-Nov-99
Maturity date	14-Dec-08
Coupon rate %	6.5000
Number of periods/year (1, 2 or 4)	2
Current yield to maturity	7.2500
Repo rate till fwd settlement	8.0000
Repo rate day count basis (360 or 365)	360
30/360 days count (y or n)	n
Dirty forward price	97.8629
Clean forward price	95.3765
Forward yield % pa	7.1988

On September 20, interest rates have risen and you decide to mark the position to market (i.e., calculate it's present value). The forward price is now as follows:

Forward price on September 20

Valuation date	20-Sep-99
Forward settlement date	02-Nov-99
Maturity date	14-Dec-08
Coupon rate %	6.5000
Number of periods/year (1, 2 or 4)	2
Current yield to maturity	7.7000
Repo rate till fwd settlement	8.4000
Repo rate day count basis (360 or 365)	360
30/360 days count (y or n)	n
Dirty forward price	94.8213
Clean forward price	92.3350
Forward yield % pa	7.6829

In general, the forward value is calculated excluding the effects of accrued interest; that is, using the "clean" price.

Forward value = (Forward price – Contract price)/100 × Face value
= (92.335 – 95.3765)/100 × 100,000,000
= (3,041,500)

Present value = Forward value/(1 + Repo rate × f/D)
= –3.041,500/(1 + 0.084 × 43/360)
= (3,011,287)

Figure 5.14
Repurchase and Reverse Repurchase Agreements

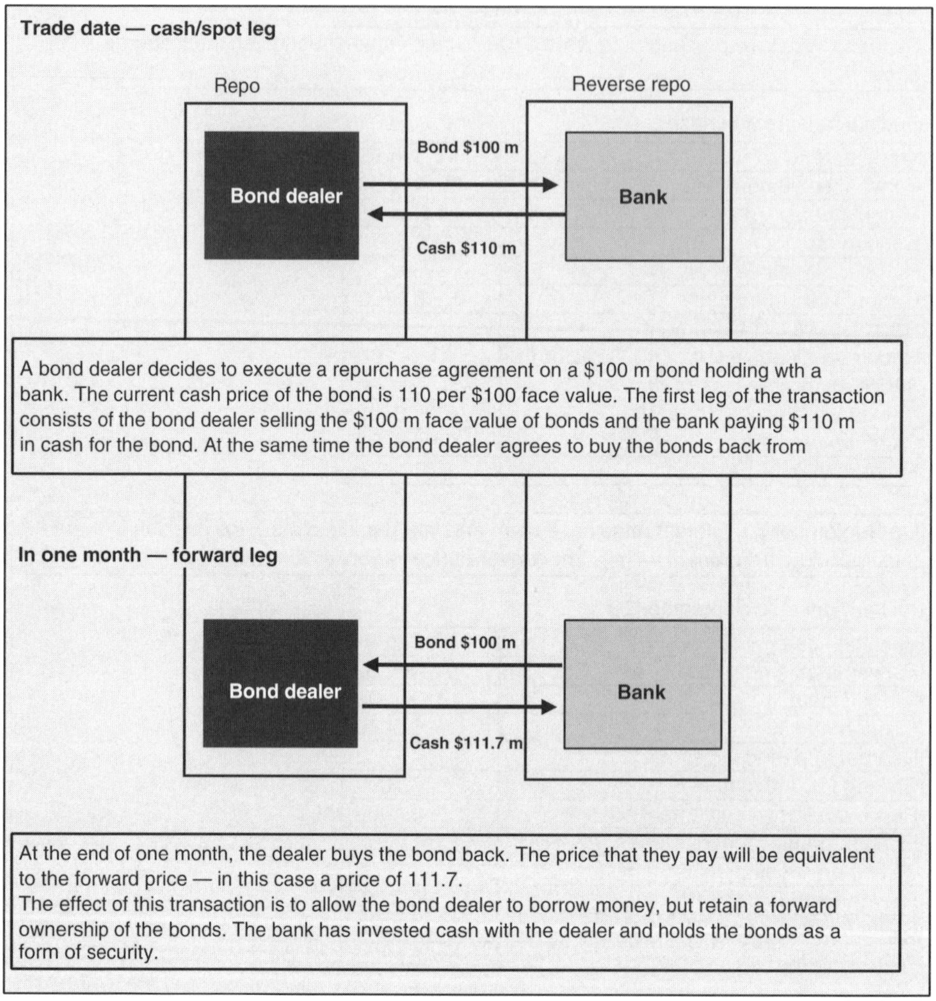

Trade date — cash/spot leg

Repo | Reverse repo

Bond dealer → Bond $100 m → Bank

Bank → Cash $110 m → Bond dealer

A bond dealer decides to execute a repurchase agreement on a $100 m bond holding wth a bank. The current cash price of the bond is 110 per $100 face value. The first leg of the transaction consists of the bond dealer selling the $100 m face value of bonds and the bank paying $110 m in cash for the bond. At the same time the bond dealer agrees to buy the bonds back from

In one month — forward leg

Bank → Bond $100 m → Bond dealer

Bond dealer → Cash $111.7 m → Bank

At the end of one month, the dealer buys the bond back. The price that they pay will be equivalent to the forward price — in this case a price of 111.7.
The effect of this transaction is to allow the bond dealer to borrow money, but retain a forward ownership of the bonds. The bank has invested cash with the dealer and holds the bonds as a form of security.

changes in the value of bonds. In *Figure 5.14*, the repo provides a very efficient method of funding the dealer's bond positions, as it retains the same long exposure to bond price movements; however, the dealer is able to finance this bond holding at a rate that is usually lower than its normal funding rate. Notice that by continually using repos; that is, executing a new repo as soon as each repo matures, the dealer could fund its bond holding over long periods at an attractive rate. This explains why the judicious use of repos is a fundamental aspect of dealing in bonds.

Some of the reasons for entering into repos and reverse repos are summarized as follows:

Repos

- funding can be obtained at an attractive rate;
- investment returns can be "grossed up," where bonds are sold into a repo and then, the cash is used to invest in more securities;
- both repos and reverse repos offer a method of liquidity management to central banks. Repos are widely used to manage the cash position of the banking system. A repo allows the central bank to withdraw cash from the economy today and then reinject that cash at a date in the future, when it will be required.

Reverse Repos

- investors can invest cash and obtain the underlying bond as security;
- often banks are required to hold government bonds for regulatory reasons. Under a reverse repo, the bank could obtain ownership of the bond. However, it is not exposed to the potential price volatility of the underlying bond;
- an organization that has created a short position in bonds (for example, from the maturity of a forward sale or from an option transaction) could cover this position temporarily through a reverse repo.

Another feature of repos is that, for any term to maturity, there are multiple repo rates. Every bond series issued has its own characteristics, such as the issuer, the maturity date, the coupon payment dates and the coupon amounts. As we saw in *Figure 5.14*, varying the size of the coupon changes the forward yield to maturity on otherwise identical bonds. If a particular bond series is in demand, the cost of financing it will be lower than a less desirable bond series. This is because reverse repo counterparties will be willing to invest cash at a lower rate to obtain temporary ownership of highly favored bonds.

The US Treasury bond market is the most liquid cash and forward bond market in the world. While the issuer is constant and the terms are similar, the repo rate on different bond issues can vary substantially depending on the level of demand for specific issues. As an example, while the overnight US dollar interest rate might be 5.75% pa at any given point in time, the repo rate for Treasury bonds might vary from 5.50% pa down to 1.75% pa for the series that are in heavy demand. Reasons for these very low repo rates reflect the existence of large short positions in these securities relative to their supply. These short positions are covered with reverse repos, and as the availability of bonds declines the short-position holders are willing to accept a lower return on the cash invested in a reverse repo.

We can calculate the repo rate implied in a forward bond transaction by rearranging the formula from Section 5.4.3 as follows (if we assume r_1 and r_2 are the same):

Calculating the Implied Repo Rate

The repo rate in the forward leg of a repo can be solved for as follows:

$$r_1 = \frac{F - S + c}{S \times f_1/D - c \times f_2/D}$$

Where:

F = forward price per US$100 face value including accrued interest at futures date (dirty price)
S = cash bond price including accrued interest
r_1 = repo rate to the forward expiry date
D = day count basis (360 or 365)
f_1 = number of days to the forward expiry date
f_2 = number of days between the coupon payment and forward expiry dates
c = periodic coupon payment per US$100 of face value.

Figure 5.15 calculates the implied repo rate on a forward bond transaction using this formula.

5.5 BOND FUTURES

5.5.1 General Description

Bond futures represent a standardized, exchange-traded forward bond contract. Like short-term interest rate futures contracts, they have become an integral part of most financial markets, and they typically represent a benchmark for long-term interest rate transactions.

The pricing and valuation of these instruments is derived from the forward bond calculations in Section 5.4. As with all futures contracts, adjustments may need to be made for margin funding costs. The users of both bond futures and forward bonds are usually very similar and the reasons for which both products are used is closely related. In those countries, where the underlying cash market is liquid, the volume in bond futures is substantial.

Figure 5.15
Repo Rate Calculation

Calculate the implied repurchase rate in the following forward bond transaction:

Cash bond details

Trade date	20-Dec-98
Forward settlement date	16-Jun-99
Maturity date	15-Jul-02
Coupon rate %	8.0000
Number of periods/year (1, 2 or 4)	2
Current yield to maturity	6.0000
Dirty cash price	109.7708
Day count basis	Act/Act

Forward details

Dirty forward price	108.2864
Repo rate day count basis (360 or 365)	365
Number of days in forward period	178
Coupon payment on 15-Jan-99	4.0000
Number of days from coupon date to fwd date	152

Repo calculation

Inputs:

S = 109.7708 f_1 = 178
F = 108.2864 f_2 = 152
c = 4.0000 D = 365

Formula:

$$r = \frac{F - S + c}{(S \times f_1/D - c \times f_2/D)}$$

= 4.8500%

Two important differences among various futures contracts relates to the quote method and the delivery method used:

- **Quote method** The price of most bond futures contracts is quoted as the current price per 100 units of face value. For these contracts, the futures price is essentially the same as the forward price calculated in Section 5.4.3. The other alternative is the yield method. Futures prices are quoted as 100 minus the yield to maturity of the underlying forward bond. The futures quotation method is usually a reflection of the local bond market convention for quoting cash bond prices.

- **Delivery method** There are two alternative methods with which bond contracts are terminated: physical delivery and cash settlement. As its name implies, physical delivery requires that all open contracts at expiry must deliver (the futures contract seller), or take delivery (the buyer) of, a defined amount and type of bond. In the case of cash settlement, at expiry, all open contracts are reversed at the final settlement price of the contract (usually on the last day of trading); that is, all obligations under the futures contract are cancelled upon payment or receipt of the cash difference between the original traded price and the final settlement price of the futures contract.

Some contracts, notably A$ futures, are quoted using the yield method and are cash settled against a basket of underlying bonds. This creates some additional pricing complexities for the forward bond formula, which are highlighted below.

5.5.2 Pricing and Valuing Bond Futures

Conceptually, the pricing and valuation tools developed in Section 5.4 can be applied directly to bond futures with the same sort of adjustments as were applied to short-term interest rate futures:

$$\begin{aligned}\text{Futures price} = {} & \text{Forward price} + \text{Funding adjustment} \\ & + \text{Convexity adjustment}\end{aligned}$$

As with all futures, there is no distinction between forward and present values and this should incorporated into any hedging transaction using the PVBP in the same manner as the short-term futures contract.[12]

While the funding and convexity adjustments discussed in relation to short-term futures should be strictly applied, they are often ignored by market participants. The reason for this is twofold:

- **Short forward period** Most of the traded volume in bond futures across all contracts has a relatively short forward period (up to six months). As we have seen in earlier sections, the funding and convexity adjustment calculations are usually extremely small for forward periods of less than one year.
- **Long forward period** If the funding or convexity adjustment is calculated and spread over the long life of the underlying bond, the impact of the adjustment tends to be relatively small.

[12] See Section 5.3.3 for an example of dealing with the constant PVBP characteristics of futures contracts.

Unfortunately, while it describes the conceptual relationship, deriving the final quoted futures price is not quite as simple as the formula above implies. In all bond futures, additional adjustments are required depending on the nature of the delivery process. We can divide the futures price calculations into two general groups:

- delivery and conversion factors
- yield quotes and basket bonds.

For more information on this see the bond contract specifications from the relevant futures exchange.

SUMMARY

This chapter examined the pricing and valuation of forwards. Forwards is a large group and consists of a variety of OTC and ET transactions. We developed a general model for valuing forwards. We compared OTC to ET forwards, and in particular, we looked at the impact of initial margins and mark-to-marking on the valuation of ET futures, in order to incorporate these factors in valuation modeling. This chapter also looked at synthetically replicating FRAs and we discussed the mechanics of repos and calculating the implied repo rate.

FURTHER READING

- Morgan, J.P. *Futures and Options Guide*, published annually.
- Labuszewski, J.W. and Nyhoff, J.E. *Trading Financial Futures: Markets, Methods, Strategies and Tactics*, John Wiley, 1988.
- Futures exchanges' web sites (e.g., cme.com, liffe.com, eurexchange.com and sfe.com.au).

SELF-TEST QUESTIONS

1. Damien is the borrower in a 1×4 FRA transaction at 7.05%. The 1-month rate is 6.50% and the 3-month rate is 7.01%. Calculate the current forward value of the FRA using the full face value method.
2. Assume you are the buyer of an FRA and you have agreed on the interest rate of a 6-month borrowing commencing in six months' time. How would you synthetically replicate your position in this transaction? *Note:* Use a cash flow diagram to illustrate your answer.
3. Explain what is meant by a "convexity adjustment."
4. Futures contracts have a constant PVBP. What affect does this have on valuing futures contracts?

5. Calculate the implied repo rate for the following forward bond transaction:

Bond

Trade date	Feb 20, 2001
Forward settlement date	Aug 15, 2001
Maturity date	July 15, 2004
Coupon rate	7.0000%
Number of periods/year	2
Current yield to maturity	5.7500%
Clean cash price	103.8061
Day count basis	A/A

Forward

Dirty clean price	104.5353
Repo rate day count basis	365
Number of days in forward period	180
Coupon payment	3.5000

6. Explain the impact of coupons on forward bond yields.

7. Royal Pensions is a large fund manager that will be receiving $500 million worth of funds in three months' time. The CFO, however, would like to purchase bonds now. Create a synthetic replication of buying the bonds forward. *Note:* Assume that the borrowing rate for three months is 5.75% pa and that you can buy the bonds today for $500 million. Use a cash flow diagram to illustrate your answer.

CHAPTER 6

FOREIGN EXCHANGE FORWARDS

The models developed in this chapter are saved as Microsoft Excel™ files in the enclosed disk.

OVERVIEW

Foreign exchange (FX) transactions represent the largest OTC market with daily turnover in excess of one trillion dollars a day. While there has been considerable innovation in FX derivatives, FX forwards remain the "bread and butter" transactions. This chapter develops pricing and valuation models for the following forms of FX forwards:

- short-term FX forwards
- long-term FX forwards
- par forwards
- currency futures.

As well as pricing and valuation models, the generation of risk characteristics of these instruments is also discussed.

6.1 INTRODUCTION

FX transactions are purely about cash flows, as opposed to interest rate transactions that typically involve underlying securities with specific interest-paying and maturity characteristics, which may be in limited supply. With an FX transaction, there is no specific underlying instrument and any organization can create its own tailor-made FX transaction.

6.2 FOREIGN EXCHANGE (FX)

Foreign exchange transactions are a homogenous product and completely fungible;[1] that is, if a company enters into an FX transaction that settles in two days' time

[1] If two financial instruments are fungible, they are perfect substitutes and can be used to replace one another.

with a bank, this can be offset by entering into an opposite transaction with another bank—the only difference will be the profit or loss due to differences in the exchange rate on the original and offsetting deals.

The enormous size and success of the OTC FX market can be explained by the underlying demand to execute FX deals for trade and capital transactions, with the flexibility to create and manage FX positions. While currency futures exist, their volume is small relative to the OTC market.

The global FX market is the epitome of the "global financial village," the huge marketplace spread across numerous financial centers and time zones. No matter what the time of day, it is possible to execute FX transactions involving major currencies. This has been further promoted by the advent of the Euro since 1999, with a fixed relationship between major European currencies (e.g., DM, FFR, ITL etc.,) volume and price discovery has been focused on considerably fewer currencies globally (i.e., US$, EUR and JP¥). The appendix in Chapter 1 is a reproduction of the Bank for International Settlements' (BIS) triennial survey on foreign exchange and this has more information on the size of the global foreign exchange forward market.

6.2.1 Foreign Exchange as an Asset

A spot FX transaction may not appear to be a financial asset. It represents an agreement today to exchange one currency for another in, usually, two business days at an agreed rate. This does not seem to share the same "asset" characteristics as an interest-bearing security, which provides an interest income and a repayment of principal at maturity.

However, assets come in a variety of forms and interest-bearing securities represent one form. In the case of an FX deal, cash in the two currencies in the transaction form the assets. Pricing a spot foreign exchange transaction, that is, the foreign exchange rate, involves determining the rate at which we are willing to exchange one asset for another. For example, the current share price of a stock reflects the rate at which one asset (the stock) will be exchanged for another (cash).

> ***Note***
> In essence, this is a general definition for all financial market securities: the cash price is the rate at which one asset is exchanged for another.

While an FX transaction does not generate income directly, it is generally considered that there is an asset income. This is because the asset created in an FX transaction is cash. It is generally considered that cash can be invested in risk-free securities, at least overnight, and still retain its key characteristic of high liquidity. Once executed, the income arising from an FX transaction is the overnight cash interest rate in the currency purchased.

6.2.2 Foreign Exchange Quotation Conventions

Even experienced market practitioners make mistakes when pricing FX transactions. To correctly value FX derivatives, it is essential to understand the nuances of exchange rate quotations, particularly when dealing with unusual currency combinations. This section will review some of the key quotation concepts.

Since the float of most major currencies in the early 1970s, most exchange rate quotations have been expressed in terms of the US dollar. In recent years, a number of other "cross rates" have become important, particularly against the Euro (EUR) such as the JP¥/EUR and GBP/EUR. However, in general, the US dollar remains the quotation benchmark. For most currencies the quotation of exchange rates on information services is expressed as the number of units of currency per one US dollar. This is the case for most currencies except the Australian dollar, British pound, and New Zealand dollar, where the exchange rate is often expressed as the number of US dollars per one unit of currency.

When reviewing any exchange rate quotation it is essential to know which currency is the "base" currency and which is the "terms" currency. In any quote, the *base* currency is the unit or currency that is held constant and the *terms* currency is the variable part of the quote. Or to put it another way, the exchange rate quotation is the price of the base currency in "terms" of the terms currency. Usually profits and losses arise in the terms currency. If we receive a quote of US$1 = A$1.61, then the price of one US dollar is 1.61 Australian dollars. The base currency is the US dollar and the commodity currency is the Australian dollar. If the exchange rate moves to 2.10, then the US$ has strengthened against the Australian dollar. In practice, a quotation is given by writing the base currency first, followed by a slash, then the terms currency and then the exchange rate. For example, US$/JP¥ 103.50 means that one US dollar is exchanged for 103.50 Japanese yen.

A quotation usually includes a bid and offer rate. For example, suppose a bank quotes US$/EUR 1.1364–74, where the bid rate is 1.1364 and the offer is 1.1374. In determining which rate will apply to the transaction we need to go back to basics. A quote is always the *terms* currency value of one unit of the base currency, and the bid is where the bank will buy and the offer is where it will sell. Combining these two rules, the bid of 1.1364 is the rate at which the bank will buy the base currency and the offer of 1.1374 is where it will sell the base currency.[2] Conversely, we *sell* the base currency at their *bid* rate and we *buy* the base currency at their *offer* rate.

If we look at a bank page of FX quotations on a quote vendor screen, each currency pair is quoted against the US dollar as is shown in *Figure 6.1.* This primarily reflects the interbank markets that exist between FX dealers. It would

[2] A useful "rule of thumb" is that the bank will always provide a quote that will make them money—they will buy the base currency at a lower rate than they will sell it.

Figure 6.1
FX Quotes Against the US Dollar

Interbank exchange rates
World spot currency rates against the US dollar (Updates in GMT)

-----UK sterling-----			----Deutsche mark----			-----Japanese yen----		
01:24	SPM	1.5789-94	01:24	SPM	1.4120-30	01:25	SER	100.90-00
01:24	SPM	1.5796-01	01:24	SPM	1.4116-21	01:25	SER	100.92-02
01:22	SPM	1.5789-94	01:22	SPM	1.4122-27	01:25	SER	100.90-00

-----Swiss franc-----			----French franc-----			---Canadian dollar---		
01:24	SPM	1.1364-74	01:24	SPM	4.8695-25	01:14	CTY	1.3536-46
01:24	SPM	1.1358-68	01:24	SPM	4.8673-03	00:56	CTY	1.3530-40
01:22	SPM	1.1363-73	01:22	SPM	4.8693-23	00:46	CTY	1.3530-40

-Netherlands guilder-			----Belgian franc----			----Australian dollar-----		
22:55	RBC	1.5773-09	21:50	CCN	28.98-01	22:54	RBC	1.5247-1.5252
22:54	RBC	1.5773-09	21:44	CCN	28.99-02	21:53	RBC	1.5253-1.5258
21:53	RBC	1.5773-09	21:37	CCN	29.00-03	21:49	CCN	1.5255-1.5261

Source: Compuserve

The format of the quote is time, bank and bid-offer.

be too difficult for dealers to provide live quotes to one another in all possible currency combinations. Instead quotes are made in the most commonly traded and understood combinations of currencies that typically still include the US dollar.

There is considerable volume of FX transactions in currency combinations that do not involve the US dollar—these are usually referred to as *cross rates*. Where there is significant volume in a cross rate, such as the EUR/JP¥, dealers provide direct live quotes to one another. However, in other less traded currency combinations, such as A$/CA$, the quotation can be determined using the chain calculation. This is a useful 4-step calculation to ensure the exchange rates are not accidentally inverted and that the bids and offers are correctly incorporated. The four steps are as follows:

1. Identify the desired base and terms currency in the exchange rate quote and which currency will be bought and sold.
2. Obtain the US$ quote for the base currency according to whether it is to be bought or sold. If it is not already the base currency, take the inverse of the US$ quote.
3. Obtain the US$ quote for the terms currency based on whether it is to be bought or sold. Make sure it is the terms currency in this quote.

4. Multiply the number in step 2 by the number in step 3.

Using the quotes from *Figure 6.1* we construct a A$/CA$ cross rate quote where we sell A$ and buy CA$ using the chain rule:

1. Desired exchange rate: Sell A$1 = Buy (−) CA$
2. Current US$/A$ rate: Buy US$1 = Sell 1.5252
   Make A$ base rate: Sell A$1 = Buy US$0.6556
3. Current US$/CA$ rate: Sell US$1 = Buy CA$1.3536
4. Cross rate (2 × 3): Sell A$1 = Buy CA$0.8874

We can see that in calculating the cross rate, the spread on both the US$/A$ and the US$/CA$ has lowered the exchange rate at which we can buy A$. In fact if we calculate the rate at which A$ can be bought against the CA$ the complete cross rate quotation is:

A$/CA$ = 0.8874 – 20

Not surprisingly, the spread has almost doubled from the direct quotes to the US$. This is an important feature of cross rates—the spread is much wider than on a directly quoted exchange rate making cross rates more expensive to trade.

6.3 SHORT-TERM FORWARD FX TRANSACTIONS

6.3.1 General Description

Short-term forward FX transactions represent the bulk of FX turnover. They are an agreement between two parties on an exchange of currency cash flows at some date after the cash, or spot, FX transactions settle. In most currency combinations, a forward is any transaction settling in three business days or more.

The market for forward FX is very liquid and has been in existence since the floating of exchange rates in the 1970s. With the floating of exchange rates came the desire by organizations with FX exposures to fix the exchange rate on future foreign currency cash flows using forward instruments. They represent a "plain vanilla" transaction; that is, they are a simple transaction, have substantial liquidity at low spreads and are widely available from a range of financial institutions.

A forward FX contract usually represents a commitment to undertake physical delivery; that is, full currency cash flows at settlement. It is common practice, however, for banks to agree to offset, or net the cash flows arising from more than one FX transaction settling in the same currency. For example, if a customer has the following two transactions settling with a bank:

1. buy US$50 million/sell DM71 million
2. sell US$50 million/buy DM69.5 million,

the bank may agree to net the two transactions so that there are no US dollar cash flows and a net payment of DM1.5 million by the customer. This type of offsetting regularly occurs where forward FX transactions are used for trading purposes.

The same quotation conventions discussed in Section 6.1.2 apply to forward FX transactions. An additional feature applied to forward FX quotations is that rather than quoting an outright rate, it is often expressed as the differential in exchange rate points between the prevailing spot rate and the forward rate, termed "forward points." For example, if the spot exchange rate is 0.7230 and the forward rate is 0.7110 then the forward points would be a discount of 120 points. As we will see in the following section, forward points can be added or subtracted from the spot rate, referred to as premium or discount points respectively. Often a bank quote does not indicate whether points are at a premium or discount. This has to be determined by examining the relationship between the forward point bid and offer. If the forward points appear to be the wrong way around, that is, the bid is higher than the offer, then the forward rate is at a discount. If the bid and offer seem to be correct, the forward rate is at a premium.

Figure 6.2 shows the usual presentation of forward FX quotations using the spot rate and forward points. As is shown in this example, forward points are often expressed as whole integers rather than in their decimal equivalent. To determine the decimal equivalent, count the number of digits to the right of the decimal points in the spot quote and apply this to the forward points. The actual forward exchange rates implied by these quotes are also provided.

6.3.2 Synthetic Replication of Forward FX Transactions

To understand the pricing of a forward FX deal, we will look at how it can be synthetically replicated using cash instruments. Forward FX transactions are comprised of the simultaneous execution of a spot FX transaction and a money market borrowing and lending. As can be seen from *Figure 6.3*, a forward sale of the domestic currency can be replicated by a spot FX deal to buy the foreign currency and sell the domestic currency, combined with a domestic currency borrowing and foreign currency investment.

Traditionally forward FX has been explained in terms of "domestic" and "foreign" currencies and money markets. While a useful explanation, it is a limited view of foreign exchange transactions. Often both currencies in a foreign exchange deal are "foreign" to both counterparties. For this reason, we will avoid referring to "domestic" and "foreign" currencies for the remainder of this book.

Figure 6.2
Spot Rates and Forward Points

Market quotation

Time GMT	CCY	SPOT	Forward maturity date 1 mth	3 mths	6 mths
15:30	GBP	1.5525-35	1.5514-25	1.5499-11	1.5469-81
15:30	DEM	1.4385-95	1.4364-76	1.4319-30	1.4257-69
15:30	CHF	1.1580-90	1.1546-58	1.1472-85	1.1367-82
15:30	JPY	101.45-55	101.00-12	100.05-17	98.77-90
15:30	FRF	4.9345-55	4.9318-31	4.9275-92	4.9248-68
13:29	NZD	0.6513-20	0.6500-07	0.6474-82	0.6438-47
15:35	HKD	7.7355-65	7.7363-83	7.7390-10	7.7453-83
15:39	SGD	1.4120-25	1.4090-98	1.4019-27	1.3933-47

Implied forward points

CCY	Spot	1 mth	3 mths	6 mths
GBP	1.5525-35	11/0	26/114	56/44
DM	1.4385-95	21/9	66/55	128/116
CHF	1.1580-90	34/22	108/95	213/198
JPY	101.45-55	45/33	140/128	268/266
FRF	4.9345-55	27/14	70/53	97/77
NZD	0.6513-20	13/6	39/31	75/66
HKD	7.7355-65	8/28	35/45	98/128
SGD	1.4120-25	30/22	101/93	187/173

Comment: If forward offer > bid then forward points are a premium.
If forward offer < bid then forward points are a discount.

An interesting feature of forward FX is the relatively simple method of constructing a synthetic forward—all it relies on is the ability of an organization to execute simple financial transactions. The ease with which short-term forwards can be executed makes forward markets in most freely floating exchange rate economies efficient and arbitrage opportunities minimal.

Figure 6.4 provides an illustration of how a synthetic replication can be constructed. A company will receive US$ in six months' time that it wants to convert immediately into JP¥. It is concerned that the JP¥ will rise against the US$ over the next few months and decides to buy JP¥ forward against the US$. It is not permitted to use derivatives so it must create the forward using only cash instruments. To synthetically create the FX forward, the company buys JP¥ against the US$ at a spot rate of 103. The settlement of this spot transaction in

Figure 6.3
Forward FX: Three Deals in One

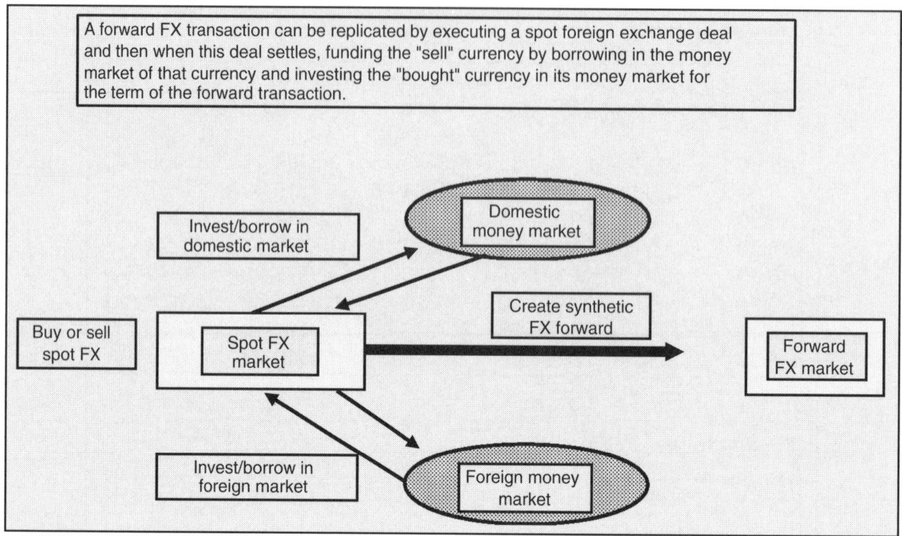

two days requires the company to pay its counterparty US$ and receive JP¥. To fund the US$ settlement, the company borrows in the US$ money market for six months and it invests the JP¥ received for six months. At the end of six months the US$ are received and used to repay the money market borrowing and the JP¥ money market investment matures.

The implied forward FX rate is then given by the respective currency balances at the end of six months, in this case US$1 = JP¥100.99. Because the interest rate on the US$ borrowing is higher than the JP¥ investment interest rate, the US$ currency balance is higher than the JP¥ balance and as a result, the FX rate is at a discount to the spot exchange rate.

The synthetic example demonstrates that, as with any forward transaction, the key variables are the current cash price and the cost of carry. In this case, the cost of carry is 4% pa—the difference between the interest rates for each currency (commonly referred to as the interest differential). However, there is one key difference in the forward FX calculation: the two cash currency balances on which interest is accrued are different. In the interest rate models the value of the asset and the cash required to finance that asset were the same. We will need to incorporate this difference into the pricing model developed in Section 6.2.3.

6.3.3 A Model for Forward FX Prices

In this section we will convert the generalized price formulae from Chapter 4 into a formula that generates a forward FX rate.

Figure 6.4
Synthetic Forward Purchase Example

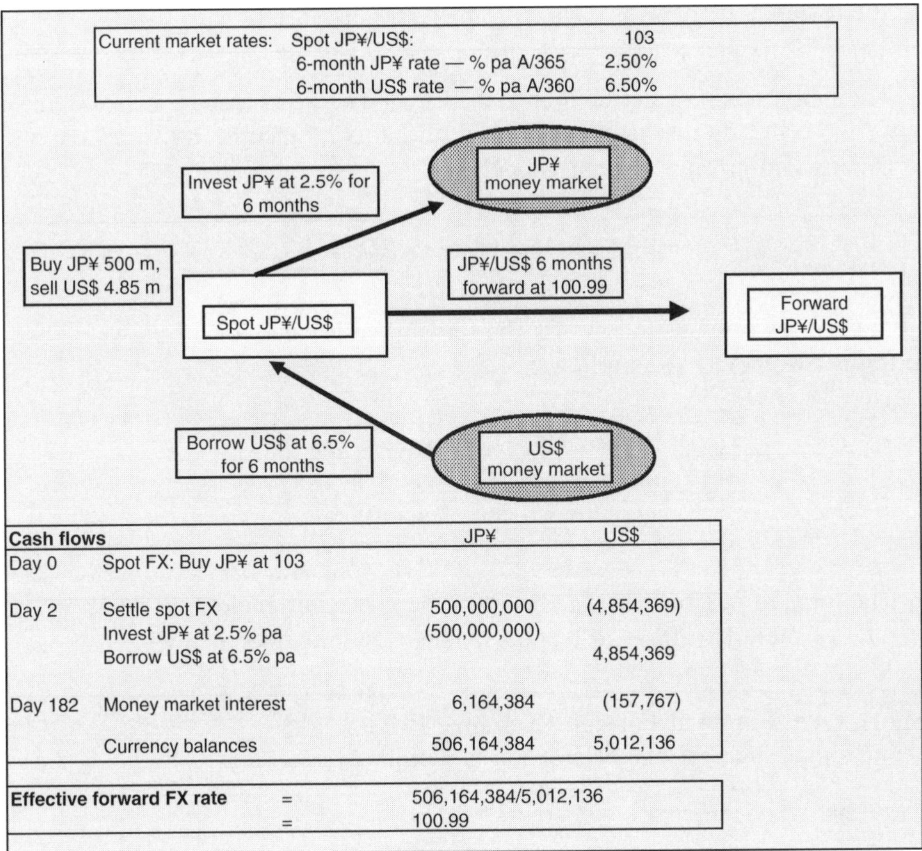

Cash flows		JP¥	US$
Day 0	Spot FX: Buy JP¥ at 103		
Day 2	Settle spot FX	500,000,000	(4,854,369)
	Invest JP¥ at 2.5% pa	(500,000,000)	
	Borrow US$ at 6.5% pa		4,854,369
Day 182	Money market interest	6,164,384	(157,767)
	Currency balances	506,164,384	5,012,136

Effective forward FX rate	=	506,164,384/5,012,136
	=	100.99

A forward FX transaction is an instrument in which cash in one currency is exchanged for cash in another currency. Either currency can be thought of as the underlying asset. These assets provide constant and known incomes in the form of interest payments. We know that these assets can be exchanged on a spot basis at a rate of one unit of the base currency for S units of the terms currency.

The spot exchange rate is the current rate of exchange of two currencies. The synthetic replication above indicates that the forward exchange rate of two currencies is dependant on their respective interest rates. The FX pricing formula has a lot in common with the general forward models developed in Chapter 4. However, the formula needs to be adjusted because interest amounts, r and q, are calculated on different currency amounts—one unit of the base currency for every S units of the terms currency. We also need to incorporate the possibility that the calculation basis underlying each interest rate may differ. Generally for short-term forwards the main differences between money market interest rates are:

- the assumed number of days pa (either 360 or 365);
- whether the rate is based on a discount or yield calculation.[3]

The simplest approach is to look at the forward value of cash in each currency. As we have already discussed, cash by itself earns no income, so we can apply the general "no-income" pricing model:

$$F = S \times (1 + r) \times f/D$$

This can be rewritten as follows for the forward cash value for the base (F_B) and the terms currency (F_T) as follows:

Base currency: $F_B = 1 \times (1 + r_B) \times f/D_B$
Terms currency: $F_T = S \times (1 + r_T) \times f/D_T$
where S is the exchange rate.

The forward rate of exchange between these two currencies will be given by the ratio of these two forward amounts. This is summarized below:

Short-Term Forward Foreign Exchange Price

Using simple interest, the calculation is as follows:

$$F = \frac{S \times (1 + r_T) \times f/D_T}{(1 + r_B) \times f/D_B}$$

Where:

F = Forward exchange rate
S = Spot exchange rate
r_T = Terms currency interest rate to forward date
r_B = Base currency interest rate to forward date
D_T = Terms currency day count basis (365 or 360)
D_B = Base currency day count basis (365 or 360)
f = Number of days to the forward expiry date from the spot settlement date.

An example of this calculation is set out in *Figure 6.5*.

[3] See Chapter 3, Section 3.3 on valuing short-term money market instruments for more detail on yield and discount interest rates.

Figure 6.5
Forward Pricing Example

The current spot rate for US$/CAD is 1.3513. Calculate the rate of a forward FX deal settling in 30 days from the spot date. The 1-month US$ interest rate is 6.25% pa and the CAD rate is 8.2% pa. Calculate the implied forward FX rate.

$S = 1.3513 \qquad f = 30$

$r_T = 8.20\% \qquad D_T = 365$

$r_B = 6.25\% \qquad D_B = 360$

$$F = \frac{S \times (1 + r_T) \times f/D_T}{(1 + r_B) \times f/D_B}$$

$$= \frac{1.3513 \times (1 + 0.082) \times 30/365}{(1 + 0.0625) \times 30/360}$$

$$= \mathbf{1.3534}$$

Forward points = 0.0021 premium

There are a number of assumptions underlying this calculation. If the assumptions are inappropriate, adjustments need to be made to the formula:

- **Simple interest** There is assumed to be no compounding in the interest calculation. This can be adjusted by applying the compound interest calculation formula from Section 3.2.2.
- **Zero-coupon** The interest rates are assumed to be zero-coupon rates. This is generally an appropriate assumption for forward FX deals of up to six months; most interest rates longer than that contain reinvestment risk. This assumption is relaxed in the section on long-term FX below.
- **Interest rates are yields** The formula assumes that interest rates are yields; that is, the interest amount is given by multiplying the principal value today. If an interest rate is from a discount security that calculates interest on a discount basis, then the discount-to-yield formula should be used from Section 3.3.4.
- **Calculations from spot date** The forward period is from the spot settlement date to the forward settlement date. Strictly speaking, the interest rates

that should be used are the two-day forward interest rates. However, this is usually ignored as the impact is minimal.

Bids and Offers

A forward FX rate is derived from three market rates: the spot FX rate and the interest rates in both currencies. In each case, the appropriate bid and offer rate has to be identified. In FX markets, the bid is the rate at which a dealer is willing to buy the base currency, the offer is where the dealer will sell the base currency; the bid rate is lower than the offer rate. Conversely, we sell the base currency at the bid and buy it at the offer. As noted earlier, from an end-user's point of view, we will always lose money from the bid-offer spread; that is, we should buy high and sell low.

Unfortunately in money markets, bids and offers can have two meanings depending on the underlying money market instrument. If the underlying instrument is a direct term deposit with a bank, then the bid will be where you can invest funds with the bank and the offer is where you can borrow from the bank—the bid interest rate is lower than the offer interest rate. However, if the instrument is a tradeable security, such as a bank bill, where the underlying security is bought and sold according to its present value, the bids and offers are expressed in terms of interest rates. As a lower price implies a higher yield, the bid interest rate is higher that the offer interest rate. One way of avoiding confusion with these conventions is to apply the "rule of thumb" to interest rates, i.e., an end-user will invest at the lower interest rate and borrow at the higher interest rate.

Assuming that we are end-users rather than FX dealers, the simplest method of identifying the appropriate rates is to make use of the synthetic replication concept to identify whether to use the bid or offer. If we wish to buy the base currency forward in three months, the synthetic replication is to buy the base currency in the spot FX market, borrow in the terms currency and invest in the base currency. In this case, the appropriate rates are as follows for a forward purchase or sale:

Calculating Forward Rates (End-User Perspective): Bids and Offers

Leg	Buy base currency forward	Sell base currency forward
Spot foreign exchange	offer	bid
Base money market[1]	bid (low rate)	offer
Terms money market[1]	offer (high rate)	bid

[1]The quote convention in this table assumes underlying instruments are bank deposits.

An example of using the correct bids and offers is set out in the first part of *Figure 6.6*.

6.3.4 A Forward FX Valuation Model

The forward value of a forward FX transaction is the difference between the original contract price and the prevailing market forward price. A forward FX transaction is usually expressed in terms of a constant amount of the base currency, while the terms currency varies and all gains and losses are generated in the commodity currency. The forward value in the terms currency of a forward FX contract, where the base currency is purchased and the terms currency is sold, can be expressed as follows:[4]

$$\text{Forward value}_{\text{TERMS}} = \text{Base amount} \times F_M - \text{Base amount} \times F_C$$

Where

F_M is the prevailing forward market rate
F_C is the contract rate.

If the terms currency is constant, the situation is inverse, as follows, for a bought base currency position:

$$\text{Forward value}_{\text{BASE}} = \text{Terms amount}/F_C - \text{Terms amount}/F_M$$

The mark-to-market on a forward FX position is calculated by present-valuing these forward value calculations. It is essential to correctly identify the currency in which the forward value is generated. As the interest rate usually differs between the two currencies, the present value of a forward cash flow in either currency will be different. So, if the forward value is calculated in the terms currency it should be present valued using the terms currency interest rate:

$$\text{Present value}_{\text{TERMS}} = \text{Forward value}_{\text{TERMS}}/(1 + r_T \times f/D)$$

otherwise if the forward value is in the base currency:

$$\text{Present value}_{\text{BASE}} = \text{Forward value}_{\text{BASE}}/(1 + r_B \times f/D)$$

[4] A sold base currency/purchased terms currency has the same formula with the forward rates F_M and F_C reversed.

Figure 6.6 provides an example of the current mark-to-market revaluation of a forward FX position.

For some discussion on the risk characteristics of forward FX transactions, see Section 6.4.2 below.

6.3.5 FX Swaps

The BIS survey, an extract of which forms the appendix for Chapter 1 of this book, identified that a very large percentage of global foreign exchange volume is in the form of FX swaps—the simultaneous execution of offsetting spot and forward foreign exchange transactions.[5] These transactions are distinct from cross-currency interest rate swaps (currency swaps). FX swaps are generally short-term in nature and consist of just a spot and forward leg. Currency swaps are longer term instruments, typically in the range of one to ten years and involve a series of periodic interest exchanges. While they are different instruments, the overall economics of the two transactions have the same effect of switching one currency exposure to another, for the life of the instrument.

The popularity of FX swaps is a reflection of the functions they perform:

- the temporary conversion of one currency to another without creating an exposure to foreign exchange movements;
- extending existing forward FX positions;
- a vehicle for trading the pure interest differential of two currencies without an exposure to exchange rates;
- a vehicle for arbitrage-related activities, such as covered interest arbitrage.

Like a bond repurchase agreement, an FX swap allows the two counterparties to temporarily exchange one asset for another; in this case, one currency for another. By itself, the transaction does not create an outright foreign exchange exposure, because any gains or losses on the initial spot currency exchange are offset by gains and losses on the final forward exchange.

The mechanics of an extension or rollover of an existing FX position consist of two legs:

1. **The spot leg** A spot FX deal is executed, which offsets the cash flows from the original forward deal. This will typically realize a gain or loss equivalent to the difference between the original forward rate and the current spot rate.[6]

[5] An FX swap can also be the simultaneous execution of offsetting forward transactions with different terms.
[6] Some countries still allow "historic rate rollovers." In these transactions, the gain or loss is not liquidated on the rollover date but is carried until the forward transaction finally matures. This introduces another component to calculating the forward FX price—an interest adjustment for any gains or losses funded by the FX dealer. In many countries, these transactions have been banned, due to the possibility of concealing trading losses for long periods of time.

Figure 6.6
Forward FX Transaction

You currently hold a forward FX position where you buy GBP/sell US$10 m at 1.5340. This contract will settle in 92 days' time. Given the market rates below, calculate the current revaluation of this position.

Market rates

	bid	offer
Spot GBP/US$:	1.5629	1.5634

3 month money market rates (Deposit rates)

	Bid	Offer
GBP	6.55	6.65
USD	5.53	5.75

1. Calculate current forward FX price

We wish to revalue a bought GBP forward FX position. The current market value will be given by the forward FX price at which an offsetting position can be put in place. Consequently, we need to generate a 3-month forward price to sell GBP/buy US$. The inputs to the forward price model will be the FX spot rate bid, the GBP money market offer and the US$ money market bid.

S = 1.5629 f = 90
r_T = 5.53% D_T = 360
r_B = 6.65% D_B = 365

$$F = \frac{S \times (1 + r_T) \times f/D_T}{(1 + r_B) \times f/D_B}$$

$$= \frac{1.5629 \times (1 + 0.0553) \times 90/360}{(1 + 0.0665) \times 90/365}$$

$$= 1.5589$$

2. Calculate the forward and present values

The principal value of the transaction is expressed in the terms currency; that is, US$ 10 million, so we use the formula:

Forward value = Terms amount/F_c – Terms amount/F_m

Where:

Terms amount = 10,000,000 US$
F_c = 1.5340
F_m = 1.5589

Forward value = 10,000,000/1.5340 – 10,000,000/1.5589
= 104,125 US$
= 66,794 GBP

Present value = Forward value/(1 + $r_T \times f/D_T$)
= 102,705 US$
= 65,715 GBP

The mark-to-market revaluation on this position is a profit of US$ 102,705.

2. **The forward leg** A forward FX deal is executed at the prevailing forward rate. The net cost of this transaction will be the spot and forward spreads and the forward points.

If these two legs are executed separately, there is a risk that the spot FX rate will change between executing the spot and forward legs. An FX swap reduces a rollover to one deal and removes the FX risk by simultaneously executing both legs. In an FX swap, the transaction becomes insensitive to the spot exchange rate used and the important variable in the transaction is the forward points—it is for this reason that forward points are also referred to as swap points or the swap rate.

Figure 6.7 demonstrates how a forward FX position expiring in two days can be extended for another three months with one FX swap transaction.

6.3.6 Covered Interest Arbitrage

As previously mentioned, unlike other derivative instruments, forward FX transactions can be easily replicated. Therefore, many market participants look for mispricing in foreign exchange and money markets and then take advantage of this by executing arbitrage transactions. Given the development and liquidity of FX markets, these arbitrage opportunities are now limited in the major currencies.

FX arbitrage involves the ability to identify a discrepancy between current market quoted forward points and the synthetic cost of creating that transaction. These arbitrage opportunities are often referred to as covered interest arbitrage. The mechanics and cash flows of this type of arbitrage transaction are outlined in *Figure 6.8.*

6.4 LONG-TERM FORWARD FX TRANSACTIONS

6.4.1 General Description

As the name implies, long-term forward foreign exchange (LTFX) transactions are a longer term version of the forward FX transaction. They are an agreement between two parties on an exchange of currency cash flow at some date in the future. For our purposes, we will consider an LTFX as any forward contract *longer* than six months.

LTFX contracts are a relatively small proportion of total FX market volume. While most FX dealers will quote LTFX transactions out to five years, given the lower liquidity of these instruments, the bid-offer spread is wider than for short-term forwards, and reversing the position can be complicated.

Typically, LTFX contracts are associated with hedging FX exposures created by long-term borrowings, or income streams created by assets in foreign currencies. Often LTFX transactions and currency swaps are used interchangeably, and an advantage of LTFX transactions is that they can be more easily tailored to meet uneven future cash flows.

Figure 6.7
Extending a Forward FX Deal with an FX Swap

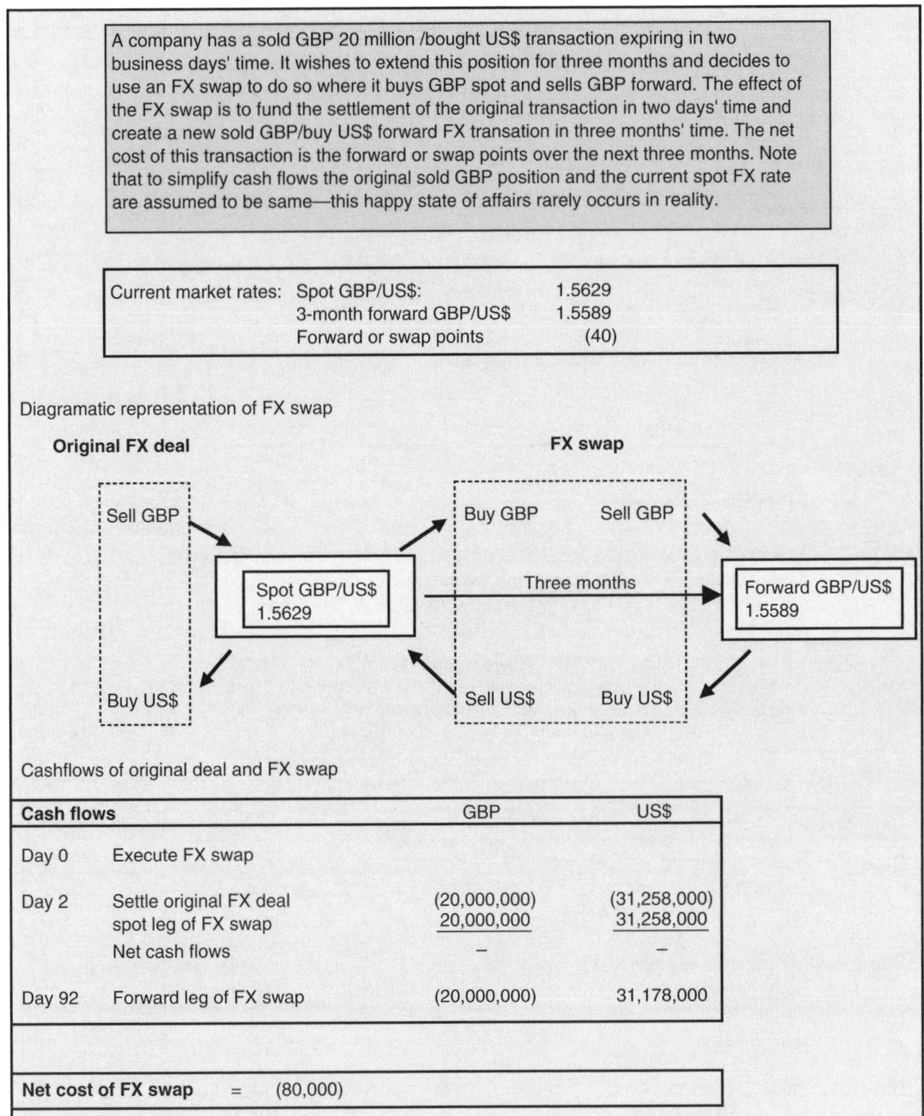

Cash flows		GBP	US$
Day 0	Execute FX swap		
Day 2	Settle original FX deal	(20,000,000)	(31,258,000)
	spot leg of FX swap	20,000,000	31,258,000
	Net cash flows	–	–
Day 92	Forward leg of FX swap	(20,000,000)	31,178,000

Net cost of FX swap = (80,000)

6.4.2 Pricing and Valuing LTFX Transactions

The synthetic replication of an LTFX is the same as a forward FX transaction—the borrowing and lending legs are just for a longer term. Likewise, the valuation procedure is identical. However, the valuation of LTFX is complicated by the following two factors:

Figure 6.8
Covered Interest Arbitrage

Suppose you work at the foreign exchange arbitrage desk of a fund manager and you identify an arbitrage opportunity in 6-month forward DM/US$. Using the market data below identify the arbitrage strategy and the cash flows resulting from this strategy. You decide to execute a transaction with a spot leg of US$ 10 m.

Market rates	bid	offer
Spot DM/US$:	1.4120	1.4130
6-month forward:	1.3972	1.3983
Forward points:	−0.0148	−0.0147

6-month money market rates (Deposit rates)

	Bid	Offer
DM	4.00	4.13
US$	5.75	5.88

Arbitrage strategy

The forward price implies a wider interest differential than from prevailing money market rates. This makes the forward price "cheap" relative to the forward price that can be generated synthetically. The strategy is as follows:

1. Buy the US$/sell DM forward at 1.4000 for 180 days; the face value covers both US$ principal and interest.
2. Create a synthetic sold US$/bought DM position at an effective rate of
3. Earn an arbitrage profit of in 182 days' time.

Cash flows		**DM**	**US$**
Day 0	Buy US$/Sell DM forward		
	Sell US$/Buy DM spot		
	Arrange money market deals		
Day 2	Borrow US$ at 5.88% pa		10,000,000
	Settle spot FX deal	(14,120,000)	(10,000,000)
	Invest DM at 4% pa	14,120,000	
	Net cash flows	–	–
Day 182	Settle forward FX deal	(14,394,100)	10,294,000
	Repay US$ borrowing		(10,294,000)
	Receive DM investment	14,398,532	
	Net cash flows	4,431	–

Net arbitrage gain	=	4,431.31	DM
		0.00044	Points

- **Zero-coupon yield** The forward pricing and valuation models assume that there are no interest cash flows during the forward period—that is, the interest rates are zero-coupon rates. This is a reasonable assumption when using money market interest rates. However, the quoted yields in most currencies that have a term to maturity of more than one year are usually coupon-paying interest rates. The difficulty with coupon-paying interest rates is that there is a reinvestment risk associated with each coupon payment. To price LTFX, this risk has to be removed by deriving zero-coupon interest rates.
- **Compounding** Longer term interest rates are expressed typically as compound interest rates; accordingly, compounding also needs to be incorporated into the model.

If we ignore either of the above factors, the LTFX price will be inaccurate—particularly if the yield curves in each currency have opposite shapes, as this will exacerbate the difference between the zero-coupon and coupon-interest differentials. *Figure 6.9* highlights the difference in the forward price of a 1-year A$/US$ LTFX example, when correctly calculated and when the short-term model is used.

Figure 6.9
LTFX Pricing: Using Zero-Coupon Yields

To demonstrate the impact of using zero-coupon versus coupon yield curves, calculate the LTFX using the two sets of interest rates provided below.

Current market rates

FX Rate	0.7202
1 year, US$ coupon (sa)	5.50%
1 year, US$ zero-coupon (sa)	5.56%
1 year, A$ coupon (ann)	7.60%
1 year, US$ zero-coupon (ann)	7.79%

Correct forward price

Using zero-coupon rate and compounding sa rate **0.7063**

The three components of a short-term forward FX model are a spot exchange rate and two money market instruments. The LTFX model is comprised of a spot FX deal and two zero-coupon bond transactions. LTFX purchase of the base currency can be synthetically replicated by buying the base currency in the spot market, funding the spot settlement of the terms currency by borrowing using a zero-coupon bond and investing the base currency proceeds in a zero-coupon bond that expires on the forward settlement date.

To incorporate this into our forward pricing model, the interest rate legs will use the forward value of a single amount formula (see Chapter 3) for compounding interest and the interest rates entered into the model will be zero-coupon rates.[7] If we incorporate these concepts into a the forward pricing model, we can express the LTFX model as follows:

Long-Term Forward Foreign Exchange (LTFX) Price

Using compounding interest, the calculation is as follows:

$$F = \frac{S \times (1 + r_T / m_T)_T^n}{(1 + r_B / m_B)_B^n}$$

Where:

F = forward exchange rate
S = spot exchange rate
r_T = terms currency zero-coupon interest rate to forward date
r_B = base currency zero-coupon interest rate to forward date
m_T = terms currency payment frequency (i.e., 1, 2, 4, 12)
m_B = base currency payment frequency
n_T = terms currency # of payment periods to the forward date
n_B = base currency # of payment periods to the forward date.

An important characteristic of LTFX contracts is the impact of the interest differential on the forward price. Compared to a short-term forward FX contract, the interest rate legs of LTFX have considerably more impact on the forward price.

Figure 6.10 calculates the LTFX price of a 5-year JP¥/US$ transaction and then graphs the sensitivity of the forward price to movements in the interest differential and the spot price. In this example, a movement of 1% in the exchange rate has the same impact as a 0.20% pa. change in the interest differential.

[7] Zero-coupon rates are often not observable as a market quote, so the rates will need to be generated from coupon-paying, or par, yields such as prevailing swap rates. To see how to generate zero-coupon yield, see the section on yields in Chapter 8.

The forward value of an LTFX contract is the same as for a short-term forward FX contract, i.e., the difference between the contract value and the current market value. However, when calculating the present value, we need to take account of the same yield considerations as the LTFX price. As a result, we

Figure 6.10
LTFX Pricing and Sensitivities

The graph below shows the sensitivity of a 5-year JP¥/US$ LTFX deal to changes in both the interest differential and the spot exchange rate. A feature of LTFX transactions is the increasing importance of the interest differential the longer the term to expiry. In this 5-year deal the impact of a move in the exchange rate of 1% is approximately equal to a change in the interest differential of 0.20% pa.

Market data	
Spot FX rate	101.00
US$ 5-year rate % pa (sa)	6.20
JP¥ 5-year rate % pa (sa)	2.50
Interest differential % pa	3.70

$$\text{LTFX price} = \frac{S \times (1 + r_T/m_T)\wedge n_T}{(1 + r_B/m_B)\wedge n_B}$$

$$= \frac{101 \times (1 + 0.025/2)\wedge 10}{(1 + 0.062/2)\wedge 10}$$

$$= 84.2723374$$

The sensitivities of this position in foreign exchange points are as follows:

PVBP = –0.0368
That is, a 1 bp rise in the interest differential will decrease the present value of the position by 0.0368 fx points.

PVFP = 0.0074
That is, a 0.01 change in the spot FX rate will alter the present value by 0.0074

PVD = 0.0075
Each day that passes increases the present value by 0.0075 fx points.

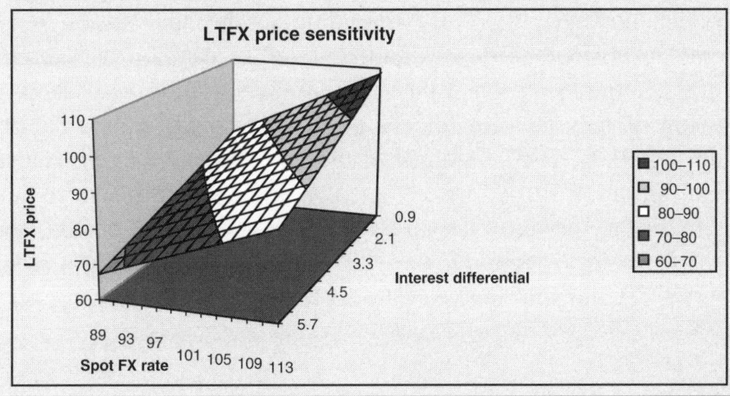

calculate the present value of the LTFX contract using a zero-coupon yield and apply the following, compound interest, present value formula:[8]

$$\text{Present value}_{\text{BASE}} = \text{Forward value}_{\text{BASE}}/(1 + r_B/m_B)_B^n$$

Risk Characteristics: PVBP, PVFP and Time

As with interest rate derivatives, the risk characteristics of a forward FX transaction can be summarized using the PVBP concept. However, we need to alter how the definition is applied so that we can highlight the key sensitivities of a forward FX transaction, the spot FX rate and the interest differential. While a PVBP can be calculated with respect to each interest rate, if the interest rate in both currencies moves the same way then, to a large extent, the impact will be offsetting. What we are particularly interested in is where interest movements are *not* offsetting; that is, where the interest differential changes. For this purpose, when we calculate the PVBP in the following example, it is actually the present value of a one basis point change in the interest differential.

As PVBP refers specifically to "basis point," which is an interest rate expression, we need to be careful how it is used in relation to exchange rates. For our purposes, we will use the term "present value of one FX point," or PVFP, to describe the sensitivity of the present value of an instrument to a change in the exchange rate by one FX point. An FX point is the minimum unit to which an exchange rate is quoted. For most exchange rates, this single point will be at the fourth decimal point (0.0001). For example, in DM/US$ quote it is the change from 1.4000 to 1.4001. However, for the JP¥/US$ it will be the second decimal point (0.01), while for ITL/US$ it will be a whole integer.

With long-term forwards, the time remaining to expiry of the forward has a substantial impact upon the forward price. When generating the sensitivity of a forward FX transaction, we need to incorporate the sensitivity of the present value of a contract to the passing of time. This is often discussed with respect to options models; however, it is also important in the analysis of long-term forwards where the cost of carry is significant. It is common to express this sensitivity as the change in present value of a contract to buy the base currency due to the passing of one day—so for our purposes, we will call it the present value of one day, or PVD. The magnitude of the time effect is heavily dependant on the interest differential. If the forward rate is at a discount, then each day that passes will increase the forward rate, so there is a positive relationship between the time and the forward FX rate. However, if the forward rate is at a premium, there is a negative relationship between the forward FX rate and time.

[8] This is the base currency present value, to generate the terms currency present value, substitute terms currency variables for the base currency variables used.

In *Figure 6.10*, the three sensitivities of the 5-year LTFX contract, to interest differential, spot FX rate and time are provided. *Figure 6.11* revalues this same position after three months and analyzes the effectiveness of the sensitivity measures. The estimated valuation based on the original sensitivities proves to be a substantial over-estimate. The main cause of this over-estimate is the fact that the pricing inputs are related, and in this example, an increase in the interest differential also increases the interest effect. The lesson from this example is that sensitivities should be recalculated regularly and, if possible, the inter-relationships between these factors re-estimated.

6.5 PAR FORWARDS

6.5.1 General Description

Another form of LTFX is the par-forward. It is a series of LTFX contracts with regularly spaced settlement dates (e.g., monthly or quarterly) at a constant exchange rate. *Figure 6.12* compares the exchange rate of a 5-year CHF/US$ par-forward transaction with a series of LTFX contracts that would achieve the same effect. The benefit for an end-user is that it allows the benefit or cost of a forward discount or premium to be spread out over the life of the transaction. In the example provided, US$ can be bought at a substantially lower exchange rate in the first two years of the transaction than implied by traditional forward instruments. The downside, of course, is that after year two the exchange rate is higher.

In terms of the present value of these transactions, the economics of a par-forward and a series of LTFX transactions are the same. In terms of the FX transaction, there seems to be little added value in a par-forward. The advantage of these instruments is that they can be very useful for cash flow management and tax planning.

For example, suppose a Swiss-based distribution company is about to commence importing equipment from the US. It has signed a 5-year contract that will require it to buy US$ 10 million of equipment every quarter. The initial set-up costs associated with selling this equipment will be substantial, and at current exchange rates the company is likely to have negative CHF cash flows for the first two years, after which time cash flows will turn positive. The company talks to its bank and the bank is concerned about financing the new project given its long lead time and currency exposures. A solution is for the Swiss company to cover the exposures using the forward FX rates outlined in *Figure 6.12*. From the Swiss manufacturer's point of view, a par-forward would be more beneficial than a series of LTFX contracts. Par forwards provide an immediately lower CHF cost for the equipment imports and possibly create a positive cash flow in the first two years. The downside is that the CHF cost of the equipment is relatively higher than a series of LTFX contracts. The par-forward allows the Swiss company to obtain forward FX cover and also to smooth out its cash flows.

A par-forward has some similarities with fixed-to-fixed cross currency interest rate swaps. It involves a constant exchange of currency cash flows as opposed to the variable cash flows of LTFX contracts. We will see in the discussion of currency swaps that par forwards can be a useful tool in managing swap exposures.

Figure 6.11
LTFX Revaluation and Sensitivities

You have executed the 5-year LTFX transaction from *Figure 6.10.* Three months later you are interested in determining the present value of the transaction and also the current risk characteristics of the transaction.

Original deal data	
Term	5 Years
US$ amount	US$100 m
Transaction	Buy US$
Original rate	84.27

Current market data	
Term remaining	4.75 Years
Spot FX rate	108.00
US$ 5-year rate % pa (sa)	7.50
JP¥ 5-year rate % pa (sa)	2.00
Interest differential % pa	5.5

1. Calculate current forward price

$$\text{LTFX price} = \frac{S \times (1 + r_T/m_T)\wedge n_T}{(1 + r_B/m_B)\wedge n_B}$$

$$= \frac{108 \times (1 + 0.02/2)\wedge 9.5}{(1 + 0.07/2)\wedge 9.5}$$

$$= 83.67$$

While the spot rate has moved nearly 7% in favor of the position, the widening of the the interest differential has more than offset this positive effect and the LTFX price is now lower than when originally executed.

2. Calculate value of position

Forward value = Base amount × F_m – Base amount × F_c

Where:

Base amount = 100,000,000 US$
F_c = 84.27
F_m = 83.67

Forward value = 100,000,000 × 83.67 – 100,000,000 × 84.27
= (60,000,000) JP¥
= (717,103) US$

Present value = Forward value/(1 + r_T/m_T)^n_T
= –60,000,000/(1 + 0.02/2)^9.5
= (54,588,128) JP¥
= (505,446) US$

Figure 6.11 Continued

The current mark-to-market value of this position is a loss of JP¥ 54.588 m or US$0.505 m. The PVBP and the PVFP calculated at the orginal time of the transaction would suggest a loss as follows.

Change in differential	=	180 basis points
PVBP	=	−0.0368
Estimated effect	=	−6.624
Change in FX rate	=	700 FX points
PVFP	=	0.0074
Estimated effect	=	5.18
Change in time	=	90 days
PVD	=	0.0075
Estimated effect	=	0.675
Estimated net effect	=	−0.769 FX points
	=	(76,900,000) JP¥
Over-estimate of loss	=	(22,311,872)

The PVBP, PVFP and time decay substantially over-estimates the loss. The main cause of this is that the each of these factors has been estimated while the other factors remained constant. There is in fact a correlation between these factors. In this case the time effect is positively correlated with the interest differential and the time effect has increased substantially—see below. If the average time effect over the past three months were incorporated then the estimated loss closely approximates the actual loss. To overcome these estimation problems the sensitivities need to be assessed at least daily and estimates of the correlations between each of these factors is required.

3. Revised sensitivities at three months

PVBP	=	−0.0358
PVFP	=	0.0070
PVD	=	0.0114

6.5.2 Pricing and Valuing Par Forwards

A par-forward is a "smoothed" series of LTFX contracts. Pricing a par-forward involves determining the cash flows from a similar series of LTFX transactions and then making an adjustment for the funding cost or benefit of evenly spreading out the currency cash flows. As is the case for any forward transaction, the present value of executing a par-forward should be zero.

Figure 6.13 shows how to calculate the par-forward rate for the CHF/US$ example from Section 6.5.1. The first step is to calculate the LTFX rates for each periodic par-forward date. We then need to determine what constant CHF delivery amount has an equivalent net present value to the CHF delivery amounts

Figure 6.12
Par-Forward Rate versus Series of LTFX Rates

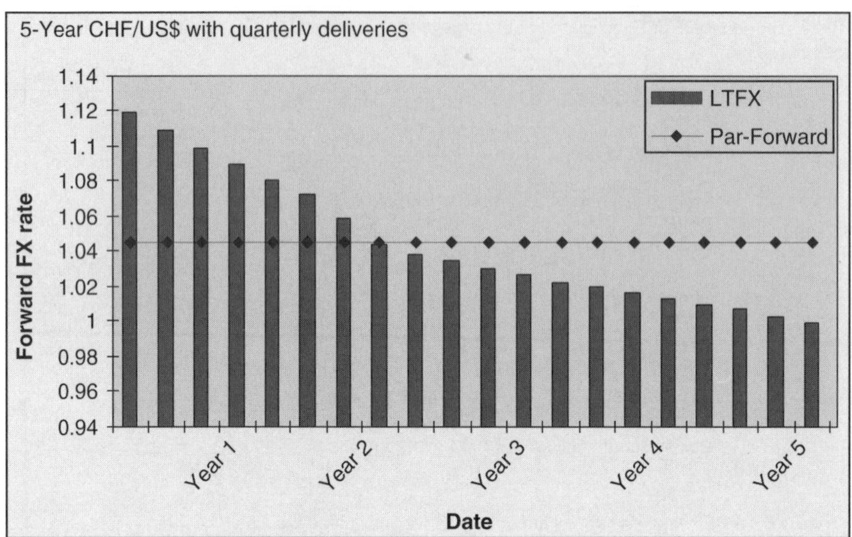

from the series of LTFX amounts. The CHF par forward amounts will save the end-user substantial CHF amounts. In effect, the FX dealer is *lending* the *difference* between the LTFX rate and the par forward rate, and having it repaid in the later delivery amounts. The dealer expects a return on the money it has loaned to the end-user, and the par-forward rate will include a funding cost. The solution is to calculate a par-forward rate which ensures that the total net present value of all the funding differences is equal to zero. In this case, while the average of the LTFX rates is 1.0447, there is a funding cost of 23 points—the correct par-forward rate is 1.0470. Money lent in the early par-forward deliveries is recouped, with interest, in the later deliveries.[9]

To build a similar spreadsheet to this example see the box at the bottom of *Figure 6.13* titled "How This Spreadsheet Works."

Once a par-forward price can be generated, then the valuation procedures are identical to an LTFX contract. However, while a series of LTFX positions can be valued individually, all of the par-forward legs should be valued together due to the interdependence between the series of deliveries.

[9] In practice, FX dealers will want to ensure that the interest rates used reflect market bids and offers and that they earn a positive funding NPV on the transaction. This can be achieved in this model by setting the target NPV at a rate that provides the dealer's required return. For example, in *Figure 6.13*, if the required NPV was CHF100,000 then the par-forward rate would be 1.0476.

Figure 6.13
Pricing a Par-Forward Transaction

Transaction details	
Spot FX rate	1.13
Term (Yrs)	5
Delivery frequency	Quarterly
Quarterly amount	10,000,000

Solution		
Unrounded par forward	1.04701178	change

A	B	C	D	E	F	G	H	I
	Market parameters			LTFX cash flows		Par-forward	Net CHF	Net CHF
	Zero US$ rate	Zero CHF rate	Forward FX rate	US$ amount	CHF amount	CHF amount	funding difference	funding NPV
1	5.7500	2.0000	1.1196	10,000,000	11,195,564	10,470,118	−725,446	(721,837)
2	5.7500	2.0000	1.1092	10,000,000	11,092,093	10,470,118	−621,975	(615,802)
3	5.7817	2.0628	1.0992	10,000,000	10,992,155	10,470,118	−522,037	(514,043)
4	5.8134	2.1257	1.0895	10,000,000	10,894,820	10,470,118	−424,702	(415,793)
5	5.8358	2.2508	1.0810	10,000,000	10,809,644	10,470,118	−339,526	(330,133)
6	5.8582	2.3759	1.0731	10,000,000	10,730,621	10,470,118	−260,504	(251,409)
7	6.6166	2.8575	1.0589	10,000,000	10,588,703	10,470,118	−118,585	(112,821)
8	7.3751	3.3391	1.0435	10,000,000	10,434,820	10,470,118	35,297	33,026
9	7.2463	3.4347	1.0383	10,000,000	10,383,014	10,470,118	87,104	80,653
10	7.1175	3.5304	1.0343	10,000,000	10,342,908	10,470,118	127,210	116,508
11	7.0405	3.6254	1.0300	10,000,000	10,299,796	10,470,118	170,322	154,230
12	6.9634	3.7205	1.0266	10,000,000	10,265,579	10,470,118	204,539	183,032
13	6.9159	3.8062	1.0227	10,000,000	10,227,428	10,470,118	242,690	214,577
14	6.8685	3.8920	1.0196	10,000,000	10,196,121	10,470,118	273,997	239,261
15	6.8380	3.9668	1.0161	10,000,000	10,161,093	10,470,118	309,025	266,506
16	6.8076	4.0416	1.0131	10,000,000	10,131,450	10,470,118	338,668	288,347
17	6.7881	4.1057	1.0098	10,000,000	10,097,918	10,470,118	372,200	312,883
18	6.7686	4.1697	1.0069	10,000,000	10,068,646	10,470,118	401,472	333,110
19	6.7534	4.2142	1.0032	10,000,000	10,032,394	10,470,118	437,724	358,691
20	6.7382	4.2587	0.9999	10,000,000	9,999,221	10,470,118	470,897	381,012
						Net CHF NPV (Target)		(0)

Summary of results	
Average LTFX rate =	1.0447
Funding cost =	0.0023
Par-forward rate =	**1.0470**

How this spreadsheet works

1. Generate the zero-coupon interest rates (on a quarterly basis for columns B and C).
2. Calculate the LTFX rates in column C.
3. Calculate the US$ and CHF cash flows for each quarterly roll for column E and F.
4. Enter a "guess" of the par-forward rate an enter into the cell labelled "unrounded par-forward."
5. Calculate the par-forward CHF amount in column H by multiplying the US$ amount by the unrounded par-forward amount.
6. The Net CHF amount is simply the difference between columns F and G.
7. Calculate the NPV in column I by taking the present value of column H using the CHF zero interest rates and the compound interest present value formula.
8. From the tools menu invoke the "Goal Seek" or "Solver" function.
9. Make the net NPV cell (column I) the target by changing the cell with the unrounded par-forward rate so that the target becomes zero and then press solve, this will iteratively solve for the unrounded par-forward rate that makes the NPV zero.

6.6 CURRENCY FUTURES

6.6.1 General Description

Currency futures are an exchange-traded forward FX instrument. The FX market primarily involves OTC transactions. As a result, the volume in currency futures is low compared to interest rate futures contracts and relatively few of the contracts listed could be considered to be liquid. Despite the lower volume, currency futures can be a useful alternative for smaller users of the FX market, such as small importers or exporters or retail currency speculators. Currency futures provide lower transaction spreads, easier execution and fewer credit issues than dealing with a bank.

6.6.2 Pricing and Valuing Currency Futures

Most currency futures are US dollar exchange rates and in the case of the CME contracts are quoted so that the US dollar is the terms currency. As a result, the currency futures prices reciprocate the exchange rate quoted in the OTC foreign exchange market. The main reason for making the US dollar contract the terms currency is so that all profits and losses, mark-to-markets and initial margins can be calculated and paid in US dollars. This simplifies the cash flow management and accounting for US-based market-users. Foreign currency cash flows occur if the contracts are delivered at expiry.

The pricing model underlying currency futures is the short-term forward FX model from Section 6.3.3. However, like all exchange-traded contracts there are funding costs associated with initial margin and mark-to-market requirements, which are unknown when a futures contract is executed. As a result, the effective forward FX rate of a currency futures contract will not be known until the contract is terminated. This can be expressed as follows:

$$\boxed{\text{Effective forward price} = \text{Futures price} + \text{Funding adjustment}}$$

Figure 6.14 calculates the price of a futures contract and then compares the risk characteristics with an equivalent forward FX transaction. The example shows the forward and futures pricing is quite consistent, with only a small implied arbitrage difference that is likely to be less than transaction costs.

For contracts with a forward period of up to six months, the funding adjustments tend to be small and currency futures and forward FX can be considered perfect substitutes. However, for currency futures with a longer forward term, consideration should be given to incorporating the possible funding consequences of a futures contract.[10]

[10] The convexity adjustment discussed in relation to interest rate contracts is not usually considered in currency futures. In an interest rate futures contract there is a strong positive correlation between a short position and futures funding costs; however, this type of relationship is not as apparent in currency futures.

Figure 6.14
Using Currency Futures

Let us suppose the data below summarizes the market conditions during US trading hours on July 28, 2000. Calculate the theoretical forward DM/US$ rate and compare this to the current December 2000 futures price. Compare the risk characteristics of a December 2000 currency future and a forward FX contract with the same delivery date.

Today:		28-Jul-00
Current FX market data		
CME DM futures (US$/DM)		
Month	Price	Del. date
Sep-00	0.4735	20-Sep-00
Dec-00	0.4758	20-Dec-00
Mar-01	0.478	19-Mar-01
DM/US$ spot rate		2.1180
US$/DM spot rate		0.4721

DM futures contract specifications	
Contract size	DM125,000
Minimum tick	0.0001
Months	Mar, Jun, Sep, Dec

Current interest rates — LIBOR A/360		
Term (days)	US$	DM
30	6.7500	4.4800
90	6.7500	4.5600
180	6.8900	4.7700

1. Calculate current theoretical forward price

Number of days to Dec 00 delivery	=	145
Number of forward days	=	143
Interpolated US$ interest rate	=	6.8324
Interpolated DM interest rate	=	4.6837
Take reciprocal of OTC spot rate	=	0.4721
Calculate theoretical forward rate	=	0.4761
Difference between actual and theoretical	=	0.0003

A small difference does exist between the theoretical forward price and the CME currency futures price; however, after taking account of transaction costs it does not represent an arbitrage opportunity.

2. Risk characterisitcs

Factor	Sensitivity as a % Currency future	Forward FX	Difference %
PVBP	0.00162%	0.00158%	–2.71%
PVFP	0.02118%	0.02062%	–2.71%
PVD	–0.00535%	–0.00521%	–2.71%

The difference between the currency future and the forward FX sensitivities is equal to the difference between a cash flow today and a cash flow in 143 days time—a difference of 2.71%.

The implications of this analysis is that if we were hedging a forward FX contract with a face value of DM 100 m we would only use currency futures with a face value of 97.36 m (approximately 779 of the CME DM contracts).

Currency futures, like any futures contracts, have the same forward and present values. This means that the sensitivity of a currency futures contract to changes in any of the pricing inputs is greater for a forward FX contract with the same forward period. Therefore, a currency futures contract has a higher PVBP, PVFP and PVD than an equivalent forward FX position.

SUMMARY

This chapter examined the pricing and valuation characteristics of short- and long-term FX forwards, par forwards and currency futures. We reviewed standard exchange rate conventions and we created pricing and valuation models based on certain standard assumptions. We discussed FX swaps and also explained covered interest arbitrage.

FURTHER READING

- Anthony, S. *Foreign Exchange Markets.*

SELF-TEST QUESTIONS

1. What is the difference between the *base* currency and the *terms* currency in an FX quotation?
2. Big Co. Inc. will receive US$1,000,000 in three months' time and it needs to convert these funds into JP¥. However, it believes that the JP¥ will rise against the US$ during this time, so it decides to buy JP¥ forward against the US$. Explain how Big Co. Inc. could synthetically replicate this transaction using cash instruments,
3. The current spot rate for US$/JP¥ is 102. Calculate the implied FX forward rate for a transaction settling in 60 days from the spot date. *Note:* the 2-month US$ interest rate is 6.30% pa and the JP¥ rate is 8.10% pa.
4. What three elements comprise a forward FX rate?
5. Assume you want to enter a forward FX position where you sell US$ and buy JP¥ 1,000,000 at 99.20. The forward contract expires in 180 days and the 6-month money market rates are as follows:

Currency	Bid	Offer
US$	6.80%	6.85%
JP¥	2.06%	2.15%

The current spot rate is US$/JP¥ 99.20. What price will you be able to transact the forward at (you are an end-user)?

6. Identify the two factors that "complicate" LTFX transactions. Explain your answer.
7. Define a "par-forward."
8. Explain why a par-forward rate is not simply the average of the LTFX rates.
9. Explain the cashflow difference between a currency future and an FX forward.

CHAPTER 7

EQUITY FORWARDS

OVERVIEW

This chapter examines forward equity instruments. By the end of this chapter we will have developed pricing and valuation models for:

- share price index futures
- individual share futures.

7.1 INTRODUCTION

Equity forwards have gained a reputation as being a highly risky instrument in their relatively short existence. The October 1987 stock market crash, and the 1989 mini-crash, prompted considerable conjecture that stock index futures exacerbated the market fall and, given the losses sustained by long position holders, were too risky to be used by the general public.[1] Then in 1995 the collapse of UK-based Barings Bank, primarily due to unauthorized trading in share price index futures in its Singapore office, prompted more regulatory "navel gazing" with respect to these instruments.

Despite the bad press, share price index futures and all other equity derivatives volume growth has been an outstanding success since they were introduced in the US in 1982. Stock index futures are a classic example of derivatives that add value to organizations and individuals with an exposure to share markets. They provide a method of gaining an exposure to share markets or hedging an existing exposure at considerably lower cost than transacting in the physical market. However, like their underlying market, the price volatility in share index futures is generally higher than most interest rate and currency markets and as a result, they are a risky instrument in the hands of a novice user or uncontrolled trader.

[1] Possibly the most spectacular case of the damage done by stock index futures to over-leveraged users was the Hang Seng Stock Index Futures contract traded on the Hong Kong Futures Exchange. The majority of long position holders at the time of the crash were individual speculators. After the crash, most of these "longs" defaulted on payment of their losses and the market was effectively closed.

An interesting feature of derivatives on equity index futures is the high usage of options relative to both cash market volume and forward volume. In developed interest rate markets, option volume might be 10% of forward volume, but in equity index markets the option percentage is more likely to be 20% or higher. This is partly explained by the high level of volatility, which encourages market participants to take insurance in the form of options. This will be discussed more in Chapter 13.

Share price index futures dominate turnover with very small volume in individual share futures. In the US, this is partly the result of regulatory restrictions, although even where contracts have been listed on individual shares, volume has been low.[2] The bulk of the volume is in US dollar-denominated indices, followed by Japan and then Germany.

Most statistics on derivatives reveal that equity derivative turnover is considerably lower than for interest rate and currency derivatives. While this is consistent with lower volume in the physical or cash share market, many market commentators suggest that the development of equity derivatives lagged behind other asset classes in the early to mid-1990s. We have seen strong growth in equity derivatives over recent years and it is widely perceived that equity derivatives will be a high growth area for the derivatives market over the next five years.[3]

7.2 SHARE PRICE INDEX (SPI) FUTURES

7.2.1 General Description

A share price index (SPI) future is an exchange-traded contract based on a broad-based share price index. A buyer of an SPI futures contract benefits from a rise in the value of the underlying index and loses from a fall in the index; the opposite applies for the seller. SPI futures are not deliverable—at expiry they are cash settled against the underlying index. Over the life of a contract, the buyer should receive or pay the difference between the original purchase price and the final settlement price depending on whether the price has moved higher or lower.

For example, if an S&P 500 futures contract is bought at a price of 600 and the price rises to 625, the buyer will receive a gain equivalent to 25 index points. In this case, each index point is worth US$500, so the total gain is US$2,500 per contract. The seller of this position is in the opposite situation, facing a loss of US$2,500.

SPI futures contracts are more esoteric than other forward contracts we have examined, in that the underlying security is not tradeable and is not deliverable.[4]

[2] Apart from Sweden, individual share futures contracts are relatively new and this may also contribute to the low volume.

[3] See Francis, Toy, Whittaker (ed.), 1995.

[4] While the profit and loss behavior of the SPI can be replicated by a portfolio of shares, this portfolio will not have exactly the same characteristics as the SPI futures contract. For example, the SPI future price is based on an index that has a value related to its original base and the time it has been in existence.

Many market observers describe these products as purely a bet on whether the value of the underlying index will be higher or lower than the traded price on the expiry date, with a payoff linked to how right or wrong they are. In fact, when the S&P 500 contract was launched in 1982, it was considered to be a gimmick with little chance of success. By the end of the 1980s, it's notional daily volume exceeded all of the stocks traded on the NYSE. Despite its esoteric nature, the SPI future is a pure form of forward contract and its price is determined by the same cost of carry factors as any forward instrument. Further, the description of the SPI as a form of bet is just another way of defining a forward contract and can be applied equally to interest rate and equity futures.

The basic specifications developed in the original US SPI futures contracts have been applied all over the world. The value of each contract is determined by multiplying the traded futures price by a fixed multiple. For example, the multiple in the FTSE 10 is UK£25, so if, the futures price is 3,600 then the total contract value will be UK£90,000 and for every one index point change in price, the value of this contract will change by UK£25.

7.2.2 Synthetic Replication of SPI Futures

As with any forward contract, an SPI future can be replicated using cash instruments. In this case, the underlying asset is a portfolio of shares with the same weightings as the underlying index.

Example

Suppose you are a fund manager operating in a share market without an SPI futures contract.[5] You intend to buy shares in three months, but wish to buy at prices prevailing today. The synthetic replication of an SPI futures contract would be to borrow funds to buy the portfolio of shares today and then repay the borrowing in three months' time with the funds you intended to buy the shares with. The price of this forward purchase will be given by the current spot price minus the net financing cost of the portfolio. The cost of carry, therefore, is calculated by the borrowing cost minus dividends received on the portfolio.

Figure 7.1 provides an example of a synthetic purchase of SPI futures. As this example demonstrates, the index can be considered as the current value of a portfolio of shares and the forward price of that index is determined by the interest cost of financing that portfolio minus the expected dividends to be received on that portfolio.

[5] This is a problem faced in a number of countries; while they may have active share markets, an SPI futures contract does not exist and the only method of obtaining forward exposure to these markets is with a synthetic position.

Figure 7.1
Synthetic Replication of a Share Index Price Future Purchase

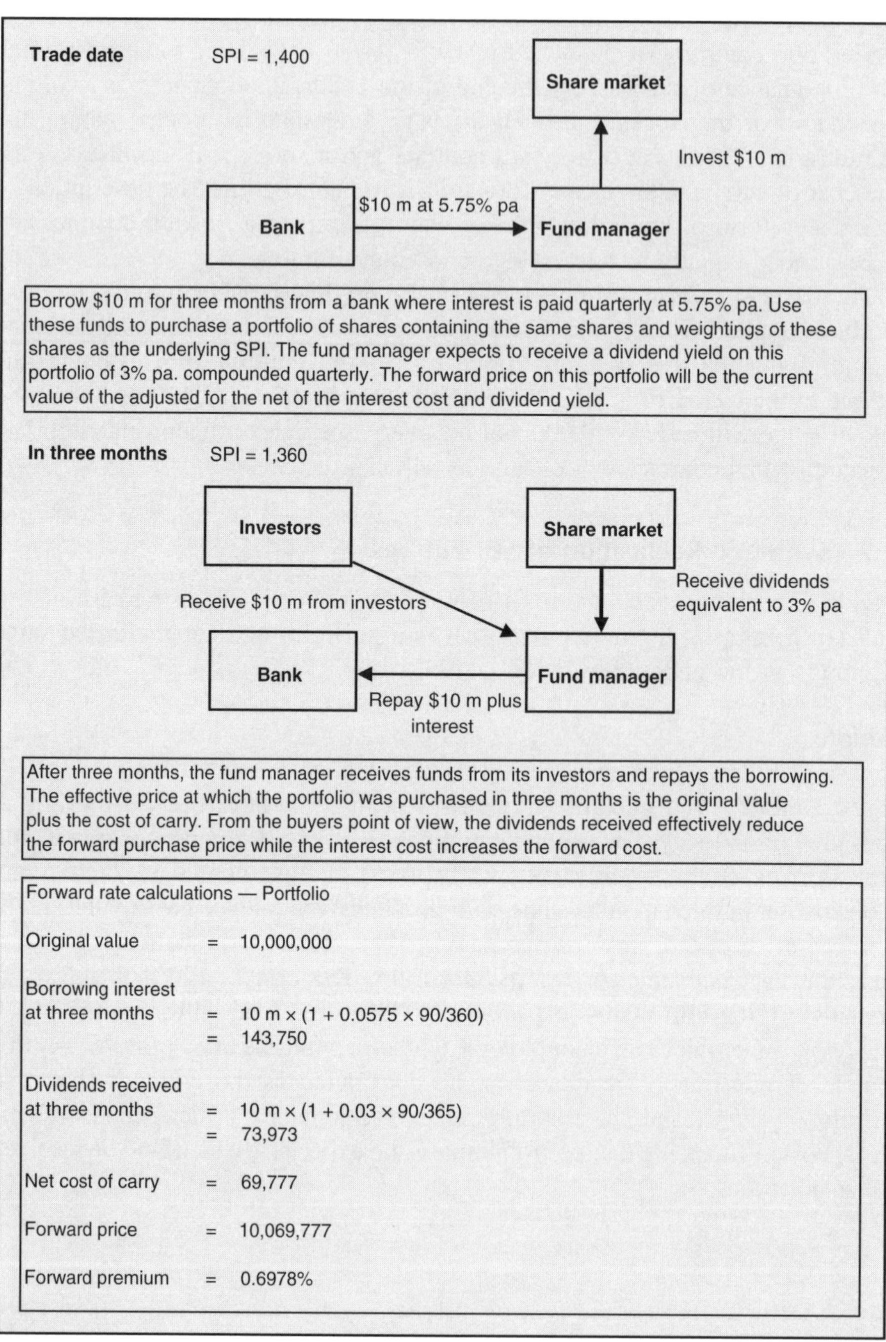

Figure 7.1 Continued

Forward rate calculations — index

Suppose we wish to express the forward price in terms of the SPI index. Essentially, the index is another way of expressing the current value of a portfolio of shares—in this case, the value is 1,400 rather than $10 m. The forward price calculation is then exactly the same as for the portfolio and is given by the net cost of carry. Using the premium as a summary of the net cost of carry, then the 3-month forward SPI price will be:

Forward SPI = Cash SPI × cost of carry
= 1400 × (1 + 0.006978)
= 1,409.77

Cost of carry = 9.77

Gain or loss on forward purchase

The actual value of the index in three months' time is 1,360—the value of the original portfolio has declined by 2.85%. The loss on your forward position is even greater because the cost of carry has increased your effective purchase price.

Loss = Index value – Forward purchase value
= 1360 – 1409.77
= 49.77 index points or −3.53%

Imperfections: Slippage, Transaction Costs and Short Selling

Most SPI futures have broad-based underlying indices; that is, the index is made up of a large number of stocks intended to replicate the performance of the whole stock market or the stock market leaders.[6] Even in the case of the "leader"-type indices, the number of shares involved can create logistical execution problems for synthetic replication. For example, executing an order for 20 shares simultaneously, even on an electronic trading network, may be difficult. It is likely that the portfolio will suffer from "slippage" as you wait for the underlying shares to be purchased, so the index value you achieve may differ from the index value at the time you commenced the strategy.

As synthetic replication is the cornerstone of arbitrage activities, the requirement to buy or sell a large number of stocks can lead to arbitrage problems. This is one of the reasons that SPI futures can trade away from "fair market value," or the forward price implied by synthetic replication (this is called slippage).

[6] For example, the All Ordinaries and All Share indices include a very large basket of shares with their market weightings, while the BEL-20 and Toronto 35 Index are based on the top 20 and 35 shares, respectively. The S&P 500, Nikkei 225 and FTSE 100 are somewhere in between.

If an arbitrage exists, it has to be of significant magnitude to overcome the risks of slippage and any other imperfections.

This deviation from fair market value is most pronounced in less liquid futures markets or underlying share markets that have not developed methods of effectively purchasing portfolios. A common complaint by fund managers is that unless they hold futures contracts until expiry (and the futures price converges with the cash price) then the hedge provided by the futures contract can over or under perform the underlying index due to this mispricing.[7] *Figure 7.2* shows the deviation from fair value of the world's largest SPI futures contract, the S&P 500, from its inception. Not surprisingly, the mispricing was greatest in the contract's early days and during the stock market crash. In the early 1990s, the discrepancy fell significantly as mechanisms for executing the cash market leg of an arbitrage improved and the market became less one-sided.

Various methods have been developed to decrease the risk of slippage including:

- **Imperfect portfolios** This involves creating a portfolio with fewer stocks than the index, but with a close correlation to the index. The risk in this strategy is that any differences in price movements between the portfolio and the index undermine the arbitrage gains.

Figure 7.2
SPI Index Future Mispricing

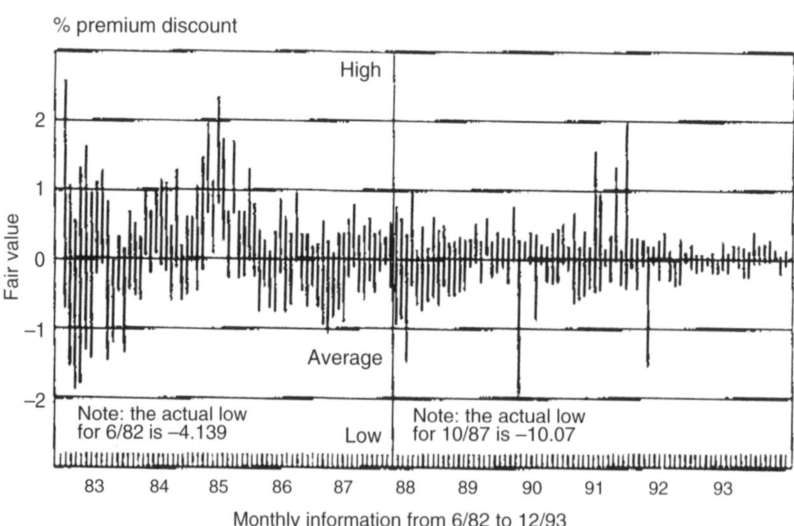

[7] A motivating factor behind the development of equity swaps was fund managers wishing to obtain a tailor-made method of linking their performance to the underlying index, without the mispricing risk with associated with futures.

- **Index portfolios** In some share markets, index portfolios are a traded instrument. Typically, these are arranged by market-makers and transaction costs are higher than for shares.
- **Portfolio trades in electronic trading networks** The development of electronic trading networks at futures and stock exchanges has improved the possibility of executing multiple stock buy and sell orders simultaneously—providing there is reasonable liquidity in each market. Many of the activities of so-called "program" traders, involves a computer program monitoring share price levels and then, if an arbitrage opportunity appears, the program automatically generates buy or sell orders for an electronic trading network. The crucial element in this type of operation is liquidity. Unless there is a corresponding sell order at the same price, the transaction will not be executed, even if a buy order can be executed instantaneously.

Another disadvantage in synthetic replication is transaction costs. As already noted, the transaction costs in stock markets tend to be higher than equity derivatives markets. While this tends to encourage the use of futures and options, it also creates an additional cost in synthetic replication and hence arbitrage opportunities. In fact, even in well-developed markets that have introduced the measures above to reduce slippage, some mispricing still occurs because of transaction costs. For example, if the share brokerage is 1%, then the futures price must move by more than 1% from fair value to make an arbitrage worthwhile.[8]

Figure 7.3 compares the mispricing of the Australian All Ordinaries Index against the transaction costs of executing an arbitrage. As the graph demonstrates, the mispricing is consistent with the transaction cost.

Another regulatory constraint on the synthetic replication of a sold forward position is limitations on short-selling and stock-lending. A synthetic sold position requires the ability to sell a portfolio of stock without owning it and then funding the settlement of this transaction by borrowing the underlying shares till the forward expiry date. Short-selling is viewed suspiciously in many share markets and is occasionally cited as a factor that leads to share price volatility and manipulation. Accordingly, short-selling and share-lending can be subject to considerable regulation. In some markets, including Asian "tigers" such as Thailand, short-selling is not permitted in any form, meaning that a forward sale cannot be replicated.

Restrictions on short-selling and stock-lending make mispricing in synthetic replication and forward contracts more likely. A market-maker buying a futures

[8] It is important to note that the mispricing tends to be less than the arbitrage gap because the major arbitrage players are often associated with share market-makers and their cost of execution is usually lower than customer executions.

Figure 7.3
SPI Index Future Mispricing and Transaction Costs

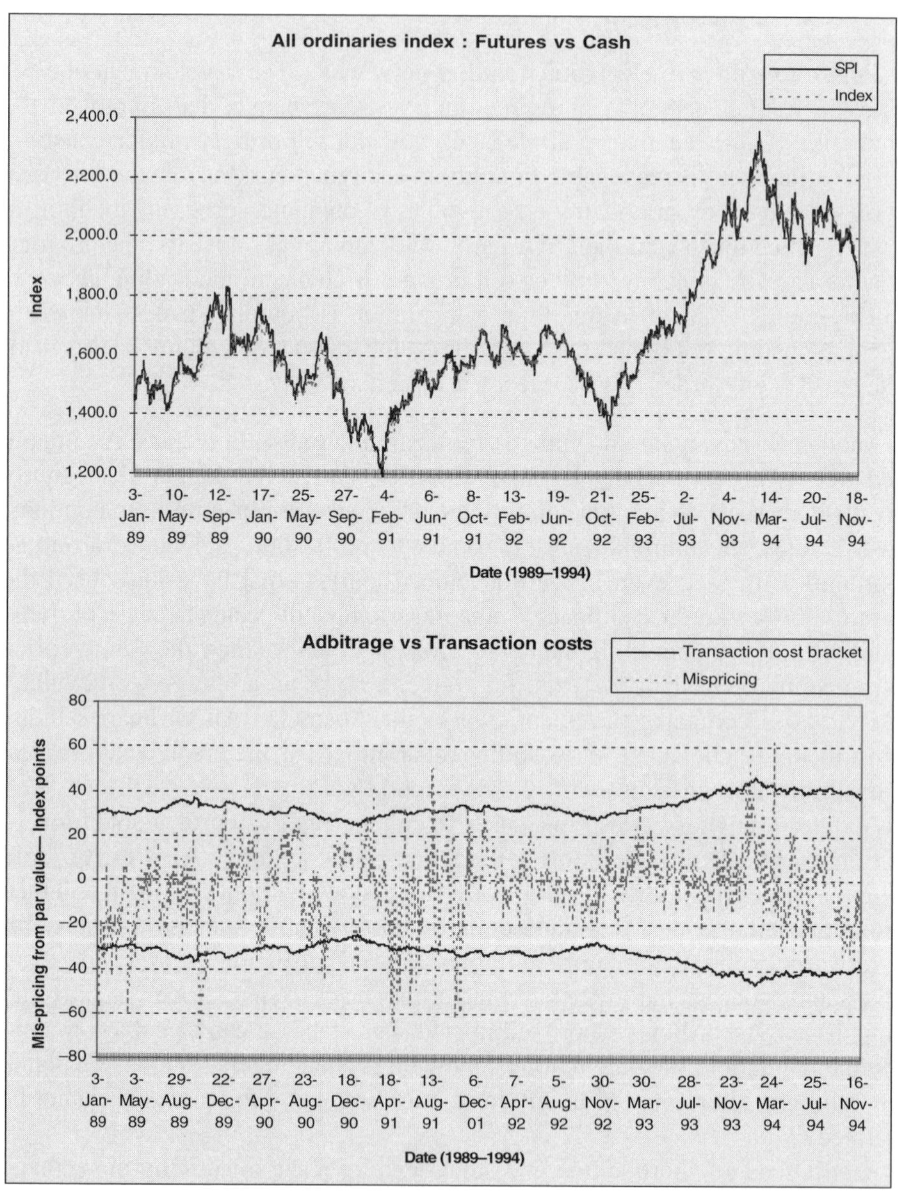

contract cannot hedge using a synthetic forward purchase and must therefore sell another futures contract. If this reduces the price relative to fair value, this mispricing is likely to persist as arbitragers will not be able to take advantage of the discrepancy.

In most markets, the restrictions that apply to short-selling are considerably less onerous and consist of the following types of requirements.

- **Eligible security** Typically, stock exchanges only allow short-selling in stock, where manipulation is difficult and there is considerable liquidity. As a result, for a share to be eligible for short-selling, it needs to meet minimum market capitalization and turnover requirements.[9]
- **Limit on short sales** To avoid manipulation, the cumulative short sales of a particular stock by a group of related companies is limited to some percentage of the outstanding shares on issue (e.g., 10% is used by a number of exchanges).
- **"Uptick" and "downtick" rules** In a number of exchanges, a short sale must be identified and it cannot be made at a price lower than the last sale price. This is referred to as both the uptick and downtick rule. Its effect is to constrain short-selling in a falling market.

These restrictions are not generally a cause of divergence between the futures prices and the fair forward price.[10] If the restrictions are onerous for a particular index, it is possible to quantify the cost to the short seller and incorporate this in another form of transaction cost.

7.2.3 A Pricing Model for SPI Futures

The forward price of a SPI future is based on the generalized price formulae outlined in Chapter 4. In this case, the asset is the share and the asset return is the dividend. The funding cost reflects the prevailing wholesale interest rate at which market-makers and arbitrageurs can borrow for the forward term.

Our generalized models can specify dividends as a constant percentage pa or as a lump sum. While dividends are generally paid at a fixed amount per share regardless of the price of that share, calculating this could become extremely complicated in an SPI futures contract, as there are potentially hundreds of dividends paid on different dates. However, this means that dividend payments can be paid throughout the year and are more like a continuous yield than a series of lumpy payments. Hence, broad-based index models often express dividends in terms rather than cents per share.

Fortunately, this task is made easier because actual historical dividend yields are provided for in most share indices and these yields tend to be quite stable.

[9] For example, in Australia, the shares must have a market capitalization in excess of A$100 million, 50 million shares on issue and a ratio of share turnover to shares on issue in excess of 7 to 8%.

[10] The downtick rule may cause some discrepancies where the price is free-falling such as in a market crash, and the short-sellers will not be permitted to execute transactions. Although in these conditions forward mispricing is generally the least of anyone's worries (!!)—as can be seen in *Figure 7.2* by the 10% discount in the futures price to fair value in October 1987.

For the purpose of pricing SPI futures, we need to be able to estimate the expected dividends over the forward period and express them as a yield on the prevailing index price. Many market practitioners simplify this, taking the historical dividend yield and using this in the forward pricing model.

If we incorporate dividends as a per annum yield, the SPI futures pricing model is an extension of the constant income model as follows:

Share Price Index Futures Price (for a Broad-Based Index)

Using simple interest, the calculation is as follows:

$$F = S \times (1 + (r - q) \times f/D)$$

Where:

F = forward SPI price
S = cash or spot price of the share price index
r = interest rate to the forward expiry date
D = day count basis (365 or 360)
f = number of days to the forward expiry date
q = dividend yield expressed as a % pa on the same day count basis as the interest rate.

This same model could be applied to a OTC share price index forward contract.

Figure 7.4 provides a spreadsheet model for calculating short-term SPI futures prices as well as any implied arbitrage opportunities. The example shown is for the FTSE100. While a mispricing of 1.81 index points is calculated, this represents a tiny proportion of the index (0.04%) and cannot be considered an arbitrage opportunity. In this example, the "arbitrage gate," or minimum mispricing requirement, is at 10 index points, reflecting our anticipated transaction costs.

While this model provides a simple and generally accurate example, some features need explanation:

- funding of margins
- continuous dividends
- forward price contango and dividend yield
- dividend seasonality
- leader indexes.

Funding of Margins

As with all futures contracts, there will be a funding impact arising from the initial margins and daily mark-to-market gains and losses. Given most SPI futures'

Figure 7.4
Share Price Index Futures Price Calculator

Spreadsheet example — Broad-based index only

Field	Cell	Cell : Formula
Inputs		
Underlying SPI index	FTSE-100	
Current cash index price	3680.4000	$E$4 :
To-day's date	01-Dec-95	$E$5 :
Forward delivery date	15-Mar-96	$E$6 :
Current interest rate (% pa)	6.4000	$E$7 :
Annual dividend yield (% pa)	4.0000	$E$8 :
Current futures price	3704.0000	$E$9 :
Arbitrage "gate" (fut price equiv)	10.0000	$E$10 :
Contract "tick size"	25.0000	$E$11 :
Outputs		
Implied futures price	3705.81	$E$13 : =E9*(1+(E12–E13)*(E11–E10)/36500)
Contract value	92,600	$E$14 : =E16*E14
Cost of carry (index points)	25.41	$E$15 : =E18–E9
Implied arbitrage opportunity (Indication only)	1.81	$E$16 : =ABS(E18–E14)
Potential arbitrage	NO ARBITRAGE	$E$17 : =IF(E21>E15,IF(E18>E14,"BUY FUTURES,SELL PHYSICAL","SELL FUTURES,BUY PHYSICAL"),"NO ARBITRAGE")

Pricing sensitivity graphs

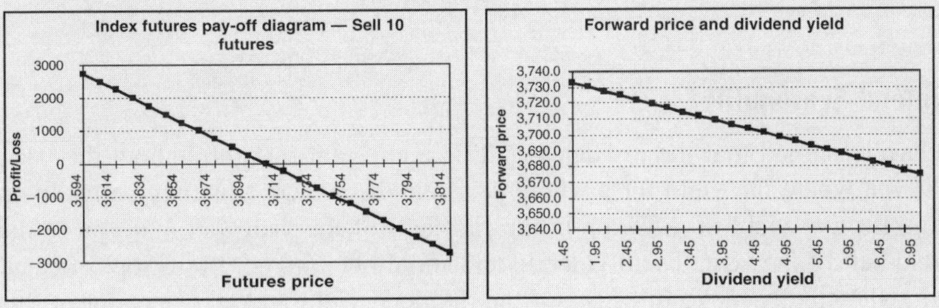

Index futures pay-off diagram — Sell 10 futures

Profit/Loss: 3000, 2000, 1000, 0, –1000, –2000, –3000

Futures price: 3,594, 3,614, 3,634, 3,654, 3,674, 3,694, 3,714, 3,734, 3,754, 3,774, 3,794, 3,814

Forward price and dividend yield

Forward price: 3,740.0, 3,730.0, 3,720.0, 3,710.0, 3,700.0, 3,690.0, 3,680.0, 3,670.0, 3,660.0, 3,650.0, 3,640.0

Dividend yield: 1.45, 1.95, 2.45, 2.95, 3.45, 3.95, 4.45, 4.95, 5.45, 5.95, 6.45, 6.95

volume is concentrated in the first delivery month, these funding issues can generally be ignored. If, however, we do wish to include the funding effects, then we should follow the same interest adjustment steps as outlined in Section 4.9.

Continuous Dividends

It is important to realize that this is a simple interest model so the interest rate has no compounding and is zero-coupon. As noted previously, this means the majority of money market interest rates can be directly entered into the model. However, a feature of most calculated dividend yields is that they are equivalent to a continuous yield. While the difference on the forward price is usually insignificant, it is sometimes necessary to convert the dividend yield from a continuous rate to a simple interest rate appropriate for the period. Use the steps provided in Section 3.2.

Forward Price Contango and Dividend Yield

The implication of this model is that as long as dividend yields are lower than prevailing interest rates, the futures prices will be higher than the cash index price, referred to as futures price "contango." As we noted in the synthetic replication discussion, the futures price can misprice relative to the fair value of the forward index. As the cash value of the index is known as well as the interest rate, this mispricing is often expressed as the expected dividend yield. This model is useful in calculating the implied dividend yield in futures prices and highlighting any pricing discrepancies. *Figure 7.5* shows the SPI futures price curve for the S&P 500 and calculates the implied dividend yield.[11] The implied dividend yield can be solved by rearranging the SPI future price formula as follows:

$$q = \frac{(1 + r \times f/D - F/S)}{f/D}$$

Dividend Seasonality

We have assumed that the dividend yield is a constant rate throughout the year. However, where the yield for a whole year may be 4% pa, this may be made up of an effective yield of 4.5% pa in the first half of the year and 3.5% pa in the second half of the year. The dividend yield should be altered. More sophisticated users will actually make forecasts of the dividend yield and take account of this seasonality. The dividend yield calculated in *Figure 7.6* illustrates very rough seasonality depending on where the forward period occurs in these dividend seasons.

The first contract month has a dividend yield of effectively zero, because the market expects no dividend effect on the index in the 11 days remaining to expiry.[12] However, the remaining three delivery months have a dividend yield of approximately 2%, which closely resembles the dividend yield over the past year calculated as a percentage of the prevailing index price. This suggests that there is little seasonality in the S&P 500 dividend yield and/or the market as a whole ignores it.

[11] This futures model and the implied "dividend yields" exercise can also be applied directly to commodity futures where the shape of the forward price can often be highly volatile. Commodities do not pay dividends, so in the case of a commodity, the asset return is referred to as the "convenience yield," which reflects the convenience of owning the asset today as opposed to some date in the future.

[12] The figure actually calculated in *Figure 7.5* is –0.05%. The prospect of a negative dividend is highly unlikely; it is a rounding error. If the futures price is reduced by the minimum tradeable unit of 0.05, then the dividend yield is 0.22%—this is the closest the market can get to a zero dividend yield.

Figure 7.5
SPI Futures and Implied Dividend Yields

CME S&P 500

Futures month	Days to expiry	Futures price	Interest rate A/365	Implied dividend yield % pa
Cash Index		613.70		
Dec-95	11	614.80	5.893	−0.05%
Mar-96	102	620.40	5.727	1.82%
Jun-96	194	625.45	5.640	2.04%
Sep-96	291	630.20	5.636	2.26%

Historical 1 year dividend yield = 2%

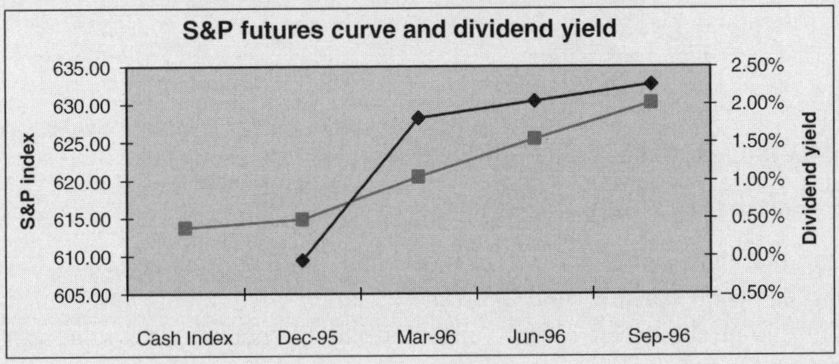

S&P futures curve and dividend yield

S&P index: 635.00, 630.00, 625.00, 620.00, 615.00, 610.00, 605.00

Dividend yield: 2.50%, 2.00%, 1.50%, 1.00%, 0.50%, 0.00%, −0.50%

Cash Index, Dec-95, Mar-96, Jun-96, Sep-96

Note: LIBOR rates used and multiplied by 365/360 to make them comparable to the dividend yield result.

Leader Indices

The assumption of the dividend as yield is reasonable for broad-based indices. However, for leader style indices with a small number of shares (e.g., 20 or less) this assumption may lead to errors as the dividend stream will start to take on a "lumpy appearance." In fact, it is possible for a short-term SPI futures contract on a narrow-based index that there may be no dividend payments at all during the forward period. Although this model can be used as an estimate, the more appropriate solution is to use the individual share price model in Section 7.3 to calculate the futures price of each share and then weight these prices using the underlying index weightings.

7.2.4 Valuation of SPI Futures

The forward valuation of an SPI futures contract is straightforward, reflecting the difference between the original contract futures price and the prevailing futures price. As with all futures contracts, profits and losses are paid as they occur. Accordingly, there is no difference between present and future values.[13] As a result, the present value sensitivities of SPI futures contracts are greater than an equivalent OTC forward by the size of the present-value discount over future values.

> ***Note***
> Determining the risk characteristics of SPI futures contracts follows the same PVBP concepts used in previous chapters, i.e., calculate the present-value impact of a 1 point change in each of the pricing variables—cash SPI, interest rates and dividend yields—as well as the impact of one day passing.

7.3 INDIVIDUAL SHARE FUTURES (ISFs)

7.3.1 General Description

Despite the fact that global volume in individual share futures contracts is minimal, there has been considerable interest by market participants and exchanges globally in this product over recent years. Individual share futures represent the basic building block for pricing equity options and narrowly based index options.

An individual share futures contract (ISF) is an agreement to buy or sell the underlying shares at an agreed date in the future. The buyer of a share futures contract is not entitled to any dividends over the forward period (i.e., the ISF trades ex-dividend). However, share futures are used to calculate bonuses, stock splits and rights issues.[14]

ISFs are listed on the Swedish Exchange (OM) and the Sydney Futures Exchange (SFE). The OM contracts have physical delivery, while the SFE contracts are currently cash settled. ISFs are directly comparable to the Low Exercise Price Option (LEPO) contracts listed on the Australian Stock Exchange (ASX) and Swiss Stock Exchange (SOFFEX). LEPOs are an option by definition; the low exercise price makes it very likely that the option will be exercised and the LEPO has features similar to a futures contract. LEPOs are discussed in greater detail in the chapter on equity options.

[13] To review the valuation of a futures contract and differences with forwards, see the discussion on short-term interest rate futures in Chapter 5.

[14] The effect of these adjustments is discussed in the chapter on equity options.

As with SPI futures, the advantage of an ISF over cash market transactions is that SPI futures provide an exposure to share price movements at a lower transaction cost. *Figure 7.6* compares the cost of trading shares versus ISFs.

Figure 7.6
Comparing ISF and Cash Market Transaction Costs

How could you have used share futures in the March quarter?

Undertake a spread trade to capitalise on Newscorp's outperformance

One of the most outstanding events that has occumed in the sharemarket in the first three months of this year has been the outperformance of News Corporation shares against the sharemarket (as illustrated in the chart on the right).

To benefit from this, a trader could have undertaken a spread trade between NCP share futures and SPI futures contracts.

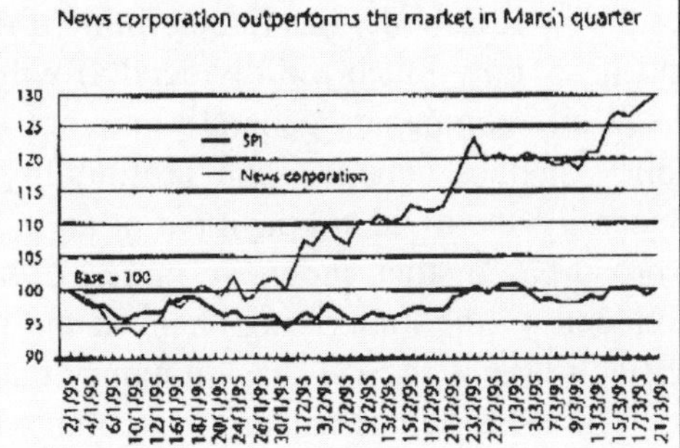

Scenario

In January, a share trader believed that News Corporation shares would perform the sharemarket during the March quarter. To benefit from this expected scenario, the trader undertakes a spread transaction by buying News Corporation (NCP) share futures contracts and simulataneously selling share price index (SPI) futures and later closing not the futures position by undertaking a reserve spread transaction.

Spread implementation

On January 3, NCP share futures were trading at $5.12 and the SPI was trading at 1927.

As illustrated in the table, this produces a contract value of $7,270 ($5.12 × 1,420°) for one SPI contract. This means that 6.6 NCP share futures contracts will be required for every on SPI contract sold (i.e., $48,175/$7,270).

The trader must, however, allow for the volatility of NCP shares versus the overall market, i.e., the beta of NCP. At the time of implementing the spread transaction, NCP had a beta of 1.02. Therefore, the number of share futures contract required would be less and is calculated as 6.5 (6.6/1.02 – 6.5). The trader therefore buys six NCP share futures contracts at $5.12 with a value of $43,622 ($5.12 × 1,420 × 6) and simultaneously sells 1 SPI contract at 1927 with a value of $48,175.

Closing the spread

On March 21, the trader's expectation comes to frutition, with NCP share futures rising $1.49 to $6.61 (an increase of 0.3%). The share trader closes out the futures position by undertaking a reserve spread by selling six NCP shares contracts and buying one SPI contract.

Calculations required		NCP share futures	SPI
Actual prices:	3/1/95	$5.12	1927
	21/3/95	$6.61	1932
	%change	+29.1%	+0.3%
Contract value:	@ 3/1/95	$7,270 ($5.12 × 1,420)	$48,175 (1927 × $25)
No. of contracts required		6.6 ($48,175/$7,270)	
Adjusted for NCP beta @ 1.02		6.5 (6.2/1.02)	
Nearest whole contracts required		6	

Result of the spread

The trader realises a profit of 149 cents on each NCP share futures contract and given that each 1 cent movement = $14.20, this represents a profit of $12,695 (i.e., 149 cents × $14.20 × 6 contracts). This more than offsets the 5-point loss incurred on the SPI contract, which given each 1 point movement = $25, translates into a loss of $125 (i.e., 5 points × $25 × 1 contract).

Overall the trader realised a net profit on this spread transaction of $12,570 (before transaction costs). The trader has thus benefited from trading relative performance that has less risk than trading absolute performance.

7.3.2 An ISF Pricing Model

The synthetic replication of an ISF is the same as for an SPI future, although as the underlying asset is a portfolio of shares, it forms a single stock. The major impact from a pricing point of view is a lumpy dividend payment. Depending on the dividend payment policy of the underlying company, the owner of shares will receive a dividend amount on a quarterly, semi-annual or annual basis. As a result, the ISF model has to determine if a dividend is paid in the forward period, and if so, how much the dividend(s) will be.

While companies generally attempt to maintain a stable dividend payment policy, it does depend upon profitability and internal cash flow requirements. Generally, the dividend payment of an individual company is not as stable as for a broad-based stock index, so more effort is required in estimating the expected dividend on the underlying share in the forward period. This can prove to be a difficult task if the ISF has an expiry date longer than one year.

The ISF pricing structure is similar to a forward bond contract and the same type of lumpy asset income model can be applied:

Individual Share Future Pricing Model

Using simple interest and one income payment, the calculation is as follows:

$$F = S \times (1 + r_1 \times f_1/D) - c \times (1 + r_2 \times f_2/D)$$

Where:

F = forward price
S = cash share price
r_1 = interest rate to the forward expiry date
r_2 = interest rate between the dividend "ex" and forward expiry dates
D = day count basis (365 or 360)
f_1 = number of days to the forward expiry date
f_2 = number of days between the dividend "ex" and forward expiry dates
c = dividend expressed in the same units as the cash price.

Note: this model is also applicable to OTC share forwards.

In this model, the dividend adjustment takes place on the date, the underlying share is deemed to be ex-dividend and shares purchased on that date are no longer entitled to that dividend. The dividend received then earns interest between the "ex" date and the futures expiry date.

Figure 7.7
Costs of Hedging an SFE ISF

How to calculate the hedge price of SFE's share futures?

On May 1, 1995 assume a futures broker, who is also a market-maker received a call from a client interested in buying June BHP share futures (going long). As a market-maker (which means they also take principal positions), the broker will take the other side of the deal and thus will sell (go short) BHP share futures. To protect his/her futures position, the market-maker will simultaneously for long on physical BHP shares.

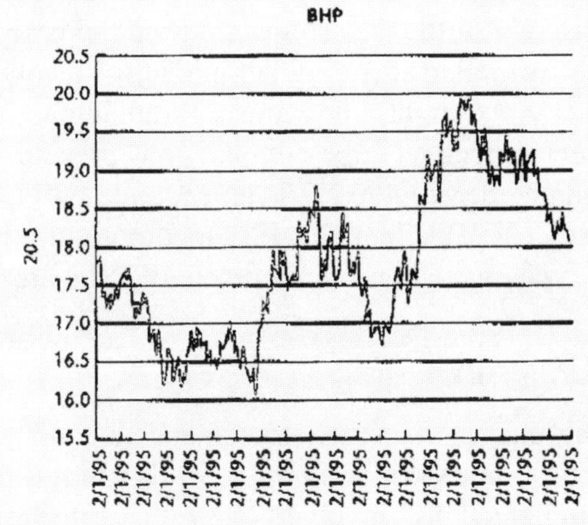

To quote the BHP share futures price, the market-maker needs to calculate the fair price of the BHP share futures contract. There are two pricing formulae used to calculate the fair price of share futures, which are based on two standard arbitrage positions that a market-maker can establish:

(1) long the underlying shares and short the share futures.

(2) short the underlying shares and or long the share futures.

In this particular example, the market-maker has established position (1) and therefore will calculate the effective hedge price on the basis of being long shares and short share futures using the following formula.

Share futures effective price =
(SP + (SP*CC*Dqys/365)) – DIV + Stamp duty Y. F.C. + T

Where by:

SP	=	PURCHASE PRICE OF THE UNDERLYING SHARES
	=	ON MAY 1 BHP SHARES WERE TRADING AT $18.18
CC	=	THE COST TO CARRY THE POSITION FOR THE DURATION OF THE TRANSACTION EXPRESSED AS AN ANNUAL PERCENTAGE RATE (SIMPLISTICLY THIS IS THE RISK-FREE RATE OF RETURN AVAILABLE IN THE MONEY MARKET FOR AN INVESTMENT WITH A SIMILAR DURATION)
	=	60%
DAYS	=	THE NUMBER OF DAYS THE CAPITAL IS INVESTED
	=	59 DAYS [MAY 1 TO JUNE 29 (DAY OF EXPIRY OF JUNE BHP SHARE FUTURES CONTRACT)]
DIV	=	THE AMOUNT OF CASH DIVIDEND WAS PAID ON THE LAST DAY OF THE CONTRACT
STAMP DUTY	=	THIS IS THE 0.3% STATE GOVERNMENT LEVY ON THE PRINCIPAL SHARE VALUE
	=	$18.18*0.003*2 (ROUND TURN)
	=	$0.11 PER SHARE
F.C.	=	THE AMOUNT OF FRANKING CREDITS ATTACHED TO THE CASH DIVIDEND
	=	GIVEN THE 26 CENT DIVIDEND IS FULLY FRANKED AND THE TAX RATES IS 33%, THE AMOUNT OF FRANKING CREDIT IS:
	=	$0.26 * 0.33/(1 – 0.33) * 100%
	=	$0.1281 PER SHARE
T	=	TOTAL TRANSACTION COST PER SHARE
	=	ARE APPROXIMATELY $0.023 ROUND TURN

Based on the above factors, the "all-up" price for a hedge for the June 1995 BHP Share Futures contract as at 1 May 1995 would thus be:

$18.18 * 6% * 59/365 – 0.26 + 0.11 – 0.1281 + 0.023 – $18.10

As expected the fair value of the June 1995 BHP share futures is priced at a discount to the physical shares due to the fact that the cash settlement process means share futures do not attract dividends and thus are quoted on an ex-dividend basis.

As with SPI futures, longer term ISFs should take account of potential funding costs associated with holding the futures position.

Another interesting feature of ISFs is that they have to reflect the pricing structure of the underlying share in the case of a dividend payment. A feature of the Australian share market is that for a company that pays the full company tax rate, a tax credit, known as a "franking credit," is attached to the dividend payment. Effectively, the company has prepaid some tax owing on the share for the shareholder. *Figure 7.7* is an example provided by the SFE calculating the effective cost of hedging an ISF, incorporating the "franking credit."

The valuation requirements of ISFs are the same as for SPI futures.

SUMMARY

This chapter examined pricing and valuation of equity forwards, specifically share price index futures and individual share futures. We discussed the "imperfections" involved in synthetically replicating equity forwards, e.g., slippage, transaction costs and regulatory restrictions on short-selling.

FURTHER READING

Francis, J.C., Toy, W.W. and Whittaker, J.G. *The Handbook of Equity Derivatives*, Irwin 1995.

SELF-TEST QUESTIONS

1. Terry is a fund manager for a medium-sized managed funds operation. Company policy prohibits the use of derivatives. Terry wishes to buy equity in one month's time, at current prices. How could Terry synthetically replicate this transaction using cash instruments?
2. What is "slippage" in the context of SPI futures?
3. Identify two regulatory constraints on a sold forward position.
4. What is meant by "forward price contango"?
5. In the context of the general forward pricing models developed in Chapter 4, discuss the impact on forward pricing of treating dividends as a constant yield or a single discrete payment amount.
6. Explain the difference between SPI futures and an ISF.

Part 3

SWAPS

CHAPTER 8

SWAP FUNDAMENTALS

OVERVIEW

In this chapter, we will discuss the key factors involved in valuing swap transactions. By the end of this chapter we will have:

- described the characteristics of the swap market;
- appreciated the relationship between forwards and swaps;
- developed models for pricing and valuing swaps.

8.1 INTRODUCTION

A financial swap transaction typically involves an agreement to exchange financial assets today and to re-exchange those assets at the termination of the swap. In most swaps, the parties repay any income on the asset they received at the commencement of the swap. The most common form is a fixed-to-floating interest rate swap, where the two parties agree to exchange a fixed interest cash flow over the life of the swap, for a variable money market interest rate.

The swap market has expanded rapidly since its inception in the late 1970s from a highly structured, special-purpose capital market; to an extremely liquid and flexible market in the late 1990s and early 2000s.[1] Over the years, the swap market has remained almost exclusively an OTC market, despite a number of exchange-traded initiatives.[2] There is currently very little data on the magnitude of the equity swap market; however, anecdotal evidence indicates it is substantial, but smaller than both the interest rate and currency swap markets.

While the use of swaps is often described in terms of arbitrage strategies, this does not give the whole picture. A key reason for using interest rate swaps is to manage interest rate exposures of assets and liabilities, to either minimize the

[1] For an excellent overview of the development of the swap market, see Das, *Swaps and Financial Derivatives, 2nd Edition*, LBC (1994) pp. 14–36.

[2] The CME launched a 3- and 5-year US dollar interest rate swap contract in 1991 that failed to attract any reasonable volume and has subsequently been delisted. The only really successful exchange-traded swap initiative has been by the Swedish exchange (OM), which provides a swap clearing and guarantee facility for swaps and related derivative such as swaptions, caps and floors.

exposure to movements in short-term interest rates or to take a strategic view on movements in interest rates. Swaps are a perfect tool to quickly and cost effectively, alter an organization's interest rate and/or currency exposure. As with all financial innovations, the success of swaps can be attributed to the fact that they represent a simple and flexible derivative that can add significant value for its users.

8.2 SWAPS REPRESENT EQUAL VALUE

A key element from the perspective of both counterparties is that a swap represents a fair exchange with no obvious benefit to either party. At the commencement of the swap, the parties to the swap transactions believe that both legs of the swap have the same value, then and throughout its life. To use the concepts developed in Chapter 2, in a liquid market, a swap transaction is an example of "equivalent value;" that is, the value of a swap should be the same as the underlying components of the swap. This is an extremely useful proposition as it assists in determining the basic pricing and valuation of swaps.

Example

Suppose Ian owns a house in the city and is considering giving up work and sailing the Caribbean for three years. Edna lives on a 40-foot yacht that she owns, but she has a demanding job for the next three years and is considering moving into a house in the city. Neither Ian or Edna want to sell their respective assets and they are both considering leasing over the next three years. Ian believes he can get a rental return of US$12,000 pa for the house, while Edna believes the boat can be rented out at around US$16,000. In both cases, they will need to employ an agent to manage these assets at a cost of US$1,000 pa.

They meet at a mutual friend's party and discover that they have opposite requirements. They decide to swap their assets for three years, but both want to make sure they are no worse off by entering into the swap than renting out the properties directly. The following table summarizes the requirements of both parties:

Item	Edna	Ian
Asset	Boat	House
Current value	$200,000	$200,000
Asset loan period	3 years	3 years
Expected value in three years	$200,000	$200,000
Annual rental	$16,000	$12,000
Rental payment frequency	Quarterly	Quarterly

Both parties have promised to keep the assets in original condition—no depreciation is expected in either asset.

The rentals are current market indications of the rent potential for both assets. The boat rental is higher reflecting the fact that Edna's boat is currently in high demand.

Let us work through the components of the swap and determine how the swap can be transacted to meet both Ian and Edna's requirements:

- **Initial exchange** The initial values of the two assets are the same, allowing an exchange of the two assets without any adjustment. At the start of the swap, Ian would hand over the house keys to Edna and sign a 3-year tenancy agreement. In exchange, Edna would give Ian the boat keys and sign a 3-year rental agreement.
- **Periodic rental agreements** To ensure that both parties receive a "fair" return on the assets they have loaned, the borrowing party will pay the market rental for the asset. For this condition to be met, Ian will pay Edna a rental of US$4,000 per quarter over the next three years and Edna will pay Ian US$3,000 per quarter for three years. To save on bank charges, the two parties could agree to net out the two payments, so Ian will just pay Edna the net rental of US$1,000 pa.
- **Re-exchange in three years** At the end of three years, Ian returns from his trip and Edna finishes her job and is looking forward to a sailing holiday. They re-exchange the assets and the swap has been completed.

The swap is graphically illustrated in *Figure 8.1.*

The swap meets the requirement of both parties' perception of equivalent value. They receive what they believe to be fair market value for their assets. If Edna had not used the swap, then she would have rented the boat at US$16,000 pa and then searched for a house and paid US$12,000 pa. With the swap, she just receives the net US$4,000 pa. Ian's position is the exact opposite. Further, by using a swap transaction, both parties have reduced the transaction costs associated with employing an agent as well as bank charges on the gross cash flows—approximately US$1,000 pa for the three years.

In this case, the *price* of the swap is determined by the rate at which the boat and house have been exchanged. This price has two components: the rate at which the assets were exchanged (the principal) as well as the asset returned (the interest). The principal price in this example is one boat equals one house, while the interest is equivalent to US$16,000 on the boat and US$12,000 on the house.

The value of the swap at the start date is zero as both the house and boat "legs" have equivalent value. Suppose, however, that after one year, the price of the house increased to US$250,000, while the boat price remained the same. Now the values of the two legs are not the same, as a swap would have started with a principal price of 1.25 boats to 1 house. Effectively, the initial exchange of the swap gives Edna a house at a considerably cheaper price than prevailing market

Figure 8.1
A Nonfinancial Swap Example: A House and a Boat

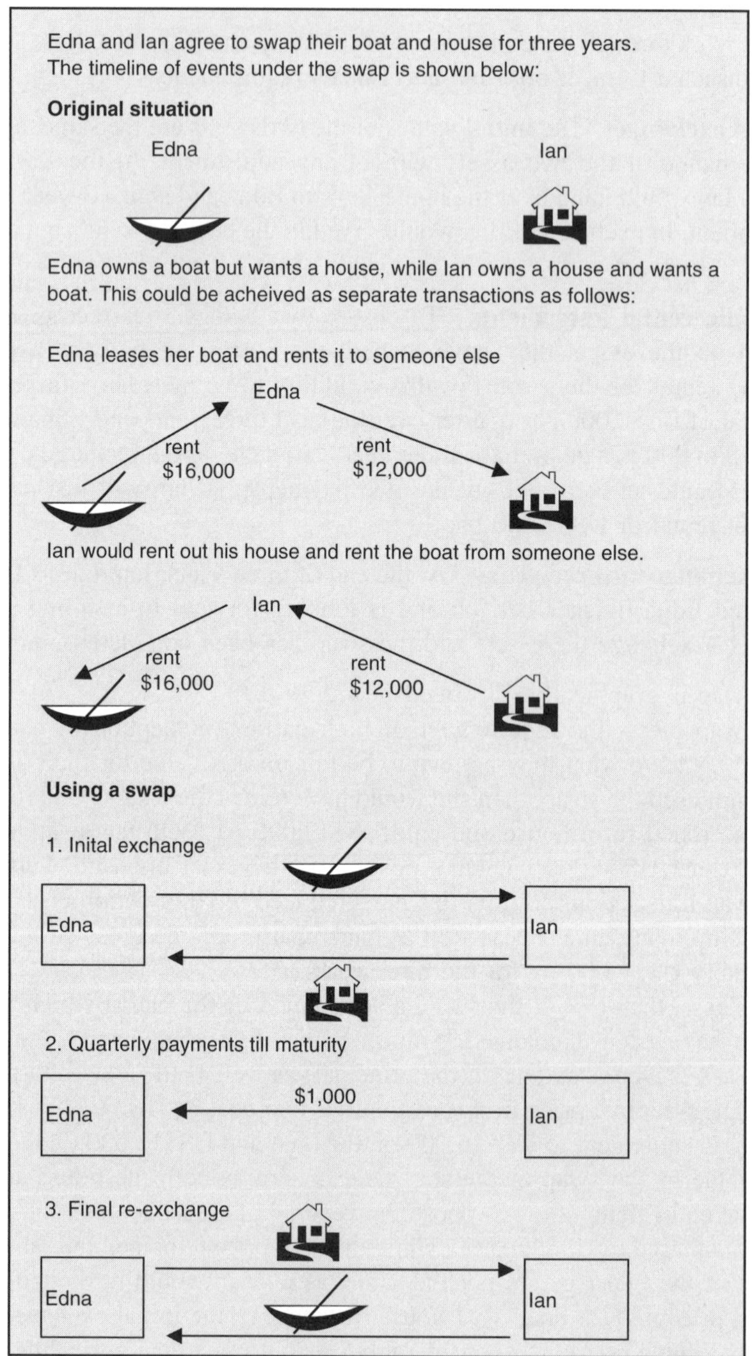

rates. However, this gain is only for the term of the swap, as at expiry Edna will re-exchange the house for the relatively cheap price of US$200,000 or one boat.

The aim of this exercise is to show that swaps are a tool and regardless of the underlying assets being swapped, the basic characteristics are the same. The boat and house in the above example could easily be replaced by deposits in two different currencies as is the case in a currency swap or portfolio of shares and a cash deposit in an equity swap. Regardless of the assets under consideration, the following characteristics are fundamental in a swap:

- **Equivalent value** The value of the swap is the same as the sum of its components. At commencement of the swap, the two assets swapped have the same market value. What's more, the two parties agree to re-exchange these assets at this value at maturity—so the initial exchange value will be retained.
- **Market asset returns** The key to maintaining the equivalent value of the asset is that each party receives the market return on that asset during the life of the swap. In the example, this is achieved by paying the current market rental for "borrowing" the asset. It is worth noting that the reason a swap does not have a cost of carry is because the asset returns are paid during the life of the transaction rather than at maturity, as is the case with a forward transaction.
- **Temporal shift** In a swap, which involves an exchange of assets at commencement and at maturity, the swap represents a shift in ownership of assets across time. The owner of an asset prior to the start of the swap will own that asset again at the end of the swap; they remain exposed to the price of that asset through the life of the swap. This was shown in the above example, where the benefit to Edna from the rise in the price of the house is offset by the loss on the final exchange. From Edna's point of view, the swap principal exchanges net out and she remains exposed to the price of the boat.

Note

Being able to "strip" a swap into its components and then look for a situation that creates equivalent value is a key to pricing and valuing swaps, particularly when considering some of the more esoteric swaps such as zero-coupon structures or mortgage swaps. Regardless of the complexity of the transaction, the starting point will always be the same, i.e., what is a "fair" exchange?

8.3 SWAPS AS A GENERAL FINANCIAL CONCEPT

While interest rate and currency swaps are a relatively new innovation in financial markets, the concept of swaps has always been a fundamental component of financial markets. As discussed in Part 2, security repurchase agreements and FX swap transactions had existed for some time prior to the commencement of the interest rate and currency swap markets in the early 1980s. Even more importantly, the idea of exchanging different asset types today and re-exchanging them in the future is what underpins all financial transactions. For example, when a bank lends money to a customer, it is providing cash for a promise to repay the cash in the future. In exchange of this cash, the bank receives a financial asset or security from the customer that includes the promise to repay the cash at a date in the future, a regular payment of interest, and perhaps some form of collateral. At maturity, the customer repays the cash and in exchange the bank agrees to terminate the security. To put it another way, a traditional lending transaction can be thought of as a "liquidity swap" where the lender is willing to exchange cash or liquidity today and have it returned at some date in the future. The price or cost of this liquidity swap is the interest rate on the loan.

In the case of a loan, the driving force for the "swap of liquidity" is that the two counterparties have offsetting requirements. The bank is a holder of cash; however, it needs to invest this cash in financial assets, which will provide it with a return in excess of its cost of funds. The customer, on the other hand, needs cash today to fund its lifestyle or business operations and is willing to pay for that need to be met. It is these offsetting requirements that will allow the loan to take place.

The price of that liquidity swap will depend on the nature of the assets being swapped. The cash leg of the swap is regarded as the highest quality financial asset, carrying a government guarantee and no risk of capital loss. The quality of the security will depend largely on the borrower: a government entity is a high-quality financial asset compared to a loan to a small company. As a result, the bank will be willing to exchange its cash for the government security at a lower interest rate than the small business.

This simple analogy of a loan as a liquidity swap is the basis of the swap concept. A swap is not just an exchange of LIBOR for a fixed interest rate, it is an exchange of different "things" for a limited period of time. These different "things" may be different financial assets (e.g., interest rates and currencies), commodities or even ideas (e.g., an author granting copyright to a publisher for a limited time in exchange for a fee). Our interest as financial mathematicians is in the *price* at which these different "things" are swapped and the current cash *value* of swaps that have already been executed. While we will only review financial swaps in this book, the concepts and methods developed can be applied to any form of swap.

8.4 SWAP PRICES AND VALUATION

As with all financial instruments, determining the present value of a swap is comprised of two steps:

- **Pricing the swap** Obtaining the current prices and interest rates that the market is willing to enter into a swap transaction.
- **Valuing a swap** Applying the market prices to an outstanding swap to determine the amount of cash or present value that would have to be paid or received to terminate the swap.

In this section, we will consider some of the pricing characteristics of swaps and develop the general procedures for determining the present value of a swap.

A basic swap can generally be replicated by cash market transactions. In a basic or "plain vanilla" swap there are none of the potential complexities of calculating the cost of carry, as in a forward contract, or the probability of a contract being exercised as with options. In the case of a plain vanilla swap there is a quoted market interest rate at which an end user can pay or receive for the term of the swap in exchange for a money market interest rate. All interest cash flows are calculated on a straightforward interest accrual basis.

> ***Note***
> Conceptually, swap pricing and valuation is straightforward. In practice, it is complicated by the underlying cash instruments or by the large number of future cash flows that can be created.

8.4.1 The Components of a Swap and Synthetic Replication

A swap contract involves the obligation to pay and receive a stream of cash flows between today and the maturity date of the swap. Each of these cash flow legs can be conceptually decomposed into two types of financial assets or securities. From the perspective of either counterparty, one leg will have the characteristics of an investment, while the other leg will be like an issued security; in accounting terms, one leg will be an asset and the other the liability. In fact, a swap is often described as a simultaneous execution of an asset and liability.

For example, the synthetic replication of a fixed-to-floating interest rate swap can be created from a fixed-rate bond (the "fixed" leg) and a floating-rate note (FRN) (the floating leg). The price and value of the swap will depend on the value of these component transactions. As the law of equivalent value tells us, the value of a swap should be equivalent to the sum of its components.

For example, in the case of a fixed-to-floating interest rate swap, the value will be the net value of the underlying FRN and bond.[3] However, these underlying instruments are only notional—typically the two decomposed securities will not actually be available in the marketplace. These underlying instruments are a conceptual device to assist in the pricing and valuation of swaps.

The decomposition of a swap is illustrated in *Figure 8.2* where a US$100 million 3-year fixed-to-floating interest rate swap is divided into a bond and FRN. The swap is viewed from the perspective of a fixed rate payer, so under the

Figure 8.2
The Component Values of an Interest Rate Swap

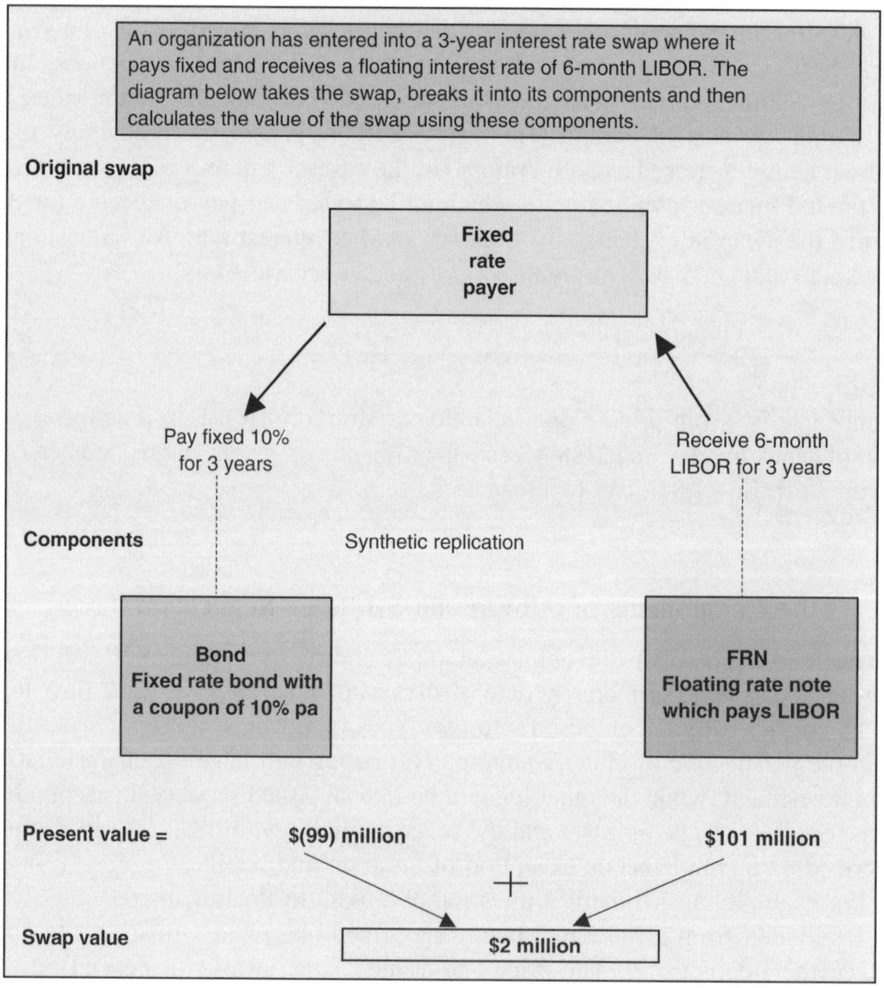

An organization has entered into a 3-year interest rate swap where it pays fixed and receives a floating interest rate of 6-month LIBOR. The diagram below takes the swap, breaks it into its components and then calculates the value of the swap using these components.

Original swap

Fixed rate payer

Pay fixed 10% for 3 years

Receive 6-month LIBOR for 3 years

Components

Synthetic replication

Bond
Fixed rate bond with a coupon of 10% pa

FRN
Floating rate note which pays LIBOR

Present value = **\$(99) million** + **\$101 million**

Swap value **\$2 million**

[3] For detail on valuing bonds and FRNs, see Chapter 3.

swap he or she will pay a fixed rate of 10% pa for three years and receive 6-month LIBOR. The fixed leg is like a liability and the floating leg is like an asset. The characteristics of the two components are summarized below:

Underlying Components of a "Payer" Interest Rate Swap (see *Figure 8.2*)

Item	Fixed leg	Floating leg
Underlying instrument	Bond	FRN
Asset/Liability	Liability	Asset
Face Value	$100 million	$100 million
Term	3 years	3 years
Coupon	10% pa	6-mth LIBOR
Coupon Payment frequency	Semi-annual	Semi-annual
Current market value of underlying instrument	$99 million	$101 million

The current market value is calculated by determining the present value of each instrument at prevailing market yields for both underlying instruments. The value of the swap is given by the net value of these two instruments. As the bond is, in effect, a liability, and the FRN is an asset, the market value of these instruments is offsetting. If we sold the underlying FRN today we would receive US$101 million. If we repurchased the issued bond, it would cost US$99 million. The present or cash value of the swap will then be the difference between these two cash flows, i.e., a gain of US$2 million.

Note

This same component value idea underlies all swaps. In the case of an equity swap, the underlying components will be a portfolio of shares and an FRN. The value of the swap will be determined by the net value of these two legs. In the case of a fixed-to-fixed currency swap the underlying components can be viewed as two fixed-rate bonds in different currencies.

Looking at the components of a swap is also useful in highlighting where the value to a swap user can arise:

- **Arbitrage** If the value of a swap is not the sum or equivalent of its cash market components, then an arbitrage opportunity exists. The evolution of the swap market can be attributed to this type of mispricing between swap and cash markets.

- **Low cost** A swap transaction simultaneously creates an asset and liability at a considerably lower transaction cost and in a much shorter time than creating the equivalent physical asset and liability.
- **Off-balance sheet** A swap transaction is not considered a balance sheet item and as such does not "build" the balance sheet in the same way as the equivalent asset and liability.

8.4.2 Swap Pricing and Default Risk

From our discussion so far we know that the price of a swap will reflect the price of its underlying financial instruments. The fixed and floating interest rates on an interest rate swap will reflect the current yields on its underlying components and an equity swap will reflect the dividend yield on the underlying equity portfolio. However, we cannot just apply prevailing market yields and prices of the underlying components. There is an important distinction between the derivative and its underlying synthetic replication with respect to default risk.

The cash flow economics are the same as between a swap and its component financial assets, *provided that neither party defaults on its obligations*. However, what about the prospect of a default by a counterparty? What are the differences then between a swap and its synthetic replication?

Using the example from *Figure 8.2*, if the other side of the swap, the floating-rate payer, defaulted, what is the maximum loss that is faced by the fixed-rate payer? In both the swap and the synthetic replication, the loss will be the equivalent of replacing the defaulting party's obligations. In the case of the swap, the defaulting party was facing a loss of US$2 million. The new counterparty will only take part in this swap if he or she receives an upfront payment equivalent to this loss, so the loss on the swap will be US$2 million. However, in the case of the synthetic replication, the issuer of the FRN has defaulted. The replacement cost of this security is US$101 million. As the bond has been issued to another party, he or she still requires its repayment. The loss on the synthetic replication is the full investment value of US$101 million.

As the example shows, swaps are considerably more efficient in their creation of counterparty exposures than their synthetic replication. Effectively, an asset and a liability is created with the one counterparty; if they default on the asset side of the swap, this matches out with the liability. The only loss will be due to any difference between the asset and liability—a credit exposure is created if the asset component of the swap is greater than the liability as in the example used.

In terms of pricing, the nature of this default risk needs to be incorporated into our model. While the cash flows of the fixed leg in an interest rate swap are like a bond, the loss arising from a default will be considerably smaller than that of an outright bond. So, the fixed interest rate in a swap will incorporate only a minimal component reflecting the risk of default. This is quite different to the yields on most nongovernment bond issues that incorporate a component for the risk that the bond issuer will default on the full value of the issue. If we think of a bond yield as being comprised of two components—the expected floating rate yield over the life of the swap *plus* a yield spread for default risk—then the swap yield is almost purely based on just the first component expected floating rate yields.

This has interesting implications for determining the appropriate fixed rate to pay in a swap transaction. In most interest rate, currency and equity swap transactions involving a floating leg, the reference interest rate is determined using a bank credit quality money market rate, such as LIBOR or bank bill swap (BBSW). So, in the case of a fixed-to-floating interest rate, the fixed rate will almost purely reflect the current expected average floating rate over the term of the swap. As a result, the yield curve of fixed swap interest rates (the swap curve) is generally above the central government bond yield curve and below the bank bond yield curve. This is diagrammatically illustrated in *Figure 8.3*.

The implications of the difference in default risk with other instruments will be discussed in more detail in the following chapters.

8.4.3 Valuing Swap Transactions

As a swap price changes, so does the value of the swap. Swap valuation involves calculating the *present value* of all remaining *future* cash flows created by a swap.

Figure 8.3
Various Fixed Interest Rate Yield Curves

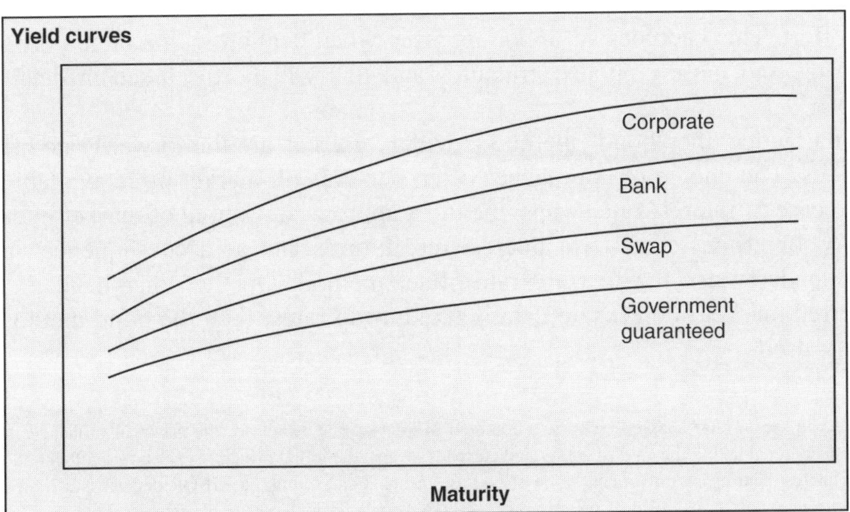

So, after a swap has been executed and the initial exchange has already taken place, or was treated as a notional exchange, then valuation will take into account all remaining interest rate and principal cash flows.[4]

There are a number of methods of generating swap present values; however, they can be divided into two general approaches:

- **The bond methods** Under this methodology we break a swap into its underlying components, described in general terms as "bonds," and then calculate the present value of each cash flow in a similar manner to the bond valuation formula.[5] The value of the swap is given by the net present value in each leg. The example in *Figure 8.3* is essentially based on the bond method.

- **The offset method** In this case, an existing swap is valued by offsetting it with a swap starting today. This creates a stream of future cash flows that are then present valued. A variant of the offset swap is the forward pricing model, which offsets the swap with a series of forward transactions matching the interest rate swap payment dates. The relationship between forwards and swaps is discussed more in the following section.

Both approaches determine the extent to which the future cash flows created by a swap differ from current market rates.

The offset method actually determines the difference between the existing swap and a swap starting today and then converts these to a present value amount.

The bond method asks the question: what amount of cash today, at prevailing market prices, would create the cash flows in the existing swap?

The differences between these two methods are illustrated in *Figure 8.4*. In the example given, the current value of the swap is identical for each valuation method. It is worth noting that the bond method takes considerably less calculation effort. This becomes an important issue when dealing with a large portfolio of swaps and more complex structures and this will be discussed in detail in Chapter 9.

In practice, the "bond" method is widely used as are the forward rate offset methods. The choice of approaches often depends on market price availability. In the case of interest rate swaps, the most appropriate source of market interest rate is sometimes short-term interest rate futures and as a consequence valuation tends to use the forward rate offset method. On the other hand, if the preferred market interest rate data is fixed swap rates, then the bond method is widely used.

[4] As we will see in later chapters, it is very common in interest rate swaps for the principal exchanges to be treated as notional and in the case of equity and currency swaps, the initial principal exchange is often notional.

[5] Most interest-bearing securities can be described as a bond. For example, a LIBOR deposit is a short-term bond with one coupon payment at maturity and an FRN is a bond with a variable interest rate.

Figure 8.4
Comparing the Bond and Offset Valuation Approaches

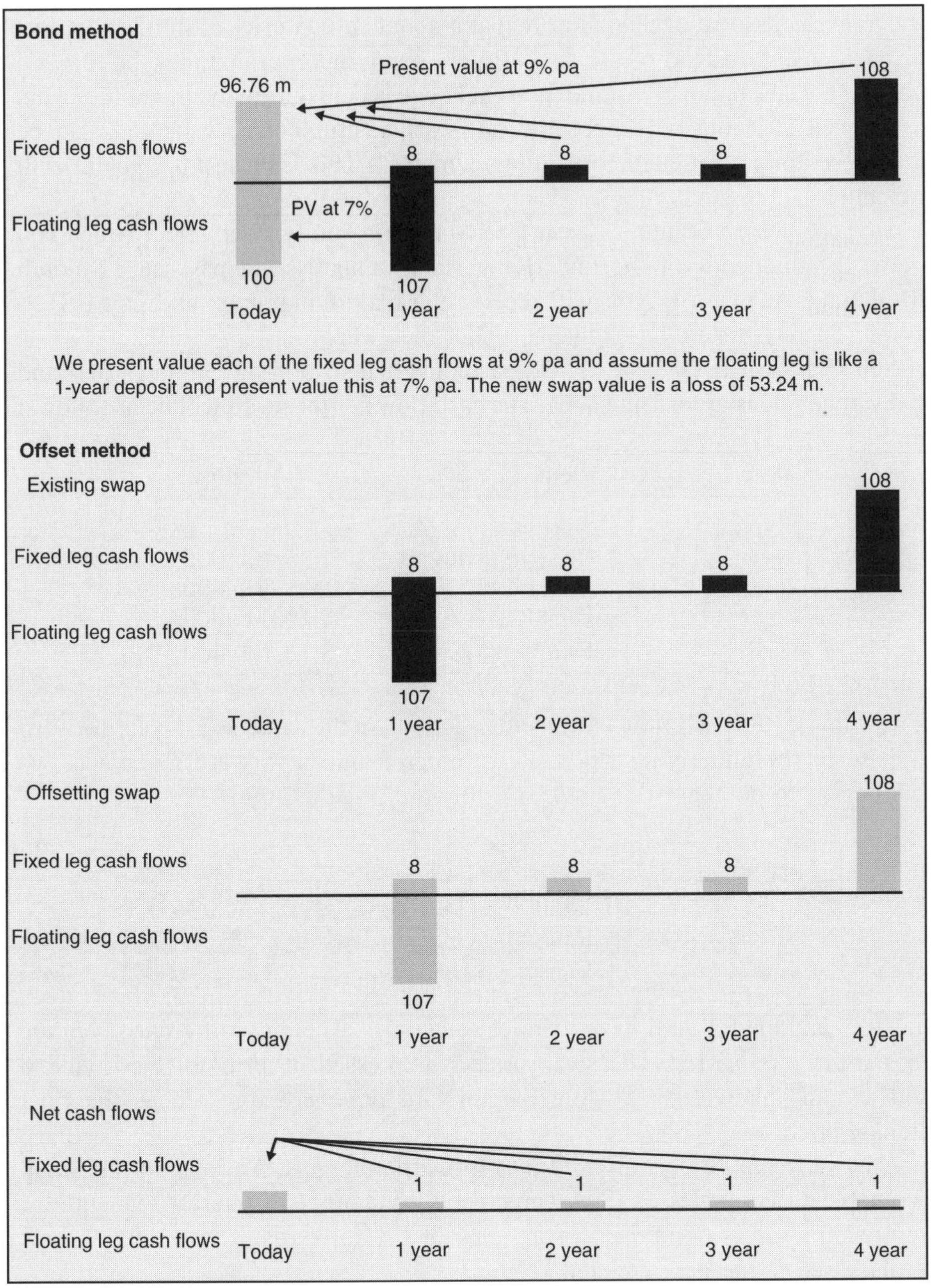
Bond method
Present value at 9% pa
108
96.76 m
Fixed leg cash flows
8
8
8
PV at 7%
Floating leg cash flows
100
107
Today
1 year
2 year
3 year
4 year
We present value each of the fixed leg cash flows at 9% pa and assume the floating leg is like a 1-year deposit and present value this at 7% pa. The new swap value is a loss of 53.24 m.
Offset method
Existing swap
108
Fixed leg cash flows
8
8
8
Floating leg cash flows
107
Today
1 year
2 year
3 year
4 year
Offsetting swap
108
Fixed leg cash flows
8
8
8
Floating leg cash flows
107
Today
1 year
2 year
3 year
4 year
Net cash flows
Fixed leg cash flows
1
1
1
1
Floating leg cash flows
Today
1 year
2 year
3 year
4 year

8.5 SWAPS AND FORWARDS

Swaps have similar features to forwards. After the initial exchange has taken place, the commitment to re-exchange principal amounts at maturity is similar to a forward agreement. Instead of the cost of carry being incorporated into the forward price, the net cost or benefit of the final exchange is paid during the life of the swap.

As well as being decomposable into cash instruments, swaps can also be decomposed into a series of forward agreements.[6] This is easiest to explain with an example.

Suppose you enter into a 1-year US$10 million equity swap under which you receive the dividends of the underlying stock annually and pay the 12-month LIBOR rate. At maturity you will receive the underlying stock and pay US$10 million. There is no initial exchange under the swap.

Suppose the LIBOR rate is 8% pa (converted to 365-day count basis) and the dividend rate is agreed at 4% pa. The cash flows of the swap will be as follows:

Date	Item	Cash flow
Today	Start swap	$ 0
1-year	Receive dividend	$ 400,000
	Pay LIBOR	– $ 800,000
	Pay for shares	– $ 10,000,000
	Net cashflow	– $ 10,400,000

As we can see, the cash flows of this transaction are the same as a 1-year forward purchase of the underlying stock. If we entered into a forward agreement we would agree to purchase the stock at a forward price as follows:

$$\begin{aligned}\text{Forward price} &= \text{Spot price} \times (1 + (r - q) \times f/D \\ &= 10{,}000{,}000 \times (1 + (0.08 - 0.04) \times 365/365) \\ &= 10{,}400{,}000\end{aligned}$$

The swap and the forward have identical outcomes. The only difference is *in the way the price is quoted.* The swap price is expressed in terms of the dividend yield and the interest rate, while the forward price is expressed as the final purchase price.

All swaps can be decomposed into forward contracts. An interest rate swap is comprised of a series of FRA agreements or short-term interest rate futures. A currency swap is comprised of a series of FX forwards. These relationships are discussed in the next chapter.

[6] This is not really a surprising result when we know that we can replicate forward contracts with cash instruments.

8.6 SWAP TERMINOLOGY

In the following three chapters, standardized terminology will be used to describe the major characteristics of a swap agreement. These terms are described in the following table:

Term	Description
Principal amount	The principal face value of the swap. This may be a notional amount, as in an interest rate swap, or it may actually be exchanged in a currency swap.
Fixed rate	The fixed interest rate paid over the life of a swap.
Floating rate	The variable interest rate on a swap, usually expressed in terms of a money market reference interest rate, such as LIBOR.
Fixed-rate payer	The party that pays a fixed rate and receives the floating rate in an interest rate swap.
Fixed-rate receiver	The party that receives the fixed rate and pays the floating rate in an interest rate swap.
Trade date	The date on which a swap contract is executed.
Valuation date	The date on which a valuation is being performed (usually today).
Commencement or start date	The date on which the swap contract commences. It is on this date that the initial exchange will take place and interest accruals will start. This may be the same as the trade date (e.g., for A$ interest rate swaps) or two business days after the trade date (e.g., for US dollar swaps).
Payment frequency	The frequency with which interest payments are made (i.e., monthly, quarterly, semi-annually, annually). This maybe different for the two legs of the swap (e.g., the fixed leg may pay interest annually, while the floating leg pays interest semi-annually).
Payment dates	A list of all of the dates on which interest will be paid on the swap.
Termination or maturity date	The date on which the swap terminates. All interest accruals stop and any exchange of principal will take place on this date.
Day count basis	The formula used for calculating interest rates. See Chapter 3 for more discussion on day count conventions.
Interest amount	The interest amount to be paid at each payment date taking account of the interest rate, the number of days elapsed since the last payment date and the day count basis.
Net settlement	An agreement to offset the interest payments and receipts under a swap. Whichever counterparty has the larger interest amount to pay will pay just the net interest amount to the other party.
ISDA agreement	A standard swap contract developed by the International Swap Dealers Association.

SUMMARY

This chapter explained the mechanics of swap transactions. We discussed the fundamental aspects of a swap transaction; namely:

- equivalent value
- market asset returns
- temporal shift.

We discussed synthetically replicating a swap transaction and we looked at how to factor in default risk in a swap valuation model. We identified the relationship between swaps and forwards and saw how swaps can be broken down into forward transactions. We also explained basic swap terminology to lay the foundations for the following chapters.

FURTHER READING

- Das, Satyajit. *Swaps and Financial Derivatives*, 2nd edition, LBC 1994.
- Das, Satyajit. *Global Swap Markets*, 2nd edition, IFR 1991.
- For general information on OTC swap markets go to the ISDA web page at www.isda.org.

SELF-TEST QUESTIONS

1. Identify the two methods of generating the present value of a swap. What determines which one of these two methods is used and why?
2. Martin enters into a 1-year A$1,000,000 equity swap, under which he receives semi-annual dividends on the underlying stock at 4.50% pa and he pays 3-month BBSW (the first rate set is 7.00% pa). Illustrate, by using a cash flow diagram, the cash flows involved in this equity swap.
3. How is the price of a swap quoted, compared to the price of a forward?
4. A company enters into a US$100 million, 2-year fixed to floating interest rate swap. It pays a fixed rate of 8.00% and it receives a floating interest rate based on the 6-month LIBOR rate. Identify the two components of this transaction and calculate the value of the swap on the initial transaction date assuming the transaction occurred at fair market value for both components.
5. Identify three advantages of using swaps, from a *value* point of view.

CHAPTER 9

INTEREST RATE SWAPS

The models developed in this chapter are saved as Microsoft Excel™ files in the enclosed disk.

OVERVIEW

In this chapter, we expand on the themes established in Chapter 8 and develop swap pricing and valuation models. We examine the importance of the yield curve and its impact upon swap valuation. By the end of this chapter, we will have explained the:

- single-rate bond valuation method
- simple offset valuation method
- zero-coupon yields: bootstrapping
- zero-coupon yields: forward rate reinvestment
- futures strip swap pricing
- forward rate offset valuation method
- zero-coupon bond valuation method.

9.1 INTRODUCTION

As mentioned in Chapter 1, interest rate swaps represent the bulk of turnover in the swap market. In most major currencies, they represent a liquid market with low transaction costs. While the US dollar represents the largest interest rate swap market, the Japanese yen has been growing in relative importance.

The advantages of swaps are:

- they can be tailor-made to a client's requirements;
- they involve one fixed rate as opposed to a series of rates with a strip of FRAs and futures;

- there are fewer concerns with the liquidity of an interest rate swap than distant short-term interest rate futures;
- the cash flow and administration requirements of a swap are considerably less than for a strip of short-term interest rate futures.

9.2 THE PLAIN INTEREST RATE SWAP

9.2.1 General Description

A plain fixed-to-floating interest rate swap is an agreement between two parties to exchange interest cash flows in the same currency for an agreed period of time. Although data is limited, it is generally recognized that plain fixed-to-floating interest rate swaps represent the bulk of all total swap volume. *Figure 9.1* illustrates a simple fixed-to-floating interest rate structure.

Another form of plain interest rate swap is a floating-to-floating or basis swap. In this case, two floating interest rates are determined using different floating indices in the same currency. Common examples of these transactions include swapping between indices, such as from LIBOR to commercial paper swaps, or swapping different floating maturities, such as 1-month to 3-month LIBOR. The term "basis swap" arises from the fact that the swap involves changing from one floating interest calculation basis to another. While fixed-to-fixed interest rate swaps do occur, they are very rare and will not be considered in this book.

> ***Note***
> In most interest rate swap markets, the principal cash flows are purely notional, therefore no exchange of principal occurs. This is because, at commencement and termination of the swap, the principal amounts on both legs are the same.[1]

Interest rate swaps have a wide range of uses and applications:

- **Asset/liability management** Interest rate swaps are the prime method for organizations to match asset and liability cash flows.
- **Liability interest rate management** Using swaps to convert debt to fixed or floating.
- **Asset interest rate management** Using swaps to alter the interest profile of investments.
- **Synthetic securities** Combining physical assets with swaps to create a "synthetic" financial instrument.

[1] A principal exchange introduces the prospect of settlement risk; that is, your organization pays its principal amount, but the other party fails to make the settlement payment. So, by not having the principal exchange, the swap is more credit efficient.

Figure 9.1
The General Interest Rate Swap Structure

Swap bank	Fixed → / ← Floating	Company A

Company A is a fixed rate receiver/floating rate payer.

Fixed rate
An interest rate set for the term of the swap. It is closely related to bond rates with a similar term to expiry.

Floating rate
The floating rate will vary over the term of the swap and will be reset periodically based on a floating index like LIBOR or BBSW.

- **Leveraged speculation** Interest rate swaps have no upfront cash cost, yet they have an interest rate pay-off similar to a bond contract. As a result, they offer a leveraged method of obtaining a bond exposure.[2]
- **New issue arbitrage** Interest rate swaps can be used to take advantage of discrepancies in yield between different securities to make an arbitrage gain in the form of a profit or lower borrowing costs.

9.2.2 Mechanics of Interest Rate Swaps

Most swap transactions consist of three types of periodic cash flow:

- initial principal exchange
- periodic interest exchange
- final principal exchange.

Figure 9.2 summarizes these three categories of cash flow.

As mentioned previously, in the case of an interest rate swap, most principal exchanges are notional, so the only cash flows that take place are the periodic interest payments; therefore, an interest rate swap is generally an exchange of interest cash flows only.

[2] A swap exposure gives a very similar risk profile to the forward bond contracts discussed in Chapter 5 and they are often used as substitutes by speculative position-takers, such as "hedge" funds.

Figure 9.2
The Mechanics of an Interest Rate Swap

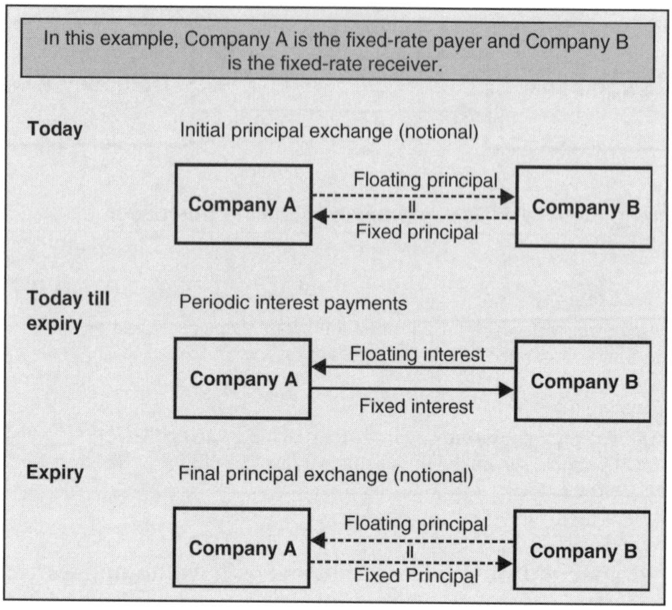

In this example, Company A is the fixed-rate payer and Company B is the fixed-rate receiver.

Today Initial principal exchange (notional)

Company A — Floating principal → Company B
Company A ← Fixed principal — Company B

Today till expiry Periodic interest payments

Company A ← Floating interest — Company B
Company A — Fixed interest → Company B

Expiry Final principal exchange (notional)

Company A ← Floating principal — Company B
Company A — Fixed Principal → Company B

Example

If we entered into a 3-year US$100 fixed-to-floating interest rate swap, where we paid a fixed rate of 7.0% pa and received 6-month LIBOR, the cash flows arising from this swap can be summarized as follows:

Years	Fixed payments (US$ m)	Floating receipts
0.5	– $3.5	LIBOR
1.0	– $3.5	LIBOR
1.5	– $3.5	LIBOR
2.0	– $3.5	LIBOR
2.5	– $3.5	LIBOR
3.0	– $3.5	LIBOR

The LIBOR rate for the first interest payment in six months will be set on the trade date of the swap and then start accruing interest from the commencement date (usually two business days after the start date for a LIBOR swap). If the first LIBOR rate is set at 6.0% pa and the number of actual days elapsed in the first six months is 181 days, then the floating leg interest receipt will be:[3]

$$\text{Floating interest payment amount} = 100{,}000{,}000 \times 0.06 \times 181/360 = 3{,}016{,}666.67$$

As a result, the interest settlement at the first half-year will consist of a US$3,500,000.00 fixed-rate payment and a $3,016,666.67 floating interest receipt. Most interest rate swaps pay interest on a "net settlement basis." The two interest amounts are offset and whichever party has the larger interest payment will settle just the net interest amount. In this example, our fixed payment is higher than the floating receipt, so we will make a net payment of US$483,333.33. These net settlements take place over the life of the swap and as the last payment is made at the end of the three years, the swap terminates.

Interest rate swaps are essentially a bet on interest rates. In this case, the bet is on what fixed interest cash flow we will pay for the next three years in exchange for an uncertain 6-month LIBOR cash flow.

The fixed interest rate will reflect the expected average LIBOR rate over three years. Given that the yield curve is primarily a reflection of market expectations of cash interest rates, the fixed rate will be closely tied to prevailing market yields for the term of the swap.

9.2.3 Synthetic Replication of Interest Rate Swaps

The cash flows created by a fixed-to-fixed interest rate swap can be replicated by the simultaneous borrowing and lending through bond and money market-linked instruments. For example, to create a paying fixed/receive floating swap for a 5-year term with quarterly payments, we would take the following steps:

1. Issue a 5-year bond at 10%.
2. Invest the proceeds of the issue in an FRN with quarterly payments based on the 3-month LIBOR rate for five years.
3. Pay the net interest on each roll, which will be equivalent to an interest rate swap.

The net cash flow column in *Figure 9.3* illustrates the cash flow from this synthetic swap. While principal cash flows occur at commencement and maturity, the net cash flows are the same as an interest rate swap.

In terms of pricing interest rate swaps, this synthetic replication example suggests that the fixed interest rate will be closely related to prevailing bond

[3] The day count basis for most LIBOR interest calculations is actual/360 and this is used in this calculation. There is more discussion on day count conventions later in the chapter.

Figure 9.3
A Synthetic Interest Rate Swap

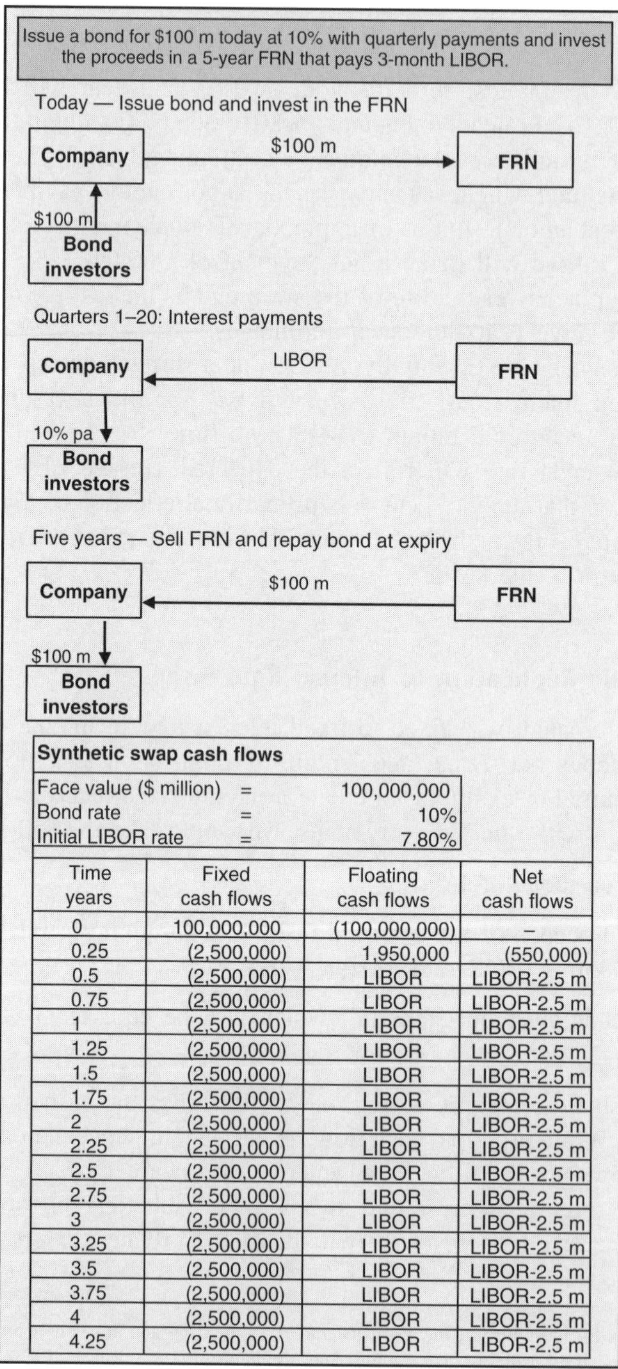

Synthetic swap cash flows

Face value ($ million)	=	100,000,000
Bond rate	=	10%
Initial LIBOR rate	=	7.80%

Time years	Fixed cash flows	Floating cash flows	Net cash flows
0	100,000,000	(100,000,000)	–
0.25	(2,500,000)	1,950,000	(550,000)
0.5	(2,500,000)	LIBOR	LIBOR-2.5 m
0.75	(2,500,000)	LIBOR	LIBOR-2.5 m
1	(2,500,000)	LIBOR	LIBOR-2.5 m
1.25	(2,500,000)	LIBOR	LIBOR-2.5 m
1.5	(2,500,000)	LIBOR	LIBOR-2.5 m
1.75	(2,500,000)	LIBOR	LIBOR-2.5 m
2	(2,500,000)	LIBOR	LIBOR-2.5 m
2.25	(2,500,000)	LIBOR	LIBOR-2.5 m
2.5	(2,500,000)	LIBOR	LIBOR-2.5 m
2.75	(2,500,000)	LIBOR	LIBOR-2.5 m
3	(2,500,000)	LIBOR	LIBOR-2.5 m
3.25	(2,500,000)	LIBOR	LIBOR-2.5 m
3.5	(2,500,000)	LIBOR	LIBOR-2.5 m
3.75	(2,500,000)	LIBOR	LIBOR-2.5 m
4	(2,500,000)	LIBOR	LIBOR-2.5 m
4.25	(2,500,000)	LIBOR	LIBOR-2.5 m

interest rates for a similar term to the swap. Likewise, the value of the swap will be closely related to the combined value of the two underlying components: the issued bond and the FRN investment.

Therefore, recognizing the underlying components of a swap is an important starting point in the analysis of any swap transaction, as it assists in determining the following:

- **Swap rate** The current fixed swap interest rate is a contrived yield; however, we know it will be related to current government bond rates.
- **Valuation** The current market value of a swap will comprise the net market value of the underlying components.
- **Risk profile** The risk profile of a swap will be the net of the sensitivity of the underlying components.
- **Financial engineering** A swap can be broken into its components and repackaged.

> ***Note***
> This synthetic replication model can also be easily extended to a basis swap. The only difference is that the two underlying instruments are both FRNs, which have a different floating rate calculation. Correspondingly, the interest rate risk of basis swaps tends to be considerably lower than fixed-to-floating interest rate swaps.

9.2.4 Interest Rate Swap Pricing

The key pricing question in an interest rate swap is: what is the interest rate on the fixed leg?

As the synthetic replication indicates, the swap rate is related to the fixed interest rate on issued medium- to long-term securities. In most currencies, the benchmark bond yields are government bond yields. Reflecting the relationship between bond and swap yields, in some currencies, such as the US dollar, swaps are quoted as a spread to prevailing central government bond yields. This is referred to as a "spread quotation" as opposed to quoting the swap rate as an absolute yield or "outright" quote.

The table in *Figure 9.4* is an indication of a spread quote for US dollar swaps, showing the Treasury yield, the swap spread and the outright swap yield. As the table demonstrates, all swap yields are higher than Treasury yields. While the swap and Treasury yields are related, they are not exactly the same. To understand a little more about the determinants of swap rates, we need to adjust the synthetic replication example, so that it closely replicates all of the characteristics of an interest rate swap.

Figure 9.4
Interest Rate Swap Yields: Simple Quotation

US$ interest rate swaps Interbank rates 12-May-XX 20:59 NYC							
	US$ treasuries			Swap spread		Fixed swap rate semi (30/360)	
Term	Bid price	Offer price	Yield midpoint	Bid	Offer	Bid	Offer
2 Year	100.00+ –	01+	5.348	0.153	0.138	5.501	5.486
3 Year	100.08+ –	09+	5.387	0.212	0.197	5.599	5.584
4 Year	101.07+ –	08+	5.45	0.251	0.235	5.701	5.685
5 Year	100.12 –	13	5.53	0.268	0.257	5.798	5.787
7 Year	104.04+ –	05+	5.613	0.324	0.307	5.937	5.92
10 Year	101.08+ –	09+	5.702	0.389	0.371	6.091	6.073

While a synthetically replicated swap may have the same net cash flows as an interest rate swap, for most organizations there are some differences between this structure and a true interest rate swap:

- **Investment risk** In Chapter 8, we identified the fact that the credit risk of a swap was related to its current market value, not the full principal value of the swap. Synthetic replication creates a full principal credit risk on the receive leg (the FRN in the above example). As a result, the yield on the FRN is likely to be higher than is required on the floating leg of a swap, due to this difference in credit risk.
- **Borrowing rate** The fixed rate in the synthetic example above will specifically reflect the rate at which we can borrow, depending on our own credit standing and the liquidity of the secondary market for this issue. As highlighted in Section 9.2.2, the fixed rate on a swap should be based purely on the expected value of the floating index over the life of the swap. The fixed rate in our bond issue is likely to include adjustments for credit risk and liquidity.
- **Separate instruments** The fact that the synthetic replication is two physical transactions has the following impact on the pricing of a swap:
  - the synthetic replication will have transaction costs on both legs; while these will be low on the asset leg, the issuance cost on the liability leg could be significant;
  - there is greater risk of market "slippage" when executing two transactions compared to one;

- the synthetic replication will "gross-up" the balance sheet and the capital required under the capital adequacy directive (CAD) is likely to be considerably higher than an interest rate swap.

So, while the synthetic replication example in the previous section has the general characteristics of an interest rate swap, it needs to be fine-tuned in order to determine the appropriate levels of fixed swap interest rates (generally referred to as swap rates). The swap rate is the expected floating rate over the life of the swap. The floating rate in most interest rate swaps is based on short-term deposit rates of a referenced set of banks such as LIBOR. So, the swap rates are related to the medium- to long-term fixed-rate bond yields of the reference banks. However, the swap rate will not include any adjustment for principal credit risk. It is almost a "pure" expectation rate—so the swap rate will typically be lower than the prevailing bank bond rate.

The interest rates on a swap are a market-determined variable and the relationship between bond yields and the swap rate will change as market conditions change. Prevailing bond yields can provide a useful reference point for understanding swap rates, although we should never assume a static relationship. Depending on the level of interest rates, the balance between fixed-rate receivers and payers and the availability of hedge instruments, the swap rate yield curve could be equivalent to prevailing bank bond yields or substantially below them.[4]

In practice, interest rate swap rates generally lie somewhere between bank bond rates and "default free" central government bond yields. In some countries, there are active markets in government agency and regional government debt (often referred to as "semi-government" issues). These securities are not default-free; however, they are generally viewed as a better credit, and usually more liquid, than bank or highly rated corporate bond issues. Often the yields on these securities are used as an approximation of swap rates and trading in these securities can often be related to swap hedge transactions.

Figure 9.5 plots three US dollar yield curves: the Treasury curve, the swap curve and a Eurodollar bank deposit curve.[5] The Eurodollar deposit curve is taken as an approximation of a bank fixed interest rate curve, while the Treasury curve reflects the "default-free" interest rate yield curve.

As we will see later in this chapter, the spread between swap rates and other similar fixed interest securities becomes a key element of any swap hedging strategy. In fact, for a swap dealer, this spread is typically one of the primary

[4] Another way of viewing the bond element of a swap is that it is like a bank bond issue that has been collaterized, i.e., government securities with a market value at the commencement date equivalent to the notional value of the swap. There are very few of these securities on issue, but it does indicate that the swap rate should be lower than the current yield on bank bonds.

[5] Observations for the Eurodollar deposit curve were only available out to a 5-year maturity.

Figure 9.5
Comparative US Dollar Yield Curves

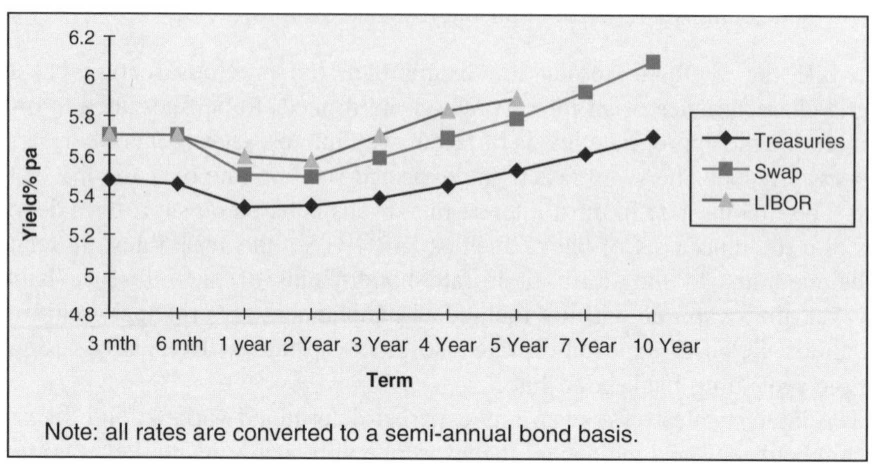

Note: all rates are converted to a semi-annual bond basis.

exposures and a profitable operation is dependant on taking advantage of changes in this spread.

Swap interest rates are different to bond interest rates in that they are not based on the yield to maturity of a specific security. While swap rates are closely related to bond market rates they can be influenced by factors other than bond markets. From this point of view, it is worth remembering that a swap rate is a quoted interest rate determined by the same type of market forces as any interest rate. While the swap rate will be heavily influenced by changes in government bond yields, the correlation between the two rates will not always be perfect and hedging a bond with a swap creates an exposure to basis risk.[6]

It is worth noting that, if the floating reference rate is a short-term government interest rate, such as a 3- or 6-month Treasury bill, then the complexities described above are reduced. The fixed rate will become the expected default-free Treasury bill rate over the life of the swap.

9.2.5 The Simple Offset and Single Rate Valuation Methods

Interest rate swaps create a stream of future interest cash flows. One leg, the fixed leg, has known interest cash flows, until the swap maturity. While the interest on the other, floating leg, is only known till the next interest payment date. As with any derivative contract, valuation involves converting both the known and unknown future cash flows to a single, known, cash value today.

[6] That is, an exposure emerges because there is a possibility that the spread between the two interest rates (determined on a different basis) will change.

> ***Note***
> The cash value of the swap reflects the amount of cash we would be willing to pay or receive, to terminate the swap today.

In this section, we will examine the following two models:

- simple offset model
- single rate bond model.

Simple Offset Model

This valuation method generates the present value of a swap by offsetting an outstanding swap with an offsetting swap executed at prevailing market interest rates. The cash flows of the original and offset swap take place on the same day so the floating-rate payments will offset and the fixed-rate payments will leave a residual according to the difference in the fixed interest rates. The value of the swap is calculated by present valuing these residual cash flows. This model replicates the net interest cash flows of an interest rate swap and ignores all principal amounts. The formula can be summarized as follows:

> **Swap Valuation: Simple Offset Model**
>
> The value of a swap from the fixed-rate receiver's point of view on an interest payment date:
>
> $$PV_{REC} = [(r - r^*)/(1 + r^*/m) \cdots + (r - r^*)/(1 + r^*/m)^n + (r_1^* - r_1)/(1 + r_1^*/m)] \times FV$$
>
> $$PV_{PAY} = \text{Value}_{REC} \times -1$$
>
> This formula assumes even interest periods and compound interest rates.
> Where:
>
> r = original swap yield to maturity in original swap (% pa)
> r^* = current swap yield to maturity in offsetting swap (% pa)
> r_1 = original floating yield to next interest payment date (% pa)
> r_1^* = current floating yield to next interest payment date (% pa)
> n = the number of periods to maturity excluding the next n payment date
> m = the number of interest payments pa
> FV = the notional face value of the swap.

Single Rate Bond Method

In this case, we make use of the synthetic replication of a swap and break the two legs into two "bonds"—one with a fixed interest rate and one with a floating interest rate. The current value of these bonds is calculated and the value of the swap is determined by the net value of these two instruments. It is called the "single rate" method because the fixed leg is present valued with just one yield—the prevailing swap rate for the remaining term to maturity. The model is summarized as follows:

Swap Valuation: Single Rate Bond Method

The value of the swap is the net of the underlying fixed and floating bonds on an interest payment date:

$$PV_{REC} = PV_{FIXED} - PV_{FLOATING}$$
$$PV_{PAY} = \text{Value}_{REC} \times -1$$

Where:

$$PV_{FIXED} = [r/m \times (1 + a_n) + v^n] \times FV$$
$$PV_{FLOATING} = [(r_1/m + 1)/(1 + r_1^*/m)] \times FV$$

Where:

r = original swap yield to maturity in original swap (% pa)
r^* = current swap yield to maturity in offsetting swap (% pa)
r_1 = original floating yield to next interest payment date (% pa)
r_1^* = current floating yield to next interest payment date (% pa)
n = the number of periods to maturity excluding the next n payment date
m = the number of coupon payments pa
v = $1/(1 + r^*/m)$
a_n = $(1 - v^n)/(r^*/m)$.

Related MS Excel functions:

PV_{FIXED}: PRICE (settlement, maturity, rate, yld, redemption, frequency, basis)

A feature of these models is the formula for the floating-rate bond, $PV_{FLOATING}$. The fixed-rate leg assumes that the notional principal value cash flow occurs at maturity of the swap, while the floating-rate leg of the swap looks as if it assumes that principal cash flow occurs on the next interest payment date. While, it may look unusual, the fixed and floating legs are being valued consistently.

The floating leg bond is valued by first present valuing the only known interest payment occurring on the next floating payment date. The next step is to ask what will be the value of the remaining cash flows on the next interest payment date. The problem is that apart from the final notional principal payment, all remaining interest cash flows are unknown. Suppose we make an estimate of the future floating interest rates, r_e, then combined with the principal payments, we can express the remaining cash flows as a bond. However, regardless of the floating rates, the bond will have a value of par or face value. This is because the yields we will use to present value the bond will be the same as the estimated rate, r_e. We know that on an interest payment date a bond with equal coupon and yield will have a value of par; that is, on the next interest date, the floating-rate bond will have the following value:

$$PV = FV \times [(r_e/m)/(1+r_e/m) \cdots\cdots + (1+r_e/m)/(1+r_e/m)^n] = FV$$

Both models assume that the valuation takes place on an interest payment date in order to keep the valuation simple.

While not "perfect" valuation models, the results provided are a reasonable indication of the present value of a swap. More importantly, the calculations required are considerably simpler and quicker to perform than the models developed later in this chapter.

As we would expect, both models indicate that at the time a swap is executed its value will be zero. At commencement of the swap, the original and offset swap rates will be the same, $r_s^* = r_s$, and the two floating rates will be the same, $r_f^* = r_f$. Under these conditions, both models will result in a present value of zero. As interest rates change, the influence on the model is the same. If fixed interest rates rise, $r_s^* > r_s$, the PV_{REC} becomes negative and vice versa for a decline in fixed rates. Also, the influence of fixed and floating rates is always opposite—consistent with the notion that one leg is an asset and the other is a liability.

To demonstrate these two approaches, *Figures 9.6* and *9.7* are spreadsheet models that value the same swap using the simple offset model and the single rate bond model respectively. The original swap has a face value of US$100 million; we pay a fixed rate of 7.00% pa on a semi-annual bond basis and receive 6-month LIBOR. Today is an interest payment date and the swap has exactly six months to maturity. The LIBOR rate set for the next floating interest payment is 5.60% pa and the current 4-year swap rate is 5.75% pa.

We know the swap value will be a loss for the fixed-rate payer: as we pay a fixed rate of 7.00% pa and the current swap rate is 5.75% pa—if we enter into an offsetting swap, we will create a "locked-in" loss equivalent to 1.25% pa or a total of US$5 million over the remaining four years. The aim of these models is to determine the present value of these cash flows.

The calculation table in *Figure 9.6* clearly demonstrates operation of the simple offset model. It essentially follows the same steps as the intuitive

Figure 9.6
Simple Offset Model Example

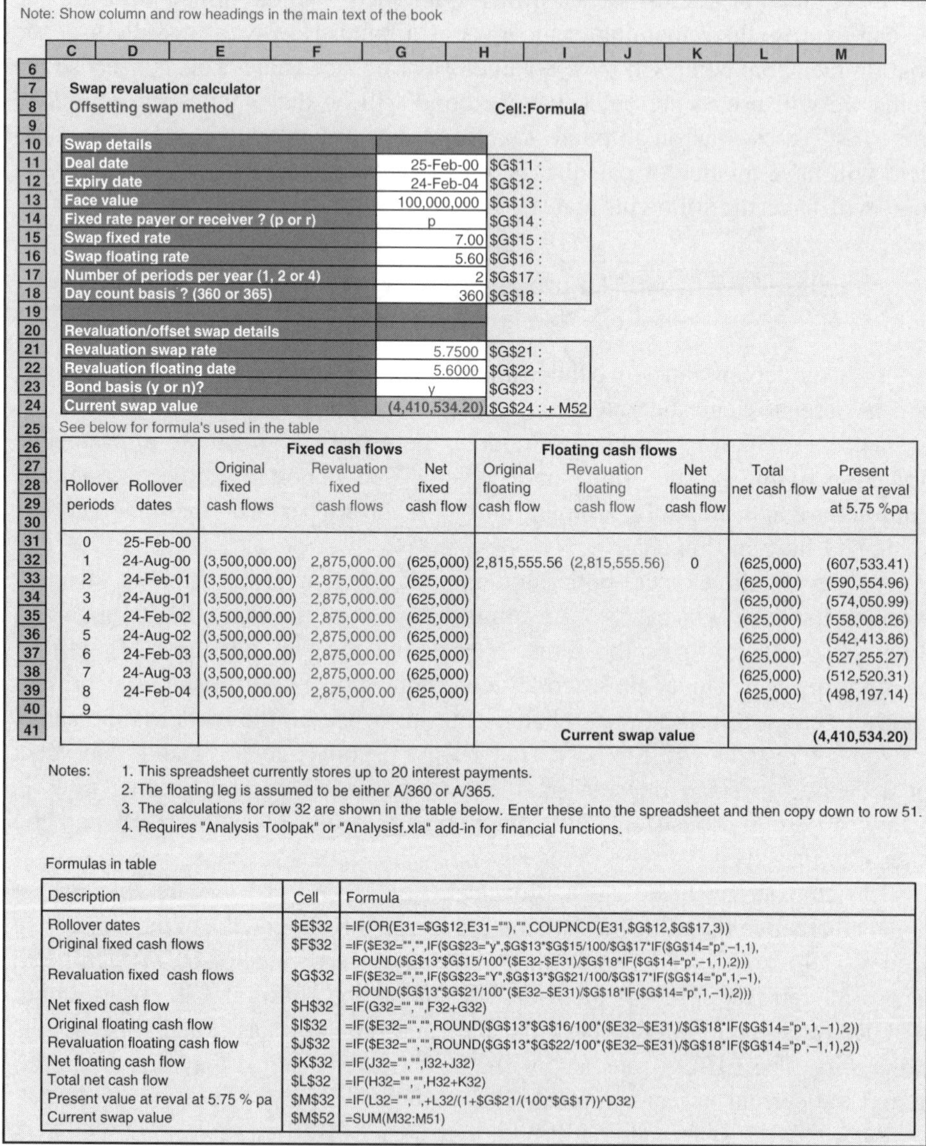

Note: Show column and row headings in the main text of the book

Row	Item	Value (G)	Cell:Formula
7	**Swap revaluation calculator**		
8	Offsetting swap method		**Cell:Formula**
10	Swap details		
11	Deal date	25-Feb-00	`$G$11 :`
12	Expiry date	24-Feb-04	`$G$12 :`
13	Face value	100,000,000	`$G$13 :`
14	Fixed rate payer or receiver ? (p or r)	p	`$G$14 :`
15	Swap fixed rate	7.00	`$G$15 :`
16	Swap floating rate	5.60	`$G$16 :`
17	Number of periods per year (1, 2 or 4)	2	`$G$17 :`
18	Day count basis ? (360 or 365)	360	`$G$18 :`
20	Revaluation/offset swap details		
21	Revaluation swap rate	5.7500	`$G$21 :`
22	Revaluation floating date	5.6000	`$G$22 :`
23	Bond basis (y or n)?	y	`$G$23 :`
24	Current swap value	(4,410,534.20)	`$G$24 : + M52`

See below for formula's used in the table

Row	Rollover periods	Rollover dates	Fixed cash flows: Original fixed cash flows	Revaluation fixed cash flows	Net fixed cash flow	Floating cash flows: Original floating cash flow	Revaluation floating cash flow	Net floating cash flow	Total net cash flow	Present value at reval at 5.75 %pa
31	0	25-Feb-00								
32	1	24-Aug-00	(3,500,000.00)	2,875,000.00	(625,000)	2,815,555.56	(2,815,555.56)	0	(625,000)	(607,533.41)
33	2	24-Feb-01	(3,500,000.00)	2,875,000.00	(625,000)				(625,000)	(590,554.96)
34	3	24-Aug-01	(3,500,000.00)	2,875,000.00	(625,000)				(625,000)	(574,050.99)
35	4	24-Feb-02	(3,500,000.00)	2,875,000.00	(625,000)				(625,000)	(558,008.26)
36	5	24-Aug-02	(3,500,000.00)	2,875,000.00	(625,000)				(625,000)	(542,413.86)
37	6	24-Feb-03	(3,500,000.00)	2,875,000.00	(625,000)				(625,000)	(527,255.27)
38	7	24-Aug-03	(3,500,000.00)	2,875,000.00	(625,000)				(625,000)	(512,520.31)
39	8	24-Feb-04	(3,500,000.00)	2,875,000.00	(625,000)				(625,000)	(498,197.14)
40	9									
41								Current swap value		(4,410,534.20)

Notes:
1. This spreadsheet currently stores up to 20 interest payments.
2. The floating leg is assumed to be either A/360 or A/365.
3. The calculations for row 32 are shown in the table below. Enter these into the spreadsheet and then copy down to row 51.
4. Requires "Analysis Toolpak" or "Analysisf.xla" add-in for financial functions.

Formulas in table

Description	Cell	Formula
Rollover dates	`$E$32`	`=IF(OR(E31=$G$12,E31=""),"",COUPNCD(E31,$G$12,$G$17,3))`
Original fixed cash flows	`$F$32`	`=IF($E32="","",IF($G$23="y",$G$13*$G$15/100/$G$17*IF($G$14="p",–1,1), ROUND($G$13*$G$15/100*($E32-$E31)/$G$18*IF($G$14="p",–1,1),2)))`
Revaluation fixed cash flows	`$G$32`	`=IF($E32="","",IF($G$23="Y",$G$13*$G$21/100/$G$17*IF($G$14="p",1,–1), ROUND($G$13*$G$21/100*($E32–$E31)/$G$18*IF($G$14="p",1,–1),2)))`
Net fixed cash flow	`$H$32`	`=IF(G32="","",F32+G32)`
Original floating cash flow	`$I$32`	`=IF($E32="","",ROUND($G$13*$G$16/100*($E32–$E31)/$G$18*IF($G$14="p",1,–1),2))`
Revaluation floating cash flow	`$J$32`	`=IF($E32="","",ROUND($G$13*$G$22/100*($E32–$E31)/$G$18*IF($G$14="p",–1,1),2))`
Net floating cash flow	`$K$32`	`=IF(J32="","",I32+J32)`
Total net cash flow	`$L$32`	`=IF(H32="","",H32+K32)`
Present value at reval at 5.75 % pa	`$M$32`	`=IF(L32="","",+L32/(1+$G$21/(100*$G$17))^D32)`
Current swap value	`$M$52`	`=SUM(M32:M51)`

assessment of the loss above. The calculation steps can be summarized as follows:

- calculate the known interest cash flows of the original swap (fixed and floating cash flows in columns F and I respectively);
- calculate the interest cash flows on the original interest payment dates using prevailing market interest rates (columns G and J);

- determine the net cash flows for both fixed and floating (columns H and K) and the combined net cash flow for each interest payment date (column L);
- present-value the net cash flow for each interest payment date using the compound interest present-value formula and the prevailing swap rate;[7]
- the value of the swap is given by the sum of each of the interest payment dates (shown as the "current swap value"). In this case, the swap value is a loss of US$4,410,534.20.

The single rate bond method takes a different, more general approach. After dividing the swap into its two component legs, the bond method asks the question: How much must I pay or receive today to create the cash flows of each component in the existing swap at current market interest rates?

In this case, reflecting the fact that we view the swap value as the combined value of its two bond components, we include the principal cash flows. The calculation steps followed in the model in *Figure 9.7* can be summarized as follows:

- convert the swap into its two underlying fixed- and floating-bond components (the fixed component is shown from cell D27 and the floating component from cell H27);
- using bond mathematics, calculate the value of the fixed leg (shown as the "total fixed leg value"). If the fixed leg is the pay leg, multiply this value by negative one;
- using money market pricing, determine the value of the floating leg (shown as the "total floating leg value"). If the floating leg is the pay leg, multiply this value by negative one;
- the value of the swap is given as the sum of the two component values calculated in steps 2 and 3—in this example a loss of US$4,410,534.20.

Not surprisingly, the results from the two models are identical. This highlights the fact that the two methods are different ways of doing the same thing—calculating the cost of replacing known interest rate cash flows. The choice of which approach to adopt is often based on the:

- calculation complexity;
- nature of the interest rate swap being hedged;
- form and availability of revaluation exchange rates.

Both these models can be applied to basis swaps also. The only difference is that both legs will be priced and valued as a floating-rate leg.

[7] See Chapter 3 for more detail on compound interest present-value formulae.

Figure 9.7
Single Rate Bond Method Example

	C–F	G	H–J	K
6				
7	**Swap revaluation calculator**			
8	**Single rate bond method**		**Cell:Formula**	
9				
10	Swap details		$G$10 :	
11	Deal date	24-Feb-00	$G$11 :	
12	Expiry date	24-Feb-04	$G$12 :	
13	Face value	100,000,000	$G$13 :	
14	Fixed rate payer or receiver ? (p or r)	p	$G$14 :	
15	Swap fixed rate	7.00	$G$15 :	
16	Swap floating rate	5.60	$G$16 :	
17	Number of periods per year (1, 2 or 4)	2	$G$17 :	
18	Fixed day count basis (0, 1, 2, 3, 4)	0	$G$18 :	
19	Floating day count basis ? (360 or 365)	360	$G$19 :	
20				
21	Revaluation details			
22	Revaluation swap rate	5.7500	$G$22 :	
23	Revaluation floating date	5.6000	$G$23 :	
24	Revaluation floating date			
25	Current swap value	(4,410,534.20)	$G$25 : +G36+K36	
26				
27	**Component 1 — Fixed leg**		**Component 2 — Floating leg**	
28	Payer or receiver	Payer	Payer or receiver	Receiver
29	Revaluation date	24-Feb-00	Revaluation date	24-Feb-00
30	Last coupon date	24-Feb-00	Last coupon date	24-Feb-00
31	Next coupon date	24-Aug-00	Next coupon date	24-Aug-00
32	Expiry date	24-Feb-04	Expiry date	24-Aug-00
33	Coupon	7.0000%	Coupon	5.6000%
34	Current yield to expiry	5.7500%	Current yield to expiry	5.6000%
35	Current clean Value	104,410,534.20	Current clean value	100,000,000.00
36	Accrued interest	–	Accrued interest	–
37	Total fixed leg value	(104,410,534.20)	Total floating leg value	100,000,000.00

Notes:

1. This spreadsheet uses the standard excel bond pricing functions. The "Analysis Toolpak" add-in must be loaded.
2. The fixed leg day count basis uses the standard Excel definitions:
   - 0 US 30/360
   - 1 Actual/Actual
   - 2 Actual/360
   - 3 Actual/365
   - 4 European 30/360
3. The floating leg is assumed to be either A/360 or A/365.
4. The formulae used in the calculation of the two components are shown in the table below.

Description	Cell	Formula
Fixed leg		
Payer or receiver	$G$28	=IF(G14="P","Payer","Receiver")
Revaluation date	$G$29	=+G11
Last coupon date	$G$30	=COUPPCD(G$29,G$32,G$17,G18)
Next coupon date	$G$31	=COUPNCD(G$29,G$32,G$17,G18)
Expiry date	$G$32	=+G12
Coupon	$G$33	=+G15/100
Current yield to expiry	$G$34	=+G22/100
Current clean value	$G$35	=(PRICE(G29,G32,G33,G34,100,G17,G18))/100*G13
Accrued Interest	$G$36	=IF(G29>G30,ACCRINT(G30,G31,G29,G33,100,G17,G18)/100*G13,0)
Total fixed leg value	$G$37	=ROUND((G36+G35)*IF(G14'="p",–1,1),2)
Floating leg		
Payer or receiver	$J$28	=IF(G14'="r","Payer","Receiver")
Revaluation date	$J$29	=+G29
Last coupon date	$J$30	=+G30
Next coupon date	$J$31	=+G31
Expiry date	$J$32	=+K31
Coupon	$J$33	=+G16/100
Current yield to expiry	$J$34	=+G23/100
Current clean value	$J$35	=G13*(1+K33*(K31–K30)/G19)/(1+K34*(K31–K29)/G19)
Accrued interest	$J$36	=IF(K29>K30,G13*K33*(K29–K30)/G19,0)
Total floating leg value	$J$37	=ROUND((K36+K35)*IF(G14'="r",–1,1),2)

Figure 9.7 Continued

Steps
1. Obtain *fixed leg bond pricing inputs.*
2. Determine fixed leg bond price.
3. Divide fixed leg bond price by 100 and multiply by swap face value (total fixed leg value).
4. Obtain *floating leg bond pricing inputs.*
5. Determine floating leg bond price.
6. Divide floating leg bond price by 100 and multiply by swap face value (total floating leg value).
7. Determine which is the "paying" leg and multiply the total value by −1.
8. Determine which is the receiving leg.
9. Swap market value is given by adding together the amounts in Steps 7 and 8.

In these two simple models, the single rate bond method involves considerably fewer calculations than the simple offset model. Part of this is related to the fact that in a simple model like this, we can use standard bond formulae. However, underlying this formula is a present-value calculation similar to that used for the net cash flows in the offset model. It is always the case that a bond method involves calculating one set of interest payments for each leg and one present-value calculation; that is, the calculations are always lower in the bond method by the number of interest calculations in the offset method. As we will see in the next chapter, this ease of calculation becomes more pronounced in the case of currency swaps.

While the single rate bond method has some advantages over the simple offset method, both of these models are for simple valuations on interest payment dates. There are a number of common features that need to be incorporated into the more advanced models. These are outlined later in this chapter.[8]

Interest Accrual

The valuations in the two examples in *Figures 9.6* and *9.7* that follow are calculated on an interest payment date. As this situation is only valid for two days

[8] See the zero-coupon bond model and forward rate model in Section 9.5.

a year in the example, the model needs to be able to incorporate the passing of time and the accrual of interest.

The interest accrual on most interest rate swaps is very similar to a bond. Interest is paid at the end of the current interest period with the calculation based on the particular day count basis of the swap. In terms of valuing the swap, the original interest payment should be the full interest payment for the period. However, this should only be present valued over the number of days remaining in the current interest period. Compared to bonds, the swap value is based on the dirty price, i.e., accrued interest is included.

In terms of the two models developed earlier, the single rate bond method requires no amendment as it incorporates interest accruals without any adjustment. The simple offset model, however, assumes that the minimum increment in time is one interest period (in this case six months). To be able to value this on noninterest payment dates, the logic for the first interest payment needs to be altered so that the offset interest amount is only for the days remaining in the interest period and the present value has to be based on the number of days rather than the number of interest periods.

Day Count Basis

In Chapter 3, we reviewed the impact of day count conventions on the valuation of bonds (see Section 3.4.1). This same range of day count conventions may emerge in the interest calculation of the fixed leg. The widest variety of day count conventions can be found in the US dollar; in other currencies, the preferred day count convention is more clearly defined.

The examples in this section assumed that the fixed leg pays interest on a semi-annual bond basis. As a result, all interest payments are the same whole number. While this day count basis is quite common in US dollar interest rate swaps, it is less common in other currencies. In Europe, the 30/360-day count is quite common and in Asia a "money market basis" or actual/365 is often used.

A summary of the major day count conventions is provided in *Figure 9.8*. The single rate bond method model in *Figure 9.7* will support most of these conventions.

It is possible in some structures that another day count basis may be used in a swap. For example, a swap may have uneven interest periods and "odd" interest payment dates that cannot be replicated by any of these conventions. These types of transactions cannot be valued properly using a generic bond valuation function. It is often worthwhile then to develop models that allow for some modification of when interest payment dates occur and the amount of interest accrued between these dates. In the case of spreadsheet models, this involves using a "table" approach as in the simple offset model. In the case of the bond

Figure 9.8
Common Day Count Conventions

1. Annual bond basis (AIBD or COUPON basis)

This calculation assumes a year of 360 days with 12 months each of 30 days. A normal security under this interest basis will pay interest in equal annual amounts (if fixed rate) irrespective of when the payment is made. Thus a security of $100 m with a coupon of 8% will pay $8 m on each anniversary prior to maturity. If a payment date falls on a nonbusiness day, for example, the $8 m will be paid on the next business day without additional interest in respect of the delay.

Example:	Last coupon date	=	18.2 × 5
	Settlement date	=	23.8 × 5
	Number of bond days	=	10 + 150 + 23 = 183

The accrued interest on the above security would be:

$8,000,000 × 183/360 = $4,066,666.67

It is important in swaps to clarify the payment calculation as there is a difference between coupon basis and 30/360 basis.

2. Annual money market (annual cash)

Interest is calculated on an Actual/360 day basis. For example, an annual money market rate of 5% of $100 m would produce an annual coupon of $5,069,444.44 for a normal year of 365 days.

3. Semi-annual bond basis

As in 1. above the interest calculation is on the basis of a year of 360 days and 12 months of 30 days. Thus, in the case of a semi-annual rate of 6% on a $100 m, interest would be calculated as $3 m per period.

The difference between semi-annual bond and 30/360 would be apparent on those occasions when the payment date is a nonbusiness day. For example, if payment dates are the 5th of January and June, and July 5 falls on Saturday the interest would be calculated as 182 bond days (180 days for January 5 to July 5 plus 2 days for settlement on July 7).

4. Semi-annual money market

As in 3.0 above the interest calculation is worked on an actual/360 day basis. For example, assuming a semi-annual interest rate of 5% for the period January 5 to July 5 the interest due would be $2,513,888.89 [$100 m × 5% × 181/360].

valuation method, this means present-valuing each interest and principal cash flow individually.

Cash Flow Valuation

In both models, we had present values of individual future cash flows using a single interest rate. In the case of the offset model, a stream of future cash flows is created and these are present valued using the interest rate prevailing until maturity of the underlying swap. While this is a reasonable approach to valuing these cash flows, it could result in inaccuracies.

When we calculate the present-value, we are determining what amount of cash today could produce the future offset swap cash flows. If we reversed or terminated the swap today, the present-value represents the amount we would pay or receive from our swap counterparty. In our example, the offset produces a net loss on each of the eight interest payment dates of US$625,000, which we calculate to have a present-value loss of US$4,410,534.20. Another way of looking at the swap value is that if we invested the present-value amount at the present-value interest rate, we would replicate the offset swap cash flows.[9] For the present-value to be accurate, if we invested the present-value amount and then received eight US$625,000 instalments over the next four years, the original investment principal as well as all interest owing should be repaid exactly. However, in these simple, single-rate models, we cannot be sure that this is the case.

The interest rate used in both models is the current swap rate to maturity of the original swap. This is effectively a "bullet" interest rate, i.e., it assumes only interest is paid during the life of the instrument and that the principal is repaid wholly at maturity. This does not fit the cash flow profile of the offset swap that effectively spreads both interest and principal payments over the life of the swap, very much like a mortgage repayment on a house.

Figure 9.9 demonstrates the gap between the offset future swap cash flows and the assumed cash flows from a bullet security. The cash flows from the assumed bullet investment leave substantial cash flow mismatches over the life of the offset swap. If the yield curve is flat and interest rates stay at 5.75%, then the cash flow shortfall in the first seven periods will be exactly offset by the large excess cash flow on the eighth period. This is shown by the fact that the present values of the net cash flows exactly match out in the column titled "PV@5.75%." However, if interest rates were to change and average 6.75% pa over the life of the swap, then the present-value would show a shortfall. Likewise, if interest rates fall, then the present-value amount will be larger than required (column titled PV@4.75%).

Figure 9.9
Using Single Interest Rates to Present-Value Swap Cash flows

Using offset model cash flows from *Figure 9.6*
Assumed present-value rate in swap models = 5.75%

Rollover periods	Rollover dates	Simple model valuation	The cash flows created by a bullet interest rate	Difference	PV@5.75% Present-value of the difference at 5.75%	PV@6.75% Present-value of the difference at 6.75%	PV@4.75% Present-value of the difference at 4.75%
0	25-Feb-00	(4,410,534.20)	4,410,534.20	-	(0.00)	(60,572.85)	64,184.60
1	24-Aug-00	(625,000.00)	126,802.86	(498,197.14)	($484,274.26)	($481,931.94)	($486,639.45)
2	24-Feb-01	(625,000.00)	126,802.86	(498,197.14)	($470,740.47)	($466,197.76)	($475,349.89)
3	24-Aug-01	(625,000.00)	126,802.86	(498,197.14)	($457,584.90)	($450,977.28)	($464,322.24)
4	24-Feb-02	(625,000.00)	126,802.86	(498,197.14)	($444,796.99)	($436,253.72)	($453,550.42)
5	24-Aug-02	(625,000.00)	126,802.86	(498,197.14)	($432,366.45)	($422,010.85)	($443,028.49)
6	24-Feb-03	(625,000.00)	126,802.86	(498,197.14)	($420,283.31)	($408,232.99)	($432,750.66)
7	24-Aug-03	(625,000.00)	126,802.86	(498,197.14)	($408,537.85)	($394,904.95)	($422,711.27)
8	24-Feb-04	(625,000.00)	4,537,337.06	3,912,337.06	$3,118,584.22	$2,999,936.64	$3,242,537.04

[9] This is a good way of understanding the cash flows that take place when a swap is reversed. When a swap is reversed, the counterparty facing a loss pays the other counterparty the present-value of this loss. If the counterparty with a profit executed another identical swap at current market rates and invested this cash in an appropriate security, it should be able to exactly replicate the future cash flows of the reversed swap.

This same problem exists with the single-rate bond model, as we assume that we can replicate each of the cash flows under the swap using the prevailing swap rate. This is only the case when the original swap rate and the current swap rate are the same. At all other times, there are likely to be cash timing discrepancies.

The only way to be confident about the accuracy of the present value is if we know that each of the cash flows can be replicated from the present-value amount. There can be no timing mismatches and no exposure to changes in interest rates. The only way this outcome can be assured is by using zero-coupon interest rates, as they are free of interest rate risk and each rate provides an unambiguous relationship between the date of the present value and each interest payment date.

The use of zero-coupon interest rates and their relationship to par and forward rates is investigated in the following section.

9.2.6 A Comparison of Interest Rate Swaps and FRAs

Earlier in this chapter, we conceptually broke down an interest rate swap into two cash market instruments: a fixed and floating bond. However, a fixed-to-floating interest rate swap can also be replicated by a series of short-term interest rate forwards, such as FRAs.

Like an interest rate swap, the cash flows of a FRA are a net settlement of interest cash flows given by the difference between the fixed FRA rate and the relevant floating index. In most FRA markets, the floating index is usually the same as the interest rate swap (e.g., LIBOR). The main difference between the two instruments is that an FRA involves a single interest payment period while a swap covers a series of future interest periods and FRAs typically pay the net settlement amount at the beginning of the interest period as opposed to the end of an interest period. However, this difference in timing can be easily accommodated by a future value adjustment.

Let us test this by examining actual market data. If an interest rate swap can be replicated by a series of FRAs, then for a given term the swap rate should be the same as the strip of FRA rates.

Example

Suppose we are comparing the expected cash flows of a 2-year US$100 million fixed-to-floating interest rate swap with a series of FRAs covering the same interest periods. Under the swap, we pay a fixed interest rate for two years and receive 3-month LIBOR quarterly. To replicate this swap, we need to enter into a series of eight consecutive FRAs. One unusual feature of replicating the swap cash flow with an FRA strip is that the first FRA has no forward period—the FRA is transacted today and the first LIBOR rate set will occur today. Effectively, this first FRA will have an interest rate that is equivalent to 3-month LIBOR. The prevailing market interest rates are summarized below:

Trade date: Dec 14, 2000
Interest rate swap

Term	2 years
Frequency	Quarterly
Index	3-month LIBOR
Fixed rate	5.47% pa (qtrly)

Forward rate agreements

Term	Forward rate
0 × 3	5.79
3 × 6	5.44
6 × 9	5.22
9 × 12	5.20
12 × 15	5.31
15 × 18	5.33
18 × 21	5.42
21 × 24	5.51
Average	5.43

While calculating the strip "average" price is not strictly an accurate method of converting the FRA strip to a swap equivalent, it does support the idea that strip and swap rates are closely related—the swap rate and the average FRA strip price are within three basis points of one another.

This relationship between forward and swap rates is widely followed in financial markets for pricing and valuing swap transactions. In terms of pricing, forward contracts provide another method of determining the appropriate swap interest rate. If the swap rate and the forward strip are sufficiently different it implies the existence of an arbitrage. In terms of valuation and trading, this forward rate/swap rate relationship indicates that a swap can be valued and hedged by treating each of the cash flows as a forward contract. This is the basic underpinning of the "forward offset" valuation model.

We shall investigate the correct method of comparing FRAs and short-term futures prices to swap rates when we investigate the forward offset valuation method. Apart from adjusting for any differences in the day count basis, much of the adjustment between forward and swap rates relates to cash flow replication. *Figure 9.10* shows that while, on average, the swap and FRA strip

Figure 9.10
Swap Rates versus FRA Rates

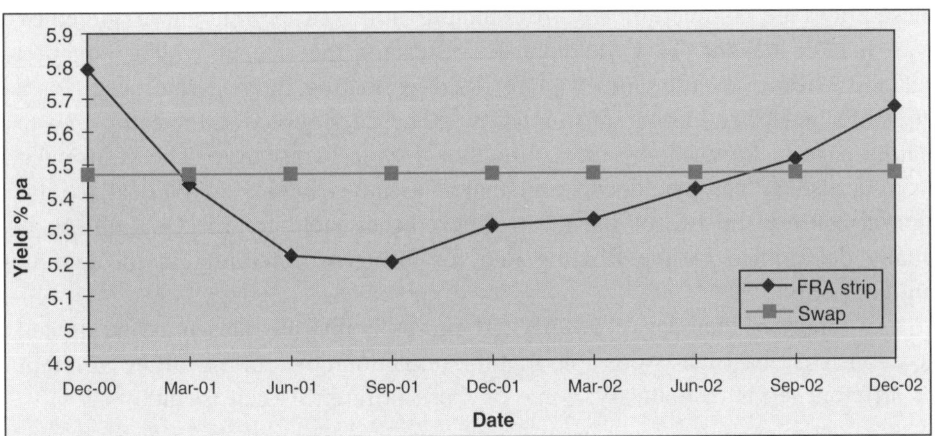

rates are similar during the life of the strip, the timing of interest cash flows is quite different. The strip requires a higher fixed-rate cash flow at the beginning and end, but a lower cash flow in the middle. To correctly compare the FRA strip to a swap we need to adjust for any funding consequences caused by the difference in cash flows.[10]

9.3 SWAP YIELD CURVES: PAR, FORWARD AND ZERO-COUPON

If we wish to improve the simple models developed in the previous section, we need to be able to understand and incorporate zero-coupon and forward swap yields. In this section, we will review the relationship between the standard coupon-paying, or par yield, curve and these two other less obvious yield curves.[11]

9.3.1 Creating Par Yield Curves Using Interpolation

All swap valuation models require accurate market prices, i.e., a method of converting these prices so that they can be applied to open swap contracts and then a process for determining the present-value impact of these prices on open swaps.

[10] In a flat yield curve environment these differences tend to be small, but they become more exaggerated as the yield curve moves to a positive or inverted shape.

[11] We focus on the structural aspects of the yield curve and take its shape as given. If you wish to examine the determinants of yield curve shape, see Van Horne (1990), Chapter 5.

In the case of an interest rate swap, the key prices required are the prevailing market interest rates to be applied to the fixed and floating legs of the swap. These prices are obtained mostly from the prevailing swap yield curve quoted by swap market-makers. This yield curve represents the rate at which a market maker is willing to enter into a plain fixed-to-floating interest rate swap for a series of standardized terms starting today.[12] The rates quoted in the sample swap dealing page in *Figure 9.4* is an example of a swap yield curve. The swap yield curve is also a "par" yield curve in that it assumes interest is paid at regular intervals during the life of the swap. The current yield for the floating leg is usually determined by the floating rate for the term remaining in the current rollover period.

An important element of swap yield curves is that all rates must be quoted on a consistent basis. It is possible that the quotation convention can be different for different terms to maturity; some of these differences can include:

- **Payment frequency** In some markets shorter term (e.g., less than three years) swap rates are quoted on a quarterly compounding rate, while longer term swaps are quoted on a semi-annual or annual basis. All yields should be converted to a consistent compounding basis using the compounding formulae from Chapter 3.
- **Day count basis** In some currencies, particularly US dollars, there are a range of commonly used day count bases. The swap rate will change according to the particular bases. For example, an A/360 day rate will always appear lower than a 30/360 day rate.
- **Floating index** While unusual, it is possible that the underlying floating index used in swap quotations could be different. This will lead to mispricing. For example, a swap rate quoted against LIBOR will be higher than a swap rate quoted against a Treasury bill rate. The swap rates should reflect a consistent floating index.

Figure 9.11 plots a yield curve for swap rates showing some possible quotation conventions. In this case, all swap rates are quoted against the same floating reference rate (e.g., LIBOR). However, the 7- and 10-year rates assume a semi-annual compounding versus quarterly for the shorter term rates. To make the rates on the curve consistent, they have all been standardized to a quarterly rate before being plotted.

The quoted swap rates do not provide a continuous swap curve, instead it is six or seven used to make a curve. In *Figure 9.11*, a curve was drawn simply by joining the dots. This method is referred to as straight-line or linear interpolation because it assumes that any swap rate between two observed swap yields will lie

[12] In most markets, these standardized points on the swap yield curve are for 2, 3, 4, 5, 7 and 10 years.

on a straight line between two observed points. We can express it mathematically as:

$$Y_i = Y_n + (Y_{n+1} - Y_n) \times (t_i / t_{n+1})$$

Where:

Y_i = the yield at time I

Y_n = the last observed yield point with a shorter term to expiry than Y_I

Y_{n+1} = the next observed yield point with a longer term to expiry than Y_I

t_i = the length of time from n to I

t_{n+1} = the length of time from n to $n+1$.

As an example, in the yield curve example in *Figure 9.11*, the swap rate at four years and 91 days would be calculated as follows:

$$\begin{aligned} Y_{4y91d} &= 7.955 + (8.150 - 7.955) \times (91/365) \\ &= 7.955 + 0.049 \\ &= 8.004 \end{aligned}$$

Figure 9.11
A Par Swap Curve

Market quotes			Standardized
Term	Rate % A/365	Quote frequency	Rate % qtrly A/365
1 yr	7.4200	4	7.4200
2 yr	7.5900	4	7.5900
3 yr	7.7600	4	7.7600
4 yr	7.9550	4	7.9550
5 yr	8.1500	4	8.1500
7 yr	8.5750	2	8.4850
10 yr	9.0000	2	8.9010

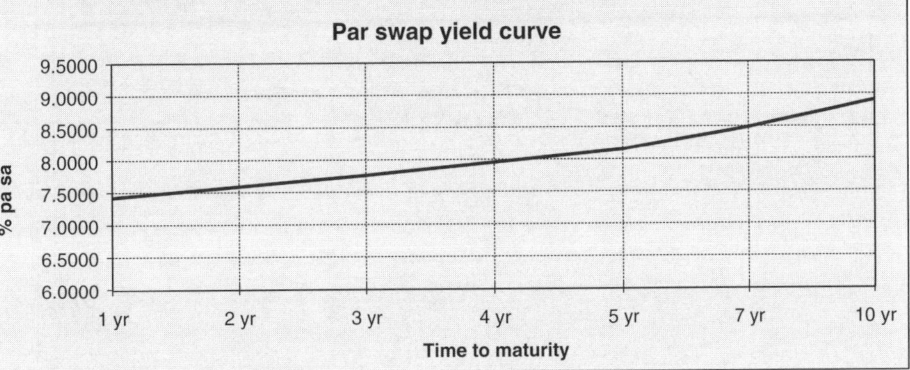

While a straight line interpolation is a very simple approach, it is widely used and is very common in derivative valuation systems.

A feature of straight-line interpolation is that it does not create a smooth yield curve, as it is typically a series of unrelated discrete straight lines that happen to join together. The impact of this is that it can lead to sudden changes in the implied yields for only a small move on either side of an observation point.

For example, in *Figure 9.11* the slope of the curve steepens after year five. A swap with a term of four years 11 months would be two basis points lower than the 5-year rate, while a swap with five years and one month would have a yield of four basis points more than the 5-year rate. While the difference is small in basis points, the rate of change in yield has doubled over two months. This type of sudden change in the slope of the curve creates problems for pricing and valuing swap transactions as they become magnified into discontinuities in forward and zero-coupon yields.

Figure 9.12 illustrates this point by taking the par yield curve from the previous example and generating zero and forward yield curves. These discontinuities are reflected in the "saw-tooth" shape of the forward yield curve, where the absolute level of the forward rate falls around an observation point. These sudden changes or "steps" do not reflect the market value of the swap and represent modeling errors. An unambiguously upward-sloping yield curve should have a consistent increase in par, forward and zero yields—the sudden drop in rates around observation points does not reflect market reality.

From an end-user's perspective, the impact of these discontinuities is relatively minor and is one reason behind the continuing popularity of straight-line

Figure 9.12
The Impact of Straight-Line Interpolation on the Yield Curve

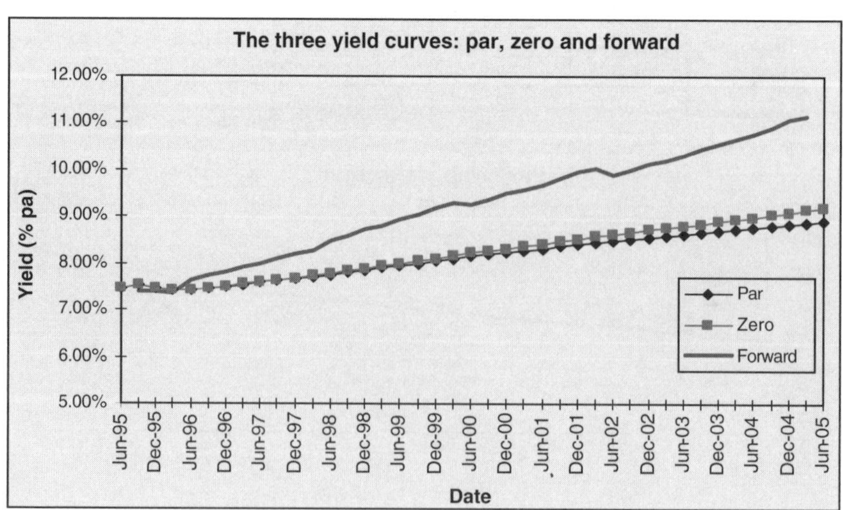

interpolation. However, from a market-maker's perspective, the more accurate the models, the more profitable their operations. Considerable effort has been put into finding a way of deriving smooth yield curves that are consistent with observed market yields. A number of line drawing models have been "borrowed" from scientific numerical analysis models. Some of these are described in *Figure 9.13.*

Drawing smooth yield curves has been a preoccupation of fixed interest market participants at least since the early 1970s. The models developed to assist in predicting the relative yield of "off-the-run" bond issues, included nonlinear regression models, such as the Bradley-Crane or the Elliot-Echols models. Although these models can quickly estimate yield curves, the yield curves will not generally pass through each of the market observations. This implies that an arbitrage opportunity exists between the actual market data and the curve fitted data. From a valuation view point, this is not satisfactory as all positions with a

Figure 9.13
Yield Curve Interpolation Models

Mathematical interpolation of yield curves

1. **Bradley-Crane model**[1]
   The Bradley-Crane model has the form
   $\ln(1+R_M)=a+b_1(M)+b_2\ln(M)+e$
   This implies values equal to the natural logarithm (ln) of one plus the observed yields for term to maturity of length *M* are regressed on two variables, the term to maturity and the natural log of the term of maturity. The last term represents the unexplained yield variation. Once the estimated values of *a*, b_1 and b_2 are obtained, specific maturities of interest can be substituted to obtain estimated yields at these maturity points.

2. **Elliot-Echols model**[2]
   The Elliot-Echols model has the form:
   $\ln(1+R_1)=a+b_1(1/M_1)+b_2(M_1)+b_3(C_1)+e_1$
   Where R_1, M_1, and C_1, are the yield to maturity, term to maturity, and coupon rate of the 1st bond.

   The Elliot-Echols Model is useful where it is sought to fit yield curves directly to yield data for individual bonds, rather than to homogenized yield series. This might be desirable as a means of avoiding possible distortions created in the process of arriving at the synthetic yield series.

3. **Laguerre functions**[3]
   Laguerre functions consist of a polynomial multiplied by a polynomial decay function. For example,
   $1(t)=(a_0+a_1{}^*t+a_2{}^*(t^2+\cdots+a_4{}^*\ln)^*eb^*t$
   is a Laguerre function where, a_1 *s* and *b* are parameters and t is a measure of time.

   One obvious advantage of using Laguerre functions for term structure modeling is that as the decay function eventually dominates the polynomial component, the long-term rates as predicted by a Laguerre function stabllizes. This property provides Laguerre models with an advantage over many other models whose long-term predicted rates continued to either increase or decrease with time.

   The justification for the use of Laguerre functions in terms structure studies is that they provide a range of flexible shapes that are consistent with observable interest rate data and there is some theoretical justification for their applicability to interest rate data.

1. Stephen P Bradley and Dwight B Crane, "Management of Commercial Bank Government: Security Portfolios: An Optimization Approach Under Uncertainty" (1973) (Spring) *Journal of Bank Research* 18.
2. Michael E Echols and Jan Walter Elliott, "A Quantitative Yield Curve Model for Estimating the Term Structure of Interest Rates" (1976) *Journal of Financial and Quantitative Analysis* 87.
3. B F Hunt, "Modeling The Term Structure" (paper presented at Conference on Options on Interest Rates (organized by IIR Pty Ltd) at Sydney, March 1992).

Source: S Das (1994) and Gerald and Wheatley (1994) p. 233.

term to expiry exactly equal to one of the quoted market yields will be incorrectly marked-to-market.

This weakness in these nonlinear regression models prompted the development of "arbitrage free" yield curve models. One model which has received considerable attention in recent years is a concept borrowed from drafting techniques—the "cubic spline." This is mathematically equivalent to making a single flexible rod bend around nails on a board, where the position of the nails is equivalent to the market observed yields. The advantage of this model is that, it provides a smooth curve and ensures that the line passes through all market observations, making it arbitrage free. The downside is that if the yield curve shows any substantial changes in gradient between two points, the curve may require extreme "twists and turns" to remain arbitrage free.[13]

Figure 9.14 indicates the differences between these models by interpolating a yield curve using three techniques:

- straight-line
- Bradley-Crane
- cubic spline.

As *Figure 9.14* shows, the change in direction of the yield curve during the first year creates difficulties for the two curve-fitting techniques. Although the Bradley-Crane model provides a smooth curve, it only comes close to the market observations for years 3 and 4 and misses out on most of the fluctuations in the first year.

The cubic spline is a closer fit to the observed market data than Bradley-Crane; however, the "bulge" in the curve between years 1 and 2 tends to give values that are a little lower than we would expect. This "wobbliness" is apparent in a cubic spline when there is any sharp change in direction in the yield curve. In this particular example, the simple straight-line interpolation gives the results that would be the most consistent with market expectations.

The example yield curve is unusual in that it contains two changes in direction, but it does highlight the fact that, while curve fitting models provide an effective tool for generating smooth curves, they should be used with some caution, particularly with "odd"-shaped yield curves. In fact, some market participants see these models as a form of "black-box" analysis and continue to use straight-line interpolation, regardless of the possibility of discontinuities.

As a practical note for implementing these curve-fitting models, the programming requirements of cubic splines are quite complex. It is often cheaper and easier to purchase commercially available curve-fitting software. Many of the

[13] For more information on interpolation techniques see Das (1997). Another curve-drawing model is the LOWESS or locally weighted regression curve. It attempts to reduce the "wobbliness" of the cubic spline by passing close to the observed data points rather than through them.

Figure 9.14
A Comparison of Interpolation Techniques

Table of yield calculations.

Term (yrs)	Market data	Straight line	Bradley & Crane	Cubic spline
0.5	7.450	7.450	7.469	7.560
0.5	7.540	7.540	7.469	7.540
1.0	7.420	7.420	7.503	7.420
1.5		7.505	7.560	7.457
2.0	7.590	7.590	7.628	7.590
2.5		7.675	7.700	7.691
3.0	7.760	7.760	7.777	7.760
3.5		7.858	7.855	7.859
4.0	7.955	7.955	7.936	7.955
4.5		8.053	8.017	8.064
5.0	8.150	8.150	8.100	8.150

Full yield curve from 0 to 10 years.

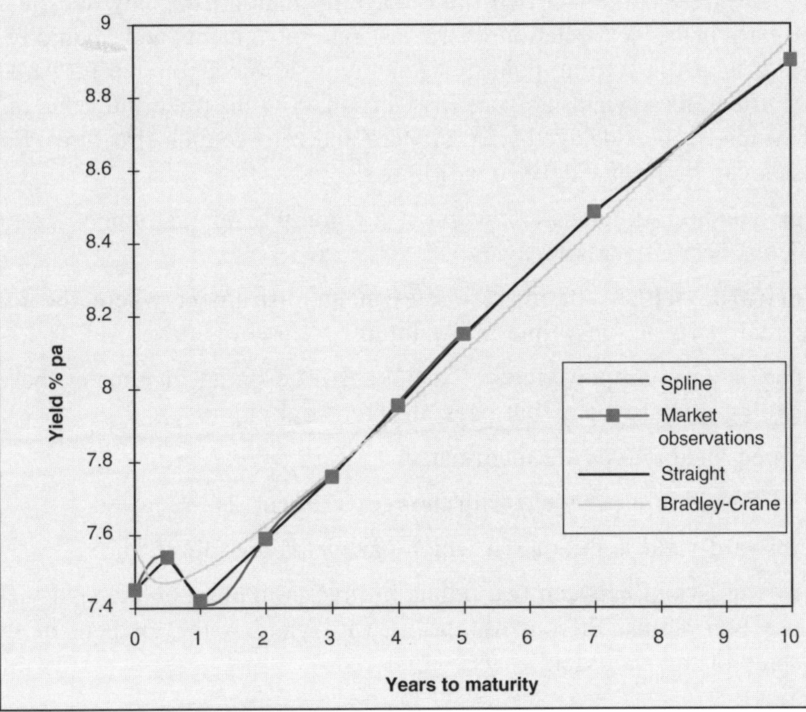

packages available can be integrated into existing pricing and valuation systems and cost less than a few hours of a programmer's time.[14]

Another alternative to the curve-fitting dilemma is to obtain more market observations; the more points we have, the smoother the curve. For example, swap rates quoted quarterly for maturities for one to ten years would provide a good indication of curvature, and simple straight-line techniques would be an adequate method of interpolation between these points. However, it is unlikely that swap market participants will start quoting 36 swap rates on a live basis, so we need to go to other sources such as the futures market; in particular, the short-term futures, such as the Eurodollar and Euroyen. The process of using these prices is investigated in the next section.

9.3.2 Three Curves in One: Par, Zero and Forward

The par swap yield curve is the usual starting point because it is observable and the observations are generally a reflection of the prices at which transactions take place. Once we have obtained an accurate and adequately interpolated par swap yield curve we can use this as the basic market price input to our pricing and valuation programs.

The par yield curve is a rich source of information. Not only does it reflect market participants' expectation of interest rate movements and "liquidity preference," it is also a starting point for generating zero-coupon and forward swap yields. Further, these yields are a main determinant of the price and value of more exotic swaps, such as delayed start, forward and zero-coupon structures. Each of the yields can be briefly defined as follows:

- **Par yields** An interest rate on a coupon-paying instrument where the interest accrual starts today.
- **Forward yields** An interest rate on an instrument where the interest accrual starts at some time in the future.
- **Spot or zero-coupon yields** An interest rate on an instrument that starts accruing interest today, but pays all interest at expiry.

These three yield curves are interrelated:

- a spot yield is a par yield with the reinvestment risk removed;
- a forward yield is the rate at which par yields are reinvested;
- a forward yield between two points in time is implied by the spot yields at those two points. Effectively, the forward yield is the gradient or rate of change of the spot yield curve.

[14] This statement is made from personal experience. There are a number of excellent statistical curve-fitting packages that can be purchased at a very reasonable cost. The curves in this book were built using GraphPad Software Inc's *Prism*™.

What is special about zero-coupon and forward yields? The important feature of zero-coupon rates is that they provide a guaranteed return between commencement and the date of expiry. A par yield assumes that as coupons are received over the life of an instrument they will be invested at the original par yield. With a zero-coupon yield, this reinvestment risk is removed. Forward yields are important because they are the rates at which the reinvestment risk on par interest rates can be hedged. So, if a zero-coupon security is not available, it can be created by combining a par security with forward interest rate contracts, where each of the coupons will be reinvested at forward rates.

The relationship among the three yields also represents the "equivalent value" concept in financial mathematics. For a given term to maturity, each of these yield types is related. If one yield is synthetically replicated by combining the two other yields, then the combined yield should be identical to the outright yield. By combining forward and par yields, the combined yield should equal the outright spot yield. If this relationship does not hold, it implies an arbitrage opportunity. Many sophisticated bond-issuers make use of these interrelationships and take advantage of any mispricing between actual traded market yields and the theoretical yields. For example, some zero-coupon bond issues are undertaken to take advantage of the mispricing of zero-coupon yields by bond investors. To take advantage of this, the zero-coupon bond is issued and then swapped back to a par yield using a zero-coupon swap to give a final par borrowing rate that is lower than the issuer's usual par borrowing rate.

9.3.3 Generating Zero-Coupon Yield Curves

As the zero-coupon yield is the least obvious, yet the most interesting from a valuation perspective, we will examine these yield curve interrelationships by generating zero-coupon yield curves in two ways:

- the forward rate reinvestment method;
- the bootstrapping method.

Forward Rate Reinvestment Method

This is an extension of the relationships discussed in the previous section. If we have observable par and forward yields, then we can create a zero-coupon yield. Essentially, the process is to invest each coupon as it is received, at the forward rate. The coupons received are accumulated and are reinvested at the forward rate on each payment date. At maturity of the par instrument, the total accumulated coupons and the interest earned on those coupons will be the same as the lump-sum interest paid by a zero-coupon instrument.

We can use a simple example to demonstrate the relationship between the three yields.

Example

Suppose we wish to determine a 1-year zero-coupon rate, when the following rates are known:

1-year rate (semi-annual) = 7.5% pa 6-month forward for six months = 9.00% pa

To create a zero-coupon rate, we can reinvest our coupon at the forward rate and create a guaranteed amount of interest at the end of one year. This is shown in the calculation below:

1-year rate (sa)	7.50%
6-month forward	9.00%

Time (Yrs)	Coupon per $100	Forward rate	Coupon interest
0.5	3.75	9.00%	
1	3.75		0.16875
Total	7.5		0.16875
Total interest	7.66875		

Zero rates
Annual rate = 7.669% Semi-annual rate = 7.527%

Note that the rate initially calculated as the total interest is a simple interest number and in this case is effectively an annual interest rate as all interest is received at maturity. To convert this back to a semi-annual rate, we use the interest compounding conversion calculations from Chapter 3.

This example raises the question—given interest payments are not made in a zero-coupon security—why distinguish between an annual and semi-annual rate? While a zero-coupon security has no cash flows to be compounded during its life, we can see from the above example that compounding plays a part in deriving the zero-coupon curve. The frequency of assumed compounding will determine the final interest amount at maturity. The greater the assumed compounding, the greater the amount of interest at maturity. Further, to make a zero-coupon rate and a par rate comparable, they need to be expressed with the same compounding frequency. So, when using a zero-coupon rate, we must remember the assumed compounding frequency and ensure this is incorporated into all calculations.

The Bootstrapping Method

This approach to generating zero-coupon yields is often available for medium-term swap rates because the implied forward yields from short-term futures contracts can be used to reinvest the coupons on the par yield curve. For longer term maturities, accurate forward interest rates are not as easily obtainable and the bootstrapping model allows us to derive spot yields from a "standard" par yield curve.

> ***Note***
> The term "bootstrapping" derives from the fact that zero-coupon rates are incrementally generated in a manner that is similar to "pulling yourself along by the bootstraps". It starts with short-term money market yields that are already zero-coupon rates and then works their way along the yield curve in equidistant steps (usually quarterly, semi-annually or annually).

The concept of bootstrapping is consistent with the law of equivalent value. For a given term, the current yield on a par security is the same as the combined yield of the spot rates of which it is comprised. If we have a par security with two coupons and we know the par yield and the spot yield to the first-coupon, then we can determine the spot yield to the second coupon. This is made clearer by using an example.

Example

Imagine that we have the following interest rates for two securities that are identical except for term and interest payment convention:

6-month spot rate = 10% pa
Par 1-year spot rate = 12% pa semi-annual

The par instrument is a bond and we know it will pay two semi-annual coupons of US$6 per US$100 of face value and it repays the principal after one year. The present value of this security is par, i.e., the present value is equal to the future value of the security:

$$
\begin{aligned}
PV_{\text{par1y}} &= 6/(1+0.12/2)+106/(1+0.12/2)^2 \\
&= 100
\end{aligned}
$$

This par security can be broken down into two zero-coupon securities: the first has a total value of US$6 in six months' time and the second has a value of US$106 in one year's time. We know the first 6-month bond will be present valued at its prevailing market yield of 10% pa. However, the yield of the 1-year bond is not known:

$$PV_{\text{spot6m}} = 6/(1+0.10/2)$$
$$PV_{\text{spot1y}} = 106/(1+r_{\text{spot1y}}/2)^2$$

Where:

r_{spot1y} is the 1-year spot rate expressed as a semi-annual compounding interest rate.

Something we do know is that if the two zero-coupon bonds are combined, then the cash flows are identical to the par 1-year bond. In this situation, the concept of equivalent value illustrates that the sum of the value of these two component bonds will have the same total value as the 1-year par bond; that is,

$$PV_{\text{par1y}} = PV_{\text{spot6m}} + PV_{\text{spot1y}}$$

Or:

$$100 = 6/(1+0.10/2) + 106/(1+r^*/2)^2$$

when rearranged this can be solved to equal;

$$r^* = 0.1206 \text{ or } 12.06\%$$

The zero-coupon rates derived from either method should be identical. In practice, there is some divergence between the two methods, which is discussed in the yield curve modeling section below.

Discount Factors

These zero-coupon, or spot, interest rates provide a complete description of the yield that prevails from today to a single date in the future equal to the maturity date of the zero-coupon rate. In the simple models developed in Section 9.2, it is this yield that we require for accurate calculation of present values.

To express the relationship between the value of the US dollar today and in the future, zero-coupon interest rates are used to determine present value "discount factors." An individual discount factor can be calculated for each day in the future and used to convert future cash flows into future value amounts. Essentially, the discount factor is a standardized expression of the compound interest present value interest rate:[15]

$$DF = \frac{1}{(1 + r_{spotn}/m)^n}$$

Where:

r_{spotn} = spot or zero rate to period n
n = number of periods
m = assumed frequency pa.

In the example above, where the 6-month and 1-year semi-annual spot rates were 10% pa and 12.06% pa respectively, the discount factors are:

$$DF_{0.5y} = \frac{1}{(1+0.10/2)^1} = 0.952381$$

$$DF_{1y} = \frac{1}{(1+0.1206/2)^2} = 0.889492$$

Once we have generated the discount factors, they can be directly applied to any present valuation models (e.g., the bond and offset swap methods) as the method of discounting the future cash flows on each leg of the swap. For example, if the bond in the previous leg was the fixed leg of a 1-year swap, then the present-value calculation using discount factors would be:

$$\begin{aligned} PV_{bond} &= 6 \times 0.952381 + 106 \times 0.889492 \\ &= 5.714 + 94.286 \\ &= 100 \end{aligned}$$

[15] Note this discount factor is calculated using compounded interest rates. In many derivatives articles, the interest rates are assumed to be continuously compounded which means that the discount factor can be calculated using the exponential function $DF = \exp(r_{spotn} \times n)$. This form of discount factor is often used in options pricing model present-value calculations.

9.3.4 Zero-Coupon Yield Curve Modeling

A useful component of any valuation system is that for all currencies where interest rate exposures exist, a yield curve model takes available market data such as swaps and futures yields and then builds par, forward and zero-coupon yields.

In this section, we look at a simple combination of interrelated spreadsheets that provide the following:

- **Market observations** Provides prevailing money market yields, futures prices and par swap yields.
- **Bootstrapping** Generates a 10-year zero-coupon swap yield curve using bootstrapping with quarterly compounding.
- **Forward rate reinvestment** Generates a zero-coupon yield curve that uses the forward rate reinvestment model by applying current futures prices.

We will look at each of the steps involved building this model.

Market Observations

It is important that the model is capable of reflecting the different characteristics of the interest rate markets in each currency. While money market and swap rates are available in most currencies in standardized blocks, the compounding frequency underlying the swap rates may vary from quarterly, to semi-annual to annual. Also, the futures expiry dates may occur on different dates for different markets.

In the model, we examine an example of an Australian dollar swap curve. This is based on actual market data that has been rebased to start in 2001. *Figure 9.15* shows the data entry screen for the model that can be divided into three components:[16]

- **Bank bill curve** These are the standard short-term money market interest rates used in a swap. For US dollars, the US dollar LIBOR curve would be used, while for the Euro, Frankfurt Interbank Offered Rate (FIBOR) rates might be used.
- **Bank bill futures curve** All listed short-term futures months are provided. In this case, it is the SFE's bank bill contract with 12 delivery months. For the US dollar, the CME's Eurodollar contract would be used with up to ten years or 40 contract months available. If we are not satisfied that the prices in the "back" futures months are sufficiently accurate, we can elect to leave these delivery months out of the model. It is important that the model incorporates when the futures contract will expire. In most cases, this can vary as

[16] These rates are loaded automatically from a quote vendor, using standard MS Windows "DDE" links supplied by the quote vendor.

Figure 9.15
Yield Curve Model Input Screen

Sample data

Start date	26-Jun-01
Currency	A$

Bank bill (BBSW) curve		Bank bill futures curve			Swap curve		
Term	Interest %	Month	Expiry date	Futures price	Term	Interest %	Frequency
Cash	7.4500	Sep-95	8-Sep-95	92.6700	1 yr	7.4200	4
1 mth	7.4900	Dec-95	8-Dec-95	92.7100	2 yr	7.5900	4
2 mth	7.5680	Mar-96	8-Mar-96	92.6600	3 yr	7.7600	4
3 mth	7.5290	Jun-96	14-Jun-96	92.5600	4 yr	7.9550	4
4 mth	7.5317	Sep-96	13-Sep-96	92.3900	5 yr	8.1500	4
5 mth	7.5343	Dec-96	13-Dec-96	92.2300	7 yr	8.5750	2
6 mth	7.5370	Mar-97	14-Mar-97	92.0700	10 yr	9.0000	2
		Jun-97	13-Jun-97	91.9100			
		Sep-97	12-Sep-97	91.8400			
		Dec-97	12-Dec-97	91.7400			
		Mar-98	13-Mar-98	91.6100			
		Jun-98	12-Jun-98	91.4800			

the futures contract closes out on a particular day in the month (e.g., the second Friday) as opposed to a specific date. This can be done by manually entering the dates, or as in this model, you can use the date functions in Excel to work out which day is the first day of the month and then work out how many days till the standard futures expiry date.

- **Swap curve** This is the prevailing par swap curve from one to ten years. Note the change in convention from quarterly to semi-annual from years five to seven. As we will be building zero-coupon curves with assumed quarterly compounding, these semi-annual rates will need to be converted to a quarterly rate before being included in either of the following models.

Bootstrapping Model

The first zero-coupon yield curve is generated by bootstrapping the par yield curve, by combining the bank bill and swap yields from the market observations. A precondition of bootstrapping is that the yield curve is divided into equal periodic iteration steps. In this case we wish to make a quarterly yield curve, so we construct a par yield curve with 40 quarterly rests. In this case we have used straight-line interpolation, although one of the curve fitting techniques could also be used.

Figure 9.16 reproduces a bootstrap spreadsheet model.[17] The procedure followed in this spreadsheet is the same as in the 2-coupon model in

[17] The model used is a "long hand" approach designed to show the mechanics of the boot-strap. For those looking to optimize the calculation, the process can be easily adapted to a spreadsheet macro or Visual Basic script with a "for" loop.

Figure 9.16
Yield Curve Model: Bootstrapping Calculation

	C	D	E	F	G	H	I	J	K	L	M	N	O	P	Q	R	S	T	U
6				Interpolated	Quarterly	Quarterly													
7	Date	Number	Number	quarterly	par	zero	Each periodic coupon discounted at the relevant spot rate												
8		days	of periods	par yield	coupon	yield		2	3	4	5	6	7	8	9	10	11	12	13
9																			
10	26-Jun-01	0	0																
11	26-Sep-01	92	1	7.5290%	$1.88	7.5290%													
12	26-Dec-01	183	2	7.4673%	$1.87	7.4673%	1.83												
13	26-Mar-02	274	3	7.4436%	$1.86	7.4428%	1.83	1.79											
14	26-Jun-02	366	4	7.4200%	$1.86	7.4187%	1.82	1.79	1.76										
15	26-Sep-02	458	5	7.4625%	$1.87	7.4631%	1.83	1.80	1.77	1.73									
16	26-Dec-02	549	6	7.5050%	$1.88	7.5075%	1.84	1.81	1.78	1.74	1.71								
17	26-Mar-03	639	7	7.5475%	$1.89	7.5522%	1.85	1.82	1.79	1.75	1.72	1.69							
18	26-Jun-03	731	8	7.5900%	$1.90	7.5970%	1.86	1.83	1.80	1.76	1.73	1.70	1.66						
19	26-Sep-03	823	9	7.6325%	$1.91	7.6422%	1.87	1.84	1.81	1.77	1.74	1.71	1.67	1.64					
20	26-Dec-03	914	10	7.6750%	$1.92	7.6877%	1.88	1.85	1.82	1.78	1.75	1.72	1.68	1.65	1.62				
21	25-Mar-04	1004	11	7.7175%	$1.93	7.7334%	1.89	1.86	1.83	1.79	1.76	1.73	1.69	1.66	1.63	1.59			
22	25-Jun-04	1096	12	7.7600%	$1.94	7.7795%	1.90	1.87	1.84	1.80	1.77	1.74	1.70	1.67	1.64	1.60	1.57		
23	25-Sep-04	1188	13	7.8088%	$1.95	7.8331%	1.92	1.88	1.85	1.81	1.78	1.75	1.71	1.68	1.65	1.61	1.58	1.55	
24	25-Dec-04	1279	14	7.8575%	$1.96	7.8870%	1.93	1.89	1.86	1.83	1.79	1.76	1.72	1.69	1.66	1.62	1.59	1.56	1.53
25	25-Mar-05	1369	15	7.9063%	$1.98	7.9414%	1.94	1.90	1.87	1.84	1.80	1.77	1.73	1.70	1.67	1.63	1.60	1.57	1.54
26	25-Jun-05	1461	16	7.9550%	$1.99	7.9962%	1.95	1.92	1.88	1.85	1.81	1.78	1.74	1.71	1.68	1.64	1.61	1.58	1.55
27	25-Sep-05	1553	17	8.0038%	$2.00	8.0515%	1.96	1.93	1.89	1.86	1.82	1.79	1.76	1.72	1.69	1.65	1.62	1.59	1.56
28	25-Dec-05	1644	18	8.0525%	$2.01	8.1073%	1.98	1.94	1.90	1.87	1.84	1.80	1.77	1.73	1.70	1.66	1.63	1.60	1.56
29	26-Mar-06	1735	19	8.1013%	$2.03	8.1637%	1.99	1.95	1.92	1.88	1.85	1.81	1.78	1.74	1.71	1.67	1.64	1.61	1.57
30	26-Jun-06	1827	20	8.1500%	$2.04	8.2205%	2.00	1.96	1.93	1.89	1.86	1.82	1.79	1.75	1.72	1.68	1.65	1.62	1.58
31	26-Sep-06	1919	21	8.1919%	$2.05	8.2694%	2.01	1.97	1.94	1.90	1.87	1.83	1.80	1.76	1.73	1.69	1.66	1.63	1.59
32	26-Dec-06	2010	22	8.2338%	$2.06	8.3188%	2.02	1.98	1.95	1.91	1.88	1.84	1.81	1.77	1.74	1.70	1.67	1.63	1.60
33	26-Mar-07	2100	23	8.2756%	$2.07	8.3687%	2.03	1.99	1.96	1.92	1.89	1.85	1.82	1.78	1.74	1.71	1.68	1.64	1.61
34	26-Jun-07	2192	24	8.3175%	$2.08	8.4192%	2.04	2.00	1.97	1.93	1.90	1.86	1.82	1.79	1.75	1.72	1.68	1.65	1.62
35	26-Sep-07	2284	25	8.3594%	$2.09	8.4702%	2.05	2.01	1.98	1.94	1.91	1.87	1.83	1.80	1.76	1.73	1.69	1.66	1.62
36	26-Dec-07	2375	26	8.4013%	$2.10	8.5218%	2.06	2.02	1.99	1.95	1.91	1.88	1.84	1.81	1.77	1.74	1.70	1.67	1.63
37	25-Mar-08	2465	27	8.4431%	$2.11	8.5741%	2.07	2.03	2.00	1.96	1.92	1.89	1.85	1.82	1.78	1.74	1.71	1.68	1.64
38	25-Jun-08	2557	28	8.4850%	$2.12	8.6269%	2.08	2.04	2.01	1.97	1.93	1.90	1.86	1.82	1.79	1.75	1.72	1.68	1.65
39	25-Sep-08	2649	29	8.5197%	$2.13	8.6704%	2.09	2.05	2.02	1.98	1.94	1.91	1.87	1.83	1.80	1.76	1.73	1.69	1.66
40	25-Dec-08	2740	30	8.5543%	$2.14	8.7144%	2.10	2.06	2.02	1.99	1.95	1.91	1.88	1.84	1.80	1.77	1.73	1.70	1.66
41	25-Mar-09	2830	31	8.5890%	$2.15	8.7590%	2.11	2.07	2.03	2.00	1.96	1.92	1.88	1.85	1.81	1.78	1.74	1.70	1.67
42	25-Jun-09	2922	32	8.6237%	$2.16	8.8042%	2.12	2.08	2.04	2.00	1.97	1.93	1.89	1.85	1.82	1.78	1.75	1.71	1.68
43	25-Sep-09	3014	33	8.6583%	$2.16	8.8501%	2.12	2.09	2.05	2.01	1.97	1.94	1.90	1.86	1.83	1.79	1.75	1.72	1.68
44	25-Dec-09	3105	34	8.6930%	$2.17	8.8965%	2.13	2.09	2.06	2.02	1.98	1.94	1.91	1.87	1.83	1.80	1.76	1.72	1.69
45	26-Mar-10	3196	35	8.7276%	$2.18	8.9436%	2.14	2.10	2.06	2.03	1.99	1.95	1.91	1.88	1.84	1.80	1.77	1.73	1.70
46	26-Jun-10	3288	36	8.7623%	$2.19	8.9914%	2.15	2.11	2.07	2.04	2.00	1.96	1.92	1.88	1.85	1.81	1.77	1.74	1.70
47	26-Sep-10	3380	37	8.7970%	$2.20	9.0399%	2.16	2.12	2.08	2.04	2.01	1.97	1.93	1.89	1.85	1.82	1.78	1.75	1.71
48	26-Dec-10	3471	38	8.8316%	$2.21	9.0891%	2.17	2.13	2.09	2.05	2.01	1.97	1.94	1.90	1.86	1.83	1.79	1.75	1.72
49	26-Mar-11	3561	39	8.8663%	$2.22	9.1391%	2.18	2.14	2.10	2.06	2.02	1.98	1.94	1.91	1.87	1.83	1.80	1.76	1.72
50	26-Jun-11	3653	40	8.9010%	$2.23	9.1898%	2.18	2.14	2.11	2.07	2.03	1.99	1.95	1.91	1.88	1.84	1.80	1.77	1.73

Note: Summary of calculations

1. The date is simply calculated as exactly one calender quarter on from the previous quarter.
2. The number of days is the difference between today and the rollover date.
3. The "par" yields for periods 1 and 2 are already zero coupon rates so the "par" yields are entered directly as zero-coupon yields.
4. The calculation from periods 3 to 40 are identical; the only difference is that the number of coupons rises by one for each extra period.
5. The main calculations for period 3 (row 13) are as follows:

Description	Cell	Formula
Quarterly par coupon	G13	=100*F13/4
Quarterly zero-coupon	H13	=4*(((100+G13)/(100–SUM(I13:AU13)))^(1/E13)–1)
Coupon 1	I 13	=$G13/(1+$H$11/4)^$E$11
Coupon 1	J13	=$G13/(1+$H$12/4)^$E$12

Note: for each extra period add one more coupon following the same sequence in the first two columns. So the third coupon will be calculated for period 4 which will discount; the par quarterly coupon (G14) by the zero-coupon rate prevailing up to period 3, that is, $G14/(1+H$13/4)^$E$13.

V	W	X	Y	Z	AA	AB	AC	AD	AE	AF	AG	AH	AI	SJ	AK	AL	AM	AN	AO	AP	AQ	AR	AS	AT	AU
14	15	16	17	18	19	20	21	22	23	24	25	26	27	28	29	30	31	32	33	34	35	36	37	38	39
1.50																									
1.51	1.48																								
1.52	1.49																								
1.53	1.50	1.47	1.43																						
1.54	1.51	1.48	1.44	1.41																					
1.55	1.52	1.48	1.45	1.42	1.39																				
1.56	1.52	1.49	1.46	1.43	1.40	1.36																			
1.57	1.53	1.50	1.47	1.43	1.40	1.37	1.34																		
1.57	1.54	1.51	1.47	1.44	1.41	1.38	1.35	1.32																	
1.58	1.55	1.51	1.48	1.45	1.42	1.38	1.35	1.32	1.29																
1.59	1.56	1.52	1.49	1.46	1.42	1.39	1.36	1.33	1.30	1.27															
1.60	1.56	1.53	1.50	1.46	1.43	1.40	1.37	1.34	1.30	1.27	1.24														
1.61	1.57	1.54	1.50	1.47	1.44	1.41	1.37	1.34	1.31	1.28	1.25	1.22													
1.61	1.58	1.55	1.51	1.48	1.45	1.41	1.38	1.35	1.32	1.29	1.26	1.23	1.20												
1.62	1.59	1.55	1.52	1.48	1.45	1.42	1.39	1.35	1.32	1.29	1.26	1.23	1.20	1.17											
1.63	1.59	1.56	1.52	1.49	1.46	1.42	1.39	1.36	1.33	1.30	1.27	1.24	1.21	1.18	1.15										
1.63	1.60	1.56	1.53	1.50	1.46	1.43	1.40	1.37	1.33	1.30	1.27	1.24	1.21	1.18	1.15	1.12									
1.64	1.61	1.57	1.54	1.50	1.47	1.44	1.40	1.37	1.34	1.31	1.28	1.25	1.22	1.19	1.16	1.13	1.10								
1.65	1.61	1.58	1.54	1.51	1.47	1.44	1.41	1.38	1.34	1.31	1.28	1.25	1.22	1.19	1.16	1.13	1.11	1.08							
1.65	1.62	1.58	1.55	1.51	1.48	1.45	1.41	1.38	1.35	1.32	1.29	1.26	1.23	1.20	1.17	1.14	1.11	1.08	1.06						
1.66	1.62	1.59	1.55	1.52	1.49	1.45	1.42	1.39	1.36	1.32	1.29	1.26	1.23	1.20	1.17	1.14	1.11	1.09	1.06	1.03					
1.67	1.63	1.60	1.56	1.53	1.49	1.46	1.43	1.39	1.36	1.33	1.30	1.27	1.24	1.21	1.18	1.15	1.12	1.09	1.06	1.04	1.01				
1.67	1.64	1.60	1.57	1.53	1.50	1.46	1.43	1.40	1.37	1.33	1.30	1.27	1.24	1.21	1.18	1.15	1.12	1.10	1.07	1.04	1.01	0.99			
1.68	1.64	1.61	1.57	1.54	1.50	1.47	1.44	1.40	1.37	1.34	1.31	1.28	1.25	1.21	1.19	1.16	1.13	1.10	1.07	1.05	1.02	0.99	0.97		
1.69	1.65	1.61	1.58	1.54	1.51	1.48	1.44	1.41	1.38	1.34	1.31	1.28	1.25	1.22	1.19	1.16	1.13	1.10	1.08	1.05	1.02	1.00	0.97	0.94	
1.69	1.66	1.62	1.59	1.55	1.52	1.48	1.45	1.41	1.38	1.35	1.32	1.29	1.26	1.22	1.19	1.17	1.14	1.11	1.08	1.05	1.03	1.00	0.97	0.95	0.92

Section 9.3.3 above, the only difference is that it has been extended to cover 40 periods. There are no calculations in period 1 or 2 as the bank bill rates entered are already zero-coupon rates. The first calculation occurs in period 3. The par rate for 274 days is converted into a quarterly coupon (cell G13). We already know the spot rates for periods 1 and 2, so the coupon is present-valued at the zero rate for these two periods (cells I and J13). The third period zero yield (cell H13) is then calculated by the third period spot rate, which will give the present value of par. This process is repeated for every extra period with the addition of one extra discounted coupon per period.

This zero-coupon curve has been generated purely by prevailing par or cash market rates without the use of forward rates. This type of zero curve is sometimes called the "cash" zero-coupon yield curve.

While this zero-coupon yield curve has been created with a quarterly compounding frequency, zero-coupon rates for other interest payment frequencies can be determined from this curve simply by using the interest rate compounding formula. For example, the 1.5 year zero-coupon rate is 7.5075% pa. If we use the interest rate conversion formula, we can see that this is equivalent to a 7.5780% pa semi-annual and 7.7216% pa annual zero-coupon rate. This indicates that once you have built a zero-coupon curve for one compounding frequency it can be easily applied to any swap interest payment frequency. A quarterly compounding curve is useful because it allows greater scope for reflecting the true shape of the yield curve.

Forward Rate Reinvestment Model

The forward reinvestment calculation is considerably easier than the bootstrapping approach. However, as most short-term interest rate futures contracts are only listed for a few years, the yield curve can only be derived for medium-term swaps.[18]

In the model displayed in *Figure 9.17*, the futures prices and the expiry date of each contract are input from the market observation date. The forward interest rate reflects the rate of change between two spot interest rates. So, if we know the spot rate for the first period and the forward rate between the first and second period, then the spot rate for the second quarter is calculated by the interest on the first period multiplied by the forward interest rate. We simplify this calculation by working in terms of discount factors, where the discount factor for the second period will be the discount factor for the first period present valued at the forward rate. The zero-coupon yield is then calculated by solving for the quarterly compounded rate that will give the calculated discount rate.

[18] The exception to this situation is CME's Eurodollar contract, which is listed out to ten years. Even with this contract, the back-month contracts tend to have very low volume and as a result, the prices may not always reflect fair value.

Figure 9.17
Yield Curve Model: Forward Rate Reinvestment Calculation

	C	D	E	F	G	H	I	J	K	L	M
6											
7											
8	Assumed compounding frequency				4						
9	Day count				365						
10											
11	Zero rates to futures expiry dates								Zero rates to cash curve dates		
12	Futures curve				Implied			Quarterly	Cash		Interpolated
13	Month	Expiry date	Futures	Days to	forward	Discount	Quarterly	zero	curve	Days	zero
14			price	expiry	yield(2)	factor	periods	yield(3)	dates	difference	yield
15	Today	26-Jun-01			7.5524%	1.000000			26-Jun-01		
16	Sep-01	8-Sep-01	92.6700	74	7.3300%	0.984919	0.810959	7.552%	26-Sep-01	18	7.5293%
17	Dec-01	8-Dec-01	92.7100	91	7.2900%	0.967243	1.808219	7.436%	26-Dec-01	18	7.4256%
18	Mar-02	9-Mar-02	92.6600	91	7.3400%	0.949977	2.805479	7.384%	26-Mar-02	17	7.3817%
19	Jun-02	15-Jun-02	92.5600	98	7.4400%	0.931617	3.879452	7.370%	26-Jun-02	11	7.3722%
20	Sep-02	14-Sep-02	92.3900	91	7.6100%	0.914651	4.876712	7.385%	26-Sep-02	12	7.3898%
21	Dec-02	14-Dec-02	92.2300	91	7.7700%	0.897621	5.873973	7.423%	26-Dec-02	12	7.4297%
22	Mar-03	15-Mar-03	92.0700	91	7.9300%	0.880563	6.871233	7.473%	26-Mar-03	11	7.4804%
23	Jun-03	14-Jun-03	91.9100	91	8.0900%	0.863491	7.868493	7.531%	26-Jun-03	12	7.5395%
24	Sep-03	13-Sep-03	91.8400	91	8.1600%	0.846419	8.865753	7.594%	26-Sep-03	13	7.6023%
25	Dec-03	13-Dec-03	91.7400	91	8.2600%	0.829543	9.863014	7.651%	26-Dec-03	13	7.6593%
26	Mar-04	13-Mar-04	91.6100	91	8.3900%	0.812804	10.86027	7.707%	26-Mar-04	13	7.7154%
27	Jun-04	12-Jun-04	91.4800	91	8.5200%	0.796151	11.85753	7.765%	26-Jun-04	14	

Notes:
(1) All interpolations are on a straight-line basis.
(2) The interest rate for the first period (cell G15) is the spot rate interpolated from the cash bank bill curve.
(3) The first rate is left as a 74-day zero rate.
(4) The calculations are summarized below for the second period (row 17):

Description	Cell	Formula
Days to expiry	F17	=+D17–D16
Implied forward Yield	G17	=(100–E17)/100
Discount factor	H17	=+H16/(1+G16*F17/$G$9)
Quarterly periods	I17	=(SUM($F$16:F17)/$G$9)*4
Quarterly zero yield	J17	=((1/H17)^(1/I17)–1)*4
Days difference	L17	=+K17–D17
Interpolated zero yield	M17	=+J17+(J18–J17)*L17/F18

A complicating factor of the futures curve is that the futures expiry dates can be different from the quarterly rollover periods in our cash zero curve. In this case, each of the futures expiry dates are between 12 and 18 days earlier than the quarterly rollover cycle of the cash zero-coupon curve. To make the two curves comparable we need to interpolate from the futures date, zero-coupon yields to cash rollover date zero-coupon yields.

Figure 9.18 graphs the cash and futures generated zero-coupon curves, labeled "cash-zero" and "futures-zero" respectively. The results are close though even the futures zero curve is consistently below the cash zero curve. The largest difference in this example is eight basis points, which is close to the market bid-offer spread and would only represent an arbitrage opportunity for a market-maker with low transaction costs.

When we discussed the relationship between short-term interest rate futures and FRAs in Chapter 5, we noted two potential causes of pricing discrepancy: funding costs and convexity adjustments. The same potential source of discrepancy

Figure 9.18
Comparison of Zero-Coupon Curves

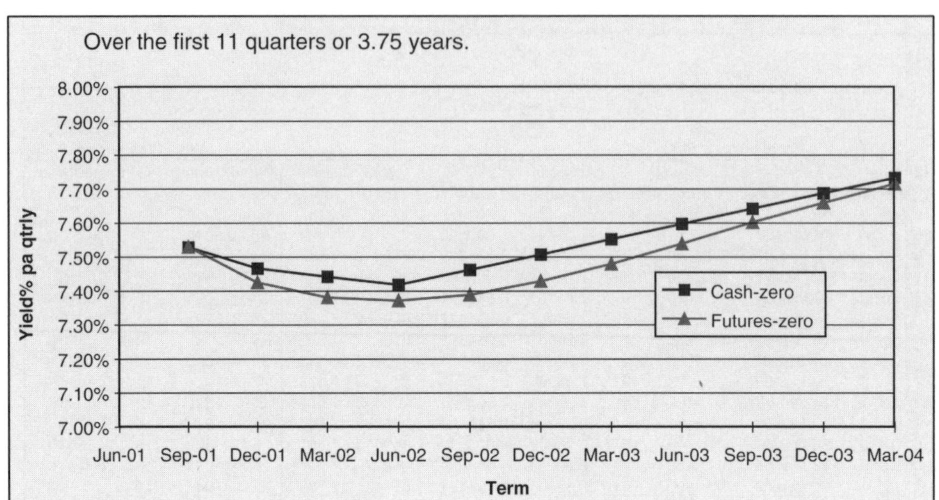

exists between futures contracts and swap contracts. The funding cost associated with a futures position may, if sufficiently large, change the effective forward rates. The convexity adjustment stems from the fact that a short futures position-taker is in a better position from a move up or down in interest rates than by taking the same position in an FRA or a swap. Typically, the adjustment is to reduce the implied forward yield of futures contract by one to two basis points when they are being compared to OTC derivatives (see *Figure 5.9*). In this case, the convexity adjustment will cause the gap between the cash and futures zero curves to widen slightly.

9.4 ZERO-COUPON SWAP MODELS

In the previous section, we developed the necessary tools to develop zero-coupon yields. The benefit of using zero-coupon yields is that these yields provide the "true" yield prevailing between two points in time. We can now incorporate these yields into the simple valuation models developed in Section 9.2. In this section, we will develop two zero-coupon pricing models:

- the forward rate offset method;
- the zero-coupon bond method.

As the names imply, they are both more complex versions of the simple bond and offset models developed earlier in this chapter.

9.4.1 The Forward Rate Offset Method

This model recognizes that swaps can be decomposed into a series of FRAs or short-term interest rate futures contracts. This relationship is important for the pricing and valuing swaps.

- **Par swap pricing** The prevailing par swap rates will be closely related to the prevailing strip of forward interest rates. We will use this approach to determine "futures strip" estimates of swap yields.
- **Swap valuation** An existing swap contract can be terminated using forward contracts. Consequently, the value of a swap will be given by the difference between the forward rate implied by the swap and the prevailing forward rate. Using this as our conceptual basis, the "futures" strip model will be extended to develop the forward rate offset model.

Pricing Swaps Using Futures Strips

As we saw from the forward rate reinvestment zero-coupon yield curve calculator in the previous section, futures prices can be converted into zero-coupon yields. We now want to convert these futures prices into estimates of current par swap yields.

We know that at the commencement of the swap, the fixed leg and floating legs should have the same value; that is, the present value of the cash flows on the fixed and floating legs should be the same. The current set of forward interest rates is the current market estimate of the floating leg of a swap for each forward period. Since we have estimates of the forward rate in the form of futures prices, we can estimate the value of each of the floating legs in the swap. What is more, we can present value these amounts using the zero-coupon yields determined in the forward reinvestment zero-coupon model. If we can present value the floating leg, then we know the present value of the fixed leg of a par swap should be the same. Therefore, the current par swap rate, with rollover dates corresponding to the futures dates, will be the fixed-leg interest rate that will create the same present value as the floating leg. This is demonstrated in *Figure 9.19* where all the futures prices used in *Figure 9.17* are used to solve for the estimated swap rate.

The example in *Figure 9.19* is known as a futures strip swap. The actual swap rate determined for a particular period is in line with the futures expiry dates. As a result, this swap is for a term of slightly less than three years and the first rollover period is a "stub" period of only 74 days, as opposed to around 90 days for the remaining interest periods. We want to determine swap rates with regular quarterly interest payments dates, so we need to interpolate the strip rates between futures dates to compare them to the current cash swap rates.

Figure 9.19
Pricing Par Swaps Using Futures Strips

Ignoring futures cash/adjustments
Requires solver add-in to be loaded

	C	D	E	F	G	H	I	J	K	L	M
6	Swap details										
7	Start date	26-Jun-01		Face value				100,000,000.00			
8	Expiry date	12-Jun-04		Compounding frequency				4	Solution		
9	Years	2.96		Fixed-leg day count				365	Swap rate		7.7408%
10				Floating-leg day count				365			
11	Zero rates to futures expiry dates										

Row	Bank bill futures curve Month	Expiry date	Futures price	Days to expiry	Implied forward yield(2)	Discount factor	Floating leg Interest cash flows	Floating leg Present value	Floating leg Interest cash flows	Floating leg Present value
15	Today	26-Jun-01			7.5524%	1.000000		20,384,904.84		20,384,904.84
16	Sep-01	8-Sep-01	92.6700	74	7.3300%	0.984919	1,531,171.51	1,508,080.21	1,569,370.17	1,545,702.81
17	Dec-01	8-Dec-01	92.7100	91	7.2900%	0.967243	1,827,479.45	1,767,616.76	1,929,901.16	1,866,683.45
18	Mar-02	9-Mar-02	92.6600	91	7.3400%	0.949977	1,817,506.85	1,726,589.94	1,929,901.16	1,833,361.97
19	Jun-02	15-Jun-02	92.5600	98	7.4400%	0.931617	1,970,739.73	1,835,975.37	2,078,355.10	1,936,231.72
20	Sep-02	14-Sep-02	92.3900	91	7.6100%	0.914651	1,854,904.11	1,696,590.77	1,929,901.16	1,765,186.93
21	Dec-02	14-Dec-02	92.2300	91	7.7700%	0.897621	1,897,287.67	1,703,045.29	1,929,901.16	1,732,319.84
22	Mar-03	15-Mar-03	92.0700	91	7.9300%	0.880563	1,937,178.08	1,705,807.24	1,929,901.16	1,699,399.45
23	Jun-03	14-Jun-03	91.9100	91	8.0900%	0.863491	1,977,068.49	1,707,181.11	1,929,901.16	1,666,452.54
24	Sep-03	13-Sep-03	91.8400	91	8.1600%	0.846419	2,016,958.90	1,707,192.75	1,929,901.16	1,633,505.41
25	Dec-03	13-Dec-03	91.7400	91	8.2600%	0.829543	2,034,410.96	1,687,631.15	1,929,901.16	1,600,935.79
26	Mar-04	13-Mar-04	91.6100	91	8.3900%	0.812804	2,059,342.47	1,673,842.75	1,929,901.16	1,568,632.28
27	Jun-04	12-Jun-04	91.4800	91	8.5200%	0.796151	2,091,753.42	1,665,351.48	1,929,901.16	1,536,492.65
28										

Notes:
(1) All interpolations are on a straight-line basis.
(2) The interest rate for the first period (cell G15) is the spot rate interpolated from the cash bank bill curve.
(3) The first rate is actually the spot rate for 74 days and the last forward rate is not actually used.
(4) This model ignores convexity and funding adjustments.
(5) The calculations are summarized below for the second period (row 17):

Description	Cell	Formula
Days to expiry	F17	=+D17–D16
Implied forward yield	G17	=(100–E17)/100
Discount factor	H17	=+H16/(1+G16*F17/$G$9)
Floating interest cash flows	I17	=+G16*F17/$I$10*$I$7
Floating present value	J17	=+I17*H17
Fixed interest cash flows	K17	=+$L$9*F17/$I$9*$I$7
Fixed present value	L17	=+K17*H17

(6) The total present values in cells J17 and L 17 are given by summing the cells immediately below each of these totals.
(7) The Excel solver function (Solver.xla) was used in this calculation using the following inputs:

Input description	Cell
Target cell	L15
By changing cells	L9
Equal to value of cell	J15

After replicating this calculation for a range of maturities, the swap rates implied by the futures strip rate is compared with the actual par swap rates for the sample period in *Figure 9.20.* As with the zero-coupon curve calculation in the previous section, the par swap yield curve is *above* the futures strip swap curve, with the discrepancy varying from two to eight basis points. Differences can be expected between the two curves as the two markets trade separately and also perhaps due to slight timing differences in the collection of the cash and

Figure 9.20
Comparison of Par Swap Curves and Swap Rates Implied in the Futures Strip Curve

In this example the calculation undertaken in *Figure 9.19* for a 3-year swap is replicated for a range of maturities. The 3-month rate is not shown as this is the same as the underlying spot curve.

Number of years	Cash swap curve Swap expiry	Rate qtrly	Futures strip curve Strip expiry	Rate qtrly	Days difference	Interpolated strip yield(1)	Cash/strip difference
0.5	26-Dec-01	7.4673%	8-Dec-01	7.4307%	18	7.4210%	0.0463%
0.75	26-Mar-02	7.4436%	9-Mar-02	7.3816%	17	7.3796%	0.0640%
1	26-Jun-02	7.4200%	15-Jun-02	7.3703%	11	7.3720%	0.0480%
1.25	26-Sep-02	7.4625%	14-Sep-02	7.3841%	12	7.3889%	0.0736%
1.5	26-Dec-02	7.5050%	14-Dec-02	7.4207%	12	7.4271%	0.0779%
1.75	26-Mar-03	7.5475%	15-Mar-03	7.4687%	11	7.4753%	0.0722%
2	26-Jun-03	7.5900%	14-Jun-03	7.5234%	12	7.5312%	0.0588%
2.25	26-Sep-03	7.6325%	13-Sep-03	7.5824%	13	7.5901%	0.0424%
2.5	26-Dec-03	7.6750%	13-Dec-03	7.6359%	13	7.6434%	0.0316%
2.75	26-Mar-04	7.7175%	13-Mar-04	7.6879%	13	7.6955%	0.0220%
3	26-Jun-04	7.7600%	12-Jun-04	7.7408%	14	7.7412%	0.0188%
	26-Sep-04	7.8088%	26-Sep-10	7.8088%			

Notes: (1) To allow an interpolation out to three years the last futures strip swap rate is actually the cash swap rate for 3.25 years.

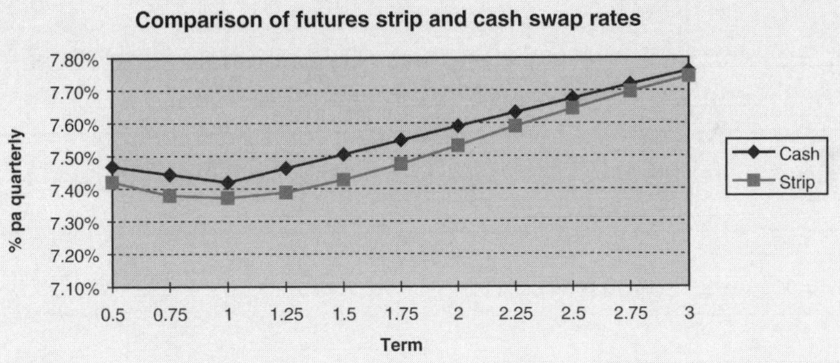

futures data. As with the example in the previous section, if we make a convexity adjustment, then the differential between the two curves will widen slightly. The potential impact of funding futures mark-to-market losses is unknown at the start of the swap and market participants will often estimate the possible additional cost and incorporate this estimate as a transaction cost. In the US dollar swap market, most swap market-makers and brokers commonly provide quotes for a swap related to a futures strip swap known as an "IMM swap." This swap has rollover dates that are equivalent to the Eurodollar contract traded on the international money market division of the CME and its expiry date coincides with a futures expiry date. Because of the very close relationship between an IMM swap and a Eurodollar strip, market participants are able to measure the prevailing convexity adjustment as the difference between these two swap rates.

The Forward Rate Offset Method

The futures strip approach to pricing par swaps can be extended to valuing existing swap transactions. In this case, the fixed swap rate has been set and changes in the swap's value will arise from changes in the relative values of the fixed and floating legs. To value the swap, we assume that we are terminating the swap by offsetting the floating leg of the swap with a strip of futures contracts. Extending the model developed for the simple offset model we have the following:

Swap Valuation Forward Rate Offset Model

The value of a swap from the fixed rate receiver's point of view on an interest payment date:

$$PV_{\text{REC}} = [(r - r_{f1})/(1 + r_{s1}^{*}/m) \cdots + (r - r_{fn}^{*})/(1 + r_{sn}^{*}/m)^{n}] \times FV$$

$$PV_{\text{PAY}} = \text{Value}_{\text{REC}} \times -1$$

This formula assumes even interest periods and compound interest rates.

Where:

r = original Swap Yield to maturity in original swap (% pa)
$r_{s1..n}^{*}$ = spot Yield to periods 1 through to n (% pa)
$r_{f1..n}$ = forward yield to periods 1 to n for 1 period (% pa)
n = the number of periods to maturity excluding the next n payment date
m = the number of interest payments pa
FV = the notional face value of the swap.

Figure 9.21 on page 244 is an example of a forward rate offset model. The formula shown above has been rearranged in order to separate the values of the fixed and floating legs. The futures yield curve is the same as the previous example. However, we have a swap that was executed some time ago at a fixed interest rate of 9% pa and has exactly two and a half years until expiry. This creates a timing mismatch between the swap interest payment dates and the futures strip dates. In the model in *Figure 9.21*, we have to create the offsetting futures contracts by interpolating between futures dates. Another difference in this model is that the floating leg interest rate has been set for the current interest period.

We know from *Figure 9.20* that a two-and-a-half-year par swap rate will have a current yield of 7.64% pa and as this swap pays a fixed rate of 9% pa, then there is loss equivalent to approximately 1.36% pa. The forward rate offset model used here indicates that this equates to a value of approximately US$3.06 million.

Risk Characteristics: PVBP and Hedge Ratios

From a risk management perspective, the forward rate offset model provides a tool for directly linking the interest sensitivity of a swap to short-term interest rate futures prices.

To quantify the risk characteristics of the swap, we determine the PVBP of the swap to each contract in the underlying futures strip. To calculate the PVBP, we determine how much the swap changes value from a one basis point change in each futures price. Using the model developed in *Figure 9.21*, the PVBP is calculated by changing each futures price individually and determining the net change in the present value of both the fixed and floating legs. The PVBPs calculated this way are summarized in *Figure 9.22* on page 246.

It is interesting to note that the PVBP of the first and second futures contracts is lower than the other expiry months. In the case of the first period, this reflects the fact that the first floating interest rate has been fixed. The last futures contract price impact is significantly reduced as, strictly speaking, it exists after the swap has expired and is only included in order to interpolate between the second-last futures expiry date and the swap expiry date.

These PVBPs are a powerful tool as they allow us to model the behavior of and manage the exposure created by a swap with considerable precision. In particular, if we wish to hedge a swap using short-term interest rate futures contracts, then the appropriate hedge ratio is given by dividing the series of PVBPs by the PVBP of the futures contract. These calculations are shown in *Figure 9.22* where the underlying futures contracts are assumed to have a PVBP of US$25.[19]

The total PVBP is influenced by two effects: a change in forward value and a net present value effect. The forward value is the difference between the forward interest cash flow at the original forward rate and at the adjusted forward rate—this makes up most of the value of the floating leg PVBP. The floating leg has a net present value effect as well, resulting from the discounting of the forward value amounts. The net present value (NPV) effect causes the decline over time in the floating-leg PVBP. The PVBP on the fixed leg is purely a net present value effect, as it results purely from a change in the discounting factor. This is quite different to the bond model that is examined next, as it relies purely on NPVs.

[19] Note that the underlying futures curve is the SFE's bank bill futures contract, which is based on a discount yield formula and gives a variable PVBP of around $25. In this example, we are aiming to provide a generalized approach to hedging, so we assume that the underlying futures contract is a Eurodollar-style contract, with a face value of $1 million and a constant PVBP of $25. To apply the SFE's bank bill futures contract to this example, the PVBP of each delivery month will have to be calculated at the prevailing market price.

Figure 9.21
Valuing Plain Swaps Using Futures Strips: The Forward Rate Offset Model

This calculation ignores potential convexity adjustments between futures positions and swaps.

	C	D	E	F	G	H	I	J	K	L	M	N
6	Swap details											
7	Start date	26-Jun-01		Face value			100,000,000.00					
8	Expiry date	26-Dec-03		Compounding frequency			4		Interest rates set in swap		Net swap value	**(3,062,191.71)**
9	Years	2.50		Fixed-leg day count			365		Floating rate	7.5200%		(71,705.54)
10	Pay leg:	Fixed		Floating-leg day count			365		Swap rate	9.0000%		
11												
12	Bank bill futures curve				Swap	Days	Interpolated		Floating-leg		Floating-leg	
13	Month	Expiry date	Futures	Days to	interest	difference	forward	Discount	Interest	Present	Interest	Present
14			price	expiry	dates		yield(2)	factor	cash flows(3)	value	cash flows	value
15	Today	26-Jun-01			26-Jun-01		7.5524%	1.000000		17,286,971.30		(20,349,163.00)
16	Sep-01	8-Sep-01	92.6700	74	26-Sep-01	18	7.3221%	0.981319	1,895,452.05	1,860,043.91	(2,268,493.15)	(2,226,116.38)
17	Dec-01	8-Dec-01	92.7100	91	26-Dec-01	18	7.2999%	0.963727	1,825,506.85	1,759,289.38	(2,243,835.62)	(2,162,443.91)
18	Mar-02	9-Mar-02	92.6600	91	26-Mar-02	17	7.3573%	0.946686	1,799,972.90	1,704,009.92	(2,219,178.08)	(2,100,865.77)
19	Jun-02	15-Jun-02	92.5600	98	26-Jun-02	11	7.4605%	0.929450	1,854,454.57	1,723,623.16	(2,268,493.15)	(2,108,451.40)
20	Sep-02	14-Sep-02	92.3900	91	26-Sep-02	12	7.6311%	0.912295	1,880,467.26	1,715,540.49	(2,268,493.15)	(2,069,534.49)
21	Dec-02	14-Dec-02	92.2300	91	26-Dec-02	12	7.7911%	0.895262	1,902,547.95	1,703,278.88	(2,243,835.62)	(2,008,820.77)
22	Mar-03	15-Mar-03	92.0700	91	26-Mar-03	11	7.9493%	0.878387	1,921,092.88	1,687,463.71	(2,219,178.08)	(1,949,297.99)
23	Jun-03	14-Jun-03	91.9100	91	26-Jun-03	12	8.0992%	0.861133	2,003,669.43	1,725,426.07	(2,268,493.15)	(1,953,474.55)
24	Sep-03	13-Sep-03	91.8400	91	26-Sep-03	13	8.1743%	0.843905	2,041,449.95	1,722,790.23	(2,268,493.15)	(1,914,393.17)
25	Dec-03	13-Dec-03	91.7400	91	26-Dec-03	13	8.2286%	0.827050	2,037,972.60	1,685,505.54	(2,243,835.62)	(1,855,764.58)
26												
27												
28												

Notes: (1) All interpolations are on a straight-line basis.
(2) The interest rate for the first period (cell G15) is the spot rate interpolated from the cash bank bill curve.
(3) The first rate used in the floating cash flows is fixed at the rate displayed in cell L8.
(4) This model ignores convexity and funding adjustments.
(5) The calculations are summarized below for the second period (row 17):

Description	Cell	Formula
Interpolate forward yield	I17	=(100–(E17+(E18–E17)*(H17/(D18–D17))))/100
Discount factor	J17	=+J16/(1+I16*(G17-G16)/$I$10)
Floating-leg interest cash flows	K17	=+I16*(G17-G16)/$I$10*$I$7*IF($D$10'="Floating",-1,1)
Floating-leg present value	L17	=+K17*J17
Fixed-leg interest cash flows	M17	=+$L$10*(G17-G16)/$I$9*$I$7*IF($D$10'="Fixed",-1,1)
Fixed-leg present value	N17	=+M17*J17

(6) The total present values in cells J17 and L 17 are given by summing the cells immediately below each of these totals.
(7) The Excel solver function (Solver.xla) was used in this calculation using the following inputs:

Input description	Cell
Target cell	L15
By changing cells	L9
Equal to value of cell	J15

Figure 9.22
Forward Rate Offset Model: PVBP and Futures Hedge Ratios

PVBP of swap example in *Figure 9.21*

Assumed PVBP of underlying futures: 25.00

Futures expiry month	Swap rollover date	PVBP to a 1 bp rise in futures price Floating leg	Fixed leg	Total	Futures hedge ratio
Sep-01	26-Sep-01	1,624.05	356.35	1,980.40	79
Dec-01	26-Dec-01	2,024.59	401.76	2,426.35	97
Mar-02	26-Mar-02	2,070.81	357.32	2,428.13	97
Jun-02	26-Jun-02	2,151.71	315.31	2,467.02	99
Sep-02	26-Sep-02	2,151.71	315.31	2,467.02	99
Dec-02	26-Dec-02	2,003.60	192.90	2,196.50	88
Mar-03	26-Mar-03	2,059.50	149.26	2,208.77	88
Jun-03	26-Jun-03	2,020.07	98.45	2,118.52	85
Sep-03	26-Sep-03	2,001.24	51.66	2,052.90	82
Dec-03	26-Dec-03	310.82	6.97	317.79	13
		18,418.11	2,245.30	20,663.41	827

Notes: (1) The PVBP for each expiry date is calculated by changing only the price of the futures contract associated with that contract month.
(2) While not shown, the swap also has a sensitivity to the prevailing money market interest rate between June 26 and September 26.

Applying hedge ratios should be treated with some caution where swap interest rollover dates differ from futures expiry dates. As time passes, the front month futures contract will expire prior to the next interest rollover date. As these expiries occur, the model has to be adjusted and the front month positions will be effectively "stacked" into the new front expiry month. Likewise, when a swap expires, no contracts should be left open in the contract months that expire after the swap.

While the forward rate offset model creates a "neat" method of hedging open swap contracts, in practice, even US dollar swaps futures strips are generally only used to hedge short-term swaps, or the first few rollovers of a longer term swap. The reason for this is the lack of liquidity in distant future months. In even the most active futures markets such as the Eurodollar, turnover is relatively low in delivery months with expiry greater than three years. This can make putting in place, and closing out, a futures strip hedge slow and subject to price "slippage."[20]

[20] For more on the use of futures as a swap hedge, see Richard Leibovitch's chapter in S. Das (1991).

Furthermore, there is another mismatch between futures and swaps due to the fact that short-term interest rate futures have zero (dollar) convexity while swaps exhibit convexity. This means that as yields change, the PVBP of swaps will alter while the futures PVBP will remain constant. The result of this mismatch is that the hedge ratio will alter, requiring regular adjustments to the number of contracts held as hedges.

9.4.2 The Zero-Coupon Bond Method

The zero-coupon model is an extension of the single-rate bond model. The major change is that the present values are now determined using zero-coupon interest rates:

Swap Valuation: Zero-Coupon Bond Method

The value of the swap is the net of the underlying fixed and floating bonds on an interest payment date:

$$PV_{REC} = PV_{FIXED} - PV_{FLOATING}$$
$$PV_{PAY} = \text{Value}_{REC} \times -1$$

Where:

$$PV_{FIXED} = [r/(1 + r_{s1}^{*}/m) \cdots + (1 + r)/(1 + r_{sn}^{*}/m)^{n}] \times FV$$
$$PV_{FLOATING} = [(r_1/m + 1)/(1 + r_1^{*}/m)] \times FV$$

Where:

r = original swap yield to maturity in original swap (% pa)
$r_{s1..n}^{*}$ = spot yield to periods 1 through to n (% pa)
r_1 = original floating yield to next interest payment date (% pa)
r_1^{*} = current floating yield to next interest payment date (% pa)
n = the number of periods to maturity excluding the next n payment date
n = the number of coupon payments pa.

Note that the *PV* calculation for the fixed leg is now a “long-hand” bond price calculation as we need to be able to identify each cash flow separately.

The model shown in *Figure 9.23* assumes that we have developed a bootstrapping zero-coupon yield curve model from Section 9.2.4 and that we have included a methodology for interpolating between the calculated yield curve points. The same swap example used in *Figure 9.21* is revalued using the bond method.

The zero-coupon bond method calculates a value of US$2.99 million—a difference of around US$70,000 to the forward rate offset model. This discrepancy arises from the difference in the swap yield curves implied by the two

Figure 9.23
Zero-Coupon Bond Method

Swap revaluation calculator

Zero-coupon bond method

Row	Item	Value	Cell:Formula
10	Swap details		
11	Deal date	26-Jun-01	$G$11 :
12	Expiry date	26-Dec-03	$G$12 :
13	Face value	100,000,000	$G$13 :
14	Fixed rate payer or receiver ? (p or r)	p	$G$14 :
15	Swap fixed rate	9.0000	$G$15 :
16	Swap floating rate	7.5200	$G$16 :
17	Number of periods per year (1,2 or 4)	4	$G$17 :
18	Day count basis ? (360 or 365)	365	$G$18 :
19			
20	Revaluation swap details		
21	Revaluation swap date	See zero curve	$G$21 :
22	Revaluation floating date	below	$G$22 :
23	Bond basis (y or n)?	n	$G$23 :
24	Current swap value	(2,990,486.17)	$G$24 : + H31+J31

See below for formulas used in the table

Row	Rollover periods	Rollover dates	Zero-coupon interest rate	Discount factor	Fixed cash flows: Original fixed cash flows	Fixed cash flows: Fixed present value	Floating cash flows: Original floating cash flow	Floating cash flows: Floating present value
31	0	26-Jun-01				(103,003,444.32)		100,012,958.15
32	1	26-Sep-01	7.5290%	0.9815252	(2,268,493.15)	(2,226,583.29)	101,895,452.05	100,012,958.15
33	2	26-Dec-01	7.4673%	0.9636836	(2,243,835.62)	(2,162,347.55)		
34	3	26-Mar-02	7.4428%	0.9461937	(2,219,178.08)	(2,099,772.22)		
35	4	26-Jun-02	7.4187%	0.9291292	(2,268,493.15)	(2,107,723.33)		
36	5	26-Sep-02	7.4631%	0.9117138	(2,268,493.15)	(2,068,216.53)		
37	6	26-Dec-02	7.5075%	0.8944299	(2,243,835.62)	(2,006,953.68)		
38	7	26-Mar-03	7.5522%	0.8772780	(2,219,178.08)	(1,946,836.14)		
39	8	26-Jun-03	7.5970%	0.8602647	(2,268,493.15)	(1,951,504.57)		
40	9	26-Sep-03	7.6422%	0.8433885	(2,268,493.15)	(1,913,221.11)		
41	10	26-Dec-03	7.6877%	0.8266541	(102,243,835.62)	(84,520,285.92)		

Notes: 1. The zero-coupon interest rates come from the model developed in *Figure 9.19*.
2. The floating-leg is assumed to be either A/360 or A/365.
3. The calculations for row 32 are shown in the table below. Enter these into the spreadsheet and then copy down to row 51.
4. Requires "Analysisf.xla" add-in for financial functions.

Formulas in table

Description	Cell	Formula
Rollover dates	$D$32	=IF(OR(E31=$G$12,E31=""),"",COUPNCD(E31,$G$12,$G$17,3))
Discount factor	$F$32	=1/(1+E32/$G$17)^C32
Original fixed cash flows	$G$32	=(IF($D32="","",IF($G$23="y",$G$13*$G$15/100/$G$17, ROUND($G$13*$G$15/100*($D32-$D31)/$G$18,2)))+IF(D33="",$G$13,0))*IF($G$14="p",–1,1)
Fixed present value	$H$32	=+G32*F32
Original floating cash flow	$I$32	=IF($D32="","",ROUND(($G$13*$G$16/100*($D32–$D31)/$G$18+G13)*IF($G$14="p",1,–1),2))
Floating present value	$J$32	=+I32*F32

methods. We know that the futures strip rate used in the forward rate offset method is approximately three basis points below the cash swap rate for a two-and-a-half-year par swap and the valuation is a reflection of this difference.[21] This proposition is proved by replacing the discount factors with those derived from

[21] Although the swap in this example is not a par swap, because it pays a fixed interest rate that is higher than the current market interest rate, the discrepancy in valuation actually equates to a difference in fixed yield of 2.2 basis points.

the interpolated futures strip discount factors in *Figure 9.21*. If this is done, the zero-coupon bond value is identical to the forward rate offset method.

Risk Characteristics: PVBP and Hedge Ratios

Just as the forward offset model allows us to derive swap risk characteristics relative to short-term interest rate futures, the bond method presents the risk characteristics of the swap in terms of bonds and bond futures contracts. It is usual to calculate the PVBP for a change in the yield of the fixed leg of the swap.

While short-term interest rate futures are widely used to hedge interest rate swaps, in most markets it is common practice to use bond-related instruments, particularly in medium- to long-term swaps for hedging purposes. The problem created by this approach is that given the range of bonds on issue, the range of potential hedge instruments available can be very broad. The selection of instruments is generally based on correlation between the bond yield and the swap rate and secondary market liquidity.

As we have seen in the swap quotation methods earlier in this chapter, US dollar swap rates are quoted relative to US Treasury note issues (Treasuries). While the correlation between swap rates and Treasuries is not perfect, as is demonstrated by the change in swap spreads over time, it is close and the Treasury market offers considerable liquidity. As a result, short-term physical or forward sales and purchases of Treasuries are commonly used by market-makers to hedge the interest rate risk of a swap. The hedge ratio is calculated by matching the PVBP of the swap with that of the Treasury.

In other markets, bond futures have become a benchmark method of hedging swaps. While there may be some mismatch between the term of the swap and term of the underlying bond, this is often compensated for by the substantial liquidity of bond futures.

While hedging swaps with bond instruments creates an effective method of matching the volatility of the swap, it typically creates a number of risks:

- **Spread risk** This is the possibility that the overall spread between the swap rate and the bond yield alters. Even though the PVBP of a swap and bond are matched, a change in the spread will create nonoffsetting gains and losses on both instruments.

- **Yield curve risk** Despite the range of bonds on issue, there is usually several months' difference between liquid issues of the desired bond. This will create mismatches between the maturity of the fixed leg of the swap and the bond used and, if the shape of the yield curve changes between these two maturity dates, the bond hedge will be less than perfect. This mismatch is often illustrated by bond futures where an 8-year swap may have to be hedged with a 10-year bond future.

- **Interest accrual risk** At each interest rollover date on a swap there is a net settlement reflecting the difference between the fixed and floating rate. A similar net interest cost will be reflected in the forward bond sale or purchase as the cost of carry.[22] If the swap net interest cost and the bond cost of carry differ, it will generate a cash gain or loss. This risk is often exacerbated by the fact that swaps are often hedged with short-term forward sales and purchases, leaving the hedge exposed to changes in the shape of the yield curve between rollover dates. A factor in favor of bond futures is that they provide a fixed cost of carry until their expiry date.

In *Figure 9.24*, the PVBP of the zero-coupon bond model is calculated for the remaining term till expiry. In this case, the swap has a term of two and half years. However, the bond used to hedge the swap has a term to expiry of three years, a coupon of 12.5% and a current yield of 7.45% pa. The PVBP of the bond is \$286 per \$ m of face value.

In this case, to hedge a swap where we are paying fixed we would short sell \$72.25 million of the bond today. This would expose us to the hedging risks

Figure 9.24
Zero-Coupon Bond Method PVBP and Futures Hedge Ratios

PVBP of swap example in *Figure 9.23.*

Assumed PVBP of underlying bond: \$286 per \$ m of face value.

Futures expiry month	Swap rollover date	PVBP to a 1 bp rise in futures price Floating leg	Fixed leg	Total
Sep-01	26-Sep-01	1,624.05	356.35	1,980.40
Dec-01	26-Dec-01	2,024.59	401.76	2,426.35
Mar-02	26-Mar-02	2,070.81	357.32	2,428.13
Jun-02	26-Jun-02	2,151.71	315.31	2,467.02
Sep-02	26-Sep-02	2,151.71	315.31	2,467.02
Dec-02	26-Dec-02	2,003.60	192.90	2,196.50
Mar-03	26-Mar-03	2,059.50	149.26	2,208.77
Jun-03	26-Jun-03	2,020.07	98.45	2,118.52
Sep-03	26-Sep-03	2,001.24	51.66	2,052.90
Dec-03	26-Dec-03	310.82	6.97	317.79
		18,418.11	2,245.30	20,663.41
		Bond PVBP per \$ m		286
		Face value of bond required (\$ m)		**72.25**

[22] The bond cost of carry will be equivalent to the differential between the yield on the bond and the prevailing repo rate of that bond—which is very similar to the difference between the fixed and floating rate in the swap. To revise the determinants of the cost of carry on a bond, see Chapter 5.

outlined above; in particular, the bond has a longer term to maturity and higher coupon than the swap. This requires ongoing monitoring of the required hedge ratio and occasional rebalancing of the amount of bonds held to hedge the swap.

9.5 NONGENERIC INTEREST RATE SWAP TRANSACTIONS

While the bulk of interest rate swap transactions are plain vanilla fixed-to-floating structures, there are a wide range of variations. In this section, we will examine characteristics of three nongeneric swaps:

- forward swaps
- amortizing and accreting swaps
- zero-coupon swaps.

As we will see, the pricing and valuation tools developed in previous sections of this chapter for plain swaps can be relatively easily applied to more exotic structures. In fact, the approach to valuing these nongeneric swaps is very similar to the present-value calculations used for plain vanilla interest rate swaps. Complications arise when determining the pricing of these other swap structures. Accordingly, most of the following discussion will focus on pricing issues.

9.5.1 Forward Swaps

A forward interest rate swap represents an exchange of interest cash flows in the same currency for a set period of time, where the start date of the swap interest accrual is delayed. The cash flows of a forward swap are illustrated in *Figure 9.25* on page 252. The delay may vary from a number of weeks to a number of years. There are no exchanges of the principal on the start date or at maturity as the principal amounts of both legs of the swap are identical. As with a plain interest rate swap, the only cash flows are the net of the fixed and floating interest payments. Other names for forward start swaps include deferred and delayed start interest rate swaps.

The synthetic replication of a forward swap is similar to a plain swap, consisting of a forward start bond for the fixed leg and a forward start FRN for the floating leg. As with any forward instrument, the current yield on a forward swap is driven by the cost of carry. In fact, the general pricing formula for a forward interest rate swap can be represented as an extension of the models developed for FRAs:[23]

$$rf = \frac{q \times d / D - r \times f / D}{d / D - f / D}$$

Where:

rf = forward fixed swap interest rate % pa
r = spot start swap rate to forward start date % pa
q = spot start swap rate to the maturity date % pa
D = day count basis (365 or 360)
f = number of days to the forward start date
d = number of days to the swap maturity date.

Figure 9.25
The Mechanics of a Forward Interest Rate Swap

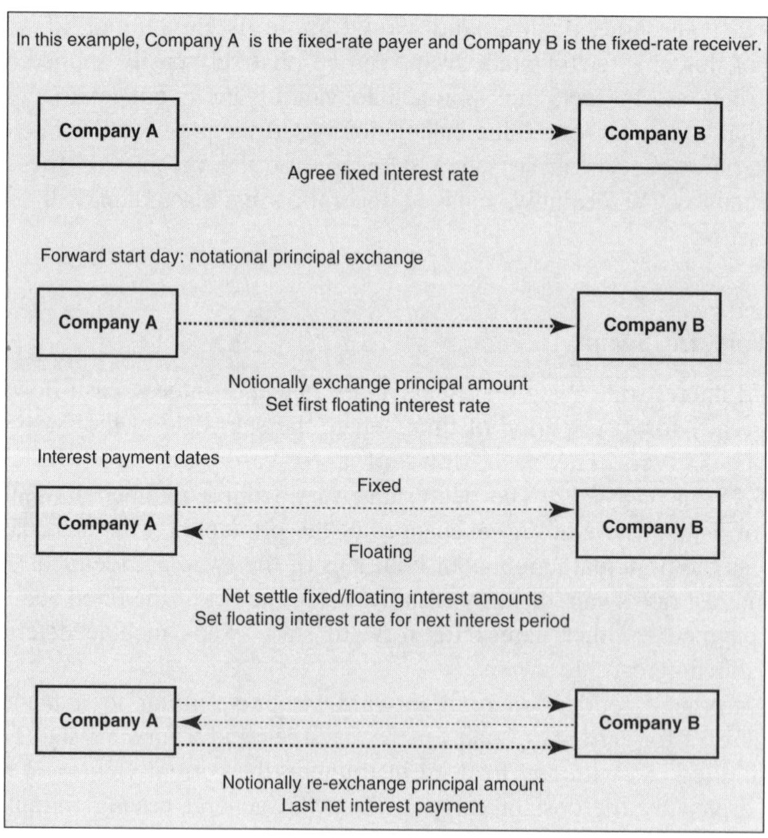

[23]See Chapter 4.

Example

Using the swap yield curve derived in *Figure 9.20*, suppose we want to price a forward start A$ interest rate swap with the following characteristics:

Trade date	=	June 26, 2001
Forward start date	=	March 9, 2002
Maturity date	=	June 26, 2004
Floating index	=	3-month bank bill

Applying the forward rate formula from above, the inputs would be as follows:

r	=	7.3816%
q	=	7.7408%
D	=	365
f	=	274
d	=	1096

which gives a forward rate calculation as follows:

$$rf = \frac{0.077408 \times 1096/365 - 0.073816 \times 274/365}{1096/365 - 274/365}$$
$$= 7.8606\%.$$

While providing a quick estimate of forward interest rates, this method assumes that the interest rates are zero-coupon and it ignores differences in compounding frequency. A more accurate approach is to make use of the traded forward interest rate prices from FRA and futures markets and to extend the futures strip model developed in *Figure 9.21*.

Figure 9.26 on page 254 prices the forward swap from the example above using the futures strip model. Our inputs are almost identical to a spot start strip model; however, in this case the interest accrual does not start until March 9, 2002. The forward rate calculated using this model is 7.8563% pa assuming quarterly compounding.

Just as the forward swap rate can be calculated using the futures strip, the valuation and PVBP calculations can use exactly the same process as illustrated in *Figure 9.22* and *Figure 9.24*.

The zero-coupon model is required to calculate the zero-coupon yields that are entered into the forward rate formula above where a forward yield curve is not available. Valuing the swap then requires applying the zero-coupon model from *Figure 9.23* with the interest accrual commencing at the start date.

Figure 9.26
Pricing Forward Start Swaps Using Futures Strips

Ignoring futures cash/adjustments
Requires solver add-in to be loaded

	C	D	E	F	G	H	I	J	K	L	M
6	Swap details										
7	Trade date	26-Jun-01		Face value			100,000,000.00				
8	Fwd start	9-Mar-02		Compounding frequency			4		Solution		
9	Expiry date	12-Jun-04		Fixed-leg day count			365		Swap rate	7.8653%	
10	Years	2.96		Floating-leg day count			365				
11	Zero rates to futures expiry dates										
12	Bank bill futures curve				Implied		Floating-leg		Floating-leg		
13	Month	Expiry date	Futures	Days to	forward	Discount	Interest	Present	Interest	Present	
14			price	expiry	yield(2)	factor	cash flows	value	cash flows	value	
15	Today	26-Jun-01			7.5524%	1.000000		15,382,617.92		15,382,617.00	
16	Sep-01	8-Sep-01	92.6700	74	7.3300%	0.984919		–		–	
17	Dec-01	8-Dec-01	92.7100	91	7.2900%	0.967243		–		–	
18	Mar-02	9-Mar-02	92.6600	91	7.3400%	0.949977		–		–	
19	Jun-02	15-Jun-02	92.5600	98	7.4400%	0.931617	1,970,739.73	1,835,975.37	2,111,778.17	1,967,369.24	
20	Sep-02	14-Sep-02	92.3900	91	7.6100%	0.914651	1,854,904.11	1,696,590.77	1,960,936.87	1,793,573.79	
21	Dec-02	14-Dec-02	92.2300	91	7.7700%	0.897621	1,897,287.67	1,703,045.29	1,960,936.87	1,760,178.15	
22	Mar-03	15-Mar-03	92.0700	91	7.9300%	0.880563	1,937,178.08	1,705,807.24	1,960,936.87	1,726,728.34	
23	Jun-03	14-Jun-03	91.9100	91	8.0900%	0.863491	1,977,068.49	1,707,181.11	1,960,936.87	1,693,251.60	
24	Sep-03	13-Sep-03	91.8400	91	8.1600%	0.846419	2,016,958.90	1,707,192.75	1,960,936.87	1,659,774.63	
25	Dec-03	13-Dec-03	91.7400	91	8.2600%	0.829543	2,034,410.96	1,687,631.15	1,960,936.87	1,626,681.25	
26	Mar-04	13-Mar-04	91.6100	91	8.3900%	0.812804	2,059,342.47	1,673,842.75	1,960,936.87	1,593,858.25	
27	Jun-04	12-Jun-04	91.4800	91	8.5200%	0.796151	2,091,753.42	1,665,351.48	1,960,936.87		
28											

See *Figure 9.19* for calculation details.

Figure 9.27
Pricing an Amortizing Swap

The amortizing swap is a series of bullet swaps equivalent to the amortizing principal amounts.

Year	Notional principal DM m	Amortizing amount DM m	Plain swap rate	Year × Amount	Year × Rate × Amount
0	100.00				
1	80.00	20.00	3.40	20.00	68.00
2	60.00	20.00	3.90	40.00	156.00
3	40.00	20.00	4.32	60.00	259.20
4	20.00	20.00	4.49	80.00	359.20
5	0.00	20.00	5.45	100.00	545.00
			Weighted average =		4.6247%

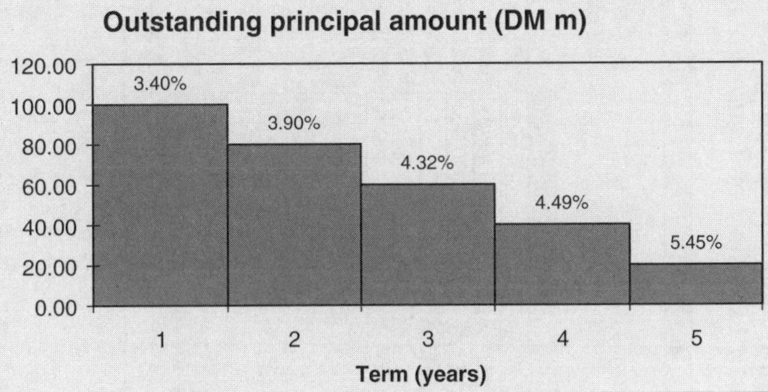

9.5.2 Amortizing and Accreting Swaps

Amortizing and accreting interest rate swaps are similar to plain interest rate swaps except that the *notional principal amount changes over time*. In the case of an amortizing swap, the principal amount reduces over time, while with an accreting swap the principal amount increases over time. Combinations of these two types of principal swaps include "rollercoaster" swaps. These "variable principal swaps" are often associated with large specific asset financings. The amount by which the principal changes over the life of the swap is usually referred to as the "amortization schedule."

Typically, the principal amortization is a predetermined amount that occurs on each interest payment date. The change in principal is usually identical for both fixed and floating legs. If there is a different amortization schedule for fixed and floating legs, the swap takes on an element of

Figure 9.28
Valuing a Zero-Coupon Swap Using the Bond Method
(An Extension of *Figure 9.23*)

	C	D	E	F	G	H	I	J	K
6									
7		Zero-coupon swap revaluation calculator							
8		Zero-coupon bond method				Cell: Formula			
9									
10		Swap details							
11		Deal date			26-Jun-01	$G$11 :			
12		Expiry date			26-Dec-03	$G$12 :			
13		Face value			100,000,000	$G$13 :			
14		Fixed-rate payer or receiver ? (p or r)			p	$G$14 :			
15		Zero-coupon swap fixed rate			8.2500	$G$15 :			
16		Swap floating rate			7.5200	$G$16 :			
17		Number of periods per year (1,2 or 4)			4	$G$17 :			
18		Day count basis ? (360 or 365)			365	$G$18 :			
19									
20		Revaluation swap details							
21		Revaluation swap rate			See zero curve below	$G$21 :			
22		Revaluation floating date				$G$22 :			
23		Bond basis (y or n)?			n	$G$23 :			
24		Current swap value			(1,374,875.81)	$G$24 : + H31+J31			
25									
26									
27					Fixed cash flows			Floating cash flows	
28–30	Rollover periods	Rollover dates	Zero-coupon interest fate	Discount factor	Original fixed cash flows		Fixed present value	Original floating cash flow	Floating present value
31	0	26-Jun-01					(101,387,833.95)		100,012,958.15
32	1	26-Sep-01	7.5290%	0.9815252	–		–	101,895,452.05	100,012,958.15
33	2	26-Dec-01	7.4673%	0.9636836	–		–		
34	3	26-Mar-02	7.4428%	0.9461937	–		–		
35	4	26-Jun-02	7.4187%	0.9291292	–		–		

36	5	26-Sep-02	7.4631%	0.9117138	–	–
37	6	26-Dec-02	7.5075%	0.8944299	–	–
38	7	26-Mar-03	7.5522%	0.8772780	–	–
39	8	26-Jun-03	7.5970%	0.8602647	–	–
40	9	26-Sep-03	7.6422%	0.8433885	–	–
41	10	26-Dec-03	7.6877%	0.8266541	(122,648,437.78)	(101,387,833.95)
42	11					
43	12					
44	13					
45	14					
46	15					
47	16					
48	17					
49	18					
50	19					
51	20					
52						

Notes:
1. The zero-coupon interest rates come from the model developed in *Figure 9.19.*
2. The floating leg is assumed to be either A/360 or A/365.
3. The calculations for row 32 are shown in the table below. Enter these into the spreadsheet and then copy down to row 51.
4. Requires "Analysisf.xla" add-in for financial functions.

Formula's in table

Description	Cell	Formula
Rollover dates	$D$32	=IF(OR(E31=$G$12,E31=""),"",COUPNCD(E31,$G$12,$G$17,3))
Discount factor	$F$32	=1/(1+E32/$G$17)^C32
Original fixed cash flows	$G$32	=IF(D33="",$G$13*((1+($G$15/(100*$G$17)))^C32),0)*IF($G$14="p",–1,1)
Fixed present value	$H$32	=+G32*F32
Original floating cash flow	$I$32	=IF($D32="","",ROUND(($G$13*$G$16/100*($D32–$D31)/$G$18+G13)*IF($G$14="p",1,–1),2))
Floating present value	$J$32	=+I32*F32

a borrowing for the party that pays interest on the leg with the larger principal amount.

Swap rates on plain swaps cannot be applied directly to an amortizing or accreting swap. Effectively, an amortizing swap is a series of plain "bullet" swaps with different maturities. Reflecting this, the amortizing swap rate is given by the weighted average of the underlying series of bullet swaps.

Calculating an amortizing swap requires breaking each fixed interest rate leg of the swap into an underlying series of plain vanilla (i.e., bullet) swaps and then for each of these swaps, identifying the prevailing swap rate for each term. The amortizing swap rate is calculated by taking the weighted average of these component swaps (using the principal of each underlying swap as the weight).

An accreting swap is a little more complicated because the component swaps consist of a plain vanilla swap as a series of forward swaps, equating to the rising principal face value over time.

An amortizing swap rate is calculated in *Figure 9.27.* In the example, the original swap principal is DM100 million 5-year fixed-to-floating swap that amortizes by US$20 million at the end of each year. Effectively, this is made up of five US$20 million "bullet" swaps with terms from one to five years.

The effective swap rate given by the weighted average calculation is 4.6247%.

> ***Note***
> The easiest method of valuing an amortizing or accreting swap is to break it down into its underlying plain and forward swap components, value these individually and then aggregate the total variable swap value.

9.5.3 Zero-Coupon Swaps

A zero-coupon swap has no periodic interest payments on the fixed leg (i.e., no "coupons"). All fixed interest amounts are paid on the maturity date of the swap, while interest payments on the floating leg are usually made at the end of each floating interest rate calculation period. As with most interest rate swaps, there is no exchange of principal, only the payment of floating-rate interest over the life of the swap and a single lump-sum fixed-rate interest payment at maturity. From a credit risk perspective, this creates an asymmetry between the fixed and floating interest rate payer. The floating-rate payer builds up a credit exposure equivalent to the unpaid zero-coupon interest amount.

In terms of synthetic replication, a zero-coupon swap is comprised of a zero-coupon bond for the fixed leg and a floating-rate note for the floating leg.

The pricing of a zero-coupon swap revolves around the fixed zero-coupon rate, as the floating leg is equivalent to the short-term interest rate index underlying the swap. The fixed zero-coupon rate can be determined using the zero-coupon yield curve calculators already discussed in this chapter (see *Figures 9.16* and *9.17*). The valuation of a zero-coupon swap can be incorporated into the model developed in *Figure 9.23*.

The only adjustment necessary is to convert the fixed-leg interest payment amounts into a single lump-sum amount at maturity.

Figure 9.28 provides an example of valuing a zero-coupon swap. The calculation in the original fixed cash flow involves a future value calculation (see Chapter 3) using the original fixed zero-coupon interest rate.

> ***Note***
> The assumed interest payment frequency underlying the fixed rate has a substantial impact on the valuation calculation due to the impact of compounding and therefore special care should be taken to use the *correct* frequency.

SUMMARY

In this chapter, we examined the importance of the yield curve and its impact upon the pricing and valuation of swaps. We analyzed swap valuation models, such as the single rate bond valuation method, simple offset valuation method, the forward rate offset and the zero-coupon bond valuation methods of swap valuation. We also examined the concepts of bootstrapping, forward rate reinvestment and futures strip swap pricing.

SELF-TEST QUESTIONS

1. Describe how you would synthetically replicate a pay fixed/receive floating swap with a 10-year term to maturity and semi-annual payments.
2. Describe three uses of interest rate swaps within an organization.
3. Identify three yield curve interpolation models. Critically evaluate each model.
4. Explain the importance of the par yield curve in derivative valuation modeling.
5. Assume that the 1-year rate is 6.90% semi-annually and a 6-month forward for six months is 8.00%. Using the forward rate reinvestment method, calculate the 1-year zero-coupon rate.
6. What is meant by "bootstrapping?"

7. Assume that the 6-month spot rate is 8.00% pa paid semi-annually and the par 1-year spot rate is 9.00% pa paid semi-annually. Calculate the forward yield in six months for a 6-month period.

8. Describe how the forward rate offset model can be applied to hedging an interest rate swap.

9. Following the methodology used to derive swap rates from futures strip data in *Figure 9.20*, show how the calculation of the 1 and 2-year interpolate swap rates were derived.

10. If you are a swap dealer about to execute a swap transaction with a Federal Government agency against 3-month LIBOR, should the fixed rate be based on current government bond curve or the swap curve?

CHAPTER 10

CROSS CURRENCY SWAPS

The models developed in this chapter are saved as Microsoft Excel™ files in the enclosed disk.

OVERVIEW

This chapter extends the discussion in Chapter 9 to apply to currency swaps. By the end of this chapter we will have:

- developed a model to price currency swaps;
- applied the single-rate bond method for fixed-to-floating currency swap valuation;
- applied the zero-coupon bond method for all combinations of currency swap valuation;
- developed a model for evaluating swaps as a tool for new issue arbitrage.

10.1 INTRODUCTION

The first currency swap transactions resulted from a need to exchange medium-to-long-term currency cash flows at a reasonable cost without breaching regulatory barriers, particularly currency exchange controls.[1] Although exchange controls have largely been removed from most floating exchange rate economies, the requirement to exchange cash flows at a reasonable cost still exists.

Many early currency swap transactions were executed as a part of a new issue arbitrage (NIA) strategy. An organization could issue debt in a foreign currency and then use a currency swap to convert the debt into the domestic currency at a lower rate than borrowing the funds directly in the domestic currency. The arbitrage gain was the difference between the borrowing costs. These NIA strategies were achieved because of a discrepancy in the pricing of debt in two different currencies relative to the "true" interest differential achievable under a swap.

[1] To read more about the origins of the swap market, see S. Das (1994), chapters 2 and 3.

Increasing integration of international capital markets has reduced the scope for NIA transactions. While NIA opportunities still exist, the size of the gains are considerably smaller than in the early 1980s. Consequently, the functions of currency swaps have broadened since then, with uses including:

- management of long-term foreign exchange exposures;
- diversification of sources of funding, which can then be swapped into the borrower's domestic currency;
- creation of foreign currency synthetic securities by combining a domestic investment with a currency swap;
- speculation on movements in exchange rates and interest rate differentials.

The appendix in Chapter 1 summarizes the major currencies used in currency swaps. The US dollar is the most important currency in both the currency swap and the foreign exchange markets; however, less so in the currency swap market. This reflects the tendency to use a US dollar leg in a transaction involving two non-US dollar currencies in the foreign exchange market, but not in the currency swap market. It is also a reflection of the fact that the currency swap market is linked closely to the hedging of international bond issues that include a significant volume of issues in a variety of relatively high-yielding currencies.

In this chapter, we will extend the pricing and valuation models developed in the last chapter to cover currency swaps. We will describe the relationship between interest rates and currency swaps and then develop a range of models based on the zero-coupon bond method models. We will examine the pricing and valuation requirements of some more esoteric swap structures including:

- forward swaps
- variable principal interest rate swaps
- zero-coupon swaps.

10.2 CHARACTERISTICS OF A PLAIN CURRENCY SWAP

10.2.1 General Description

A plain currency swap is an agreement between two parties to exchange interest and principal cash flows in different currencies for an agreed period of time. A more strict definition would be "cross currency interest rate swaps" but they are commonly referred to as "currency swaps" in order to avoid confusion with FX swaps.[2]

[2] See Chapter 6 for more information on FX swaps.

While the inclusion of an exposure to FX rate movements adds another level of complexity, we will see that the general interest rate models developed in the previous chapter can easily be extended to cover currency swaps.

The interest cash flows may be fixed or floating in either currency. This gives rise to three different combinations of interest payment:

- fixed-to-fixed currency swap
- fixed-to-floating currency swap
- floating-to-floating or basis swap.

Figure 10.1 illustrates some simple examples of plain currency swaps.

The predominant structures are plain vanilla fixed-to-fixed and fixed-to-floating swaps. Floating-to-floating, or "basis," currency swaps are predominantly an inter-dealer market. The main functions are FX and interest rate risk management, as well arbitrage transactions linked to capital market issues.

Figure 10.1
Plain Currency Swap Structures

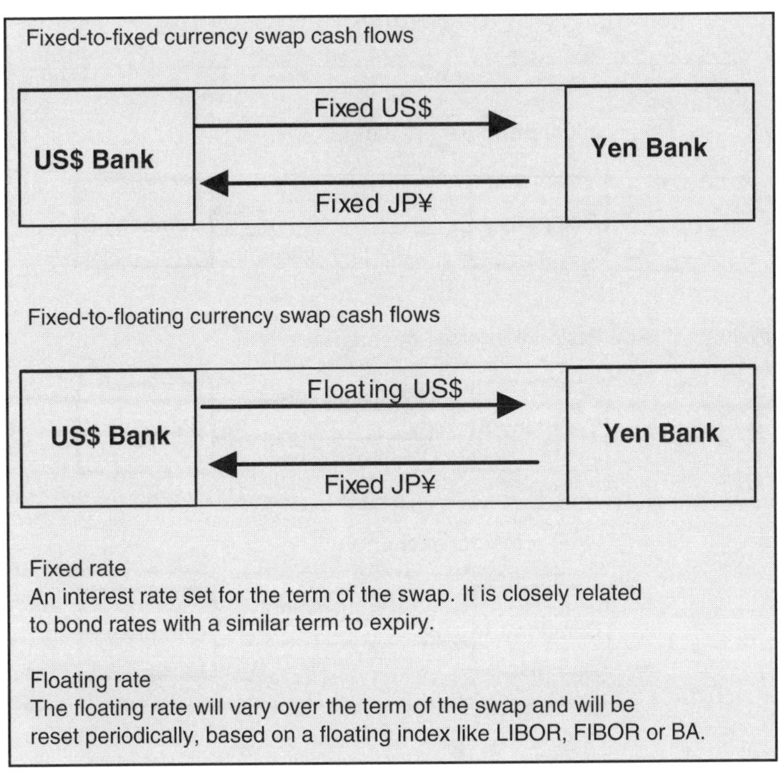

10.2.2 Mechanics of Currency Swaps

The mechanics of a currency swap are very similar to an interest rate swap. The swap can be broken down into three stages:

- initial principal exchange
- periodic interest payments
- final principal exchange.

These periodic cash flows are highlighted in *Figure 10.2.*

An important difference between currency and interest rate swaps is that, unlike plain vanilla interest rate swaps, the principal cash flows have an impact on the value of currency swaps. This is because the swap principal amounts are in different currencies. As a result, the relative value of each principal amount may change between the commencement and termination of the swap—creating the possibility of FX gains and losses.[3]

Figure 10.2
The Mechanics of a Currency Swap

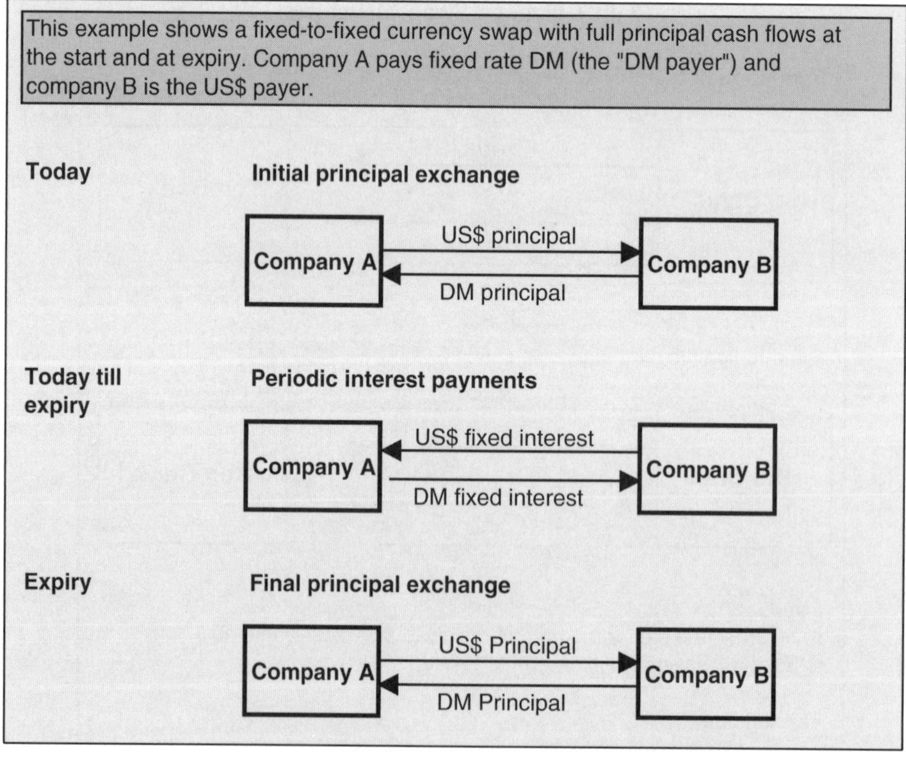

[3] The gain or loss arises where the actual market exchange rate differs from the rate agreed in the swap.

In most currency swaps, the principal exchanges occur at expiry, whereas the first exchange is often notional. One reason for a notional initial exchange is because a foreign exposure already exists and an initial cash flow would "double up" that FX exposure.

10.2.3 Synthetic Replication of Currency Swaps

A fixed-to-fixed currency swap can be created synthetically by simultaneously borrowing and lending in different currencies. This is shown in *Figure 10.3*, where a company synthetically creates a pay fixed US$/receive fixed-DM currency swap.

The company issues a US$100 million bond, converts this to DM at the prevailing spot exchange rate and invests the proceeds in a bond. Over the term of the transaction, the company will receive a fixed rate of DM and pay a fixed rate of US dollar. At maturity of the bonds, the company will receive the DM 140 million and have to repay the US$100 million. A gain or loss will be realized depending on the change in the exchange rate over the swap term. A gain will be realized if the US dollar has depreciated against the DM as the conversion of the DM will generate more than US$100 million. An appreciation in the US dollar will result in a loss.[4]

> ***Note***
> The synthetic replication illustrates how currency and interest rate swaps can be priced and valued. The two legs can be thought of as a bond in each currency, where the relative values of these bonds will vary as exchange rates change.

The price, or interest rate, on each leg of the swap will be closely related to the interest rate swap rate in each currency. The value of the swap will be closely related to the relative values of the two underlying bond components at prevailing market exchange rates. If we extend this idea to fixed-to-floating currency swaps, we can see that the underlying components will be a bond and an FRN in different currencies. A floating-to-floating currency swap is composed of two FRNs.

Currency Swaps and Foreign Exchange Forwards

As well as a "physical" synthetic replication, a currency swap can also be replicated by combinations of other derivatives, including foreign exchange forwards.

A fixed-to-fixed currency swap can also be viewed as a form of LTFX contract. The two contracts are economically similar in that they both require the

[4] Given the fixed link between the Euro and the DM, then the cause of any appreciation or depreciation in the DM will be due to movements in the Euro.

Figure 10.3
A Synthetic Currency Swap

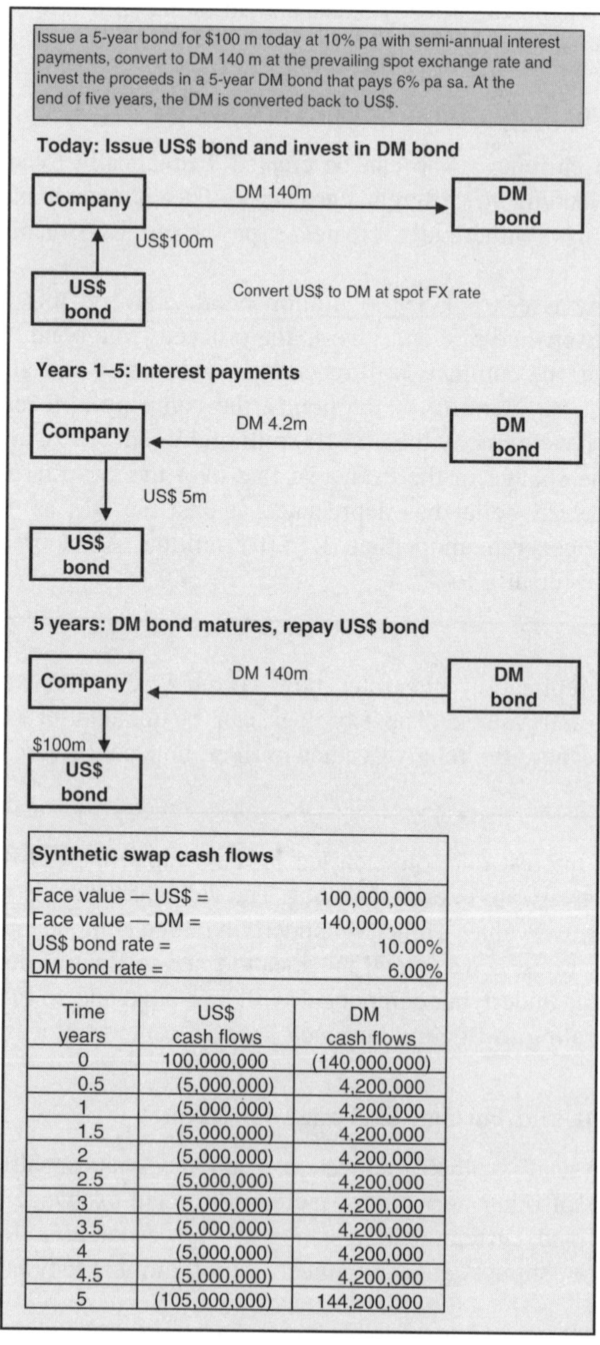

Synthetic swap cash flows

Face value — US$ =	100,000,000
Face value — DM =	140,000,000
US$ bond rate =	10.00%
DM bond rate =	6.00%

Time years	US$ cash flows	DM cash flows
0	100,000,000	(140,000,000)
0.5	(5,000,000)	4,200,000
1	(5,000,000)	4,200,000
1.5	(5,000,000)	4,200,000
2	(5,000,000)	4,200,000
2.5	(5,000,000)	4,200,000
3	(5,000,000)	4,200,000
3.5	(5,000,000)	4,200,000
4	(5,000,000)	4,200,000
4.5	(5,000,000)	4,200,000
5	(105,000,000)	144,200,000

delivery of an agreed amount of two currencies at a future date. The key difference is that the cost of carry is incorporated into the forward price of an LTFX contract, while in a currency swap, the cost of carry is paid as time passes in the form of the regular interest payments. Given this relationship, forward FX contracts are commonly used by swap dealers to hedge currency swap transactions.

There will be a difference in the timing of cash flows between LTFX and currency swap contracts that can produce present-value discrepancies. In an effort to overcome these differences, the currency swap can be decomposed into a series of LTFX contracts, which attempts to replicate each interest and principal cash flows. This replication of cash flows is usually not perfect as it is unlikely that the interest amounts exchanged under a currency swap will be the same as the amounts generated by a forward FX contract. From a swap dealer's point of view, this creates a hedging imperfection that is often reflected in currency swap pricing.

> ***Note***
> These two methods of synthetically replicating currency swaps are very similar to interest rate swaps. The physical replication reflects the "bond" approach to pricing and valuation while the LTFX replication is an extension of the forward offset model (both approaches are explained in Section 9.4). Accordingly, these two models can be extended to develop currency swap pricing and valuation models.

In this chapter, we will focus on developing models based on the bond approach. The reason for this is that the approach is simpler and also the basic market prices underlying the calculations are easier to obtain than LTFX prices.

10.2.4 Currency Swap Pricing

As with any derivative, pricing involves obtaining the key market prices that determine value. First, we need to determine the key pricing parameters and then obtain current market estimates.

There are three important pricing variables in a currency swap:

- the swap exchange rate;
- the pay currency interest rate;
- the receive currency interest rate.

In the case of plain vanilla currency swaps, the exchange rate is set at the spot rate prevailing at the time the swap is executed. For most of our valuation requirements, we can use a current market quote of the spot exchange rate.

Determining the appropriate interest rate is more complex. The pay and receive interest rates may be fixed or floating. An effective swap model must be able to incorporate four possible combinations:

- pay a fixed interest rate, receive a fixed interest rate;
- pay a floating interest rate, receive a fixed interest rate;
- pay a fixed interest rate, receive a floating interest rate;
- pay a floating interest rate, receive a floating interest rate.

As with an interest rate swap, the synthetic replication scenarios from the previous section suggest that these fixed and floating interest rates will be related to bond and FRN rates respectively in each currency. However, as we have previously identified, the credit risk and obligations created by a swap are different to a physical security, giving rise to an interest rate swap yield curve that is independent, but related, to the yield on physical securities.[5] This interest rate swap curve is our starting point for the fixed rates in currency swaps.

While the interest rates used in a currency swap are closely related to the rates on fixed-to-floating interest rates, they are not usually identical. This is because the obligations in an interest rate swap and a currency swap are not identical. The differences are illustrated below:

- **Full cash flow payments** Unlike an interest rate swap, in a currency swap, there is usually full payment of interest and principal amounts in each currency, which substantially increases the settlement risk.
- **Hedging different currency cash flows** The currency swap creates forward obligations to exchange currencies; any hedging costs associated with replicating the currency exchanges will typically be reflected in the currency swap rates.
- **A term commitment** A currency swap obliges both counterparties to exchange different currencies over a number of years, the term nature of this commitment may be reflected in the swap interest rates.

In general, interest rate swap rates can be used as a close indication of currency swap rates. More accurate pricing requires obtaining currency swap rate quotations from a swap dealer. The dealer will obtain currency swap quotes from its own internal pricing models. A common method of modeling currency swap quotes is to use more simplistic swaps. The following section examines one of these models.

[5] See Section 9.4.2 for a detailed discussion on the differences between swaps and physical securities.

10.2.5 Constructing Currency Swap Prices from Simpler Swaps

When a swap dealer provides a quote on a fixed-to-fixed currency swap, it is often broken down into three underlying swaps:

- a pay fixed, receive floating interest rate swap;
- a pay floating, receive fixed interest rate swap;
- a currency basis swap—receive floating in one currency and pay floating in another currency.

By converting the fixed rates to floating and then using a currency basis swap, the dealer is able to overcome the differences created by the two fixed cash flows occurring in different currencies. It also highlights that the difference between a currency and interest swap rate will be equivalent to the net cost of executing a currency basis swap. For example, if a 3-year US$/CA$ currency basis swap creates a net cost of ten basis points per annum, the price of a fixed-to-fixed US$/CA$ currency swap will be given by adjusting either of the interest rate swap fixed rates up or down by ten basis points.

> ***Note***
> The advantage of this "components" approach to pricing a currency swap is that currency basis swap rates are commonly available on quote vendor swap pages. So by combining interest swap rates with the currency basis swap, we can obtain an accurate indication of currency swap interest rates.

Figure 10.4 shows how to derive a currency swap price from interest rate and basis swap quotations. As this example shows, the difference between interest rate swap rates and currency swap rates is given by the prevailing currency basis swap margin. In this example, the basis swap results in a 10-basis point margin below the DM floating index—this translates into a DM fixed rate in the currency swap that is ten basis points below the DM swap rate.[6] Once we have obtained these adjusted swap rates they can be applied directly to the valuation of a currency swap.

The margins in a currency basis swap are influenced by the prevailing demand and supply for currency swaps. In the example in *Figure 10.5* on pages 274–5 the basis swap requires the payment of US dollar LIBOR flat and DM (i.e., Euro)

[6] In this case, the impact of the currency basis swap is shown as a margin below the DM fixed rate, it could also be calculated as a margin above the US dollar fixed rate.

LIBOR minus ten basis points—the swap market is indicating that there is an imbalance between DM payers and receivers. Specifically, there is an excess demand to receive DM. The swap market is counteracting this imbalance by reducing the DM interest rate, making receiving DM less attractive than paying DM.

Figure 10.4
The Components Approach to Pricing a Currency Swap

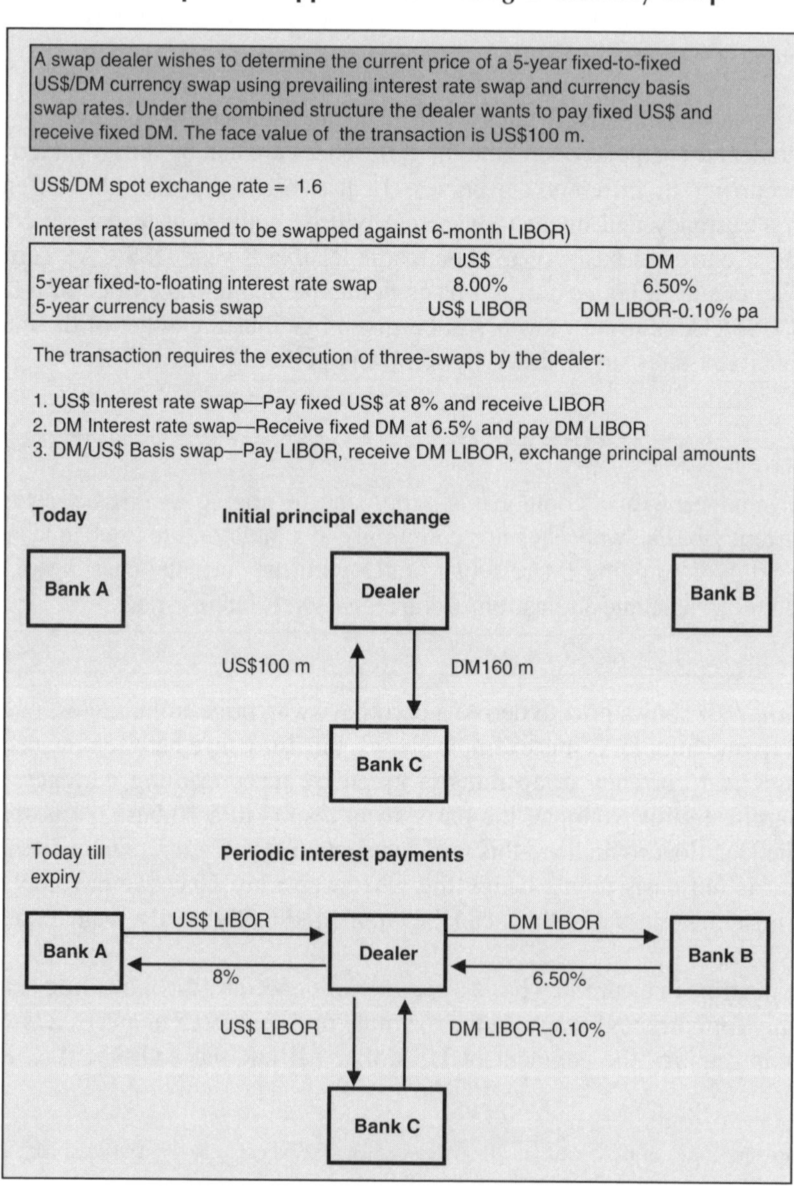

Figure 10.4 Continued

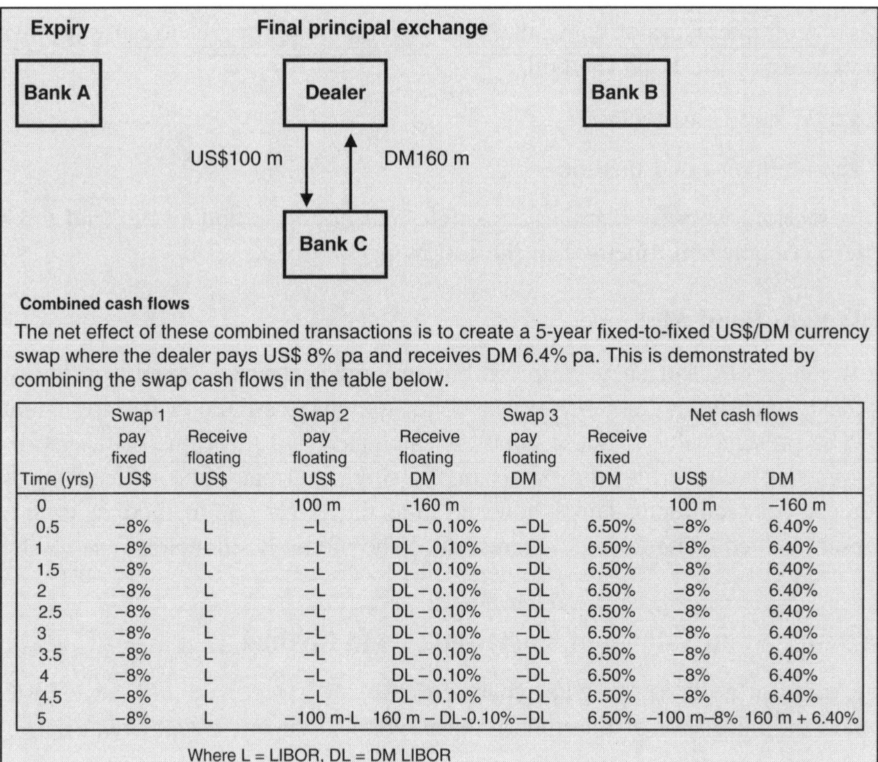

Combined cash flows

The net effect of these combined transactions is to create a 5-year fixed-to-fixed US$/DM currency swap where the dealer pays US$ 8% pa and receives DM 6.4% pa. This is demonstrated by combining the swap cash flows in the table below.

	Swap 1		Swap 2		Swap 3		Net cash flows	
	pay fixed	Receive floating	pay floating	Receive floating	pay floating	Receive fixed		
Time (yrs)	US$	US$	US$	DM	DM	DM	US$	DM
0			100 m	-160 m			100 m	–160 m
0.5	–8%	L	–L	DL – 0.10%	–DL	6.50%	–8%	6.40%
1	–8%	L	–L	DL – 0.10%	–DL	6.50%	–8%	6.40%
1.5	–8%	L	–L	DL – 0.10%	–DL	6.50%	–8%	6.40%
2	–8%	L	–L	DL – 0.10%	–DL	6.50%	–8%	6.40%
2.5	–8%	L	–L	DL – 0.10%	–DL	6.50%	–8%	6.40%
3	–8%	L	–L	DL – 0.10%	–DL	6.50%	–8%	6.40%
3.5	–8%	L	–L	DL – 0.10%	–DL	6.50%	–8%	6.40%
4	–8%	L	–L	DL – 0.10%	–DL	6.50%	–8%	6.40%
4.5	–8%	L	–L	DL – 0.10%	–DL	6.50%	–8%	6.40%
5	–8%	L	–100 m-L	160 m – DL-0.10%	–DL	6.50%	–100 m–8%	160 m + 6.40%

Where L = LIBOR, DL = DM LIBOR

10.2.6 Simple Valuation: The Single Rate Bond Method

As we have seen from the synthetic replication, a currency swap can be viewed as an extension of the interest rate swap. However, the underlying asset and liability are now in different currencies.

Using this concept, we can extend the valuation models derived for interest rate swaps in Chapter 9.[7] In the case of currency swaps, the offset approach to valuation becomes more complex as it requires three offsetting transactions:

- interest cash flows in each currency
- principal cash flows at the start date
- principal cash flows at expiry.

It usually requires more complex inputs such as the LTFX rate that applies to the expiry date of the swap.

[7] See Section 9.2.5 for a description of the basic interest rate swap valuation models.

The bond method of valuation is considerably easier to adapt to currency swaps because it relies on bond mathematics and the prevailing spot exchange rate. As with interest rate swaps, there are two main approaches to currency swap valuation using the bond method:

- single rate bond method;
- zero-coupon bond method.

In this section, we will examine the single-rate bond method and extend this to the zero-coupon bond method in the following section.

Single-Rate Bond Method

The two legs of a currency swap are broken down into two "bonds" in the two currencies underlying the swap—these bonds may have a fixed or floating interest rate. The present value of these bonds is calculated and the value of the swap is determined by converting the bonds into a single currency and then taking the difference between them. This is referred to as the single rate method, as each leg is present valued using a single interest rate. The model is summarized as follows:

Currency Swap Valuation: Single-Rate Bond Method

The value of a currency swap where currency A is received and currency B is paid the net value of the underlying bonds (on an interest payment date):

$$PV_{AREC} = PV_A - PV_B/E$$
$$PV_{APAY} = PV_{REC} \times -1$$

Where:

PV_A = present value of currency A cash flows
PV_B = present value of currency B cash flows
E = spot exchange rate.

These present values are determined using the following formulae depending on whether they are fixed or floating:

$$PV_{FIXED} = [r/m \times (1 + a_n) + v^n] \times FV$$
$$PV_{FLOATING} = [(r_1/m + 1)/(1 + r_1^*/m)] \times FV$$

Where:

r = original swap yield to maturity in original swap (% pa)
r^* = current swap yield to maturity in offsetting swap (% pa)
r_l = original floating yield to next interest payment date (% pa)
rl^* = current floating yield to next interest payment date (% pa)
n = the number of periods to maturity excluding the next n payment date

m = the number of coupon payments pa
$v = 1/(1+r^*/m)$
$a_n = (1-v^n)/(r^*/m)$.

Related MS Excel functions:
PV_{FIXED}: PRICE(settlement, maturity, rate, yld, redemption, frequency, basis)

This is an extension of the interest rate swap single rate valuation model—we have introduced an exchange rate and the possibility that both legs may be fixed. As a result, the same adjustments that can be made to the interest rate swap models with respect to interest accrual and day count basis also apply to this currency swap model (see Section 9.2.5 for a discussion on these adjustments).

In *Figure 10.5*, we develop a single-rate bond method currency swap model for a fixed-to-fixed currency swap.[8] In this case, we have executed a US$/DM 5-year fixed-to-fixed swap. Since it was executed the market prices of the swap have changed: both US dollar and DM/Euro fixed interest rates have fallen by 1% and the exchange rate has risen from 1.6000 to 1.7000. The current market value of the swap is a loss of US$6.454 million or DM10.972 million.

Risk Characteristics: PVBP, PVFP and Time

A feature of fixed-to-fixed currency swaps is that the primary interest rate exposure is to the *interest differential* as opposed to outright interest rates. For example, if the loss in the example used in *Figure 10.5* is broken down into an FX and interest rate effect, almost all of the valuation change is due to the change in the exchange rate:

Valuation Effects

FX value effect	(6,368,718.93)
Interest rate value effect	(85,862.81)
Total value – US dollar	(6,454,581.74)

This is very similar to the risk characteristics of LTFX contracts discussed in Chapter 6. LTFX contracts are often used as a vehicle for hedging fixed-to-fixed currency swaps.

As with a forward FX transaction, the main risk characteristics of a currency swap can be broken down into the impact of interest rate, FX and time.

[8] This model is an extension of the interest rate in *Figure 9.7*.

Figure 10.5
Single Rate Bond Method Example

	C	D	E	F	G	H	I	J	K
6									
7		Currency swap revaluation calculator — Fixed-to-fixed							
8		Single-rate bond method				Cell:Formula			
9									
10		Swap details							
11		Revaluation/deal date			24-May-00	$G$11 :			
12		Expiry date			24-Feb-05	$G$12 :			
13		Base currency face value			100,000,000	$G$13 :			
14		Original swap exchange rate			1.6000	$G$14 :			
15		Base currency (p)ayer or (r)eceiver			p	$G$15 :			
16		Base currency swap rate			8.00	$G$16 :			
17		Terms currency swap rate			6.40	$G$17 :			
18		Number of periods per year (1, 2 or 4)			2	$G$18 :			
19		Base day count casis (0, 1, 2, 3, 4)			0	$G$19 :			
20		Terms day count basis (0, 1, 2, 3 ,4)			0	$G$20 :			
21		Revaluation details							
22		Revaluation base swap rate			7.0000	$G$22 :			
23		Revaluation terms swap rate			5.4000	$G$23 :			
24		Revaluation exchange rate			1.7000	$G$24 :			
25		Revaluation fating date							
26		Current swap value - base currency			6,454,581.74	$G$26 : +G38+K38/G24			
27									
28		Component 1 — Base currency				Component 2 — Terms currency			
29		Payer or receiver			Payer	Payer or receiver			Receiver
30		Revaluation date			24-May-00	Revaluation date			24-May-00
31		Last coupon date			24-Feb-00	Last coupon date			
32		Next coupon date			24-Aug-00	Next coupon date			
33		Expiry date			24-Feb-05	Expiry date			24-Feb-05
34		Coupon			8.0000%	Coupon			6.4000%
35		Current yield to expiry			7.0000%	Current yield to expiry			5.4000%
36		Current clean value			103,965,396.87	Current clean value			
37		Accrued interest			2000,000.00	Accrued interest			
38		Total base leg value			(105,965,396.87)	Total terms leg value			

Figure 10.5 Continued

Notes:
1. This spreadsheet uses the standard excel bond pricing functions. The Analysisf.xla add-in must be loaded.
2. This model assumes that the interest rate rollover dates are the same on both legs. This is often not the case; to extend the model, insert additional fields for terms currency interest frequency and use these fields to determine the intermediate values used in the "Component 2" calculations.
3. The formulae used in the calculation of the two components are shown in the table below.

Description	Cell	Formula
Base currency leg		
Payer or receiver	$F$29	=IF(G15="P","Payer","Receiver")
Revaluation date	$F$30	=+G11
Last coupon date	$F$31	=COUPPCD(G$30,G$33,G$18,G19)
Next coupon date	$F$32	=COUPNCD(G$30,G$33,G$18,G19)
Expiry date	$F$33	=+G12
Coupon	$F$34	=+G16/100
Current yield to expiry	$F$35	=+G22/100
Current clean value	$F$36	=(PRICE(G30,G33,G34,G35,100,G18,G19))/100*G13
Accrued interest	$F$37	=IF(G30>G31,ACCRINT(G31,G32,G30,G34,100,$G18,$G19)/100*$G13,0)
Total base leg value	$F$38	=ROUND((G36+G37)*IF(G14'="p",–1,1),2)
Terms currency leg		
Payer or receiver	$J$29	=IF(G15="r","Payer","Receiver")
Revaluation date	$J$30	=+G30
Last coupon date	$J$31	=+G31
Next coupon date	$J$32	=+G32
Expiry date	$J$33	=+G33
Coupon	$J$34	=+G17/100
Current yield to expiry	$J$35	=+G23/100
Current clean value	$J$36	=(PRICE(K30,K33,K34,K35,100,G18,G20))/100*G13*G14
Accrued interest	$J$37	=IF(K30>K31,ACCRINT(K31,K32,K30,K34,100,$G18,$G19)/100*$G13*$G14,0)
Total terms leg value	$J$38	=ROUND((K36+K37)*IF(G14'="r",–1,1),2)

Steps
1. Obtain fixed-leg bond pricing inputs.
2. Determine fixed-leg bond price.
3. Divide fixed-leg bond price by 100 and multiply by swap face value (total fixed-leg value).
4. Obtain floating-leg bond pricing inputs.
5. Determine floating-leg bond price.
6. Divide floating-leg bond price by 100 and multiply by swap face value (total floating-leg value).
7. Determine which is the "paying" leg an multiply the total value by –1.
8. Determine which is the receiving leg.
9. Swap market value is given by adding together the amounts in Steps 7 and 8.

In Chapter 6, we extended the PVBP concept to incorporate sensitivities to the FX rate and time—PVFP and PVD respectively.[9]

In the example in *Figure 10.6*, these sensitivities are calculated by changing each of the pricing variables by one point and increasing time by one day. Each of the risk characteristics is calculated below:

Exposure	Sensitivity	US$
Base interest rate	$PVBP_{BASE}$	40,820.85
Term interest rate	$PVBP_{TERM}$	(39,959.84)
Interest differential	$PVBP_{DIFF}$	861.01
FX rate	PVFP	(581,934.59)
Time	PVD	(5,524.18)

These sensitivities provide the data to determine the appropriate hedging strategy for a fixed-to-fixed currency swap. The aim of the hedge transaction should be to offset each of these risks as closely as possible. The perfect hedge would be an exactly offsetting currency swap; however, from the point of view of a dealer, it is highly unlikely that another counterparty will be available with exactly offsetting requirements.

As a result, the hedge will require the breaking of the swap into components. This may involve executing two interest rate swaps and a basis swap as discussed in Section 10.2.5; the two interest rate swaps will match the PVBP of the term and base currencies and the basis swap will have a PVFP which is close to that of the original currency swap.

> ***Note***
> Another alternative would be to execute a 5-year LTFX transaction—the sensitivities will be similar to the currency swap; however, the cash flow timing differences will result in some hedge imperfections.

10.2.7 Zero-Coupon Valuation of Currency Swaps

As with interest rate swaps, the zero-coupon model for currency swaps is an extension of the single-rate bond model:

[9] See Section 6.4.2.

Currency Swap Valuation: Zero-Coupon Bond Method

The value of a currency swap where currency A is received and currency B is paid the net value of the underlying bonds (on an interest payment date):

$$PV_{AREC} = PV_{A} - PV_{B}/E$$
$$PV_{APAY} = PV_{REC} \times -1$$

Where:

PV_A = present value of currency A cash flows
PV_B = present value of currency B cash flows
E = spot exchange rate.

These present values are determined using the following formulae depending on whether they are fixed or floating:

$$PV_{FIXED} = [\, r/(1 + r_{s1}^{*}/m) \cdots + (1 + r)/(1 + r_{sn}^{*}/m)^{n} \,] \times FV$$
$$PV_{FLOATING} = [\, (r_l/m + 1)/(1 + r_l^{*}/m)] \times FV$$

Where:

r = original swap yield to maturity in original swap (% pa)
$r_{s1..n}^{*}$ = spot yield to periods 1 through to n (% pa)
r_l = original floating yield to next interest payment date (% pa)
r_l^{*} = current floating yield to next interest payment date (% pa)
n = the number of periods to maturity excluding the next n payment date
n = the number of coupon payments pa.

Note that the *PV* calculation for the fixed leg is now a "long-hand" bond price calculation as we need to be able to identify each cash flow separately.

The main additional complexity of the zero-coupon bond method is the requirement to generate zero-coupon interest rates for each swap cash flow in both currencies. The simplest solution to this is to derive a zero-coupon yield curve from the par swap yield curve in each currency using the bootstrapping model from Section 9.2.4. This produces standardized zero-coupon yield curve points from which the zero-coupon rates for each cash flow date can be determined by some form of interpolation.

Suppose we wish to value a GBP/DM 3-year fixed-to-floating currency swap using the zero-coupon bond method. Under the swap, we receive fixed-rate sterling at 9% on a quarterly basis and pay DM on a 6-month floating rate basis.

Figure 10.6
Generating a GBP Zero Yield Curve Bootstrapping on a Quarterly Basis

	C	D	E	F	G	H	I	J	K	L	M	N	O	P	Q	R	S
6				Interpolated	Quarterly	Quarterly											
7	Date	Number	Number	quarterly	par	zero	Each periodic coupon discounted at the relevant spot rate										
8		days	of periods	par yield	coupon	yield		2	3	4	5	6	7	8	9	10	11
9																	
10	25-Oct-95	0	0														
11	25-Jan-96	92	1	6.8846%	$1.72	6.8846%											
12	25-Apr-96	183	2	6.8264%	$1.71	6.8264%	1.68										
13	25-Jul-96	274	3	6.8339%	$1.71	6.8337%	1.68	1.65									
14	25-Oct-96	366	4	6.8415%	$1.71	6.8415%	1.68	1.65	1.63								
15	25-Jan-97	458	5	6.8759%	$1.72	6.8771%	1.69	1.66	1.63	1.61							
16	26-Apr-97	549	6	6.9103%	$1.73	6.9129%	1.70	1.67	1.64	1.61	1.59						
17	25-Jul-97	639	7	6.9447%	$1.74	6.9488%	1.71	1.68	1.65	1.62	1.59	1.57					
18	25-Oct-97	731	8	6.9791%	$1.74	6.9849%	1.72	1.69	1.66	1.63	1.60	1.57	1.55				
19	25-Jan-98	823	9	7.0528%	$1.76	7.0634%	1.73	1.70	1.68	1.65	1.62	1.59	1.56	1.54			
20	26-Apr-98	914	10	7.1265%	$1.78	7.1423%	1.75	1.72	1.69	1.66	1.64	1.61	1.58	1.55	1.52		
21	25-Jul-98	1004	11	7.2002%	$1.80	7.2218%	1.77	1.74	1.71	1.68	1.65	1.62	1.60	1.57	1.54	1.51	
22	25-Oct-98	1096	12	7.2739%	$1.82	7.3018%	1.79	1.76	1.73	1.70	1.67	1.64	1.61	1.58	1.55	1.52	1.49
23																	

Note: Summary of calculations

1. The date is simply calculated as exactly one calender quarter on from the previous quarter.
2. The number of days is the difference between today and the rollover date.
3. The "par" yields for periods 1 and 2 are already zero-coupon rates so the "par" yields are entered directly as zero-coupon yield.
4. The calculation from periods 3 to 40 are identical, the only difference is that the number of coupons rises by one for each extra period.
5. The main calculations for period 3 (row 13) are as follows:

Description	Cell	Formula
Quarterly par coupon	G13	=100*F13/4
Quarterly zero-coupon	H13	=4*(((100+G13)/(100–SUM(I13:AU13)))^(1/E13)–1)
Coupon 1	I 13	=$G13/(1+$H$11/4)^$E$11
Coupon 1	J13	=$G13/(1+$H$12/4)^$E$12

Note: For each extra period, add one more coupon following the same sequence in the first two columns. So the third coupon will be calculated for period 4, which will discount the par quarterly coupon (G14) by the zero-coupon rate prevailing up to period 3; that is, $G14/(1+H$13/4)^$E$13.

The steps in the valuation calculation are to:

1. generate a GBP zero-coupon yield curve;
2. generate a DM zero-coupon yield curve;
3. calculate the present value of the GBP cash flows;
4. calculate the present value of the DM cash flows;
5. convert the DM present value to GBP and net against the GBP present value.

Figures 10.6 and *10.7* generate the zero-coupon yield curves for each currency (steps 1 and 2) using the same method developed in *Figure 9.16.* Notice that we require quarterly compounded zero-coupon rates for GBP and semi-annual rates for DM.

Figure 10.8 takes these zero-coupon yield curves and applies them to the cash flows generated by a fixed-to-floating GBP/DM currency swap using the zero-coupon bond model. This involves first taking the present value of the GBP and DM amounts (steps 3 and 4) and then converting the DM amount to GBP and netting this with the GBP present value to give the final profit (step 5).

Figure 10.8 provides a robust model for valuing plain vanilla currency *and* interest rate swaps. This model will support all combinations of fixed and floating legs in a currency swap, and if the original swap exchange rate and the revaluation exchange rate are both set to equal one, then the model will be able to value interest rate swaps as well.

10.2.8 Valuation of Nongeneric Currency Swaps

In Chapter 9, we developed pricing and valuation models for a range of nongeneric swaps such as forward, amortizing and zero-coupon structures. The extension of these structures to currency swaps involves applying the interest rate bond method model directly to currency swaps.

Using the bond method, we can replicate each currency leg as a bond. In the example above, we have assumed these to be plain vanilla, spot start, coupon paying bonds with a bullet principal payment. If we have a forward start currency swap, each of the underlying bonds is priced and valued as a forward bond.

In the case of an amortizing currency swap, each of the component bonds has an amortization schedule and the present value is taken based on the interest payments and periodic principal repayments. One important feature of an amortizing currency swap is that the amortization of both legs is identical. If one leg is repaid at a slower rate than another, one counterparty is effectively lending money to the other—making the transaction a combination of a loan and a swap.

We can apply the models developed in Chapter 9 with a zero-coupon swap. In this case, the interest payment basis of each leg can differ and it is relatively

Figure 10.7
Generating a DEM Zero Yield Curve

Bootstrapping on a quarterly basis and then compounding to semi-annual

	C	D	E	F	G	H		I	J	K	L	M	N	O	P	Q	R	S
6				Interpolated	Quarterly	Quarterly	Semi-annual											
7	Date	Number	Number	quarterly	par	zero	zero	Each periodic coupon discounted at the relevant spot rate										
8		days	of periods	par yield	coupon	yield	yield		2	3	4	5	6	7	8	9	10	11
9																		
10	25-Oct-95	0	0															
11	25-Jan-96	92	1	4.0000%	$1.00	4.0000%												
12	25-Apr-96	183	2	4.0792%	$1.02	4.0792%	4.1000%	1.01										
13	25-Jul-96	274	3	3.9059%	$0.98	3.9045%		0.97	0.96									
14	25-Oct-96	366	4	3.7326%	$0.93	3.7291%	3.7465%	0.92	0.91	0.91								
15	25-Jan-97	458	5	3.7635%	$0.94	3.7613%		0.93	0.92	0.91	0.91							
16	26-Apr-97	549	6	3.7945%	$0.95	3.7934%	3.8114%	0.94	0.93	0.92	0.91	0.91						
17	25-Jul-97	639	7	3.8255%	$0.96	3.8254%		0.95	0.94	0.93	0.92	0.91	0.90					
18	25-Oct-97	731	8	3.8564%	$0.96	3.8574%	3.8760%	0.95	0.94	0.94	0.93	0.92	0.91	0.90				
19	25-Jan-98	823	9	3.9646%	$0.99	3.9699%		0.98	0.97	0.96	0.96	0.95	0.94	0.93	0.92			
20	26-Apr-98	914	10	4.0727%	$1.02	4.0827%	4.1036%	1.01	1.00	0.99	0.98	0.97	0.96	0.95	0.94	0.93		
21	25-Jul-98	1004	11	4.1809%	$1.05	4.1961%		1.03	1.02	1.02	1.01	1.00	0.99	0.98	0.97	0.96	0.94	
22	25-Oct-98	1096	12	4.2890%	$1.07	4.3100%	4.3332%	1.06	1.05	1.04	1.03	1.02	1.01	1.00	0.99	0.98	0.97	0.96
23																		

Note: Summary of calculations

1. All calculations are the same as *Figure 10.6*.
2. The semi-annual rates are generated using the standard periodic compounding functions.

common to have one leg paying zero-coupon interest and the other paying a floating rate.

In order to build valuation models for these nongeneric structures, we can take the model from *Figure 10.8* and insert the nongeneric features from these same structures in interest rate swaps.

10.3 VALUATION CASE STUDY: HEDGING A EUROBOND ISSUE

Our focus so far has been on developing pricing and valuation models of individual instruments. In practice, most risk managers and financial engineers are faced with determining the value of transactions that combine a range of financial instruments. In this section, we apply some of the valuation models we have developed, to analyze the combined value generated by a hedged Eurobond issue.

10.3.1 New Issue Arbitrage (NIA)

A relatively common combined transaction is the use of currency swaps to hedge bond issues in foreign currencies. Typically, these transactions are driven by NIA, where an organization combines fund-raising in a foreign currency with a currency swap to give a combined cost of funds, which is lower than borrowing the same funds. These arbitrage opportunities arise for a number of reasons, including incomplete information on the part of foreign investors or difference in tax and regulatory treatments of these issues in different countries.

> ***Note***
> NIA is effectively an exercise in applied equivalent value, because an organization is able to synthetically create a bond in another currency by combining a bond and a currency swap. While the characteristics of the synthetic bond are the same as a physical bond issue, due to imperfections in financial markets, the issuer is able to achieve a lower issue cost.

In the following case study we examine an NIA transaction undertaken by an Australian issuer in the mid-1990s. In this case study, the transaction involved issuing a US dollar Eurobond issue that was then swapped into A$. There are a number of key points to address in the analysis:

- how to accurately price an NIA;
- NIA is an application of equivalent value;
- the gains of an NIA can be quantified using the models we have developed for financial instrument valuation;
- the risks associated with an NIA can be analyzed using our valuation tools.

Figure 10.8
Zero-Coupon Bond Method

Currency swap revaluation calculator
Zero-coupon bond method

Swap details		Cell:Formula
Deal date	25-Oct-00	$G$11 :
Expiry date	25-Oct-03	$G$12 :
Base currency face value	100,000,000	$G$13 :
Original swap exchange rate	2.7200	
Base currency (p)ayer or (r)eceiver	p	$G$15 :
Base currency swap rate	9.0000	$G$16 :
Base currency (f)ixed or f(l)oating	f	$G$17 :
Base currency payment frequency	4	$G$18 :
Terms day count basis ? (360 or 365)	365	$G$19 :
Terms currency swap rate	7.5200	$G$20 :
Terms currency (f)ixed or f(l)oating	l	$G$21 :
Terms currency payment frequency	2	$G$22 :
Terms day count basis ? (360 or 365)	365	$G$23 :
Revaluation swap details		
Revaluation exchange rate	2.6000	
Revaluation GBP swap rate	See zero curve below	$G$27 :
Revaluation DM fixed rate		$G$28 :
		$G$29 :
Current swap value - base currency	1,727,782.09	$G$30 : + H31+J31/G26

— See below for formulae used in the table.

	Base currency PV factors			**Base currency cash flows**		Terms currency discount factors			**Terms currency cash flows**	
Rollover periods	Rollover dates	Zero-coupon interest rate	Discount factor	Original base currency cash flows	Base present value	Rollover dates	Zero-coupon interest rate	Discount factor	Original terms currency cash flow	Terms present value
0	25-Oct-00				(104,630,029.04)	25-Oct-00				276,530,308.94
1	25-Jan-01	6.8846%	0.9830797	(2,268,493.15)	(2,230,109.53)	25-Apr-01	4.1000%	0.9799118	282,199,180.27	276,530,308.94
2	25-Apr-01	6.8264%	0.9667224	(2,219,178.08)	(2,145,329.25)	25-Oct-01	3.7465%	0.9635620		
3	25-Jul-01	6.8337%	0.9504497	(2,243,835.62)	(2,132,652.91)	25-Apr-02	3.8114%	0.9449411		
4	25-Oct-01	6.8415%	0.9344129	(2,268,493.15)	(2,119,709.32)	25-Oct-02	3.8760%	0.9260947		
5	25-Jan-02	6.8771%	0.9182978	(2,268,493.15)	(2,083,152.23)	25-Apr-03	4.1036%	0.9034351		
6	25-Apr-02	6.9129%	0.9023010	(2,219,178.08)	(2,002,366.66)	25-Oct-03	4.3332%	0.8793184		
7	25-Jul-02	6.9488%	0.8864247	(2,243,835.62)	(1,988,991.30)					
8	25-Oct-02	6.9849%	0.8706707	(2,268,493.15)	(1,975,110.60)					
9	25-Jan-03	7.0634%	0.8542432	(2,268,493.15)	(1,937,844.91)					
10	25-Apr-03	7.1423%	0.8377940	(2,219,178.08)	(1,859,214.18)					
11	25-Jul-03	7.2218%	0.8213325	(2,243,835.62)	(1,842,935.13)					
12	25-Oct-03	7.3018%	0.8048678	(102,268,493.15)	(82,312,613.03)					
13										

Figure 10.8 Continued

51	14				
52	15				
53	16				
54	17				
55	18				
56	19				
57	20				
58	13				

Notes:
1. The zero-coupon interest rates come from the model developed in *Figure 9.19.*
2. The floating leg is assumed to be either A/360 or A/365.
3. The calculations for row 38 and 39 are shown in the table below. Enter these into the spreadsheet and then copy from row 39 down to row 57.
4. Requires "Analysis Toolpak" add-in for financial functions.

Formulae in Table

Description	Cell	Formulae
Row 38		
Base currency		
Rollover dates	$D$38	=IF(OR(D37=$G$12,D37=""),"",COUPNCD(D37,$G$12,$G$18,3))
Discount factor	$F$38	=1/(1+E38/$G$18)^C38
Original base currency cash flows	$G$38	=(IF(D38="","",ROUND($G$13*$G$16/100*(D38-D37)/$G$19,2))+IF(OR(D39="",$G$17="L"),$G$13,0))*IF($G$15="p",-1,1)
Base present value	$H$38	=IF(G38="","",+G38*F38)
Terms currency		
Rollover dates	$I$38	=IF(OR(I37=$G$12,I37=""),"",COUPNCD(I37,$G$12,$G$22,3))
Discount factor	$K$38	=1/(1+J38/$G$22)^$C38
Original terms currency cash flows	$L$38	=(IF(I38="","",ROUND($G$13*$G$14*$G$20/100*(I38-I37)/$G$23,2))+IF(OR(I39="",G21="L"),$G$13*$G$14,0))*IF($G$15="p",1,-1)
Terms present value	$M$38	=IF(L38="","",+L38*K38)
Row 30 (copy down to row 57)		
Base currency		
Rollover dates	$D$39	=IF(OR(D38=$G$12,D38=""),"",COUPNCD(D38,$G$12,$G$18,3))
Discount factor	$F$39	=1/(1+E39/$G$18)^C39
Original base currency cash flows	$G$39	=(IF(D39="","",IF($G$17="L","",((ROUND($G$13*$G$16/100*(D39-D38)/$G$19,2))+IF(D40="",$G$13,0))*IF($G$15="p",-1,1))))
Base present value	$H$39	=IF(G39="","",+G39*F39)
Terms currency		
Rollover dates	$I$39	=IF(OR(I38=$G$12,I38=""),"",COUPNCD(I38,$G$12,$G$22,3))
Discount factor	$K$39	=1/(1+J39/$G$22)^$C39
Original terms currency cash flows	$L$39	=IF($G$21="L","",(IF(I39="","",((ROUND($G$13*$G$14*$G$20/100*(I39-I38)/$G$23,2))+IF(I40="",$G$13*$G$14,0))*IF($G$15="p",1,-1))))
Terms present value	$M$39	=IF(L39="","",+L39*K39)

10.3.2 Pricing the Arbitrage: The Simple Analysis

Suppose an Australian-based issuer requires A$100 million to finance a new project. It would like to structure this transaction as an Australian dollar 5-year fixed-rate debt and is currently investigating two methods of achieving that goal:

1. issuing a domestic A$100 million 5-year fixed-rate bond; or
2. issuing a US$75 million Eurobond and swapping to A$ at the current exchange rate of A$1 = US$0.75.

We know that issuing the A$ bond meets the company's requirements. This can then be used as a benchmark for determining whether or not the swapped US dollar Eurobond is worthwhile.

The first step in examining an NIA is to determine the current market price of the swapped Eurobond. This involves combining the interest costs of all of the legs to the transaction and determining an equivalent A$ borrowing cost.

The current market conditions, the structure of the swapped Eurobond and the "simple" arbitrage opportunity are presented in *Figure 10.9*. The net A$ interest rate given by the swapped Eurobond is found by netting out the interest rates across different currencies. This analysis suggests that the effective A$ borrowing cost of the swapped Eurobond will be 9.43% pa—an interest cost saving of 0.15% pa.

One of the problems with the "simple" analysis is that it assumes that the value of interest paid in US dollars is the same as interest paid in Australian dollars. In fact, in the simple analysis, the "all-up" interest rate is A$ 8.78% pa plus US$ 0.65% pa. If we want to add these interest amounts, we need to convert the US dollar interest payment into an A$ interest amount.

10.3.3 The "True" Arbitrage: Using Conversion Factors

The swapped Eurobond structure will create a net US dollar interest margin of 0.65% pa that will have to be paid on each interest payment date. The "simple" arbitrage analysis assumes that this US dollar margin payment is funded in US dollars. This is inconsistent with our objective of converting all aspects of the US dollar Eurobond into Australian dollars so that it can be compared to the domestic bond issue.

The US dollar margin can be thought of as a regular US dollar payment that has to be made by the Australian company. In order to convert these to Australian dollars, the company will have to enter into a series of forward sell Australian dollar/buy US dollar forward FX contracts for each interest payment. As a result, the cost of converting the US dollar margin to A$ will be the same as the forward discount on the Australian dollar/US dollar—which in turn is determined by the interest rate differential.

Figure 10.9
Current Market Conditions and Simple Arbitrage Analysis

Current market rates	% pa
A$ 5-year bond issuance yield (sa)	9.58
A$ 5-year swap rate (sa)	8.78
US$ 5-year Eurobond issuance yield (sa)	7.35
US$ 5-year swap rate (sa)	6.70
A$/US$ spot exchange Rate	0.7500

Simple arbitrage analysis

Is a swapped Eurobond issue worthwhile?

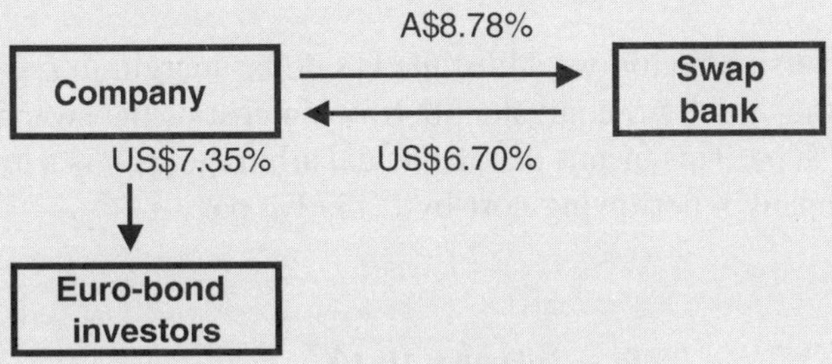

Company → Swap bank: A$8.78%
Swap bank → Company: US$6.70%
Company → Euro-bond investors: US$7.35%

Net interest cash flows

Currency	US$	A$
Pay fixed	7.35%	8.78%
Receive fixed	–6.70%	
Net	0.65%	8.78%

Simple A$ borrowing cost	9.43%
Simple saving	0.15%

In order to compare, we need to convert all of the swapped Eurobond interest cash flows to Australian dollars and then we can determine the difference in funding in Australian dollar and US dollar (i.e., the interest differential) and adjust the US dollar margin using the "conversion factor."

As the interest differential between the Australian dollar and US dollar varies, depending on the term to maturity, a conversion factor should be determined for each separate US dollar margin payment using zero-coupon interest rates:

$$\text{Adjusted margin} = m_1 \times CF_1 + m_2 \times CF_2 \cdots m_2 \times CF_n$$
$$CF = [(1 + r_{a1} \times t_1)/(1 + r_{u1})]$$
$$CF^{\cdot} = [(1 + r_{an} \times t_n)/(1 + r_{un} \times t_n)]$$

While this is the correct method, it is common practice to simplify this calculation to the "simple" conversion factor, which uses the prevailing par yield to maturity of the underlying instrument:

$$\text{Simple adjusted margin} = m\% \text{ pa} \times CF$$
$$CF = \frac{(1 + \text{A\$ interest rate})}{(1 + \text{US\$ interest rate})}$$

Using this conversion factor, we adjust the US dollar margin in *Figure 10.10* and we determine the "true" A$ equivalent borrowing cost of the swapped Eurobond issue is 9.4427% pa. This means that the actual arbitrage gain is a lowering of the Australian company's borrowing cost by 0.1373% pa.

Figure 10.10
Conversion Factors

◄

Simple conversion factor

Calculate the simple conversion factor

CF = (1 + A$ swap rate)/(1 + US$ swap rate)
= (1 + 8.78%)/(1 + 6.7%)
= 1.0195

True A$ equivalent borrowing cost of NIA

NIA A$ borrowing cost = (US$ margin) * *CF* + A$ swap rate
= (0.65%) × 1.0195 + 8.78%
= 9.4427 % pa

True NIA = A$ bond rate – NIA A$ borrowing cost
= 0.1373% pa

10.3.4 Analysing the Value of an NIA

Often the analysis of the swapped Eurobond ceases when the arbitrage has been determined. Then there is a flurry of activity by corporate bankers and the combined structure is put in place. The Australian company views the transaction as effectively an A$ borrowing and may even treat it as a "synthetic" 5-year $100 million Australian dollar bond issued with a coupon of 9.4427%.

However, it is interesting to take the analysis a little further in order to test the assumption that the NIA has "equivalent value" to an A$ 5-year fixed-rate bond. In the pricing analysis above, we have assumed that the arbitrage gain is risk-free. In this case, this implies the combined value of the NIA is insensitive to movements in interest rates and exchange rates.

While the exposures have been reduced, there are a number of residual exposures that while small, can have an impact on the magnitude of the arbitrage gain achieved. These imperfections often become apparent if an NIA issuer decides to buy back the combined swap and bond structure and discovers that the gain or loss realized is somewhat different to what was expected.

In the case where the arbitrage gain is small, it is important to investigate the key residual risks and determine the capacity for an adverse movement in any of these exposures to undermine the arbitrage gain. These exposures arise from mismatches in the characteristics of the bond and the swap. *Figure 10.11* summarizes the initial characteristics of the NIA transaction.

If we compare the Eurobond and the swap, we can see that the key parameters such as face value, interest payment dates and maturity dates all match. However, we know that the mismatch between the Eurobond coupon and the US dollar interest receipt under the swap creates a net US dollar payment of the US$487,500 pa. While we determined the cost of hedging this exposure, it was not actually hedged—so we have a short US$/long A$ exposure on this margin.

We can also see that there is a difference in the absolute coupon levels on the Eurobond, the swap and the synthetic bond. We know from our bond pricing models that bonds with different coupons have different duration and convexity characteristics. As a result, any change in market interest rates is likely to affect each of the components of the swap differently.

In the following section, we examine the sensitivity of the structure to interest rate and exchange rate movements and then quantify these sensitivities.

10.3.5 The Value Sensitivity of an NIA

A perfect arbitrage would be a gain that, regardless of changes in market prices, would continue to give the same arbitrage gain. In the previous section, we identified two potential sources of exposure and now we will examine the actual *sensitivity* of the structure to changes in market rates.

Figure 10.11
Initial Value of the Arbitrage

The initial terms of the transaction are illustrated below:

Initial terms of NIA issue

Eurobond

Face value — US$	75,000,000
Start date	24-Jul-95
Expiry date	24-Jul-00
Coupon	7.35%
Interest frequency (1, 2 or 4)	2
Market value — US$	75,000,000

Swap

US$ face value	75,000,000
Swap FX rate	0.7500
A$ face value	100,000,000
Start date	24-Jul-95
Expiry date	24-Jul-00
Receive fixed US$ (% pa)	6.70%
Pay fixed A$ (% pa)	8.78%
Interest frequency (1, 2 or 4)	2
Swap market value — A$	–

Combined structure — synthetic A$ bond

Face value — A$	100,000,000
Start date	24-Jul-95
Expiry date	24-Jul-00
Synthetic 5-yr bond rate coupon	9.4427%
Interest frequency (1, 2 or 4)	2
Market value — A$ value of Eurobond	100,000,000
Market value — A$ value of swap	–
Market value — combined A$ value	100,000,000

Comparative issue — domestic A$ bond

Face value —A$	100,000,000
Start date	24-Jul-95
Expiry date	24-Jul-00
Synthetic 5-yr bond rate coupon	9.5800%
Interest frequency (1, 2 or 4)	2
Revaluation interest rate (synthetic yield)	9.4427%
Arbitrage market value — A$	100,537,300

Present value of arbitrage gain — A$

Market value of NIA synthetic bond	100,000,000
Market value of domestic bond	100,537,300
Present value of NIA	537,300

Using the bond valuation models from Chapter 3 and the simple bond method currency swap valuation model developed in Section 10.2.6, we will revalue the swapped Eurobond given a set of changes in market interest rates and exchange rates. The NIA is assumed to have the same risk characteristics as the synthetic A$ 5-year bond set out in *Figure 10.11*. Using this as our benchmark, we will determine whether the valuation sensitivity of the NIA structure changes.

Let us suppose US dollar interest rates rise by a flat 1% pa and that Australian dollar interest rates fall by 1% pa, while the Australian dollar depreciates against the US dollar immediately after the NIA has been put in place. The revised market prices are set out in *Figure 10.12*.

Our analysis requires three valuations to be performed using these revised market prices:

- the benchmark synthetic bond (*Figure 10.14*);
- the US dollar Eurobond converted to Australian dollars (*Figure 10.15*);
- the Australian dollar US dollar currency swap in Australian dollars (*Figure 10.16*).

The table in *Figure 10.16* compares the combined value of the NIA with the synthetic bond and shows that the change in value of the NIA is a loss of A$4,154,426, and the synthetic bond changed in value by A$4,011,100—a difference of A$143,326. Whereas this is not a large amount relative to the face

Figure 10.12
Revised Market Prices

In order to understand the sensitivity of the transactions, it is useful to undertake a "what if" calculation. Suppose on *n* the start date (July 24, 1995) the exchange rate falls, US interest rates rise by 1% pa and A% interest rates fall by 1% pa to give the following set of revaluation rates:

Revaluation rates (Eurobond and swap)	
Date	**24-Jul-95**
FX rate	**0.7100**
5-year Eurobond rate %	**8.35%**
US$ 5-year swap rate	**7.70%**
A$ 5-year swap rate	**7.78%**

Revaluation rates (synthetic A$ bond)

We want to see how closely the synthetic bond approximates a straight bond, so we will deduct 1% pa from the synthetic yield.

New synthetic yield on the bond	**8.4427%**

Figure 10.13
Revised Benchmark Synthetic Bond Value

The change in value of the synthetic security provides the benchmark for the change in value of the NIA.

Revaluation date	24-Jul-95
Expiry date	24-Jul-00
Coupon	9.4427
Frequency pa	2
Current yield to expiry	8.4427

Initial bond market value	(100,000,000)
Revaluation bond market value	(104,011,100)
Profit/loss on synthetic bond	(4,011,100)

Figure 10.14
Revised Eurobond Value

The value of the Eurobond is determined in US$ and then converted into A$.

Revaluation date	24-Jul-95
Expiry date	24-Jul-00
Coupon	7.3500
Frequency pa	2
Current yield to expiry	8.3500

1. Initial bond market value — US$	(75,000,000)
2. Issue exchange rate	0.7500
3. Initial bond market value — A$	(100,000,000)

4. Revaluation bond market value — US$	(71,984,775)
5. Current exchange rate	0.7100
6. Revaluation bond market value — A$	(101,387,007)

7. Total A$ P/L on Eurobond (6–3)	(1,387,007)
8. Interest P/L — A$ (4–1)/2	4,020,300
9. Interest P/L — A$ (7–8)	(5,407,307)

value of the transaction, it is 27% of the present value of the arbitrage gain calculated in *Figure 10.11*. While the magnitude of this market price change is unlikely over one day, it could easily occur over several months and this highlights the importance of doing this type of analysis on low margin arbitrage transactions.

In summary, while the NIA and the synthetic bond are *similar* they are *not identical*. This may be the reason why equivalent value did not hold. It is possible

Figure 10.15
Revised Currency Swap Value

Cross currency swap calculations

Revaluation date	24-Jul-95	
Expiry date	24-Jul-00	
Revaluation exchange rate	0.7100	
	Base currency	Terms currency
Payer/receiver (P or R)	P	R
Currency	A$	US$
Face value	100,000,000	75,000,000
Deal fixed swap rate %	8.78	6.70
Number of payments per year (1, 2 or 4)	2	2
Principal flows (y or n)	y	y
Day count basis (365, 360)	365	365
Revaluation swap rate %	7.78	7.70
Next rollover date	24-Jan-96	24-Jan-96

Total swap profit/loss — A$	(2,767,419)
Interest P/L — A$	(8,170,784)
FX P/L — A$	5,403,366

Figure 10.16
Comparing the Revised Values

Market rates used

	Original	Revaluation
US$ Eurobond yield	7.350%	8.350%
US$ swap yield	6.700%	7.700%
A$ swap yield	8.780%	7.780%
A$ bond benchmark	9.443%	8.443%
A$/US$ FX rate	0.7500	0.7100

Benchmark A$ straight issue — valuation

1. A$ bond profit/loss — A$	(4,011,100)

NIA components — valuation

2. Eurobond profit/loss — A$	(1,387,007)
3. Currency swap profit/loss — A$	(2,767,419)
4. Combined profit/loss — A$	(4,154,426)

Difference in values

5. Difference in profit/loss (4 —1)	(143,326)

that the arbitrage gain is purely the return made for assuming the risk of the NIA structure.

The two sources of exposure identified earlier, the US dollar margin and the coupon effect, both have a role to play in the valuation difference. The fall in Australian dollar and the US dollar will create an FX loss as it will cost more Australian dollars than expected to cover the US dollar margin.

Figure 10.17
The Margin and Coupon Effects

The US$ interest margin

The US$ margin has not been hedged. The fall in the FX rate increases the cost of the spread; however, the fall in the interest differential has partly offset this—so the total impact is quite small.

Annual value of the spread	487,500.00
Original present value of spread — US$	1,735,993.50
Original exchange rate	0.7500
Original present value of spread amount — A$	2,314,658.01
Revaluation present value of spread — US$	1,657,947.14
Revaluation exchange rate	0.7100
Reval. present value of spread amount — A$	2,335,136.82
Spread effect — A$	**(20,478.81)**

The coupon effect

The different coupons of each instrument gives them slightly different interest sensitivities and has meant that the overall lower coupon NIA issue slightly under-hedges.

A$ coupons	
Change in A$ leg of swap — interest only in A$	(4,081,119)
Change in A$ Straight Bond — interest only in A$	4,011,100
	(70,019)
US$ coupons	
Change in US$ leg of swap — interest only in A$	(4,089,266)
Change in US$ leg of Eurobond — interest only in A$	4,020,300
	(68,966)
Total coupon effect	**(138,985)**

Note that these effects cannot be added because what they measure is partly overlapping.

These effects are quantified in *Figure 10.17*. Both factors contribute to the imperfection. The two effects combined are greater than the total valuation difference because both the valuation and margin effects are interrelated. This is shown by the fact that the possible FX loss caused by the fall in the exchange rate is offset by the reduction in the margin exposure due to the rise in US dollar interest rates.

If these exposures are considered significant, they should be hedged as part of the NIA and the hedging cost should be incorporated into the arbitrage calculation. In the case study, we have examined possible hedges might include:

- **Par-forward FX transactions** The US dollar margin exposure creates a constant requirement to purchase US dollars and sell Australian dollars. In order to spread the hedging cost evenly across the NIA, a par-forward would effectively provide a constant forward FX rate for each margin payment and the net par-forward cost could simply be used as the conversion factor in the arbitrage calculation.

- **Bond futures** The coupon effect tells us that the swap leg of the NIA has a higher PVBP than either the Eurobond or the synthetic bond. One way of offsetting this higher PVBP would be to enter into a sufficient number of Australian dollar and US dollar bond futures to reduce the swap PVBP on both legs to the same as the underlying bonds.

SUMMARY

In this chapter, we extended upon the swap models developed in Chapter 9 to price and value cross currency swaps. This has involved and applied the single-rate bond method to value fixed-to-floating currency swaps and the zero-coupon bond method for all combinations of currency swaps. We also developed a model for evaluating swaps as a tool for new issue arbitrage.

SELF-TEST QUESTIONS

1. Assume a large French or France-based company has a floating rate debt of US$100 million, and wishes to convert this to fixed-rate Euro. Answer the following questions (with the use of diagrams):
   a. Using the concept of synthetic replication, explain how the company could achieve the desired outcome using physical assets and liabilities.
   b. Show how the same transaction could be achieved using a cross-currency swap.
2. Identify the three main pricing variables in a cross-currency swap.

3. Assume the following information:

A$/US$ = 0.55	US$	A$
3-year fixed to floating swap interest rate	7.00%	6.00%
3-year currency basis swap	US$ LIBOR	BBSW — 0.08% pa

Jody, a swap dealer, wishes to pay fixed A$ and receive fixed US$. Calculate the current price of a 3-year fixed-to-fixed US$/A$ currency swap. Use cash flow diagrams to help illustrate your example.

4. You are the risk manager of a financial institution. Your swap dealer has just executed a Euro/JP¥ fixed-to-fixed cross currency swap. The dealer has hedged the risk by executing a strip of interest rate futures in both currency. The dealer claims to have mitigated all major risks associated with the swap—do you agree? If not, what other hedging needs to be undertaken?

CHAPTER 11

EQUITY SWAPS

The models developed in this chapter are saved as Microsoft Excel™ files in the enclosed disk.

OVERVIEW

In this chapter, we examine the valuation of equity swaps. At the end of this chapter we will have:

- explained the underlying price and value drivers of equity swaps;
- developed models to value plain vanilla equity swaps.

11.1 INTRODUCTION

As mentioned in Chapter 1, the equity swap market is substantially smaller than both the interest rate and currency swap markets. Even in the major markets, such as North America, liquidity is relatively low.

The major end-users of equity swaps are fund and portfolio managers. Rather than purchasing a portfolio of physical shares in order to replicate a broad-based stock index, the fund manager retains the cash and enters into a swap that will generate gains and losses according to movements in the index.

Reasons for using swaps rather than directly investing in shares include:

- **Reduced execution and administration costs** The costs of initially purchasing a broad-based portfolio can be substantial in terms of brokerage and slippage. Also, on an ongoing basis, there is a requirement to rebalance the portfolio for changes in the underlying index weightings. A swap is a single transaction that always reflects the gains and losses of the index. This is, particularly, useful in emerging markets where stock markets may be less liquid, transaction costs high and the fund manager may have no local presence to manage a physical portfolio.
- **Suitable for index funds** Where a portfolio manager deliberately attempts to replicate an index, the swap provides a return directly linked to the stock index; there is no room for slippage.

- **Regulatory constraints** There are often regulatory constraints or tax issues that limit the ability of an investor to purchase shares, a swap allows an investor to gain a stock market exposure without contravening regulatory requirements.
- **Foreign exchange risk** Where the stock market is in a different currency to the investor's home currency, a cross currency equity swap allows the investor to gain a foreign stock market exposure and also hedge the FX exposure.

While these potential advantages do exist there a number of factors that have constrained the market development:

- **Low liquidity** The low liquidity in the market means that the bid and offer spreads can be wide and the range of counterparties is limited, increasing the cost of reversing an equity swap.
- **Limited requirement for "off-balance sheet" exposures** In interest rate and currency markets, executing swap transactions is an efficient, low cost means of transforming balance sheet exposures. Typically, a swap is considerably more effective than creating on balance sheet assets and liabilities (i.e., synthetic replication). In equity markets, investors are typically asset holders who switch between cash and equity holdings at relatively low cost. In many instances, the use of a swap to create equity exposures or to modify the basket of stocks held may often be more expensive and slower to execute than the physical market transactions.
- **Availability of substitutes** As we will see later in this chapter, an equity swap can be closely replicated by stock price index futures. The existence of a more liquid and transparent economic equivalent has the effect of reducing volume from the swaps market.
- **Nonindex portfolios** Most equity swaps are offered on market benchmark stock portfolios. If an investor wishes to construct a nonindex weighted portfolio, then, an equity swap may appear expensive.

11.2 CHARACTERISTICS OF AN EQUITY SWAP

11.2.1 General Description

Equity swaps have the same structure as interest rate and currency swaps. They are based on a notional face value at the start of the swap and there is a regular exchange of cash flows based an agreed term to maturity. The unique feature of an equity swap is that the cash flows are based on two different underlying markets: one cash flow is based on the total return on an agreed equity benchmark (e.g., a stock index) and the other is based on a return on an interest rate index (e.g., LIBOR). The equity return often is a total return reflecting both dividend and share price movements, but the swap can be based on price movements only. As with interest rate swaps, there is usually no initial exchange or re-exchange of principal amounts at maturity.

There are four general forms of equity swap in a single currency:

- **Equity/floating rate swaps — variable principal** An equity index is exchanged for a floating interest rate and the principal amount is adjusted each payment date.
- **Equity/floating rate swaps — fixed principal** An equity index is exchanged for a floating interest rate with a constant notional principal amount.
- **Equity/fixed rate swaps — variable principal** An equity index is exchanged for a fixed interest rate and the principal amount is adjusted each payment date.
- **Equity/fixed rate swaps — fixed principal** An equity index is exchanged for a fixed interest rate with a constant notional principal amount.

These four combinations outlined above also apply to cross currency equity swaps, where the equity and interest rate indices are in different currencies. Another cross currency variation is to enable the foreign exchange risk hedged—leaving the swap cash flows to be determined purely by the relative performance of the two indices. Currency hedging costs also have to be incorporated into this type of structure.

Although, there are a range of variants, all the swaps are based on single currency equity-to-floating swaps, with interest rate and cross-currency swaps incorporated into the structure. For example, an equity-to-fixed swap is an equity-to-floating swap combined with a fixed-to-floating interest rate swap. Given our already extensive discussion of interest rate and currency swaps in this chapter, we will focus on the pricing and valuation of the "core" single-currency equity-to-floating swaps.

11.2.2 Mechanics of Equity Swaps[1]

The most common form of equity swap is a single currency equity to floating interest index. For example, the swap may consist of the exchange of cash flows

[1] For more information on the mechanics of equity swaps, see the *IFR Self Study Workbook on Swaps*, Part 3, "Equity Swaps." This provides a very thorough grounding in each of the various structures available and the cash flows that they generate.

based on the return generated by an S&P 500 index against US dollar LIBOR. In most equity swaps, the notional principal amount varies over the life of the swap, to reflect the change in capital value that would occur to a physical equity investment. Equity swaps with fixed notional face values do exist, but are less common.

Figure 11.1 illustrates this variable notional floating-rate equity swap. In this case, an investor wishes to invest US$100 million, which is linked to the S&P 500 index and decides to execute an equity swap with a swap counterparty. To construct the synthetic equity investment, the investor deposits US$100 million in a money market security that pays 6-month LIBOR. Under the equity swap, the investor agrees to pay 6-month LIBOR in exchange for the return on the S&P 500 at each 6-monthly payment dates. The investor is the equity receiver and LIBOR payer. An equity swap may also contain a requirement to pay or received a fixed margin as part of the swap counterparties spread and it may also reflect any hedging gains or costs arising from the equity swap structure. In this example, the investor receives a fixed margin equivalent to 0.05% pa of the notional face value over the life of the swap.

> **Note**
> Unlike an interest rate swap, where the receiver always receives cash, because equity returns can be negative the investor will be in the position of paying the S&P return if it is negative for a 6-month period.

Figure 11.1
Payment Cash Flows of a Single-Currency Floating-Rate Equity Swap

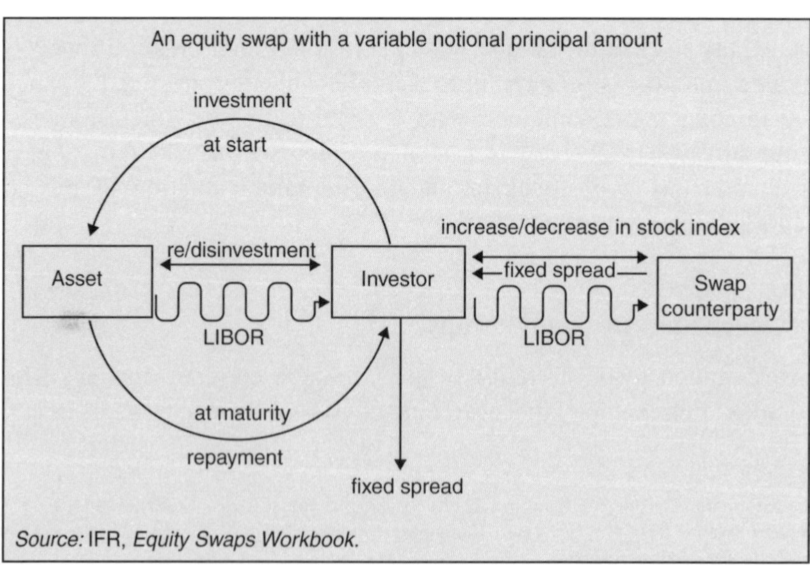

Source: IFR, *Equity Swaps Workbook.*

On each payment date, the investor uses the interest from the money market deposit to make the LIBOR payments under the swap. As equity gains or losses arise, the investor will invest or divest the principal value of the swap. For example, if in the first six months the equity return was US$7 million, then this would be added to the money market deposit to increase the principal amount to US$107 million. Accordingly, the notional principal value of the swap is also increased to US$107 million. In a constant notional principal swap, all principal amounts are kept the same on each payment date.

Assuming the swap described above had a maturity of two years and we know the outcome of each payment date, *Figure 11.2* summarizes the actual cash flows generated for the investor over the life of the swap.

Figure 11.2
Equity Swap Cash flows

Suppose that the equity swap desdfcribed in *Figure 11.1* was executed for a term of two years and that the actual S&P 500 and LIBOR outcomes were as follows:

	S&P 500		6-mth LIBOR
Years	Accum index	% chg.	
0	513.00		3.5000%
0.5	585.03	14.04%	4.2500%
1	560.28	–4.23%	5.8750%
1.5	594.57	6.12%	5.3750%
2	628.22	5.66%	

The details of the equity swap were as follows:

Notional principal	100,000,000
Equity index	S&P 500 — incl. dividends
Fixed spread	0.05% paid to investor
Interest rate index	6-month US$ LIBOR
Term	2 years

The details of the money market deposit are as follows:

Original investment	100,000,000
Interest rate	6-month US$ LIBOR

The resulting combined cash flows for the investor are as follows:

Investor cash flows

	Deposit		Equity swap					
Term yrs	Principal	Interest	Notional principal	Equity return	Fixed spread	LIBOR payment	Net swap	Combined cash flow
0	100,000,000		100,000,000					
0.5	114,040,000	1,750,000	114,040,000	14,040,000	28,510	(1,750,000)	12,318,510	14,068,510
1	109,216,108	2,423,350	109,216,108	(4,823,892)	27,304	(2,423,350)	(7,219,938)	(4,796,588)
1.5	115,900,134	3,208,223	115,900,134	6,684,026	28,975	(3,208,223)	3,504,778	6,713,001
2	122,460,081	3,114,816	122,460,081	6,559,948	30,615	(3,114,816)	3,475,746	6,590,563
Totals		10,496,389		22,460,081	115,404	(10,496,389)	12,079,096	22,575,485

Total return = 22,575,485
or 10.441% pa compounded semi-annually

11.2.3 Synthetic Replication of Equity Swaps

An equity swap can be created synthetically by using either the physical assets and liabilities, or using stock price index futures contracts. For example, we can create a physical replication of a receiving equity/paying floating by simultaneously borrowing the notional principal amount on a floating interest rate basis and investing the proceeds into an index-weighted portfolio of shares. At the end of each payment period, the equity portfolio is sold in order to crystallize the return on the equity portfolio and the floating interest is paid on the borrowing. An example of synthetically replicating a 2-year equity receiver S&P 500 swap is provided in *Figure 11.3*. If we wished to make this, a receiving equity/paying fixed equity swap, the borrowing would be at a fixed rate rather than a floating rate.

In the case of the fixed notional principal swap, the equity return is distributed and the original notional face value is reborrowed at the floating interest rate and reinvested in the share portfolio. In the case of the variable notional principal swap, the equity return is redistributed at each payment date; however, the amount reborrowed is equivalent to the notional face value of the equity portfolio on that payment date. As a result, while the percentage returns will be the same, the actual magnitude of the equity gains or losses and interest amount will be different depending on whether the notional face value is variable or fixed.

Another point worth noting, is that if the swap excludes dividends from the equity return, the cash flows of the swap will differ. In the synthetic example above, the dividend was distributed on each payment date. If the dividend is not included in the return, only the capital gain or loss is distributed and the dividend is retained. The amount that needs to be borrowed at each rollover date is reduced by the dividend received, which effectively reduces the interest cost of the strategy. As a result, when comparing a dividend paying and nondividend paying equity swap, the amount of floating interest paid should be lower for the nondividend paying swap. This lower interest amount can take the form of a fixed margin below the floating interest rate paid or a fixed margin above the equity return received.

> ***Note***
>
> A receiving equity/paying floating equity swap could also be replicated by buying index futures. While an index future does not actually pay a dividend, the forward price is adjusted for the payment of dividends so that the forward purchase price is reduced by the future value of any dividend payment.

The synthetic equity swap structure outlined could also be created by purchasing a stock index futures contract with six months to expiry and then rolling that futures contract for another six months on each expiry date.

Figure 11.3
A Fixed Notional Principal Synthetic Equity Swap

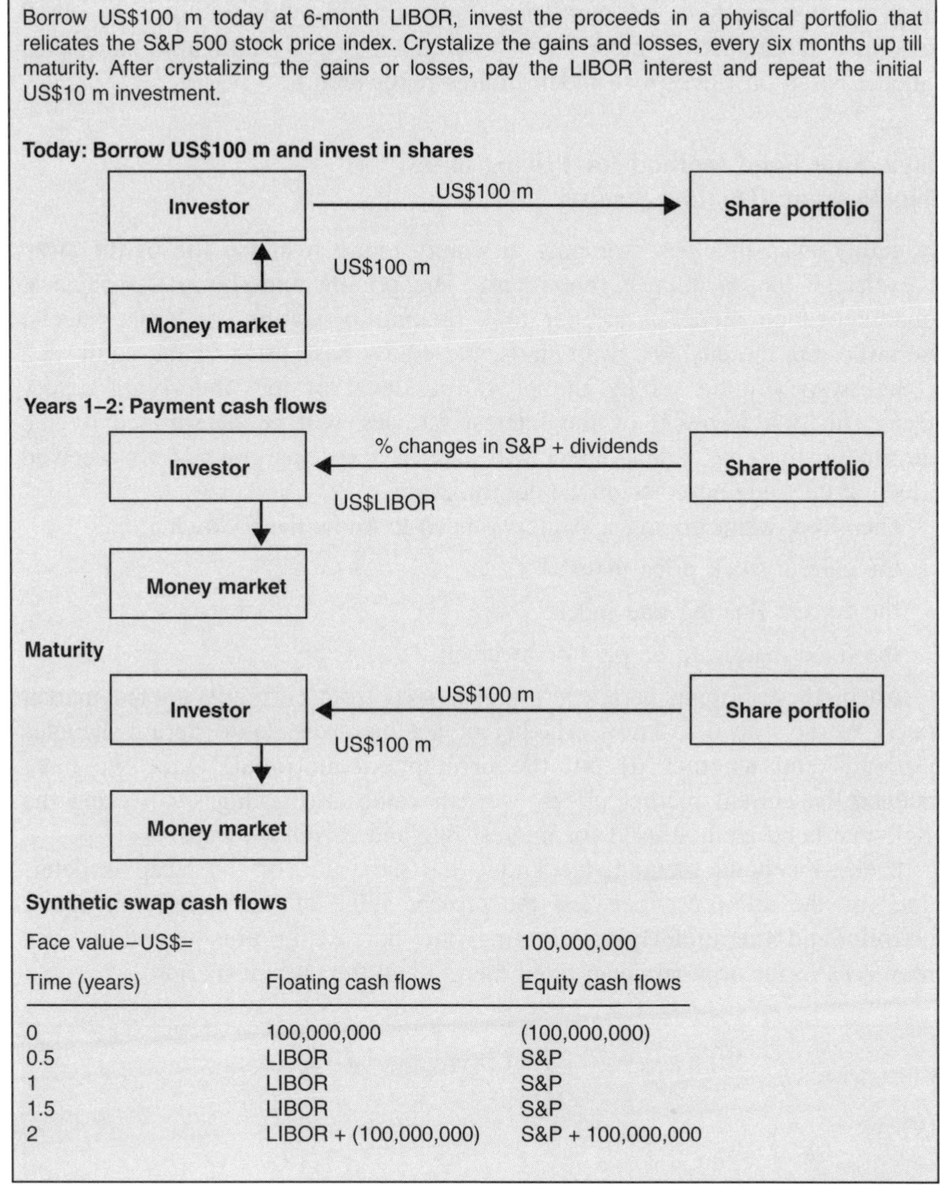

Time (years)	Floating cash flows	Equity cash flows
0	100,000,000	(100,000,000)
0.5	LIBOR	S&P
1	LIBOR	S&P
1.5	LIBOR	S&P
2	LIBOR + (100,000,000)	S&P + 100,000,000

While the economics is very similar to an equity swap, the usual funding cost differences emerge between the futures contract and swap.

The adjustment for an equity swap *without* dividends is identical to the adjustment made for equity forwards in Chapter 7.

11.2.4 Pricing and Valuing a Simple Equity Swap

As with interest rate swaps, pricing and valuation models can be derived from the two methods of synthetic replication. In this section, we shall develop a bond pricing model based on the physical replication and then a model based on stock price index futures replication.

Single-Rate Bond Method for Pricing and Valuing Equity/Floating Swaps[2]

An equity swap involves swapping an equity return over the life of the swap in exchange for an interest rate return. The pricing underlying the physical bond replication model is similar to a floating-to-floating, or basis, interest rate swap. On the day the swap starts, the equity base price of the equity leg of the swap will be set by the prevailing level of the underlying equity index. The first payment of the interest rate leg will be determined by the relevant floating-rate index. There will also be fixed margin paid or received reflecting the hedging costs of the equity swap.

Therefore, when pricing a swap, we need to know the following:

- the current stock price index;
- the current floating rate index;
- the fixed margin to be paid or received.

All of these pricing parameters are derived from currently quoted market prices. We also need to know whether or not the swap equity return includes dividends and whether or not the principal is notional. Once we have obtained the current market prices, we can value an existing swap using the single-rate bond method used for interest rate and currency swaps.

Under the bond method, we know that the value of the swap is determined by the difference between the present value of the underlying equity portfolio and the underlying floating-rate borrowing plus or minus any differences in the original swap fixed margin and the current margin:

$$PV_{\text{EQREC}} = PV_{\text{EQ}} - PV_{\text{FLOATING}} + PV_{\text{MARGIN}}$$

Where:

PV_{EQ} is the current value of the underlying equity portfolio.
PV_{FLOATING} is the current present value of the underlying floating rate borrowing.

[2] For a refresher on the bond valuation method, see Chapter 9.

A feature of the equity portfolio is that on any given day, all aspects of the future return are floating. The present value of the portfolio is determined by the current price at which the portfolio can be liquidated (i.e., the current stock index price) plus any dividends accrued since the last payment date. The gain or loss on the fixed margin is calculated by the difference on each rollover date between the traded and current margin, present valued.

Figure 11.4 provides an example of revaluing a US$100 million one-and-half-year equity swap with quarterly rollovers and an equity return that incorporates dividends. The swap is valued from the point of view of the equity receiver/floating-rate payer. Since the swap was executed, the stock index has moved higher, resulting in a substantial gain on the equity leg of the swap of around US$4.885 million. However, both the fixed margin and the floating interest rates have moved against the position and resulted in small revaluation loss of US$0.191 million—creating a net gain on the swap of US$4.693 million.

Figure 11.4 on page 304 provides a valuation based on the single-rate bond method. Extending this to a zero-coupon method involves generating a zero-coupon yield curve and then performing all of the present values using these rates. Furthermore, extending the model to an equity-to-fixed swap requires replacing the floating-rate leg present valuation calculations with fixed-rate leg calculations as in *Figure 9.23*.

A problem with the pricing and valuation approach used above is that it leaves most of the pricing complexity, namely, the determination of the margin, as an external calculation. While this is satisfactory for an end-user, a market-maker needs to be in a position to determine all aspects of the price of a swap, including any fixed margins. Using the physical asset and liability approach, this involves determining all of the costs associated with hedging; particularly, where the hedge involves short-selling of stock, which can be very expensive in some markets.

Futures Pricing Approach to Pricing and Valuing Equity Swaps

A more simplistic approach to price and value equity swaps is by synthetic replication using forward markets as a conceptual base. In Chapter 9, we devised methods of determining par swap rates based on short-term interest rate futures prices.[3] In those interest rate models, we recognized that the forward interest yield curve could be used to determine both spot and par yields. The same relationship is applicable for stock index futures. We already know (see Part 2) that the fair value of a stock index price forward is given by:

[3] See *Figures 9.18* and *9.20*.

Figure 11.4
Valuing an Equity Swap Using the Bond Method

	C	D	E	F	G	H	I	J	K
6									
7		Swap revaluation calculator — single-rate method							
8						Cell:Formula			
9		Swap details							
10		Revaluation date			20-Apr-00				
11		Expiry date			30-Sep-01	$G$10 :			
12		Face value			100,000,000	$G$11 :			
13		Equity payer or receiver			r	$G$12 :			
14		Traded stock index price			3000.0000	$G$13 :			
15		Swap floating rate			7.5200	$G$14 :			
16		Margin (+ for receive, – for pay)			0.1000	$G$15 :			
17		Dividend yield			4.0000	$G$16 :			
18		Number of periods per year (1, 2 or 4)			4	$G$18 :			
19		Day count basis ? (360 or 365)			365	$G$19 :			
20									
21		Revaluation swap details							
22		Revaluation index price			3140.0000	$G$22 :			
23		Revaluation floating rate			7.2000	$G$23 :			
24		Revaluation margin			0.2000	$G$24 :			
25		Revaluation swap rate to maturity			7.5000	$G$25 :			
26		Current swap value			4,693,937	$G$26 : +E34 + H34+J34			

See below for formulas used in the table.

Row	Rollover periods	Rollover dates	Equity PV	Fixed margin cash flows: Original margin cash flows	Current margin cash flows	PV of margins	Floating cash flows: Original floating cash flow	Floating present value
33	Deal date	31-Mar-00						
34	0	20-Apr-00	104,885,845			(130,521)		(100,061,386.82)
35	1	30-Jun-00		24,932	38,904	(13,772)	(101,462,794.52)	(100,061,386.82)
36	2	30-Sep-00		25,205	50,411	(24,383)		
37	3	31-Dec-00		25,205	50,411	(23,930)		
38	4	31-Mar-01		24,658	49,315	(22,985)		
39	5	30-Jun-01		24,932	49,863	(22,814)		
40	6	30-Sep-01		25,205	50,411	(22,637)		
41	7							
42	8							
43	9							
44	10							
45								

Notes:
1. Requires Analysis Toolpack add-in for financial functions.
2. One method of removing dividends from the calculation is simply to set the dividend yield to zero.
3. A more accurate calculation of the margin present values would be achieved by using zero-coupon rates.

Formulae in table

Description	Cell	Formula
Deal date	$D$34	=COUPPCD(D34,$G$11,$G$18,3)
Equity PV	$E$34	=+G12*(G22/G14+(D34–D33)/G19*G17/100)*if(g13="p",–1,1)
Rollover dates	$D$35	=IF(OR(D34'=$G$11,D34'=""),"",COUPNCD(D34,$G$11,$G$18,3))
Original margin cash flows	$F$35	=IF($D35="","",$G$12*$G$16/100*(D35–D33)/$G$19)
Current margin cash flows	$G$36	=IF($D35="","",$G$12*$G$24/100*(D35–D34)/$G$19)
PV of margin	$H$35	=(F35–G35)/(1+$G$25/(100*$G$18))^(($D35–$D$34)/$G$19*$G$18)
Original floating cash flow	$I$35	=IF($D35="","",ROUND(($G$12*$G$15/100*($D35–$D34)/$G$19+G12)*IF($G$13'="p",1,–1),2))
Floating present value	$J$35	=I35/(1+G23/100*(D35–D34)/G19)

$$F = S \times (1 + (r - q))$$

Where:

F is the forward price
S is the spot index price
r is the cost of financing the index
q is the dividend yield.

Each futures price contains all of this information and given that we know S and we are willing to estimate q, we can calculate r. In this case, r represents the zero-coupon interest rate from today until the futures expiry date and, more specifically, it represents the "all-in" cost of financing a stock index-weighted portfolio. From a market-maker's point of view, this financing cost or stock lending rate will drive the equity swap price, as it reflects the hedging cost of the swap. In terms of our earlier examples, it is this component of the forward price that determines the fixed margin earned above or below the actual index return.

The futures prices can be applied directly to equity swap pricing as the two are economically equivalent and the concept of equivalent value means that the prices should also be equivalent. For example, suppose we entered into a short-term receive stock index/pay LIBOR swap with two months to expiry as follows:

Start date	April 15, 2001
Maturity date	June 20, 2001
Days to expiry	61
Current stock price index	637.1
Include dividends	Yes
Floating interest rate % pa	5.25%
Expected dividend yield % pa	2.00%
Fixed margin % pa	0.00%

As we are the fixed-rate receiver, we will gain from this swap, if the index value rises. At the end of two months, the index will have to have risen far enough to offset the net of the interest rate and the dividend yield over 66 days:

$$
\begin{aligned}
\text{Interest payment} &= 637.1 \times 0.0525 \times 61/360 \\
&= 5.667 \text{ index points} \\
\text{Dividend receipts} &= 637.1 \times 0.02 \times 61/365 \\
&= 2.129 \text{ index points} \\
\text{Break-even index level} &= 637.1 + 5.667 - 2.129 \\
&= 640.638.
\end{aligned}
$$

If the index is above 640.638 on June 20, the swap will realize a net gain, while if it is below this level, then it will realize a loss.

This looks very much like a forward pricing calculation and if we apply the standard continuous asset income forward pricing model, the forward price is as follows:

$$
\begin{aligned}
F &= S \times (1 + (r - q)) \\
&= 637.1 \times (1 + (0.0525/360 - 0.02/365) \times 61) \\
&= 640.638
\end{aligned}
$$

If we are a market-maker and we are asked to price an equity swap, we know that we can hedge ourselves effectively using a share price index futures contract. When quoting this price, we need to ensure that the interest amount paid over, or under the swap, actually reflects the forward financing cost, r, in the futures contract. This financing cost is likely to be different than the usual floating-rate money market indices, such as LIBOR, for a number of reasons:

- **Forward mispricing** SPI futures often trade away from fair value. As a result, for a given index price and dividend yield, the implied financing cost can vary significantly from current money market rates and even be negative.
- **Risk differences** The two indices in an equity swap have different credit and market risk characteristics. The interest rate index is a high-quality bank deposit with a fixed return and very low probability of default, while the equity index is a broad-based portfolio of shares with uncertain return with some possibility of some shares in the portfolio defaulting. This suggests that the receiver of the equity index should receive an extra return (i.e., fixed margin) relative to the interest rate receiver for holding an inherently risky position.[4]
- **Structural influences** Any regulatory or institutional constraints on the borrowing and lending of shares will move stock lending rates away from money market yields. For example, if short selling is severely constrained, stock lending rates will have to fall to relatively low levels to make it worth a short-seller borrowing stock. As a result, in many markets, the implied financing rates are often below money market interest rates.

These factors, combined with the existence of stock index futures, create an opportunity for option market-makers. They can effectively hedge using futures and, because of the possibility that the implied financing rates are

[4] For more on this idea, see L. Chew, "Sex, Swaps and Arbitrage," *Risk*, June 1991.

Figure 11.5
Calculating an Equity Swap Price from Share Price Index Futures

Ignoring futures cash/adjustments
Requires Solver Add-in to be loaded

	C	D	E	F	G	H	I	J	K	L	M	N
6	**Swap details**											
7	Start date		18-Aug-00		Face value			10,000,000.00				
8	Expiry date		31-Dec-01		Compounding frequency			4		**Solver solution**		
9	Years		1.37		Equity leg day count			365		Swap rate	5.7515%	
10	Projected dividend yield		3.00%		Interest leg daycount			365		Current swap rate	6.3692%	
11										implied margin	0.6177%	
12										paid to	Equity receiver	
13	Underlying S&P/ASX 200				Implied		Implied	Implied forward financing cost		Coupon financing costs		
14	Month	Expiry date	Futures	Days	financing	Discount	forward	Forward	Present	Coupon	Coupon	
15			price	in period	rate	factor	yield	cash flows	value	cash flows	present value	Difference
16	Today	18-Aug-00	3344.2			1.000000			7,527,662.92		7,527,662.92	–
17	Sep-00	30-Sep-00	3354.0	43	5.4875%	0.993577	5.487%	646,469.33	642,316.95	677,576.68	673,224.50	
18	Dec-00	31-Dec-00	3377.0	92	5.6518%	0.979524	5.692%	1,434,647.74	1,405,272.05	1,449,698.95	1,420,015.08	
19	Mar-01	31-Mar-01	3397.0	90	5.5613%	0.966855	5.314%	1,310,384.22	1,266,951.01	1,418,183.76	1,371,177.49	
20	Jun-01	30-Jun-01	3425.0	91	5.7908%	0.952260	6.148%	1,532,673.09	1,459,502.63	1,433,941.36	1,365,484.38	
21	Sep-01	30-Sep-01	3460.0	92	6.0978%	0.936188	6.811%	1,716,688.33	1,607,143.26	1,449,698.95	1,357,190.97	
22	Dec-01	31-Dec-01	3479.0	92	5.9425%	0.924723	4.919%	1,239,805.40	1,146,477.03	1,449,698.95	1,340,570.50	
23												
			1.0029	0.0249	5.4875%							

Implied equity swap pricing

Swap type	Equity leg	Interest leg	Margin	
Equity-to-fixed (qtrly)	All ords	5.7515%		
Equity-to-floating (qtrly)	All ords	Bank bill	0.618%	margin paid to equity receiver

Notes:

(1) This model ignores convexity and funding adjustments.

(2) The calculations are summarized below for the second period (row 17):

Description	Cell	Formula
Days to expiry	F17	=D17–D16
Implied financing yield	G17	=(E17/$E$16–1+$E$10/$J$9*(D17–$D$16))*$J$9/(D17–$D$16)
Discount factor	H17	=+$H$16/(1+G17*(D17–$D$16)/$J$10)
Implied forward yield	I17	=+(H16/H17–1)*$J$10/F17
Forward cash flows	J17	=+I17*F17/$J$10*$J$7
Present value	K17	=+J17*H17
Coupon cash flows	L17	=+$M$9*F17/$J$9*$J$7
Coupon present values	M17	=+L17*H17
Difference	N16	=+M16–K16

(3) The total present values in cells J17 and L 17 are given by summing the cells immediately below each of these totals.

(4) The Excel solver function (Solver.xla) was used in this calculation using the following inputs:

Input description	Cell
Target cell	N16
Equal to value of	0
By changing cells	M9

different from the floating index, there are opportunities to make substantial returns from equity swaps. Most noticeably, if the financing rates are below floating rates, then the dealer can possibly arbitrage this pay equity/receive floating without any margins and hedge by selling SPI futures.

In the remainder of this section, we will examine first, how to price an equity swap using futures prices and then we will determine the existence of any fixed margins. These pricing inputs can then be applied to the valuation model developed in *Figure 11.4.*

Figure 11.5 takes the strip of prevailing futures prices on the Sydney Futures Exchange's Share Price Index futures contracts and determines the implied financing cost of a security with a little less than one and a half years to expiry. Effectively, this calculation uses the forward pricing formula to determine the implied financing cost for each futures rollover date. These rates are zero-coupon financing rates to each futures expiry date. However, an equity swap is effectively a series of payments, in this case on each futures expiry date. Therefore, we need to determine the coupon-based financing rate that would apply from today, until expiry of the swap with quarterly rollovers.

This is where we apply the forward pricing logic previously used for short-term interest rate contracts. We have calculated the zero-coupon financing rates and we know from this, we can generate discount factors. From this, we can generate the forward financing yields (see the formula in column H and I). Once these are calculated, we can directly apply the logic from *Figure 9.19* to determine the coupon-paying financing rate that has an equivalent present value to the present value of the stream of financing charges implied by the forward financing charges. (That is, we calculate a yield which makes the value in cell M16 equivalent to K-16.) The result of this calculation is a par coupon financing rate for the term of the swap. This is effectively the fair value of the fixed rate for an equity-to-fixed swap. To determine the pricing of an equity-to-floating swap we need to enter into an offsetting fixed-to-floating interest rate swap at the prevailing 1.37-year swap rate of 6.3692%. This will convert the interest rate leg into a floating-rate leg based on bank bill minus a margin of 0.6177% pa. Normally, the margin is expressed against the equity leg of the swap, so in this case the equity receiver would receive the equity return plus this fixed margin of 0.6177% pa.

Using this technique, we can determine a range of equity swap prices for each major maturity category and this can be used by market-makers as the basis of their price-making to clients. In this example, the implied margin is probably overstated, as the liquidity in the back month SPI futures is very low and executing a transaction of this size would probably move the market against a market-maker executing a hedge and significantly erode the margin. Even in more liquid markets such as the S&P 500, a buffer should be added for likely slippage in the futures market and additional transaction and funding costs.

> ***Note***
> An important point to note when hedging an equity swap is that the only outright futures position should be in the front futures expiry month. In this example, if we entered into outright hedges in all expiry months, we would "overhedge" the swap by a factor of six. There is an exposure to the price spread between expiry months and this should be hedged with inter-month spread positions, i.e., simultaneously buying and selling consecutive delivery months.

In order to value swaps, we can load the outputs from the futures pricing model into the single-rate bond model developed in *Figure 11.4* or else we can extend the forward pricing model to include valuation.

FURTHER READING

- Francis, J.C., W.W. Toy, and J.G. Whitaker. *The Handbook of Equity Derivatives*, Irwin 1995 (see Chapter 7).

SUMMARY

In this chapter, we examined features and the underlying price and value drivers of equity swaps. We discussed synthetic replication of equity swaps and we developed models to value plain vanilla equity swaps.

SELF-TEST QUESTIONS

1. Describe the four main forms of equity swaps.
2. Describe a distinguishing feature of equity swaps, compared to interest rate and FX swaps, in terms of cashflow.
3. Assume you are valuing a US$100 million 2-year equity swap with quarterly rollovers and an equity return that incorporates dividends. The traded stock index price is 2120 and the swap floating rate is 5.85% pa plus 0.10%. Calculate the value of the swap from the perspective of the equity

receiver and the floating rate payer one month later, if the index is now 2000, the floating rate is 6%, the margin is 0.20% and the swap rate is 6.5%? Dividends accrue at a rate of 4% pa.

4. Assume the following information and calculate the break even index level of the equity swap.

Start date	August 15, 2001
Maturity date	November 12, 2001
Days to maturity	89
Current stock price index	600
Include dividends	Yes
Floating interest rate % pa	5.90%
Expected dividend yield % pa	2.80%
Fixed margin % pa	0.00%

Part 4

Options

CHAPTER 12

OPTION FUNDAMENTALS

The models developed in this chapter are saved as Microsoft Excel™ files in the enclosed disk.

OVERVIEW

In this chapter we discuss the key determinants of the price and value of options. We outline the importance of expected price distributions and volatility and we examine the Black-Scholes option pricing model and look at how it can be used to price a generic asset. At the end of this chapter we will have examined the following pricing and valuation models:

- simple binomial option model;
- normal and log-normal distributions;
- the Black-Scholes model for an asset which pays no income;
- models for calculating the "Greek letters," i.e., delta, gamma, lambda, theta and rho.

Option pricing introduces a substantial valuation complexity—uncertainty. To value an option we need to estimate the likely future behavior of the underlying asset. This chapter will focus on the key variables driving option prices and values.[1]

12.1 INTRODUCTION

In the two decades since the commencement of trading in options on the Chicago Board Options Exchange (CBOE), the range of underlying instruments and option types has expanded enormously. As we saw in Chapter 1, while the level of turnover in options generally remains lower than that of forwards, futures and swaps, there is a longer term trend that has the proportion of option volume rising relative to total derivative turnover. Further, the volume statistics tend to

[1] In accordance with the aims of this book, we will focus on pricing and valuation of options rather than their uses and applications. For an excellent, non-mathematical view of the practical use and trading of options see Sheldon Natenberg's *Option Volatility and Pricing*, Probus 1994.

understate the use of options because options tend to be "bought and held" and are traded less often during their lifetime than forward-based instruments.

> **Note**
> Options tend to be used as specific, often complex risk management tools for end-users, whereas futures, forwards and swaps represent the tools used by financial intermediaries to manage their day-to-day market risk.

As we will see in the following chapters, the use of options reflects uncertainty about the future price of an asset or the interest rate on a borrowing. The greater this uncertainty, or risk, the more likely it is an option will be used to manage that risk. As a consequence, the use of options relative to other derivatives is higher in riskier assets such as the equity and commodity markets. As the turnover in all instruments in the market is dwarfed by the volume in the 'less-risky' short-term interest rate markets, then it stands to reason that options' share of total derivative business will be lower.

12.2 WHAT IS AN OPTION?

12.2.1 General Description

The definitions of the two basic types of options are:

- a call option is the right, but not the obligation, to buy a specified quantity of an underlying asset at an agreed exercise price on (or before) an agreed expiration date;
- a put option is the right, but not the obligation, to sell a specified quantity of an underlying asset at an agreed exercise price on (or before) an agreed expiration date.

In exchange for this right, the buyer of an option will pay an upfront premium to the option writer or grantor (seller of the option). If the option can be exercised only on the expiration date it is a *European option*, if it can be exercised *prior or on* the expiration date it is an *American option*.

These definitions illustrate the mechanics of an option contract, and also explain the economics of the pricing and valuation of an option. An option contract is like a "soft" or one-sided forward contract. A forward purchase is a commitment to buy an underlying instrument at a future date. A call option gives the same right to purchase the underlying instrument, *but only if the option buyer chooses to exercise*. Therefore, the option buyer is obliged only to exercise the forward purchase if the *market price* of the underlying instrument is *higher* than the *exercise* price, otherwise the option buyer will abandon the call and purchase the underlying instrument at the lower market price. The buyer of an option gets the best of both worlds, protected if the price rises but benefitting if the price falls. This protection element is often used to describe purchasing options as equivalent to taking out insurance.

12.2.2 The Value of an Option at Expiry

This "one-sided," or asymmetric feature, of an option is important for pricing and valuation. In the case of a forward contract, an option's forward value is equivalent to the profit or loss calculated by the difference between the value of the contract at the *traded forward price* and the value at the prevailing *market forward price*. However, with an option, the forward value will never be a loss—the option buyer will not exercise an option if he or she will lose money. As a result, the forward value of an option will either be zero or positive. This is summarized as follows:

- **Call Options** Calls will only be exercised if the underlying price (S) is *above* the exercise price (E), otherwise it is cheaper to buy the underlying security directly from the market. At expiry, the value of the call will be $S - E$, if it is positive or zero.

$$\boxed{\text{Value at expiry} = \text{Maximum}(0, S - E)}$$

- **Put Options** Puts will only be exercised if the underlying price (S) is *below* the exercise price (E), otherwise it is more beneficial to sell the underlying security at the higher market price. So, at expiry, the value will be either $E - S$, if it is positive or zero.

$$\boxed{\text{Value at expiry} = \text{Maximum}(0, E - S)}$$

The value of an option at expiry can be illustrated using payoff diagrams. In *Figure 12.1*, we look at the value of a call option on one share with an exercise price of US$10. If the price at expiry is *less* than US$10 then the option value is zero; if the price is *more* than US$10, the value is a positive number equal to $S - E$.

12.2.3 The Price of an Option: The Expected Forward Value

Estimating the market price of an option prior to its expiry revolves around the question—how much would an option buyer pay for a one-sided forward contract? The answer is related to the forward price of the underlying instrument. However, the relationship is not just to the current forward price, but also the expected underlying price at expiration of the option. This is the complicating feature of an option versus a forward—expected movements in the underlying price will influence the current price of an option.

Figure 12.1
The Value of a Call Option at Expiry

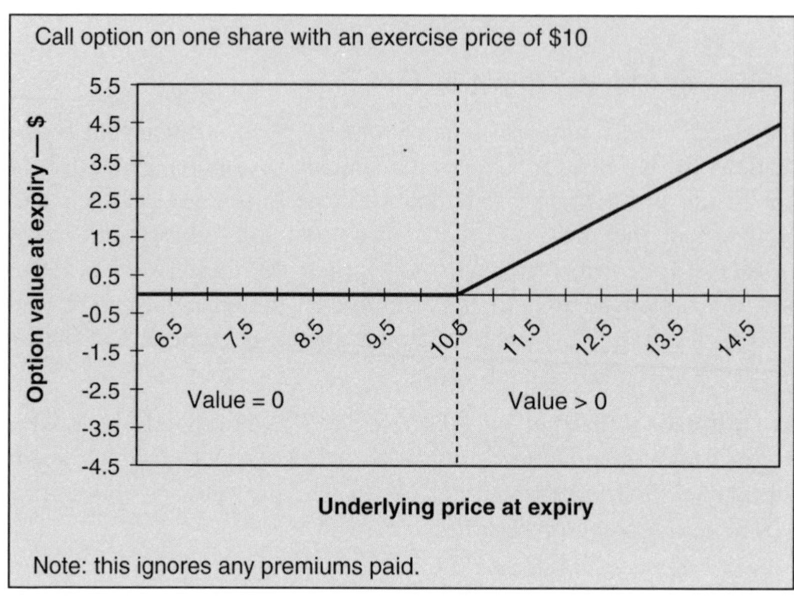

For most financial instruments, the forward price is determined purely by the prevailing cash price of a financial instrument and the cost of carry. An assumption behind this pricing formula is that there is an equal chance at expiry of the underlying price being *above* or *below* where it is today. So, at expiry there is an even possibility that the value of the forward will be a gain or a loss. Given this assumption, the expected value of the forward at expiry is the same as the time it is executed—zero.

In the case of a forward, this assumption allows us to separate the forward pricing calculation from any expectation of the future value of the contract. This is not valid for an option because, as we saw in Section 12.1.2, the value of an option at expiry is asymmetrical, or "lopsided" and it is either zero or positive. So, in the case of a call, provided there is time to expiry and some possibility that the price will be above the exercise price, the expected value of the option today will be positive; that is, we will pay an amount of money today, the premium, which is equivalent to the present value of the expected forward value of the option. We can express these relationships for a call option mathematically as follows:

$$\text{Expected forward value} = E[\text{Max}(0, S - E)] \geqslant 0$$
$$\text{Option premium} = PV\,(\text{Expected forward value}) \geqslant 0$$

Unlike other forwards and swaps, there is a direct relationship between the option premium or price and the expected forward value of the option. Essentially, option pricing theory revolves around estimating the expected forward value. Given that the expected forward value is unknown when the option is executed, we need to model the likely forward value outcomes of the option in order to derive the *expected* forward value.

> ***Note***
> At any given time, the market price of an option, its premium, will be related to its expected forward value. This differs from the actual forward value of an option contract that, like any derivative, is determined by the difference between the dollar value of the price at which the option was traded and the current market price.

12.3 OPTION PRICING: MODELING UNCERTAINTY

In the previous section we identified the essence of the option pricing problem: estimating price movements in uncertainty. In the case of option pricing, *uncertainty* is defined as the fact that we do not know what the price of the underlying instrument will be on the option expiry date. Given that it is possible that a price could be anywhere between zero and infinity by the time an option expires, this is a difficult estimation problem. In order to develop option pricing models, we need to be able to make some assumptions regarding the nature of the distribution of the underlying instrument price.

The first assumption we make about the distribution of this uncertainty is that the movement in the underlying price is random, but that its potential range of outcomes can be defined with specific probabilities.

There has been considerable effort put into the distribution of underlying prices and incorporating these into option pricing models—this is particularly the case with interest rate and energy market options.[2] Given that the objective of this book is not that of an option theory text, but more a pragmatic approach to building robust models for nonmathematicians, most of these models are outside our scope. However, it is useful to review the concepts underlying all option pricing models in the following chapter.

[2] If you are interested in a review of these more complex interest rate models, see John Hull (1993) Chapter 15. The development of non-oil energy markets since the mid-1990s has seen the creation of options with extremely complex price dynamics (particularly electricity). An excellent text on these new markets is Les Clewlow and Chris Strickland, *Energy Derivatives: Pricing and Risk Management*, Lacima (2000).

In Sections 12.3.2 and 12.3.3, we shall examine the approaches to modeling uncertainty by analyzing:

- a very simplistic discrete time, or binomial, approach to defining the distribution;
- a continuous time model underlying the Black-Scholes model.

First we look at the requirements of an option pricing model.

12.3.1 The Requirements of an Option Pricing Model

Option pricing models are required to determine both the price and value of an option contract, thereby deriving an estimate for the current price of an option. The *value* of an open option contract is the present value of the difference in the traded option price and the current option price.

Depending on the requirements of the organization, the option pricing model can range in complexity from a simple binomial model, to Black-Scholes, to sophisticated analytical and simulation models. However, regardless of the complexity of the underlying calculations, the process of modeling an options price requires the following steps to be performed:

- determine a range of possible underlying prices at option expiry;
- assign probabilities to each price outcome;
- using these prices and probabilities, determine the expected value of these outcomes;
- calculate the present value of the expected value.

12.3.2 Discrete Time: A Simple Binomial Model

A very simple approach to describing the distribution of the underlying price is to say that:

> *At any point in time, the underlying price can only move up or down by a discrete amount.*

This is referred to as the *binomial approach* because it consists of breaking the time to expiry of an option into discrete points, each of which consists of two possibilities: the price going up or the price going down.

The simplest, and the least likely to be realistic of the binomial models is the 1-step model; that is, there is only one time period till the expiry of the option and the underlying price can only move up or down from its current position.

A Simple 1-Step Model

Suppose we buy a European call option on a share that expires tomorrow and has an exercise price of US$141. Given that the underlying price is US$140 today and on any day we know that share prices have an equal chance of moving up or down by US$5, what is the premium of the call today?

The pricing problem is presented in *Figure 12.2*. If the share price can only be US$135 or US$145 tomorrow, then the forward value of the option will be either US$0 or US$4 respectively; that is, if the price tomorrow is US$135 then it is not worth exercising the call and it expires worthless. If the price is US$145, then the call can be exercised at US$14, offering a gain of US$4. Given that there is an equal chance of the price going up as there is of it going down, the price of the call is:

$$\begin{aligned}\text{Call premium} &= \$4 \times 50\% + \$0 \times 50\% \\ &= \$2\end{aligned}$$

This model is extremely simplistic as the possible range of price movements by tomorrow is far wider than US$5, and the frequency with which these price movements is made is much greater than one per day. Furthermore, with this analysis, the price cannot stay the same (i.e., US$140).

A Simple 2-Step Model

We can improve the accuracy of the model by increasing the number of binomial "nodes," i.e., the number of points at which the price moves up or down. *Figure 12.3* extends the previous example to a 2-step binomial model: the

Figure 12.2
A Simple 1-Step Binomial Model

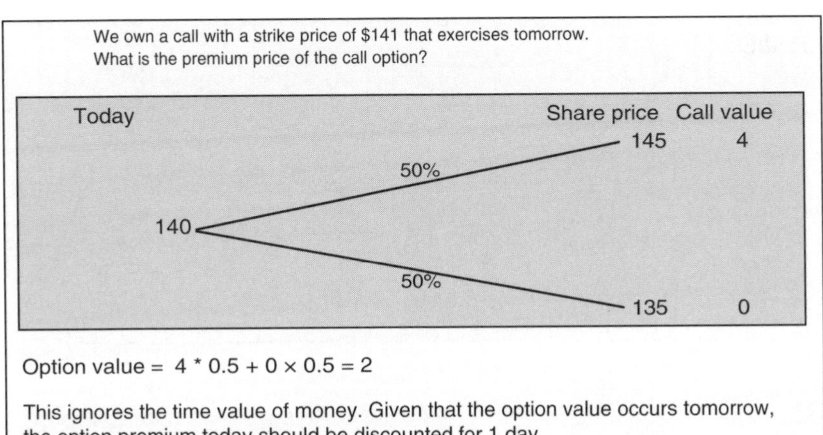

Figure 12.3
A Simple 2-Step Binomial Model

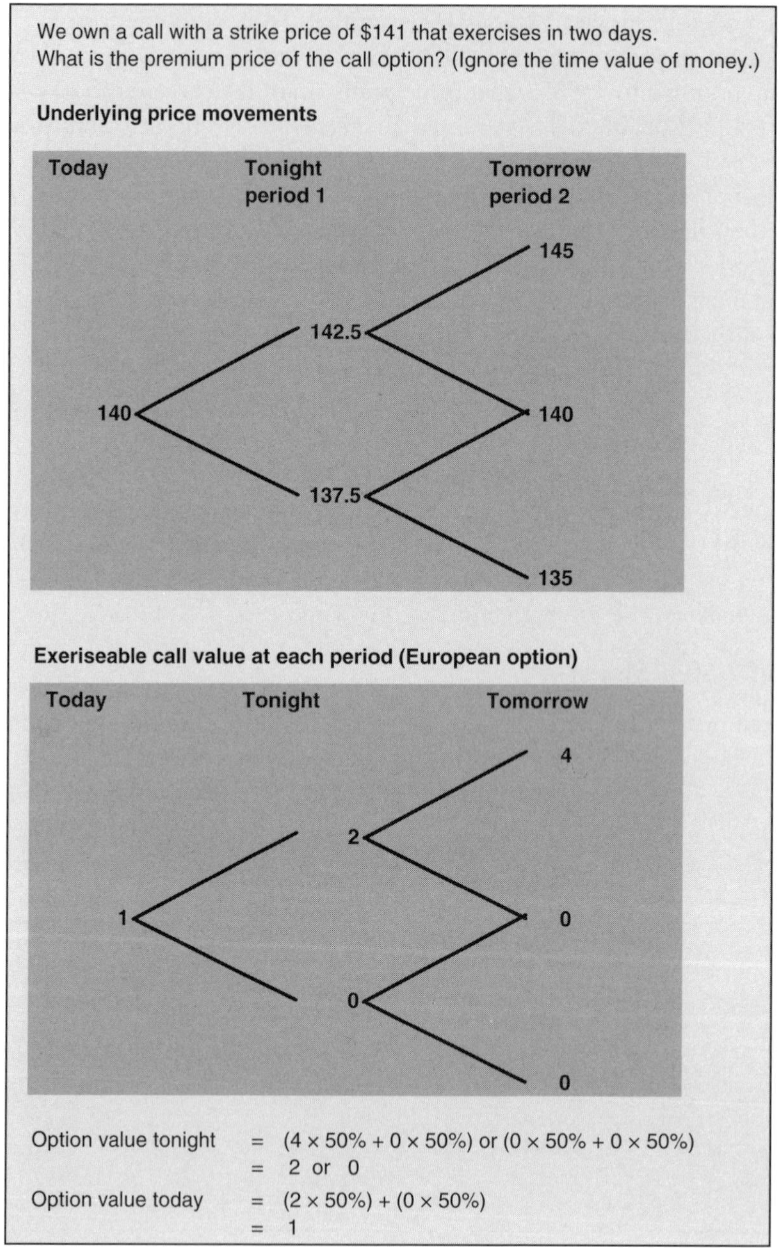

option still expires tomorrow; however, time has been broken into two and the periodic price movements have been halved. This increases the range of potential price outcomes over the life of the option giving four potential price results at expiry (two of which are US$140).

By increasing the number of discrete time periods, we move closer to providing a range of outcomes at expiry that is close to reality. In general, the greater the number of observations, the more accurate is the estimate of the call option value. In this example, the call premium at one step is US$2 and at two steps it is US$1. If we used a 30-step model the value is approximately US$1.50.

Using this process, we can create a model that creates a predefined pattern of potential outcomes. As we shall see in later chapters, this binomial approach can be employed successfully to price most options. The only constraint with the binomial model is that it is computationally intensive. In the 2-step model, the underlying price can follow four paths, and if we have 30 periods then we have more than one billion potential price paths.

> ***Note***
> Something that has been ignored in these simple examples is the time value of money. In both cases, the option values calculated are values that occur tomorrow. As the option premium is paid today, the forward values calculated above need to be present valued. Furthermore, most asset price movements are proportional to the current price rather than an absolute dollar value.

12.3.3 Continuous Time: Using the Normal Distribution

In the previous section, we saw that between using the binomial model the possible path of future underlying prices is built in discrete units of time and price movement; hence, it is described as a *discrete* time model.

The price distribution assumption underlying the Black-Scholes model is at the other end of the spectrum: time is assumed to be *continuous*; that is, the time to expiry is divided into an infinite number of time periods. At any point in time, the price movements are in infinitesimal increments and there are an infinite number of paths that the underlying price can follow to maturity. It can be thought of as using the binomial model with an infinite number of time periods.

Whereas the binomial model is unlike reality in that it describes price movements in discrete steps, the Black-Scholes model assumes that the underlying price is always trading and that there are no "gaps" in the price path followed. While the Black-Scholes assumption also seems somewhat unrealistic, the nature of the price behavior it describes does reasonably approximate the nature of liquid financial markets.

When we combine this continuous time approach with an assumption that the distribution of percentage changes in the underlying price are normally distributed, we can create an expected distribution of the underlying price until expiry of an option.[3] The advantage of the normal distribution is that it can be described purely by its mean and standard deviation.

Figure 12.4 plots a normal distribution of a series of continuous numbers with a mean of zero and a standard deviation of one. The mean is the center point of the distribution and we know that for any set of numbers, 66% of the observations will fall within one standard deviation movement up and down in price.

> ***Note***
> It is important to remember that Black-Scholes assumes that the percentage change, or "return," of the underlying price is normally distributed. This means that the underlying price distribution is slightly different, as the lower the absolute price, the lower the change in absolute price given by a 1% change in the underlying price. As a result, the underlying price distribution tends to favor larger price increases than decreases. The distribution of the underlying price is usually described as log-normal. *Figure 12.8* contrasts a normal and log-normal distribution.

Figure 12.4
The Normal Distribution

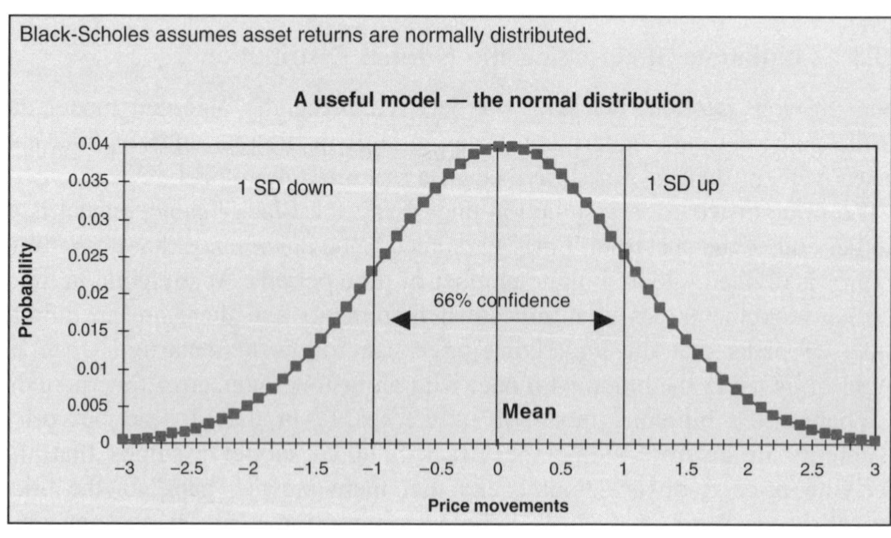

[3] This is usually described as the random walk assumption.

Figure 12.5
Comparing Normal and Log-Normal Distributions

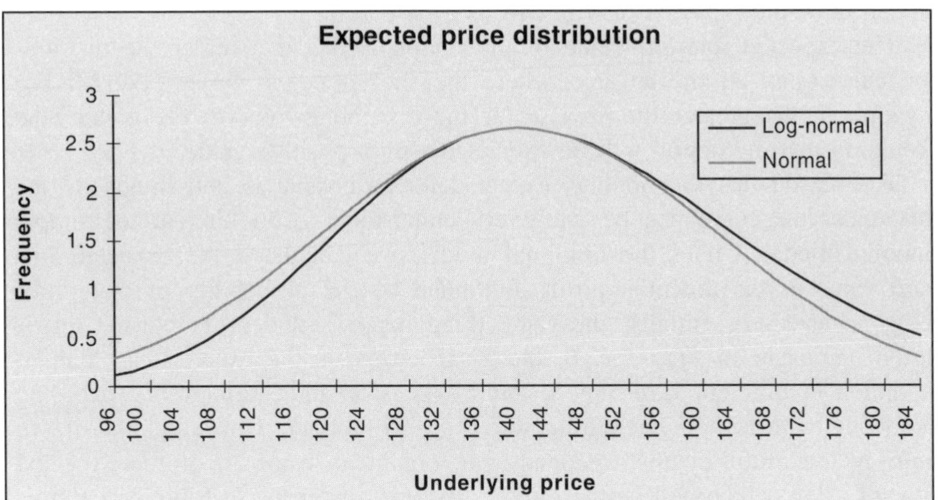

Fortunately, this log-normal assumption regarding asset prices is a reasonable assumption. There is considerable evidence to show that asset prices in many financial markets are log-normally distributed over time. It is important to note that these log-normal distributions usually require a considerable number of price observations; that is, the observed price distribution is moving toward being continuous. In the situation where the option has a very short time to expiry, the likely distribution of price changes is difficult to predict.

In terms of modeling the future, this normal distribution is extremely convenient. Provided we are willing to make an estimate of the standard deviation, or volatility, of the price distribution, we can determine the price we would pay for the option. We will use the following example to explain this concept.

Example

Assume the current price of a financial asset is US$100. We believe the asset price is log-normally distributed and that over the next year, volatility will be 10% pa. If we buy a 1-year European call with an exercise price (X) of US$112, how can we use the log-normal distribution assumption to determine the price of the option?

We know that at expiry of the option in 1-year's time, the value of the option will be zero if the underlying price (S) is *less* than X, and $S-X$ if S is *greater* than X. If we say that this asset has no cost of carry, then the expected future value of the asset price in one year's time is the same as the current spot price of US$100. This tells us that the mean of the expected change in price is zero, i.e., no change in price is expected. If we combine this with the 10% volatility as our estimate of the standard deviation, then we can draw the expected distribution as *Figure 12.6*.

The expected forward value of the option is the area under the distribution curve, i.e., all of the area where the spot price is above US$112. For any option, the greater the area under the distribution curve, the greater the likelihood that the option will be exercised with a positive value.

The reason that the option's expected forward value is determined by the area under the curve can be intuitively understood by looking at the simple binomial model. Under the binomial model, we calculated the expected forward value as the potential profit multiplied by the probability of that profit being achieved. Essentially, the same thing happens under the normal distribution approach. In *Figure 12.6*, the x-axis gives us the exercisable value of an option at different levels of S, the y-axis is an indication of the expected frequency with which each outcome of S will occur. Consequently, if we multiply the profit by the frequency, we obtain an estimate of the expected forward value, which will be the same as the area under the distribution curve.

> ***Note***
> An important point to note about using the normal distribution approach is that we are relying on the underlying price being a normal distribution. While over a long time period this can be approximately the case in a shorter time frame, the distribution can deviate from a "normal" shape. The premium given by an option pricing model should be treated as an *estimate of future outcomes* and all models rely on key assumptions about the uncertain future.

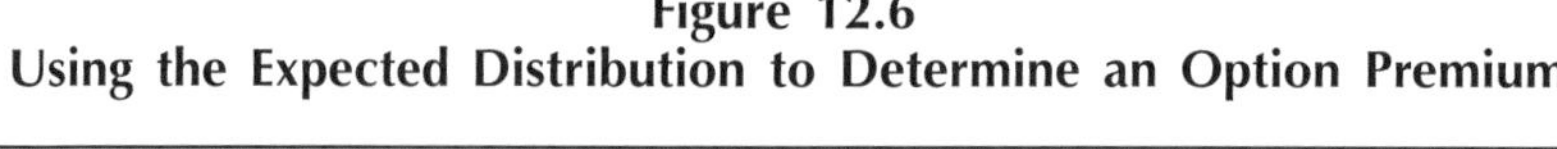

Figure 12.6
Using the Expected Distribution to Determine an Option Premium

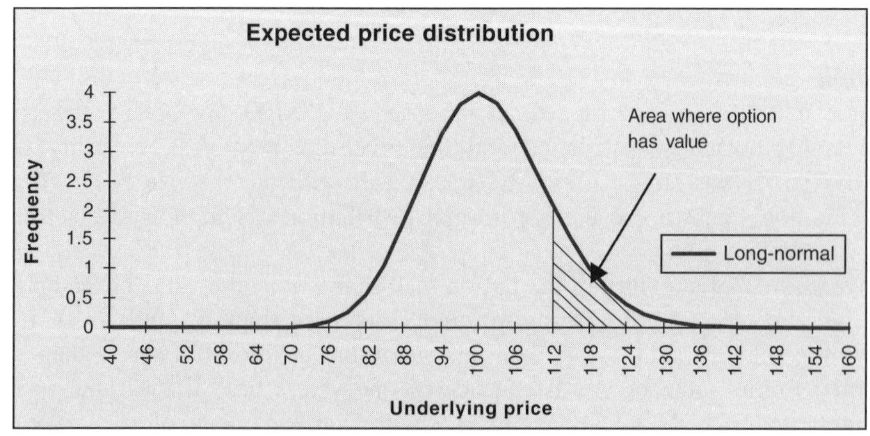

When we build an option pricing model using the continuous log-normal assumption, it must be able to convert this area under the curve into a dollar figure—this is what the Black-Scholes model achieves.

12.4 AN INTRODUCTION TO THE BLACK-SCHOLES FORMULA

12.4.1 The Black-Scholes Model

Before considering the requirements of specific asset classes, we will develop a generic version of the Black-Scholes model that can be applied to any asset class. This generic underlying asset is assumed to have the following characteristics:

- the underlying cash market is liquid and the underlying price is continuous in time (i.e., there are no jumps in price);
- there are no restraints on transacting in the cash market;
- the asset provides no income (this will be expanded upon later);
- there is an identifiable cost of funding the asset;
- the return on the asset for any period is normally distributed, making the distribution of the underlying asset price log-normally distributed;
- the interest rate and volatility are constant over time.

A further assumption we make about the option is that it is European; that is, it can only be exercised on its expiry date. While Black-Scholes can often be used as an estimate of the price of American-style options we have to be careful with how it is applied. American options are examined in Chapter 13.

Based on these assumptions, the Black-Scholes options pricing model for this generic asset is set out in *Figure 12.7.* Although the model appears complex, if we simplify some of the parameters, we can see the driving forces behind the value. In the case of the call formula, we can divide the formula into two components:

- the present value of the benefit of exercising the option $[S \times N(d_1)]$;
- the present value of the cost of exercise $[X \times \exp(-r \times t) \times N(d_2)]$.

That is, the price of a call is dependant on the relative position of the spot price, S, to the fixed cost of exercising that call at the strike price, X. Essentially, the model determines the likelihood of S being above X at expiry and potentially by how much. This is shown where S is above X and the time

Figure 12.7
The Black-Scholes Model

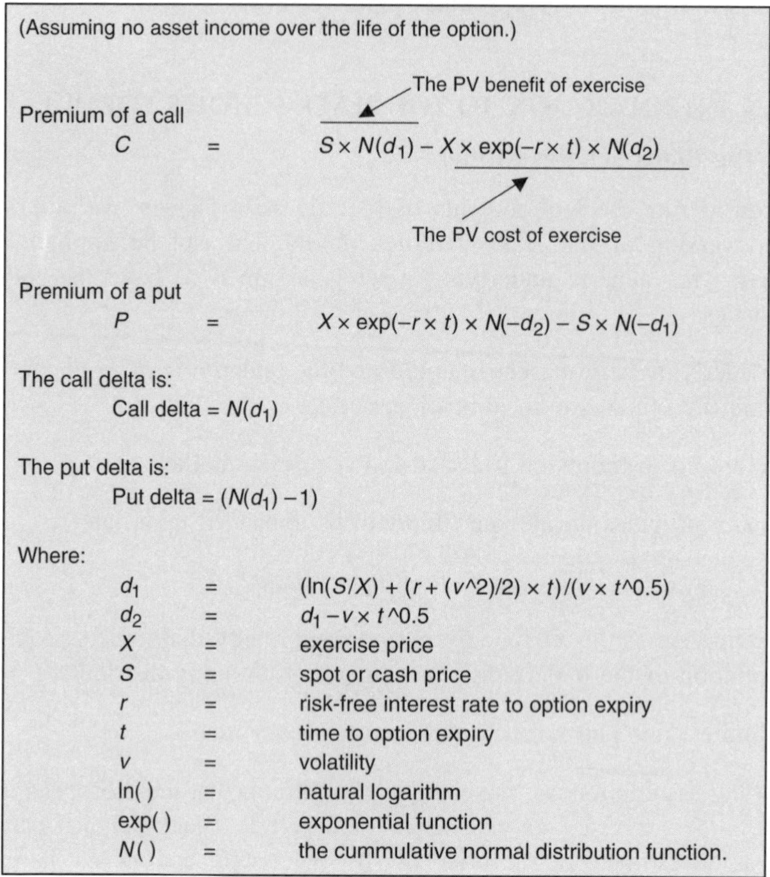

to expiry, t, to zero;[4] the terms $N(d_1)$ and $\exp(-r \times t) \times N(d_2)$ both have a value of 1 and the price of the option becomes $S - X$.

12.4.2 Using Black-Scholes to Price an Option

The main complication in Black-Scholes is the method used for estimating the cumulative normal distribution function. Spreadsheet software usually provides a normal distribution function;[5] however, if you are calculating "by hand," the most commonly used method is set out below.

[4] Strictly speaking, the value of t has to be fractionally greater than zero, because setting t to zero in the Black-Scholes model will produce an error.

[5] Within Microsoft Excel use the function "Normdist."

Cumulative Normal Distribution Estimation

The cumulative distribution for any variable z, which is greater than zero, can be approximated by:

$$N(z) = 1 - (1/\sqrt{2\pi})\exp(-z^2/2)(b_1k + b_2k^2 + b_3k^3 + b_4k^4 + b_5k^5)$$

Where:

$k = 1/(1+az)$
$a = 0.2316419$
$b_1 = 0.319381530$
$b_2 = -0.356563782$
$b_3 = 1.781477937$
$b_4 = -1.821255978$
$b_5 = 1.330274429.$

Source: Cox and Rubenstein (1985), p. 261.

Using this estimation, constructing a longhand option model is possible.[6]

Figure 12.8 provides a detailed step-by-step calculation example of the Black-Scholes model. In this case, we are pricing a European call option with exactly half a year to expiry. The underlying asset price, S, is US$25 and the exercise price, X, is US$26. The anticipated volatility (or standard deviation of the future distribution of price movements), V, is 35% pa and the risk-free interest rate over the next half year is 10% pa. The option premium given by the Black-Scholes model is US$2.54.

This option price can be divided into two components:

- **Intrinsic value** This is the current expected value of exercise or the amount the option is "in-the-money." This is given by the difference between the forward price and the exercise price.
- **Time value** This is the part of the price arising from the possibility that the underlying price might move further in-the-money over the remaining life of the option.

While this option looks to be out-of-the-money because the exercise price is above the current spot price, this is not the case. An option is, in fact, a form of forward contract and the underlying asset price is actually the current forward price. Black-Scholes assumes continuous compounding so the current forward price is given by:

$$\begin{aligned}\text{Forward price} &= S \times \exp(r \times t)\\ &= \$25 \times \exp(0.1 \times 0.5)\\ &= \$26.28.\end{aligned}$$

[6] Note that in the following models π is calculated by dividing 22 by 7.

Figure 12.8
Calculating the Price of a Call

(Note: this spreadsheet model also prices puts.)

Inputs

Row	Inputs		G
10	Option type (*P* or *C*)	*C*	
11	$S =$		\$25
12	$E =$		\$26
13	$v =$		35.00%
14	$t =$		0.5
15	$r =$		10.00%

Normal distribution constants

Row	Constant	J
10	$a =$	0.2316419
11	$b_1 =$	0.31938153
12	$b_2 =$	−0.356563782
13	$b_3 =$	1.781477937
14	$b_4 =$	−1.821255978
15	$b_5 =$	1.330274429

Row	Calculations		Result	Formula used
19	ln(*S*/*E*) =		−0.03922	=LN(G11/G12)
20	*v*^2**t*/2 =		0.030625	=(G13^2)/2*(G14)
21	*v***t*^0.5 =		0.247487	=G13*(G14^0.5)
23	d_1:	$d_2 =$	−0.03473	=(G19+G20)/G21
24		Adjust for *P* or *C* =	−0.03473	=IF(UPPER(LEFT(\$G\$10,1))="C",G23,−G23)
26	d_2 :	$d_2 =$	−0.28222	=G23–G21
27		Adjust for *P* or *C* =	−0.28222	=IF(UPPER(LEFT(\$G\$10,1))="C",G26,−G26)
29	$N(d_1)$:	*k* =	0.99	=1/(1+ABS(\$J\$10*G24))
30		1/(2*22/7)^0.5 =	0.398862	=1/(2*22/7)^0.5
31		EXP((−*z*^2)/2) =	0.999397	=EXP(((G24)^2*−1)/2)
32		Calculation =	0.4860	=(G30*G31*(\$J\$11*G29+\$J\$12*G29^2+\$J\$13*G29^3
33				+\$J\$14*G29^4+\$J\$15*G29^5))
34		$N(d_1) =$	0.486049	=IF(G24>0,1−G32,G32)
36	$N(d_2)$:	*k* =	0.94	=1/(1+ABS(\$J\$10*G27))
37		1/(2*22/7)^0.5 =	0.398862	=1/(2*22/7)^0.5
38		EXP((−*z*^2)/2) =	0.960959	=EXP(((G27)^2*−1)/2)
39		Calculation =	0.3888	=(G36*G37*(\$J\$11*G35+\$J\$12*G35^2+\$J\$13*G35^3
40				+\$J\$14*G35^4+\$J\$15*G35^5))
41		$N(d_2)) =$	0.38881	=IF(G27>0,1−G38,G38)
42		$N(d_2) \times \text{Exp}(-r \times t)$	0.369847	=+G39*EXP(−G15*G14)

Row	Results			
47	Option premium	– \$	2.54	=ROUND(ABS((G11*G33–G12*G40)),4)
48		– %of spot	10.14%	=G45/G11
49	Option delta =		48.60%	=G32

Therefore, the intrinsic value of this option is 28 cents and the time value is US$2.26.

The spreadsheet model underlying *Figure 12.9* can also be used to price puts and it will provide a robust model for pricing most plain vanilla options that do not pay any income over the life of the option.[7]

The relative simplicity of generating an option price using Black-Scholes makes it a useful and popular model for financial market participants. Other discrete time models, such as the binomial model, can represent a considerable processing task.

12.5 BLACK-SCHOLES RISK CHARACTERISTICS AND THE GREEK LETTERS

12.5.1 Option Risk Characteristics

The sensitivity of options to changes in key pricing parameters is considerably more complex than it is for forwards and swaps. Both price and value of options are highly sensitive to the underlying asset price, time and volatility. Furthermore, the nature of this sensitivity to one input can change substantially as any of the inputs change.

The best way to understand the sensitivity of an option to each of its inputs, or risk drivers, is by calculating the derivatives of the Black-Scholes model—referred to as the "Greek letters." These Greek letters summarize the change in the option price resulting from a small change in the relevant input with all other inputs kept constant.

Figure 12.9 summarizes the risk characteristics of the US$26 call from *Figure 12.8*, and identifies the relevant Greek letter. While the magnitude of the Greek letters depends on the characteristics of each option, the general influence of each input on an option is identified in the table at the bottom of *Figure 12.9.*

We shall briefly investigate the calculations behind these characteristics in the remainder of this chapter.

12.5.2 Sensitivity to Underlying Price: Delta and Gamma

The delta of an option is determined by the cumulative normal distribution calculation associated with the spot price and can be summarized as follows:

Delta formula:

$$\text{Call delta} = N(d_1)$$
$$\text{Put delta} = 1 - N(d_1)$$

[7] This means the model can be used to price instruments that pay "lumpy" income such as bonds and shares as long as the option expires prior to the next income payment date. This is discussed in more detail in the following chapter on equity options.

Figure 12.9
Option Risk Characteristics and the Greek Letters

By rearranging the Black-Scholes model, the risk sensitivities of the call option priced in *Figure 12.8* are presented in the following table.

Risk sensitivity	Greek letter	Black-Scholes value	Explanation
Premium sensitivity to spot price	Delta	56.65%	A $1 increase in *S* will change premium by = $ 0.5665
Delta sensitivity to spot price	Gamma	6.28%	A $1 increase in *S* will change delta by = 6.28%
Premium sensitivity to time	Theta	−3.4836	Divide by 365 to get daily time decay = $(0.0095)
Premium sensitivity to volatility	Vega or Lambda	6.8657	A 1% rise in *v* will change the premium by =$ 0.0687
Premium sensitivity to the interest rate	Rho	5.6963	A 1 % rise in *r* will change by premium by =$ 0.0570

The General influence of each input can be summarized as follows:

Influences on option value

Parameter	Call	Put
Price	+	−
Exercise price	−	+
Volatility	+	+
Time	−	−
Interest rates	+	−
Dividends	−	+

+ = Positive relationship
− = Negative relationship

Dividends and asset income will be discussed in the next chapter.

The delta value provides an estimate of how much the option premium will change due to a change in the underlying price. In our example the delta is 48.60%, meaning that a US$1 change in the underlying price will cause the option premium to change by 48.6 cents. In the case of a call, the underlying price and premium move in the same direction, while for a put there is a negative relationship (i.e., a rise in the underlying price will result in a fall in the put premium).

Some of the characteristics of a delta include:

- **Delta = 100%** Option value change is the same as the underlying price change and is likely to be exercised. The option is deeply "in-the-money."
- **Delta = 50%** Each change in the underlying price will cause half that price change in the option. The option is "at-the-money" and there is an equal chance that the option will be exercised or abandoned.

- **Delta = 0%** The option is insensitive to underlying price changes and is unlikely to be exercised—it is deeply "out-of-the-money."
- Bought calls and sold puts have positive deltas; bought puts and sold calls have negative deltas.

> ***Note***
> The delta of an option is equivalent to the hedge ratio concept we have already developed for forwards and swaps. Just as we used the dollar duration and PVBP to determine hedge strategies, the delta can be used to determine the appropriate hedge for an option.

The delta can be interpreted as the number of units of the underlying asset that are equivalent to the option position. So, in our example, if the call option entitled the buyer to purchase 1,000 units of the underlying asset upon exercise, then this is currently equivalent to owning 486 units of the underlying asset. If we wanted to hedge the option against changes in the underlying asset price, then we would sell 486 units of the underlying asset. This creates a "delta neutral" position, as changes in the option premium will be offset by a change in the value of the hedge. For example, a US$1 rise in the underlying asset would cause the value of the option to rise by US$486, which in turn would cause a US$486 loss on the hedge—giving a net change of US$0. This is the basic methodology of "delta hedging;" an option is hedged by an offsetting, but delta equivalent, position in the underlying asset. We will discuss this concept in more detail in later chapters.

The delta represents the first derivative of the Black-Scholes model with respect to price. If we plot the sensitivity of the option price to changes in the underlying price, the delta is the tangent to this curve at the prevailing price. This is shown in *Figure 12.10.*

As *Figure 12.10* shows, the option price sensitivity graph is curved; the tangent becomes steeper as the price rises. This is a unique characteristic of options: the delta can fall anywhere between zero and one; that is, the price sensitivity can vary from being insensitive to spot price movements, to the other extreme, of the spot price and the option price being perfectly correlated. What is more, this sensitivity and the underlying price are interrelated, as changes in the underlying price will change the delta. The sensitivity of the delta to changes in the underlying price is shown in *Figure 12.11* with the original half a year until expiry and also with just one week until expiry.

The delta sensitivity becomes more pronounced as an option approaches expiry. This creates considerable difficulty for those attempting to delta hedge an option position. As *Figure 12.11* shows, with only one week to

Figure 12.10
Sensitivity to Underlying Price — Delta

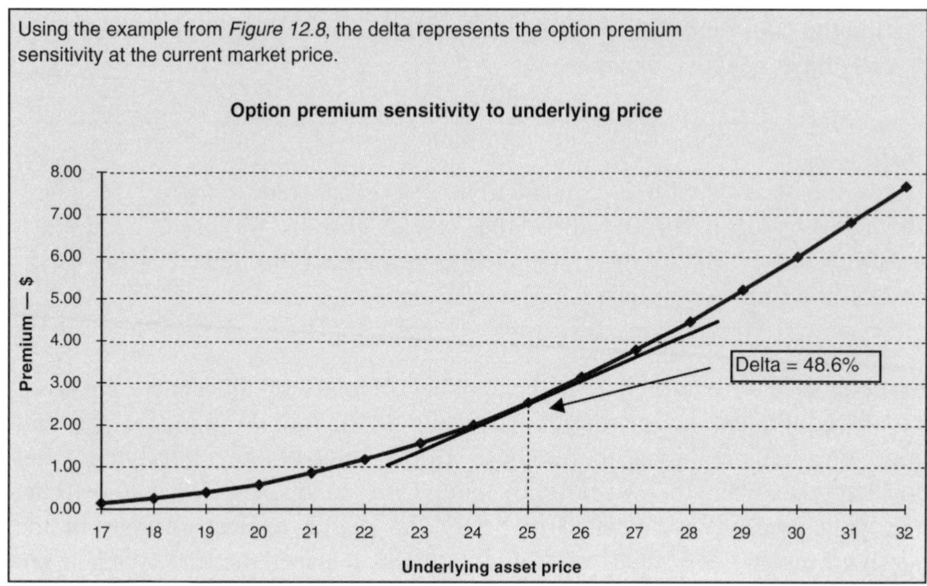

expiry, the option delta becomes extremely sensitive to small changes in the underlying price around the exercise price. For example, if the price rises from US$25 to US$26 the delta changes from 23% to 80%—an almost quadrupling of the amount of the underlying required to hedge the option.

This sensitivity of the delta to the underlying price is referred to as "gamma risk." The gamma is the second derivative of the Black-Scholes formula with respect to the underlying asset price and is calculated using the following rearrangement of the Black-Scholes formula:

Gamma formula for a call or put:

$$\text{Gamma} = [(1/\sqrt{2\pi}) \times \exp(-d1^2/2)]/(S \times v \times \sqrt{t})$$

A low gamma (e.g., less than 1%) indicates a stable delta that only changes slowly in response to movements in the underlying price. A high gamma option has a delta that is very sensitive to movements in the underlying price. High gammas are associated with "at-the-money" options with only a short time to expiry. In our US$26 call example, the option has a moderate gamma of 6.28% with half a year to expiry. However, with only one week to expiry, if the underlying price was still US$25, the gamma jumps to 25%.

Figure 12.11
Delta Sensitivity

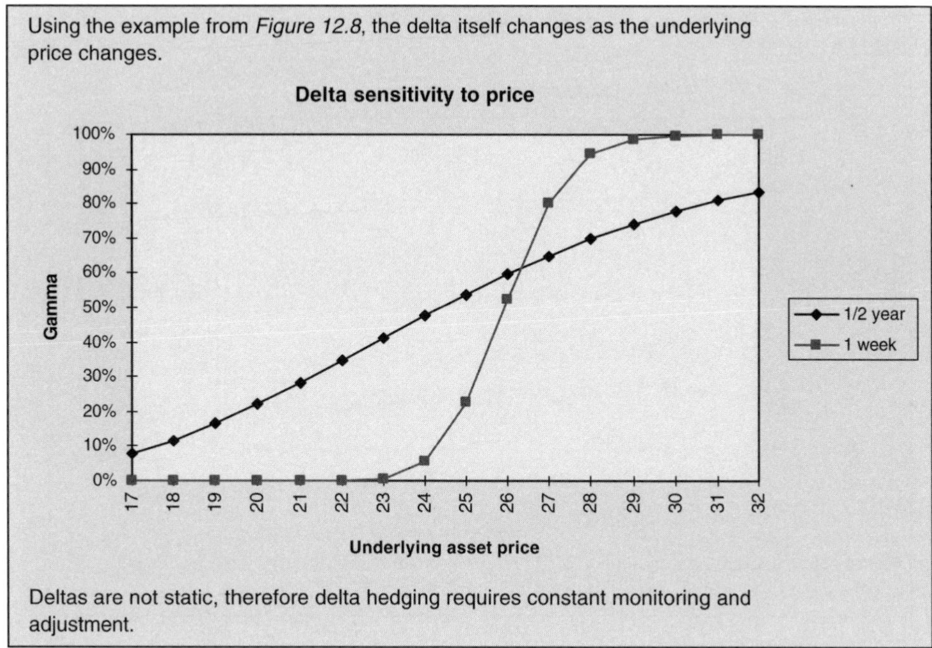

The option gamma is plotted for a range of underlying asset prices in *Figure 12.12.*

Bought options have positive gammas and sold options have negative gammas. In general, sold options with high gammas are viewed as undesirable as it is extremely uncertain as to whether or not they will be exercised and they are very difficult to hedge. It is common market practice by option traders to avoid option positions with less than one month to expiry.

> ***Note***
> As the delta of an option can be compared to duration and PVBP of a bond, gamma is a similar concept to bond convexity. Both are a measure of the stability of the relationship between the underlying asset price behavior and the value of its derivative instruments.

12.5.3 Sensitivity to Volatility: Vega or Lambda

As we saw earlier in this chapter, the price of an option is linked to the expected future distribution of the underlying asset price. When using

Figure 12.12
Gamma Sensitivity

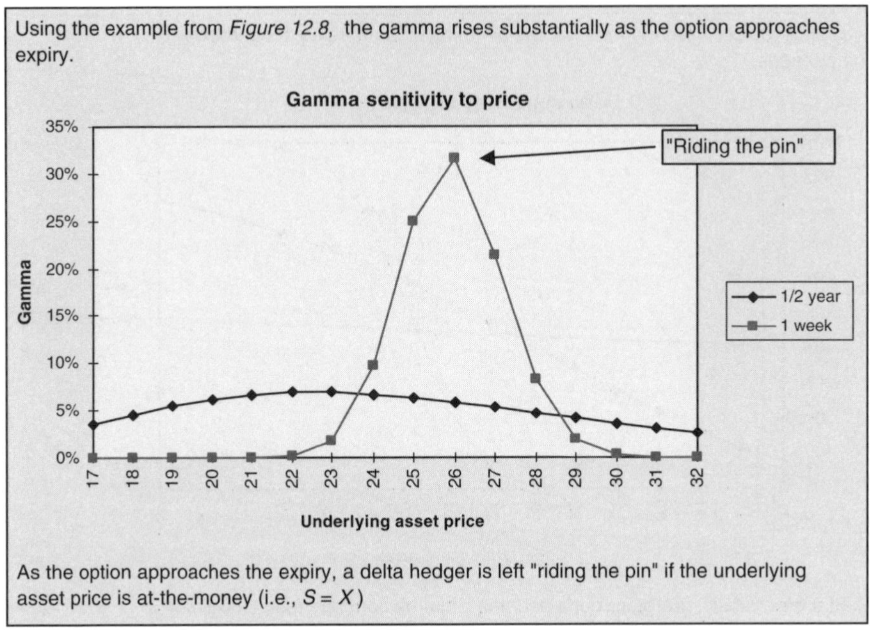

Black-Scholes, this distribution is summarized by the volatility. The volatility represents the annualized expected standard deviation of the return, or change, in the underlying asset price. As expectations of volatility change, so will the option premium. The Greek letter used to describe the sensitivity of the option premium to volatility can either be termed vega or lambda—we will use lambda. The volatility sensitivity of the US$26 call is shown in *Figure 12.13*.

The formula for calculating lambda can be expressed as follows:

$$\text{Lambda} = [(1/\sqrt{2\pi}) \times \exp(-d1^2/2)]/(S \times v \times \sqrt{t})$$

Bought options have positive lambda (long volatility) and sold options have negative lambda (short volatility). In our example, the option has a lambda of +6.8657, which implies that a 1% rise in volatility will increase the option premium by 6.87 cents.

Volatility only influences the time value component of the option price. So, volatility is more important for options with a significant proportion of

Figure 12.13
Volatility Sensitivity

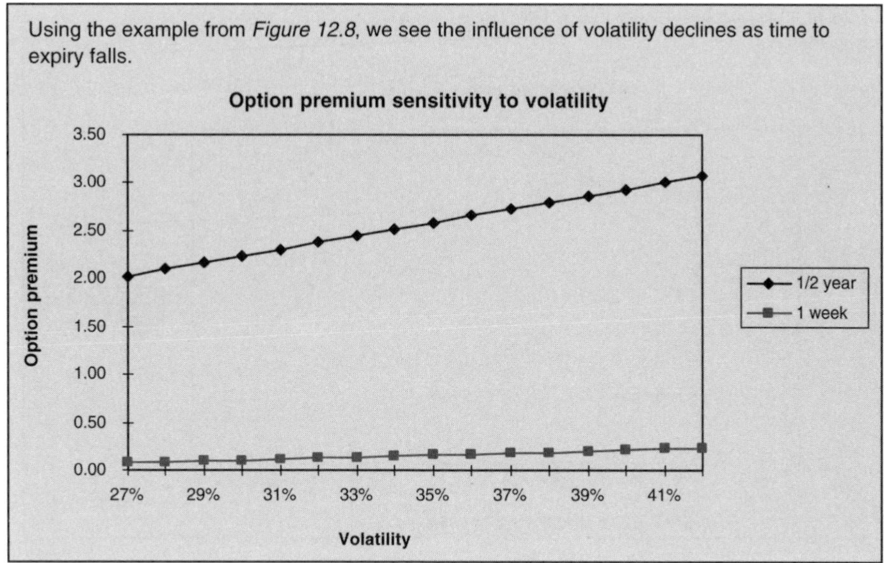

time value. As a result, volatility has a bigger impact on an option premium, the longer the term to expiry and the closer it is to being "at-the-money." This is demonstrated in *Figure 12.14*, which plots lambda against the underlying price. The impact of volatility close to expiry can be quite low. A common phenomenon with options is that there is an increase in volatility in the last weeks to expiry, in order to ensure that the option retains some time value.

12.5.4 Sensitivity to Time — Theta

Time gives an option value other than the current intrinsic value. The combination of volatility and time determines the range of potential underlying asset prices at expiry of an option. For a given level of annualized volatility, different time horizons will give a different range of outcomes; that is, the longer the time period, the more chance of larger price movements from the current underlying asset price.

This relationship between time and volatility is highlighted in *Figure 12.15* on page 340. It plots the log-normal distribution of the underlying asset price with volatility kept constant at 12% pa, but over different time horizons of three months, six months and one year. This implies the longer the term to expiry, the greater the value of out-of-the-money options. For example,

Figure 12.14
Lambda Sensitivity to Price

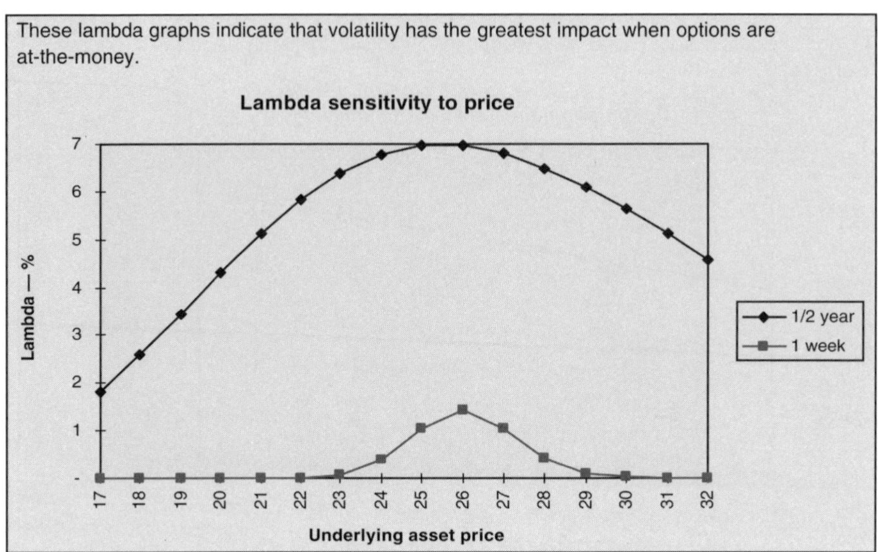

in *Figure 12.15* with only three months to expiry, a call option with a strike price of US$31 will have practically no expected future value and a premium of approximately zero. With one year to expiry, there is a strong possibility of a US$31 call being exercised and correspondingly, it will have a premium considerably greater than zero.

The passing of time decreases the value of both calls and puts; this process is referred to as time decay. Time decay is not a linear process and the closer to expiry of an option, the more rapid is the loss of an option's time value. The time decay of the option in our example over its remaining term to expiry is shown in *Figure 12.16* on page 340.

The rapid time decay of options with a relatively short time to expiry is another reason why option traders tend to avoid buying options with a term to expiry of under one month.

Theta is the Greek letter used to describe the rate of change of an option premium with respect to the passing of time. The formula for calculating theta is as follows:

$$\text{Theta}_{\text{call}} = -N'(d_1) \times S \times v/(2 \times \sqrt{t}) - r \times X \times \exp(-r \times t) \times N(d_2)$$

Where:

$$N'(d_1) = [(1/\sqrt{2\pi}) \times \exp(-d_1^2/2)]$$

Figure 12.15
Time, Volatility and Price Distributions

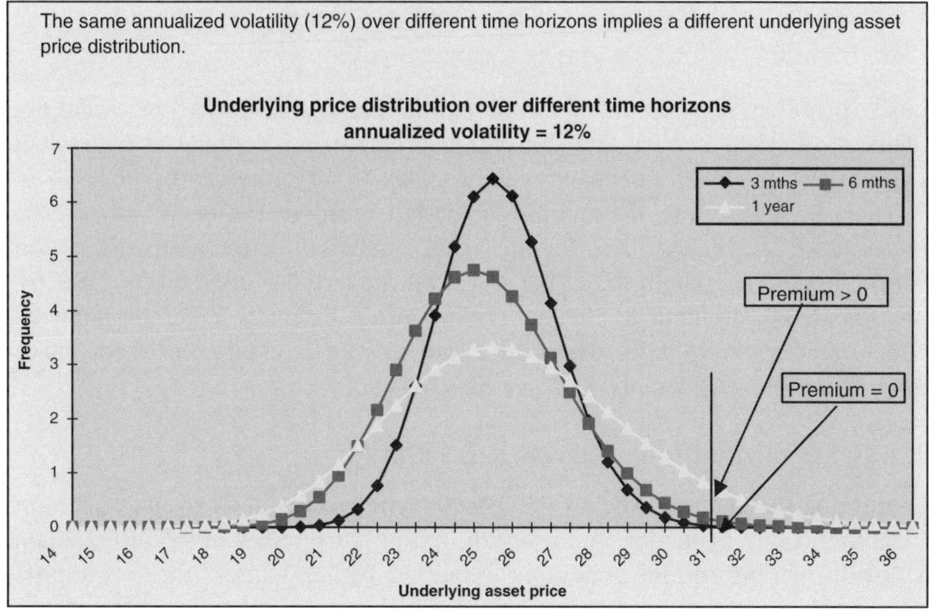

Figure 12.16
Option Time Decay

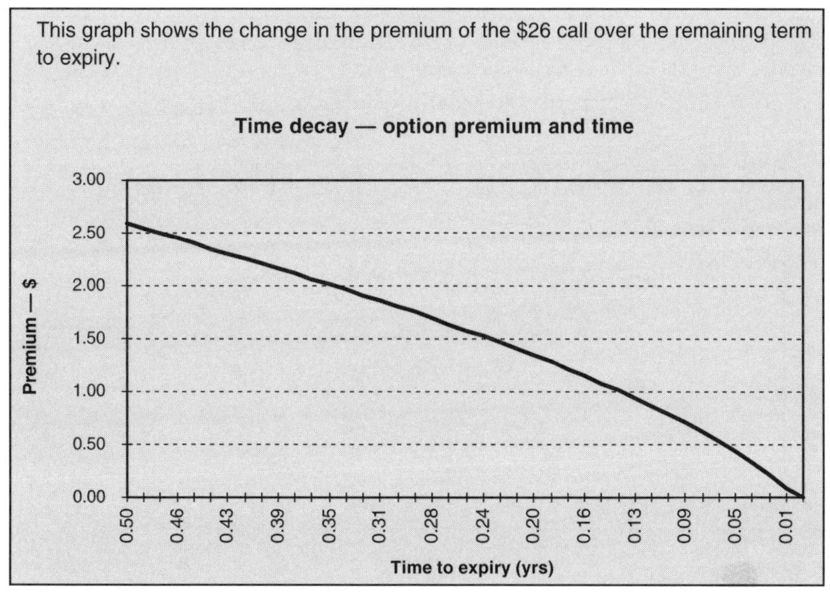

The theta formula for a put is:

$$\text{Theta}_{\text{put}} = -N'(d_1) \times S \times v/(2 \times \sqrt{t}) + r \times X \times \exp(-r \times t) \times N(-d_2)$$

These formulae provide theta as an annualized amount. In our example, a theta of –3.4836 implies that the option premium is declining at equivalent to US$3.4836 pa or 0.95 cents per calendar day (3.4836 divided by 365).

Theta is sensitive to the amount an option is in- or out-of-the money. As *Figure 12.17* shows, the theta for the US$26 call is greatest when the option is at-the-money (i.e., both the strike price and underlying price are at US$26). This sensitivity of theta to the underlying price becomes more pronounced as the time to expiry falls. With only one month to expiry the theta curve shown becomes considerably more variable.

12.5.5 Sensitivity to the Interest Rate: Rho

The role of the interest rate in the Black-Scholes model is to take account of the time value of money. A European option is exercised at maturity. When an option pricing model generates expected future values, these amounts are forward values that need to be converted to a present-value amount to determine the premium. In the Black-Scholes formula for a call, the first term, the

Figure 12.17
Theta Sensitivity to Underlying Price

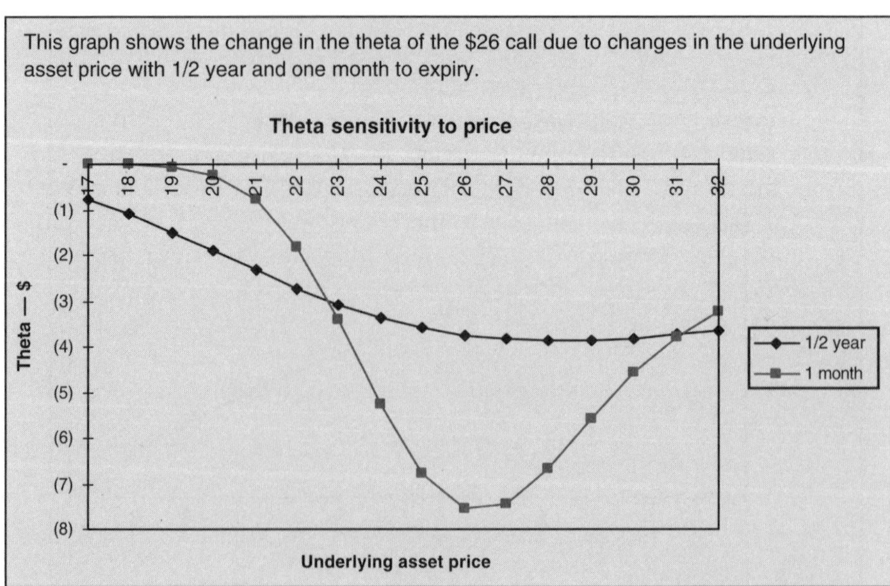

present-value benefit of exercising, is expressed as a present-value amount today, while the second term, the present-value cost of exercising, contains a present-value component, $\exp(-r \times t)x$, which converts the exercise value to an amount today.

> ***Note***
> It is worth noting that this present-value calculation uses the exponential approach. As we saw in Chapter 3, this type of approach to present value implies that the interest rate used in the formula is a continuously compounded zero-coupon interest rate. As most observed interest rates have a specific compounding frequency, we should convert the observed interest rates to a continuously compounded basis before entering them into the Black-Scholes model. In practice, this step is often ignored and traders enter observed market data directly, as the impact on the option value is viewed as minimal. While this is the case for short-dated options, the impact on longer dated options (e.g., longer than one year) can be important. If we are using continuously compounded zero-coupon rates, we must generate a zero-coupon yield curve using the methods described in Chapter 5 and then convert to a continuously compounded basis using the formula from Chapter 3, Section 3.2.3.

Another way of viewing the interest rate in the Black-Scholes formula is that it determines the cost of carry in the forward instrument underlying the option calculation. It does this by reversing the usual forward calculation, where it determines the present value of the forward exercise price. We will look at changing this to a more typical forward calculation when we consider options on futures. Furthermore, when we introduce assets that pay income in the next chapter, we will enter the asset income into the model in order to correctly determine the underlying asset's cost of carry.

The relationship of a call option to the interest rate is a positive one. As the interest rate rises, the implied forward price rises and the option moves further into-the-money. The interest sensitivity of the US$26 call is plotted in *Figure 12.18*. The sensitivity of a put to the interest rate is negative, as a higher interest rate tends to push the implied forward price further out-of-the-money.

As *Figure 12.18* reveals, the option premium tends to be substantially less sensitive to changes in the interest rate than to changes in the underlying price, volatility and time.

The Greek letter covering sensitivity to the interest rate is rho:

> Rho formula for a call:
> $$\text{Rho}_{\text{call}} = X \times t \times \exp(-r \times t) \times N(d_2)$$
> Rho formula for a put:
> $$\text{Rho}_{\text{put}} = -X \times t \times \exp(-r \times t) \times N(-d_2)$$

Figure 12.18
Option Premium Sensitivity to Interest Rates

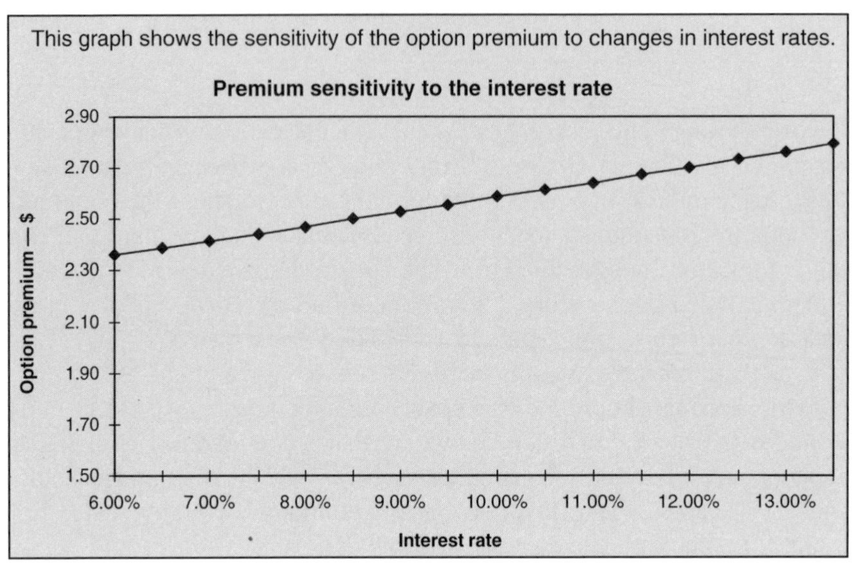

The value of rho given by Black-Scholes is expressed as the impact of a 1% change in the interest rate on the premium value. In the US$26 call example, a rho of 5.6963 can be interpreted as a 1% rise in the interest rate will increase the premium by 5.6963 cents.

12.6 THE RELATIONSHIP BETWEEN OPTIONS AND FORWARDS

In the introduction to option pricing (Section 12.1), options were described as a "one-sided" forward transaction. This section examines the relationships between forwards and options a little further by examining:

- the synthetic replication of an option;
- put-call parity.

12.6.1 Synthetic Replication of an Option

In our discussions on forwards and swaps in previous chapters, we developed approaches for synthetically replicating derivative transactions. We were then able to use these synthetic relationships to determine the "building blocks" for our pricing and valuation models. In this section, we examine an approach for synthetically replicating an option. However, it is worth noting upfront that synthetically replicating an option is open to considerable imperfections.

We know that the current sensitivity of an option to movements in the underlying price is determined by its delta. Suppose we have sold a call option with six months to expiry on 100 shares. If the delta is 50%, a US$1 rise or fall in the underlying price will result in a US$50 rise or fall in the premium of the option (US$0.50 × 100). This change in price can be replicated, for small changes in price, by purchasing 50 shares. So if the underlying share price rose by US$1 change then the estimated US$50 loss on the call option will be offset by a US$50 gain on the purchased shares.

Although this is a reasonable replication, purchasing physical shares fails to capture the forward element of the option behavior and will not be sensitive to changes in the cost of carry. This can be improved by purchasing 50 shares forward with an expiry date equivalent to the option expiry date.[8] As the underlying price changes, the delta of the option will also change. As the delta changes, the number of forward shares required to replicate the option will also change. If the delta rises to 60%, ten additional forward shares would have to be purchased in order to keep the replication valid.

This type of synthetic replication strategy is demonstrated in *Figure 12.19*. In this case, a US$10 call is replicated over a 5-day period, by adjusting the number of forward shares purchased in line with the option delta. The total loss over the five days on the option and the synthetic replication are roughly similar. The discrepancy arises because the replication strategy is only adjusted after the delta and underlying price have changed significantly. For example, at the end of the first day, the delta has risen from 70% to 78%. However, the synthetic replication strategy only makes a profit on 70 shares. As a result the profit on the synthetic replication is less than the option. This "lagged" gain and loss structure on the synthetic replication continues over the remaining four days. This difference between the behavior of the option and the synthetic replication is often referred to as "tracking error."

To improve synthetic replication, the frequency with which the strategy is adjusted has to be increased from one day, to second by second, if possible.[9] While this increases the accuracy of the replication, it remains exposed to "gaps" in price movement. In a gap, the price moves substantially in an extremely short time period without trading (e.g., after the announcement of important economic data).

[8] In practice, option traders will replicate options using positions in the underlying physical instrument, rather than a forward in the underlying instrument. This is due to the fact that a liquid forward market may not exist (often the case in equity markets) or else the trader views the cost of carry effects to be minimal and they aim to hedge the underlying price risk.

[9] There have been a number of commercial ventures offering option synthetic replication strategies using forwards for underlying assets or portfolios where options are not readily available. These systems require sophisticated and extremely powerful computing capacities in order to significantly to minimize the "tracking" error.

Figure 12.19
An Example of Synthetic Replication

Suppose we wish to replicate the behavior of a call option on 100 shares with a strike price of $10. The current underlying price is $10 and the delta is 50%.

The synthetic replication would involve buying forward the delta equivalent number of shares.

The table below compares the behavior of the option with a synthetic replication where the replicaton strategy is adjusted at the end of each day.

Note in particular the profit and loss of the replication.

Day	Underlying price	Option premium	Option P&L	Delta	Replication no. of shares	Replication P&L
0	10.00	0.63		70%	70	
1	10.25	0.82	$ 19.52	78%	78	$ 17.50
2	10.35	0.91	$ 8.36	81%	81	$ 7.80
3	9.90	0.56	$ (35.05)	66%	66	$ (36.45)
4	9.70	0.43	$ (13.05)	58%	58	$ (13.20)
5	9.60	0.37	$ (5.84)	53%	53	$ (5.80)
Total			$ (26.05)			$ (30.15)
Difference			$ (4.10)			

While the total P&L on the synthetic replication is close to the replicated option P&L, there is a tracking error of $4.10. This tracking error primarily arises from the replication porfolio not being rebalanced sufficiently frequently to capture the changing delta of the option.

This concept of synthetic replication underlies the process of delta hedging that is discussed in detail in the following chapters.

12.6.2 Put-Call Parity

A concept frequently used by options traders is put-call parity. It describes the basic arbitrage-related interrelationships between puts, calls and the underlying asset. Traders monitor the current market prices of all three and if there is any divergence from put-call parity they execute arbitrage strategies to take advantage of the discrepancy.

Put-call parity recognizes the payoff characteristics of a put and a call and the combination of these characteristics can create forward contracts. For example, we know that the payoff of a bought call option at maturity is a maximum of max($-C$, $S-X-C$) where C is the traded call premium. The payoff of a sold put with the same exercise price is max(P, $S-X+P$), where P is the traded put premium. If we bought the call and the put, the combined payoff is given by:

$$\text{Combined payoff: } S \geqslant X: S-X-C+P$$
$$S \leqslant X: S-X-C+P$$

Regardless of the relative values of S or X, the payoff is identical and this payoff is linked to the value of S, as X, C and P will be constant over the remaining life of the option. If the option is at-the-money, then the values of C and P will be the same giving:

$$\text{Combined payoff: } S-X$$

which is the same payoff as a forward executed at a price of X. Therefore, a bought call, combined with a sold put (with the same exercise price), has the same payoff behavior as a bought forward; that is, if F is the payoff of a forward contract then:

$$F=S-X-C+P$$

This can then be rearranged to solve for the call premium as follows:

$$C=P+F-X$$

This illustrates that a call premium is determined by the put premium plus the difference between the forward and strike prices.

The formula can be rearranged to determine the put premium:

$$P=C+X-F$$

These are invaluable tools if we know the forward price and the put premium because we can use put-call parity to calculate the call premium. In addition, if we know the forward price and the call premium, we can determine the put premium.

These relationships also provide important arbitrage trading opportunities, as put-call parity is effectively another synthetic replication method. We can synthetically replicate a long call by buying a put and buying a forward. A synthetic put can be created by buying a call and selling forward. Therefore,

Figure 12.20
Put-Call Parity

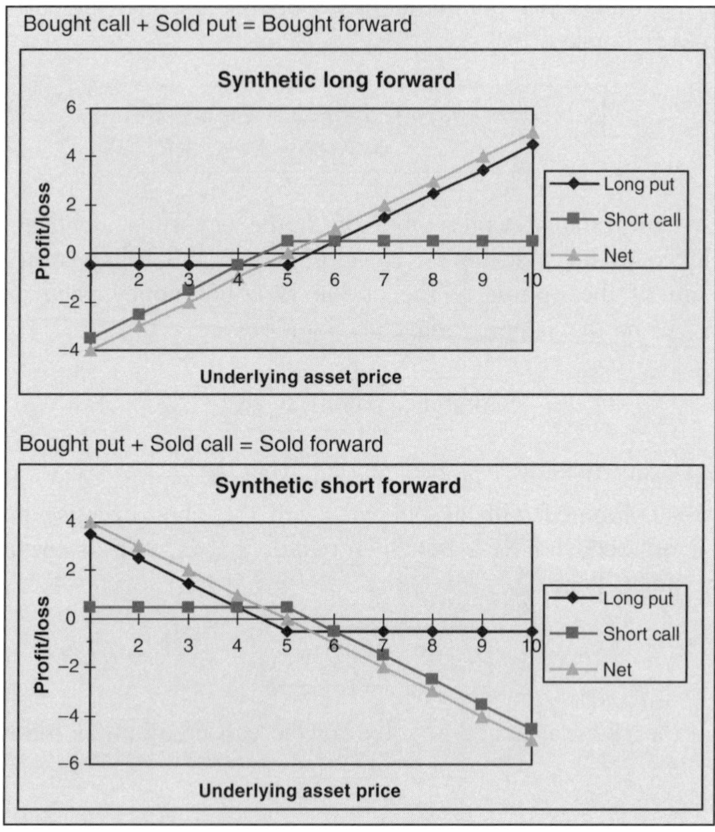

if the current market call premium is *higher* than the premium implied by put-call parity, an arbitrage can be created by selling the call and buying the synthetic call (bought put and bought forward).

The diagrams in *Figure 12.20* show these put-call parity relationships in terms of payoff diagrams.

FURTHER RESOURCES

- Hull, John. *Futures, Options and Other Derivatives* (latest edition).
- Clewlow, Les and Chris Strickland. *Energy Derivatives: Pricing and Risk Management*, Lacima 2000.
- Natenberg, Sheldon. *Option Volatility and Pricing*, Probus 1994.

SUMMARY

In this chapter we discussed the key determinants of the price and value of options. We outlined the importance of expected price distributions and volatility and we examined the Black-Scholes option pricing model. We also discussed the simple binomial model and looked at models for calculating the "Greek letters."

SELF-TEST QUESTIONS

1. Draw an option payoff diagram for a call and put with an exercise price of US$5.
2. Explain why the value of an option can be described as "lopsided."
3. Describe the relationship between the option premium and the forward value of the option.
4. You are a risk manager and one of your traders has just learned about put-call parity. He has just bought forward and "hedged" this by selling an at-the-money call and put. Is this a perfect hedge? Has the trader correctly understood put-call parity?
5. Bob buys a European equity call option, which expires tomorrow and has an exercise price of US$80. Assume that the price of the underlying stock is US$79 today and that on any given day, share prices move up or down by exactly US$2. Calculate the value of the option premium today. Ignore the time value of money.
6. Why is the binomial model classified as a discrete time model?
7. Explain the underlying price distribution assumption in the Black-Scholes model.
8. Assume we are pricing a 6-month European call option using the Black-Scholes model. The underlying asset price is US$20 and the exercise price is US$21. The expected volatility is 30% pa and the risk-free interest rate over the next half year is 8.00% pa. Calculate the option premium.
9. Suppose you are a trader and your portfolio is described by your risk manager as being delta neutral but with significant negative gamma and short theta. Explain what this means about the risk characteristics of your portfolio.
10. By way of an example, explain how you would replicate the behavior of a 1 month bought $75 put on 100 shares with a delta of 40% on a stock currently trading at $80.

CHAPTER 13

EQUITY OPTIONS

The models developed in this chapter are saved as Microsoft Excel™ files in the enclosed disk.

OVERVIEW

In this chapter we develop options pricing models that extend upon the generic Black-Scholes model. We formulate pricing tools that identify and adapt the characteristics of the underlying stock index or share. By the end of this chapter we will have addressed the following valuation issues:

- a model for pricing stock price index options;
- incorporating dividends into the valuation model;
- volatility skews;
- American options and early exercise;
- margining methodologies for exchange-traded instruments.

13.1 INTRODUCTION

Reasons for the popularity of using equity options, as opposed to equity forwards and swaps, include the following:

- **High absolute levels of volatility** It is common in equity markets for the implied volatility of individual stocks to range from 20% to 60%, while in interest rate and currency markets this range can be from 1% to 20%. As volatility is a measure of future uncertainty, and the reason options are purchased is to remove uncertainty, equity market participants have more to gain by trading options.
- **Less need for forwards and swaps** Traditionally the buyers of shares wish to own the physical asset today rather than purchase shares forward. They buy the shares today and fund the purchase with borrowings, effectively creating a synthetic forward.

- **Shares are perpetual** Unlike debt instruments, which have a limited life, shares are perpetual; this tends to blur the distinction between a share and a forward share.
- **Options were first!** Equity option markets developed before equity futures, forwards and swaps. In financial markets, often the market that develops first retains a competitive advantage over products introduced later.
- **Regulatory Constraints** In the US, equity derivatives' regulation explicitly prohibits futures contracts on individual shares. In addition, confusion is caused by the split in regulatory authority between the Securities and Exchange Commission (SEC) for equity options and the Commodities and Futures Trading Commission (CFTC) for options and equity futures.

13.1.1 Types of Equity Options

A number of models have been developed to efficiently and accurately price the different types of instruments underlying an equity option. In this chapter we will develop models, mainly based on Black-Scholes, for the following:

- options on stock price indexes (SPI options);
- options on individual shares (share options).

Although all related, each option type has slightly different characteristics. In the case of SPI options and share options, the difference is the nature of the underlying instrument.[1] An SPI option is the right to buy or sell a basket of shares, rather than a single share. While warrants and convertibles are usually on an individual share, they usually have a much longer term to expiry than SPI or share options and the mechanics of the option exercise can be quite different.

We also need to consider the differences in American and European options and the possibility of early exercise. This is discussed in the section on share options below.

This chapter will show that pricing all of these types of equity options can be achieved by extending the generalized Black-Scholes model from Chapter 12.[2] The first step is to incorporate an asset income or dividend and then allow for the possibility of "lumpy" asset payments.

13.1.2 Synthetic Replication of Equity Options

As we identified in the previous chapter, the synthetic replication of options is achieved by creating an option-equivalent position in the underlying

[1] The only futures contract permitted is futures on share price indices.

[2] See Section 12.4 and 12.5.

instrument.[3] The underlying instrument is usually a forward contract on the cash instrument for which the option can be exercised.

> ***Note***
> If we are applying the Black-Scholes model to an option pricing problem, the synthetic replication is largely unchanged.[4] The major question in building each model is how to incorporate the characteristics of the underlying forward contract. As a result, when we construct a pricing model in the following chapters, we will not repeat the same synthetic replication argument each time, instead we will consider the characteristics of the underlying forward contract and then determine *how* this should be incorporated into our generalized Black-Scholes model.

13.2 OPTIONS ON STOCK PRICE INDICES

13.2.1 General Description

Options on stock price indices are generally exchange-traded and take the form of an American option, an option on an SPI future or a European option on the cash value of the index at expiry date (i.e., option on a cash SPI).

Most options on SPI futures are American style, although it is rare to see an option exercised prior to expiry. Usually the option and futures expiry occurs on the same day.

An option on a cash SPI is usually a European option. Notionally, the buyer of a call can buy a portfolio of shares equivalent to the index at the exercise price. Taking delivery of the underlying index would be difficult and expensive, so in practice, if the option is in-the-money, the buyer of a call receives a cash gain equivalent to the difference between the closing stock index price on the option expiry date and the option expiry price. The buyer of a put receives a cash gain equivalent to the strike price minus the closing index price if the option expires in-the-money.

While the pay-off of an option on a cash SPI or SPI future is identical at expiry, there may be small pricing differences prior to expiry, due to the difference in type (American versus European) and also because the SPI future can deviate from a fair forward value (see Chapter 7).

The total face value of SPI options traded is approximately the same as SPI futures. While this high option usage is characteristic of equity markets, the usage is not as high as for individual shares. Also, while SPI futures are the predominant forward instrument for share index trading, cash settled

[3] See Section 12.6.1.

[4] This rather general statement applies to "plain vanilla" options; once you move into the more complex interest rate option models and exotic options, these synthetic replication relationships can change.

options are the predominant SPI option (representing 87% of total SPI option trading).

13.2.2 The Underlying Instrument

In the case of an option on an SPI future and on a cash SPI index, the value at expiry is determined as the difference in contract value at the exercise price and the closing value of the cash index. At expiry, the underlying instrument is the cash stock price index. Prior to expiry, the underlying instrument is the forward SPI contract. In the case of the option on an SPI future, this forward price is the prevailing futures price.

In order to build an option pricing model we need to accommodate the characteristics of the underlying instrument:

- a share price index replicates the pricing pattern of an underlying portfolio of shares;
- the underlying portfolio of shares pay regular dividends, while these are not paid to holders of forward contracts, on the ex-dividend date the price of the underlying shares falls, which in turn reduces the share price index;
- on a broad-based index, such as the S&P 500, dividend payments on the underlying shares are very frequent and can be viewed as approximately a continuous asset return. This allows us to use the continuous return assumptions of Black-Scholes;
- on a more narrowly defined index (e.g., ten underlying shares) the dividend payment pattern is more "lumpy" and it is more accurate to calculate the forward price accordingly and is similar to pricing an option on an individual share (Section 13.3).

13.2.3 A Pricing Model for an Option on Cash SPI

The generic Black-Scholes model can be extended to cover options on a cash SPI. The major difference is that we must now incorporate an asset income in the form of dividends. We will assume the underlying index is broad-based and that the payment of dividends is approximately continuous.

If we consider the Black-Scholes model derived in *Figure 12.7*, we divided the formula into two components—the present value benefit of exercising an option and the present value cost of exercising an option. We know from our earlier discussions on forward pricing, that the influence of an asset income is to *reduce* the forward price.[5] In the case of an SPI forward, with everything else constant, the payment of dividends between today and

[5] See Chapters 4–7.

Figure 13.1
The Black-Scholes Model Including Continuous Asset Income

(Assumes a continuously compounded asset return.)

Premium of a call

$$C = S \times \exp(-q \times t) \times N(d_1) - X \times \exp(-r \times t) \times N(d_2)$$

Premium of a put

$$P = X \times \exp(-r \times t) \times N(-d_2) - S \times \exp(-q \times t) \times N(-d_1)$$

The call delta is:

$$\text{Call delta} = \exp(-q \times t) \times N(d_1)$$

The put delta is:

$$\text{Put delta} = \exp(-q \times t) \times (N(d_1) - 1)$$

Where:

d_1	=	$(\ln(S/X) + (r - q + (v\text{^}2)/2) \times t)/(v \times t\text{^}0.5)$
d_2	=	$d_1 - v \times t\text{^}0.5$
X	=	exercise price
S	=	spot or cash price
r	=	risk-free interest rate to option expiry (% pa)
q	=	asset return to option expiry (% pa)
t	=	time to option expiry (in years)
v	=	volatility (% pa)
ln( )	=	natural logarithm
exp( )	=	exponential function
$N(\,)$	=	the cummulative normal distribution function.

the option expiry date will *reduce* the forward price and in turn the present value on option exercise. Accordingly, to incorporate dividends, we need to deduct the value of dividends from the benefit of exercising an option. This adjustment is reflected in the Black-Scholes model including continuous asset income in *Figure 13.1*.[6] The key new requirement in pricing an option on a cash SPI is the ability to forecast the expected dividend over the life

[6] We will see in Chapter 15 that this model we have developed is essentially the same as the Garman-Kolhagen model developed for currency options.

of the option. Given the generally stable nature of dividends on broad-based indices, it is common to use an historical dividend yield.

Figure 13.2 builds a pricing spreadsheet based on this pricing model. This is essentially an extension of the program devised in *Figure 12.7* with the addition of an asset return in accordance with the adjusted model above. In this case, we price a put option on a broad-based share price index that has one year to expiry. Here, the historical dividend is 3% pa and this is used to determine the option premium.

This model can be used to create the generic Black-Scholes model from Chapter 12. By setting the asset income to zero, $q=0$, the model immediately

Figure 13.2
A Put Option on a Share Price Index
(Note: this spreadsheet model also prices calls)

Row	Inputs		Cell:Formula
10	Option type (*P* or *C*)	p	$F$10
11	*S* =	644.00	$F$11
12	*E* =	600.00	$F$12
13	*v* =	21.00%	$F$13
14	*t* =	1	$F$14
15	*r* =	10.00%	$F$15
16	*q* =	3.00%	$F$16

Normal distribution constants	
a =	0.23164
b_1 =	0.31938
b_2 =	–0.35656
b_3 =	1.781478
b_4 =	–1.82126
b_5 =	1.330274

Row	Calculations		Result	Cell address: Formula used
19	ln(*S*/*E*) =		0.070769	$F$19:=LN(G11/G12)
20	(*r* – *q* + 0.5*v^2)*t =		0.09205	$F$20:=(G15–G16+(G13^2)/2)*(G14)
21	v*t^0.5 =		0.21	$F$21:=G13*(G14^0.5)
23	d_1:	d_1 =	0.775329	$F$23:=(G19+G20)/G21
24		Adjust for *P* or *C* =	–0.77533	$F$24:=IF(UPPER(LEFT($G$10,1))="C",G23,–G23)
26	d_2:	d_2 =	0.565329	$F$26:=G23-G21
27		Adjust for *P* or *C* =	–0.56533	$F$27:=IF(UPPER(LEFT($G$10,1))="C",G26,–G26)
29	$N(d_1)$:	*k* =	0.85	$F$29:=1/(1+ABS($L$10*G24))
30		1/(2*22/7)^0.5 =	0.398862	$F$30:=1/(2*22/7)^0.5
31		EXP((–z^2)/2) =	0.740398	$F$31:=EXP(((G24)^2*–1)/2)
32		Calculation =	0.2190	$F$32:=(G30*G31*($L$11*G29+$L$12*G29^2+$L$13*G29^3 +$L$14*G29^4+$L$15*G29^5))
34		$N(d_1)$ =	0.219029	$F$33:=IF(G24>0,1–G32,G32)
35		$N(d_1)$ × Exp (–*q* × *t*) =	0.212555	
37	$N(d_2)$:	*k* =	0.88	$F$36:=1/(1+ABS($L$10*G27))
38		1/(2*22/7)^0.5 =	0.398862	$F$37:=1/(2*22/7)^0.5
39		EXP((–z^2)/2) =	0.852316	$F$38:=EXP(((G27)^2*-1)/2)
40		Calculation =	0.2859	$F$39:=(G37*G38*($L$11*G36+$L$12*G36^2+$L$13*G36^3 +$L$14*G36^4+$L$15*G36^5))
42		$N(d_2)$ =	0.285867	$F$40:=IF(G27>0,1–G39,G39)
43		$N(d_2)$ × Exp (–*r* × *t*) =	0.258664	$F$41:=+G40*EXP(-G15*G14)

Row	Results			
48	Option premium	— $	18.31	$F$46:=ROUND(ABS((G11*G34–G12*G41)),4)
49		— % of spot	2.84%	$F$47:=+G46/G11
50	Option delta =		21.26%	$F$48:=G34

provides an option with an underlying instrument that will pay no income over the life of the option.

Another feature of this model is that the asset income also becomes incorporated into the delta calculation for the option. Whereas in the generic Black-Scholes model the delta for a call is given by $N(d_1)$, in this continuous asset income model the delta becomes:

$$\text{Call delta} = \exp(-q \times t) \times N(d_1).$$

The effect of this is to slightly reduce the delta sensitivity of the option for both puts and calls relative to the generic Black-Scholes model.

13.2.4 Building a Black-Scholes Macro Function

In the example in *Figure 13.2*, we have built a long-hand, formula-based option pricing model for a spreadsheet. Although accurate, it is clumsy to use and when we wish to simultaneously assess an option value it tends to be slow even on a very powerful personal computer. A useful addition to any "financial engineer," a market professional who creates tailored financial solutions by applying derivative pricing principles.

Within Microsoft Excel (and Visual Basic) we can create user-defined macro programs that operate like any other customized function. Once created, these macros can be used potentially hundreds of times in one spreadsheet and can easily be copied between applications.

To give an example of a function macro we will adapt the formula-based Black-Scholes model with continuous asset income from *Figure 13.2.* The steps in creating the program in Excel 4.0 and 5.0/95 are listed below:

1. Create a new spreadsheet called "Input.xls" and one macro sheet called "Option.xlm." Combine these into a workbook called "Option.xlw." (In Excel 5.0 just create one workbook called "Option.xls" with a worksheet called "input" and macro sheet called "option.")
2. In the input spreadsheet, enter the pricing parameters: type, S, X, v, t, r, q.
3. In the macro sheet, enter the option pricing function macro called "option" set out in *Figure 13.3.*
4. Insert the function "option" into the input spreadsheet and use the pricing parameters.
5. Create payoff tables by creating a column of underlying prices and then apply the function "option" to each of these prices keeping the other variables constant. Use the graph wizard to create a payoff graph.

This macro will also operate in version 7.0/97 but it is more effective to apply the same macro logic to the VBA programming language used in more recent versions of Excel.

An example of an option pricing workbook is provided in *Figure 13.3*. This also gives the details of the macro commands in the function "option." The reason it is called "option" is because the function macro in the generic pricing model based on *Figure 12.7* has been called "option."

This example gives an idea of the flexibility that a function macro offers. In this case, we have performed ten option price calculations and essentially put it

Figure 13.3
Creating a Black-Scholes Function Macro

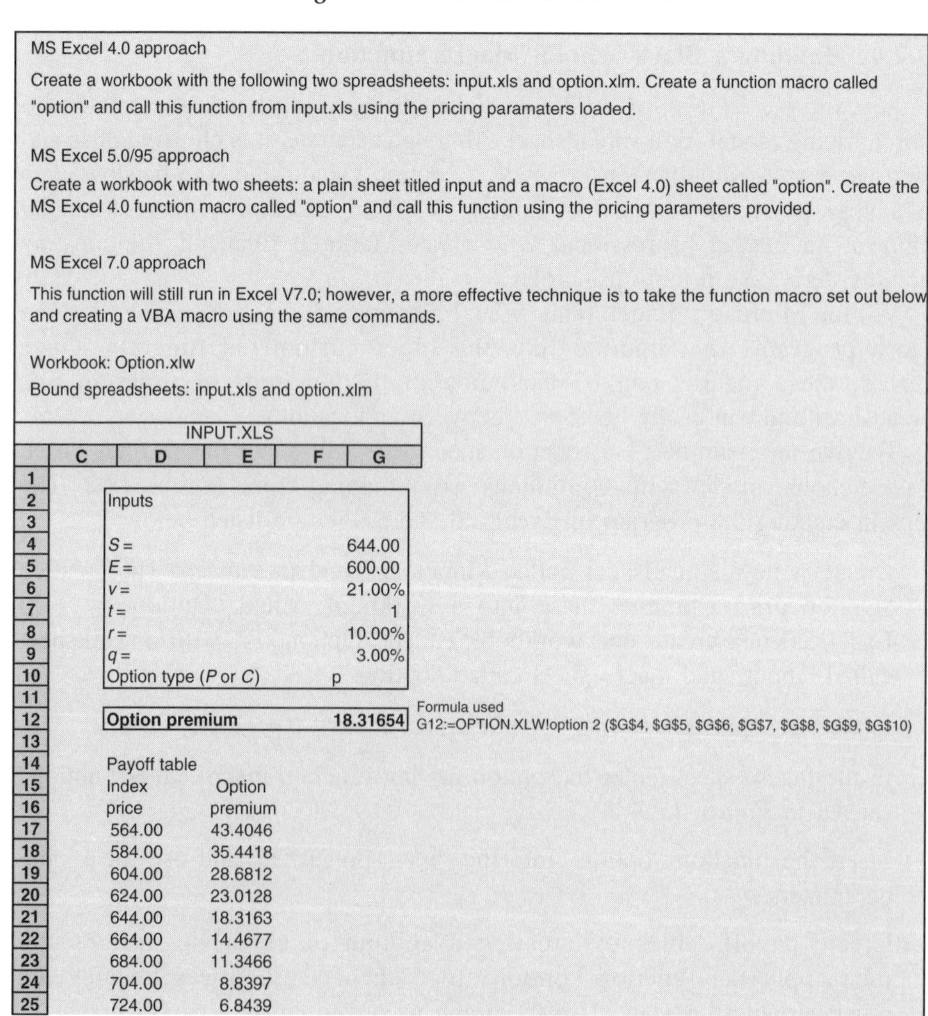

MS Excel 4.0 approach

Create a workbook with the following two spreadsheets: input.xls and option.xlm. Create a function macro called "option" and call this function from input.xls using the pricing paramaters loaded.

MS Excel 5.0/95 approach

Create a workbook with two sheets: a plain sheet titled input and a macro (Excel 4.0) sheet called "option". Create the MS Excel 4.0 function macro called "option" and call this function using the pricing parameters provided.

MS Excel 7.0 approach

This function will still run in Excel V7.0; however, a more effective technique is to take the function macro set out below and creating a VBA macro using the same commands.

Workbook: Option.xlw

Bound spreadsheets: input.xls and option.xlm

INPUT.XLS

	C	D	E	F	G
1					
2		Inputs			
3					
4		*S* =			644.00
5		*E* =			600.00
6		*v* =			21.00%
7		*t* =			1
8		*r* =			10.00%
9		*q* =			3.00%
10		Option type (*P* or *C*)		p	
11					
12		**Option premium**			**18.31654**
13					
14		Payoff table			
15		Index	Option		
16		price	premium		
17		564.00	43.4046		
18		584.00	35.4418		
19		604.00	28.6812		
20		624.00	23.0128		
21		644.00	18.3163		
22		664.00	14.4677		
23		684.00	11.3466		
24		704.00	8.8397		
25		724.00	6.8439		

Formula used
G12:=OPTION.XLW!option 2 ($G$4, $G$5, $G$6, $G$7, $G$8, $G$9, $G$10)

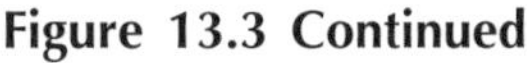

Figure 13.3 Continued

Payoff diagram (using data from table)

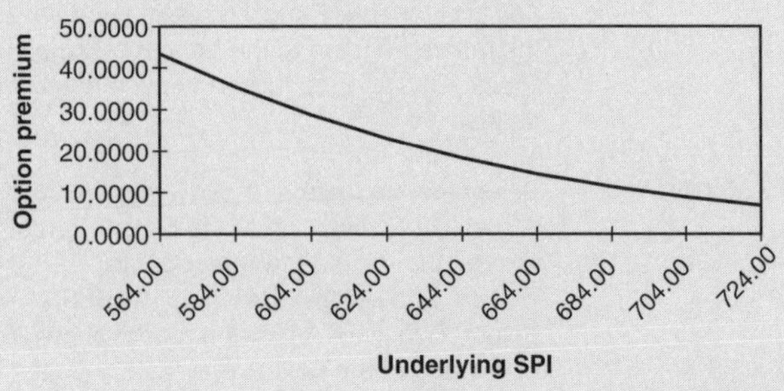

OPTION.XLM

	A	B	C
1			
2			
3		**option()**	
4		=ARGUMENT("sp",1)	
5		=ARGUMENT("x",1)	
6		=ARGUMENT("s",1)	
7		=ARGUMENT("t",1)	
8		=ARGUMENT("a",1)	
9		=ARGUMENT("q",1)	
10		=ARGUMENT("cccc",1)	
11		ddd1=(LN(sp/x)+(a-q+0.5*s^2)*t)/(s*(t^0.5))	
12		ddd= ddd1-s*(t^0.5)	
13		ndd1=NORMSDIST(ddd1)	
14		ndd=NORMSDIST(ddd)	
15		call1=sp*EXP(-q*t)*ndd1-x*EXP(-a*t)*ndd	
16		put1=-sp*EXP(-q*t)*(1-ndd1)+x*EXP(-a*t)*(1-ndd)	
17		=IF(UPPER(cccc)="C")	
18		optiona=call1	
19		=ELSE()	
20		optiona=put1	
21		=END.IF()	
22		=RETURN(optiona)	
23			

Comments:

1. The function macro must be entered into a macro sheet. Create a range name called "option" at cell B3. This name has to be defined as a "function". The procedure for doing this differs between version 4 and 5:

Figure 13.3 Continued

MS Excel 4.0	Select the menu item "Formula" and select "Define Name". In the Define Name box set the Name to "option" that refers to "$B$3" and click on the "Function" option under the macro heading at the bottom of the box. Press "OK" and the function option has been defined.
MS Excel 5.0	Select the menu item "Insert", then "Name" and select "Define....". In the Define Name box set the "Name in Workbook" to "option" and set the "Refers to" as $B$3. Select "Function" under the macro heading at the side of the box. Press "OK" and the function option has been defined.

through one formula—the function macro. If we used the long-hand method we would have had to copy the formula used in *Figure 13.4* nine times, which means extra processing time required and increased scope for error.

Once you have developed one function-like "option," it is a relatively simple matter to adjust it to price options using the other derivatives (i.e., the Greek letters) of the Black-Scholes model.

13.2.5 A Pricing Model for an Option on SPI Futures

The major distinction between the option on a cash SPI or SPI future is that the forward price is already given by the underlying traded futures price. As a result, when using a derivative of Black-Scholes we do not need to calculate the underlying forward price and the futures price is entered directly into the option pricing model.

However, whether or not we still need to have a present-value calculation in the formula depends on the particular contract specifications of each option. While most options on SPI futures require an option premium to become due for payment on the day it is executed, a few exchanges actually do not require the payment of a premium until the option expiry.[7] The premium upfront options are referred to as "premium"-style options and the others are called "futures"-style options. The label of "futures" style applies because options are marked-to-market on a daily basis and an initial margin is required from both the buyer and seller.

[7] Although the premium is due for payment on the trade date, because of the daily processing cycles of exchanges, the premium is not actually paid until the following morning.

Figure 13.4
The Black Model

For premium-style options

$C = F \times \exp(-r \times t) \times N(d_1) - X \times \exp(-r \times t) \times N(d_2)$

$P = X \times \exp(-r \times t) \times N(-d_2) - F \times \exp(-r \times t) \times N(-d_1)$

Call delta $= \exp(-r \times t) \times N(d_1)$

For futures-style options

$C = F \times N(d_1) - X \times N(d_2)$

$P = X \times N(-d_2) - F \times N(-d_1)$

Call delta $= N(d_1)$

Where:

d_1	=	$(\ln(F/X) + ((v\text{^}2)/2) \times t)/(v \times t\text{^}0.5)$
d_2	=	$d_1 - v \times t\text{^}0.5$
X	=	exercise price
S	=	futures price
r	=	risk-free interest rate to option expiry (% pa)
q	=	asset return to option expiry (% pa)
t	=	time to option expiry (in years)
v	=	volatility (% pa)
ln( )	=	natural logarithm
exp( )	=	exponential function
$N(\,)$	=	the cummulative normal distribution function.

The two main exchanges that offer the futures-style option are the Hong Kong Futures Exchange and the Sydney Futures Exchange. It is worth noting that this distinction applies to all options traded on these exchanges. There are also initial margin considerations for all exchange-traded options and this is discussed later in the chapter and also in the appendix.

The Black Model

The Black Model is used to price both the premium and futures style options. The Black model takes the futures price as a given and this is used to determine the cost of carry of the underlying instrument—so there is no requirement to enter the asset income. The Black model then effectively prices the option based on forward values on the option expiry date, and then takes a present value of this amount for premium-style options and leaves it as a forward amount for "futures"-style options.

The basic structure of the Black model is set out in *Figure 13.4*.

The Black model is an extremely important model for all exchange-traded options. It is still widely used by the world's major futures exchanges to generate options quoted and option settlement premiums.

Figure 13.5 provides a long-hand formula for the calculation of a Black model on a premium style option on an SPI future.

If this were a futures style option, the premium could be calculated by setting the interest rate input, r, to zero, in which case the premium would be 27.08 index points and the delta 40.05%.

Whereas the model used for options on a cash index has a delta that is influenced by the asset return, in the case of the Black model for premium style options, the delta is influenced by the interest rate:

$$\text{Call delta} = N(d_1) \times \exp(-r \times t)$$

13.3 OPTIONS ON INDIVIDUAL SHARES

13.3.1 General Description

Volume in options on individual shares is spread across both exchange-traded and OTC markets. Exchange-traded options on individual shares, generally referred to as stock options, probably have the longest trading history of any derivative since their successful launch on the CBOE in 1973. Most OTC options on individual shares have very similar characters to stock options except there is no margining. We will focus on stock options although the pricing models developed can be applied to OTC individual share options as well.

The bulk of the stock option trading still takes place on US exchanges where there are more than 1,000 contracts.

While there is a very diverse range of stocks underlying stock options, the characteristics are all similar and are summarized below:

Stocks underlying stock options	
Type	American
Underlying number of shares	Ranges from 100 to 1,000
Expiry dates	Standardized—generally on a quarterly cycle
Premium quotation	In terms of the underlying stock price
Exercise prices	Listed in standard intervals around the current stock price
Adjustments	Most stock options are adjusted for corporate events such as bonuses and splits
Expiration method	Most stock options require delivery; however, some are cash settled
Margin methodology	TIMS for most markets except LIFFE, which uses SPAN
Premium payment	All premiums are paid upfront (i.e., premium-style options)
Contract value	No. of shares × Premium

Figure 13.5
Using the Black Model to Calculate the Price of a Premium Style Call

(Note: this spreadsheet model also prices puts)

	C	D	E	F	G	H	I	J	K	L	M	N	O
6													
7													
8		**Inputs**				Cell:Formula			**Normal distribution constants**				
9													
10		Option type (*P* or *C*)		c		$G$10			a =	0.23164			
11		F =			$665	$G$11			b_1=	0.31938			
12		E =			$700	$G$12			b_2 =	–0.35656			
13		v =			22.00%	$G$13			b_3 =	1.781478			
14		t =			0.5	$G$14			b_4 =	–1.82126			
15		r =			10.00%	$G$15			b_5 =	1.330274			
16													
17		**Calculations**			**Result**	**Cell address: Formula used**							
18													
19		ln(*F*/*E*) =			–0.05129	$G$19:=LN(G11/G12)							
20		*v*^2***t*/2 =			0.0121	$G$20:=(G13^2)/2*(G14)							
21		*v***t*^0.5 =			0.155563	$G$21:=G13*(G14^0.5)							
22													
23		d_1:	d_1 =		–0.25194	$G$23:=(G19+G20)/G21							
24			Adjust for *P* or *C* =		–0.25194	$G$24:=IF(UPPER(LEFT($G$10,1))="C",G23,–G23)							
25													
26		d_2:	d_2 =		–0.40751	$G$26:=G23-G21							
27			Adjust for *P* or *C* =		–0.40751	$G$27:=IF(UPPER(LEFT($G$10,1))="C",G26,–G26)							
28													
29		$N(d_1)$:	k =		0.94	$G$29:=1/(1+ABS($L$10*G24))							
30			1/(2*22/7)^0.5 =		0.398862	$G$30:=1/(2*22/7)^0.5							
31			EXP((–*z*^2)/2) =		0.96876	$G$31:=EXP(((G24)^2*–1)/2)							
32			Calculation =		0.4005	$G$32:=(G30*G31*($L$11*G29+$L$12*G29^2+$L$13*G29^3+$L$14*G29^4+$L$15*G29^5))							
33			$N(d_1)$ =		0.400462	$G$33:=IF(G24>0,1–G32,G32)							
34													
35		$N(d_2)$:	k =		0.91	$G$35:=1/(1+ABS($L$10*G27))							
36			1/(2*22/7)^0.5 =		0.398862	$G$36:=1/(2*22/7)^0.5							
37			EXP((–*z*^2)/2) =		0.920322	$G$37:=EXP(((G27)^2*–1)/2)							
38			Calculation =		0.3417	$G$38:=(G36*G37*($L$11*G35+$L$12*G35^2+$L$13*G35^3+$L$14*G35^4+$L$15*G35^5))							
39			$N(d_2)$ =		0.341749	$G$39:=IF(G27>0,1–G38,G38)							
40													
41													
42													
43		**Results**											
44													
45		Option premium		– $	25.76	$G$45:=ROUND(ABS((G11*G33-G12*G39)*EXP(-G15*G14)),4)							
46				– % of spot	3.87%	$G$46:=G45/G11							
47		Option delta =			38.09%	$G$47:=G33*EXP(-G15*G14)							

13.3.2 The Underlying Instrument

Upon exercise of a stock option, the seller of a call or buyer of a put must deliver the underlying parcel of shares in return for payment that is equivalent to the exercise price. Prior to expiry, the underlying instrument is a forward contract on this parcel of shares.

Unlike an SPI option, we cannot assume a known and continuous asset return. Dividends on shares are "lumpy" and the forward pricing model needs to be able to incorporate this. In order to build an option pricing model, we need to accommodate the following characteristics of the underlying instrument:

- the shares underlying a stock option pay regular dividends. While these are not paid to holders of forward contracts, on the ex-dividend date the price of the underlying shares falls;
- dividend payments are made in discrete amounts, with the dividend payment taking place on a known date and then a forecast of the dividend can be made;
- there are no significant restraints on trading in the underlying instrument and any delivery requirements can always be met.

13.3.3 A Stock Option Pricing Model

As stated above, because the underlying contract has lumpy asset income, the forward pricing component of the Black-Scholes model has to be modified to incorporate the discrete payment of dividends. If we ignore the potential for early exercise, there are two approaches that we can take:

- **Discrete time** Develop a discrete time (e.g., binomial) model that incorporates the dividend payment at one of the nodes on the binomial tree;
- **Continuous time** Extend our existing Black-Scholes models to cater for the lumpy dividend.

This "dividend-adjusted" Black-Scholes model is shown in *Figure 13.6*. In this case, we have taken the model from *Figure 12.7* and adjusted the value of *S* by the present value of future dividends. If no dividends are paid over the remaining life of the option, it is unnecessary to make the dividend adjustment.

The advantage of the discrete time approach is that we can replicate the actual payment of the dividend on a particular date (i.e., replicate its lumpy nature). Whereas in the Black-Scholes model we are not able to distinguish between remaining days to expiry, and the dividend adjustment tends to be spread over the remaining term to expiry (i.e., the influence of the dividend is smoothed). This distinction will become more important when we discuss the possibility of early exercise.

Figure 13.6
The "Dividend-Adjusted" Black-Scholes Model

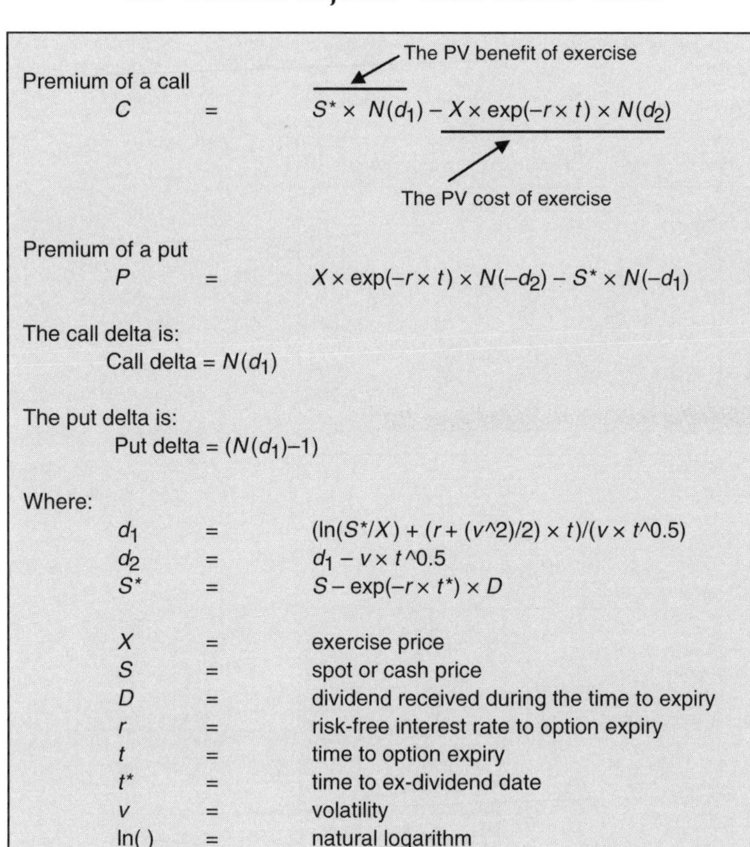

As a first step, we will look at adjusting the Black-Scholes model for dividends. If we follow the approach we used for individual share futures in Chapter 7, we can incorporate lumpy dividends by reducing the current forward price by the future value of dividends to be paid between today and the forward date.[8] As the underlying price inputs into Black-Scholes are in terms of the current cash price, the simplest approach is to deduct the present value of all dividends over the life of the option from the current cash share price.

Example

Suppose you wish to buy an option on a stock with an underlying price of US$30 expiring in 180 days. A dividend of US$2/share will be paid in 90 days and the 3-month interest rate is 12% pa.

[8] See Chapter 7, Section 7.3.2.

Figure 13.7
A Dividend Adjustment Model

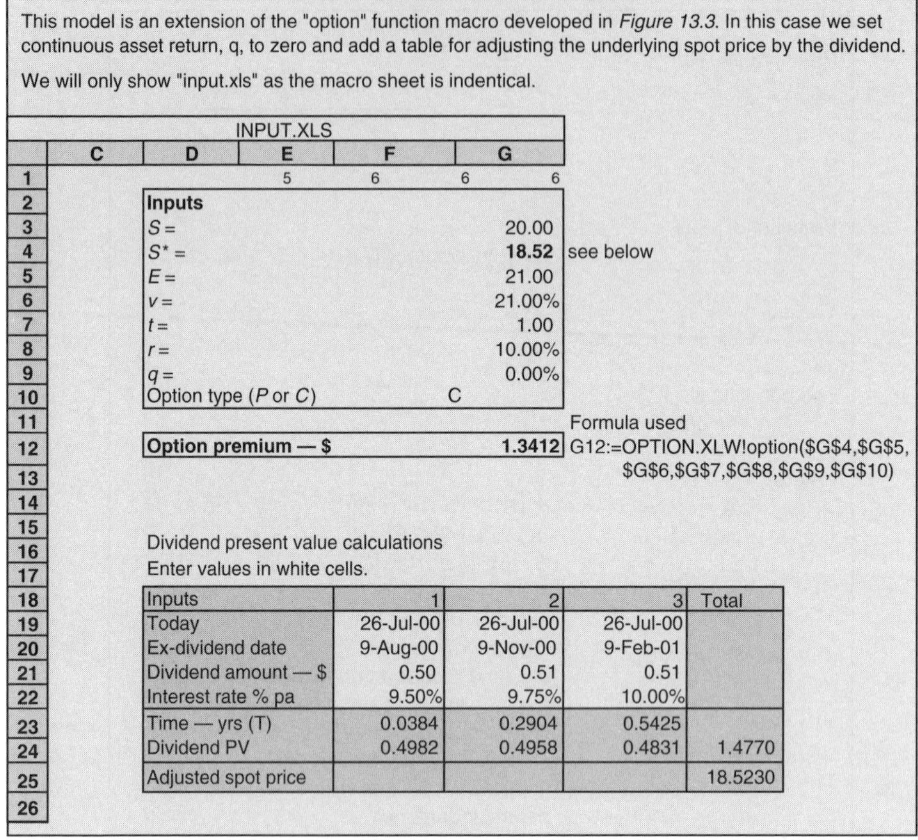

This model is an extension of the "option" function macro developed in *Figure 13.3.* In this case we set continuous asset return, q, to zero and add a table for adjusting the underlying spot price by the dividend.

We will only show "input.xls" as the macro sheet is indentical.

INPUT.XLS

	C	D	E	F	G	
1			5	6	6 6	
2		**Inputs**				
3		*S* =			20.00	
4		*S** =			**18.52**	see below
5		*E* =			21.00	
6		*v* =			21.00%	
7		*t* =			1.00	
8		*r* =			10.00%	
9		*q* =			0.00%	
10		Option type (*P* or *C*)		C		
11						Formula used
12		**Option premium — $**			**1.3412**	G12:=OPTION.XLW!option($G$4,$G$5, $G$6,$G$7,$G$8,$G$9,$G$10)
13						
14						
15						
16		Dividend present value calculations				
17		Enter values in white cells.				

Row	Inputs	1	2	3	Total
18	Inputs	1	2	3	Total
19	Today	26-Jul-00	26-Jul-00	26-Jul-00	
20	Ex-dividend date	9-Aug-00	9-Nov-00	9-Feb-01	
21	Dividend amount — $	0.50	0.51	0.51	
22	Interest rate % pa	9.50%	9.75%	10.00%	
23	Time — yrs (T)	0.0384	0.2904	0.5425	
24	Dividend PV	0.4982	0.4958	0.4831	1.4770
25	Adjusted spot price				18.5230
26					

To calculate the dividend adjusted price:

$$
\begin{aligned}
S^* &= 30 - 2 \times \exp(-0.12 \times 0.4932) \\
&= 30 - 2 \times 0.9425 \\
&= 30 - 1.8851 \\
&= 28.1149
\end{aligned}
$$

This model only allows for the existence of one interest rate; another extension of this model is to enter a separate interest rate to present value the dividend payment. Also, the model provided allows for the payment for one dividend during the life of the option. This was done to simplify the formula. Including additional dividends requires present valuing of each of the dividends as follows:

$$S^* = S - PV \text{ of dividends}$$

$$PV \text{ of dividends} = D_1 \times \exp(-r_1 \times t_1) + D_2 \times \exp(-r_2 \times t_2) \cdots\cdots$$

Where:

D_1 = the first dividend
t_1 = the time until the first ex-dividend date
r_1 = the interest rate for period t_1
D_1 = the second dividend
t_1 = the time until the second ex-dividend date
r_1 = the interest rate for period t_2.

13.3.4 Is a Portfolio of Stock Options the Same as an SPI Option?

A feature of equity markets is that implied volatilities on SPI options are often lower than implied volatility on stock options. Lower volatility suggests that the cost of purchasing an SPI option for a given portfolio is cheaper than purchasing stock options. Does this create an incentive for hedgers to use SPI options rather than stock options? To answer this question we will look at the forces behind the volatility differential.

Most share price indices represent a well-diversified portfolio. From portfolio theory we know that by diversification we can lower the risk associated with the return of a portfolio, i.e., lower the volatility of the portfolio. As a result, the volatility of an SPI option is often considerably lower than that of a stock options due to this diversification benefit.[9] *Figure 13.8* compares the volatility of some Australian equity options and compares the implied volatility of options on the All Ordinaries Share Price Index against stock options on some major corporations based on two different maturity dates.

As well as a generally lower absolute level of volatility, another difference is that the implied volatility of SPI options is generally more stable over time than stock options; that is, the volatility of SPI options is less volatile. While a simple example, this is illustrated by the change in implied volatility over the 6-month period shown in *Figure 13.8*.

[9] There is a connection here to the capital asset pricing model (CAPM). In fact, the comparison of the implied volatility of the SPI versus a stock option is a related concept to the beta of a share. And the phenomenon described in this subsection is essentially the same discussion as the stability of the beta of a share.

Figure 13.8
Comparison of Implied Volatilities

At-the-money implied volatility			
As at	March	Sep	Difference
SPI	15.5%	15.5%	0.00%
BHP	20.0%	20.3%	0.30%
NAB	18.0%	18.1%	0.10%
MIM	32.0%	29.0%	−3.00%
PDP	22.0%	22.0%	0.00%
NCP	45.0%	26.5%	−18.50%
FBG	35.0%	20.0%	−15.00%
TNT	45.0%	32.0%	−13.00%

The lower volatility of SPI options reflects the nature of the underlying instrument. Accordingly, if we wish to hedge the price risk of a diversified portfolio, we should use SPI options—because a combined portfolio of stock options would be more expensive. However, if we are using SPI options to hedge less well diversified risk, such as a portfolio of shares in just one company, then we are faced with the prospect of a very imperfect hedge due to, first, the higher volatility of an individual share and, second, the variability in this level of volatility. If we hedge a portfolio of News Corporation shares (NCP) with SPI options, the volatility savings is substantial—a 45% versus a 15.5% implied volatility. However, if NCP does actually display 45% volatility over the life of the option we will be grossly underhedged as we will have failed to capture the bulk of the underlying price distribution of NCP shares. Effectively, the diversification has worked against the hedge and we have failed to capture the specific risk of the underlying portfolio.

Note

There may be a temptation to use SPI options because they appear "cheaper;" however, this is only the case when the exposure we wish to hedge is a diversified portfolio similar to the instrument underlying the SPI. An SPI option is really a form of basket option and it only provides a cost saving when we are a rehedging a similar "basket." When hedging the specific risk of a share, the stock option on that share is generally much more effective.

13.3.5 Equity Options and Volatility Skews

A feature of all options markets, but particularly with equity options, is a phenomenon known as a "volatility skew." So far, we have only discussed the prospect of one volatility for an underlying instrument. In practice, for a given option series on a futures contract, there can be different volatilities for different exercise prices. This is shown in *Figure 13.9*, which plots the volatility skew of a BHP stock option—all of the options have the same underlying instrument and the same expiry date.

The volatility curve shown is a common skew in equity markets where the lower strike prices have a higher volatility than strikes prices that are around or above the current strike price. This shape is often referred to as a "smirk." In interest rate markets it is common for the skew to have the shape of a "smile" where volatility is lowest at-the-money and then it rises as the strike price is above or below the current underlying price.

Often our first reaction to a volatility skew is that it seems to imply some type of arbitrage using the put-call parity relationships in Chapter 12. However, put-call parity arbitrage relationships only apply to options with the same strike price, so we cannot execute an arbitrage to take advantage of the skew.

The next question then becomes: how is it possible that the market simultaneously believes that the BHP share price will exhibit a volatility anywhere between 17% and 29%? The answer is that the market is not actually being inconsistent, but it is saying something about the expected future distribution of the BHP share price. In fact, by increasing the volatility on the lower strike prices, the market is saying that there is a higher chance

Figure 13.9
Volatility Skew by Exercise Price

The graph below plots the volatilities a of stock option with the same expiry date but different exercise prices. The underlying share price was $17.26.

BHP share option — implied volatility curves by exercise price

Implied volatility %

29%
27%
25%
23%
21%
19%
17%
15%

At-the-money

Sep-95

14.57 15.02 15.47 15.92 16.37 16.82 17.27 17.72 18.17 18.62 19.07 19.52 19.97

Exercise price (underlying price = $17.26)

of the underlying share price falling by $3 than is implied by the at-the-money volatility of 19%.

We know Black-Scholes assumes a log-normal distribution of the underlying asset price. However, actual price distributions are not perfectly log-normal and the Black-Scholes model does not easily allow us to alter the shape of the underlying distribution. The next best thing is to force Black-Scholes to recognize the true value of none—at-the-money options by changing the volatility used in the pricing model.

For example, we know from history that share prices are occasionally subject to large price falls (such as October 1987). The impact of this type of distribution is to increase the value of out-of-the-money puts relative to the value implied by a log-normal distribution. As a result, the market bids up the price of out-of-the-money put options, which in turn forces up the implied volatility of these options relative to the at-the-money volatility.

No matter what the shape of the skew, the basic motivation of market participants is to over- or under-value traded option premiums relative to Black-Scholes. If we take the at-the-money volatility as the "true" implied volatility over the life of an option, then the other volatilities are "tweaked" to give all option strike prices a value that reflects the expected underlying price distribution.

The skew is not just across strike prices, there are also skews across time. So, an option with the same strike price but different expiry dates can also have a different volatility. This is linked to both the possibility of particular events occurring between expiry dates, which will change volatility and also the fact that the shape of the price distribution may change over time. In particular, Black-Scholes tends to underestimate the possibility of large price moves close to expiry. As a result, volatility skews typically become more pronounced the closer an option is to expiry—in fact, longer term options often show no skew at all. This is illustrated by comparing the BHP volatility skew over three different expiry dates in *Figure 13.10*. This shows relatively little skew in the second and third expiry months relative to the front month.

> ***Note***
> Essentially, the volatility skew becomes a "de facto" method of adjusting the probability of particular outcomes to meet the market's view of the expected underlying price distribution over the life of the option.

13.3.6 Stock Options and Early Exercise

A feature of most stock options is that they are American, i.e., they can be exercised prior to expiry. The Black-Scholes models we have developed are

Figure 13.10
Volatility Skew by Time

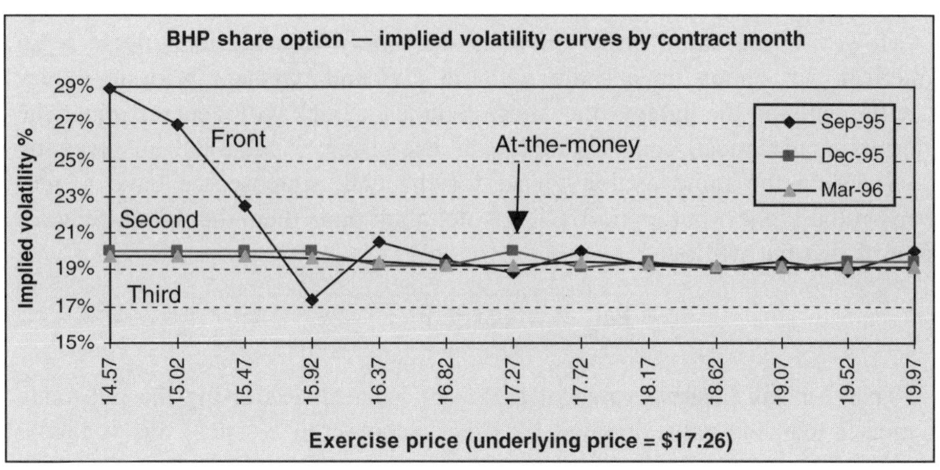

designed for European options. The European model often can be used as a reasonable approximation of the American model, because if an option is exercised prior to the expiry date, the time value, or insurance element of the option is not applicable. In general, American options are held until expiry and effectively operate like a European option. However, there are some exceptions, notably when an option has very high intrinsic value relative to time value and when asset income payments are lumpy, as is the case with stock options.

Early Exercise with No Dividend Payment

The net benefit of exercising a call option today is given by the difference between the current spot price and the exercise price, $S - X$. An American option will be exercised early if the current option price is *less* than the net benefit of exercising the option today. On an instrument that pays no income this is highly unlikely, as it will always be beneficial for an option buyer to delay having to pay for an option, even for an option that has practically zero time value. If we portray the payoff of exercising at the expiry of the option as:

$$S - X \times \exp(-r \times t)$$

then as long as $t > 0$, this net amount will always be greater than $S - X$.

So, an American call option on a stock option with no dividend payment prior to expiry is highly unlikely ever to be exercised early and the Black-Scholes model is appropriate.

However, the same situation does not apply to American puts. If an American put option on a share with no dividend payment prior to expiry is sufficiently in-the-money, the Black-Scholes model will underestimate the price of an American call. The value of exercising a put today is given by $X - S$. Using the same analogy used for the call, suppose we have a very deep in-the-money put option with a delta of one, then the Black-Scholes price of that put will be:

$$\text{Put}_{\text{BS}} = X \times \exp(-r \times t) - S$$

Then for any positive value of t, the net value of exercising the put today is greater than the value implied by Black-Scholes. In essence, this is taking advantage of a time value of money differential—the early exerciser obtains the interest early on the proceeds of selling the underlying shares at the exercise price.

To overcome this potential anomaly, when pricing in-the-money American put options we need to ensure that the current price is at least equivalent to the exercise price minus the current spot price. *Figure 13.11* gives an example of the potential underpricing of American options by Black-Scholes.

In summary, the adjustment for pricing American put options using Black-Scholes is as follows:

$$\text{Put}_{\text{AMERICAN}} = \text{Max}(X - S, \text{Put}_{\text{EUROPEAN}})$$

Where:

$\text{Put}_{\text{EUROPEAN}}$ is the generic Black-Scholes model.

Early Exercise and Dividend Payments

The payment of dividends over the life of an option adds a new element to the possibility of exercising an American option early. We know the payment of dividends are lumpy and that the day the underlying share loses its rights to the next dividend payment (the "ex-dividend" date), the share price falls by an amount the market equates to the value of the dividend. In the case of a European option, this does not present any difficulty, as the option trades on an ex-dividend basis; that is, because the option can only be exercised at expiry, all dividends over the life of the option are stripped from the option price.[10]

[10] This is effectively what is occurring in the dividend-adjusted Black-Scholes model from Section 13.3.3.

Figure 13.11
Early Exercise Example without Dividends

Black-Scholes — European option pricing		
Spot price (S)		22
Exercise (X)		26
Volatility (V)		35%
Time — yrs (T)		0.5
Interest rate (r)		12.5%
Type — p or c	p	
Outputs		
Price — points		3.698
Value of early exercise		
$X - S =$		4
Net benefit of early exercise		0.302
The value of an American put is given by max(BS price, $X - S$) = 4		

Because an American option can be exercised at any time, this process of adjusting for dividends may not reflect the full exerciseable value of a stock option for call options, which are very deeply in-the-money.

Example

Suppose we have an underlying share trading at a price of US$200, the share goes ex-dividend tomorrow and there is an expected fall in the price of US$4.

Assume we own a deep-in-the-money call option with a strike price of US$160, one month to expiry and a delta of 0.99. The value of exercising the option today is US$40. However, tomorrow it will be US$36. As the adjusted Black-Scholes model will effectively be removing the dividend payment, it will already be reflecting the ex-dividend price of US$196. This is demonstrated in *Figure 13.12* where the Black-Scholes European call premium for this option US$37.33. If the call can be purchased for US$37.33 today and then exercised, there is a net benefit of US$2.67.

However, by exercising early we are removing the insurance element of an option. So, in the case above, if the call is exercised and then the price of the underlying share falls to US$140 over the next month, the trader will suffer a substantially greater loss on the underlying share holding it created by the exercise than if it had kept the call option. Essentially, by exercising

Figure 13.12
Early Exercise of American Calls

Today is Sep 1, 2000 and we have an American call stock option with an exercise price of $160. The underlying price is $200 and there is one month to expiry. The underlying share will go ex-dividend tommorrow, the dividend will be $4 and the share price is expected to fall by $4 at tommorrows opening. We know the value of exercising the option today is $40 plus we receive the underlying shares.

How does this intrinsic value compare against the Black-Scholes model?

Using the model from *Figure 13.7* we compare the premium value of an option using Black-Scholes and comparing it against the current value of exercising the option today.

Inputs	
Current share price =	200.00
PV of dividends =	4.00
Adjusted share price =	**196.00**
Exercise price =	160.00
Volatility =	20.00%
Time =	1/12
Interest rate =	10.00%
Option type (*P* or *C*)	C

Option premium — $	**37.33**
Option delta	99.16%

Early exercise value	**40.00**
Difference	**2.67**

Dividend present value calculations
Enter values in white cells.

Inputs	
Today	1-Sep-00
Ex-dividend date	2-Sep-00
Dividend amount $	4.00
Interest rate % pa	9.50%
Time yrs	0.0027
Dividend PV	3.9990
Adjusted spot price	196.0010

early, there is a trade-off between the future insurance value and the value of the dividend today. This is the reason early exercise of calls is only ever likely on very deep-in-the-money calls where the time, or insurance value, is very low and they effectively have the same characteristics of the underlying share (i.e., a delta close to one). For any option with a delta of around 0.95 or lower, the benefit of time value is likely to offset the benefit of early exercise.

The adjustment for the early exercise of a call is the same used for a put: we need to ensure that the value of the call is at least equivalent to its exercisable value. In order to derive a "pseudo-American" formula using Black-Scholes we adjust it as follows:

$$\text{Call}_{\text{AMERICAN}} = \text{Max}(S - X, \text{Call}_{\text{EUROPEAN}})$$

Where:

$\text{Call}_{\text{EUROPEAN}}$ is the dividend adjusted Black-Scholes model.

13.4 EXCHANGE-TRADED OPTIONS AND MARGINING

As is the case with exchange-traded futures contracts, exchange-traded options are subject to margining by a centralized clearinghouse. In the case of "premium-style" options, the buyer of the option is not affected as he or she pays the premium upfront and that is effectively the only cash flow until the options are sold.[11] However, reflecting the lopsided risk profile of options, the seller is subject to the imposition of margins which are equivalent to the current option premium plus an initial margin or performance bond. When an option contract is executed, the seller receives the premium from the buyer, but this is held by the clearinghouse until the contract is closed.

Although the seller receives the premium from the buyer, the seller must fund a margin requirement—effectively decreasing the value of the premium received under the option equivalent to the funding cost of the margin. As a result, an option seller may receive a slightly higher premium from a stock option than an equivalent OTC equity option, in order to assist in the recouping of the funding cost.

In the case of futures-style margining, both the buyer and seller are subject to a daily mark-to-market as well as an initial margin. When a transaction is executed, both parties must pay an initial margin rather than the payment of a premium. This margin will reflect a worst case one day loss for the option holders. As the option premium changes over time, both the buyer and seller will be marked-to-market on a daily basis. The premium is not paid until exercise of the contract, and, because of the mark-to-market, this will be equivalent to the premium at the time of exercise.

This margining system creates a bias toward the buyer, as in most situations the premium payment is delayed. The seller faces similar problems as encountered with the premium-style options in that they do not receive the premium today and they must fund an initial margin. Not surprisingly, the margining results for a seller under both futures and premium-style margining is basically the same.

In those markets that offer futures-style margining, the pricing model used by the SFE is the Black model, but without a present value calculation applied to the exercise price; that is, the model recognizes that if nothing else changes, the premium will be paid at expiry. This model was shown in *Figure 13.4*.

While this does adjust for the pricing bias in futures-style margining transactions, it is on the basis that all payments take place at expiry of the option. However, like futures, all mark-to-market gains and losses occur today

[11] Most equity options are "premium-style." The only exceptions are "futures-style" SPI options.

rather than at expiry date. This has the same outcome as futures, whereby there is no difference between forward and present values.[12]

The mechanisms for deriving the initial margin, or performance bonds, is provided in some detail in the appendix to this chapter. It is important to note that the margining procedures and the impact upon options outlined above apply equally to all exchange-traded options.

SUMMARY

This chapter developed options pricing models that expand upon the generic Black-Scholes model. We formulated pricing tools to enable us to adapt the specific characteristics of the underlying stock index or share, by taking into account dividend, volatility skews and early exercise of options. We also discussed margin methodologies for exchange-traded options.

SELF-TEST QUESTIONS

1. Explain the difference between an option on a cash SPI and an option on an SPI futures contract.

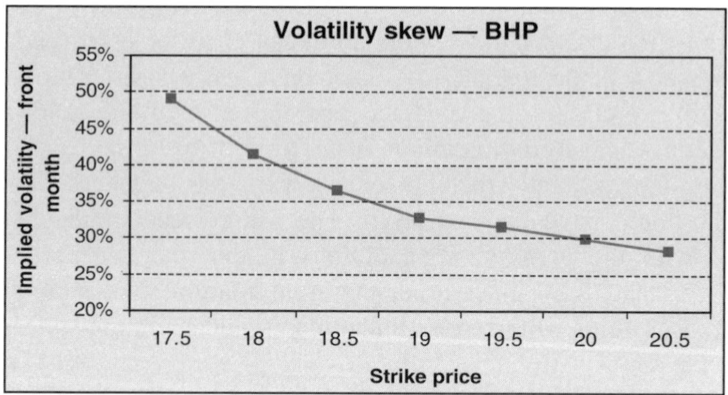

2. Analyze the above diagram. How do you interpret the information given in this diagram?
3. Toby holds an American call stock option with an exercise price of US$125. The underlying price is US$150 and there are two months until expiry. The underlying share goes ex-dividend tomorrow and the dividend

[12] Convexity adjustments are not usually applied to equity options; however, we can see from this reasoning that futures-style interest rate options will exhibit the same convexity biases as interest rate futures.

will be US$3 and the share price is expected to fall by US$3 tomorrow as a result. Calculate the option's intrinsic value.

4. Use the Black-Scholes method to calculate the value of the option in Question 3 above. How do the values compare?

5. Explain the reason why early exercise of calls is only likely on deep-in-the-money calls.

6. What variable(s), which do not apply to the seller of an OTC option, should the seller of an ET option factor into their option valuation model?

APPENDIX

EXCHANGE-TRADED MARGINING SYSTEMS

1 INTRODUCTION[13]

This appendix provides an overview of the two main ET margining systems, SPAN and TIMS.[14] The objective of this appendix is to explain why clearing-houses set initial margins and how they have reacted in terms of devising margining systems that protect them against risk without pricing an undue burden on market-users.

This appendix develops a framework for understanding the magnitude of initial margins in order to determine the potential funding impact on futures and options.

> **Note**
> While the appendix is part of the equity options chapter, the margining procedures described are equally applicable to exchange-traded interest rate and currency instruments.

[13] Some of this Appendix is based on an article written by the author titled "Managing Risk: Exchange Style," in *Financial Derivatives and Risk Management*, Issue 3, November 1995.

[14] SPAN and TIMS are respectively registered trademarks of the Chicago Mercantile Exchange and The Options Clearing Corporation (OCC). All comments and calculations in this article reflect the author's understanding of these two systems and are provided purely for exposition purposes.

2 THE RISK FACED BY A CLEARINGHOUSE

2.1 The Guarantee

The clearinghouse plays a key role in the operation of an exchange and is one of the distinguishing features between exchange-traded and OTC markets. The primary role of a clearinghouse is to register all contracts traded on an exchange with its clearing members and to guarantee the performance of these contracts to both buyers and sellers until the contract expires. The nature of this guarantee can be on a net or gross basis. Internationally, 30 clearinghouses guarantee on a net basis, while around ten provide some form of gross guarantee.

In a net clearing market, the clearinghouse provides a guarantee on the net position held by each clearing member. The guarantee does not extend to the clearing member's clients. There are various alternative forms of gross clearing, but in its pure form, it involves the clearinghouse providing a guarantee to all clearing members and their clients. Other forms of gross clearing include collecting initial margins at a client level, but only providing a guarantee to the clearing member.

While most clearinghouses guarantee only the clearing member, it is common for the clearing members to separate positions into "house" and "client" accounts. While the clearinghouse does not recognize the underlying clients, there are restrictions placed on the rights of the clearinghouse to use client funds to offset house account losses.

Whether the clearinghouse provides a net or gross guarantee has a substantial impact upon the magnitude of the risk it assumes; a clearinghouse with a net guarantee faces less risk than if it provided a gross guarantee. This is because a net clearinghouse benefits if a clearing member has clients with offsetting positions. From the clearinghouse point of view, it only provides a guarantee on the net of these clients' positions, while the clearing member carries a counterparty exposure for each of the client positions. A net clearinghouse essentially shifts part of the guarantee requirement to its clearing members.

Example

Figure 13.13 shows the difference between a net and gross clearinghouse. Suppose Client A holds 100 long futures contracts and Client B holds 60 short futures contracts through Clearing Member XYZ. In a gross clearing environment, the clearing house faces an exposure to loss if Client A and Client B default and so it carries a risk of loss equivalent to $+100$ and -60 contracts.

However, under a net clearing scenario, the clearinghouse has a substantially reduced exposure to loss of $+40$ contracts held by XYZ. The degree of netting is not always this extreme, but a rough estimate is that the guarantee risk of a gross clearinghouse is three times that of a net clearinghouse.

Figure 13.13
Clearinghouse Exposure — Market and Credit Risk

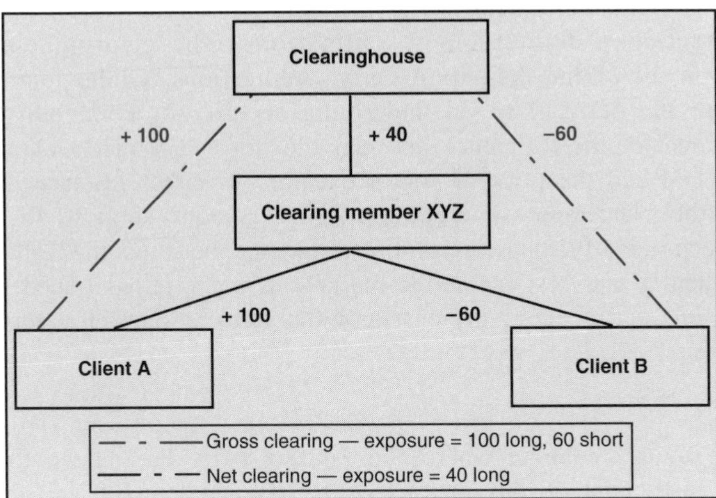

The form of the guarantee will have a substantial impact on the size of the financial backing required by the clearinghouse and the magnitude of total margins it holds. Although there are no data available providing net and gross initial margins for a clearinghouse, it is fair to say that initial margin levels for gross clearinghouses are higher than for net clearinghouses. We can make a general comparison between CME, which collects initial margins on a gross basis, and CBOT, which collects initial margins on a net basis.[15] Both markets have a similar level of volume in lots; however, the end of the CME often holds more than three times the level of initial margins of the CBOT.[16]

Clients of clearing members are also affected by the nature of the guarantee. It is still a common presumption by users of futures and options markets that their counterparty risk is to the exchange clearinghouse. In fact this is not the case with a net clearinghouse; the client's counterparty exposure is directly to the clearing member.

2.2 The Exposure of a Clearinghouse: Market and Credit Risk

By guaranteeing the performance of all registered contracts, the clearinghouse is a central and highly creditworthy counterparty. However, by providing

[15] Although the CME collects initial margins on a gross basis, it provides a net guarantee.

[16] This is only a loose comparison because the nature of the underlying contracts on both exchanges is very different and the relationship between volume and open position is likely to differ.

this service, the clearinghouse creates substantial exposures that need to be managed.

The clearinghouse is exposed to the possibility that one of the parties to a contract may default on its obligations. The clearinghouse must then perform all of the defaulting party's obligations. Obligations under a contract are the delivery of an underlying security or commodity, or the cash settlement of the difference between the price at which a contract was bought or sold and the price at contract expiry. In either instance, the magnitude of the clearinghouse credit exposure is equivalent to the market risk of a counterparty's positions—the difference between the value of the position when it was last marked-to-market or, the original traded value of the defaulting party's commitment, and the current market value of that commitment.

Example

Consider a futures contract where a defaulting party has agreed to buy an underlying instrument on the contract expiry date of US$100 and the actual value on the expiry date is US$80. The exposure the clearinghouse has to the buyer is US$20; if the buyer defaults, the clearinghouse will still pay the seller US$100 and when it sells the delivered instrument back to the market it will only receive US$80. The clearinghouse's risk is always the market replacement, or liquidation, cost of a defaulting position.

In terms of categories of risk, the clearinghouse has a credit risk to each buyer and seller of open contracts equivalent to the current market risk of the derivative instrument. The aim of all clearinghouses is to offset this credit risk to the greatest extent possible by collecting sufficient collateral from open position holders.

However, when determining the amount of collateral it collects, the clearing house needs to ensure that it does not place an unreasonably large financial burden on position holders. To some degree, the amount of collateral held represents a trade-off between covering a clearing house's risk and maintaining a reasonable level of transaction costs for market users.

3 THE MARGINING PROCESS

In order to offset counterparty credit exposures, clearinghouses have developed a margining process that marks positions to market and collects collateral in the form of initial margins. Reflecting the growing size and complexity of derivative markets, these systems have continued to evolve in terms of processing capabilities and modeling accuracy.

The aim of this margining process is to reduce the magnitude of clearinghouse exposure. The clearinghouse is only exposed to a counterparty loss where the price movement exceeds the amount of initial margins held since the last mark-to-market.

3.1 Mark-to-Market

The first step in margining is the mark-to-market. A set of current market prices is applied to each clearing member's portfolio at the close of trading and a total profit or loss is crystallized. The cash flows arising from these profits and losses are typically settled before the commencement of trading the following day. Any failure by a clearing member to pay its losses will result in the clearing house liquidating the member's portfolio.

> ***Note***
> The longer the time horizon of a clearinghouse's guarantee, the larger its exposure. For example, the market risk of a position for one day is substantially less than for one month. The more frequently positions are marked-to-market, the lower the market risk faced by a clearinghouse.

Most clearinghouses mark-to-market, at least, at the close of business each day. A number of clearinghouses, including CME and CBOT, perform a second mark-to-market at the end of morning trading. Other clearinghouses perform intra-day mark-to-markets on an ad hoc basis when there is significant market volatility. When the mark-to-market is performed it should reflect the true liquidation cost of a counterparty's portfolio and its accuracy depends on the accuracy of the market prices used in the calculation. As a consequence, in most markets the clearinghouse pays close attention to the generation of closing market prices.

3.2 Initial Margins

The second step is to determine the initial margin to be applied to each clearing member's portfolio.[17] This initial margin amount represents a "worst case" loss on each counterparty's portfolio over one full trading day. In other words, the initial margin represents the portfolio's daily value at risk. While the initial margin period is one trading day for most clearinghouses, New York-based NYMEX assume that it will take two trading days to liquidate a portfolio and initial margins are set accordingly.

After defining the initial margin period, the next decision is to determine what represents a "worst case" movement in each of the parameters that

[17] The terms "performance bond," "initial margin," "additional margin" and "deposit margin" tend to be used interchangeably within futures and options markets. For the remainder of this article we will use "initial margin."

can affect the market value of a portfolio. The primary value driver in most portfolios is the underlying contract price. This is calculated by determining the historical distribution of price movements and setting the initial margins at a required frequency. This frequency is usually defined as a confidence interval; generally this falls somewhere between a 95% level and the 99.7% used by Options Clearing Corporation (OCC). A confidence level of 95% means that the initial margins are set to cover the absolute level of price movements for every 95 trading days out of 100.

This distribution will vary according to the historical time period used. The nature of the results depends on the term of the sample: distributions over a long time frame provide a good indication of the range of possible movements, while short-term distributions are a good indicator of current market conditions. Clearinghouses tend to be flexible in terms of the historical period used as a benchmark for initial margins and generate distributions ranging anywhere from three months to ten years.

The confidence level underlying the initial margin tends to be traded off against the frequency of mark-to-markets and the number of trading days assumed necessary to liquidate the portfolio. For an organization like CME, using a 95% confidence level is higher than it appears because the mark-to-market occurs every half day, but the initial margin is still set to cover a full day's price movement.

The nature of the historical distribution also has a bearing on the initial margin level. If price distributions are assumed to be normal, initial margins can be calculated as a multiple of the historical standard deviation. For example, a 99% confidence level equates to three times the standard deviation. However, as most financial asset prices exhibit a "fat-tailed" distribution this approach tends to underestimate the true historical confidence level. As a consequence, many clearinghouses generate historical frequency distributions to calculate a more accurate confidence level.

Figure 13.14 plots the actual distribution of daily price movements in the Australian dollar ten-year bond futures price traded on the Sydney Futures Exchange (SFE). The actual distribution is plotted against an assumed normal distribution for the same data series. A confidence level using a normal distribution will significantly underestimate the actual confidence level due to the relatively high number of large price changes in the actual distribution.

While this historical analysis plays an important part in setting initial margins, it is not mechanically applied. In most clearinghouses, there is some subjectivity in setting initial margins—the historical volatility is used as a minimum level and then a buffer is added for the influence of other factors, such as expected future price volatility, market concentration and liquidity. Traditionally, this means that clearinghouses are quick to increase initial margins and slow to decrease them. Also, in many markets, the

Figure 13.14
Historical SFE 10-year Bond Price Distribution

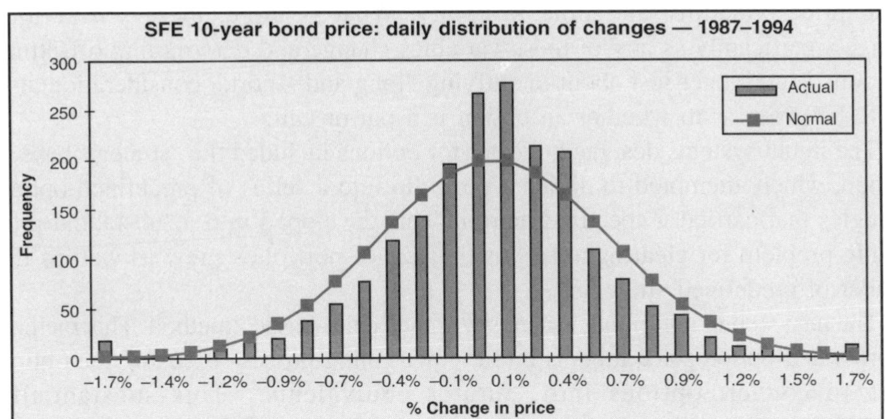

clearinghouse is subject to minimum initial margin levels set by the board, the exchange or regulators.

The clearinghouse is not just exposed to outright movements in price. Any factors that influence the value of a portfolio need to be incorporated into the measurement of this exposure. Depending on the positions in a portfolio, it may be influenced by movements in time, the price spread between delivery months, the correlation between different contracts and also changes in implied volatility. All of these factors are monitored in a similar fashion to outright price movements and, when an initial margin is generated, it also takes account of a worst case movement in these parameters.

Once the initial margin parameters have been identified, a system is required that will apply these "worst case" parameters to portfolios of clearing members and clients and accurately model their impact. There has been considerable change over the past decade in the systems used to model portfolio behavior, with the transition from simple strategy and delta-based systems to the current portfolio-based simulation methodologies such as SPAN and TIMS.

4 MARGINING SYSTEMS

The systems for generating initial margins on ET derivatives up until the 1970s were quite straight forward. Volume was relatively small and the contracts were primarily futures, which meant that the current initial margin and the maximum loss on a futures contract were the same. The situation became considerably more complicated with the development of options contracts. In the case of an option, the influence of the initial margin is variable, depending on the absolute level of the underlying price, the option's strike price, volatility and time to expiry. What is more, these sensitivities change significantly as any of these variables change and determining offsetting positions is no longer just about identifying "long and 'short;" consideration also has to be given as to whether an option is a put or call.

The initial systems designed to cater for options included the "strategy-based" method, which attempted to divide a portfolio into a series of predefined option strategies that carried a specified margin. This developed into a substantial processing problem for clearinghouses as the size of portfolios grew as well as the number of predefined strategies.

The next step in margining systems was the "delta-based" method. This method incorporated option price models into the margining process by using the option delta to convert options into "futures equivalents." This substantially reduced the processing burden of the strategy method but because of its inaccuracies in modeling option pricing behavior, it often led to significant under- or overmargining of portfolios. For example, a delta neutral strategy involving a sold put and call may not have been subject to a margin when in fact the position carried a significant risk of loss. Various "work-arounds" were developed to overcome the majority of the undermargining scenarios, but the overall inaccuracy of this method persisted.

In the early 1980s, both CME and OCC were working on methods of overcoming the problems with the strategy-based and delta-based systems. While the underlying markets for both clearinghouses were different—agricultural and financial futures and options for CME and equity options for OCC—their aim was the same: to build a system that would accurately model the profit and loss risk profile of a complex portfolio over a range of defined movements in market prices. A feature of these margining systems was that while they would provide an accurate measure of risk, they also needed to be capable of processing large volumes of transactions in a short time frame to meet the clearinghouses daily processing schedule.

After considerable development work, OCC implemented TIMS in 1986 and CME introduced SPAN in 1988. Since then, both systems have continued to be enhanced and have been adopted by clearinghouses around the globe. TIMS has been adopted by seven clearinghouses and SPAN by 12 clearinghouses. While both systems are used on a range of markets, SPAN has been adopted by futures and options markets while TIMS has primarily been introduced to equity options markets.

Reasons behind the success of SPAN and TIMS include:

- a willingness on behalf of CME and OCC to provide the systems to other clearinghouses and strong support from both groups;

- the development of low-cost personal computer versions of the software that could be used by clearing members and their clients;
- the substantially lower cost for a clearinghouse of introducing SPAN or TIMS instead of developing a similar system internally;
- a desire by clearinghouses to develop a standardised risk benchmark;
- the need to reduce the development workload of clearing members, by providing a standardized margining system.

Clearinghouses not using SPAN or TIMS use a form of strategy-based margining or have their own in-house risk-based margining systems. Most of these risk-based approaches share a similar general methodology to SPAN and TIMS; differences relate to the calculation of the risks associated with spread positions across months and contracts.

5 SIMILARITIES AND DIFFERENCES BETWEEN SPAN AND TIMS

Given their similar development history, it is not surprising that the margining methodology of SPAN and TIMS is similar. The pricing behavior of the instruments they cleared had similar characteristics and they were influenced by developments in over-the-counter risk management systems. The matrix approach to calculating risk in both SPAN and TIMS has a lot in common with the emerging use "what-if" risk management evaluation by OTC option market-makers in the early 1980s. Furthermore, both organizations are based in Chicago and while there is a degree of competition between the two systems, OCC and CME share quite a close working relationship.

The similarities of SPAN and TIMS are highlighted by the margining practice of the Hong Kong Futures Exchange Clearing Corporation. Clearing members are margined by the clearinghouse using TIMS but are permitted to use SPAN to margin clients. This occurs without undue distortion in the margins calculated.

The table below provides a summary of some of these similarities and differences between the two methodologies:

Area	SPAN	TIMS
Main market users	Futures and options	Equity options
Methodology	Portfolio risk-based	Portfolio risk-based
Type of system	Documented algorithm	Full clearing system
PC version available	Yes	Yes
Scanning parameters	Underlying price and volatility	Underlying price
Inter-contract spread	Delta equivalent offset	Scanning approach

Figure 13.15
Clearinghouses using SPAN and TIMS

Clearinghouse	Country	1994 volume Millions of contracts	Total initial Margins Dec 94 - US$ m	Exchanges cleared
SPAN users				
1 Chicago board of trade clearing corporation	US	222.6	2,300	CBOT, MIDAM
2 COMEX clearing association	US	20.4	n/a	COMEX
3 Commodity clearing corporation	US	4.7	119	NYCE, FINEX
4 Commodity futures clearing corp. of New York	US	13.4	681	CSCE
5 Chicago mercantile exchange, clearing division	US	225.2	9,180	CME
6 Kansas city board of trade clearing corporation	US	1.7	n/a	KCBT
7 London clearinghouse*	UK	219.0	3,476	LCE, LIFFE, LTOM, LME
8 MATIF S.A., Paris**	France	93.4	2,743	MATIF
9 New York mercantile exchange, clearing division	US	58.3	1,700	NYMEX
10 Sydney futures exchange clearinghouse**	Australia	32.4	284	SFE, NZFOE
11 Singapore international monetary exchange	Singapore	24.1	n/a	SIMEX
12 Winnipeg commodity clearing Ltd	US	1.6	n/a	WCE
Total		**916.8**	**20,482**	
TIMS users				
1 EOCC clearing corporation	Italy	6.4	62	EOE
2 Cassa di compensazione Garanzia	Germany	59.2	805	MEF, IDEM
3 Deutsche terminborse***	Netherlands	13.7	728	DTB
4 HKFE clearing corporation	Hong Kong	4.8	295	HKFE
5 Options clearing corporation	US	282.3	8,610	CBOE,AMEX,NYSE,PSE,PHLX
6 Options clearinghouse	Australia	10.2	155	ASX
7 Trans Canada options Inc***	Canada	5.8	138	ME,TSE,VSE,TFE
Total		**382.4**	**10,794**	

Notes:
* LME is margined using a delta-based methodology
** MATIF and NZFOE commenced using SPAN in 1995
*** Modified version of TIMS

Source: McGaw(1995).

5.1 Margining Methodology

SPAN and TIMS are not actually computer systems—they represent frameworks, or algorithms, for calculating initial margins. In the case of SPAN, CME does not sell a SPAN clearing system. It provides detailed documentation to assist the implementing clearinghouse to program its clearing system and a PC-based program called "PC-SPAN." TIMS on the other hand is offered more as an "off-the-shelf" product, designed to run on an IBM AS/400™. Alternatively, there is a PC-based version of the software (PC-TIMS™).

Both algorithms rely on generating the worst case loss on a contract portfolio, adjusting this loss for the net premium cost or benefit from liquidating any options positions, and then adjusting for any offsetting profits generated by closely correlated portfolios in other contracts.

The algorithm for generating initial margins can be summarized for both SPAN and TIMS as follows:

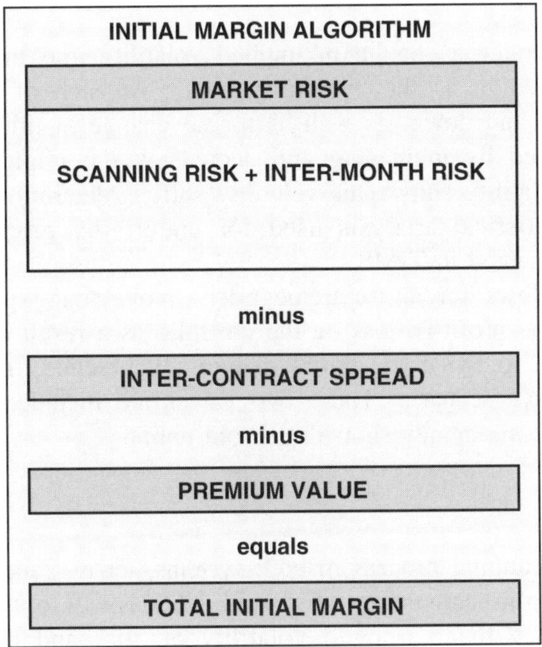

5.2 Scanning Risk

The scanning risk reflects the maximum loss (referred to as the "active scenario") of the portfolio in each contract given a range of worst case movements in the initial margin parameters—price, volatility and time (this range of outcomes is the "scanning array"). While the portfolio scanned usually contains just the delivery months in a single contract, both SPAN and TIMS allow scanning to occur for a defined "combined commodity" or "class group." This allows the combination of highly correlated contracts into one portfolio for margining purposes. Perfect underlying price correlation is assumed in the initial scanning phase for all instruments in a portfolio.

In both SPAN and TIMS, the underlying price is moved up or down by the initial margin amount (referred to as the "scanning range" in SPAN and the "margin interval" in TIMS) and time is reduced by one trading day. As well as valuing the portfolio at this extreme price movement up and down, both systems also value the portfolio at equal intervals between these initial margin amounts to pick up strategies where the largest loss occurs between the two extreme moves (e.g., bought straddles and strangles). TIMS divides the price move up and down into ten intervals, while SPAN divides it into three. In TIMS the margin interval is expressed as a percentage and in SPAN the price move is expressed in terms of the underlying instrument's contract value change. In the case of a futures contract the scanning risk will be the same as the price movement.

SPAN incorporates a change in implied volatility into the scanning risk calculation, referred to as the "volatility shift." At each of the three price movements go up and down, as well as for no change in price, the portfolio value is determined by increasing and decreasing the implied volatility of options by the volatility shift. This volatility shift is determined by using the same type of statistical analysis used for underlying price. The implied volatility is not changed in TIMS.

SPAN also allows for an "extreme price" move that typically is calculated as 35% of the profit or loss on the portfolio as a result of a price move up or down equal to twice the initial margin—in practice, these two values are rarely the active scenario. These two values are included to capture the risk of deep out-of-the-money short dated sold options.

Example

To illustrate the scanning process in both systems, let us generate a scanning array for a portfolio consisting of a sold US$21 call option on a stock trading at US$20 with an implied volatility of 30% and three months to expiry. Suppose the initial margin is US$2 (or 10% of the stock price) and the volatility shift is a flat change of 5%. An estimate of scanning arrays under a "TIMS-like" and "SPAN-like" methodology is summarized in *Figure 13.16*. The scanning risk is obtained by identifying the largest loss across all scenarios in the scanning array. Both systems generate the loss based on the same price scenario of US$22; however, the SPAN scanning risk is higher because of the increase in volatility to 35%.

Note

A common misconception about both systems is that they support only one option pricing model: SPAN uses the Black model and TIMS uses the Cox Ross Rubenstein Binomial model. In fact *both* methodologies will adapt to any option model(s) the implementing clearinghouse wishes to use.

Figure 13.16
An Example of SPAN and TIMS Margining

Option details	
Number of shares	1,000
Underlying price	20
Strike	21
Volatility	30%
Premium	$ 788

SPAN scanning array*				**TIMS scanning array***		
Scanning range			$ 2,000	Margin interval		10%
Volatility shift			5%			
Scenario	Price	Volatility	Portfolio profit/loss	Scenario	Price	Portfolio profit/loss
1	20.00	35%	$ (194)	1	20.20	$ (82)
2	20.00	25%	$ 191	2	19.80	$ 77
3	20.67	35%	$ (501)	3	20.40	$ (170)
4	20.67	25%	$ (90)	4	19.60	$ 150
5	19.33	35%	$ 63	5	20.60	$ (263)
6	19.33	25%	$ 405	6	19.40	$ 217
7	21.33	35%	$ (858)	7	20.80	$ (366)
8	21.33	25%	$ (440)	8	19.20	$ 280
9	18.67	35%	$ 272	9	21.00	$ (469)
10	18.67	25%	$ 559	10	19.00	$ 337
11	**22.00**	**35%**	**$ (1,261)**	11	21.20	$ (578)
12	22.00	25%	$ (855)	12	18.80	$ 390
13	18.00	35%	$ 436	13	21.40	$ (687)
14	18.00	25%	$ 661	14	18.60	$ 439
15	24.00	30%	$ (894)	15	21.60	$ (805)
16	16.00	30%	$ 262	16	18.40	$ 483
				17	21.80	$ (928)
				18	18.20	$ 523
				19	**22.00**	**$ (1,056)**
				20	18.00	$ 558
Scanning risk			**$ 1,261**			**$ 1,056**
Active scenario:		Price up 3/3, vol up			Price up 10/10	

Note: * These are estimates only.

5.3 Inter-Month Risk

The scanning process initially assumes perfect correlation between all contracts within a portfolio. In many products, such as agricultural products or short-term interest rate futures, the price correlation between different contract delivery months is less than perfect and the spread between delivery months can be subject to considerable volatility.[18] To take account of the possibility of a portfolio losing money due to movements in inter-month spreads, an extra initial margin is added on for all offsetting positions between delivery months.

The inter-month spread methodology used in SPAN has developed a complexity of its own. For example, in short-term interest rate contracts, it is possible to build a matrix of inter-month spread relationships between every delivery month. So, in a contract with 40 delivery months like the Eurodollar, it is possible to set up to 780 individual spread initial margins! In practice, clearinghouses limit the number of spreads by grouping together the more closely correlated delivery months and setting spreads between these groups.

5.4 Inter-Contract Spread

Another potentially complex area of the initial margin algorithm is the assessment of deductions to market risk due to offsetting positions in closely correlated contracts. This is known as inter-contract spread or inter-commodity concession. The practice of providing inter-contract spreads varies widely across clearinhouses. It is in a clearinghouse's interest to hold as much collateral as possible, so providing spread concessions is treated with considerable caution. The contracts need to show a high and very stable level of correlation before any inter-commodity spread will be considered.

Examples of inter-contract spreads include offsetting bought and sold positions between medium- and long-term bond futures contracts, between equity options in similar industry groups, or between closely correlated currency contracts.

Both SPAN and TIMS offer sophisticated approaches to providing inter-contract concessions. The idea in SPAN is to identify closely correlated portfolios, determine the quantity of offsetting positions between portfolios (identified by the delta equivalent futures position) and then provide a percentage deduction to the scanning risk based on the number of offsetting positions. TIMS, on the other hand, compares the profit and loss profile of two

[18] For example, in short-term interest rate futures such as the Eurodollar contract, the correlation co-efficient between the first and last delivery months can be in the order of 0.60.

correlated portfolios at each of the scenarios in the scanning process when determining the inter-contract concessions.

5.5 Premium Value

The premium value reflects the current market value of option positions. Most exchanges require that option premiums be paid upfront.[19] This means liquidating a long option position will generate cash equivalent to the premium, while liquidating a short option position will have a cash cost equal to the current premium. If a portfolio is net long options, then liquidating the portfolio will generate cash equivalent to the net long option value of the portfolio. On the other hand, a net short option portfolio will have an additional cost equivalent to the net short option value.

In terms of the clearinghouse's market exposure, a net long option position effectively represents additional collateral that can be credited against the market risk calculation.[20] For a portfolio containing only long options the premium value will always be at least the equivalent of the market risk so no initial margin collateral will be required.

5.6 Total Initial Margin

The outcome of both the SPAN and TIMS approach to the margining algorithm is to generate a total initial margin figure that reflects the true risk profile of a clearing member or client across all portfolios.

The total initial margin for each clearing member can be added together to provide an estimate of the clearinghouse's total market risk. Using the data from *Figure 13.15*, the total market risk of all positions cleared using SPAN and TIMS clearinghouses in the mid-1990s was US$15.6bn![21]

The two methodologies have deliberately been designed as a generalized solution to derivative risk management. This is primarily to cater for the development of new exchange traded products but it also allows for the incorporation of OTC products; provided the pricing characteristics can be modeled and the primary "risk-drivers" are price, volatility and time, any type of instrument can be integrated into either SPAN or TIMS.

[19] An exception to this is options on futures traded on the Sydney Futures Exchange and the Hong Kong Futures Exchange, where options are marked-to-market and the premium is paid at expiry. In these markets the premium value is always zero.

[20] The maximum amount of this premium value credit is the amount of the market risk.

[21] It is common practice to halve the total initial margin collected by the clearinghouse when calculating its market risk, as the initial margins are held from equally offsetting long- and short-position holders. In a market crash, prices will only move one way—causing a loss for only one side (or half) the market.

CHAPTER 14

INTERESTING RATE OPTIONS

🖫 The models developed in this chapter are saved as Microsoft Excel™ files in the enclosed disk.

OVERVIEW

This chapter outlines the complexity of modeling the distribution of interest rates and examines various valuation models for both ET and OTC interest rate options. By the end of this chapter we will have developed valuation models for the following instruments:

- caps and floors;
- options on short-term futures: Eurodollar, Euro, A$ bank bill;
- bond options;
- options on bond futures: US T-bond, Bund, A$ 3/10 year bond;
- swaptions.

14.1 INTRODUCTION

14.1.1 Types of Interest Rate Options

The range of interest rate options products is broader than other categories, reflecting the variety of underlying interest-bearing instruments. It is usual to distinguish between interest rate options by the type of market in which they are traded; that is, whether they are OTC or exchange-traded.

A brief description of the main types of interest rate option are provided below:

OTC Interest Rate Options

- **Caps** An option to "cap" a borrower's level of interest against an agreed floating interest index (e.g., LIBOR). A cap is often thought of as a call on interest rates.[1] A cap can consist of a single option to cover one floating

[1] We have to be wary of the use of put and call with interest rate options, as the price of the instrument can be expressed in terms of yield or price. The movement of price and yield are opposite and an interest rate call is a price put.

interest rate rollover period (often referred to as a "caplet") or it can be a series of options to cover multiple rollovers (a "strip" of caps). The underlying instrument determines the pricing of a cap is an FRA.

- **Floors** This is equivalent to a put on short-term interest rates. It is an option to ensure an investor's level of interest does not fall below an agreed level (the "floor") of an interest index for a period of time. The underlying instrument is also an FRA.
- **Collars** A combination of a cap and a floor. The level of interest is agreed to remain within a predefined band or collar (i.e., between a cap and floor rate) for a period of time.
- **Swaptions** An option to enter into a swap at an agreed rate at some date in the future. The underlying instrument is a forward start swap.
- **Bond options** An option to buy or sell physical bonds at an agreed price and date in the future. The underlying instrument is a forward bond.

ET Interest Rate Options

- **Option on short-term interest rate futures** An option to buy the underlying short-term futures contract at an agreed exercise price and usually just prior to, or on, the underlying futures expiry date (e.g., Eurodollar, Euroyen or bank bill).[2]
- **Option on bond futures** An option to buy the underlying bond futures contract at an agreed exercise price and agreed expiry date.

The largest participants of interest rate options are end-users, as opposed to financial intermediaries. End-users tend to use these products depending on the part of the yield curve to which they are exposed. In general, volume in options on short-term underlying instruments is higher than options on long-term underlying instruments (e.g., bonds). *Figure 14.1* provides a method of classifying interest rate options by the term of the underlying interest rate exposure.

14.2 SPECIAL CONSIDERATIONS

The pricing of interest rate options is more complex than pricing currency and equity options. This is due to the fact that there are elements in the value

[2] Many exchanges now list serial options on futures contracts (e.g., Eurodollar and bank bill). In this case, there is a series of up to three options listed on the front contract of the underlying futures contract. The first option expires two months prior to the underlying futures contract, the next options expires one month prior and the last expires at approximately the same time as the underlying futures contract.

Figure 14.1
Use of Interest Rate Options

Interest rate options general hedging categories		
Interest rate exposure	**OTC**	**ETO**
Short-term debt issuer	Buy caps	Buy puts on S/T futures
Short-term investor	Buy floors	Buy calls on S/T futures
Medium-term debt issuer	Buy payer swaptions Buy cap strips	Buy series of puts on S/T futures
Medium-term investor	Buy receiver swaptions Buy floor strips	Buy series of puts on S/T futures
Long-term debt issuer	Buy bond option puts	Buy puts on bond futures
Long-term investor	Buy bond option calls	Buy calls on bond futures

of interest-bearing assets that are non-random. Given that the basic assumption underlying the Black-Scholes model is that the spot price of the underlying instrument is a random variable, we need to build models that incorporate all the characteristics of the underlying price behavior.

The scope of this book is limited to a Black-Scholes environment; however, it is important to appreciate some of the potential sources of pricing imperfection. Some of these imperfections include:

- **Multiple yields** When valuing an option on an interest-bearing security, we are not only exposed to the volatility of the yield on the underlying instrument but also the "funding" interest rate to the expiry date of the option. These two interest rates are of different terms and will have different volatilities; however, they will be correlated to some extent. How do we incorporate both price distributions in the option price and also take account of correlation? Most practitioners avoid this problem by modeling forward yields; that is, they use a yield that has already incorporated both interest rates and then price the option based on this yield. This forward yield can be applied directly to the Black model developed in Chapter 13.

- **"Pull to par"** As time passes, the price of an interest-bearing security always moves towards its par value. For example, a bond that is currently priced at a price of 95 with two years to maturity will have a price at maturity of par or 100, and every day that passes will pull the bond price toward par. If we buy a bond option that is aging, we need to somehow incorporate this price "drift." We have limited capacity to incorporate this into a Black-Scholes environment because we cannot control the evolution of price behavior over time. However, it does suggest that using Black-Scholes is less prone to error where the time to expiry of the option relative to the term of the underlying instrument is short, or where the underlying instrument does not start aging or accruing interest till the option expires.

- **Changing price volatility** Associated with the "pull to par" is the fact that the price sensitivity of an interest-bearing instrument declines as time passes. For example, the sensitivity of the price of a 10-year bond to a one basis point change in yield is considerably higher than for a 5-year bond. This undermines the Black-Scholes assumption of constant volatility—the price volatility of a bond systematically declines as it moves towards maturity. This provides a warning when using Black-Scholes to price long-term options on aging interest-bearing securities.

- **Mean reversion** Interest rates tend to be pulled back to a long-term average. If short-term rates are historically very high, they tend to move back toward the long-term average and vice versa, if rates are historically very low. This undermines the idea of interest rates moving randomly regardless of their absolute level. Further, it also implies that interest rate or yield volatility declines with the term to expiry as the longer the term to expiry of an option, the more likely it is that the yield will move to the long-term average.

- **American options and early exercise** As we have seen with equity options, if Black-Scholes cannot correctly model all of the possible underlying price outcomes, it is liable to misprice American options. Given the pricing complexities outlined above, it is highly probable that Black-Scholes may misprice American options and create the possibility of profitable early exercise. We need to be particularly careful when pricing American interest rate options in a Black-Scholes environment.

> ***Note***
> These difficulties have led to the development of a range of models that can be used to model the behavior of the yield curve over time. A binomial or trinomial tree can then be applied to solve for an option price. These models include Rendleman and Bartter; Cox Ingersol and Ross; Heath, Jarrow and Morton; Ho and Lee; and Hull and White.[3]

A key characteristic of these models is that they are computationally complex and there is relatively little material available on how to put these models into practice. Further, in some cases, the yield curve outcomes generated by the model are not consistent with the currently observed yield curve.

While there are a number of constraints on using a Black-Scholes model to price interest rate options, it is still widely used by market participants. This is because most interest rate options that are traded have a short-term relative to the time to maturity of the underlying instrument (e.g., bond options), or else they are on forward instruments that do not begin to age until the option expires (caps, floors, swaptions and options on short-term futures).

Some useful "rules of thumb" when applying Black-Scholes to interest rate options are:

1. When building an interest rate option model based around Black-Scholes:
   - always price options off an underlying forward instrument;
   - use the forward volatility of the instrument;
   - be wary of any aging or interest accrual behavior of the underlying security;
   - use European options.
2. Treat with caution:
   - long-term options on bonds;
   - options on any instrument that starts accruing interest prior to the option expiry;
   - American options.

In the remainder of this chapter, we will focus on models that price and value interest rate options in a Black-Scholes environment. The emphasis will be on producing relatively straight-forward models with commentary on possible pricing imperfections. The models will be satisfactory for end-users of these instruments. However, as market-makers need greater accuracy, they should develop the more complex yield curve models described above.

[3] For a description of these models, see Chapter 15 of John Hull's book, *Options, Futures and Other Derivative Securities.*

For the purpose of pricing, we will divide the instruments into short-term and long-term models as follows:

- short-term options
- options on short-term futures
- caps, floors and collars
- long-term options
- bonds options
- options on bond futures
- swaptions.

14.3 PRICING AND VALUING SHORT-TERM INTEREST RATE OPTIONS

14.3.1 The Underlying Instrument

We can price options on short-term futures (e.g., Eurodollars) and caps and floors using an extension of the Black model. The basic pricing premise is that the underlying instrument for both options is a forward interest rate contract: a short-term interest rate future and an FRA respectively. As we found, when we compared futures and FRAs in Part 2 of this book, the forward pricing was essentially the same. In the case of option pricing, we can extend this to the distribution of the forward price—it should be essentially the same for both instruments.

As with all options, the synthetic replication is to create a portfolio of the underlying instruments that exhibits the same pricing characteristics as the option.[4] Using this as our starting point, we derive a Black-Scholes pricing model that can be applied to the particular characteristics of each market.

In this section, we will develop a model for pricing caps and floors and then apply this to options on simple interest-based futures contracts such as the Eurodollar. We will also extend this to options on short-term instruments based on discount security pricing such as bank bill futures.

14.3.2 Pricing Caps and Floors

A cap is usually expressed in terms of a floating rate short-term interest rate index, such as 3-month LIBOR. On the expiry date of the option, if the index is above the strike interest rate (the cap) then the buyer of the option

[4]See Chapter 12 for a description of this process, or Chapter 15 for a detailed example of synthetic replication by delta hedging.

receives a cash amount equivalent to L minus the cap. In most markets, the cap is assumed to be European unless otherwise requested by the option buyer.

The cash flow generated is the same as a borrower FRA position except that if LIBOR is below the cap rate, then the option is abandoned. We can express the cap payoff in terms of yield at expiry as follows:

$$\text{Cap payoff} = \text{Max}(r_f - r_x, 0).$$

Where:

r_f = LIBOR rate at expiry
r_x = Cap or Strike interest rate.

The payoff is the same as the payoff of a call option on the variable r_f. The price of a cap prior to expiry is the same as any call option—how likely is it that the option will expire "in-the-money?"

Providing we are satisfied that the Black-Scholes assumptions about the forward short-term interest rate, r_f, are adequate, we can transform the Black model for pricing a call option discussed in Chapter 13, into a cap pricing model by entering r_f as the current forward price and, r_x as the strike price. A Black model for pricing caps and floors is provided in *Figure 14.2*. The output of the Black model is in terms of a yield percentage pa. To convert this into a dollar amount, we need to multiply the yield by interest sensitivity of the option. This interest sensitivity will be determined by the principal amount of the option and the term of the underlying interest period. As most caps and floors are executed on similar terms to FRAs, the same calculations that apply at an FRA settlement apply to a cap or floor settlement.

When we considered FRA pricing in Chapter 5, we made use of the full face value method for the major currencies or discounted face value method for Australian dollars, New Zealand dollars and some discount securities in other currencies.[5] Applying the full face value method is straightforward, as we just need to multiply the premium in yield by the face value times the term of the underlying security. The discounted face value is not as straight forward because the basis point magnitude of the intrinsic value of an option *changes* depending on the difference between the forward interest rate and the cap rate; that is, the instruments display convexity.[6] We can attempt to model the behavior of the discount face value method by approaches such as determining

[5] See Chapter 5, Section 5.2.4 for more discussion on this point.
[6] That is, there is variable tick size.

Figure 14.2
The Black Model for Caps and Floors

Option premium calculation

Cap	=	$[r_f \times \exp(-r \times t) \times N(d_1) - r_x \times \exp(-r \times t) \times N(d_2)] \times B$
Floor	=	$[r_x \times \exp(-r \times t) \times N(-d_2) - r_f \times \exp(-r \times t) \times N(-d_1)] \times B$
Cap delta	=	$\exp(-r \times t) \times N(d_1)$

Interest sensitivity calculation

B	=	$(d_c/D \times FV) \times \exp(-r_f \times d_c/D)$

Where:

B	=	underlying instrument interest sensitivity
FV	=	face value of the option
d_1	=	$(\ln(r_f/r_x) + ((v\text{^}2)/2) \times t)/(v \times t\text{^}0.5)$
d_2	=	$d_1 - v \times t\text{^}0.5$
r_x	=	exercise interest rate
r_f	=	forward interest rate
r	=	risk-free interest rate to option expiry (% pa)
t	=	time to option expiry (in years)
v	=	volatility (% pa)
ln( )	=	natural logarithm
exp( )	=	exponential function
$N(\,)$	=	the cumulative normal distribution function.

Note: all interest rates assume continuous compounding.

the "tick size" of the contract at the current futures price and multiplying this by the premium expressed as a yield. Given that the full face value method does discount the premium to the option expiry date, and that the differences are quite small, it is relatively common to apply the same formula to both forms of contract settlement calculation.

Figure 14.3 provides a "long-hand" calculation of a cap premium using the Black model and yield volatility. In this particular example, we are pricing a caplet against 3-month LIBOR (91 days) expiring in one year at a cap rate of 7% pa. The current 1-year forward 3-month rate (12 × 15 in FRA terms) is 6% pa and the 1-year rate is 6.25% pa (all rates are continuously compounded). The implied volatility of the forward yield is 25% per annum. In this case, we are calculating the premium of a cap, a floor premium can be calculated using the same model, by setting the "option type" to "F."

Figure 14.3
Using the Black Model to Price Caps and Floors Using Yields (Note this spreadsheet model also prices floors)

Inputs			Cell address
FV	=	1,000,000	\$G\$7
d_c	=	91	\$G\$8
D	=	360	\$G\$9
Option type (*F* or *C*)	=	C	\$G\$10
r_f	=	6.0000%	\$G\$11
r_x	=	7.0000%	\$G\$12
v	=	25.00%	\$G\$13
t	=	1	\$G\$14
r	=	6.25%	\$G\$15

Normal distribution constants	
a =	0.23164
b_1 =	0.31938
b_2 =	−0.35656
b_3 =	1.781478
b_4 =	−1.82126
b_5 =	1.330274

Calculations		Result	Cell address: Formula used
ln(*F/E*) =		−0.15415068	\$G\$19:=LN(G11/G12)
v^2**t*/2 =		0.03125	\$G\$20:=(G13^2)/2*(G14)
*v***t*^0.5 =		0.25	\$G\$21:=G13*(G14^0.5)
d_1:	d_1 =	−0.491602719	\$G\$23:=(G19+G20)/G21
	AdLust for F or C =	−0.491602719	\$G\$24:=IF(UPPER(LEFT(\$G\$10,1))="C",G23,−G23)
d_2:	d_2 =	−0.741602719	\$G\$26:=G23–G21
	AdLust for F or C =	−0.741602719	\$G\$27:=IF(UPPER(LEFT(\$G\$10,1))="C",G26,−G26)
$N(d_1)$:	*k* =	0.90	\$G\$29:=1/(1+ABS(\$L\$10*G24))
	1/(2*22/7)^0.5 =	0.398862018	\$G\$30:=1/(2*22/7)^0.5
	EXP((−*z*^2)/2) =	0.886178734	\$G\$31:=EXP(((G24)^2*−1)/2)
	Calculation =	0.3114	\$G\$32:=(G30*G31*(\$L\$11*G29+\$L\$12*G29^2+\$L\$13*G29^3 +\$L\$14*G29^4+\$L\$15*G29^5))
	$N(d_1)$ =	0.311437438	\$G\$33:=IF(G24>0,1−G32,G32)
$N(d_2)$:	*k* =	0.85	\$G\$35:=1/(1+ABS(\$L\$10*G27))
	1/(2*22/7)^0.5 =	0.398862018	\$G\$36:=1/(2*22/7)^0.5
	EXP((−*z*^2)/2) =	0.759581772	\$G\$37:=EXP(((G27)^2*−1)/2)
	Calculation =	0.2291	\$G\$38:=(G36*G37*(\$L\$11*G35+\$L\$12*G35^2 +\$L\$13*G35^3+\$L\$14*G35^4+\$L\$15*G35^5))
	$N(d_2)$ =	0.229117859	\$G\$39:=IF(G27>0,1−G38,G38)

Results				
Option premium	−% pa		0.2488%	\$G\$45:=ROUND(ABS((G11*G33−G12*G39)*EXP(−G15*G14)),4)
	−\$	\$	618.94	\$G\$46:=G45*G7*G8/G9*(EXP(−G8/G9*G15))
	−% flat		0.0619%	\$G\$47:=+G46/G7
Option delta =			29.26%	\$G\$48:=G33*EXP(−G15*G14)

The Black model in *Figure 14.3* expresses the premium as a percentage pa amount. However, market convention usually quotes the premium as a flat percentage upfront amount to reflect the way that premiums are paid.[7] The role of the "interest sensitivity" calculation is to convert the percentage pa into an upfront dollar amount that, when divided by the face value, gives the upfront premium amount.

[7] Premiums are typically paid as an upfront dollar amount rather than being paid as an ongoing pa amount.

Another feature of this model is that the underlying pricing variable is expressed as a percentage pa yield. As a result, the option pricing model is determining the expected future distribution of this yield and the volatility describes the standard deviation of this distribution. As we know, the price of interest-bearing instruments can be expressed in terms of both yield and present value or "price per 100." As a result, the option price can be calculated using the forward yield as an input or forward price. This creates some potential confusion:

- **Yield and present value move in opposite directions** A rise in yield causes a fall in present value. Although we viewed a cap to be a call option because the premium rises when yields rise, it is actually a put option in price per 100 terms. Likewise a floor is a call option in price per US$100 terms. So, if we are pricing any interest rate options, we need to recognize a cap is a yield call and price put, while a floor is a yield put and a price call. We will see a price-based calculation in the option on bank bill futures example below.
- **Yield and price volatility** When calculating an option premium using yield or price, the volatility used will be a yield or price volatility respectively. While we can calculate historical volatilities separately for each variable, we know that regardless of whether price or yield is used, the resulting premium must be the same. If this was not the case, it would imply an arbitrage exists purely based on calculation method. We need to determine a relationship between the price and yield volatility and this is done in the section on bond options.

The model provided above prices individual caplets. Both caps and floors are often executed as a series of options on a short-term interest rate indices with consecutive expiry dates. In order to price the strip of options we need to break the strip of options into individual caplets or floorlets, price each option individually and then add these together to determine the total upfront premium. It is worth noting that the interest sensitivity calculation assumes that the underlying instrument pays interest on a zero-coupon basis.

As *Figure 14.4* shows, a strip of caps is a portfolio of options. While a strip of caps and floors is packaged and traded as one parcel, each option has its own risk characteristics, which are related to the particular segment of the forward yield curve where they are exercisable. In the example shown, a strip of 10 caps is priced with a strike rate of 5% pa. In this model, we generate the forward rates for each option expiry date and then enter these into the option function macro, "option," developed in Chapter 13. As this example shows, the characteristics of these caplets change significantly over time. Reflecting the strongly positive forward yield curve, the delta on each option increases from zero for the first caplet to a delta of close to one for the last.

14.3.3 Pricing Options on Euro-Style Short-Term Futures Contracts

Options on short-term futures contracts where interest is calculated on a simple interest accrual basis, such as the Eurodollar and Euro, are economically very similar to caps and floors. In this section, we will develop a model that extends upon the Black model to price options on Euro style futures.

An option on a short-term interest rate futures contract is typically an American-style option that can be exercised any time up until expiry. The last day of trading is usually just prior to, or on, the last day of trading in the underlying futures contract.

> ***Note***
> The major difference between a cap and a floor is that the underlying instrument is traded in terms of an index price of 100 minus the current forward yield. This creates an inverse relationship between the option on a future and a cap: a cap is equivalent to a Eurodollar put and a floor is equivalent to a Eurodollar call. While the option is expressed in terms of index prices, the volatility is expressed in terms of the implied forward yield; that is, a yield volatility is used. To price an option on these contracts, we need to convert the inputs into a yield-based model and then use the cap pricing model.

Example

Suppose it is March 2000 and we wish to buy a 95.75 put on March 14, 2001 Euro short-term interest rate futures contract. The current futures price is 96.08 and the volatility is 27.09%. The pricing model provided in *Figure 14.5* generates the premium of the option using a modified version of the Black model used to price the cap in *Figure 14.3*. The resulting premium of 0.28 index points is expressed in terms of yield pa. To convert this into a Euro amount, we need to multiply this index value by the contract tick value or interest sensitivity.

A Quick Note on Margins

As with all exchange-traded contracts, options on futures are subject to margins, which can create additional funding costs for the seller. The margining procedures for most options on interest rate futures are covered by either the SPAN or TIMS systems discussed in the appendix to Chapter 13.

As with futures, margining can create a convexity difference between options on futures and OTC options. In most US markets, the buyer pays the

Figure 14.4
Pricing a Strip of Caps

This model uses the Black-Scholes function macro devised in Chapter 13 to price a strip of 10 caplets.

Strip cap/floor calculator

Option details

Face value	10,000,000
Cap or floor ? (*C* or *F*)	*C*
Trade date	01-Jan-00
Days count (360 or 365)	360
Rollover frequency	2
First option expiry	01-Feb-00
Last option expiry	02-Aug-04
Cap rate %	5.00%
Volatility %	12.0000

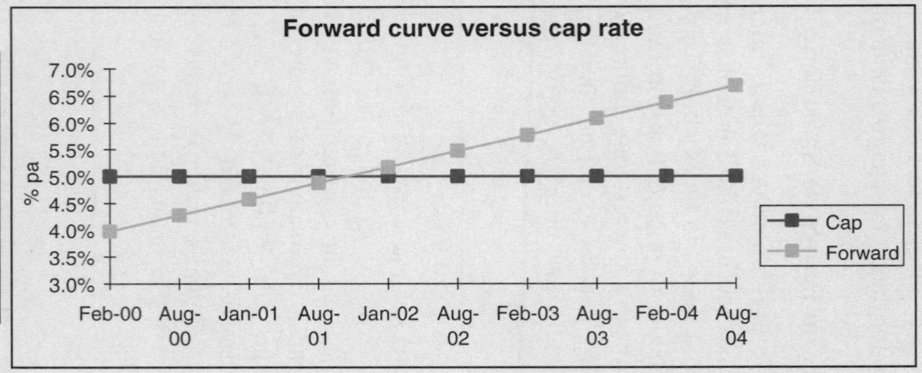

Calculations

	Option expiry date	Zero rate*	Forward volatility	Forward rate	Time	Interest sensitivity	Option premium — $	Option delta
1	01-Feb-00	3.80%	12.00%	3.98%	0.08	5,082,306.18	0.00	0%
2	02-Aug-00	3.95%	11.70%	4.28%	0.59	5,054,462.69	342.51	4%
3	31-Jan-01	4.10%	9.20%	4.57%	1.08	5,109,916.67	2,214.39	19%
4	03-Aug-01	4.25%	9.00%	4.88%	1.59	5,026,544.17	8,481.83	44%
5	31-Jan-02	4.40%	8.50%	5.17%	2.08	5,109,760.61	17,522.04	63%
6	03-Aug-02	4.55%	8.55%	5.48%	2.59	5,054,155.43	29,676.39	77%

27	6	03-Aug-02	4.55%	8.55%	5.48%	2.59	5,054,155.43	29,676.39	77%
28	7	01-Feb-03	4.70%	7.50%	5.77%	3.09	5,109,604.34	41,770.88	88%
29	8	04-Aug-03	4.85%	7.50%	6.09%	3.59	5,026,239.44	56,006.95	93%
30	9	01-Feb-04	5.00%	7.50%	6.37%	4.09	5,081,686.81	70,633.25	95%
31	10	02-Aug-04	5.15%	7.50%	6.68%	4.59	5,053,848.40	85,390.09	97%
32		31-Jan-05	5.30%						
33	Totals					Premium — $	upfront	312,038.33	
34						Premium — % upfront		3.1204%	
35									
36									
37									

* Rates are continuously compounded zero-coupon rates with the same compounding frequency as the underlying interest rate rollover. It is essential that the zero-coupon interest rate for the rollover date after the last expiry date is entered in order to determine the last forward rate.

Formulas in table

Description	Cell	Formula
Forward rate	G22	=IF(D22>0,(E23*(D23-$F$11)-E22*(D22-$F$11))/(D23-D22),0)
Time	H22	=+(D22-$F$11)/365
Interest sensitivity	I22	=(D23-D22)/$F$12*$F$9*EXP(-G22/100*(D23-D22)/$F$12)
Option premium — $	J22	=option(G22,$F$16,$F22,$H22,0,0,$F$10)*EXP(-E22/100*H22)*I22

Note: the option function macro has been converted to the Black model by setting the values of *a* and *r* to zero in Black-Scholes and then present valuing the resulting premium using *r*.

Figure 14.5
Pricing Options on "Euro" Short-term Futures

This model uses the Black version of the "option" function macro developed in *Figure 13.3.*

Row	Label	G
6		
7	Inputs	
8	Contract size =	1,000,000
9	Futures price =	96.08
10	Strike price =	95.75
11	Volatility =	27.09%
12	Today's date =	14-Mar-00
13	Futures expiry date =	14-Mar-01
14	Time to expiry (yrs) =	1.00
15	Interest rate to expiry =	3.75%
16	Option type (*P* or *C*) =	*P*
17		
18	Intermediate calculations	
19	Implied forward yield =	3.92
20	Implied forward strike =	4.25
21	Tick size =	25
22	Adjusted option type =	*C*
23		
24	Option premium calculation	
25	• Index points — raw	0.2836
26	• Index points — rounded	0.28
27	• Value per contract	700

Formula used

Cell	Formula
$G$19	=100-G9
$G$20	=100-G10
$G$21	=0.01*90/36000*G8
$G$22	=IF(G16="C","P","C")
$G$25	=OPTION.XLW!option(G19,G20,G11,G14,0,0,G22)*EXP(-G15*G14)
$G$26	=ROUND(G25,2)
$G$27	=+G26*G21*100

This formula can be used for all of the "Euro"-style short-term futures contracts that assume the underlying instrument is a 90-day Euro market deposit. These instruments include:

Instrument	Currency	Exchange
3-month Euro-Swiss Franc	CHF	LIFFE
3-month Euro	Euro	LIFFE
3-month Sterling interest rate	GBP	LIFFE
3-month Euro-Yen	JP¥	TIFFE
3-month Euro-Yen	JP¥	SIMEX
1-month Eurodollar	US$	CME
3-month Eurodollar	US$	CME
3-month Eurodollar	US$	SIMEX

option premium upfront and there is no difference between the OTC and ET option.[8] However, while the seller of an option receives their premium today, he or she is required to leave an initial margin with the clearinghouse equivalent to the current premium of the option, plus an amount equivalent to a large 1-day loss—effectively the clearinghouse takes back the premium plus a little extra. The amount the clearinghouse holds varies over time depending on the market premium and the risk profile of the option. All amounts held are repaid on the expiry date of the option.

Strictly speaking, this creates a funding cost that is not shared by granted OTC options and effectively any change in the premium results in a cash flow today rather than on the option expiry date. Option sellers should receive a premium that is higher than received from an OTC option, which will compensate them for having to fund the daily margin requirement. In practice, the pricing of options on futures and caps and floors is very similar.

14.3.4 Pricing Options on Discount-Style Short-Term Futures Contracts

While the Euro-style model used above applies to most of the traded volume in options on short-term interest rate futures, it does not apply to discount-style short-term interest rate futures contracts like the Australian dollar and New Zealand dollar bank bill contract traded on the SFE. The underlying futures contract value is determined as the discounted proceeds of the notional face value of the contract. As a result, the dollar value of each basis point, or the tick value, changes as the futures price changes.

Unlike the Euro-style contracts, we cannot just enter the implied yield directly into the Black model as the actual dollar value of each index point differs according to the absolute levels of the futures price and strike price. In order to calculate the option premiums, the SFE contract needs to be priced using the underlying contract dollar values. As the options are traded in terms of index points, a method has to be found for converting the dollar values back into index points.

The procedure developed by the SFE to price options is as follows:

1. convert the futures and exercise price into contract values;
2. obtain an implied volatility in terms of these contract values;
3. enter the values obtained in steps 1 and 2 into the Black pricing model to give a premium expressed in dollar values;

[8] This is referred to as a premium-style margining. See the appendix to Chapter 13 for more detail. If margining uses the futures-style system (LIFFE interest rate contracts, HKFOE and SFE), where both buyers and sellers are marked-to-market on a daily basis, then there is a potential funding requirement for both of them—see the option on bank bill futures section below.

4. determine the tick value of the contract at the strike price;
5. divide the dollar value premium from Step 3 by the tick value from Step 4 to express the premium.

A further complication in pricing these options is that both exchanges margin options on a futures-style basis. Both buyers and sellers must put up an initial margin and are subject to daily mark-to-market based on the change in market premiums. The premium is not actually paid by the purchaser of the option, until it is exercised or expires. As a result, the pricing formula for SFE bank bill futures assumes that the premium is paid at expiry.[9] This is simply incorporated into the Black model by no longer present valuing the premium calculation to give the following call formula:

$$\boxed{C = F \times N(d_1) - X \times N(d_2)}$$

While it is technically true that the premium is paid in arrears, it is only the prevailing market premium on the last day of trading that is paid. Prior to this date, depending on how the premium changed after the option was traded, there is likely to have been significant premium cash flows. For example, if the underlying futures price had moved so that the option premium fell to zero well before the option expires, then the option premium will effectively have been paid prior to expiry. So, while the formula above is a representation of the fair value of the option on the day it is traded, the total premium value will depend on funding gains or costs arising from the daily mark-to-market prior to expiry.

Figure 14.6 provides an example of calculating the premium value of an option on a bank bill futures contract following the five steps outlined above. It is interesting to note the very low level of volatility in this contract (0.22%) versus the level of volatility in Euro-style contracts, where volatility ranges from 5% to 30%. The reason for this is that the bank bill volatility is expressed in terms of the total contract or present value, whereas the Euro contract volatility refers to the yield on the instrument.

14.3.5 Short-Term Interest Rate Futures and Volatility Curves

In Chapter 13, we discussed the role of volatility curves in allowing equity option market participants to fine tune their expectations on the distribution of the forward price. In that case, we discussed intra-month curves; that is, the volatility on options with the same expiry date, but different strike prices. Similar factors drive volatility curves in interest rate markets.

[9] In fact, all options traded on the SFE assume that the premium is paid at expiry.

Figure 14.6
Pricing SFE Options on Bank Bill Futures

Row	Inputs	Underlying SPI
8	Contract size =	1,000,000
9	Futures price =	92.01
10	Strike price =	92.25
11	Volatility (contract value) =	0.22%
12	Today's date =	15-Apr-01
13	Futures expiry date =	13-Sep-01
14	Time to expiry (yrs) =	0.41
15	Option type (*P* or *C*) =	*c*

Row	Intermediate calculations	
19	Futures contract value =	980,679.27
20	Strike contract value =	981,248.74
21	Strike contract value – .01=	981,272.48
22	Tick value at strike =	23.74

Row	Option premium calculation	
25	• Contract value — $	314.99
26	• Index points	0.13

Formula used

Cell	Formula
$G$19	=+$G$8/(1+(100-G9)/100/365*90)
$G$20	=+$G$8/(1+(100-G10)/100/365*90)
$G$21	=+$G$8/(1+(100-G10-0.01)/100/365*90)
$G$22	=ROUND(G21-G20,2)
$G$25	=OPTION.XLW!option(G19,G20,G11,G14,0,0,G15)
$G$26	=ROUND(G25/G22/100,2)

Note: the contract value of the SFE bank bill contract is A$1 m while the NZFOE contract is NZ$0.5m.

Another form of volatility curve is inter-month curves; that is, a curve which plots the volatility of options on the same underlying instruments, but across different expiry dates. An aspect of options on short-term interest rate futures contracts is that, in the major contracts at least, there is a "true" inter-month forward volatility curve.

In most exchange-traded options contracts, almost all of the volume is concentrated in the front delivery month and the volatilities in back months tend not to reflect true market prices. While most of the volume in options on interest rate futures is concentrated in the front months, the back-month volumes show reasonable liquidity and the volatilities tend to reflect a true forward volatility curve.

Forward volatility curves provide an insight into market expectations regarding the likely distribution of the forward price over time. These curves can take on all types of shapes reflecting market expectations and also the manipulation of volatilities to produce appropriate price distributions. For example, it is very common in short-term interest rate markets to see a curve with a low front-month volatility followed by a sharp rise in volatility over the next two to three quarterly expiries. If there are more than four quarterly deliveries listed, this can be followed by a steady decline in volatility over time. This shape reflects the fact that most short-term interest rates are anchored to the cash rate, which is in turn largely influenced by monetary policy, which in most currencies is very stable, apart from infrequent adjustments to monetary policy. As the futures expiry moves away from the cash rate, this linkage loosens and the forward rate begins to act more like a random variable along with changes in accordance to alterations in the market view of future monetary policy directions.

Some inter-month yield volatility curves are plotted in *Figure 14.7* for options contracts on the some European contracts listed on LIFFE prior to commencement of the Euro in 1999. In this case, there is a convergence of volatilities in the DM and Euro to a similar level (reflecting the move toward the single currency) and all curves display a rise in volatility over time.

Another aspect of these volatility curves is the difference in absolute magnitude of volatilities. While at first this may seem to present a trading opportunity for interest rates that we think will be reasonably closely correlated over the future, a large part of the difference arises purely from the absolute level in yields in each currency. For example, at the time these graphs were drawn the front- month implied yield for Euro-DM was 3.24% pa while short-sterling was 6.05% pa. Each 0.01% change in yield will be a substantially greater proportion of the Euromark yield than the short sterling. As yield volatility is quoted as a percentage of yield, we would expect the volatility of the lower yielding contract (the Euromark) to be higher. The change in yield implied by the front-month volatilities on both contracts is very similar to the Euromark, implying a change in yield of 0.51% pa and the short sterling 0.61% pa.

Figure 14.7
Inter-Month Volatility Curves on Some European Short-Term Interest Rate Futures

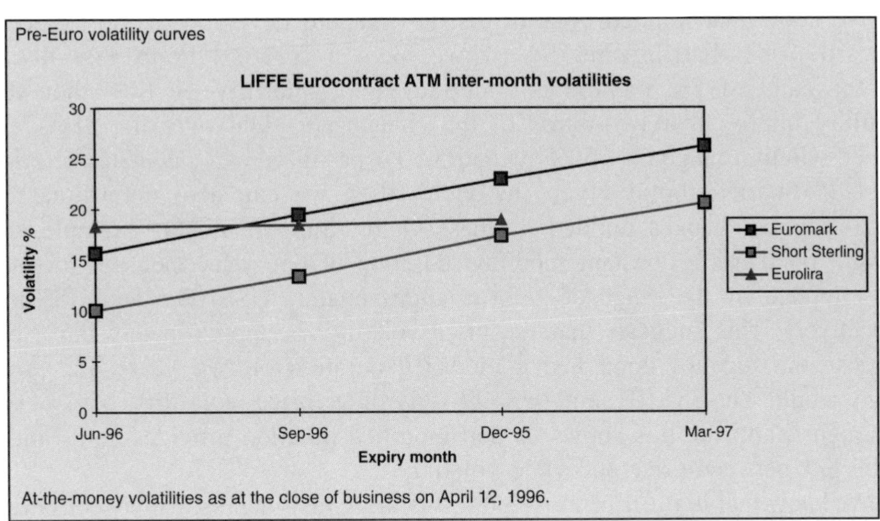

14.4 PRICING AND VALUING LONG-TERM INTEREST RATE OPTIONS

The pricing models developed for options on short-term instruments can also be extended to options on long-term instruments. As with interest rate options, most of the effort is in transforming the underlying market prices into a form that can be directly applied to the Black model. In this section, we will develop a model for the following instruments:

- OTC bond options
- options on bond futures
- swaptions.

First, however, a short discussion on the relationship between price and yield volatilities.

14.4.1 Price and Yield Volatility

As we saw, the volatility of an underlying interest-bearing instrument can be expressed in terms of its yield to maturity or the current price per US$100—referred to as yield and price volatility respectively. When pricing any given option, the concept of equivalent value tells us that the premium calculated should be the same whether we use the underlying instrument's yield or price.[10] What is the relationship between these two volatilities that ensures that equivalent value holds?

We know that implied volatility is the standard deviation of the expected forward price distribution. So, if we have a forward bond that has a current yield of 5% pa and an implied yield volatility of 10% then the volatility implies that two-thirds of the changes in yield over the next year will be within a range of 4.50% pa and 5.50% pa. If we can calculate the price per US$100 of a bond given the yield, then we can also determine the range of price changes implied by these yields. Suppose in this example, the forward bond has a constant modified duration of one year, then the forward price implied by the range of yield is approximately US$100.5 and US$99.5 respectively. This suggests that the price volatility is approximately 0.5% pa. Suppose the forward bond had a modified duration of two years; the price range would be US$101 and US$99—giving a price volatility of 1% pa. Although simplistic, this shows us that modified duration provides an estimate of the *link* between price and yield volatility.[11]

We know that in practice most interest-bearing instruments display convexity and so duration is not usually constant as in the simplified example used above. The most accurate method of determining the price volatility would be to take the implied log-normal yield distribution and convert all values to price per US$100 to create a price distribution—the price volatility is then determined by the standard deviation. However, this is a large computational undertaking and an approximation can be made using modified duration as follows:

$$V_{\text{price}} = V_{\text{yield}} \times \text{Modified duration} \times \text{Yield}$$

Where:

V_{price} = price volatility
V_{yield} = yield volatility.
Modified duration refers to the underlying forward bond:
In the example above, the calculation would be

$$V_{\text{price}} = 10\% \text{ pa} \times 1 \times 5\% \text{ pa}$$
$$= 0.5\% \text{ pa}$$

14.4.2 Pricing an OTC Bond Option

An OTC bond option is an agreement to buy or sell an underlying physical bond at an agreed price or yield in the future. In most countries, the strike

[10] See Chapter 2 for more discussion of this concept.

[11] See Chapter 3 for more discussion of modified duration.

price is expressed in terms of price per US$100; however, in a few countries, such as Australia, the market convention is to set the exercise in terms of the yield to maturity. In this section we shall concentrate on pricing the option first in terms of price per US$100. In the next section, on SFE bond options, we will incorporate exercise prices expressed in terms of the yield.

A characteristic of OTC bond options is that they are exercisable against physical securities that already exist and they pay coupons during the life of the option. In the case of caps and floors and even swaptions, the option is on an instrument that does not commence accruing interest until the expiry date of the option. Using the terminology developed in Part 2 on forwards, the underlying instrument for a bond option is a forward contract that pays "lumpy" asset returns in the form of coupons.[12]

When pricing a bond option, we can use the Black model. However, the inputs are based on the price per US$100 and the forward price used in the model must incorporate the "lumpy" coupon payment. Accordingly, the bond forward pricing model developed in Chapter 5 (in *Figure 5.11*) provides a coupon-adjusted forward price that can be entered directly into the model.

A Black model for European OTC bond options is summarized in *Figure 14.8* on page 412. It is usual practice to refer to the exercise price in terms of the "clean" price; that is, with the accrued interest removed. This model incorporates the accrued interest in the forward cost of carry calculation, but the accrued interest is removed from the forward price before it is entered into the Black model.

The Black model shown in *Figure 14.8* is suitable for European options. Pricing American options introduces the possibility of early exercise and some of the pricing complexities highlighted at the start of the chapter. In the previous chapter on equity options, we adjusted for the possibility of early exercise in American options when using the Black model by ensuring that the premium is at least always equal to the intrinsic value of the option. This same adjustment should be made when using the Black model for any American interest rate options as follows:

$$\text{Call}_{\text{AMERICAN}} = \text{Max}(S - X, \text{Call}_{\text{EUROPEAN}})$$

and

$$\text{Put}_{\text{AMERICAN}} = \text{Max}(X - S, \text{Put}_{\text{EUROPEAN}})$$

Where:

the $\text{Call}_{\text{EUROPEAN}}$ and $\text{Put}_{\text{EUROPEAN}}$ are the premiums for European calls and puts using the model in *Figure 14.8*.

[12] The instrument underlying caps and floors is a forward contract on instruments that pay no income.

Figure 14.8
The Black Model for European Bond Options

Option premium calculation (as a price per $100)

Call	=	$[F \times \exp(-r_1 \times t) \times N(r_1) - X \times \exp(-r_1 \times t) \times N(d_2)]$
Put	=	$[X \times \exp(-r_1 \times t) \times N(-d_2) - F \times \exp(-r_1 \times t) \times N(-d_1)]$
F	=	$(S + A_1) \times (1 + r_1 \times t) - c \times (1 + r_2 \times f) - A_2$

Where:

d_1	=	$(\ln(F/X) + ((v\text{^}2)/2) \times t)/(v \times t\text{^}0.5)$
d_2	=	$d_1 - v \times t\text{^}0.5$
X	=	clean exercise price (PPH basis)
F	=	clean forward price (PPH basis)
S	=	clean forward price (PPH basis)
A_1	=	accrued interest on the pricing date
A_2	=	accrued interest on the option expiry date
r_1	=	risk-free interest rate to option expiry (% pa) [the repo rate]
r_2	=	risk-free interest rate from coupon payment date to option expiry (% pa)
t	=	time to option expiry (in years)
f	=	time from coupon payment to the option expiry (in years)
v	=	price volatility (% pa)
ln( )	=	natural logarithm
exp( )	=	exponential function
$N(\,)$	=	the cumulative normal distribution function.

Note: (1) all interest rates assume continuous compounding.
(2) to include more than one coupon payment make the same adjustment for each coupon paid.

Often while the strike price of a bond option is in terms of the clean price at expiry, we want the forward pricing component of the model to start with the current yield to maturity of the underlying bond. The example in *Figure 14.9* develops a bond option pricing model that, while it calculates the forward price using the yield input, the exercise price is expressed as a price per hundred. In this example, an investor currently owns a bond that matures in June 2002 and pays a semi-annual coupon of 8.5% pa. The investor is concerned about the possibility of a rise in long-term yields over the next six months and decides to buy a European at-the-money forward put option on the bond and wishes to calculate an indicative premium. The investor knows the current yield to maturity of the bond is 6.264% pa and the 6-month repo rate is 5.242% pa. In order to generate the option premium, there are three calculations to be made:

1. determine the current spot price of the bond;
2. calculate the cost of carrying the bond and the forward price on the option expiry date;

3. calculate the premium by entering the forward price and exercise price in Step 2 into the Black model.

Each of these calculations is performed in *Figure 14.9*. At current yields, the clean spot price on February 12, 2000 is 111.5 and the forward price on August 13, 2000 is 110.2260. Using the forward price as the exercise price, the option premium calculated is 1.5886 per US$100 of bond face value.

14.4.3 Pricing Options on Bond Futures

An option on a deliverable bond futures contract gives the buyer of a call or put the right respectively to buy or sell the underlying futures contract. Most of the major bond contracts are deliverable and include the CBOT US Treasury Bond or LIFFE's gilt and European government bond contracts. In this section, we will firstly consider pricing options on deliverable bond futures and then examine the changes required to incorporate bond futures that are cash settled against a basket of underlying bonds.

Deliverable Bond Futures

In the case of options on deliverable bonds, the option is American style and expires toward the end of the month, prior to the delivery month of the underlying futures contract. Upon exercise, a position is created in the underlying futures contract and, if left open, will take part in the delivery process.

As the underlying futures contract price is driven by the "cheapest to deliver" concept and essentially pricing behavior, the futures price that is to be captured in the option pricing model is the price distribution of the cheapest to deliver bond adjusted by its conversion factor.[13] One pricing complication that can arise is the possibility of the actual cheapest to deliver bond changing over the life of the option, as it will have its own pricing characteristics. Incorporating this into the model is complex and is beyond our current scope.

Pricing an option on a deliverable bond futures contract is an extension of the OTC bond model. As the contracts are traded in terms of the price per hundred of the underlying notional contract, we do not need to perform a yield to price conversion used in *Figure 14.9*. Essentially, the pricing process consists of entering the current futures price and strike price directly into the Black model (i.e., calculation Step 3 in *Figure 14.9*). A pricing example is set out in *Figure 14.10* on page 416.

As with all futures contracts, there is an additional funding cost in the form of margining. For premium-style options, such as the US Treasury

[13] For more information on delivery and the cheapest to deliver concept, see Chapter 5.

Figure 14.9
European Bond Option Pricing Model

Uses option function macro and MS Excel bond pricing functions (analysis toolpack).

Row	Inputs	H
9	Option details	
10	Pricing/revaluation date	12-Feb-00
11	Option expiry date	12-Aug-00
12	Exercise price	110.2260
13	Price volatility	5.2500
14	Option type (*P* or *C*)	*P*
15	Underlying bond details	
16	Maturity date	15-Jun-06
17	Coupon rate %	8.5000
18	Number of periods/year (1, 2 or 4)	2
19	Current yield to maturity	6.2640
20	Repo rate till fwd settlement	5.2420
21	Repo rate day count basis (360 or 365)	365
22	30/360 days count (y or n)	n

Calculations

Row	1. Current bond spot price	H
27	Settlement date	12-Feb-00
28	Fwd date	12-Aug-00
29	Maturity date	15-Jun-06
30	Last coupon date	15-Dec-99
31	Next coupon date 1	15-Jun-00
32	Coupon rate %	8.5000
33	Number of periods/year -(1, 2 or 4)	2
34	Current yield to maturity % pa	6.2640
35	MS excel day count method	1
36	Clean price	111.5370
37	Accrued interest at trade date	1.3702

Formula used

Cell	Formula
$H$27	=H10
$H$28	=H11
$H$29	=H16
$H$30	=COUPPCD(H27,H29,H33,H35)
$H$31	=COUPNCD(H27,H29,H33,H35)
$H$32	=H17
$H$33	=H18
$H$34	=H19
$H$35	=IF(H22="n",1,0)
$H$36	=PRICE(H27,H29,H32/100,H34/100,100,H33,H35)
$H$37	=IF(H27=H30,0,ANALYSF.XLA!ACCRINT(H30,H31,H27,H32,1,H33,H35))

Row	Item	Value	Cell	Formula
38	2(a). Financing (or Repo) details			
39	Current financing rate	5.24	$H$39	=+H20
40	Repo rate day count	365	$H$40	=+H21
41	Dirty bond price on trade date	112.9072	$H$41	=+H37+H36
42	Number of coupons during repo	1	$H$42	=IF(H28>H31,1,0)
43	Number of repo days in forward period	182	$H$43	=+H28-H27
44	Number of days from coupon date to fwd date	58	$H$44	=IF(H42=1,H28-H31,0)
45	Repo finance cost of bond	115.8584	$H$45	=+H41*(1+H39/(H40*100)*H43)
46	2(b). Forward price calculation			
47	Cumulative coupon 1 value at forward date	4.2854	$H$47	=H$32/H$33*(1+H$39/(100*H$40)*H44)*H42
48	Dirty forward price	111.5730	$H$48	=+H45-H47
49	Last coupon at forward date	15-Jun-00	$H$49	=COUPPCD(H$28,H$29,H$33,H$35)
50	Next coupon date at forward date	15-Dec-00	$H$50	=COUPNCD(H$28,H$29,H$33,H$35)
51	Accrued interest at forward date	1.3470	$H$51	=ACCRINT(H$49,H$50,H$28,H$32,1,H$33,H$35)
52	Clean forward price	110.2260	$H$52	=+H48-H51
53	Forward yield % pa	6.3730	$H$53	=YIELD(H11,H16,H17/100,H52,100,H18,IF(H22="y",0,1))*100
54	3. Option premium calculation			
55	Clean forward price	110.2260	$H$55	=+H52
56	Exercise price	110.2260	$H$56	=+H12
57	Volatility	5.25%	$H$57	=+H13/100
58	Time to expiry (yrs)	0.4986	$H$58	=+(H11-H10)/365
59	Interest rate to option expiry	5.2420%	$H$59	=+H20/100
60	Option type	p	$H$60	=+H14
61				
62	Premium — price per hundred*	1.5886	$H$62	=option(H55,H56,H57,H58,0,0,H60)/(1+H59*H58)

* Note: the interest rates are not continuously compunded in this model so a standard discount function is used to present value the premium rather than an exponential model.

Figure 14.10
Options on Deliverable Bond Futures

This model prices options on deliverable bond futures contracts such as the Tbond, Bund and Long-Gilt. In this example a call option is priced in April for a June futures contract. The futures price is taken as given.

	C	D	E	F	G	H
9						
10		Inputs				
11		Option details				
12		Contract size				250,000
13		Futures price				96.150
14		Pricing/revaluation date				15-Apr-00
15		Option expiry date				25-May-00
16		Exercise price				97.0000
17		Price volatility				5.7500
18		Interest rate to option expiry				3.7500
19		Option type (*P* or *C*)				*C*
20		Margining type (*F* or *P*)				*F*
21		Minimum tick size (no. of dec. places)				2
22		Option premium calculation				
23		Time to expiry (yrs)				0.1096
24		Premium—price per hundred—raw				0.3854
25		Premium—price per hundred—rounded				0.3900
26		Premium—contract value				975.00

Formulas used

Cell	Formula
$H$23	=+(H15-H14)/365
$H$24	=option(H13,H16,H17/100,H23,0,0,H19)*IF(H20="F",1,1/(1+H18/100*H23))
$H$25	=ROUND(H24,2)
$H$26	=+H25*H12/100

Note: "margining-type" refers to whether the option is margined as a "premium-style" option (ie. premium paid upfront) or a "futures-style" option (ie. options are marked-to-market).

bond contract, the grantor of the option is subject to additional costs; however, given the relatively short term of most option volumes (three months or less) this cost is generally relatively low and is often ignored by market participants.

In the case of deliverable bond options margined on a "futures-style" basis (e.g., LIFFE bond options), the premium in arrears model devised in Section 14.4.3 should be used to calculate the value of the premium. However, there will still be a difference between the actual option on futures' outcome relative to an OTC bond option due to the funding cost that may emerge for either the buyer or the grantor over the life of the options due to the daily mark-to-markets.[14]

Cash Settled Basket Bond Futures

As we saw in Chapter 5, the bond contracts listed on the SFE are cash settled against the average yield of a known basket of cash bonds at expiry. In terms of constructing an option pricing model, the SFE contracts create a number of issues:

- the futures and exercise price is expressed in terms of an index price equivalent to 100 minus the yield of the basket bonds;
- the volatility is quoted in terms of the notional underlying contract value;
- the contract value is determined in terms of a notional forward bond with no interest accrual and either exactly three or ten years to expiry;
- the option premium is quoted in yield points.

In essence, while the futures' price is based on the underlying basket of bonds, the price volatility is expressed in terms of a notional forward bond rather than any of the bonds in the underlying basket. In order to determine the option premium we need, we must take the following steps:

1. convert the yield-based futures and strike price into a notional contract value;[15]
2. enter the futures price strike price contract values and volatility (contract price) into the Black model (premium in arrears) to calculate the dollar premium;
3. convert the dollar premium back into yield points by dividing by the tick value.

[14] For more information on option margining, see the discussion in the section on options on Euro-style short-term interest rate futures, earlier in this chapter.

[15] The contract value calculation for these contracts is covered in Chapter 5. The contract value for the 3-year and 10-year bond is given by the present value of a semi-annual coupon-paying bond with exactly three and ten years to expiry. There is no accrued interest calculation.

As with the options on the bank bill futures, the SFE assumes the tick value to be used is the tick value at the option strike price. *Figure 14.11* follows the steps outlined above to calculate an option premium for the bond contracts on both exchanges.

Figure 14.11 also highlights an additional rounding complexity in the SFE bond contracts. In the 3- and 10-year bond contracts, options' premiums are quoted to three decimal points, where the third decimal point can only change by a half tick (i.e., it can be either 0 or 5). The model provides the simple two decimal place rounding for the NZFOE contracts and the more involved three decimal point rounding for the SFE contracts.

A common mistake in the SFE market is to calculate the option premium based on the index futures price (i.e., without converting to contract values). If this approach is taken, there often appear to be arbitrage opportunities in the marketplace, as options with higher strike prices appear to be trading at below fair value. However, this is not the case, as the tick value of the options with higher strike prices is substantially greater than lower strike prices, so fewer yield points are required for any given dollar value of premium. There are a number of famous cases where large "arbitrage" transactions have been executed due to a trader erroneously calculating the premium using the index price. The end result of these transactions has been a net loss equivalent to the transaction costs (brokerage and bid-offer spreads). The moral of this story is that there are a number of market convention traps with respect to the calculation of yields and it is always safer to work in dollar values, when looking at arbitrage strategies.

14.4.4 Extending the Black Model to Price Swaptions

A swaption is an agreement between two counterparties to enter into a currency or interest rate swap at an agreed fixed rate at a date in the future. In this section, we will refer to interest rate swaptions only.

The option buyer agrees to enter into a "pay" or "receive" swap, referred to as a "payer" or "receiver" swaption respectively. The buyer of a payer swaption will exercise, if the swap rate prevailing on the option expiry date is above the exercise rate, making it an interest rate call option. The receiver swaption, on the other hand, will only be exercised if the swap rate on the option expiry date is below the swaption exercise rate and is an interest rate put option.

> ***Note***
>
> The economics of the swaption is almost identical to the option on cash settled bond futures discussed above and is very similar to the cap and floor models, except that the underlying instrument has coupon payments. The only difference is that the underlying instrument is a forward swap and the volatility is a yield rather than a price volatility.

Figure 14.11
Pricing SFE Options on 3- and 10-Year Bond Features

Row	D–F	G	H	Cell	Formula
6					
7	Inputs — Underlying SPI				
8	Contract size =	100,000			
9	Years of underlying bond (3 or 10) =	10			
10	Underlying assumed coupon =	12%	(12% for SFE, 8% for NZFOE)		
11	Futures price =	89.510			
12	Strike price =	90.000			
13	Volatility (contract vaue) =	3.75%			
14	Today's date =	8-Jan-01			
15	Futures expiry date =	15-Jun-01			
16	Time to expiry (yrs) =	0.43			
17	Option type (*P* or *C*) =	*c*			
18				Formula used	
19	Intermediate calculations			Cell	Formula
20	Futures i =	0.05245		$G$20	=(100-$G$11)/200
21	Futures v =	0.9501639		$G$21	=ROUND(1/(1+G20),8)
22	Futures contract value =	$109,216.54		$G$22	=ROUND(1000*(($G$10*50)*(1-G21^($G$9*2))/G20+100*G21^($G$9*2)),2)
23	Strike i =	0.05		$G$23	=(100-$G$12)/200
24	Strike v =	0.95238095		$G$24	=ROUND(1/(1+G23),8)
25	Strike contract value =	$112,462.21		$G$25	=ROUND(1000*(($G$10*50)*(1-G24^($G$9*2))/G23+100*G24^($G$9*2)),2)
26	Strike—.01 i =	0.05005		$G$26	=(100-($G$12-0.01))/200
27	Strike—.01 v =	0.9523356		$G$27	=ROUND(1/(1+G26),8)
28	Strike contract value—.01=	$112,394.64		$G$28	=ROUND(1000*(($G$10*50)*(1-G27^($G$9*2))/G26+100*G27^($G$9*2)),2)
29	Tick value at strike =	$67.57		$G$29	=G25-G28
30					
31	Option premium calculation				
32	• Contract value—$ raw	157.55300		$G$32	=option(G22,G25,G13,G16,0,0,G17)
33	• Index points—raw	0.0233		$G$33	=G32/G29/100
34	• Index points*—NZFOE rounding	0.02		$G$34	=ROUND(G33,2)
35	• Index points*—SFE rounding	0.025		$G$35	=TRUNC(G33,2)+IF((G33-TRUNC(G33,2))<0.0025,0,IF((G33-TRUNC(G33,2))<0.0075,0.005,0.01))
36	• Contract value—$ rounded	168.93		$G$36	=ROUND(G35*G29*100,2)

* Note: the SFE contracts trade to three decimal places but the third decimal place can only ever be 0 or 5.

To price a swaption, we can make use of the Black model developed for caps and floors, if we follow the steps below:

1. calculate the prevailing forward start swap interest rate and obtain the current market implied volatility for the desired option term;
2. enter the prices from Step 1 along with the exercise swap rate and enter into the Black model developed for caps and floors;
3. take the premium in yield points obtained from Step 2 and multiply it by the current PVBP of the swap to determine the current premium dollar value of the swaption.

SUMMARY

This chapter discussed modeling methodologies for the distribution of interest rates and examined various valuation models for both ET and OTC interest rate options, including caps and floors, options on short-term futures, bond options, options on bond futures and swaptions.

SELF-TEST QUESTIONS

1. Describe five complexities that lead to imperfections in interest rate options pricing.
2. You are given the following information:

Face value	US$5,000,000
Cap or floor	Cap
Trade date	January 1, 2000
Days count	360
Rollover frequency	2
First option expiry	February 1, 2000
Last option expiry	August 2, 2001
Cap rate %	6.00%
Volatility	9.00%

Assume the same zero rate term structure as provided in *Figure 14.4*. Using the information in the table above, price the strip of caps.

3. Assume it is December 2000 and you wish to buy a 94.65 put on 15 February 2001 short-term Eurodollar interest rate futures. The current futures price is 95.28 and the volatility is 20.00%. The interest rate to expiry is 3.75%. Calculate the option premium.

4. Calculate the price volatility of a long-term interest rate option, if the yield is 7.00%, the modified duration is 0.5% and the implied yield volatility is 10.00%.
5. You are given the following information:

Pricing date	September 10, 2000
Option expiry date	December 15, 2000
Exercise price	106.231
Price volatility	5.90%
Option type	Put
Maturity date of bond	April 15, 2006
Coupon rate %	7.50%
Number of periods	2
Current yield to maturity	6.15%
Rep rate till forward settlement	6.02%
Repo rate day count basis	365
30/360 days count	No

Using the above information, calculate the option premium.

CHAPTER 15

CURRENCY OPTIONS

🖫 The models developed in this chapter are saved as Microsoft Excel^{TM} files in the enclosed disk.

OVERVIEW

In this chapter, we examine the currency options market and discuss the valuation issues on currency options. By the end of this chapter we will have:

- described currency options and the currency options market;
- developed a model for pricing currency options, incorporating underlying assumptions;
- examined delta hedging and cross currency hedging examples.

15.1 INTRODUCTION

As stated in Chapter 1, the bulk of currency option volume is OTC, reflecting the fact that business in the underlying spot and forward FX contracts is primarily OTC.

A feature of currency options is that they are easily accessible and offered by most international banks. The markets in the major currency combinations such as US$/Euro and US$/JPY are very liquid and are generally open 24 hours a day.

15.2 OPTIONS ON FX FORWARDS

15.2.1 General Description

A currency option involves an agreement to exchange currencies at an agreed exchange rate and agreed date in the future. As both parties are simultaneously agreeing to buy and sell currencies, it is easy to become confused at to whether you are pricing a put or call—the fact is, you are pricing both. For example, suppose you wish to buy Sterling against the US dollar in three months' time at an exchange rate of 1.6000. The option used to put this strategy in place would be to purchase a call option on Sterling that specifies an agreement to buy US$1.6000 for each £1 Sterling. However, this is also a put option on the

US dollar, because you are agreeing to sell the US dollar against the Sterling. When buying and selling currency options, it is essential to know in which currency it is a put and in which it is a call.

Global FX markets have developed conventions for the quotation of FX options. In general, options are quoted in a similar manner to the underlying FX rate and the call or put refers to the base currency in this quotation. A sample quote vendor screen is provided in *Figure 15.1*.

Currency options can be either American or European, although as with most options, the percentage of American options exercised early is very low. Upon exercise, an option is usually physically settled as a spot FX contract; that is, for most exchange rates, currency cash flows occur two business days after the exercise date. Exercise is often not automatic and the seller must be contacted on the exercise date and a formal notification of exercise given.

15.2.2 The Underlying Instrument

A currency option is an option on a forward FX contract. The value upon exercise is equivalent to the difference between the prevailing FX rate and the exercise exchange rate of the option. As a result, when a currency option is executed, the underlying instrument is the prevailing forward FX rate to expiry of the option.

Figure 15.1
Sample Currency Option Quotations

Macquarie Bank – Sydney											
A$/US$	US$/DM	US$/¥	£/US$			US$/SFr				NZ$/US$	
0.7962-67											
A$ forwards						A$ options				Metals	
ON	5m 35–34		A$	US$	A$	¥	A$	DM		Gold	
TN .4–.3	6m 37–36										
1W 2.5–2.2	7m 42–40	1 month	6.1	6.3	9.5	10.0	8.7	9.7		282.20	382.50
2W 4.9–4.6	8m 46–44	2 month	6.3	6.5	10.3	10.8	9.4	10.4			
3W 7–6.7	9m 49–47	3 month	6.4	6.6	10.8	11.3	9.5	10.5		Silver	
1M 10.9	10m 52–50	6 month	6.5	6.7	11.4	11.9	10.0	11.0			
2M 18–17	11m 56–54	1 year	6.5	6.7	12.0	12.4	10.2	11.2		5.03	5.05
3M 24–23	12m 59–57	2 years									
4M 29–28											

Source Telerate page 2627

In order to build an option pricing model, we need to accommodate the characteristics of the underlying instrument:

- the underlying instrument is an FX forward contract to exchange the underlying currencies at the expiry date of the option;
- the pricing of the underlying forward instrument is based on the continuous asset income forward FX model developed in Chapter 7;
- a liquid and global market exists in the underlying forward market;
- the distribution of the underlying instrument is approximately log-normal;[1]
- borrowing and lending can occur in each currency without constraint.[2]

15.2.3 Pricing and Valuing Currency Options

The description of the underlying instrument above complies closely with the assumptions that underlie the generic Black-Scholes model. The most widely used model for currency options, the Garman Kohlhagen model shown in *Figure 15.2*, is an extension of Black-Scholes.

Figure 15.2
The Garman Kohlhagen Currency Options Model

$$C = S \times \exp(-r_b \times t) \times N(d_1) - X \times \exp(-r_t \times t) \times N(d_2)$$

$$P = X \times \exp(-r_t \times t) \times N(-d_2) - S \times \exp(-r_b \times t) \times N(-d_1)$$

$$\text{Call delta} = \exp(-r_b \times t) \times N(d_1)$$

$$\text{Put delta} = \exp(-r_b \times t) \times N(-d_1)$$

Where:

d_1	=	$(\ln(S/X) + (r_t - r_b - (v\char`^2)/2) \times t)/(v \times t\char`^0.5)$
d_2	=	$d_1 - v \times t\char`^0.5$
X	=	exercise exchange rate
S	=	spot exchange rate
r_b	=	base currency risk-free interest rate to option expiry (% pa)
r_t	=	terms currency risk-free interest rate to option expiry (% pa)
t	=	time to option expiry (in years)
v	=	volatility (% pa)
ln( )	=	natural logarithm
exp( )	=	exponential function
$N(\,)$	=	the cumulative normal distribution function.

[1] Research into the distribution of the major foreign exchange rates shows that the price distribution has a generally log-normal distribution; however, they exhibit significant kurtosis (otherwise known as a "fat-tailed" normal distribution).

[2] As with FX forwards, any currency that is still subject to exchange controls can undermine this assumption and lead to a distortion in the pricing of forwards.

This model is very similar to the model derived for stock price index options' in Section 13.2. If we replaced the asset return, q, for the base currency interest rate, r_b, and an interest rate, r, for the terms currency interest rate, r_t, the formulae are identical. Although the asset classes are quite different for currency options and SPI options, the key characteristics of the underlying instruments are very similar: both pay an almost continuous asset income, there are few restraints on trading in the underlying instrument and the distributions can be assumed to be log-normal. However, in the case of currency options, we can usually determine the base currency interest rate (effectively the asset return) with certainty—something that cannot be said of forecasting the dividend yield on a share price index.

Figure 15.3 builds a pricing spreadsheet based on this pricing model. This is essentially an extension of the program devised in *Figure 13.2* with the asset return renamed as the base currency interest rate and the terms currency interest rate replaces the interest rate. In this example, the premium of a US$ call/C$ put is calculated with an implied volatility of 6% and a term to expiry of nine months.

As with all Black-Scholes models, the Garman Kohlhagen model assumes continuously compounded zero-coupon interest rates. So, the Canadian and US dollar interest rates in this example are taken from a zero-coupon yield curve and then converted to continuously compounded rates.[3]

As we saw with previous options on assets with continuous income, the delta of the call is influenced by the asset income, in this case the base currency interest rate:

$$\text{Call delta} = \exp(-r_b \times t) \times N(d_1)$$

The effect of this is to slightly reduce the delta sensitivity of the option for both puts and calls relative to the generic Black-Scholes model.

The value of a currency option is given by the difference between the originally traded premium and today's revaluation premium. As premiums are expressed as a present value amount, no TVM adjustment is required:

$$\text{Option value} = \text{Premium}_{\text{traded}} - \text{Premium}_{\text{revaluation}}$$

[3] See Chapter 3 for the formula to adjust from periodic to continuously compounded interest rates.

Figure 15.3
A Model for Pricing Currency Options

(Note: this spreadsheet model also prices puts.)

Row	Label		Value/Result	Formula used
8	**Inputs**			
9	Amount of base currency =		1,000,000	
10	Option type (P or C) =		C	
11	Spot exchange rate (S) =		1.3600	
12	Exercise rate (E) =		1.3700	
13	Volatility (v) =		6.00%	
14	Time (t) =		0.75	
15	Terms currency interest rate (r_t) =		5.90%	
16	Base currency interest rate (r_b) =		5.50%	
18	**Calculations**		**Result**	**Formula used**
19	ln(S/E) =		−0.00732604	=LN(G11/G12)
20	($r_t - r_b$ +0.5*v^2)*t =		0.00435	=(G15 – G16+(G13^2)/2)*(G14)
21	v*t^0.5 =		0.051961524	=G13*(G14^0.5)
23	d_1:	d_1 =	−0.05727392	=(G19+G20)/G21
24		Adjust for P or C =	−0.05727392	=IF(UPPER(LEFT($G$10,1))="C",G23,–G23)
26	d_2:	d_2 =	−0.10923544	=G23-G21
27		Adjust for P or C =	−0.10923544	=IF(UPPER(LEFT($G$10,1))="C",G26,–G26)
29	$N(d_1)$:	k =	0.99	=1/(1+ABS($J$10*G24))
30		1/(2*22/7)^0.5 =	0.398862018	=1/(2*22/7)^0.5
31		EXP((–z^2)/2) =	0.998361193	=EXP(((G24)^2*–1)/2)
32		Calculation =	0.4771	=(G30*G31*($J$11*G29+$J$12*G29^2+$J$13*G29^3+$J$14*G29^4+$J$15*G29^5))
33		N(d_1) =	0.477067428	=IF(G24>0,1–G32,G32)
34		N(d_1) × Exp (–r_b × t) =	0.457788753	
36	$N(d_2)$:	k =	0.98	=1/(1+ABS($J$10*G27))
37		1/(2*22/7)^0.5 =	0.398862018	=1/(2*22/7)^0.5
38		EXP((–z^2)/2) =	0.994051571	=EXP(((G27)^2*–1)/2)
39		Calculation =	0.4564	=(G37*G38*($J$11*G36+$J$12*G36^2+$J$13*G36^3+$J$14*G36^4+$J$15*G36^5))
40		N(d_2) =	0.456415977	=IF(G27>0,1–G39,G39)
41		N(d_2) × Exp (–r_t × t) =	0.436659897	=+G40*EXP(–G15*G14)
44	**Results**			
45	Option premium			
46		—FX points	0.0244	=ROUND(ABS((G11*G34–G12*G41)),4)
47		—%of spot	1.79%	=+G46/G11
		—Terms currency	24,400	=+G46*G9
		—Base currency	17,941	=+G48/G11
48	Option delta =		45.78%	=G34

Row	Normal distribution constants	
10	a =	0.2316419
11	b_1 =	0.31938153
12	b_2 =	−0.356563782
13	b_3 =	1.781477937
14	b_4 =	−1.821255978
15	b_5 =	1.330274429

15.2.4 Using Function Macros to Price Options

> **Note**
> In Chapter 13, an MS Excel function macro called "option" was derived as an efficient method of pricing equity options.[4] This model can easily be applied to currency options, by relabeling the inputs to comply with the requirements of currency options outlined above.

Figure 15.4 provides a simple application of this function macro to pricing an A$ call/US$ put option with a face value of A$10 million. In order to use the model for currency options, relabel the inputs to the model so that S is the spot exchange rate, E is the exercise exchange rate, r is the terms currency (US$) interest rate, and q is the base currency (A$) interest rate.

As with all FX instruments, any user of currency options needs to be wary of making mistakes due to quotation conventions, as well as correctly converting currency amounts. An example of the potential mistakes that can be made in currency options relates to the quotation conventions of currency option premiums. It is usual for option quotations to be given in terms of FX points. Common confusion for traders is to mistake in which currency the FX points are quoted. For example, in *Figure 15.4* the option premium expressed as US$ per A$ (US$ points) is much lower than A$ per US$ (A$ points). While we might expect the premium to be quoted in US points, some market-makers actually quote in A$ points. So, you might accidentally execute this option expecting to receive US$195,000, when in fact you only receive A$195,000. As we have identified earlier in the book, it is safer to operate in terms of cash flows rather than points—to save confusion it is often easier to ask for an option dealer to express the quote in terms of a currency amount prior to executing a transaction.

15.3 CALCULATING OPTION VOLATILITY

The volatility figure that is entered into an option pricing model, the implied volatility, is a market-determined price. It reflects the anticipated distribution of future price changes in the underlying asset price. Like all market prices, it is determined by the forces of supply and demand. While the historical level of volatility in the underlying asset may have a bearing on implied volatility, there is no hard and fast relationship. In fact, implied and historical volatility can be very different due to an event that is expected in the future, such as a release of economic data, which did not occur in the historical sample period.

[4] See Section 13.2.4.

Figure 15.4
Using a Function Macro with Currency Options

The function macro devised in *Figure 13.3* can be applied to currency options. The following example prices an A$ put/US$ call with 1/2 a year to expiry and an exercise price which is out-of-the-money.

INPUT.XLS

	C	D	E	F	G	H
12						
13		**Inputs**				
14		FX combination =			A$/US$	
15		Spot exchange rate =			0.60	
16		Exercise rate =			0.58	
17		Volatility =			12.00%	
18		Time (yrs) =			0.50	
19		Term currency interest rate =			6.00%	
20		Base currency interest rate =			6.50%	
21		Option type (*P* or *C*) =			P	
22		Base currency amount =			10,000,000	
23						
24						Formula used
25		Option premium		—US$ points	0.0117	G14:=option($G$15,$G$15,$G$17,$G$18,$G$19,$G$20,$G$21)
26				—A$ points	0.0195	
27				—% of spot	1.9472%	
28				—% of exercise	2.0144%	
29				—US$ amount	116,833.98	
30				—A$ amount	195,000.00	

15.3.1 Historical Volatility

We can define the price volatility of an asset as the standard deviation of the log-normal returns of the asset price. Mathematically this can be expressed as follows:

$$v = \text{std}[\ln(P_t/P_{t-1})]$$

Where:

std[ ] = standard deviation function
ln( ) = natural logarithm function
P_t = asset price at period t.

This can be thought of as similar to the standard deviation of the percentage change in price.

Figure 15.5 shows the calculation of the historical volatility using daily data over 60 days on an exchange rate. This process can be applied to any asset price or yield.

The calculation is relatively straight forward; complexity lies in determining an appropriate historical time period, the frequency of observations and how to convert the standard deviation into an annualized volatility so that it can be compared directly to Black-Scholes.

Time Horizon

Just as there is no guaranteed relationship between the past and the future, there is no right or wrong historical time period. Most market participants monitor a range of standardized time periods such as 1-, 3-, 6- and 12-month historical volatilities.

Figure 15.5 calculates the historical volatility on day 60, looking back 10, 20, 40 and 60 trading days (or roughly two weeks, one month, two months and three months). Not surprisingly, the volatilities for each time horizon are quite different ranging from 11.29% to 14.09% pa.

This difference in historical volatility due to time horizons is a characteristic of all asset classes. *Figure 15.6* shows the relationship of historical and implied volatilities over time for options on the Australian dollar 3-year bond futures contract.

We can make some general conclusions about the relative nature of volatilities:

- long-term volatilities are considerably more stable than shorter term volatilities;
- short-term volatilities are much more influenced by recent events;

Figure 15.5
Calculating Historical Volatility

The spreadsheet below calculates the annualized volatility over 60 trading days of an exchange rate. The standard deviation calculated is on a daily basis; to convert it to an annualized volatility to enter into Black-Scholes the daily number is mutliplied by the square root of the assumed number of trading days in a year, 250.

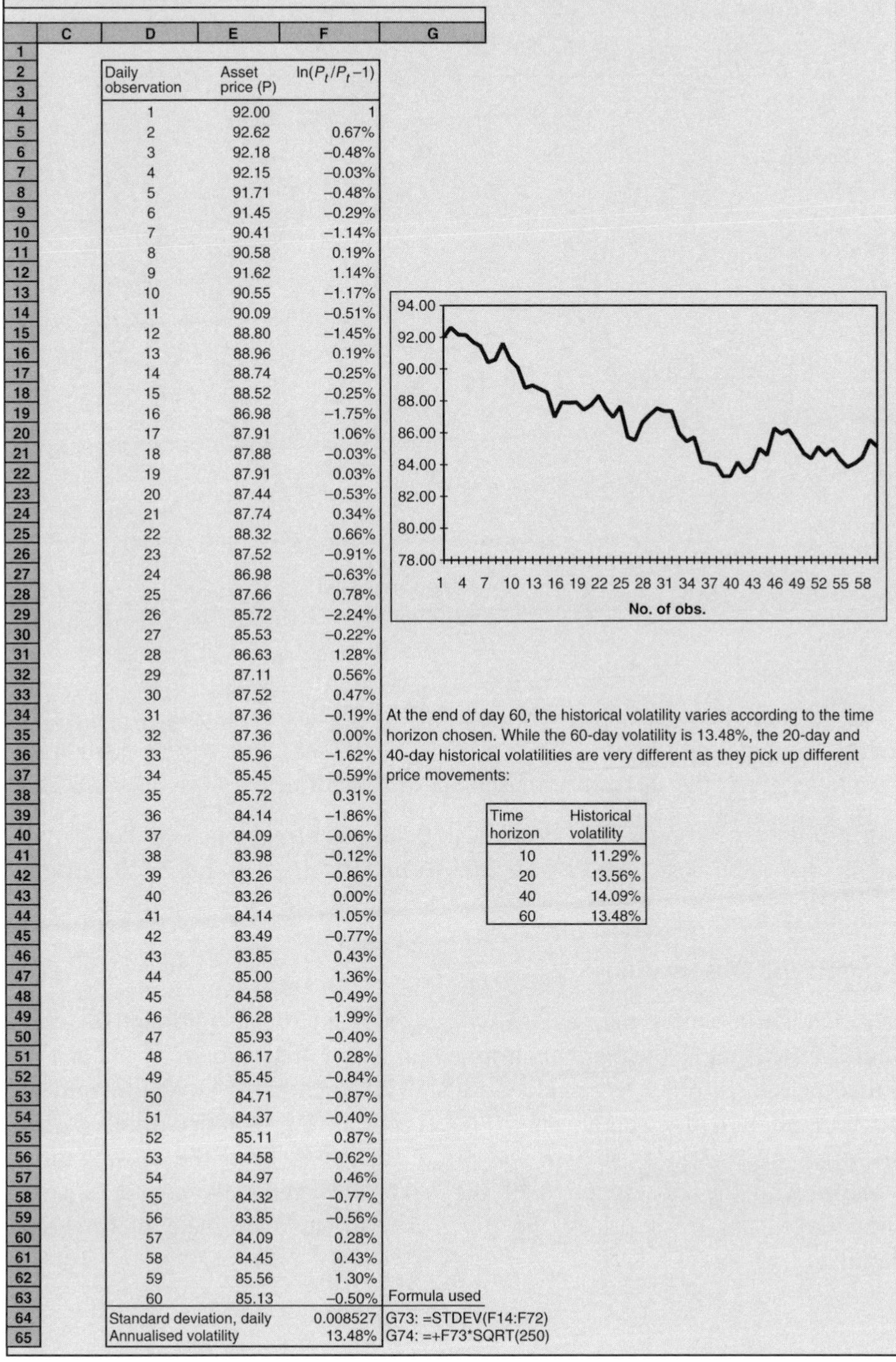

Row	D	E	F
2–3	Daily observation	Asset price (P)	$\ln(P_t/P_t-1)$
4	1	92.00	1
5	2	92.62	0.67%
6	3	92.18	–0.48%
7	4	92.15	–0.03%
8	5	91.71	–0.48%
9	6	91.45	–0.29%
10	7	90.41	–1.14%
11	8	90.58	0.19%
12	9	91.62	1.14%
13	10	90.55	–1.17%
14	11	90.09	–0.51%
15	12	88.80	–1.45%
16	13	88.96	0.19%
17	14	88.74	–0.25%
18	15	88.52	–0.25%
19	16	86.98	–1.75%
20	17	87.91	1.06%
21	18	87.88	–0.03%
22	19	87.91	0.03%
23	20	87.44	–0.53%
24	21	87.74	0.34%
25	22	88.32	0.66%
26	23	87.52	–0.91%
27	24	86.98	–0.63%
28	25	87.66	0.78%
29	26	85.72	–2.24%
30	27	85.53	–0.22%
31	28	86.63	1.28%
32	29	87.11	0.56%
33	30	87.52	0.47%
34	31	87.36	–0.19%
35	32	87.36	0.00%
36	33	85.96	–1.62%
37	34	85.45	–0.59%
38	35	85.72	0.31%
39	36	84.14	–1.86%
40	37	84.09	–0.06%
41	38	83.98	–0.12%
42	39	83.26	–0.86%
43	40	83.26	0.00%
44	41	84.14	1.05%
45	42	83.49	–0.77%
46	43	83.85	0.43%
47	44	85.00	1.36%
48	45	84.58	–0.49%
49	46	86.28	1.99%
50	47	85.93	–0.40%
51	48	86.17	0.28%
52	49	85.45	–0.84%
53	50	84.71	–0.87%
54	51	84.37	–0.40%
55	52	85.11	0.87%
56	53	84.58	–0.62%
57	54	84.97	0.46%
58	55	84.32	–0.77%
59	56	83.85	–0.56%
60	57	84.09	0.28%
61	58	84.45	0.43%
62	59	85.56	1.30%
63	60	85.13	–0.50%
64	Standard deviation, daily		0.008527
65	Annualised volatility		13.48%

At the end of day 60, the historical volatility varies according to the time horizon chosen. While the 60-day volatility is 13.48%, the 20-day and 40-day historical volatilities are very different as they pick up different price movements:

Time horizon	Historical volatility
10	11.29%
20	13.56%
40	14.09%
60	13.48%

Formula used

G73: =STDEV(F14:F72)

G74: =+F73*SQRT(250)

Figure 15.6
Comparison of Implied and Historical and Implied Volatility

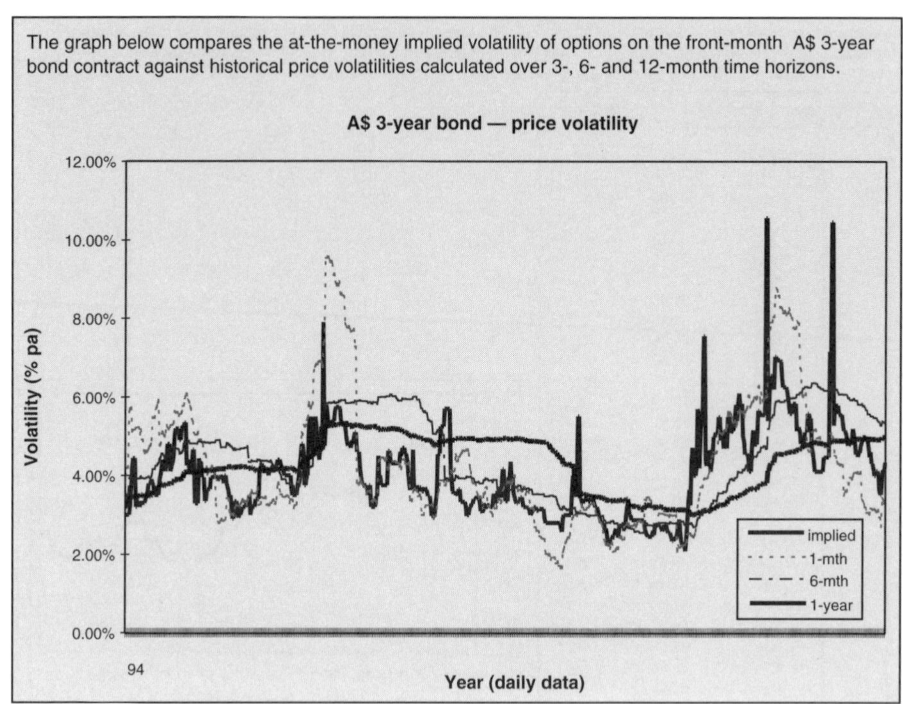

- the best indicator of long-term option volatilities is usually a long-term historical volatility—the same does not necessarily apply to short-term options given the instability of short-term volatilities.

In an effort to determine the "best" historical volatility, some market participants compare the correlation of implied to historical volatilities with different time horizons.

Frequency of Observations

Black-Scholes assumes that volatility is expressed on a continuously compounded basis; that is, there are an infinite number of observations in any historical time period. In order to calculate a historical volatility, we need to split the time horizon into a discrete set of observations—in practice this is often daily price observations, so that the price change is from the closing price on one day to the closing price of the next. This generally creates a sufficiently large sample of prices and gives a reasonable estimate of historical volatility.

It is possible to collect price data on a more frequent basis, such as hourly, but this does increase the data collection and calculation workload with little improvement in the volatility estimate.

Annualizing the Standard Deviation

Once the time horizon and the frequency of observations has been determined, we can determine the standard deviation of the logarithmic returns of the asset price. When calculated, this standard deviation will be expressed in terms of the observation frequency. So, if we have used daily observations, the standard deviation has a daily frequency.

As we have already discussed, Black-Scholes expresses volatility in terms of an annualized percentage. If we have a daily standard deviation then it will need to be annualized. In a Black-Scholes environment this is achieved by multiplying the standard deviation by the square root of the number of observations that will occur in one year. As there are approximately 250 trading days in a year, it is usual to multiply a daily standard deviation by the square root of 250, or 15.811. This explains the annualization calculation in *Figure 15.5*. The daily standard deviation of logarithmic returns is 0.008527; if this is multiplied by 15.811 then the volatility, expressed as a percentage, is 13.48% pa.

If the observation frequency is anything other than daily, then we determine the number of observations that occur pa, take the square root of that number and multiply this by the standard deviation. So, if observations are weekly then we multiply the standard deviation by the square root of 52. *Figure 15.7* summarizes these adjustment calculations.

Figure 15.7
Determining Annualized Volatility

Frequency of obs.	Number of obs. pa	Square root
Hourly*	2500	50.0000
Half days	500	22.3607
Daily	250	15.8114
Weekly	52	7.2111
Monthly	12	3.4641
Quarterly	4	2.0000

* Assume the market is open for trading for 10 hours a day.

It should be noted that this very simplistic approach to annualizing volatilities by multiplying by the square root of time, while consistent with Black-Scholes assumptions, can be misleading. For most markets, observed annual volatility is considerably lower than that implied by the square root of time calculation. This is particularly the case in commodity markets where there is a strong tendency for prices to move toward a long-term average price (referred to as "mean reversion"). In these instances, the square root of time calculation significantly overstates actual volatility.[5]

15.3.2 Solving for Implied Volatility

In most markets, option prices are expressed in terms of the current premium of the option. If we want to determine the current market volatility implied

Figure 15.8
Solving for Implied Volatility Using Black-Scholes

Using the option pricing model from *Figure 15.4* we can make use of the Goal Seek or Solver functions available in MS Excel. In the model below we use Solver.

We know the current market premium for the option shown is 0.0410 DM points. Using the model shown we invoke the solver function to determine the market implied volatility. The implied volatility is 16.09%.

INPUT.XLS

	C	D	E	F	G	H
12						
13		**Inputs**				
14		FX combination =			US$/DM	
15		Spot exchange rate =			1.40	
16		Exercise rate =			1.39	
17		Volatility =			13.00%	
18		Time (yrs) =			0.25	
19		Term currency interest rate =			5.00%	
20		Base currency interest rate =			6.00%	
21		Option type (*P* or *C*) =			P	
22		Base currency amount =			50,000,000	
23						
24						Formula used
25		Option premium		—DM points	0.0326	
26				—US$ points	0.0233	
27				—% of spot	2.3253%	
28				—% of exercise	2.3420%	
29				—DM amount	1,627,692	
30				—US$ amount	1,163,000	

[5] For more detail on this calculation, see Clewlow, L. and Chris Strickland, *Energy Derivatives: Pricing Risk Management*, Lacima Publications 2000.

Figure 15.8 Continued

How to use Solver

1. From the "Tools" menu select "Solver."
2. Set the "Target Cell" as the cell $G$14.
3. The "Equal to" field should be set to the "Value of" of 0.0410.
4. The "By Changing Cells" field should be set to $G$6.
5. Press the "Solve" button and you will be offered a range of ways of viewing the answer. If you select "Answer Report" it will be something similar to the following:

Microsoft Excel 5.0 answer report
Worksheet: [OPTION.XLW]Input.xls
Report created: 31/12/96 12:00

Target cell (value of)

Cell	Name	Original value	Final value
$G$27	—DM points P	0.0326	0.0410

Adjustable cells

Cell	Name	Original value	Final value
$G$19	Volatility = US$/DM	13.00%	16.09%

Constraints
NONE

Hint: make sure the premium you enter is at least equivalent to the intrinsic value of the options, otherwise no solution will be found.

by these premiums, we will need to be able to solve the Black-Scholes formula backwards. However, this does not provide a closed-form solution, determining the volatility requires some sort of solving or searching functions.

The most simple approach is to use the option pricing calculators already developed, such as the option function macro, entering an initial of volatility and adjusting the volatility in order to achieve the desired volatility. There are a number of mathematical search models that can be built to solve for implied volatility, however, for a spreadsheet user there are a range of solver and goal-seeking functions already available in most packages.[6]

Figure 15.8 shows how we can adapt the currency option pricing model developed in *Figure 15.4* to include an implied volatility calculation using Microsoft Excel. In this case, we invoke the solver function to adjust volatility

[6] For example, the Newton-Raphson search method described in Natenberg (1994), p. 446.

until a desired premium is determined. We do not need to alter the original option pricing model in any way, the solver makes use of the model as it is already set up.

In this example, we wish to determine the implied volatility of a DM/US$ currency option. We know the premium is DM0.0410 points, we have already tried a volatility of 13%, which is too low. By using the solver function, we are quickly able to solve for the implied volatility of 16.09%. Essentially, the solver function provides an automated and fast method of applying trial and error.

15.4 DELTA HEDGING

15.4.1 What Is Delta Hedging?

The most common approach to hedging an option is delta hedging; that is, by taking an offsetting underlying asset position equivalent to the option face value multiplied by its current delta. When an offsetting delta equivalent position is held against an option position, it is considered *delta neutral.* In this situation, the combined option and hedge position will show no profit or loss for small changes in the underlying asset price.

Note

A critical aspect of delta hedging is the *rebalancing* of the hedge as the delta of an option changes. A common mistake in delta hedging is to execute the initial hedge and then not change the hedge in accordance with the changing delta of the option. Frequent adjustments are required for the hedge, but this has to be weighed up against the transaction costs of buying and selling the underlying asset. For example, if the hedge were adjusted for every 0.0001% of a change in delta, the hedge costs are potentially enormous. So, from an option market-maker's point of view, there is a trade-off between the frequency of hedge rebalances and the cost of executing those rebalances.

A common practice among options traders is to set *hedge triggers*, where the trigger is the event that leads to a rebalance. This may be expressed in terms of a minimum change in the delta of an option, or else it may be linked to a change in the underlying asset price, volatility or time to expiry. For example, an options trader may automatically calculate the hedge requirements for every 10-point change in the exchange rate. If an underlying asset price trigger is set appropriately, a change in price will only lead to a rebalance when there has been a significant change in the price, as opposed to rebalances occurring just due to small changes in price that are within normal day-to-day trading ranges (i.e., sometimes these small price changes are referred to as "noise").

Essentially, a delta hedge of an option position aims to recreate the nonlinear valuation behavior of an option using forward (or sometimes physical) contracts. While a forward contract has linear valuation behavior, we convert this to an approximately nonlinear payoff by adjusting the face value of the forward position. If we wish to replicate small changes in value for a given change in the underlying price, we lower the face value of the forward positions held and increase the magnitude of the forward hedge as we need to replicate greater sensitivity in value to a given price change.

If we could continuously trade in forward markets with no transaction costs, and if price changes were normally distributed with volatility remaining constant, then delta hedging would perfectly replicate the pricing behavior of an option.[7] However, forward markets are not continuous and not perfectly normal, so changes in price implied by Black-Scholes will not exactly be reflected in the actual price changes that impact the delta hedge.[8] Furthermore, we know volatility is not constant and as forward instruments are not sensitive to volatility changes, this is not something that can be replicated with a delta hedge. As we will see in the following example, the major exposure created by a delta hedge is to changes in volatility.

> ***Note***
> While there are considerable risks associated with delta hedging, it generally becomes more effective the longer the term of the delta hedge. This reflects the fact that in most financial markets, the longer the time period, the more likely it is that a price distribution will become approximately normal. This also suggests we should be wary about delta hedging for short periods of time on short-term options, because not only do we face substantial gamma risk but also the prospect that the price distribution will not be approximately normal.

Currency options provide an excellent example of delta hedging because of the existence of a very liquid forward FX market, which allows frequent rebalancing at low transaction costs.

15.4.2 Creating a Delta Hedge

If we wish to create a delta hedging program, we need to create a hedging strategy which incorporates the fact that the hedge has to be managed as

[7] Note that these are some of the key assumptions of Black-Scholes.

[8] In fact, financial markets are famous for their discontinuities or "gaps" in pricing behavior following the release of important economic data or other market shocks, such as the October 1987 stock market crash.

market conditions change. Also, the strategy needs to measure the profit and loss performance of the hedge over time.

We can break the delta hedge into a number of steps:

1. Execute the option and pay or receive premium.
2. Calculate the current delta of the option.
3. Execute an offsetting delta equivalent of forward contracts. If the option has made us long the underlying asset (bought call or sold put) then the hedge is to sell forward. If the option has made us short the underlying asset (sold call or bought put) then we buy forward.
4. Set a rebalance trigger that determines under what conditions we will adjust the hedge. This might be set in terms of a change in the delta or underlying asset price or a change in the time to expiry.
5. As market conditions change and pass through the trigger, rebalance the delta hedge accordingly.
6. If the option position is closed out, then the hedge must be closed-out simultaneously. If the option expires and is exercised then the hedge should be equivalent to our obligations arising from the exercise and these should be delivered or matched against the exercise.
7. Determine the net cost of the delta hedge.
   - 7.1. Option profit/loss: this is given by the difference between the premium paid or received and any profit or loss arising from option exercise.
   - 7.2. Hedge profit/loss: this is the net gain or loss of the forward delta hedge including crystalized gains and losses.
   - 7.3. Finance costs/income: this incorporates the interest paid or received on premiums, the cost of carry in forward contracts, the interest cost or gain associated with financing hedge gains or losses and any other transaction costs such as brokerage and initial margin funding costs.

15.4.3 Creating a Delta Hedging Program

Using the guidelines developed above, we will now develop a delta hedging program and investigate its effectiveness.

Case Study

You are the currency option dealer of a bank and a customer calls you, wishing to buy a European call option on the Australian dollar against the

US dollar for A$10 million. The option will expire in 70 days with a strike price of A$ = US$ 0.72.

The A$/US$ is currently trading at 0.71. The current market implied volatility for the next ten weeks is 14% while the 70-day interest rates are 7.60% pa for the Australian dollar and 6.00% for the US dollar.[9]

As the dealer, you are required to give the client a quotation for the option premium and devise a delta hedging program to manage the risk of the option.

Premium Quotation

Using the option pricing calculator developed earlier in *Figure 15.4*, enter the market parameters provided above. This gives an option premium of 0.0119 US dollar FX points or 1.68% of face value. Given the face value of the transaction is A$10 million, the dollar value of the premium is A$168,000. As the customer is the option buyer and your bank is granting the option you will receive the premium.

Hedge Rebalance Trigger

The current delta of the option is 40%. As you will be selling an Australian dollar call option, your position is equivalent to selling A$/buying US$. The initial delta hedge is to buy A$/sell US$ forward to the option expiry data with a face value equivalent to 40% of the option face value; that is, A$4 million.

Once the hedge is in place, you need to implement a hedge rebalance trigger. In order to simplify the analysis, suppose that you decide to make the rebalance dependant purely on time—you decide to rebalance at the end of each week. This gives us ten periods over the life of the option where a rebalance occurs. On each rebalance date, the delta is recalculated and the bought A$/sold US$ hedge adjusted accordingly.

Monitoring the Delta Hedge

Suppose the customer agrees to execute the option with your bank at the quoted premium, *Figure 15.9* monitors the outcome of the hedge over the ten weeks to expiry under the FX rate scenario shown at the top of the figure.[10]

[9] As with any market price, there is a bid and offer implied volatility. The bid is where a market-maker will buy options (customer sells options) and the offer is where the market-maker sells options (customer buys options). Accordingly, this 14% volatility is the bank's offer volatility.

[10] To further simplify the analysis, we assume that the A$ and US$ interest rates remain constant and that the implied volatility remains at 14%. This makes the delta sensitive only to changes in the exchange rate and the passing of time.

Figure 15.9
Delta Hedging Case Study: Actual = Historical Volatility

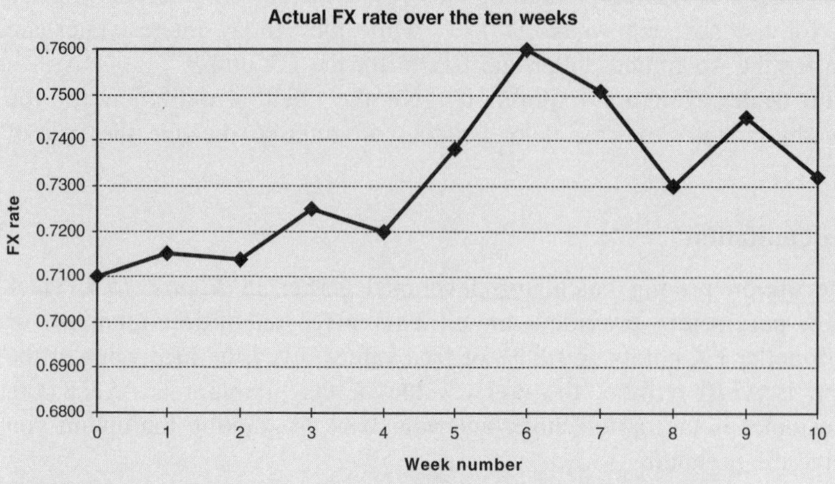

Actual FX rate over the ten weeks

FX rate: 0.6800, 0.6900, 0.7000, 0.7100, 0.7200, 0.7300, 0.7400, 0.7500, 0.7600

Week number: 0, 1, 2, 3, 4, 5, 6, 7, 8, 9, 10

Option details

Initial theoretical price		Transaction details	
Spot	0.71	Type	Call
Exercise	0.72	Strike	0.72
Volatility	14.00%	Premium — % of spot	1.68%
Time (yrs)	0.19	Buy/sell	Sell
Interest rate	6.00%	Face value A$'000	10,000
Div. yld	7.60%	Frequency	Weekly
Type	c		
Premium — FX points	0.0119	Other details	
Premium —% of spot	1.68%	US$ interest rate	6.00%
Delta	40.00%	A$ interest rate	7.60%

All dollar amounts are in '000's

Periods weeks	Actual FX rate	Option cash flows	Delta	Option Delta -A$	Delta hedge details: Delta hedge required	Delta hedge details: A$/US$ Fwd FX rate	Weekly Rebalance A$	Weekly Rebalance US$	FX hedge Balances A$	FX hedge Balances US$	Interest on premium
0	0.7100	168	40%	(4,000)	4,000	0.7078	4,000	(2,831)	4,000	(2,831)	0.002
1	0.7150		45%	(4,500)	4,500	0.7130	500	(357)	4,500	(3,188)	0.002
2	0.7137		43%	(4,300)	4,300	0.7120	(200)	142	4,300	(3,046)	0.002
3	0.7250		55%	(5,500)	5,500	0.7235	1,200	(868)	5,500	(3,914)	0.002
4	0.7200		49%	(4,900)	4,900	0.7187	(600)	431	4,900	(3,482)	0.002
5	0.7380		71%	(7,100)	7,100	0.7369	2,200	(1,621)	7,100	(5,104)	0.002
6	0.7600		92%	(9,200)	9,200	0.7591	2,100	(1,594)	9,200	(6,698)	0.002
7	0.7510		89%	(8,900)	8,900	0.7503	(300)	225	8,900	(6,473)	0.002
8	0.7300		69%	(6,900)	6,900	0.7296	(2,000)	1,459	6,900	(5,013)	0.002
9	0.7450		96%	(9,600)	9,600	0.7448	2,700	(2,011)	9,600	(7,024)	0.002
10	0.7320	(164)	0	–	–	0.7320	(9,600)	7,027	–	3	
Total		3.73						2.89			0.025
In A$		3.73								3.95	0.025

Figure 15.9 Continued

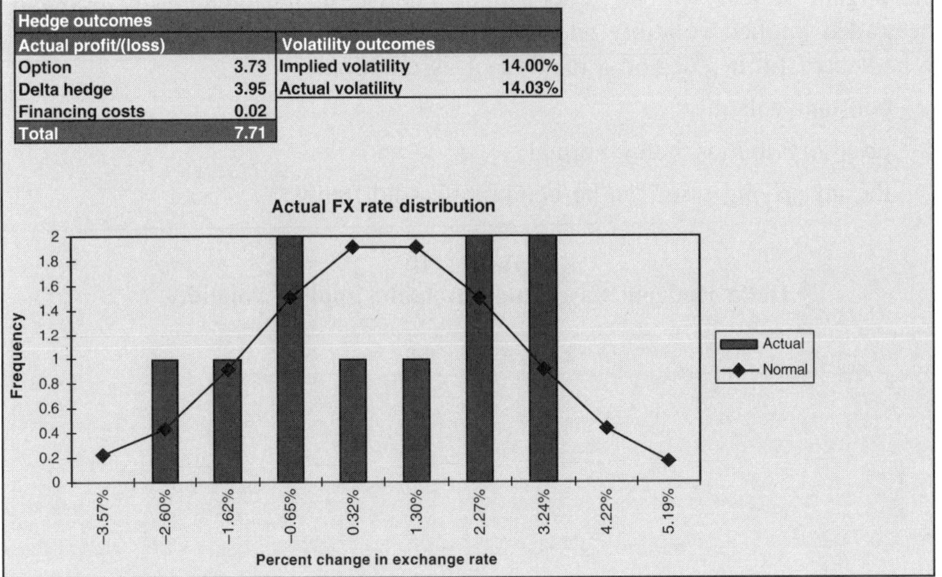

Not surprisingly, the delta hedge is not perfect, as there is a small net gain on both the option and hedge totaling 7,710. The weekly rebalance is a very loose trigger and exposes the bank to the risk of large changes in delta between rebalance dates—moving the model. Further, the distribution graph at the bottom of the figure compares the actual distribution of price changes over the ten weeks compared to the normal distribution assumed by Black-Scholes.

However, despite the imperfections of the hedge, the loss is surprisingly still relatively small. This demonstrates an important aspect regarding delta hedging a sold option in that the hedge losses incurred on the hedge are offset by the premium received. In this example, the premium received almost exactly offsets the hedge losses. This is because the implied volatility of the option when it originally traded is the same as the actual volatility over the 10-week period.

This shows a key characteristic of delta hedging—the major exposure is to changes in volatility. This is demonstrated in *Figure 15.10*, where we look at the same delta hedging exercise with a different actual price outcome. In this case, the actual volatility is higher than the original traded volatility. As expected, the hedger faces a loss on the delta hedge. In option trader jargon, the hedger is "short volatility;" that is, they will lose money from a rise in volatility and gain from a fall.

In summary, a delta hedge creates an exposure to changes in volatility and a gain or loss will be generated depending on the relationship between the traded implied volatility and the actual price outcome. For a delta hedge to be successful it relies on a number of assumptions:

- constant volatility;
- price distribution is log-normal;
- the underlying asset can be bought and sold freely;

Figure 15.10
Delta Hedging Case Study: Actual > Implied Volatility

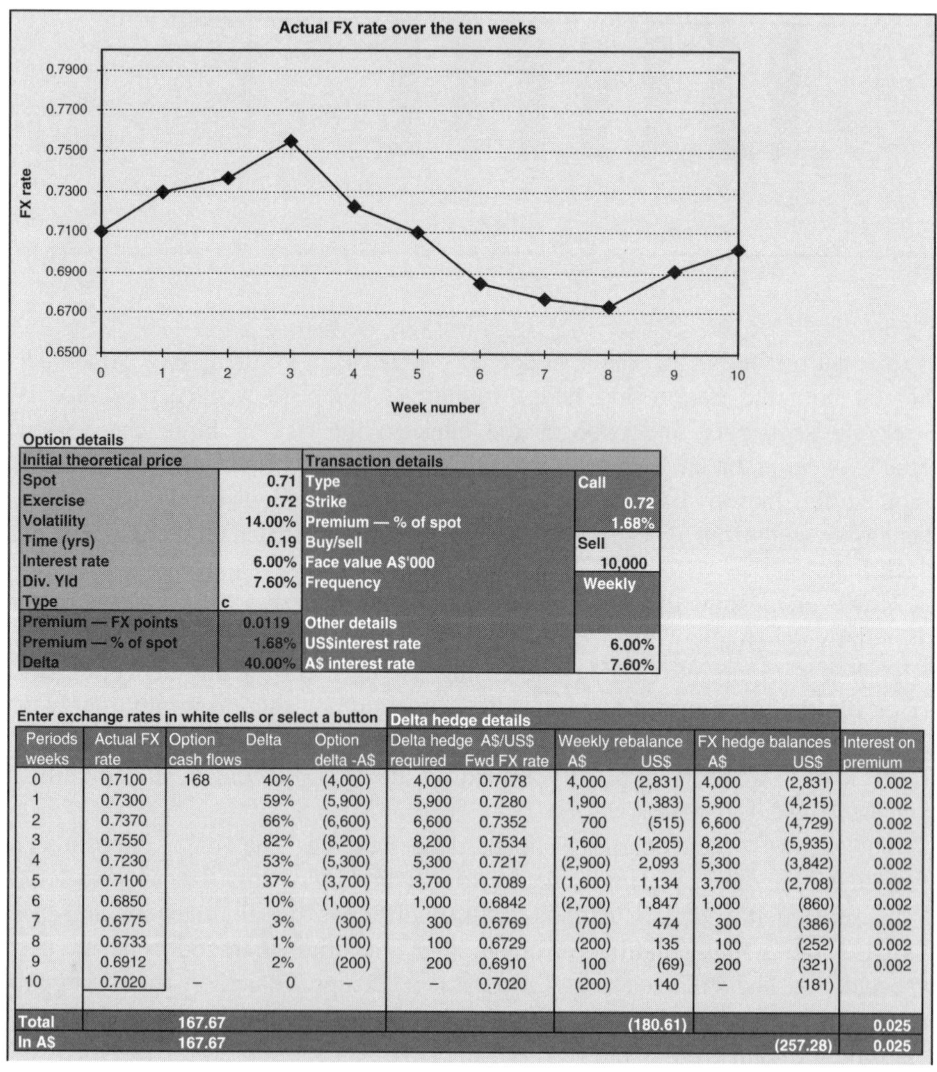

Option details

Initial theoretical price		Transaction details	
Spot	0.71	Type	Call
Exercise	0.72	Strike	0.72
Volatility	14.00%	Premium — % of spot	1.68%
Time (yrs)	0.19	Buy/sell	Sell
Interest rate	6.00%	Face value A$'000	10,000
Div. Yld	7.60%	Frequency	Weekly
Type	c		
Premium — FX points	0.0119	Other details	
Premium — % of spot	1.68%	US$interest rate	6.00%
Delta	40.00%	A$ interest rate	7.60%

Enter exchange rates in white cells or select a button

					Delta hedge details						
Periods weeks	Actual FX rate	Option cash flows	Delta	Option delta -A$	Delta hedge required	A$/US$ Fwd FX rate	Weekly rebalance A$	Weekly rebalance US$	FX hedge balances A$	FX hedge balances US$	Interest on premium
0	0.7100	168	40%	(4,000)	4,000	0.7078	4,000	(2,831)	4,000	(2,831)	0.002
1	0.7300		59%	(5,900)	5,900	0.7280	1,900	(1,383)	5,900	(4,215)	0.002
2	0.7370		66%	(6,600)	6,600	0.7352	700	(515)	6,600	(4,729)	0.002
3	0.7550		82%	(8,200)	8,200	0.7534	1,600	(1,205)	8,200	(5,935)	0.002
4	0.7230		53%	(5,300)	5,300	0.7217	(2,900)	2,093	5,300	(3,842)	0.002
5	0.7100		37%	(3,700)	3,700	0.7089	(1,600)	1,134	3,700	(2,708)	0.002
6	0.6850		10%	(1,000)	1,000	0.6842	(2,700)	1,847	1,000	(860)	0.002
7	0.6775		3%	(300)	300	0.6769	(700)	474	300	(386)	0.002
8	0.6733		1%	(100)	100	0.6729	(200)	135	100	(252)	0.002
9	0.6912		2%	(200)	200	0.6910	100	(69)	200	(321)	0.002
10	0.7020	–	0	–	–	0.7020	(200)	140	–	(181)	
Total		167.67						(180.61)			0.025
In A$		167.67								(257.28)	0.025

Figure 15.10 Continued

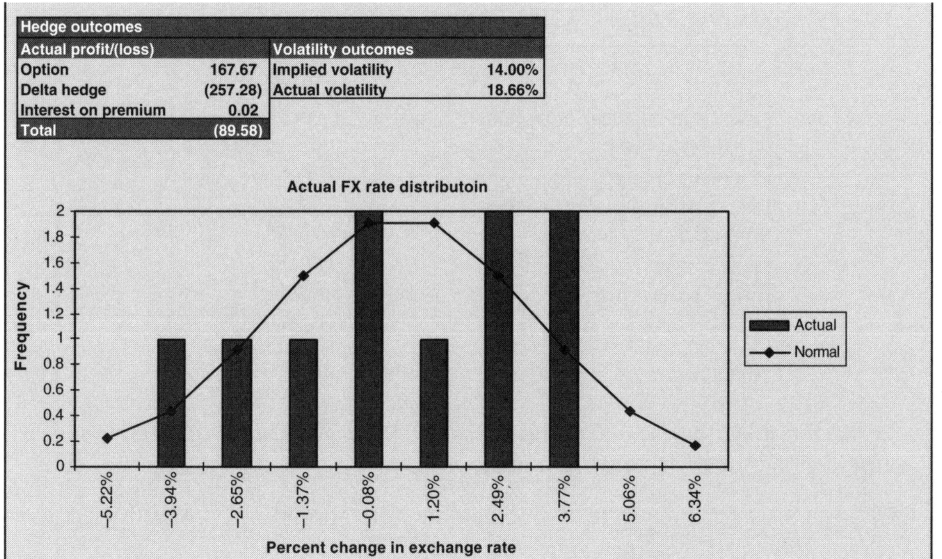

Hedge outcomes			
Actual profit/(loss)		Volatility outcomes	
Option	167.67	Implied volatility	14.00%
Delta hedge	(257.28)	Actual volatility	18.66%
Interest on premium	0.02		
Total	(89.58)		

- there are no transaction costs;
- borrowing and lending at the same rate;
- the strategy is held over time.

A delta hedge also relies on time so that the price distribution can begin to approximate a normal distribution—another form of gamma risk. As a result, delta hedges over short time frames can expose the hedger to hedging greater imperfections.

SUMMARY

In this chapter, we discussed currency options and the currency market. We examined the valuation of currency options, based on some underlying assumptions and we developed models for pricing and valuing currency options. We went through worked examples of delta hedging and cross currency hedging to illustrate how to use options in order to create an effective hedge.

SELF-TEST QUESTIONS

1. You are given the following information:

Amount of base currency	10,000,000
Option type	Put
Spot exchange rate	1.20
Exercise rate	1.30
Volatility	5.75%
Time	0.80
Terms currency interest rate	5.80%
Base currency interest rate	5.65%

   Using the information above, price the currency option, giving the result as a percentage of spot and FX points.

2. Choose an exchange rate and calculate the annualized volatility of the currency over 30 trading days.
3. Suppose you receive a quotation for an at-the-money spot put and call and the premiums are not the same. Does put-call parity imply these premiums should be the same? If not why not?
4. Suppose you are quoted a premium of 2% on the option in Question 1—what is the implied volatility? Use the solver functions in Microsoft Excel to calculate the implied volatility.
5. Explain the function of delta hedging. Why do currency options lend themselves very well to delta hedging?
6. What is a delta "trigger?"

SUBJECT INDEX

WILEY